ASPEN PUBLISHERS

Health Savings Account Answer Book
Fifth Edition

by Christine L. Keller, Gary S. Lesser, and William F. Sweetnam, Jr.

This comprehensive, authoritative volume provides up-to-date coverage of recent legislative and regulatory developments relating to health savings accounts (HSAs). It provides clear and concise guidance on the complex qualification, contribution, administration, and compliance issues that arise in connection with HSAs.

Highlights of the Fifth Edition

Health Savings Account Answer Book, Fifth Edition, offers the practitioner in-depth analysis of the full range of issues concerning these plans. Highlights include:

- Discussion and analysis of the much-anticipated "grab-bag" guidance issued in Notice 2008-59 relating to HSAs. Topics include:
  — Eligible Individuals
  — High Deductible Health Plans
  — Contributions
  — Distributions
  — Prohibited Transactions
  — Establishing an HSA
  — Administration
- Discussion of the guidance issued in Notice 2008-52 regarding the repeal of the HDHP deductible limit on HSA contributions and for treating an eligible individual on December 1, as being eligible for the entire year. The full contribution rule, testing period rules, and the consequences of failing to remain an eligible individual are examined in great detail.
- Discussion of the guidance issued in Notice 2008-51 on qualified HSA funding distribution (a one-time transfer) from an individual's IRA or Roth IRA to an HSA.
- Coverage of the prohibited transaction exemption under the Pension Protection Act of 2006 (PPA), as amended by the Worker, Retiree,

 Wolters Kluwer
Law & Business

and Employer Recovery Act of 2008 (WRERA), which allows HSA providers to offer personalized investment advice to HSA owner.

- Discussion and analysis of the proposed Department of Labor (DOL) regulations and a proposed class exemption relating to the provision of fee-level or computer model investment advice arrangements that were published on August 22, 2008.

- Analysis of changes made to the definition of dependent for HSA and other purposes by the Working Families Tax Relief Act of 2004 (WFTRA), the Gulf Opportunity Zone Act of 2005 (GOZA), and the Fostering Connections to Success and Increasing Adoptions Act of 2008 (FCSIA).

- Discussion and analysis of the improvements made by the Tax Relief and Health Care Act of 2006 (TRHCA), including:
  — The modification of the contribution rules for treating mid-year enrollees as being HSA eligible for the entire year;
  — The one-time transfer rules allowing rollovers to HSAs from HRAs and FSAs;
  — The tax-free funding transfers from an IRA;
  — Analysis of the maximum annual contribution rules that allow for the annual statutory amount to be contributed to an HSA without regard to the deductible under the HDHP associated with the HSA;
  — How employers can now make higher contributions to lower-paid workers; and
  — Discussion of the grace period rules and new exceptions that allow unused contributions in a cafeteria plan to be rolled over to an HSA and how unused contributions in a health FSA that carry over from one plan year to the next affect HSA contribution eligibility.

- Discussion of the DOL guidance for an HSA to be exempt from ERISA.

- Discussion of ERISA fiduciary rules and the consequences when an HSA is subject to ERISA, including whether a trust rather than a custodial account is required.

- Discussion of the advantages to an employer of allowing employees to contribute to HSAs on a pretax basis through an employer's cafeteria plan.

- Changes and clarifications that were made under the final employer contribution comparability regulations and their significance, as well as the new rules under the June 2007 proposed regulations (finalized in 2008) that address accelerated HSA contributions and an employee's failure to establish an HSA.

- Comparability issues for independent contractors, sole proprietors, partnerships, former employees, part-time employees, unionized employees, and others.
- Examination of the mechanics of funding, prefunding, testing periods, and categories of coverage relating to comparable contributions.
- Updated form filing requirements for HSA owners and contributing employers.
- Examination of the effect of state laws on HSA contribution eligibility and legislative proposals to address these issues.
- Discussion of ERISA fiduciary rules and the consequences when an HSA is subject to ERISA, including whether a trust rather than a custodial account is required.
- Analysis of the interaction between HSAs and other types of health coverage.

8/09

For questions concerning this shipment, billing, or other customer service matters, call our Customer Service Department at 1-800-234-1660.

For toll-free ordering, please call 1-800-638-8437.

ASPEN PUBLISHERS

Health Savings Account Answer Book

Fifth Edition

Christine L. Keller, Esq.
Gary S. Lesser, Esq.
William F. Sweetnam, Jr., Esq.

Wolters Kluwer
Law & Business

AUSTIN   BOSTON   CHICAGO   NEW YORK   THE NETHERLANDS

This publication is designed to provide accurate and authoritative information in regard to the subject matter covered. It is sold with the understanding that the publisher is not engaged in rendering legal, accounting, or other professional services. If legal advice or other professional assistance is required, the services of a competent professional person should be sought.

—From a *Declaration of Principles* jointly adopted by
a Committee of the American Bar Association and
a Committee of Publishers and Associations

Printed in the United States of America

ISBN 978-0-7355-8169-2

1 2 3 4 5 6 7 8 9 0

About Wolters Kluwer Law & Business

Wolters Kluwer Law & Business is a leading provider of research information and workflow solutions in key specialty areas. The strengths of the individual brands of Aspen Publishers, CCH, Kluwer Law International and Loislaw are aligned within Wolters Kluwer Law & Business to provide comprehensive, in-depth solutions and expert-authored content for the legal, professional and education markets.

CCH was founded in 1913 and has served more than four generations of business professionals and their clients. The CCH products in the Wolters Kluwer Law & Business group are highly regarded electronic and print resources for legal, securities, antitrust and trade regulation, government contracting, banking, pension, payroll, employment and labor, and healthcare reimbursement and compliance professionals.

Aspen Publishers is a leading information provider for attorneys, business professionals and law students. Written by preeminent authorities, Aspen products offer analytical and practical information in a range of specialty practice areas from securities law and intellectual property to mergers and acquisitions and pension/benefits. Aspen's trusted legal education resources provide professors and students with high-quality, up-to-date and effective resources for successful instruction and study in all areas of the law.

Kluwer Law International supplies the global business community with comprehensive English-language international legal information. Legal practitioners, corporate counsel and business executives around the world rely on the Kluwer Law International journals, loose-leafs, books and electronic products for authoritative information in many areas of international legal practice.

Loislaw is a premier provider of digitized legal content to small law firm practitioners of various specializations. Loislaw provides attorneys with the ability to quickly and efficiently find the necessary legal information they need, when and where they need it, by facilitating access to primary law as well as state-specific law, records, forms and treatises.

Wolters Kluwer Law & Business, a unit of Wolters Kluwer, is headquartered in New York and Riverwoods, Illinois. Wolters Kluwer is a leading multinational publisher and information services company.

ASPEN PUBLISHERS SUBSCRIPTION NOTICE

This Aspen Publishers product is updated on a periodic basis with supplements to reflect important changes in the subject matter. If you purchased this product directly from Aspen Publishers, we have already recorded your subscription for the update service.

If, however, you purchased this product from a bookstore and wish to receive future updates and revised or related volumes billed separately with a 30-day examination review, please contact our Customer Service Department at 1-800-234-1660 or send your name, company name (if applicable), address, and the title of the product to:

ASPEN PUBLISHERS
7201 McKinney Circle
Frederick, MD 21704

Important Aspen Publishers Contact Information

- To order any Aspen Publishers title, go to *www.aspenpublishers.com* or call 1-800-638-8437.
- To reinstate your manual update service, call 1-800-638-8437.
- To contact Customer Care, e-mail *customer.care@aspenpublishers .com*, call 1-800-234-1660, fax 1-800-901-9075, or mail correspondence to Order Department, Aspen Publishers, PO Box 990, Frederick, MD 21705.
- To review your account history or pay an invoice online, visit *www.aspenpublishers.com/payinvoices*.

Preface

Aspen Publishers' *Health Savings Account Answer Book, Fifth Edition*, provides an up-to-the-minute tutorial on this emerging form of consumer-directed health plan. It will benefit a wide variety of professional markets, including pension consultants, plan sponsors, health and insurance agents, financial planners and investment advisers, plan administrators, attorneys, custodians, trustees, brokers, and accountants, as well as those institutions that promote, market, service, or provide technical support to health and/or retirement plans, products, and related services.

Health Savings Account Answer Book, Fifth Edition, is a decision-making tool. Its combination of theory and practice-based advice provides a clear course of action to increase the subscriber's understanding of all aspects of the creation, administration, and operation of health savings accounts (HSAs), as mandated by the Internal Revenue Code, Treasury regulations, and IRS notices, procedures, and announcements.

Written by a team of practicing experts, preeminent in their fields, *Health Savings Account Answer Book, Fifth Edition*, provides step-by-step guidance on the creation, operation, and administration of HSAs. Topics covered include medical coverage and insurance, contributions and deductions, HSA rollovers and transfers, distributions, administration and compliance, and other federal and state laws that affect HSAs. Subscribers will find answers to such commonly asked questions as the following:

- What is an HSA?

- Who is eligible to establish an HSA?

- What are the differences between an HSA, an HRA, and a health FSA?

- Which federal government agencies regulate HSAs?

- What state laws apply to HSAs?

- How are deductions claimed? How are excludable contributions handled?

- Do the prohibited transaction provisions of ERISA and/or Code Section 4975 apply to an HSA? Does the prohibited transaction penalty tax apply to an HSA?

- What is the HDHP requirement? What is an HDHP?

- What factors should an employer consider before offering an HSA with HDHP coverage? What factors should an individual consider before enrolling?

- How does an HSA protect the owner in the event of catastrophic financial loss due to unforeseen illness or injury?

- How are Medigap policies treated?

- When are employer HSA contributions deductible, and when are they excluded from income?

- What are "comparable" employer contributions? What is the testing period used to determine "comparable" contributions?

- Are HSA contributions made under a cafeteria plan subject to the comparability rules?

- Do employer contributions count as fringe benefits under the Davis-Bacon Act?

- How are contributions made by a Subchapter S corporation treated by the corporation and the shareholders?

- What are the rules relating to rollovers and transfers? When can a trustee or custodian refuse to accept rollovers and transfers?

- How is Form 8889—*Health Savings Accounts (HSAs)*—completed?

- Is an HSA subject to HIPAA privacy regulations? Would the electronic standards apply?

- When is an HSA a security subject to regulation by the Securities and Exchange Commission?

- When are HSA distributions subject to tax—and to penalty?

- What are the special rules if one or both spouses have family coverage?

- How is the maximum deductible computed when spouses have separate health plans?

- What are the estate and gift tax aspects of an HSA, of key interest to attorneys and CPAs?

- Do community property rules affect the HSA contribution limitations?

- What are the exceptions to the rule that require that the employee not be covered under any other HDHP?

- Are penalty payments or flat dollar charges for failure to obtain provider precertification counted toward the $5,800/$11,600 out-of-pocket limits for 2009?

- How are Medicare-eligible individuals or those receiving Veteran Affairs benefits treated for contribution purposes?

- What are qualified medical expenses eligible for tax-free treatment?

- When are payments for insurance treated as qualified medical expenses?

- Do the "use it or lose it" rules apply to an HSA or affect eligibility to make contributions?

- Are HSA rollovers and transfers subject to a "one in 12-month" or "60-day" rule?

- How can Archer Medical Savings Accounts be transferred or rolled over to an HSA?

List of Questions. The detailed List of Questions that follows the Contents helps the reader to locate areas of immediate interest. The list of questions is similar to a detailed table of contents, providing the question number and the page on which the question appears. Within each chapter, section headings group and organize questions by topic.

Examples. Numerous examples and practice pointers are interspersed with textual discussion to illustrate important concepts.

Practice Pointers. These paragraphs offer tips and advice to practitioners in the effective design, implementation, and administration of employee benefit plans.

Citations. Case citations and references to statutes and authorities are included to help readers who wish to research specific issues.

Appendixes. Updated appendix material includes charts on state laws affecting HSAs, as well as coverage of pertinent legislation and regulation.

Index. A detailed topical index is provided as a further aid to locating specific information. All references are to question numbers and appendices.

Abbreviations and Acronyms. A number of the terms and statutory references that appear repeatedly in this book are referred to by their abbreviations and/or acronyms after the first mention. The most common of the abbreviations and acronyms are:

- Ann.—IRS Announcement

- BAPCPA—Bankruptcy Abuse Prevention and Consumer Protection Act of 2005

- C.B.—Cumulative Bulletin of the IRS

- Code; I.R.C.—Internal Revenue Code

- DOL—Department of Labor

- DOL Adv. Op.—Department of Labor Advisory Opinion
- ERISA—Employee Retirement Income Security Act of 1974
- FAB—Department of Labor Field Assistance Bulletin
- FCSIA—Fostering Connections to Success and Increasing Adoptions Act of 2008.
- GOZA—Gulf Opportunity Zone Act of 2005
- IR—IRS Information Release
- IRA —Individual retirement arrangement (account and annuity)
- I.R.B.—Internal Revenue Bulletin
- IRS or I.R.S.—Internal Revenue Service
- Ltr. Rul.—Private Letter Ruling
- PPA—Pension Protection Act of 2006
- Prop. Treas. Reg.—Proposed Treasury Regulation
- P.T.E.—Prohibited Transaction Exemption
- Pub. L.—Public Law
- Rev. Proc.—Revenue Procedure
- RIN—Regulation Indentification Number
- Rev. Rul.—Revenue Ruling
- Temp. Treas. Reg.—Temporary Treasury Regulation
- Treas. Reg.—Treasury Regulation
- TRHCA—Tax Relief and Health Care Act of 2006
- WFTRA—Working Families Tax Relief Act of 2004
- WRERA—Worker, Retiree, and Employer Recovery Act of 2008

It is the authors' hope that *Health Savings Account Answer Book, Fifth Edition*, will become an essential research tool for practitioners in the field of employee benefits.

Christine L. Keller
Gary S. Lesser
William F. Sweetnam, Jr.
July 2009

About the Authors

Christine L. Keller, Esq., LL.M., is a principal at Groom Law Group, Chartered. She joined the firm in 2001 after practicing for six years at the Internal Revenue Service, Office of Chief Counsel (Tax-Exempt and Government Entities Division). At the Office of Chief Counsel, Ms. Keller worked first in the qualified plans litigation branch and later in the health and welfare branch. She is one of the principal authors of two sets of final cafeteria plan regulations published by the IRS in 2000 and 2001. At Groom Law Group, Ms. Keller advises employers, insurers, and plan administrators concerning federal and state laws that affect the administration of welfare benefit plans, cafeteria plans, health savings accounts, and other employee benefit arrangements. She also assists clients with obtaining rulings from the IRS and submitting comments to the IRS and Department of Labor in response to agency guidance. She has experience with drafting various types of plan documents, including defined contribution health plans, summary plan descriptions, welfare plans, and cafeteria plans. She has published articles in *RIA Pension & Benefits Week* on USERRA & The Soldiers' and Sailors' Civil Relief Act (Dec. 2001) and Defined Contribution Health Plans (Sept. 2002) and in *Employee Benefits News* on HSA Funding Issues (January 2006).

Ms. Keller earned an LL.M. (Taxation) with distinction and a Certificate in Employee Benefits from Georgetown University Law Center in February 2000. She earned her J.D. from the State University of New York at Buffalo Law School in 1995 and graduated cum laude from Alfred University in 1990 with a B.S. in Business Administration and a minor in Industrial Engineering. She is admitted to practice in New York and the District of Columbia.

Gary S. Lesser, Esq., is the principal of GSL Galactic Consulting, located in Indianapolis, Indiana. Mr. Lesser maintains a telephone-based consulting practice providing services to other professionals and business owners. Mr. Lesser is a nationally known author, educator, and speaker on retirement plans for individuals and smaller businesses. He has broad technical and practical knowledge of both qualified and nonqualified retirement plans.

Mr. Lesser is the technical editor and co-author of *SIMPLE, SEP, and SARSEP Answer Book; Life Insurance Answer Book; Roth IRA Answer Book; 457 Answer Book;* and *Quick Reference to IRAs* (all Aspen Publishers). Mr. Lesser is also the principal author and technical editor of *The CPA's Guide to Retirement Plans for Small Businesses* (American Institute of Certified Public Accountants (AICPA)). He has developed several software programs that are used by financial planners, accountants, and other pension practitioners to design and market retirement plans for smaller businesses. His two software programs—*QP-SEP Illustrator*™ and *SIMPLE Illustrator*^SM—are marketed and distributed nationally. He has also been published in the *EP/EO Digest, Journal of Taxation of Employee Benefits, Journal of Compensation and Benefits, Journal of Pension Benefits, Life Insurance Selling, Rough Notes*, and the *NAPFA Advisor*. Mr. Lesser is an associated professional member of the American Society of Pension Professionals and Actuaries (ASPPA).

In 1974, Mr. Lesser started his employee benefits career with the Internal Revenue Service as a Tax Law Specialist/Attorney in the Employee Plans/Exempt Organizations (EP/EO) Division. He later managed and operated a pension administration and actuarial service organization, was an ERISA marketing attorney for a national brokerage firm, and was a senior vice-president/director of retirement plans for several nationally known families of mutual funds and variable annuity products. Mr. Lesser graduated from New York Law School and received his B.A. in accounting from Fairleigh Dickinson University. He is admitted to the bars of the state of New York and the United States Tax Court. Mr. Lesser can be reached at GSL Galactic Consulting, 944 Stockton St., Indianapolis, IN 46260-4925, (317) 254-0385, at QPSEP@aol.com, or at http://www.garylesser.com.

William F. Sweetnam, Jr., Esq. is a principal at the Groom Law Group, Chartered, the nation's largest employee benefits specialty law firm, and is the practice leader of its Policy and Legislation Group. Before joining Groom in May 2005, he was the Benefits Tax Counsel in the Office of Tax Policy at the U.S. Department of the Treasury. The Benefits Tax Counsel is the principal legal advisor to the Secretary of the Treasury and the Assistant Secretary for Tax Policy with regard to all aspects of employee benefits taxation and related matters, including pensions, health care, and executive compensation. Mr. Sweetnam was the Treasury's primary contact with Congress with regard to the IRA and pension provisions in the Economic Growth and Tax Relief Reconciliation Act of 2001. He also led the team at the Treasury in its guidance efforts with regard to consumer-directed health care (such as health savings accounts and health reimbursement arrangements) and the new executive deferred compensation rules.

Prior to the Treasury Department, Mr. Sweetnam was Tax Counsel on the Majority Staff of the U.S. Senate Committee on Finance under the chairmanship of Senator William V. Roth of Delaware. At the Committee, he was responsible for tax matters in the areas of employee benefits (pensions, medical plans, and executive compensation), retirement savings vehicles (such as IRAs), insurance, and tax-exempt organizations (including charitable giving). During his tenure,

Mr. Sweetnam was involved with the Retirement Savings and Security Act, the Patients' Bill of Rights, and the IRS personnel flexibility provisions in the IRS Reform and Restructuring Act.

Mr. Sweetnam is a graduate of Rutgers University and Fordham University School of Law. He is admitted to practice in the District of Columbia, New York, and Pennsylvania.

Introduction

There is a significant trend in employer-provided health care: consumer-directed health plans. In these plans, the decision of how to spend health care dollars rests more with the employee, and his or her health care provider, than with the employer or insurance company. Consumer-directed health plans are part of an overall initiative to help rein in the rising costs of health care and health insurance. This policy goal takes on added importance because an increase in the cost of health insurance means a decrease in the number of people covered by insurance. Employees who participate in consumer-driven health plans become wiser consumers of medical services as a result of their enhanced decision-making responsibility. Another advantage is that the lower costs associated with consumer-directed health plans provide more coverage options for individuals who wish to purchase health insurance outside of the employment context.

The inclusion of the health savings account (HSA) provision as part of the Medicare Modernization Act in 2003 is an important part of the trend toward consumer-directed health plans. President George W. Bush was very supportive of including HSAs in this important legislation, which modernized Medicare by adding a prescription drug feature to the Medicare program. Many members of Congress were motivated to vote for the Medicare Modernization Act because of its HSA provision. They expressed concern about rising health care costs and believed that making HSAs available to all Americans would help address those spiraling costs.

It is important to note that as one of the final acts of Representative Bill Thomas, the retiring Chairman of the powerful Committee on Ways and Means in the House of Representatives, additional HSA provisions were included in H.R. 6111, the Tax Relief and Health Care Act of 2006—must-pass legislation that the Congress enacted on December 9, 2006. This bill contained many provisions that plan sponsors and HSA advocates promoted that would make HSAs more workable. Passage of this bill in 2006 was important because leading Democrats in Congress do not believe in HSAs. With Democrats controlling Congress in 2007, there would be no opportunity to advance this pro-HSA agenda in the next few years.

In terms of developing cost-consciousness in medical spending, it is useful to review how medical insurance operates. Traditional health insurance pays for all medical costs once a deductible is met, usually requiring some sort of co-pay with each visit or prescription drug. Health maintenance organizations (HMOs) contain costs by limiting the health care professionals and procedures that the HMO will pay for. HSAs require that the HSA owner participate in a high deductible health plan (HDHP) before he or she can contribute to the HSA, and the amount of the maximum HSA contribution cannot exceed the statutory limit (which is higher than the minimum deductible under the HDHP). High deductible health insurance is less expensive than traditional health insurance and HMO coverage because it insures only major catastrophic health care expenses; the consumer pays for all other medical services, either directly or through a vehicle such as an HSA. Thus, there are two ways in which high deductible health insurance reduces costs: the premium for such insurance is lower, and there is more prudent health care spending. By their support of the HSA provision in the Medicare Modernization Act, Congress and the Bush Administration expressed their belief that the use of HDHPs and HSAs would result in more cost-conscious decisions by consumers of medical services.

The operation of HDHPs is similar to that of other types of insurance (e.g., automobile insurance or homeowners' insurance), which make payments only when there is a major problem (e.g., an automobile accident or a house fire). Traditional health insurance generally starts paying claims for medical care, whether routine or not, after a low deductible is reached. This is analogous to having an automobile insurer pay for changing a car's fluids, in addition to providing coverage in case of accidents. Because traditional health insurance pays for all medical expenses (once the low deductible is reached), the cost of such insurance is higher than the cost of an HDHP, where the consumer pays for routine medical services.

Another important change is that using the HSA with an HDHP provides a tax-effective way to pay for out-of-pocket medical costs, because all contributions made to the HSA that meet the contribution limits are fully tax-deductible by the HSA owner. Compare that to the current system of itemized deduction for out-of-pocket health care expenses. Given the restrictions on the amount of medical deduction (amounts over 7.5 percent of adjusted gross income), individuals rarely get any tax benefit for paying medical expenses themselves. Clearly, the use of an HSA to pay for these medical expenses benefits everyone, no matter what their tax bracket.

The successful implementation of the HSA legislation was an important priority of the Bush Administration. As the former Benefits Tax Counsel at the U.S. Department of the Treasury, I was involved in crafting the guidance to help implement HSAs. Our main objective was to offer guidance, consistent with the legislation, that would facilitate the offering of qualifying high deductible health insurance and the accounts themselves. We asked those individuals in the health care and financial services industry who were considering providing HSAs and HDHPs to tell us what issues needed to be addressed and when such guidance would be needed in order to provide a successful rollout of the these products. We met with many of the stakeholders to determine how to craft helpful, easy-to-understand guidance that could be used by all employees, including those who were not familiar with the process for issuing tax-related guidance. To that end, Treasury and the IRS issued eight pieces of guidance by July 2004 that addressed many of the important issues surrounding HSAs and high deductible health insurance. In addition, we heard that financial institutions were concerned about the forms that were needed for the establishment of HSAs. Treasury and the IRS provided forms that any financial institution would choose to use for their clients to establish an HSA. *Health Savings Account Answer Book* provides an excellent description of all the guidance promulgated by the federal government regarding HSAs and HDHPs.

In addition to the guidance, the Bush Administration made a very proactive effort to explain the benefits of HSAs and HDHPs to the American public. President Bush had several town-hall meetings promoting the HSA concept, as did Secretary of the Treasury John Snow. Treasury had a separate Web site that contained all the information regarding HSAs, and the Department answered and continues to answer questions from the public about HSAs. Doubtless, many subscribers to *Health Savings Account Answer Book* have heard me or my former staff talk at length about the HSA guidance at numerous meetings around the country and on countless conference calls.

Americans are taking control of their health spending. According to America's Health Insurance Plans (AHIP), approximately 8 million people were covered by HSAs and HDHPs. This is a great start. Do not let the HSA naysayers say that this take-up rate is proof that Americans do not want HSAs. I can look to the 401(k) market and the slow but steady increase in the number of people with 401(k) plans. The HSA is similar, and in time more Americans will see the value of this important innovation in health care. Many more Americans are also getting health insurance coverage with HSAs. Approximately one-third of the people with HSAs are those with new health insurance coverage. The criticisms of those against HSAs say that HSAs are solely for the healthy and wealthy have been refuted by actual market data. HSAs are important new products for controlling health care costs. I am confident that those who use the *Health Savings Account Answer Book* will find it useful in promoting HSAs.

What will happen to HSAs under the Obama Administration and the push for health insurance reform? If health insurance reform adds either an individual mandate to purchase insurance or a mandate that employers provide health insurance coverage to their employees, the fate of HSAs depends on whether a HDHP will comply with the mandate. If HDHP coverage does not satisfy the coverage mandate, it will be the end of HSAs. We should all watch the legislative process to make sure that HSAs are protected. To that end, I've given copies of the

Health Savings Account Answer Book to the relevant Congressional Staff so that they can understand what a great health care innovation HSAs are.

William F. Sweetnam, Jr.
Groom Law Group*

---

*Mr. Sweetnam was the Benefits Tax Counsel at the U.S. Department of the Treasury from April 2001 to February 2005 and was Tax Counsel on the majority staff of the U.S. Senate Committee on Finance from January 1998 to February 2001.

Contents

List of Questions xxiii

CHAPTER 1

Overview of HSAs 1-1

    Introduction 1-2

    HSA/HDHP Providers 1-3

    Other Defined Contribution Health Care
        Arrangements 1-4

    Regulation 1-5

    Advantages and Disadvantages 1-6

    Future of HSAs 1-11

CHAPTER 2

General HSA Rules 2-1

    In General 2-1

    Eligible Individual for Establishing an HSA 2-4

    Establishment and Effective Dates 2-10

Divorced Parents 2-13

Qualified Medical Expenses 2-14

Dependents 2-15

Advantages and Disadvantages of HSAs 2-21

CHAPTER **3**

Medical Coverage and Insurance 3-1

HDHP Requirements 3-2

Plan Deductible 3-6

Limitation on Benefits 3-17

Family Coverage vs. Self-Only Coverage 3-20

Other Health Plan Coverage 3-21

Miscellaneous Issues 3-44

CHAPTER **4**

Contributions and Deductions 4-1

Making HSA Contributions 4-2

Eligibility for HSA Contributions 4-12

Other Employee Health Plans 4-13

Cafeteria Plan Grace Period Rules 4-17

Interaction Between HSAs and Health FSAs 4-21

Contribution Limitations 4-23

Catch-Up Contributions 4-35

Computing Annual Contributions 4-38

Special Computation Rules for Married Individuals 4-41

Deductions for Individual Contributions 4-49

Employer Contributions in General 4-52

Employer Responsibility 4-55

Exclusion and Deductibility of Employer
  Contributions 4-56

Timing of Contributions 4-59

Excess Contributions 4-59

Employer Contributions and ERISA 4-67

Comparability of Employer Contributions 4-69

IRS Reporting by Individuals 4-101

Partnership Considerations 4-102

S Corporation Considerations 4-106

CHAPTER 5

HSA Rollovers and Transfers 5-1

Rollovers and Transfers from IRAs and HSAs 5-2

Qualified HSA Funding Distributions (IRA to HSA) 5-11

Qualified HSA Distributions (One-Time HRA and FSA
  Transfers to an HSA) 5-21

CHAPTER 6

Distributions 6-1

Taxation of HSA Distributions 6-2

Restrictions on Distributions 6-7

Medical Care Paid from an HSA 6-11

Medicine and Drugs 6-20

Distributions Used for Long-Term Care Insurance
    Premiums 6-22

Deemed Distributions Due to Prohibited
    Transactions 6-23

Transactions with Service Providers 6-35

Other Prohibited Transaction Exemptions 6-36

The 10 Percent Additional Tax 6-40

Returning Distributions Mistakenly Made 6-44

Death Distributions to Designated Beneficiaries 6-45

Income Tax Withholding on HSA Distributions 6-47

CHAPTER 7

Administration and Compliance 7-1

HSA Documents 7-2

Permissible Investments 7-5

Account Fees 7-6

Trustees and Custodians 7-7

Reports 7-10

Form Filing Requirements 7-10

CHAPTER **8**

Federal and State Laws Affecting HSAs 8-1

ERISA 8-1

HIPAA Privacy 8-18

Medicare Part D 8-19

State Benefit Mandates 8-20

State Tax Consequences 8-22

Davis-Bacon Act 8-24

USA Patriot Act 8-25

Securities Law 8-26

Use of Electronic Media 8-27

Creditor Protection 8-27

APPENDIX **A**

Extracts from Relevant Code Sections A-1

APPENDIX **B**

IRS Notices B-1

APPENDIX **C**

IRS Announcements C-1

APPENDIX **D**

IRS Revenue Rulings D-1

APPENDIX **E**

Department of Labor Releases E-1

APPENDIX **F**

Annual HSA Limitations F-1

APPENDIX **G**

How Health Savings Accounts Compare to Health Flexible Spending Arrangements (FSAs) and Health Reimbursement Arrangements (HRAs) G-1

TABLES

Table of Internal Revenue Code Sections T-1

Table of IRS Announcements and Notices T-5

INDEX IN-1

List of Questions

Chapter 1 Overview of HSAs

Introduction

Q 1:1 What is a health savings account?....................... 1-2

Q 1:2 Is the HSA an entirely new creation by Congress? 1-2

Q 1:3 What factors contributed to the enactment of the HSA
legislation? 1-3

Q 1:4 Why do proponents of HSAs consider HSAs to be an
improvement over the current health insurance system? 1-3

HSA/HDHP Providers

Q 1:5 Did companies offer HSAs with accompanying HDHPs on
January 1, 2004, the date the law became effective? 1-3

Q 1:6 Do some companies offer their services as HSA trustees or
custodians only, without offering an accompanying
HDHP?... 1-4

Other Defined Contribution Health Care
Arrangements

Q 1:7 In addition to HSAs, what types of health accounts are
considered defined contribution or consumer-driven
arrangements? 1-4

Q 1:8 What are the main differences among an HSA, an HRA, and a
health FSA? 1-4

Regulation

Q 1:9 Which federal government agencies regulate HSAs? 1-5

Q 1:10 Are states permitted to regulate HSAs?................... 1-5

Q 1:11 Which federal government agencies have issued guidance on
HSAs? 1-5

Advantages and Disadvantages

Q 1:12 What are the primary advantages to an individual of participating in an HSA? **1-6**

Q 1:13 What are the advantages to an employer of offering an HSA option to employees? **1-7**

Q 1:14 What are the advantages to an employer of allowing employees to contribute to an HSA on a pretax basis through the employer's cafeteria plan? **1-7**

Q 1:15 Will the HSA serve as a good vehicle to set aside funds for retiree health? **1-8**

Q 1:16 What are the *primary* disadvantages to an individual of participating in an HSA? **1-8**

Q 1:17 What are the disadvantages to an employer of offering an HSA? **1-9**

Q 1:18 What factors should an individual consider before enrolling in an HSA with HDHP? **1-9**

Q 1:19 How will a spouse's health coverage affect an HSA owner's ability to contribute to an HSA? **1-9**

Q 1:20 How will a domestic partner's health coverage affect the HSA contribution limits? **1-10**

Q 1:21 What factors should an employer consider before offering an HSA with HDHP coverage? **1-10**

Q 1:22 What are the potential consequences to an individual of enrolling in an HSA but failing to follow the applicable rules? **1-10**

Q 1:23 What are the potential consequences to an employer of failing to follow the applicable HSA rules? **1-11**

Future of HSAs

Q 1:24 What were some of the major issues that commentators to the IRS were concerned about with respect to HSAs in 2004 and continue to be concerned about today? **1-11**

Q 1:25 What were the Bush Administration's proposals to make additional changes that would have expanded HSAs in 2009? **1-12**

Q 1:26 What were the reasons for the Bush Administration's proposed changes to the HSA rules? **1-13**

Q 1:27 What were the proposed changes to HSAs under the Bush Administration's budget proposals? **1-14**

Q 1:28 What were the leading HSA-related legislative proposals introduced in the 109th Congress (2005–2007)? **1-17**

Q 1:29 What were the leading HSA-related legislative proposals introduced in the 110th Congress (2007–2009)? **1-19**

Q 1:30 What are the leading HSA-related legislative proposals introduced in the 111th Congress (2009–2011)? **1-20**

Chapter 2 General HSA Rules

In General

Q 2:1 What is an *HSA*? **2-1**

Q 2:2 Who is the account beneficiary, account owner, or HSA
owner?.. **2-3**

Q 2:3 How and when were HSAs created?.................... **2-3**

Q 2:4 When are the HSA rules effective?..................... **2-3**

Q 2:5 Do HSAs replace Archer Medical Savings Accounts?........ **2-3**

Eligible Individual for Establishing an HSA

Q 2:6 Who is an *eligible individual* for purposes of establishing an
HSA?.. **2-4**

Q 2:7 If an employee begins HDHP coverage midmonth, when does
the employee become an eligible individual?............. **2-6**

Q 2:8 Are there any exceptions to the rule that prohibits an employee
who is an "eligible individual" from having coverage under
any other non-HDHP?............................. **2-6**

Q 2:9 May an ineligible individual establish an HSA if his or her
spouse is an eligible individual? **2-7**

Q 2:10 May a joint HSA be established by a married couple?........ **2-7**

Q 2:11 Are HSAs available to residents of the U.S. Virgin Islands,
Guam, and the Commonwealth of the Northern Mariana
Islands? **2-7**

Q 2:12 Are HSAs available to residents of Hawaii? **2-8**

Q 2:13 Will an individual be treated as participating in an HDHP
and no other non-HDHP if he or she elects HDHP coverage
but also has the option to choose a plan that is not an
HDHP?....................................... **2-8**

Q 2:14 Are individuals who are eligible for Medicare but who are
not enrolled in Medicare Part A or B eligible to establish
HSAs? **2-8**

Q 2:15 When does eligibility to contribute to an HSA end for a
Medicare-eligible individual? **2-9**

Q 2:16 Are individuals who are eligible for medical benefits through the
Department of Veterans Affairs (VA) eligible to make
contributions to an HSA?.......................... **2-9**

Q 2:17 Is a government retiree who is enrolled in Medicare Part B (but
not Part A) an eligible individual for HSA purposes?........ **2-10**

Q 2:18 May an otherwise HSA-eligible individual who is age 65 or
older and thus eligible for Medicare, but who is not enrolled
in Medicare Part A or Part B, make the additional catch-up
contributions for individuals age 55 or older? **2-10**

Q 2:19 May active duty or retired service members receiving medical
coverage under TRICARE contribute to an HSA? **2-10**

Establishment and Effective Dates

Q 2:20   When is an HSA *established*? **2-10**
Q 2:21   Can HSA contributions be made as soon as the HSA is
         effective? **2-11**
Q 2:22   Can an HSA be *established* before it becomes effective? **2-11**
Q 2:23   May a trustee treat an HSA as established before the date of
         establishment determined under state law, such as the date
         when HDHP coverage began?. **2-12**
Q 2:24   If an individual sends in paperwork and an initial deposit to the
         HSA trustee, is the HSA considered established as of the
         date of mailing? **2-12**
Q 2:25   When is an HSA established if the funds in the HSA were rolled
         over or transferred from an Archer MSA or another HSA? . . .   **2-12**
Q 2:26   On what date is an HSA established if the owner had
         previously established an HSA?. **2-13**

Divorced Parents

Q 2:27   Which rules apply to determine whether a child of divorced
         parents may be covered under a parent's HSA or HDHP on
         a tax-free basis? **2-13**

Qualified Medical Expenses

Q 2:28   Which distributions from an HSA are excludable from gross
         income?. **2-14**
Q 2:29   What are qualified medical expenses?. **2-14**
Q 2:30   What is included in *medical care*? **2-14**
Q 2:31   Are payments for insurance qualified medical expenses? **2-14**
Q 2:32   May qualified medical expenses be incurred before the HSA is
         established?. **2-15**
Q 2:33   May an HSA be used to pay for an individual's qualified
         medical expenses on a tax-free basis even if such individual
         is not covered by an HDHP?. **2-15**

Dependents

Q 2:34   What is the significance for HSAs of the Gulf Opportunity Zone
         Act of 2005?. **2-15**
Q 2:35   How did WFTRA change the definition of *dependent*? **2-16**
Q 2:36   How did GOZA change the definition of *dependent*? **2-16**
Q 2:37   Who is a dependent for HSA purposes? **2-17**
Q 2:38   What relationship must the individual have to the taxpayer to
         be treated as a qualifying relative? **2-17**
Q 2:39   Who is a qualifying child? **2-18**
Q 2:40   Does an individual's age affect his or her status as a qualifying
         child?. **2-18**

Q 2:41   Does an individual's disability affect his or her status as a qualifying child? **2-18**

Q 2:42   When does a child attain a specified age for purposes of the qualifying child definition? **2-19**

Q 2:43   Who is a qualifying relative for purposes of an HSA? **2-19**

Q 2:44   Can a child of divorced or separated parents be claimed as a dependent of both parents if the custodial parent has not released the claim to the exemption for a dependent under Code Section 152(e)(2)? **2-20**

Advantages and Disadvantages of HSAs

Q 2:45   What are the potential advantages of an HSA to an individual? . **2-21**

Q 2:46   What are the potential disadvantages of an HSA for an individual? **2-24**

Q 2:47   Who is best suited for adopting an HSA? **2-26**

Q 2:48   How might an HSA work for an individual? **2-26**

Chapter 3 Medical Coverage and Insurance

HDHP Requirements

Q 3:1   What is a high deductible health plan? **3-2**

Q 3:2   Can an insured or self-insured medical reimbursement plan sponsored by an employer be an HDHP? **3-3**

Q 3:3   Is a limited coverage plan treated as an HDHP? **3-3**

Q 3:4   Must an HDHP provide meaningful medical coverage in order to be considered an HDHP under Code Section 223? **3-4**

Q 3:5   Does a state high-risk health plan qualify as an HDHP? **3-4**

Q 3:6   Would a health plan that negotiates discounted prices for services qualify as an HDHP if an HSA owner receives services at a discount? **3-4**

Q 3:7   Are the minimum annual deductible and maximum out-of-pocket expense amounts applicable to the HDHP under Code Section 223 adjusted for inflation? **3-4**

Q 3:8   Must an HDHP be offered on a calendar year basis? **3-5**

Q 3:9   How are changes to the deductibles and out-of-pocket expense limits applied? **3-5**

Plan Deductible

Q 3:10   What is the plan deductible? **3-6**

Q 3:11   Are plan deductibles for out-of-network services taken into account when determining the HDHP maximum out-of-pocket limitation? **3-6**

Q 3:12 What medical expenses may be taken into account in determining when the HDHP deductible is satisfied for purposes of a post-deductible HRA or post-deductible health FSA? **3-7**

Q 3:13 Can a health plan's deductible period last longer than 12 months? **3-7**

Q 3:14 How is the plan's annual deductible limit adjusted when the deductible period lasts longer than 12 months? **3-7**

Transitional Rule

Q 3:15 Can a health plan that would otherwise qualify as an HDHP but for an annual deductible that does not satisfy the rules for periods of more than 12 months be treated as an HDHP?... **3-9**

Out-of-Pocket Expenses

Q 3:16 What are out-of-pocket expenses? **3-9**

Q 3:17 What are the limits for out-of-pocket expenses? **3-9**

Q 3:18 Are amounts paid by the HSA owner toward covered medical expenses for out-of-network services required to be applied toward the out-of-pocket limit? **3-9**

Q 3:19 Must a plan specify an out-of-pocket maximum in order to be considered an HDHP? **3-10**

Transitional Rule

Q 3:20 What transitional relief was granted by the IRS to HDHPs relative to out-of-pocket expenses when the health plan does not provide any maximum on payments above the deductible? **3-11**

Q 3:21 What transitional relief was provided for a health plan that complies with state laws that mandate benefits without regard to a deductible or a deductible below the minimum annual deductible? **3-11**

Q 3:22 Why was the transitional relief provided in Notice 2005-83 extended for non-calendar-year health plans? **3-11**

Q 3:23 When did the additional transitional relief for a coverage period of 12 months or less in a non-calendar year health plan expire? **3-12**

Other Out-of-Pocket Issues

Q 3:24 Must a penalty payment or flat-dollar charge paid by the covered individual for failure to obtain pre-certification for a specific provider be treated as an out-of-pocket expense? **3-12**

Q 3:25 Are cumulative embedded deductibles under family coverage subject to the out-of-pocket maximum? **3-13**

Q 3:26   Are cumulative embedded deductibles under family coverage
subject to the out-of-pocket maximum if the plan contains
an umbrella deductible of $11,600 or less for 2009?. **3-13**

Q 3:27   Are amounts incurred by an individual for medical care for
noncovered expenses included in computing the plan's
out-of-pocket expenses? **3-13**

Q 3:28   If an employer changes health plans midyear, is the minimum
annual deductible of $1,150/$2,300 (for 2009) satisfied if the
new HDHP provides a credit toward the deductible for
expenses incurred during the previous health plan's short
plan year?. **3-14**

Q 3:29   If an eligible individual changes coverage during the plan year
from self-only HDHP coverage to family HDHP coverage,
does the individual fail to be covered by an HDHP merely
because the family HDHP coverage takes into account
expenses incurred while the individual had self-only
coverage? **3-15**

Q 3:30   If an eligible individual changes coverage during the plan year
from family HDHP coverage to self-only HDHP coverage,
does the individual fail to be covered by an HDHP merely
because the self-only HDHP coverage takes into account
expenses incurred while the individual had family
coverage? **3-15**

Limitation on Benefits

Q 3:31   May an HDHP impose a lifetime limit on benefits? **3-17**

Q 3:32   Are amounts paid by a covered individual above a lifetime limit
treated as out-of-pocket expenses?. **3-17**

Q 3:33   If a plan imposes reasonable annual or lifetime limits on
specific benefits, are amounts paid by covered individuals
beyond these annual or lifetime limits subject to the
maximum out-of-pocket limitations? **3-18**

Q 3:34   May a plan limit covered benefits?. **3-18**

Q 3:35   If a health plan imposes a separate or higher deductible for
specific benefits, are amounts paid by covered individuals
to satisfy the separate or higher deductible treated as
out-of-pocket expenses? **3-18**

Q 3:36   May a health plan meeting the minimum deductible ($1,150 for
self-only coverage and $2,300 for family coverage for 2009)
restrict benefits to expenses for hospitalization or in-patient
care out-of-pocket expenses?. **3-18**

Q 3:37   When is a restriction or exclusion on benefits reasonable? **3-19**

Q 3:38   If a plan limits benefits to UCR amounts, are amounts paid by
covered individuals in excess of UCR included in determining
the out-of-pocket expenses paid for purposes of calculating
the maximum out-of-pocket limit? **3-20**

Family Coverage vs. Self-Only Coverage

Q 3:39 What is self-only coverage under an HDHP? **3-20**

Q 3:40 What is family coverage under an HDHP? **3-20**

Q 3:41 May a family-coverage HDHP plan cover only the eligible
individual? **3-21**

Q 3:42 Can benefits under a family-coverage plan be paid before the
family incurs annual covered medical expenses in excess
of the minimum annual deductible under Code
Section 223? **3-21**

Other Health Plan Coverage

Q 3:43 Are there exceptions to the rule requiring that the eligible
individual not be covered under any other health plan? **3-21**

Permitted Insurance

Q 3:44 What is permitted insurance? **3-23**

Q 3:45 What does permitted insurance include? **3-23**

Q 3:46 May an otherwise eligible individual who is covered by both an
HDHP and insurance contracts for one or more specific
diseases or illnesses contribute to an HSA if the insurance
provides benefits before the deductible of the HDHP is
satisfied? **3-23**

Q 3:47 Must coverage for permitted insurance be provided under an
insurance contract? **3-24**

Prescription Drug Coverage

Q 3:48 May an individual who is covered by a health plan that
provides prescription drug benefits before the deductible of
the HDHP is satisfied contribute to an HSA?............. **3-24**

Preventive Care Safe Harbor

Q 3:49 What is the preventive care safe harbor? **3-24**

Q 3:50 What benefits and services are permitted under the preventive
care safe harbor? **3-25**

Q 3:51 Are prescription drugs or medications that are used to prevent
a disease or recurrence of a disease from which an HSA
owner, spouse, or dependent has recovered eligible for
safe-harbor treatment? **3-27**

Q 3:52 To what extent do drugs or medications come within the safe
harbor for preventive care services as "preventive care?" ... **3-27**

Q 3:53 Must an HDHP provide preventive care benefits?.......... **3-28**

Q 3:54 Does preventive care include the treatment of an existing
illness?.. **3-28**

Q 3:55   Does a preventive care service or screening that also includes the treatment of a related condition during that procedure come within the safe harbor for preventive care in I.R.S. Notice 2004-23?................................ **3-28**

Q 3:56   Does the characterization of a benefit required by state law determine whether health care is preventive?............ **3-37**

Medical Discount Cards

Q 3:57   May an individual who is covered by an HDHP, and also has a discount card that enables the user to obtain discounts for health care services or products, contribute to an HSA?.... **3-38**

Employee Assistance, Disease Management, and Wellness Programs

Q 3:58   Does coverage under an Employee Assistance Program (EAP), disease management program, or wellness program make an individual ineligible to contribute to an HSA?.......... **3-38**

Q 3:59   Would services provided by a nurse practitioner at an employer's on-site clinic be considered a health plan that makes an individual ineligible to contribute to an HSA?..... **3-38**

Q 3:60   Does access to free health care or health care at charges below fair market value from an employer's on-site clinic affect an individual's eligibility to contribute to an HSA?..... **3-39**

Q 3:61   May the safe-harbor screening and preventive care services be disregarded in determining whether an EAP provides significant benefits for medical care or treatment?......... **3-39**

Health Reimbursement Arrangements

Q 3:62   May an HSA owner who participates in an HDHP and a post-deductible health reimbursement arrangement (HRA) be an eligible individual?................................ **3-40**

Long-Term Care Insurance

Q 3:63   May an HSA owner pay for long-term care premiums from an HSA?.. **3-41**

Q 3:64   May an HSA owner pay for long-term care services from an HSA (i.e., services that are provided without regard to insurance)?...................................... **3-41**

HSAs Under a Code Section 125 Cafeteria Plan

Q 3:65   May an HSA be funded by salary reduction contributions through a cafeteria plan?........................... **3-41**

Q 3:66   Must a cafeteria plan document be amended to allow employees to fund an HSA with salary reduction contributions?................................... **3-41**

Q 3:67 May the employer offer negative elections for an HSA if offered through a cafeteria plan?........................... **3-42**

Q 3:68 Which requirements that apply to health flexible spending arrangements (FSAs) under a Code Section 125 cafeteria plan do not apply to HSAs?....................... **3-42**

Q 3:69 Do the Code Section 125 change-in-status rules apply to elections of HSA contributions through a cafeteria plan?.... **3-43**

Q 3:70 Can an employer place additional restrictions on the election of HSA contributions under a cafeteria plan?.............. **3-43**

Q 3:71 Can an employer permit employees to elect an HSA midyear if offered as a new benefit under the employer's cafeteria plan?....................................... **3-43**

Q 3:72 When the HSA is offered as a new benefit under the employer's cafeteria plan midyear, are there circumstances that will prevent the employee from being an eligible individual?..................................... **3-43**

Q 3:73 If an employee elects to make contributions to an HSA through the employer's cafeteria plan, may the employer contribute amounts to an employee's HSA to cover qualified medical expenses incurred by an employee that exceed the employee's current HSA balance?................... **3-44**

Retiree Health Coverage

Q 3:74 Are HSA distributions qualified medical expenses if used to pay for the retiree portion of health care coverage once the HSA owner reaches age 65?........................... **3-44**

Miscellaneous Issues

Q 3:75 Is an HSA a group health plan under Code Section 5000(b)(1) for purposes of the 25 percent excise tax on nonconforming group health plans?............................. **3-44**

Q 3:76 Do HIPAA privacy and security rules apply to an HSA?....... **3-44**

Chapter 4 Contributions and Deductions

Making HSA Contributions

Q 4:1 In what form must contributions be made to an HSA?....... **4-2**

Q 4:2 Can a transfer to an HSA be made from an employer's health FSA or HRA?................................... **4-3**

Q 4:3 Can a transfer to an HSA be made from a traditional IRA?.... **4-3**

Q 4:4 May an HSA be fully funded in the beginning of a year?...... **4-4**

Q 4:5 May the full HSA contribution be made for a year for an individual who becomes covered under an HDHP during the year or who increases coverage level during the year?..... **4-4**

Q 4:6   How is the maximum contribution determined if an individual
             was, or was considered, an eligible individual for the entire
             year, and changes their type of coverage during the year? **4-6**

Q 4:7   Is an eligible individual on December 1 considered to have
             self-only or family coverage? **4-8**

Q 4:8   What happens if the individual makes contributions under the
             exception and does not remain an eligible individual during
             the testing period? **4-8**

Q 4:9   Does the additional 10 percent tax apply if the individual does
             not remain an eligible individual during the testing period? . . .   **4-9**

Q 4:10   What is the testing period during which the individual must
             remain an eligible individual? **4-9**

Q 4:11   What is the last date for making annual contributions to an
             HSA? **4-10**

Q 4:12   May an individual who ceases to be an eligible individual during
             a year still contribute to an HSA with respect to the months
             of the year when the individual was an eligible individual? . . .   **4-10**

Q 4:13   May employer contributions to employees' HSAs made
             between January 1 and the date for filing the employee's
             return, without extensions, be allocated to the prior year? . . .   **4-11**

Q 4:14   For contributions to be made on behalf an eligible individual, is
             the individual required to have compensation? **4-11**

Q 4:15   May HSA contributions be made into an individual retirement
             arrangement (IRA)? **4-11**

Q 4:16   Must contributions be made into an HSA established at the
             same institution that provides the HDHP? **4-12**

Eligibility for HSA Contributions

Q 4:17   Who may contribute to an HSA? **4-12**

Q 4:18   May contributions to an HSA be made through a cafeteria
             plan? **4-12**

Q 4:19   May a state government make an HSA contribution on behalf
             of an eligible individual? **4-12**

Other Employee Health Plans

Q 4:20   May an employee covered by an HDHP and a health FSA or
             an HRA make contributions to an HSA? **4-13**

Cafeteria Plan Grace Period Rules

Q 4:21   May a cafeteria plan permit employees to carry over unused
             contributions to a subsequent year? **4-17**

Q 4:22   How can an employer provide a grace period in a cafeteria
             plan? **4-19**

Q 4:23   Is it permissible for a plan to impose a cap on the amount of
             benefits that are subject to the grace period? **4-19**

Q 4:24   How long may the grace period last? **4-19**

Q 4:25 May unused benefits be cashed out or converted? **4-20**

Q 4:26 How may an employer adopt a grace period? **4-20**

Q 4:27 How long does a grace period remain in effect?. **4-21**

Interaction Between HSAs and Health FSAs

Q 4:28 May an individual who is otherwise eligible for an HSA be covered under certain types of health FSAs and remain eligible to contribute to an HSA? **4-21**

Q 4:29 Who has the responsibility for verifying that the FSA has a zero balance? **4-22**

Contribution Limitations

Q 4:30 What is the maximum annual contribution that can be made to an HSA?. **4-23**

Q 4:31 Are the HSA annual contribution limitations coordinated with contributions made to an Archer MSA? **4-24**

Q 4:32 Are the maximum annual contribution amounts indexed for inflation?. **4-25**

Q 4:33 How are the statutory annual contribution limits indexed for inflation?. **4-25**

Q 4:34 May an eligible individual have more than one HSA, and do contribution limits apply?. **4-26**

Q 4:35 How are contributions treated if the eligible individual has more than one HSA?. **4-26**

Q 4:36 How do the maximum annual HSA contribution limits apply to an eligible individual with family HDHP coverage for the entire year if the family HDHP covers spouses or dependent children who also have coverage by a non-HDHP, Medicare, or Medicaid?. **4-26**

Q 4:37 How is the contribution limit computed for an individual who begins coverage under an HDHP midyear and continues to be covered under the HDHP for the rest of the year? **4-27**

Q 4:38 What is the exception for an individual who is an eligible individual on the first day of the last month of his or her taxable year (generally December 1)?. **4-27**

Q 4:39 When is the annual contribution made under the last-month rule exception subject to the additional 10 percent tax under Code Section 223(b)(8)(B)? **4-33**

Q 4:40 In what health plan is the individual treated as having been enrolled in under the exception allowing the full contribution to be made for a year? **4-34**

Q 4:41 What is the contribution limit for an eligible individual covered by an HDHP and also by a post-deductible HRA or post-deductible health FSA? **4-34**

Catch-Up Contributions

Q 4:42   Are catch-up contributions permitted?. **4-35**

Q 4:43   May an otherwise HSA-eligible individual who is age 65 or older and thus eligible for Medicare, but is not enrolled in Medicare Part A or Part B, make the additional catch-up contributions for individuals age 55 or older? **4-36**

Q 4:44   What are the catch-up contribution limits?. **4-36**

Q 4:45   Are the maximum catch-up amounts indexed for inflation?. . . .   **4-37**

Computing Annual Contributions

Q 4:46   How are catch-up contributions computed? **4-38**

Q 4:47   How is the annual contribution limit determined for an individual who is an eligible individual, or who is considered an eligible individual under the last-month rule, for the entire year? **4-38**

Q 4:48   How can the annual contribution limit be computed if the individual did not have the same coverage on the first day of every month during 2009 or was not an eligible individual on December 1, 2009? **4-39**

Special Computation Rules for Married Individuals

Q 4:49   If one or both spouses have family coverage, how is the contribution limit computed? **4-41**

Q 4:50   How do the maximum annual HSA contribution limits apply to a married couple if both spouses are eligible individuals and each spouse has family HDHP coverage that does not cover the other spouse?. **4-41**

Q 4:51   Which plan deductible limit was used before 2007 for computing contributions when each spouse had family coverage under a separate health plan?. **4-42**

Q 4:52   What is the contribution limit for spouses?. **4-43**

Q 4:53   What is an umbrella deductible? **4-44**

Q 4:54   What is an embedded individual deductible? **4-44**

Q 4:55   How was the maximum annual HSA contribution limit determined before 2007 for an eligible individual with family coverage under an HDHP that included embedded individual deductibles and an umbrella deductible? **4-45**

Q 4:56   How do the maximum annual HSA contribution limits apply to family HDHP coverage that may include an ineligible individual? **4-46**

Q 4:57   How may spouses agree to divide the annual HSA contribution limit between themselves?. **4-47**

Q 4:58   How does an employer report HSA contributions?. **4-48**

Q 4:59   How is an employer's contribution to an HSA reflected on Form W-2—*Wage and Tax Statement*? **4-49**

Deductions for Individual Contributions

Q 4:60   Are an eligible individual's HSA contributions deductible?..... **4-49**

Q 4:61   Are employer contributions to the HSA of an employee's spouse (who is not an employee of this employer) excluded from the employee's gross income and wages?.......... **4-50**

Q 4:62   How is the deduction taken on the individual's federal income tax return?..................................... **4-50**

Q 4:63   Is the deduction for contributions to a self-employed individual's own HSA taken into account in determining net earnings from self-employment under Code Section 1402(a)?...................................... **4-50**

Q 4:64   If a C corporation makes a contribution to the HSA of a shareholder who is not an employee of the C corporation, what are the tax consequences to the shareholder and to the C corporation?...................... **4-51**

Q 4:65   Must an individual itemize deductions in order to claim a deduction for HSA contributions?................... **4-51**

Q 4:66   Can HSA contributions be claimed as an itemized expense on the federal income tax return?...................... **4-51**

Q 4:67   Are contributions made by a family member or other person on behalf of an eligible individual deductible?.............. **4-51**

Q 4:68   May an individual who may be claimed as a dependent on another person's tax return deduct contributions to an HSA?.. **4-52**

Q 4:69   Do community property rules apply in determining limitations on contributions or their deductibility?................ **4-52**

Employer Contributions in General

Q 4:70   May employer contributions exceed the maximum allowable amount for the individual?......................... **4-52**

Q 4:71   How are employer payments to an HSA treated?........... **4-53**

Q 4:72   What tax advantages does an employer receive by allowing employees to make HSA contributions through the employer's cafeteria plan?........................ **4-53**

Q 4:73   Can an employer make higher contributions to the HSA accounts of participants with chronic health conditions?.... **4-54**

Q 4:74   Are contributions to an HSA subject to the nonqualified deferred compensation rules under Code Section 409A? ... **4-54**

Employer Responsibility

Q 4:75   Is the employer responsible for determining employee eligibility for an HSA?...................................... **4-55**

Q 4:76   May the employer rely on an employee's representation of their age?.. **4-55**

Q 4:77   Is the employer responsible for determining whether HSA distributions are used exclusively for qualified medical expenses? **4-55**

Q 4:78   Is an employer permitted to structure cafeteria plan elections for HSAs as negative elections? **4-56**

Exclusion and Deductibility of Employer Contributions

Q 4:79   What is the tax treatment of employer contributions on behalf of an eligible individual? **4-56**

Q 4:80   Are employer contributions on behalf of an eligible individual excluded from the employee's income? **4-56**

Q 4:81   Are contributions to an employee's HSA through a cafeteria plan treated as made by the employer or employee? **4-57**

Q 4:82   Are employer contributions subject to Railroad Retirement taxes? **4-57**

Q 4:83   Are employer contributions subject to income withholding from wages? **4-57**

Q 4:84   Are employer contributions subject to FICA taxes? **4-58**

Q 4:85   Are employer contributions made under a cafeteria plan subject to FICA taxes? **4-58**

Q 4:86   Are employer contributions subject to FUTA taxes? **4-58**

Q 4:87   May an employee deduct employer contributions made on his or her behalf on his or her federal income tax return? **4-58**

Q 4:88   What is the tax treatment of an HSA? **4-58**

Timing of Contributions

Q 4:89   When may HSA contributions be made? **4-59**

Q 4:90   Is there a deadline for contributions to an HSA for a taxable year? **4-59**

Excess Contributions

Q 4:91   How may an excess HSA contribution be created? **4-59**

Q 4:92   What is an excess contribution for purposes of the 6 percent excise tax? **4-60**

Q 4:93   Is it permissible for an individual to deduct an HSA contribution that exceeds the maximum amount that may be contributed in a taxable year? **4-61**

Q 4:94   How are employer contributions and excess employer contributions reported by the employer? **4-61**

Q 4:95   May an employer's HSA contribution to an ineligible individual be deducted by the employee? **4-62**

Q 4:96   Are excess contributions subject to penalty? **4-62**

Q 4:97   Can the excess contribution penalty be avoided? **4-62**

Q 4:98 When is the net income attributable to the excess contribution taxable?.. **4-62**

Q 4:99 What is the result if the net income is not distributed in a correcting distribution?........................... **4-62**

Q 4:100 Is the excess contribution distributed in a correcting distribution subject to tax?........................... **4-63**

Q 4:101 How are earnings attributable to the excess HSA contribution calculated?....................................... **4-63**

Q 4:102 What is the adjusted closing balance used in computing earnings on an excess contribution?.................. **4-63**

Q 4:103 What is the adjusted opening balance used in computing earnings on an excess contribution?.................. **4-63**

Q 4:104 What is the computation period used in computing earnings on an excess contribution?........................... **4-64**

Q 4:105 How is the account valued when correcting an excess HSA contribution?....................................... **4-64**

Q 4:106 May an excess contribution be corrected after the extended due date of the individual's federal income tax return?..... **4-64**

Q 4:107 How are excess HSA contributions corrected after the due date of the owner's return?........................... **4-66**

Q 4:108 May an individual who has not made excess HSA contributions treat a distribution from an HSA other than for qualified medical expenses as the withdrawal of excess HSA contributions?.................................... **4-67**

Employer Contributions and ERISA

Q 4:109 Is an HSA established in connection with an employment-based group health plan treated as an employee welfare benefit plan under Title I of ERISA?.................. **4-67**

Q 4:110 Is an employer required to make COBRA continuation coverage available with respect to an HSA?............ **4-67**

Q 4:111 Do the rules under Code Section 419 regarding funded welfare benefit plans affect contributions by an employer to an HSA?.. **4-68**

Q 4:112 Do the minimum funding standards under Code Section 412 apply to an HSA?.................................. **4-68**

Q 4:113 Are employer contributions to an HSA subject to the 10 percent tax on nondeductible employer contributions?..... **4-68**

Comparability of Employer Contributions

Q 4:114 What are the comparability rules that apply to employer contributions to an HSA?........................... **4-69**

Q 4:115 Who are comparable participating employees?........... **4-69**

Categories of Coverage Relating to Comparability

Q 4:116   What are the categories of HDHP coverage for purposes of applying the comparability rules? **4-70**

Q 4:117   What is family HDHP coverage? **4-72**

Testing Period for Comparability

Q 4:118   What is the testing period for making comparable contributions to employees' HSAs? **4-72**

The Excise Tax and Comparability

Q 4:119   What are the consequences of violating the comparability rules? **4-72**

Employer Contributions

Q 4:120   Do the comparability rules apply to amounts rolled over from an employee's HSA or Archer Medical Savings Account (Archer MSA)? **4-73**

Q 4:121   If an employee requests that his or her employer deduct after-tax amounts from the employee's compensation and forward these amounts as employee contributions to the employee's HSA, do the comparability rules apply to these amounts? **4-73**

Employee for Comparability Testing

Q 4:122   Do the comparability rules apply to contributions that an employer makes to the HSAs of independent contractors or self-employed individuals? **4-73**

Q 4:123   May a sole proprietor who is an eligible individual contribute to his or her own HSA without contributing to the HSAs of his or her employees who are eligible individuals? **4-73**

Q 4:124   Do the comparability rules apply to contributions by a partnership to a partner's HSA? **4-74**

Q 4:125   How are members of controlled groups treated when applying the comparability rules? **4-74**

Comparable Contributions

Q 4:126   What are the categories of employees for comparability testing? **4-75**

Collectively Bargained Employees

Q 4:127   Do the comparability rules apply to unionized employees or groups of collectively bargained employees? **4-75**

Coverage Requirements Under HDHPs

Q 4:128 Is an employer permitted to make comparable contributions only to the HSAs of comparable participating employees who have coverage under the employer's HDHP? **4-76**

Q 4:129 If an employee and his or her spouse are eligible individuals who work for the same employer and one employee-spouse has family coverage for both employees under the employer's HDHP, must the employer make comparable contributions to the HSAs of both employees? **4-77**

Q 4:130 Does an employer that makes HSA contributions only for one class of non-collectively bargained employees who are eligible individuals but not for another class of non-collectively bargained employees who are eligible individuals (for example, management v. nonmanagement) satisfy the requirement that the employer make comparable contributions? **4-78**

Comparability and Former Employees

Q 4:131 If an employer contributes to the HSAs of former employees who are eligible individuals, do the comparability rules apply to these contributions? **4-79**

Q 4:132 What action must an employer take to locate former employees? **4-80**

Q 4:133 Is an employer permitted to make comparable contributions only to the HSAs of comparable participating former employees who have coverage under the employer's HDHP? **4-80**

Q 4:134 If an employer contributes only to the HSAs of former employees who are eligible individuals with coverage under the employer's HDHP, must the employer make comparable contributions to the HSAs of former employees who are eligible individuals with coverage under the employer's HDHP because of an election under a COBRA continuation provision (as defined in Code Section 9832(d)(1))? **4-81**

Comparability Rules Relating to Archer MSAs

Q 4:135 How do the comparability rules apply if some employees have HSAs and other employees have Archer MSAs? **4-81**

Calculating Comparable Contributions

Q 4:136 What are comparable contributions under Code Section 4980G? **4-81**

The Comparability Rules in Relation to Full-Time and Part-Time Employees

Q 4:137   How does an employer comply with the comparability rules when some non-collectively bargained employees who are eligible individuals do not work for the employer during the entire calendar year? **4-84**

Q 4:138   How do the comparability rules apply to employer contributions to employees' HSAs if some non-collectively bargained employees work full-time during the entire calendar year, and other non-collectively bargained employees work full-time for less than the entire calendar year? **4-87**

Q 4:139   May an employer make contributions for the entire year to the HSAs of its employees who are eligible individuals at the beginning of the calendar year (on a pre-funded basis) instead of contributing on a pay-as-you-go or on a look-back basis? **4-88**

Q 4:140   Must an employer use the same contribution method for all employees who were comparable participating employees for any month during the calendar year? **4-88**

Q 4:141   How can an employer comply with the comparability rules if an employee has not established an HSA at the time the employer contributes to its employees' HSAs? **4-90**

Notice to Employees Regarding Employer Contributions to HSAs

Q 4:142   If an employer bases its contributions on a percentage of the HDHP deductible, how is the correct percentage or dollar amount computed? **4-93**

Q 4:143   Does an employer that contributes to the HSA of each comparable participating employee in an amount equal to the employee's HSA contribution or a percentage of the employee's HSA contribution (matching contributions) satisfy the rule that all comparable participating employees receive comparable contributions? **4-94**

Q 4:144   If an employer conditions contributions by the employer to an employee's HSA on an employee's participation in health assessments, disease management programs, or wellness programs and makes the same contributions available to all employees who participate in the programs, do the contributions satisfy the comparability rules? **4-94**

Q 4:145   If an employer makes additional contributions to the HSAs of all comparable participating employees who have attained a specified age or who have worked for the employer for a specified number of years, do the contributions satisfy the comparability rules? **4-94**

Q 4:146 If an employer makes additional contributions to the HSAs of all comparable participating employees who are eligible to make the additional contributions (HSA catch-up contributions), do the contributions satisfy the comparability rules?. **4-94**

Q 4:147 If an employer's contributions to an employee's HSA result in noncomparable contributions, may the employer recoup the excess amount from the employee's HSA? **4-95**

Q 4:148 What constitutes a reasonable interest rate for purposes of making comparable contributions? **4-95**

HSA Comparability Rules and Cafeteria Plans

Q 4:149 If an employer makes contributions through a cafeteria plan to the HSA of each employee who is an eligible individual, are the contributions subject to the comparability rules?. **4-95**

Q 4:150 If an employer makes contributions through a cafeteria plan to the HSA of each employee who is an eligible individual in an amount equal to the amount of the employee's HSA contribution or a percentage of the amount of the employee's HSA contribution (matching contributions), are the contributions subject to the Code Section 4980G comparability rules? **4-99**

Q 4:151 If under the employer's cafeteria plan, employees who are eligible individuals and who participate in health assessments, disease management programs, or wellness programs receive an employer contribution to an HSA and the employees have the right to elect to make pretax salary reduction contributions to their HSAs, are the contributions subject to the comparability rules?. **4-99**

Waiver of Excise Tax

Q 4:152 May all or part of the excise tax imposed under Code Section 4980G be waived? **4-100**

Tax Treatment of Contributions

Q 4:153 What are the main areas to consider relative to taxation of contributions?. **4-101**

IRS Reporting by Individuals

Q 4:154 How are HSA contributions reported to the IRS by the taxpayer?. **4-101**

Q 4:155 Who must file Form 8889—*Health Savings Accounts (HSAs)*?. . . **4-101**

Partnership Considerations

Q 4:156 May a partnership make HSA contributions on behalf of a partner or guaranteed payment partner? **4-102**

Q 4:157   Are contributions by a partnership that are treated as
distributions to the partner under Code Section 731 treated
as a contribution to an HSA?...................... **4-102**

Q 4:158   What is the tax treatment of contributions to an HSA by a
partnership that are considered distributions to the partner
under Code Section 731?...................... **4-102**

Q 4:159   How are contributions by a partnership that are treated as
distributions to the partner under Code Section 731 reported
to the partner?.............................. **4-103**

Q 4:160   Are contributions by a partnership that are treated as
distributions to the partner under Code Section 731
included in a partner's net earnings from self-employment
(NESE)?.................................. **4-103**

Q 4:161   Are contributions by a partnership that are treated as
distributions to the partner under Code Section 731
deductible by the partner?...................... **4-103**

Q 4:162   Are contributions by a partnership that are treated as
guaranteed payments under Code Section 707(c), are
derived from the partnership's trade or business, and are for
services rendered to the partnership treated as contributions
to an HSA?................................ **4-103**

Q 4:163   Are contributions by a partnership that are treated as
guaranteed payments under Code Section 707(c) deductible
by the partnership?.......................... **4-103**

Q 4:164   Are contributions by a partnership that are treated as
guaranteed payments under Code Section 707(c), are
derived from the partnership's trade or business, and are for
services rendered to the partnership included in a partner's
gross income?.............................. **4-104**

Q 4:165   How are contributions by a partnership to a partner's HSA
that are treated as guaranteed payments under Code
Section 707(c) reported by the partnership to the
partner?.................................. **4-104**

Q 4:166   Are contributions by a partnership that are treated as
guaranteed payments under Code Section 707(c), are
derived from the partnership's trade or business, and are for
services rendered to the partnership treated as net earnings
from self-employment?........................ **4-104**

Q 4:167   How are contributions by a partnership that are treated as
guaranteed payments under Code Section 707(c), are
derived from the partnership's trade or business, and are for
services rendered to the partnership included in a partner's
gross income?.............................. **4-104**

S Corporation Considerations

Q 4:168   How is an S corporation treated with respect to contributions
made by the S corporation to the HSA of a 2 percent
shareholder, who is also an employee (2 percent
shareholder-employee) in consideration for services
rendered to the S corporation?.................... **4-106**

Q 4:169   How is a 2 percent shareholder treated with respect to contributions made by the S corporation to the HSA of a 2 percent shareholder, who is also an employee (2 percent shareholder-employee) in consideration of services rendered to the S corporation? **4-106**

Q 4:170   What is the tax treatment of an S corporation's contributions to an HSA of a 2 percent shareholder who is also an employee (2 percent shareholder-employee)? **4-106**

Q 4:171   Are contributions by an S corporation to an HSA of a 2 percent shareholder-employee in consideration for services rendered deductible by the S corporation? **4-106**

Q 4:172   Are contributions by an S corporation to an HSA of a 2 percent shareholder-employee in consideration of services rendered excluded from a 2 percent shareholder-employee's gross income? **4-107**

Q 4:173   Are contributions made by an S corporation to an HSA of a 2 percent shareholder-employee subject to FICA tax? **4-107**

Q 4:174   Is there an exception relative to FICA taxes for a contribution made by an S corporation to an HSA of a 2 percent shareholder-employee? **4-107**

Q 4:175   Are contributions made by an S corporation to an HSA of a 2 percent shareholder-employee subject to SECA taxes? **4-107**

Q 4:176   May a 2 percent shareholder-employee who is an eligible individual deduct the amount of the contributions made to an HSA by his or her employer during the taxable year as an adjustment to gross income on his or her federal income tax? **4-108**

Chapter 5 HSA Rollovers and Transfers

Rollovers and Transfers from IRAs and HSAs

General Rules

Q 5:1   Are rollovers permitted between HSA accounts? **5-2**

Q 5:2   Are rollovers permitted from an Archer MSA to an HSA? **5-2**

Q 5:3   May distributions from an individual retirement account (IRA), a health reimbursement arrangement (HRA), or a health care flexible spending account (FSA) be rolled over into an HSA? **5-2**

Q 5:4   May an individual claim a deduction for the amount rolled over? **5-3**

Q 5:5   Must rollover contributions be made in cash? **5-3**

Q 5:6   Must the same property received in a distribution from an HSA or Archer MSA be rolled over? **5-3**

Q 5:7   Must all of the cash or property received in a distribution from an HSA or Archer MSA be rolled over? **5-3**

Q 5:8   Is an HSA trustee or custodian required to accept rollover
contributions?. **5-3**

Q 5:9   What are the tax consequences with respect to the portion of
an HSA distribution that is not rolled over to an HSA?. **5-4**

Q 5:10   Are rollovers from an Archer MSA or another HSA subject to
the annual contribution limits? **5-4**

Q 5:11   May an HSA holder make a rollover contribution more than
once during a one-year period?. **5-4**

Q 5:12   How is a second rollover from an HSA treated if it is made
before the one-year period has expired? **5-5**

Q 5:13   Does a rollover of a distribution from an Archer MSA into
another Archer MSA affect eligibility to roll over a distribution
from an HSA?. **5-5**

Q 5:14   If an Archer MSA is rolled over into an HSA, when does the
one-year rule pertaining to HSAs apply?. **5-5**

Q 5:15   Must the rollover be completed within 60 days?. **5-6**

Q 5:16   Must the total amount be distributed in order to roll over an
HSA to another HSA?. **5-6**

Q 5:17   Must the same property received in a distribution from an
Archer MSA be rolled over?. **5-6**

Q 5:18   May an HSA trust or custodial agreement restrict the HSA
owner's ability to roll over amounts from that HSA? **5-6**

Q 5:19   How does a taxpayer report a rollover contribution from an
Archer MSA or another HSA? **5-7**

Q 5:20   How are rollover contributions reported by the trustee or
custodian of the distributing HSA on Form 1099-SA?. **5-7**

Q 5:21   When must Form 5498-SA be provided to participants?. **5-7**

Inherited HSAs

Q 5:22   How is an HSA treated when the HSA owner dies? **5-7**

Q 5:23   May an inherited HSA be rolled over? **5-8**

Q 5:24   How is an HSA treated when the surviving spouse is not the
sole designated beneficiary? **5-8**

Q 5:25   How is the value of an HSA reported if the HSA owner's estate
is the beneficiary?. **5-8**

Q 5:26   How are earnings after the date of death treated? **5-8**

Q 5:27   Are earnings after death subject to the additional 10 percent
tax?. **5-8**

HSA Transfers

Q 5:28   Is there a limit on the number of trustee-to-trustee transfers
permitted between HSAs?. **5-8**

Q 5:29   How are trustee-to-trustee transfers between HSAs treated? . . .   **5-9**

Q 5:30   Are HSA trustees or custodians required to accept trustee-to-
trustee transfers? **5-9**

Q 5:31   May the trust or custodial agreement contain restrictions
         concerning transfers from one HSA to another?   5-9
Q 5:32   Must trustee-to-trustee transfers be made in cash?   5-9

Transfer Incident to Divorce

Q 5:33   May an HSA be transferred to a spouse or former spouse? . . .   5-9
Q 5:34   Is a transfer incident to divorce or a separation agreement
         treated as a taxable distribution?   5-9
Q 5:35   What is a divorce or separation instrument?   5-9
Q 5:36   Is a transfer incident to divorce or a separation agreement
         treated as a taxable transfer?   5-10
Q 5:37   How is an HSA treated after a transfer incident to divorce?   5-10
Q 5:38   May a trustee-to-trustee transfer be made to an HSA from an
         IRA, an HRA, or a health care FSA?   5-10

Other Issues

Q 5:39   May the health coverage tax credit be claimed for premiums
         paid with tax-free distributions from an HSA?   5-11

Qualified HSA Funding Distributions (IRA to HSA)

Q 5:40   May an individual rollover or transfer an amount from a
         traditional IRA to an HSA?   5-11
Q 5:41   Do the qualified HSA funding distribution rules apply to a Roth
         IRA?   5-12
Q 5:42   May a qualified funding distribution be made from a SEP IRA or
         SIMPLE IRA?   5-12

Tax Treatment

Q 5:43   Can a deduction be taken for the amount distributed from an
         IRA and transferred to an HSA in a qualified HSA funding
         distribution?   5-12
Q 5:44   To what extent are the amounts transferred in a qualified HSA
         funding distribution not included in the IRA owner's gross
         income?   5-13
Q 5:45   Does a qualified HSA funding distribution count towards the
         maximum annual contribution limit?   5-13
Q 5:46   What happens if the individual does not remain an eligible
         individual during the testing period?   5-13

No Pro-Rata Recovery

Q 5:47   Do the pro-rata recovery rules apply in determining how much
         of the qualified HSA funding distribution would otherwise
         have been includible in income?   5-14

Maximum Lifetime Distribution Rules

Q 5:48   Is there a limit on the amount that can be transferred to an HSA in a qualified HSA funding distribution? **5-15**

Q 5:49   May an individual make more than one qualified HSA funding distribution? **5-15**

Testing Period

Q 5:50   What is the testing period for an IRA transfer to an HSA? **5-16**

Examples of Qualified HSA Funding Distributions

Q 5:51   Must an individual that fails to remain an eligible individual during the testing period have to remove the amount transferred in the qualified HSA funding distribution? **5-21**

Qualified HSA Distributions (One-Time HRA and FSA Transfers to an HSA)

In General

Q 5:52   What is a qualified HSA distribution? **5-21**

Q 5:53   What are the steps an employer and employee must follow to transfer amounts from a health care FSA or HRA to an HSA on a tax-free basis? **5-22**

Q 5:54   May a qualified HSA distribution be made from limited purpose or post-deductible FSA/HRA arrangements? **5-22**

Q 5:55   May a qualified HSA distribution be made from a dependent care FSA? **5-23**

Q 5:56   May an employer unilaterally decide to make a qualified HSA distribution? **5-23**

Q 5:57   Must the option to make a qualified HSA distribution be offered to all employees? **5-23**

Q 5:58   May an individual request more than one qualified HSA distribution? **5-23**

Plan Amendment Required

Q 5:59   Must an employer offer a qualified HSA distribution option? . . . **5-23**

Q 5:60   Must the FSA or HRA contain provisions allowing qualified HSA distributions? **5-24**

Other Rules

Q 5:61   May the opportunity to make a qualified HSA distribution be provided on a one-time basis? **5-24**

Q 5:62   Must an employer with an FSA and an HRA who wishes to allow for qualified HSA distributions do so for both the FSAs and the HRA? **5-24**

Q 5:63 May a qualified HSA distribution be made in property? **5-25**

Treatment of Qualified HSA Distributions

Q 5:64 How are qualified HSA distributions treated? **5-25**

Q 5:65 Is a qualified HSA distribution taken into account for purposes of determining the HSA annual contribution limitation? **5-25**

Q 5:66 May an individual who makes a qualified HSA distribution claim a deduction for the amount transferred to the HSA? **5-25**

Comparability Rule

Q 5:67 Must an employer that allows any employee to make a transfer from an HRA or FSA to an HSA offer the same right to all eligible individuals? **5-25**

Transfer Amount

Q 5:68 Is there a limit to the amount that may be transferred to an HSA in a qualified HSA distribution? **5-26**

Q 5:69 May the September 21, 2006 balance be based on the balance in the FSA or HRA account of a former employer? . . **5-26**

Minimum Transfer Amount

Q 5:70 What is the minimum amount that must be transferred in a qualified HSA distribution? **5-26**

Timing Issues

Q 5:71 Is it possible for an employee to do a tax-free transfer during the year? **5-27**

Q 5:72 Is it possible to make a mid-year transfer from a limited purpose FSA or HRA? Must the transfer result in a zero balance? **5-27**

Testing Period

Q 5:73 What is the testing period for a qualified HSA distribution? **5-27**

Q 5:74 What happens if the individual does not remain an eligible individual during the testing period following a qualified HSA distribution? **5-28**

Q 5:75 Is withdrawal of the transferred amount required if an individual fails to remain an eligible individual during the testing period? **5-28**

Q 5:76 Is an employer responsible for reporting whether an employee who makes an FSA or HRA transfer remains an eligible individual during the testing period? **5-29**

Access to Funds

Q 5:77   Does an employee have immediate ability to access the HSA funds that are transferred in a qualified HSA distribution? . . .   **5-29**

Disregarded FSA Coverage

Q 5:78   Is there an exception to the zero balance requirement following a qualified HSA distribution? **5-29**

Q 5:79   What were the steps an employer had to take under the transitional relief that applied before March 15, 2007? **5-30**

Permanent Rule Under I.R.S. Notice 2007-22 (after March 15, 2007)

Q 5:80   Must an employer adopt a grace period extension and must the qualified HSA distribution result in a zero balance? **5-33**

Q 5:81   Must the participant have a zero balance after a qualified HSA distribution is made? **5-33**

Q 5:82   Is a participant with a zero balance treated as having coverage during the grace period? **5-33**

Q 5:83   What happens if the steps identified in I.R.S. Notice 2007-22 are not followed? **5-33**

Q 5:84   What must an employer do under the permanent rule of I.R.S. Notice 2007-22 to allow qualified HSA distributions? **5-34**

HRA/FSA-Compatible Coverage Rules

Q 5:85   May an employer convert a general purpose HRA or FSA to an HSA-compatible arrangement only for HSA-eligible individuals who elect to make qualified HSA distributions? . . .   **5-40**

Q 5:86   May an employer convert a general purpose HRA or FSA to an HSA-compatible arrangement? **5-41**

Treatment of Qualified HSA Distributions

Q 5:87   Are qualified HSA distributions taken into account in computing the maximum HSA contribution limit? **5-41**

Q 5:88   May a participant deduct qualified HSA distributions on their federal income tax return? **5-41**

Reporting FSA/HRA Transfers

Q 5:89   How does an employer report a qualifying HSA distribution to the trustee or custodian of the HSA? **5-41**

Q 5:90   Does an employer report a qualifying HSA distribution to the participant? **5-42**

Chapter 6 Distributions

Taxation of HSA Distributions

Q 6:1 When is an individual permitted to receive distributions from an HSA? **6-2**

Q 6:2 May an employer request a distribution from an employee's HSA? **6-2**

Q 6:3 If an employer contributes to the account of an employee who was never an eligible individual, can the employer recoup the amounts? **6-3**

Q 6:4 May an employer recover amounts contributed in excess of the maximum annual contribution limit? **6-3**

Q 6:5 If an employer contributes to the HSA of an employee who ceases to be an eligible individual during a year, can the employer recoup amounts that the employer contributed after the employee ceased to be an eligible individual? **6-4**

Q 6:6 May an HSA be administered through a debit card that restricts payments and reimbursements to health care? **6-4**

Q 6:7 Must HSA distributions commence when the HSA owner attains a specified age? **6-4**

Q 6:8 May an HSA owner authorize someone else to withdraw funds from his or her HSA? **6-5**

Q 6:9 How are distributions from an HSA taxed? **6-5**

Q 6:10 May an HSA owner claim an investment loss if his or her HSA declines in value? **6-6**

Q 6:11 Can tax-free distributions be received by an individual who is not an HSA eligible individual (e.g., an individual who does not have HDHP coverage)? **6-6**

Responsibility

Q 6:12 Is the trustee responsible for determining whether HSA distributions are used exclusively for qualified medical expenses? **6-6**

Q 6:13 Who is responsible for determining whether HSA distributions are used exclusively for qualified medical expenses? **6-7**

Restrictions on Distributions

Q 6:14 May a trustee or custodian place reasonable restrictions on withdrawals from an HSA? **6-7**

Q 6:15 May an HSA trust or custodial agreement restrict HSA distributions to pay or reimburse only the HSA owner's qualified medical expenses? **6-7**

Q 6:16 Must distributions from an HSA that are not used exclusively for qualified medical expenses be included in the HSA owner's gross income? **6-8**

Q 6:17   How are distributions from an HSA that are not used exclusively for qualified medical expenses reported by the HSA owner to the IRS? **6-8**

Q 6:18   How are distributions from an HSA that are subject to the 10 percent additional tax reported to the IRS by the HSA owner? **6-8**

Q 6:19   Are amounts distributed to an individual not currently eligible to make contributions excluded from gross income if used exclusively for qualified medical expenses? **6-8**

Q 6:20   Will tax-free treatment apply to a distribution made directly from the HSA to a third party if the distribution is used exclusively to pay for qualified medical expenses incurred by the HSA owner, spouse, or dependent? **6-9**

Q 6:21   May qualified medical expenses incurred before establishment of an HSA be reimbursed from an HSA? **6-9**

Q 6:22   Why was transitional relief provided in 2004? **6-9**

Q 6:23   Are distributions from an HSA for expenses that were already reimbursed by another health plan excludable from gross income? **6-10**

Q 6:24   In cases where both spouses have an HSA and one spouse (i.e., the HSA owner) uses distributions from his or her HSA to pay or reimburse the qualified medical expenses of the other spouse, are the distributions excluded from the HSA owner's gross income? **6-10**

Q 6:25   What is the time limit for taking a distribution from an HSA to pay for a qualified medical expense incurred during the current year? **6-10**

Q 6:26   Do the Code Section 105(h) discrimination rules, which apply to self-insured plans, apply to a distribution from an HSA? **6-11**

Medical Care Paid from an HSA

Q 6:27   Who must incur the expense in order to qualify for tax-free distributions from the HSA? **6-11**

Q 6:28   What are qualified medical expenses for purposes of an HSA under Code Section 223? **6-11**

Q 6:29   What types of expenses are deductible under Code Section 213(a) as medical expenses? **6-12**

Q 6:30   Are HSA distributions coordinated with the medical expense deduction? **6-12**

Q 6:31   May a payment or distribution from an HSA for a qualified medical expense also be deducted as an expense for medical care under Code Section 213(a)? **6-12**

Q 6:32   What requirements must medical care expenses satisfy to be deductible? **6-12**

Q 6:33   Are Medicare Part D premiums qualified medical expenses? . . . **6-14**

Q 6:34 Are premiums for continuation coverage required under federal law for the spouse or dependent of an HSA owner qualified medical expenses? **6-14**

Q 6:35 Are premiums for health coverage for a spouse or dependent during a period when the spouse or dependent is receiving unemployment compensation under any federal or state law qualified medical expenses? **6-14**

Q 6:36 Do qualified medical expenses for HSA purposes include the Code Section 213(d) medical expenses incurred by an HSA owner's child who is claimed as a dependent by the HSA owner's former spouse? **6-14**

Q 6:37 Are transportation expenses related to medical care deductible?.. **6-15**

Q 6:38 Are lodging expenses related to medical care deductible? **6-15**

Q 6:39 Are meal expenses related to medical care deductible? **6-15**

Q 6:40 Is cosmetic surgery deductible? **6-17**

Q 6:41 Are expenses for nonprescription drugs qualified medical expenses for purposes of an HSA? **6-17**

Q 6:42 Are health insurance premiums qualified medical expenses for purposes of an HSA? **6-17**

Q 6:43 Are Medicare premiums that are deducted from a retiree Medicare beneficiary's Social Security benefits considered qualified medical expenses for purposes of an HSA? **6-18**

Q 6:44 Can medical expenses paid or reimbursed by distributions from an HSA be treated as expenses paid for medical care for purposes of taking an itemized deduction under Code Section 213(a)?................................... **6-18**

Q 6:45 What are Medigap policies? **6-18**

Q 6:46 Are premiums for Medigap policies treated as qualified medical expenses? **6-18**

Q 6:47 Can accident or disability insurance premiums be paid out of an HSA?.. **6-18**

Q 6:48 Are distributions from an HSA for long-term care services considered qualified medical expenses that are excluded from the HSA owner's income? **6-19**

Q 6:49 May a retiree who is age 65 or older receive tax-free distributions from an HSA to pay the retiree's contributions to an employer's self-insured retiree health coverage? **6-19**

Q 6:50 May an individual who is under age 65 and has end stage renal disease or is disabled receive tax-free distributions from an HSA to pay for health insurance premiums? **6-20**

Q 6:51 Are amounts paid by an individual for equipment, supplies, and diagnostic devices that may be purchased without a prescription from a physician qualified medical expenses for purposes of an HSA? **6-20**

Medicine and Drugs

Q 6:52 What does the term *medicine and drugs* include? **6-20**

Q 6:53 Can an HSA reimburse the cost of prescription drugs imported
from Canada (or other countries)? **6-21**

Q 6:54 Are amounts paid by an individual for medicines that may be
purchased without a prescription of a physician qualified
medical expenses for purposes of an HSA? **6-21**

Q 6:55 What is meant by the term *prescribed drug*? **6-22**

Distributions Used for Long-Term Care Insurance Premiums

Q 6:56 May an HSA owner pay qualified long-term care insurance
premiums with a tax-free distribution from an HSA? **6-22**

Q 6:57 May an HSA owner pay qualified long-term care insurance
premiums with tax-free distributions from an HSA if
contributions to the HSA are made by salary reduction
through a Code Section 125 cafeteria plan? **6-22**

Q 6:58 Are tax-free distributions from an HSA for long-term care
insurance premiums limited in amount? **6-22**

Deemed Distributions Due to Prohibited Transactions

Q 6:59 Are account beneficiaries prohibited from engaging in any
transactions involving an HSA? **6-23**

Q 6:60 What are the results if an individual engages in a prohibited
transaction? **6-24**

Q 6:61 May an HSA owner pledge his or her HSA as security for a
loan? **6-24**

Q 6:62 Is an HSA subject to the prohibited transaction provisions of
the Code? **6-24**

Q 6:63 What is a prohibited transaction? **6-25**

Q 6:64 What are the consequences if an HSA owner or other
disqualified persons enter into a prohibited transaction with
an HSA? **6-26**

Personalized Investment Advice

Q 6:65 Is the provision of investment advice through an "eligible
investment advice arrangement" a prohibited transaction? . . .   **6-27**

Q 6:66 What is an "eligible investment advice arrangement?" **6-29**

Transactions with Service Providers

Other Prohibited Transaction Exemptions

Q 6:67 What is the prohibited transaction penalty tax rate? **6-36**

Q 6:68 May the prohibited transaction rules be waived? **6-37**

Q 6:69   What is meant by a disqualified person under the Code and by a party in interest under ERISA?. **6-37**

Q 6:70   What is meant by the term *fiduciary* for purposes of ERISA?. . .   **6-38**

Q 6:71   May an insurer offer a cash incentive to establish an HSA and an HDHP without violating the prohibited transaction rules?. **6-39**

The 10 Percent Additional Tax

Q 6:72   When is a distribution from an HSA subject to the 10 percent additional tax under Code Section 223(f)(4)?. **6-40**

Q 6:73   May a distribution that does not violate the contribution limit be treated as a distribution of an excess amount?. **6-41**

Q 6:74   What are the exceptions to the 10 percent additional tax on distributions not used exclusively to pay or reimburse qualified medical expenses of the HSA owner, his or her spouse, or a dependent? **6-41**

Q 6:75   When is an individual disabled?. **6-42**

Q 6:76   What is a substantial gainful activity for purposes of the disability exception? **6-43**

Q 6:77   What is an indefinite duration for purposes of the disability exception? **6-44**

Returning Distributions Mistakenly Made

Q 6:78   May a distribution made erroneously be redeposited into an HSA?. **6-44**

Q 6:79   What is reasonable cause that would permit a mistake-of-fact distribution from an HSA to be redeposited into an HSA? . . .   **6-44**

Q 6:80   Are trustees and custodians required to accept the return of mistaken distributions? **6-44**

Q 6:81   What is the tax treatment of a mistake-of-fact HSA distribution that is properly and timely repaid into an HSA?. **6-45**

Death Distributions to Designated Beneficiaries

Q 6:82   What happens to an HSA upon the death of the HSA owner? .   **6-45**

Q 6:83   What are the federal income tax consequences of the HSA owner's death?. **6-45**

Q 6:84   Is a surviving spouse who assumes ownership of an HSA upon the death of his or her spouse (and former HSA owner) subject to income tax upon transfer of the HSA? **6-46**

Q 6:85   How is an HSA treated for federal estate tax purposes?. **6-46**

Q 6:86   How is an HSA treated for federal gift tax purposes? **6-46**

Income Tax Withholding on HSA Distributions

Q 6:87   Is a distribution from an HSA subject to federal income tax withholding?. **6-47**

Q 6:88   Are payers required to withhold income taxes on distributions
             that are not used for qualified medical expenses?. **6-47**

Chapter 7 Administration and Compliance

HSA Documents

Q 7:1   Must an HSA be offered in the form of a trust?. **7-2**

Q 7:2   What is the difference between an HSA trustee and an HSA
             custodian? **7-2**

Q 7:3   Does federal or state law determine whether an arrangement is
             a trust or custodial account? **7-2**

Q 7:4   Has the IRS issued any documents that an individual may use
             to establish an HSA?. **7-2**

Q 7:5   Should Model Form 5305-B or Model Form 5305-C be filed
             with the IRS? **7-3**

Q 7:6   May a sponsor of a Model Form 5305-B or Model Form
             5305-C add provisions to the model forms?. **7-3**

Q 7:7   What type of additional provisions can be added to Model
             Form 5305-B and Model Form 5305-C? **7-3**

Q 7:8   What happens if the additional provisions are inconsistent with
             Code Section 223 or published IRS guidance?. **7-4**

Q 7:9   When are the model forms deemed established?. **7-4**

Q 7:10   Must the HSA be created in the United States? **7-4**

Q 7:11   What is the HSA owner's "identifying number" for use in
             establishing an HSA using Model Form 5305-B or Model
             Form 5305-C? **7-4**

Q 7:12   What documents should an HSA trustee or custodian provide
             to the HSA owner when an HSA is established? **7-4**

Q 7:13   May a plan sponsor design an IRS-approved prototype
             HSA?. **7-5**

Permissible Investments

Q 7:14   How may HSA funds be invested? **7-5**

Q 7:15   May an HSA trust or custodial agreement restrict investments
             to certain types of permissible investments?. **7-5**

Q 7:16   May HSA funds be commingled in a common trust fund or
             common investment fund? **7-5**

Q 7:17   Are HSA trustees and custodians also subject to the rules
             against prohibited transactions? **7-6**

Account Fees

Q 7:18   If HSA administration and account maintenance fees are
             withdrawn from the HSA, are the withdrawn amounts
             treated as taxable distributions to the HSA owner?. **7-6**

Q 7:19 How do HSA trustees report amounts withdrawn from the HSA to pay for HSA administration and account maintenance fees? **7-6**

Q 7:20 If HSA administration and account maintenance fees are withdrawn from the HSA, does the withdrawn amount increase the maximum annual HSA contribution limit?. **7-6**

Q 7:21 If HSA administration and account maintenance fees are paid by the HSA owner or employer directly to the HSA trustee or HSA custodian, do these payments count toward the annual maximum contribution limit for the HSA? **7-6**

Trustees and Custodians

Q 7:22 Is any insurance company a qualified HSA trustee or HSA custodian? **7-7**

Q 7:23 Can an individual qualify to be an HSA trustee or custodian? **7-7**

Q 7:24 Is there a limit on the annual HSA contribution which the HSA trustee or custodian may accept? **7-7**

Q 7:25 May an HSA trustee or custodian accept contributions of property? **7-7**

Q 7:26 Who is responsible for determining whether contributions to an HSA exceed the maximum annual contribution limit for a particular HSA owner? **7-7**

Q 7:27 Who is responsible for notifying the HSA trustee or custodian of any excess contribution and requesting a withdrawal of the excess contribution? **7-8**

Q 7:28 Is the HSA trustee or custodian responsible for accepting cash contributions?. **7-8**

Q 7:29 Is the HSA trustee or custodian responsible for filing required information returns with the IRS? **7-8**

Q 7:30 Is the HSA trustee or custodian responsible for tracking the HSA owner's age? **7-8**

Q 7:31 Must the HSA trustee or custodian allow account beneficiaries to return mistaken distributions to the HSA?. **7-8**

Q 7:32 May an HSA trust or custodial agreement restrict the HSA owner's ability to roll over amounts from that HSA? **7-9**

Q 7:33 Are HSA trustees or custodians required to accept rollover contributions or trustee-to-trustee transfers? **7-9**

Q 7:34 May an HSA trust or custodial agreement restrict HSA distributions to pay or reimburse only the HSA owner's qualified medical expenses? **7-9**

Q 7:35 May an HSA trustee or custodian restrict the frequency or minimum amount of distributions from an HSA? **7-9**

Q 7:36 May an HSA trustee or custodian that does not sponsor the HDHP require proof or certification that the HSA owner is an eligible individual? **7-9**

Q 7:37   May an HSA trustee or custodian that does not sponsor the HDHP require proof or certification that the HSA owner is covered by an HDHP?. **7-10**

Reports

Q 7:38   What reports may the IRS require in connection with an HSA?. **7-10**

Q 7:39   When must reports regarding HSA accounts be provided?. . . .   **7-10**

Q 7:40   What is the penalty if an HSA trustee, custodian, or employer fails to file a required report with the IRS?. **7-10**

Form Filing Requirements

Q 7:41   Is an employer required to provide participants in an HSA or an HDHP with an SPD?. **7-10**

Reporting HSA Contributions on Form 5498-SA

Q 7:42   What is the purpose of Form 5498-SA—HSA, Archer MSA, or Medicare Advantage MSA Information? **7-11**

Q 7:43   For whom is Form 5498-SA required to be filed? **7-11**

Q 7:44   Is Form 5498-SA required if no contributions were made and there was a total distribution made from the HSA? **7-12**

Q 7:45   When must Form 5498-SA be filed with the IRS?. **7-12**

Q 7:46   When must Form 5498-SA be provided to the recipient? **7-12**

Q 7:47   Must Form 5498-SA be filed if the owner of an HSA dies? **7-12**

Q 7:48   How are the boxes on Form 5498-SA completed for an HSA?. **7-12**

Reporting HSA Distributions on Form 1099-SA

Q 7:49   What is the purpose of Form 1099-SA?. **7-13**

Q 7:50   In what year are distributions from an HSA required to be reported? **7-14**

Q 7:51   Must Form 1099-SA be provided to the HSA owner and/or account beneficiaries?. **7-14**

Q 7:52   When is Form 1099-SA required to be provided to the recipient? **7-14**

Q 7:53   When is Form 1099-SA required to be filed with the IRS?. **7-14**

Q 7:54   What is a substitute statement for Form 1099-SA? **7-14**

Q 7:55   How are transfers between trustees and/or custodians treated for purposes of Form 1099-SA? **7-15**

Q 7:56   How is Form 1099-SA completed for an HSA? **7-15**

Form 5329: Reporting Additional Taxes on Excess HSA Contributions

Q 7:57   What is the purpose of Form 5329? **7-17**

Q 7:58   Under what circumstances must Form 5329 be filed with respect to an HSA?.................................. **7-17**

Q 7:59   If applicable, can a married couple who are filing a joint tax return file one Form 5329?.......................... **7-17**

Q 7:60   When must Form 5329 be filed?........................ **7-17**

Q 7:61   How is Part VII of Form 5329 completed for an HSA? **7-18**

Reporting Excise Tax on Prohibited Transactions

Q 7:62   What is the purpose of Form 5330? **7-19**

Q 7:63   When must Form 5330 be filed?....................... **7-19**

Q 7:64   How is Form 5330 completed when a disqualified person participates in a prohibited transaction involving an HSA? ... **7-19**

Form 8889: Health Savings Accounts (HSAs)

Q 7:65   What is the purpose of Form 8889? **7-20**

Q 7:66   Who must file Form 8889? **7-20**

Q 7:67   How is Form 8889 completed upon the death of the owner?... **7-20**

Q 7:68   How are contributions, excess contributions, and deductions reported on Form 8889?........................... **7-21**

Reporting Deemed Distributions

Q 7:69   How are deemed distributions from an HSA reported on Form 8889? **7-26**

Q 7:70   How is Form 8889 completed if a distribution is made from the account? **7-26**

Q 7:71   How is Form 8889 completed if HDHP coverage is not maintained during the testing period?................. **7-27**

Reporting Employer Contributions on Form W-2

Q 7:72   How is Form W-2, Wage and Tax Statement, completed if an employer makes contributions to an HSA?............. **7-28**

Q 7:73   How should pretax contributions made to an HSA through an employer's cafeteria plan be reported?................ **7-28**

Q 7:74   How does an employer report contributions on Form W-2 that are recouped because the employee was never an eligible individual or that exceeded the maximum annual contributions limit? **7-28**

Q 7:75   How are employer contributions to the HSA of an employee's spouse (who is not an employee of this employer) treated? **7-29**

Chapter 8 Federal and State Laws Affecting HSAs

ERISA

Q 8:1 What guidance did the DOL issue regarding HSAs and ERISA?... 8-1

Q 8:2 What conditions must be satisfied in order for an HSA to be exempt from ERISA?................................ 8-2

Q 8:3 How does the guidance issued in FAB 2006-02 differ from earlier DOL guidance with respect to other arrangements?..................................... 8-2

Q 8:4 What are the safe harbor rules that apply to determine whether Title I coverage under ERISA applies to a group or group-type insurance program offered to employees by an employer?..................................... 8-3

Q 8:5 What weight would a court give to a FAB?............... 8-4

Q 8:6 What types of employer actions would not be viewed by the DOL as "representing that an HSA is an employee welfare plan established and maintained by the employer?"....... 8-4

Q 8:7 Is FAB 2004-01 more flexible than the group insurance safe harbor with respect to "endorsement?"................ 8-5

Q 8:8 If an employer offering an HSA to employees asks the HSA provider for specific investment options, will the HSA be subject to ERISA?................................. 8-7

Q 8:9 May an employer select an HSA provider that also offers some or all of its investment options made available to employees in the employer-sponsored 401(k) plan?............... 8-7

Q 8:10 Can an employer select a single HSA trustee that offers a limited range of investment options to provide HSA services to its employees without violating the FAB prohibition against making or selecting investment options?............... 8-7

Q 8:11 May an employer encourage participation in the HSA program?..................................... 8-8

Q 8:12 May an employer that makes an HSA program available to employees pay the fees imposed by the HSA provider without causing the HSA to be subject to ERISA, or without generating adverse tax consequences for employees?..... 8-8

Q 8:13 If an employer makes arrangements with an HSA trustee to offer an HSA with a debit card to employees, can the employer specify that the debit card be used only for medical expenses without violating the FAB prohibition against imposing conditions on the use of HSA funds?..... 8-9

Q 8:14 May an HSA owner direct the payment of HSA funds to a credit line vendor to reimburse the vendor for HSA expenses paid with a credit card?........................... 8-10

Q 8:15   If an employer is in the business of providing HSAs, can it offer HSAs to its employees on the same terms as offered to the public without causing the HSA to be subject to ERISA?.... **8-10**

Q 8:16   Can an employer offer the HDHP and HSA as a single option without making the HSA subject to ERISA? **8-10**

Q 8:17   Can an employer limit an employee's HSA contributions without causing the HSA to be subject to ERISA?......... **8-10**

Q 8:18   What are the consequences if an HSA is not subject to ERISA?.. **8-11**

Q 8:19   What are the employer's legal obligations and consequences if the HSA is subject to ERISA? **8-11**

Q 8:20   If an HSA is subject to ERISA, would an employer be required to distribute a COBRA General Notice? **8-11**

Q 8:21   If an HSA is subject to ERISA, is an employer required to distribute a HIPAA certificate of creditable coverage and comply with the HIPAA nondiscrimination rules?.......... **8-12**

Q 8:22   If an HSA is subject to ERISA, is an employer required to comply with the DOL claims procedure rules that apply to group health plans? **8-13**

Q 8:23   If an HSA is subject to ERISA, could its funds be held in a custodial account rather than a trust? **8-14**

Q 8:24   If an HSA is subject to ERISA, what fiduciary standards would apply to the HSA trustee or custodian? **8-14**

Q 8:25   Does an entity incur additional risk and responsibilities as an HSA trustee as compared to an HSA custodian? **8-15**

Q 8:26   Is it possible to designate one entity as the trustee of an HSA and another entity as the custodian of an HSA? **8-15**

Q 8:27   What are the potential consequences when a fiduciary violates ERISA?.. **8-16**

Q 8:28   If an HSA is not subject to ERISA, what fiduciary standards would apply to the HSA trustee or custodian? **8-16**

Q 8:29   Has the DOL issued any guidance regarding incentive payments made into an HSA other than FAB 2004-01 relating to HSAs?.................................... **8-17**

Q 8:30   Do the prohibited transaction rules under Code Section 4975 apply if an HSA is not subject to ERISA? **8-17**

HIPAA Privacy

Q 8:31   Is an HSA subject to the HIPAA privacy regulations? **8-18**

Q 8:32   Would the HIPAA Electronic Standards Regulations apply to HSAs?.................................... **8-18**

Medicare Part D

Q 8:33   Is an HSA a plan for which an employer must issue a certificate of creditable coverage for purposes of Medicare Part D? ... **8-19**

Q 8:34   Is an HSA a plan for which an employer may apply for the
              employer subsidy under Medicare Part D? **8-20**

State Benefit Mandates

Q 8:35   What state laws could affect the HDHP that accompanies the
              HSA? **8-20**

Q 8:36   What transition relief has the IRS issued with respect to
              HDHPs that are subject to state mandates? **8-21**

Q 8:37   Can an employer make the same HDHP/HSA available to its
              employees in Hawaii as is available in other states? **8-21**

State Tax Consequences

Q 8:38   If an HSA satisfies applicable federal requirements, will a
              participant have the same favorable tax consequences
              under state law as under federal law? **8-22**

Q 8:39   Is it possible to have an HDHP in New Jersey that satisfies
              federal requirements? **8-22**

Q 8:40   Is it possible to have an HDHP in Wisconsin that satisfies
              federal requirements? **8-23**

Q 8:41   What impact did California's Assembly Bill 115 have on
              HSAs? **8-23**

Q 8:42   Does Alabama conform to Code Section 223? **8-24**

Q 8:43   What impact did the Health Savings Account Act in
              Pennsylvania have on HSAs? **8-24**

Davis-Bacon Act

Q 8:44   Do employer contributions to an HSA count as fringe benefits
              under the Davis-Bacon Act? **8-24**

USA Patriot Act

Q 8:45   Do the Customer Identification Procedures of the USA Patriot
              Act apply to HSAs for which a bank is trustee or
              custodian? **8-25**

Securities Law

Q 8:46   Is an HSA subject to regulation by the Securities and
              Exchange Commission? **8-26**

Q 8:47   Under what circumstances would an HSA be considered a
              security for purposes of the federal securities laws? **8-26**

Q 8:48   Is guidance relating to IRAs relevant for purposes of
              determining whether an HSA is a security? **8-26**

Q 8:49   What is the SEC's position regarding IRAs? **8-26**

Use of Electronic Media

Q 8:50   To what extent can an employer use electronic technologies
          for providing employee benefit notices and transmitting
          employee benefit elections and consents? **8-27**

Creditor Protection

Q 8:51   Are HSAs subject to the claims of creditors? **8-27**

Chapter 1

Overview of HSAs

The steadily rising cost of health care and premiums for health coverage in the United States presents an economic challenge for many individuals; some struggle to maintain coverage, while others remain uninsured. In addition, employers of all sizes that have traditionally provided health benefits for their workforces have become concerned about their ability to continue to offer such coverage on an affordable basis. This was the climate when, in December 2003, Congress created, as part of the Medicare Prescription Drug, Improvement, and Modernization Act of 2003 (2003 MMA), a new type of tax-favored savings vehicle for health expenses known as a health savings account (HSA). Three years later, after HSAs had gained some popularity, significant improvements were made. On December 20, 2006, President Bush signed into law the Tax Relief and Health Care Act of 2006 (Pub. L. No. 109-432) (TRHCA), which included several significant HSA provisions, such as increases to the HSA contribution limits and administrative simplifications. It is too early to tell how the Obama Administration or the 111th Congress will impact the growth of HSAs. Chapter 1 provides information about the history of HSAs, including their establishment and improvements by Congress and their regulation by government agencies, and explores the pros and cons of HSA arrangements from the perspectives of individuals and employers. Legislative proposals are also discussed in this chapter.

Introduction 1-2
HSA/HDHP Providers 1-3
Other Defined Contribution Health Care Arrangements 1-4
Regulation 1-5
Advantages and Disadvantages 1-6
Future of HSAs 1-11

Introduction

Q 1:1   What is a health savings account?

A health savings account (HSA), described in Section 223 of the Internal Revenue Code (Code), is a funded account, similar to an individual retirement arrangement (IRA). Contributions may be made within specified limits by individuals who meet certain eligibility requirements and/or by employers or others on behalf of such individuals. Amounts in an HSA grow on a tax-deferred basis and, if used for qualified medical expenses, may be distributed on a tax-free basis. In order to contribute to an HSA, an individual must be covered under a high deductible health plan (HDHP) and may not also participate in a non-HDHP, subject to certain exceptions.

Q 1:2   Is the HSA an entirely new creation by Congress?

No. The HSA is based upon and similar to the Archer Medical Savings Account (MSA) (see Q 2:5), which became available for use by self-employed individuals and employees of small employers (i.e., employers with 50 or fewer employees) in 1996. MSAs have not enjoyed widespread use, however, due in large part to a restriction that prohibits employers with more than 50 employees from making the account available to employees. When MSA legislation was passed, Congress placed a cap on the number of individuals (generally 750,000 taxpayers) who could have an MSA. That number was never reached. [I.R.S. Ann. 2007-44, 2007-19 I.R.B. 1238] In addition, MSAs were intended to be temporary and were due to expire in 2000, but since 2000 Congress extended the deadline four times. [Tax Relief and Health Care Act of 2006 (Pub. L. No. 109-432) § 117(a)-(c); I.R.C. §§ 220(i), 220(j)] No legislation, however, has been introduced to extend MSAs beyond 2008 and Congressional leaders have indicated their intent not to extend the MSA provisions.

Two substantive differences between MSAs and HSAs relate to the deductible under the HDHP and the funding of the account, as delineated below:

1. With respect to the deductible, there is a required upper limit on the deductible for MSAs under the HDHP, but for HSAs there is only a lower limit.

2. With respect to funding, MSAs are not permitted to be funded by both an employer and an employee during the same plan year, or with pretax salary reductions through an employer's cafeteria plan. HSAs may be funded by both the employer and the employee during the same plan year, as well as by any other individual on behalf of the employee. HSAs may also be funded through an employer's cafeteria plan on a pretax basis.

Q 1:3   What factors contributed to the enactment of the HSA legislation?

In the years immediately preceding the enactment of the 2003 MMA HSA legislation, *consumer-driven*, or *defined contribution*, health plans emerged. Through these plans, employers offered employees a defined amount of health care dollars to be spent or saved for future use, at the employees' discretion. Proponents of these alternative arrangements note that they can make costs more predictable and provide incentives to employees to make wiser health care spending decisions. HSAs are consistent with the consumer-driven philosophy. In addition, amounts in the HSA account may be used for medical purposes on a tax-advantaged basis as well as for nonmedical purposes (subject to income tax and 10 percent additional tax). With the exception of MSAs, existing vehicles for providing such coverage on a tax-advantaged basis do not allow that flexibility. Finally, because HSAs are based on MSAs, which had already been enacted, there was precedent for the approach.

Q 1:4   Why do proponents of HSAs consider HSAs to be an improvement over the current health insurance system?

In order to participate in an HSA, an individual must be covered by an HDHP. HSA proponents say that participants can save money by participating in an HDHP, which generally has lower premiums than a non-HDHP. In addition, HSA proponents say that if participants are given a choice to either save money in an HSA account, which can earn interest tax-free, or spend it on medical goods and services, they will confine their spending to necessary purchases and will demand lower prices and/or better value for their dollar. In contrast, the full cost of a service under traditional health plans is not as obvious to a participant because he or she typically is responsible only for the co-payment. Thus, HSA proponents argue that HSAs will re-introduce market forces to the health care system, as well as allow savings to accumulate on a tax-free basis to pay for future health care expenses.

HSA/HDHP Providers

Q 1:5   Did companies offer HSAs with accompanying HDHPs on January 1, 2004, the date the law became effective?

HSAs with *individual* HDHPs were offered effective January 1, 2004, by a few companies, many of whom had previously offered MSAs. HSAs with *group* HDHPs were not widely available on January 1, 2004, primarily because most existing HDHPs offered on the group market had to be modified to comply with the requirements under the Medicare Prescription Drug Improvement and Modernization Act of 2003 [Pub. L. No. 108-173], creating Code Section 223 (see Q 8:4). For example, many HDHPs offered on the group market were structured to provide prescription drug coverage before the deductible was satisfied. Once these products were modified, many group health insurers offered HSAs and

HDHPs that satisfied the requirements under the 2003 MMA HSA legislation effective January 1, 2005.

> **Note.** Under the Centers for Medicare & Medicaid Services (CMS) final regulations [42 C.F.R. § 423.56], all group health plan sponsors that offer prescription drug coverage are required to provide a notice to all Medicare-eligible participants that states whether prescription drug coverage under its plan is "creditable" when compared to the prescription drug coverage under Medicare Part D.

Q 1:6   Do some companies offer their services as HSA trustees or custodians only, without offering an accompanying HDHP?

Yes. There are companies that offer services as HSA trustees or custodians only. The number of HSA trustees/custodians has been growing steadily since the 2003 MMA HSA legislation passed (see Q 1:3). In order to be an HSA trustee, a company must be a bank, an insurance company, or a nonbank trustee (see Qs 2:1, 7:22). Each year the IRS publishes a list of companies that are approved as nonbank trustees. [I.R.S. Ann. 2007-20, 2007-20 I.R.B. 1260]

HSAs are expected to continue to attract banks and financial institutions to sponsor the accounts and manage the assets in them, particularly because of the increased contribution limits under TRHCA. The aggregate amounts held and invested in HSAs are expected to grow steadily each year. In addition, HSA sponsors can charge set-up fees, maintenance charges, and service fees. These factors may make the HSA as lucrative for these institutions as IRAs, which gained popularity in the mid-70s. [See "Health Savings Accounts Attract Wall Street," by Eric Dash, The New York Times (Jan. 27, 2006)]

Other Defined Contribution Health Care Arrangements

Q 1:7   In addition to HSAs, what types of health accounts are considered defined contribution or consumer-driven arrangements?

Health Reimbursement Arrangements (HRAs), Health Flexible Spending Arrangements (FSAs), and Archer MSAs are considered defined contribution or consumer-driven arrangements because they all allow employees to decide how the dollars credited or deposited to the account are spent. [I.R.S. Notice 2002-45, 2002-2 C.B. 93; Rev. Rul. 2002-41; I.R.C. §§ 106(c), 220; Prop. Treas. Reg. § 1.125-2, Q&A 7]

Q 1:8   What are the main differences among an HSA, an HRA, and a health FSA?

All three vehicles share a common purpose of making dollars available on a tax-advantaged basis for reimbursement of medical expenses. However, there are differences in the way these accounts are required to be structured under federal law. Main differences among an HSA, HRA, and FSA include the following:

1. An HSA is the only arrangement of the three that must be funded through a custodial account or trust and accompanied by an HDHP (see Q 8:23). An HSA also is the only arrangement of the three for which amounts in the HSA account may be used for nonmedical purposes, although such expenditure requires inclusion for income tax purposes and may result in a 10 percent additional tax.

2. An FSA is the only arrangement of the three in which amounts that are unused at the end of the plan year must be forfeited (subject to the two-month extension under Notice 2005-4; see Q 4:22, "Caution").

3. An HRA is the only arrangement of the three that must be paid for solely by the employer; and salary reduction contributions are prohibited.

(See appendix G for a detailed comparison of HRAs, FSAs, and HSAs.)

Regulation

Q 1:9   Which federal government agencies regulate HSAs?

HSAs are governed by Code Section 223 and are therefore regulated by the Internal Revenue Service (IRS). An HSA is also subject to prohibited transaction rules under Code Section 4975 that are regulated by the Department of Labor (DOL). (Under Reorganization Plan Number 4 of 1978, 43 Federal Register 47,713 (Oct. 17, 1978), the authority of the Secretary of the Treasury to issue rulings under Code Section 4975 has been transferred, with certain exceptions, to the Secretary of Labor.) The DOL also regulates whether a particular HSA is subject to ERISA (see Qs 8:1–8:8). Finally, to the extent that an HSA invests in securities, or is considered a security itself, the Securities and Exchange Commission (SEC) will regulate (see Q 8:46).

Q 1:10   Are states permitted to regulate HSAs?

Yes. A state may regulate an HSA for state income tax purposes (see Q 8:38), and, to the extent that the HSA is not considered an ERISA plan, state trust law will apply to the HSA (see Q 8:28). In addition, states may regulate insured HDHPs that accompany the HSAs (see Q 8:35). ERISA preemption generally precludes a state from regulating a self-funded health plan.

Q 1:11   Which federal government agencies have issued guidance on HSAs?

The IRS has issued a significant amount of guidance in the relatively short period of time since the enactment of HSAs by the 2003 MMA. Most of this guidance is in the form of revenue rulings and notices, with questions and answers, and some guidance provides transitional relief. In addition, the IRS has issued final regulations on the comparable contribution requirements under Code Section 4980G that apply to HSAs (see Qs 4:114–4:151). [Treas. Reg. § 54.4980G-1–5] The final regulations apply only to employers who make contributions to employee HSAs outside of a cafeteria plan, and generally require that an employer make similar contributions for all employees who participate in the employer's qualifying HDHP. If the employer's contributions do not satisfy these rules, the employer will be subject to a 35 percent excise tax on all HSA contributions that the employer makes for a year (see Qs 4:119, 4:152). Employers that make HSA contributions through a cafeteria plan, and/or allow employees to make contributions on a pre-tax basis through a cafeteria plan, are subject to new IRS proposed cafeteria plan regulations. The new proposed regulations require cafeteria plans to permit prospective changes to HSA salary reduction contributions on at least a monthly basis, and where applicable, permit a one-time transfer from an FSA to an HSA. The proposed regulations also describe the ability to offer a limited purpose FSA (i.e., vision and dental only), post-deductible FSA, or combination FSA (i.e., both limited purpose and post-deductible) concurrently with an HSA. [72 Fed. Reg. 43938 (Aug. 6, 2007)]

In addition, the IRS issued new tax forms and instructions (Form 1040, Form W-2, Form 8889, Form 5498-SA, Form 1099-SA), model trust and custodial account agreements (Forms 5305(c) and 5305(b)), and Publication 969, describing HSA rules.

The DOL issued Field Assistance Bulletins 2004-1 and 2006-02 (involving ERISA) and Advisory Opinion 2004-09A (involving the Prohibited Transaction Rules). (See appendix E.) The Department of Health and Human Services, and the Centers for Medicare and Medicaid Services (CMS) issued guidance on account-based plans with respect to Medicare Part D, which includes a discussion of HSAs (see Qs 8:33, 8:34). As of the time of publication, the SEC has not issued any guidance.

Advantages and Disadvantages

Q 1:12   What are the primary advantages to an individual of participating in an HSA?

From an individual's perspective, primary advantages of HSA participation include:

- Reduced premiums for health coverage (cost of HDHP coverage will be lower than non-HDHP coverage)
- More control over medical spending
- Ability to set aside money for future use on a tax-favored basis

(See Q 2:45 for a comprehensive list of possible advantages of participating in an HSA.)

Q 1:13   What are the advantages to an employer of offering an HSA option to employees?

Offering an HSA option gives the employer a more predictable financial obligation, as well as the opportunity to restructure cost sharing between the employer and employees. For some employers, particularly small ones, an HSA may provide the opportunity to offer a health plan to employees for the first time. Other employers may offer the HSA as an additional medical coverage option. In addition, an HSA, which is a defined contribution approach to health care rather than a defined benefit approach, may bring an employer's health plans in line with changes that have already been made to the employer's retirement plans. Finally, as noted above, the premium for an HDHP is generally lower than for a non-HDHP health plan, which will result in a cost savings to the employer, to the extent that the employer contributes to this cost.

Q 1:14   What are the advantages to an employer of allowing employees to contribute to an HSA on a pretax basis through the employer's cafeteria plan?

An employer may offer an HSA option as part of its cafeteria plan, allowing an individual to make HSA contributions on a pretax basis. Alternatively, contributions may be made by an individual on an after-tax basis, with a corresponding deduction available to the individual at year-end on the individual's tax return. Similarly, employers may structure employer HSA contributions through a cafeteria plan, or make contributions without using a cafeteria plan.

For an employer, there are several advantages to allowing employees to make HSA contributions through its cafeteria plan:

1. HSA contributions by an employee through a cafeteria plan (provided they are within statutory limits) are treated as employer contributions that are not subject to withholding from wages for income tax or subject to the Federal Insurance Contributions Act (FICA), the Federal Unemployment Tax Act (FUTA), or the Railroad Retirement Tax Act. Thus, by allowing employees to make HSA contributions through the cafeteria plan, the employer will reduce its liability for these taxes, as long as it is reasonable for an employer to believe at the time a contribution is made that such contribution will not exceed the HSA limits that apply to a particular employee.

2. Offering an HSA through an existing cafeteria plan provides the employer with a convenient way to integrate the HSA into existing benefit options. For example, if the employer currently offers a flex dollar system (i.e., where the employer offers employees dollars that can be allocated among different benefits), the employer could allow employees to use flex dollars to fund the HSA.

3. If the employer wants to use a creative method for establishing its level of HSA contributions (e.g., matching the amounts that an employee contributes or contributing more to employees who participate in wellness programs), an HSA must be offered through a cafeteria plan to avoid

violating the comparable contribution rules under Code Section 4980G. In that event, the nondiscrimination requirements of Code Section 125 would have to be satisfied.

Q 1:15 Will the HSA serve as a good vehicle to set aside funds for retiree health?

It is possible that funds in an HSA will accumulate and be available for use during the HSA owner's retirement, particularly because the HSA contributions are now higher, enhancing the ability of individuals to accumulate funds for retiree medical expenses. However, the fact that an individual generally must give up all other health coverage except for HDHP coverage makes it likely that a good portion of the amount deposited to the HSA may be used by the HSA owner to pay his or her medical expenses each year. This will not be true for individuals who are able to use other assets for ongoing health expenses, allowing the funds in their HSA to accumulate. It also may not be true for individuals who fund the HSA up to the maximum amount allowed by law each year. (See Qs 1:24–1:30.)

Note. The terms *HSA owner, account owner, account holder,* and *account beneficiary* are used interchangeably in IRS publications, notices, and announcements to refer to the person that established the HSA. To avoid confusion, the term *HSA owner* will be used to refer to that person.

Q 1:16 What are the *primary* disadvantages to an individual of participating in an HSA?

The primary disadvantages of an HSA to the individual include the following:

1. An HSA participant who is not accustomed to participating in an HDHP may not feel that he or she has adequate coverage, particularly if the participant is responsible for paying all costs below the deductible from his or her own funds or from the HSA. (However, HDHPs are permitted to offer *preventive care* coverage before the deductible is satisfied, so a participant in an HDHP with generous preventive care coverage may view the coverage level as adequate.)

2. If medical expenses are incurred before money is set aside in the HSA for the year, the participant is required to pay those expenses out-of-pocket.

3. If there are significant medical expenses, it will be more difficult for an individual to allow HSA funds to carry over from year to year for retiree medical or nonmedical expenses, eliminating one of the primary advantages of HSA participation.

(See Q 2:46 for a comprehensive list of possible disadvantages of participating in an HSA.)

Q 1:17   What are the disadvantages to an employer of offering an HSA?

Disadvantages of an HSA to the employer include the following:

1. Employees may view an HSA offering as a reduction of existing benefits, particularly if the employer does not contribute to the HSA on behalf of employees. (This is unlikely to be the case if the employer offers an HSA as part of its array of existing benefits, however.)

2. The employer must invest administrative resources to implement an HSA option and to educate human resources personnel regarding the benefit.

3. An employer that offers an HSA option may discover that the majority of the workforce prefers to maintain existing coverage and is unwilling to switch to an HSA.

Q 1:18   What factors should an individual consider before enrolling in an HSA with HDHP?

Factors that an individual should consider include:

1. The anticipated level of medical expenses for the year;

2. The likelihood that such expenses will be covered under a particular HDHP;

3. The level of resources available to the individual to pay for expenses before the deductible is satisfied; and

4. The existing coverage of such individual's spouse (see Q 1:19) or domestic partner (see Q 1:20).

Q 1:19   How will a spouse's health coverage affect an HSA owner's ability to contribute to an HSA?

An HSA owner's ability to contribute to his or her HSA may be affected by his or her spouse's health coverage. Specifically, if a spouse has separate health coverage, the following special rules may apply:

1. The HSA owner could be prohibited from contributing to an HSA at all.

2. The HSA owner could be required to limit the amount contributed to the HSA to the amount of the HSA owner's HSA contribution limit for family coverage less the amount allocated to the spouse.

These rules, and other variations, are described in chapter 4. Whether or not the HSA owner's spouse is covered under the HDHP and/or has other coverage, the spouse's medical expenses will be considered "qualified medical expenses," allowing the HSA owner to take a tax-free distribution from his or her HSA to pay for such expenses, as long as the expenses are not reimbursed by another health plan (see chapter 6).

Q 1:20   How will a domestic partner's health coverage affect the HSA contribution limits?

Unlike a spouse's health coverage, it appears that a domestic partner's health coverage generally will not affect an HSA owner's ability to contribute to his or her HSA, even where the employee covers the domestic partner under his or her HDHP. Because no rule requires domestic partners to divide an HSA contribution in the manner that married individuals are required to, it appears that a domestic partner covered under an HSA owner's HDHP could open his or her own HSA and contribute the full statutory maximum annual contribution.

Further, neither Treasury nor the IRS has indicated that there is any problem with an HSA owner covering a domestic partner under an HDHP and having the domestic partner's expenses count toward satisfying the family deductible under the HDHP, notwithstanding that these individuals are not related. Thus, in the absence of further guidance from IRS or Treasury, this appears permissible.

Note. Unlike a spouse's expenses, an HSA owner may not take a tax-free distribution from his or her HSA to pay for his or her domestic partner's expenses unless the domestic partner is a dependent under Code Section 152 (see Q 2:37).

Q 1:21   What factors should an employer consider before offering an HSA with HDHP coverage?

Before offering an HSA with HDHP coverage, an employer should consider (1) what proportion of its workforce is likely to be receptive to HSAs and (2) the level of resources it wishes to devote to facilitating an HSA arrangement. Employers that wish to assist employees in establishing HSAs have two options:

1. Offer an HDHP that satisfies the HSA requirements and leave it up to employees to establish HSAs on their own; or

2. Offer an HDHP/HSA package, which allows employees one-stop shopping. Also, the employer will have to decide whether to offer employees the flexibility of making HSA contributions on a pretax basis through the employer's cafeteria plan during the year rather than making contributions on an after-tax basis with an accompanying deduction on the individual's tax return.

Q 1:22   What are the potential consequences to an individual of enrolling in an HSA but failing to follow the applicable rules?

An individual who does not maintain adequate records of medical expenditures may be required to pay income tax and a 10 percent additional tax on amounts distributed from the HSA. In contrast to FSAs and HRAs, HSA owners are required to maintain their own records of medical expenditures and do not submit claims to their employer for approval. Thus, on audit, an individual would be required to prove that the level of medical expenses matched those on the tax return (Form 1040 and Form 8889) filed by the individual. In addition, if an individual makes excess contributions to an HSA for a given year and fails to withdraw those contributions by April 15 of the following year, the individual will be subject to a 6 percent excise tax on the excess contributions. Finally, if an employee fails to maintain HDHP coverage for the required 13-month testing period after making certain types of HSA contributions described in chapter 5, an individual may be required to pay income tax and a 10 percent additional tax on amounts contributed to the HSA.

Q 1:23   What are the potential consequences to an employer of failing to follow the applicable HSA rules?

An employer that fails to make comparable contributions to the HSAs of employees may be required to pay an excise tax of 35 percent of the aggregate amount contributed by the employer to the HSAs of employees for the year (see Qs 4:119, 4:152). In addition, an employer that excludes HSA contributions from employees' wages without following applicable IRS guidance, or that violates cafeteria plan nondiscrimination rules, may be responsible for paying employment taxes and penalties (see Q 4:83).

An employer could also be found in violation of ERISA rules, which could generate DOL civil penalties or participant lawsuits (see Q 8:19).

Future of HSAs

Q 1:24   What were some of the major issues that commentators to the IRS were concerned about with respect to HSAs in 2004 and continue to be concerned about today?

Issues about which commentators expressed concern to the IRS included the following:

- HSA owners' participants' eligibility to continue to participate in health care FSAs (those with $2\frac{1}{2}$ month grace periods) and HRAs (FSAs with $2\frac{1}{2}$ month grace period) or to make a one-time rollover from an HRA to an HSA (see Qs 5:40, 5:52). [Addressed by the IRS in I.R.S. Notice 2004-45, 2004-28 I.R.B. 1 and I.R.S. Notice 2005-86, 2005-49 I.R.B. 1075. Addressed by Congress in Section 305 of the 2007 TRHCRA.]
- The eligibility of HSA owners to receive prescription drug coverage before the HDHP deductible is satisfied (see Q 3:48). [Addressed in Rev. Rul. 2004-38, 2004-15 I.R.B. 717, and Rev. Proc. 2004-22, 2004-15 I.R.B. 727]
- The definition of the term *preventive care*—not defined by Congress in the 2003 MMA and significant because any item considered preventive care may be covered under the HDHP before the deductible is satisfied (see Q 3:49). [Addressed in I.R.S. Notice 2004-23, 2004-15 I.R.B. 725]
- The application of the HSA comparable contribution rules and whether the rules would prohibit employers from making matching contributions or

incentive payments to employee HSAs (see Qs 4:143, 4:149–4:151). [Addressed in I.R.S. Notice 2004-50, Q&As 46, 47, 2004-33 I.R.B. 196; Prop. Treas. Reg. § 54.4980G-1 through 5; 70 Fed. Reg. 50,233 (Aug. 26, 2005)]

- State laws that mandate that health insurance policies provide particular benefits, which could preclude an individual in a particular state from participating in an HDHP that satisfies applicable federal rules (see Q 8:35). [Addressed in I.R.S. Notice 2004-43, 2004-27 I.R.B. 1 and IRS Notice 2005-83, 2005-49 I.R.B. 1075]

- The ability of employers to restrict the use of the HSA account to medical expenses (see Q 6:15) and to recoup amounts paid into the HSA of an employee who terminates employment (see Qs 4:147, 6:2). [Addressed in I.R.S. Notice 2004-50, Q&As 79 and 82, 2004-33 I.R.B. 196, respectively]

- The ability of an employee to contribute to an HSA even if his or her spouse has an FSA. Currently, IRS guidance indicates that an individual may not contribute to an HSA if his or her spouse has a health FSA, even if the individual never seeks to be reimbursed for any medical expenses from the spouse's FSA. Commentators have requested that the IRS correct this situation by allowing the HSA owner to certify that he or she will not receive reimbursement for any health expenses from his or her spouse's FSA. The IRS has not provided any guidance on this issue other than Notice 2004-45 [2004-28 I.R.B. 1], which does not adopt this flexible approach.

- Earlier indexing of HSA/HDHP cost-of-living adjustments (COLAs). Under prior law, the current statutory provisions for calculating COLAs, the IRS could not provide information about the indexed COLA amounts that apply to HSAs and HDHPs before October of each year. Commentators asked Treasury to change this rule so that the limits could be announced earlier each year. Treasury indicated informally that this would require a legislative change. That change was made in the TRHCA, and Treasury is now required to provide notice of the indexed COLA amounts no later than June 1 of each year (see Qs 4:32–4:33).

Q 1:25 What were the Bush Administration's proposals to make additional changes that would have expanded HSAs in 2009?

As part of its fiscal year 2008 budget proposal, the Bush Administration had proposed to completely reform the tax treatment of health insurance coverage and to make additional changes to the rules that apply to HSAs. [General Explanation of the Administration's Fiscal Year 2008 Revenue Proposals (commonly known as the "Blue Book"), Dept. of Treasury (Feb. 5, 2007)] Had 2008 fiscal year revenue proposals been enacted as proposed, they would have been effective for tax years beginning after 2009.

Q 1:26   What were the reasons for the Bush Administration's proposed changes to the HSA rules?

It was the Administration's position that empowering health care consumers (rather than third-party payers) to play a more direct role in their health care decisions would help to stem the trend of rapidly rising health care costs, and that a more market-oriented and consumer-driven health care system will help control costs and result in more affordable and accessible health care. Furthermore, the U.S. Tax Code does not afford the same treatment to the self-employed, the unemployed, and workers for companies that do not offer health insurance (most of whom are small businesses) as it does to companies that do offer health insurance. Employer-based insurance receives a tax subsidy that individually purchased insurance does not. An individual may deduct the cost of individually purchased insurance only if the individual's medical expenses exceed 7.5 percent of the individual's adjusted gross income. In addition, employer-based insurance generally receives a tax subsidy, while out-of-pocket spending does not. These large tax subsidies encourage generous health insurance and health spending that is not fully valued and makes labor markets less flexible. The Administration's reasons for the proposed changes are as follows:

1. Because health care purchased through an employer insurance plan is subsidized by the Tax Code, people insure against predictable and routine expenses (not just unpredictable, catastrophic expenses) and are thus insensitive to the cost of the health care they consume.

2. The tax subsidy is generally not available to the uninsured or to individual insurance purchasers, resulting in an underdeveloped individual market.

3. Employer contributions further mask the cost of health care to employees, whose wages tend to be lower when health care costs increase.

4. Employees may be reluctant to leave their jobs for fear of losing their insurance. Portability of health insurance is increasingly important in today's dynamic labor markets, where workers choose to change jobs with increasing frequency.

The Bush Administration believed that HSAs are making health care more affordable and accessible. Since January 2004, more than 3.8 million individuals have enrolled in HSAs, which are helping make health insurance more affordable for individuals and companies while providing greater choices and flexibility in how workers and employers spend their health care dollars.

President Bush proposed to build on this success and expand HSAs by:

- *Giving individuals that purchase HSAs on their own the same tax advantages as individuals with employer-sponsored insurance.* President Bush proposed making premiums for HSA-compatible insurance policies deductible from income taxes when purchased by individuals outside of work. In addition, an income tax credit would offset payroll taxes paid on premiums paid for their HSA policies. This would level the playing field for those who currently do not have access to employer-sponsored health care plans, including the self-employed, unemployed, and workers for companies that do not offer health insurance. For Americans who are not working, especially early retirees, premiums for the purchase of non-group HSA plans would now be allowed tax-free from an HSA account.

- *Eliminating all taxes on out-of-pocket spending through HSAs.* President Bush proposed allowing individuals with HSAs and their employers to make annual contributions to their accounts to cover all out-of-pocket costs under their HSA policy, not just their deductible as provided under current law. This would allow patients to cover all their out-of-pocket expenses tax-free through their HSA. The new proposal would also provide a credit for payroll taxes paid on HSA contributions made by individuals. [General Explanation of the Administration's Fiscal Year 2008 Revenue Proposals ("Blue Book"), p. 5, Dept. of Treasury (Feb. 5, 2007)]

Q 1:27 What were the proposed changes to HSAs under the Bush Administration's budget proposals?

The general explanation of the Bush Administration's fiscal year 2008 revenue proposals included the following:

1. New Standard Deduction for Health Insurance Coverage

Current tax treatment for health insurance. Under current law, if an individual receives health coverage through his employer, the entire amount of that coverage is excludable for both income and employment tax (Social Security, Medicare, and federal unemployment) purposes. An outgrowth of the exclusion for employer-provided health care is the favorable tax treatment of expenses paid through a cafeteria plan, an FSA, or an HRA. Self-employed individuals who purchase health insurance are able to deduct the full cost of health insurance for income tax (but not employment tax) purposes. Individuals who purchase their health insurance on their own rather than through their employer can only deduct their health care premiums for income tax purposes to the extent that they itemize their tax deductions and their health care costs exceed 7.5 percent of adjusted gross income; they do not receive any tax relief for employment tax purposes. Consequently, certain lower income individuals who purchase insurance on their own may not receive any income or employment tax relief on those purchases.

Administration's proposal. The Administration proposed to add a new "standard deduction" for those who are covered by health insurance and to generally eliminate the other tax preferences that are available for health coverage. The Administration believed that providing a standard deduction to all individuals who have health insurance—regardless of whether it is acquired through one's employer—will result in an increase in the number of individuals covered by health insurance. The Administration also believed that providing a uniform standard deduction that is not based on the amount of health care coverage purchased will provide an incentive for individuals to move to less comprehensive and less costly insurance, including HDHPs with lower premiums. The Administration believed that this will promote more cost consciousness in health care decision making and make individuals more engaged consumers of health services.

New standard deduction for health insurance coverage. Effective in 2009, the Administration proposed that all individuals who have qualifying health insurance coverage be provided a standard deduction of up to $15,000 for those with family coverage and $7,500 for those with individual coverage, based on the number of months that the individual is covered by the qualifying health coverage. The deduction amount would be indexed to increases in inflation based upon the rise in the consumer price index (CPI) rather than being based upon health care cost inflation. The amount of the standard deduction would not depend on the cost of the insurance purchased, but the insurance would have to meet certain minimum coverage requirements in order to qualify, including:

- A reasonable annual and/or lifetime benefit maximum;
- A limit on out-of-pocket exposure for covered expenses that is not higher than that currently allowable for HSAs (e.g., $5,800 for single coverage and $11,600 for family coverage for 2009);
- Coverage for inpatient and outpatient care, emergency benefits and physician care; and
- Guaranteed renewability by the provider.

Meaningful coverage. Although the health coverage could contain coverage exclusions and limitations—thereby lowering the cost—it would have to "meaningfully limit individual economic exposure to extraordinary medical expenses" under regulations issued by the Treasury Department in order to be considered qualifying health coverage. Coverage under a long-term care plan or under Medicare would not count as qualifying health insurance. State laws mandating certain insurance coverage would not be preempted by the proposal.

Individuals with certain coverage ineligible. Individuals and their dependents who are enrolled in Medicare, Medicaid, or the State Children's Health Insurance Program (SCHIP) would not be eligible for the new standard deduction. If an individual pays for his health insurance through a distribution from an HSA or Medical Savings Account (MSA), or uses the health care tax credit to purchase coverage, he or she also would not be eligible for the new standard deduction.

Effect of new standard deduction. The new standard deduction would reduce an individual's income for both income tax and employment tax purposes. Qualifying individuals apparently would be permitted to reduce their tax withholding so that the deduction is reflected in their regular paycheck rather than having to wait until filing their tax return and receiving a refund. If an employee is eligible for the new standard deduction due to health care coverage acquired through the employer, the employer could reduce the employee's employment taxes to reflect the new standard deduction. If an employee purchases qualifying health insurance on his or her own outside the employment context, the employer apparently could adjust the employee's employment taxes if the employee provides proof of coverage under qualifying health insurance. Self-employed individuals also could take the standard deduction for both income and employment tax purposes and could adjust estimated tax payments accordingly.

Impact on current tax law. Under the Administration's proposal, employers could still offer their employees health coverage, but the value of that coverage would have to be included in the employee's wages for income and employment tax purposes. Employees could not purchase health coverage on a pretax basis or make contributions to a health FSA through a cafeteria plan. Amounts paid for medical expenses from an HRA would be currently taxable to the individuals, which would make HRAs less attractive and likely eliminate their use. Contributions could still be made on a pretax basis to an HSA; however, it is not clear whether a contribution could be made through a cafeteria plan. Earnings in the HSA would continue to be tax-deferred and distributions from the HSA for qualified medical expenses would still not be taxable. Self-employed individuals would no longer have a separate deduction for premiums paid for health insurance. Further, the itemized deduction for medical expenses would be eliminated, except for taxpayers enrolled in Medicare. Employers could, however, continue to deduct the premiums paid for employee health insurance as a business expense.

2. Expansion of HSAs

The Bush Administration, which had been a very strong proponent of HSAs, proposed the following series of changes to the HSA provisions to provide further incentives for individuals to purchase HDHPs and contribute to HSAs.

Expand qualifying HDHPs. Under current law, to make a contribution to an HSA, the individual must have a qualifying HDHP, defined as a plan with a deductible of at least $1,150 for self-only coverage and $2,300 for family coverage and maximum out-of-pocket expense limits of no more than $5,800 for self-only coverage and $11,600 for family coverage for 2009. The Administration's proposal would allow plans with 50 percent or more coinsurance and a minimum out-of-pocket exposure to be considered a qualifying HDHP if, under rules established by the Treasury Department, the resulting policy had the same (or lower) premiums than an already-qualifying HDHP.

Qualifying medical expenses. Under current law, qualifying medical expenses only can be paid out of the HSA tax-free if the expenses were incurred after the HSA was established. Under the Administration's proposal, expenses that were incurred after the individual was eligible to contribute to an HSA (i.e., they have enrolled in an HDHP and have no other non-HDHP coverage) could support a tax-free distribution as long as the HSA is established before the filing date of the individual's tax return for the year.

Larger employer contributions for the chronically ill. Previously, the comparable contribution rules generally precluded an employer from making contributions to HSAs on behalf of non-highly compensated employees (NHCEs) in higher amounts (or higher percentages of deductibles) than to highly compensated employees (HCEs). Under the Tax Relief and Health Care Act of 2006 (Pub. L. No. 109-432) enacted on December 20, 2006, employers are now permitted to make larger HSA contributions on behalf of NHCEs, but they must still satisfy the comparability rules with respect to contributions to NHCEs (i.e., each NHCE must get the same dollar amount (or percentage of deductible) of contributions from the employer). The Administration's proposal allows employers to make HSA contributions on behalf of employees who are chronically ill or who have spouses or dependents who are chronically ill to be excluded from the comparable contribution rules to the extent that these amounts exceed the comparable contributions to other employees.

Deductibles in family policies. Under current law, the HDHP deductible must be reached by the entire family, rather than on a per-family member basis. However, plans that have an embedded deductible (where a lesser deductible is applied to expenses incurred by each individual family member) will not be considered a qualifying HDHP for HSA purposes unless the minimum individual deductible is at least equal to the minimum deductible for family coverage ($2,300 for 2009). The Administration's proposal would allow these embedded deductibles as long as the deductible is at least the minimum deductible for individual coverage ($1,150 for 2009) and the overall family coverage deductible is at least equal to the family minimum deductible.

Catch-up contributions. Under current law, individuals who are age 55 or over are permitted to make an additional contribution to their HSA annually ($1,000 for 2009). However, if two individuals who are age 55 or over are married, both individuals must have their own HSAs to make this catch-up contribution. The Administration's proposal would permit both spouses who are eligible to make catch-up contributions to an HSA to make contributions to a single HSA owned by one spouse.

HSA contributions of individuals covered by an FSA or an HRA. Generally, individuals who are covered by a health FSA or HRA are not eligible to make contributions to an HSA. The Administration's proposal would allow such individuals to make contributions to an HSA, but the maximum allowable HSA contribution would be reduced by the health FSA or HRA coverage amount. The Administration believes that this will make it easier for an individual to transfer to HSA-eligible coverage when he or she was previously participating in a health FSA or HRA.

Political outlook. Democrats have been skeptical of the benefits of HSAs, believing them to be mainly for the benefit of the healthy and wealthy. Consequently, these proposals did not get much traction in the Democrat-controlled Congress.

[General Explanation of the Administration's Fiscal Year 2008 Revenue Proposals ("Blue Book"), p. 21, Dept. of Treasury (Feb. 5, 2007)]

Q 1:28 What were the leading HSA-related legislative proposals introduced in the 109th Congress (2005–2007)?

H.R. 6134, an HSA bill that was approved by the Ways and Means Committee on September 27, 2006, was the leading HSA-related proposal introduced in the 109th Congress. This bill was enacted on December 20, 2006 as part of TRHCA, and included several significant HSA provisions:

- Permits an individual to transfer the balance remaining in his or her FSA or HRA account as of September 21, 2006 (or, if less, the balance on the transfer date) to a new HSA. The transfer must be made before January 1, 2012 (see Q 5:52).

- Modifies the limit on contributions to HSAs, so that contributions are not limited to the annual deductible of the HDHP (see Q 4:30); instead, contributions are limited only by the indexed dollar amount ($3,000 for self-only coverage and $5,950 for family coverage for 2009; $2,900 for self-only coverage and $5,800 for family coverage for 2008).

- Requires the Secretary of Treasury to announce the cost-of-living adjustments applicable to HSAs by June 1 of each year (see Q 4:32).

- Allows individuals who become covered by an HDHP after January to contribute up to the full annual limit, even if they only were eligible individuals for a portion of the tax year (the "last-month rule"); however, if they did not maintain an HDHP for the 12-month period beginning with the last month of year (except in the case of death or disability), then they must pay tax on the HSA contributions that were made under the "last-month rule" plus a 10 percent penalty. [I.R.C. § 223(b)(8), as amended by TRHCA § 305(a)] Based on the 2007 Instructions to Form 8889—*Health Savings Accounts (HSAs)*, the *last-month rule* is interpreted to allow an individual to calculate his or her HSA contribution limit as the greater of a full-year contribution, based on the individual's HDHP coverage on the first day of the last month of the individual's taxable year (generally December 1), or a pro-rated amount based on the type of HDHP coverage the individual actually had during months when they were HSA eligible (see Q 4:6). Thus, and as interpreted by the IRS, coverage can be attributed to previous months of the year regardless of whether the individual was or was not an eligible individual during such previous months (i.e., not restricted to individuals that became eligible individual *after* beginning of year). The completion of Form 8889 is discussed in chapter 7.

- Allows employers to make contributions to HSAs on behalf of NHCEs in higher amounts (or higher percentages of deductibles) than to HCEs without violating the comparable contribution rules. Thus, an HCE (as defined in Code Section 414(q)) is not treated as a comparable participating employee (see Q 4:115). [I.R.C. § 4980(G)(d)]

- Allows coverage under a health FSA during the "2½–month grace period" to be disregarded for eligible individuals who have a zero balance in their HSA at the end of the previous calendar year (see Qs 4:14–4:19).

- Allows individuals to make a one-time distribution to rollover amounts from an IRA to an HSA, subject to the HSA contribution limit (see Qs 5:40– 5:51).

Q 1:29   What were the leading HSA-related legislative proposals introduced in the 110th Congress (2007–2009)?

Unlike the 109th Congress, Democrats held more seats in the 110th Congress. Democrats generally disfavor legislation to expand the use of HSAs. Accordingly, fewer HSA bills were proposed, and the likelihood of their passage was lower. Three notable bills were proposed in the House, and no significant bills were proposed in the Senate. None of the bills passed. The three House bills are summarized below.

- H.R. 3234, the HSA Improvement and Expansion Act of 2007, would have amended the Code to (1) permit HSAs to incorporate FSAs and HRAs; (2) increase the annual HSA contribution limit; (3) permit the use of HSA funds to purchase health insurance; (4) permit reimbursement of expenses incurred prior to establishment of an HSA; (5) permit veterans who are eligible for service connected disability benefits to establish an HSA; and (6) permit spouses to make increased catch-up contributions to a single HSA. The bill did not pass.

- H.R. 2639, the Promoting Health for Future Generations Act of 2007, would have amended the Code to expand opportunities to increase HSA utilization and includes the following provisions: (1) increase the tax deduction for HSA contributions; (2) permit Medicare and veterans health care beneficiaries to establish and contribute to an HSA; (3) permit individuals over age 50 to make increased catch-up contributions; (4) treat Medicare supplemental insurance premiums as tax-deductible; (5) create a new above-the-line tax deduction for individual high deductible health plan premiums; (6) permit individual contributions to Medicare Advantage Medical Savings Accounts; (7) permit adult children to inherit HSA and MSA account balances; and (8) permit Medicare Advantage Medical Savings Accounts to be used for wellness and fitness programs. The bill did not pass.

- H.R. 5719, the Taxpayer Assistance and Simplification Act, contained a provision that would have had a significant impact on owners and providers of HSAs. This provision would have taxed any distribution from an HSA that was not substantiated as a qualified medical expense in a manner similar to the substantiation required for payments from flexible spending arrangements (FSAs). In addition, it would have required HSA trustees and custodians to report to the IRS the aggregate amount of distributions from an HSA that have not been determined to be for qualified medical expenses through substantiation methods similar to the substantiation methods required for FSAs. The bill did not pass.

  - Currently, HSA trustees and custodians do not have any responsibility to determine whether a distribution from an HSA is used to pay for qualified medical expenses; HSA owners make a representation on their annual tax return about the extent to which they had qualified medical expenses that equaled or exceeded the HSA distribution they received. If the HSA distribution is greater than the qualified medical expenses incurred, the excess amount is taxable and, if the owner has not become

Medicare eligible, died, or become disabled, is also subject to an additional 10 percent tax. If audited by the IRS, the owner has to prove (e.g., by presenting medical records) that qualified medical expenses have been incurred. This self-determination is similar to what occurs if the taxpayer claims an itemized deduction for medical expenses on his or her tax return.

- H.R. 5719 provided that the trustee of a HSA report to the IRS and to the HSA owner (i) the name, address, and identifying number of the HSA owner, and (ii) the amount paid or distributed out of such account for the preceding calendar year that is not properly substantiated. The substantiation provisions would have applied to amounts paid or distributed out of health savings accounts after December 31, 2010.

- Had this provision been enacted, an HSA owner would be taxed on distributions from an HSA if the distribution is not substantiated as a qualified medical expense by the HSA trustee or custodian at the time the distribution is made—regardless of whether the HSA owner can later prove that he or she has qualified medical expenses that equal or exceed the amount of the distribution. This would have compelled HSA trustees and custodians to add procedures to substantiate that distributions are being used for qualified medical expenses, similar to the way that FSAs required substantiation that an expense is a qualified medical expense before payments are made.

- This proposal was expected to increase tax revenues by $485 million over 10 years (2010–2020) since it would have resulted in more distributions from HSAs being taxable and may also cause fewer employers and/or HSA providers to offer them, resulting in fewer tax-deductible contributions to HSAs.

Q 1:30   What are the leading HSA-related legislative proposals introduced in the 111th Congress (2009–2011)?

The 111th Congress will attempt to address healthcare reform in 2009. It is one of President Obama's signature issues. However, neither the Obama Administration nor any of the relevant Congressional have provided a detailed legislative proposal on how they would change the current health care system and whether any of these changes would impact HSAs and HDHPs. Based on statements made by President Obama and House Democratic leadership, they aim to have healthcare reform legislation enacted by the year of 2009.

Given that Democrats are in control of both houses of Congress and that Democratic leadership do not have a favorable view of HSAs, there is little chance that expansion of HSAs will be part of overall health care reform. In addition, there is concern that health care reform legislation could limit the use of HSAs. For example, if health care reform legislation mandates that an employer must provide health insurance coverage to all of its employees and the minimum requirement for health insurance coverage does not permit high deductible health insurance, then employees would no longer be able to contribute to an HSA, since they would be covered by insurance which was not an HDHP. In addition, HSA proponents are concerned that the HSA substantiation legislation introduced in the 110th Congress (see Q 1:29) will be introduced again in the 111th Congress. Unfortunately at the time that this book goes to press, there are few specifics on how health care reform will impact HSAs.

Chapter 2

General HSA Rules

Chapter 2 includes topics related to establishing a Health Savings Account (HSA) including determining when an HSA is established, and the establishment date for rollovers and for successive HSAs. In addition, this chapter discusses the establishment of HSAs under the Internal Revenue Code. This chapter also discusses eligibility rules for establishing an HSA and new definitions of the terms *dependent* and *qualified medical expense*.

In General 2-1
Eligible Individual for Establishing an HSA 2-4
Establishment and Effective Dates 2-10
Divorced Parents 2-13
Qualified Medical Expenses 2-14
Dependents 2-15
Advantages and Disadvantages of HSAs 2-21

In General

Q 2:1   What is an *HSA*?

An *HSA* is a trust created or organized in the United States exclusively for the purpose of paying the qualified medical expenses of the HSA owner, but only if the written governing instrument creating the trust meets all of the following requirements:

Note. The terms *HSA owner, account owner, account holder,* and *account beneficiary* are used interchangeably in IRS publications, notices, and announcements to refer to the person that established the HSA. To avoid confusion, the term *HSA owner* will be used to refer to that person.

1. Regular HSA contributions are made only in cash, although there is an exception for rollovers and trustee-to-trustee transfers (see Qs 4:1, 5:5,

5:32) [I.R.C. § 223(d)(1)(A)(i); I.R.S. Notice 2004-50, Q&A 73, 2004-33 I.R.B. 196];

2. Except in the case of a rollover contribution or a trustee-to-trustee transfer, the trustee or custodian does not accept more than the maximum annual contribution limit for the calendar year. For the 2009 calendar year, the annual contribution limit for individuals with self-only coverage is $3,000, and the annual contribution limit for individuals with family coverage is $5,950. Additionally, individuals that are 55 years old or older may make annual "catch-up" contributions up to $1,000 annually. See Q 4:30. [I.R.C. §§ 223(b)(2)-(3); (d)(1)(A)(ii); (g); Rev. Proc. 2008-29; 2008-22 I.R.B. 1039];

   Note. Although the statutory maximum contribution limit does not generally include rollovers and transfers made to an HSA from another HSA, Archer MSA, health FSA or HRA, a direct transfer that is rolled over from an IRA in a qualified funding distribution (see chapter 5) is subject to the statutory annual contribution limit when combined with regular contributions made for the year.

3. The HSA trustee or custodian must be a bank, as defined in Code Section 408(n); an insurance company, as defined in Code Section 816; or a person who the Secretary of the Treasury has determined will administer the trust in compliance with the HSA trust requirements (i.e., an IRS approved nonbank trustee) (see Qs 1:6, 7:22, 7:23). [I.R.C. §§ 223(d)(1)(B), 408(n), 816; Treas. Reg. § 1.408-2(e); I.R.S. Notice 2004-2, Q&A 9, 2004-2 I.R.B. 269];

   Note. A financial organization authorized to serve as trustee or custodian for an individual retirement arrangement (IRA) or an Archer MSA automatically is permitted to serve as trustee or custodian for an HSA without additional approval from the IRS. [I.R.C. § 223(d)(1)(B); I.R.S. Notice 2004-2, Q&A 9, 2004-2 I.R.B. 269; I.R.S. Ann. 2003-54, 2003-40 I.R.B. 761; I.R.S. Ann. 2005-59, 2005-37 I.R.B. 524, containing a list of approved nonbank trustees and custodians] An HSA is a newer type of financial product and can be offered by various types of financial organizations that qualify as an HSA trustee or custodian (see chapter 7).

4. No part of the HSA assets may be invested in life insurance contracts or collectibles [I.R.C. § 223(d)(1)(C); I.R.S. Notice 2004-50, Q&A 65, 2004-33 I.R.B. 196];

5. The balance in the HSA account must be nonforfeitable [I.R.C. § 223(d)(1)(E); I.R.S. Notice 2004-50, Q&A 82, 2004-33 I.R.B. 196]; and

6. The trust assets may not be commingled with other property except in a common trust fund, as defined in Treasury Regulations Section 1.408-2 (b)(5)(ii), or in a common investment fund, as defined in Code Section 584(a)(1). [I.R.C. § 223(d)(1)(D); I.R.S. Notice 2004-50, Q&A 66, 2004-33 I.R.B. 196].

Unless these requirements are satisfied, no contributions may be accepted by the trustee or custodian. [I.R.C. § 223(d)(1)(A)]

Q 2:2   Who is the account beneficiary, account owner, or HSA owner?

The account beneficiary, account owner, or HSA owner is the individual on whose behalf the HSA was established. The IRS model HSA forms (see Q 7:4) use the term *account owner* to refer to the account beneficiary. In general, this book refers to the individual on whose behalf the HSA was established as the "HSA owner." [I.R.C. § 223(d)(3)]

Q 2:3   How and when were HSAs created?

HSAs were created by the Medicare Prescription Drug, Improvement, and Modernization Act of 2003, which was signed into law on December 8, 2003. [Pub. L. No. 108-173, title XII, § 1201(a), 117 Stat. 2469, (2003), amending Part VII of subchapter B of chapter 1 of the Code by adding § 223, and redesignating former § 223 (a cross-reference) to § 224] See chapter 1 for more information on the history and legislation affecting HSAs.

Q 2:4   When are the HSA rules effective?

The HSA rules are generally effective for taxable years beginning after December 31, 2003. The Medicare Prescription Drug, Improvement, and Modernization Act of 2003, Section 1201(k), provides: "The amendments made by this section [amending sections 62, 106, 125, 220, 223, 224, 848, 3231, 3306, 3401, 4973, 4975, 6051, and 6693 and enacting section 4980G of the Code] shall apply to taxable years beginning after December 31, 2003." Thus, the first date on which it was permissible for an eligible individual to establish an HSA was January 1, 2004. [I.R.S. Notice 2004-2 Q&A 8, 2004-2 I.R.B. 269]

Q 2:5   Do HSAs replace Archer Medical Savings Accounts?

No. The HSA is modeled on the Archer Medical Savings Account (MSA). MSAs were permitted under a pilot program effective for years beginning after December 31, 1996. The Archer MSA program will terminate if the number of individuals establishing them exceeds numerical limits (generally 750,000 accounts). [I.R.C. § 220(j)(2), as amended by § 322(a) of the Working Families Tax Relief Act of 2004, Pub. L. No. 108-311, 118 Stat. 1166 (2004) ("WFTRA")] In general, the trustee will report the number of MSAs established through June 30 of each year to the IRS by August 1. Generally, the IRS must publish whether the threshold as been met by October 1 each year. [I.R.C. § 220(j)(4)]

Note. This limit has never been reached, and is not likely to be reached. [I.R.S. Ann. 2007-44, 2007-19 I.R.B. 1238]

Archer MSAs were extended by the Tax Relief and Health Care Act of 2006 ("TRHCA"). The extension applies through 2007. [I.R.C. § 220(i)(2); TRHCA § 117(a) and (b)] As of the writing of this book, Congress has not extended MSAs past December 31, 2007.

Note. An individual will not be treated as an eligible individual for purposes of contributing to an MSA for any tax year beginning after 2007 (the "cut-off year"), unless (1) the individual was an active MSA participant for a tax year ending on or before the close of the cut-off year, or (2) the individual became an active MSA participant for the tax year ending after the cut-off year by reason of coverage under an HDHP of an MSA-participating employer. [I.R.C. §§ 220(i)(2), 220(i)(3)(B)]

Eligible Individual for Establishing an HSA

Q 2:6   Who is an *eligible individual* for purposes of establishing an HSA?

The term *eligible individual* means, with respect to any month, any individual who:

- Is covered under a high deductible health plan ("HDHP") as of the first day of such month;
- While being covered by an HDHP, is not covered by another health plan that is not an HDHP (with certain exceptions for plans providing limited coverage—see Q 2:8);
- Is not enrolled in Medicare (generally, has not reached age 65—see Q 2:15; Qs 4:42–4:45 regarding catch-up contributions);
- Cannot be claimed as a dependent on another person's tax return.

[I.R.C. § 223(c)(1)(A); I.R.S. Notice 2004-2, Q&A 2, 2004-2 I.R.B. 269, as modified by I.R.S. Notice 2004-50, 2004-33 I.R.B. 196, see *Effect on Other Documents;* see also I.R.S. Notice 2008-59, 2008-29 I.R.B. 123]

However, an individual will be eligible to contribute to an HSA if his or her spouse has non-HDHP *family* coverage, as long as the individual is not covered under that plan. [Rev. Rul. 2005-25, 2005-18 I.R.B. 971]

Example 1. Horace and Wanda are a married couple, and both are age 35. Throughout 2009, Horace has self-only coverage under an HDHP. Horace has no other health coverage, is not enrolled in Medicare, and may not be claimed as a dependent on another taxpayer's return. Wanda has non-HDHP family coverage for herself and for the couple's two dependent children. Horace is excluded from Wanda's coverage. Therefore, Horace is an eligible individual for purposes of an HSA. He may contribute $3,000 (the maximum annual contribution limit for self-only coverage for 2009).

Note. The special rules for married individuals that treat both spouses as having family coverage (see Q 4:49) do not apply because Wanda's non-HDHP family coverage does not cover Horace. [I.R.C. § 223(b)(5)] Thus, Horace remains an eligible individual. However, Horace may not make the catch-up contribution because he is not age 55 or older in 2009. Wanda has non-HDHP coverage and is therefore not an eligible individual.

Caution. If a spouse has a health FSA that covers an HSA owner, the HSA owner's eligibility to make HSA contributions may be affected (see Q 4:20). [See I.R.S. Notice 2004-45, 2004-28 I.R.B. 1]

Example 2. The same facts as in Example 1, except that Horace has HDHP family coverage for himself and for one of the couple's dependent children. Wanda has non-HDHP family coverage for herself and for the couple's other dependent child. Horace and the child covered under Horace's HDHP coverage are excluded from Wanda's coverage. Because the non-HDHP family coverage does not cover Horace, the special rules that treat both spouses as having family coverage do not affect Horace's eligibility to make HSA contributions. Wanda has non-HDHP coverage and is, therefore, not an eligible individual.

Historical Note. A state could have laws that mandate certain benefits be included in an insured HDHP. These laws, for example, might require certain benefits to be covered under an HDHP without regard to whether the deductible is satisfied. Unless such state mandated benefits satisfy the definition of preventive care for federal purposes (see Qs 3:49, 3:55, 3:56), these state requirements would cause the HDHP to fail to satisfy the requirements of Code Section 223 because the plan would provide benefits not subject to the high deductible. Individuals in states with these types of laws could not contribute to an HSA. Other state laws may require an insurer or HMO to comply with limits on deductibles, which could similarly conflict with federal requirements for HDHPs.

The IRS has addressed this by issuing transitional guidance for months before January 1, 2006, for state requirements in effect on January 1, 2004. The guidance states that during this time period, an HDHP will not be considered to violate federal requirements if the sole reason it does not comply with federal requirements is because it is complying with state benefit mandates. However, after January 1, 2006, individuals covered by insured HDHPs or HMOs subject to state laws that conflict with Code Section 223 requirements will not be considered *eligible individuals* able to contribute to HSAs. [I.R.S. Notice 2004-43, 2004-27 I.R.B. 10]

Historical Note. Generally, a health plan may not reduce existing benefits before the plan's renewal date. Thus, even though a state may amend its laws before January 1, 2006, to authorize HDHPs that comply with Code Section 223(c)(2), non-calendar-year plans still fail to qualify as HDHPs after January 1, 2006. (See transitional relief for non-calendar-year plans in Q 3:22.)

Practice Pointer. Distributions from an HSA to pay for qualified medical expenses of the HSA owner or the HSA owner's spouse or dependents may be made without regard to their status as eligible individuals. Thus, it is not necessary for an individual to be covered by an HDHP to have his or her qualified medical expenses reimbursed from an HSA on a tax-free basis. [I.R.S. Notice 2004-50, Q&A 36, 2004-33 I.R.B. 196] However, distributions made for expenses reimbursed by another health plan are not excludable from income, whether or not the other health plan is an HDHP (see chapter 6).

Q 2:7   If an employee begins HDHP coverage midmonth, when does the employee become an eligible individual?

An eligible individual generally must have HDHP coverage as of the first day of the month. An individual with employer-provided HDHP coverage on a payroll-by-payroll basis becomes an eligible individual on the first day of the month on or following the first day of the pay period when HDHP coverage begins. [I.R.C. § 223(b)(2); I.R.S. Notice 2004-50, Q&A 11, 2004-33 I.R.B. 196]

> **Note.** For taxable years beginning after 2006, an HSA owner is permitted to make a full-year HSA contribution, if such individual is an HSA eligible individual on the first day of the last month of their taxable year (generally December 1). The "last-month rule" exception is discussed in chapter 4, Contributions and Deductions.

> **Example 1.** Omar, an unmarried employee, begins self-only HDHP coverage on August 6, 2009, the first day of a biweekly payroll period. He continues to be covered by the HDHP throughout 2009. For purposes of contributing to an HSA, Omar becomes an eligible individual on September 1, 2009. For taxable years beginning after 2006, Omar is allowed to make a full-year HSA contribution even though he became an HSA eligible individual after the first day of his taxable year (assume January 1) because he was an eligible individual on December 1, 2009. This exception is further discussed in Qs 4:5–4:16 If Omar utilizes the "last-month rule" exception, which allows him to be treated as eligible for the entire year, his maximum contribution amount will likely increase (up to the statutory limit of $3,000 for 2009). However, Omar will have to remain an eligible individual during a testing period that will not end until December 31, 2010. Omar must maintain his HDHP coverage and otherwise remain an eligible individual during the testing period (see Qs 4:8–4:10).

> **Example 2.** Same facts as in example 1, except Omar's self-only HDHP coverage ended on November 30. Because the "last-month rule" does not apply, Omar's maximum contribution limit will be prorated (see Q 4:48). He will not, however, be required to remain an eligible individual during the testing period (see Qs 4:8–4:10).

Q 2:8   Are there any exceptions to the rule that prohibits an employee who is an "eligible individual" from having coverage under any other non-HDHP?

Yes. There are two exceptions to the rule that prohibits an employee who is an eligible individual from having coverage under any other non-HDHP (see Q 2:6). These exceptions apply to:

- Coverage for any benefit provided by "permitted insurance;" and
- Coverage, whether through insurance or otherwise, for accidents, disability, dental care, vision care, or long-term care.

[I.R.C. § 223(c)(1)(B); I.R.S. Notice 2008-59, Part 1, 2008-29 I.R.B. 123, I.R.S. Notice 2004-2, Q&A 5, 2004-2 I.R.B. 269]

See chapter 3 for more information related to medical plan coverage, including a definition of "permitted insurance."

Q 2:9 May an ineligible individual establish an HSA if his or her spouse is an eligible individual?

No. Although the special rule for married individuals under Code Section 223(b)(5) generally allows a married couple to divide the maximum HSA contribution (and deduction) between spouses, if only one spouse is an eligible individual (see Q 2:10), only that spouse may contribute to an HSA. [Rev. Rul. 2005-25, 2005-18 I.R.B. 971; I.R.S. Notice 2004-50, Q&A 31, 2004-33 I.R.B. 196]

Q 2:10 May a joint HSA be established by a married couple?

No. An HSA may be established only on behalf of one individual. Thus, if a husband and wife are eligible to contribute to an HSA, they are both eligible to establish separate HSAs. Only one person may be the HSA owner of an HSA. [I.R.S. Notice 2004-50, Q&A 63, 2004-33 I.R.B. 196] (See Qs 4:49–4:52, 4:57 concerning allocating contributions, other than catch-up contributions, between spouses; Q 6:14 concerning reimbursements from a spouse's HSAs.)

Practice Pointer. If both spouses are age 55 or older and they both want to make "catch-up" contributions, they must each establish an HSA.

Q 2:11 Are HSAs available to residents of the U.S. Virgin Islands, Guam, and the Commonwealth of the Northern Mariana Islands?

Yes. Bona fide residents of the U.S. Virgin Islands, Guam, and the Commonwealth of the Northern Mariana Islands may establish HSAs. However, bona fide residents of Puerto Rico (see below) and American Samoa may establish HSAs only after statutory provisions similar to Code Sections 223 (relating to HSAs) and 106(d) (relating to employer-provided medical expense coverage) are enacted. [I.R.S. Notice 2004-50, Q&A 87, 2004-33 I.R.B. 196]

Puerto Rico. Effective for taxable years beginning after 2008, statutory provisions now permit tax deductible contributions to be made in Puerto Rico. [Act No. 156, amending the P.R. Tax Code (Aug. 4, 2008)], however, the deduction limitations under Puerto Rican law, and certain other provisions, differ from those under Code section 223. [*Compare,* PRIRC § 1169C(b)(2) contribution limits *with* the indexed limits under I.R.C. § 223(b)(2); PRIRC § 1169C(d)(2), *with* I.R.S. Pub. 502, *Medical and Dental Expenses*, with regard to treating a vaccination as a qualified medical expense for purposes of I.R.C. § 223(d)(2)(A); PRIRC § 1169C(b)(3)(B), *with* I.R.C. § 223(b)(3)(B), regarding increases to the catch-up limits; PRIRC § 1169C(c)(2)(A)(i) *with* I.R.C. § 223(c)(2)(A)(i) regarding minimum annual deductible limits to be an HDHP; PRIRC § 1169C(c)(2)(A)(ii) with I.R.C. § 223(c)(2)(A)(ii) regarding maximum out-of-pocket expense limits to be a HDHP; and PRIRC § 1169C(f), *with* I.R.C. § 223(f) regarding the 10 percent tax for individuals who are age 65 or over.

See also, PRIRC § 1169C(d)(5) regarding the enactment of legislation similar to I.R.C. § 106(d) which has not happened.] Notwithstanding the differences between the two laws, it should be possible to administer HSAs so that the minimum requirements of both Puerto Rico and U.S. laws are satisfied, and to communicate these requirements to residents of Puerto Rico.

Q 2:12   Are HSAs available to residents of Hawaii?

Hawaiian residents are not prohibited from having HSAs. However, an HDHP offered by an employer in Hawaii would have to satisfy Hawaii's Prepaid Health Care Act (PHCA), which sets forth various requirements concerning plan benefits and cost-sharing, and would have to be approved as a qualified plan by Hawaii's Prepaid Health Care Council. [Haw. Rev. Stat., ch. 393] Hawaii Department of Labor and Industrial Relations (DLIR) staff have informally indicated that, while Hawaii may be willing to approve HDHP/HSA plans as satisfying PHCA requirements, the state likely would require significant employer HSA contributions as a condition for approval. Accordingly, at the present time, HSAs are generally established only by Hawaiian residents who do not have employer-provided health coverage (e.g., sole proprietors, self-employed individuals, and those working as part-time employees) (see Q 8:37).

Q 2:13   Will an individual be treated as participating in an HDHP and no other non-HDHP if he or she elects HDHP coverage but also has the option to choose a plan that is not an HDHP?

Yes. To determine whether an employee is an eligible individual, the employee's actual health coverage election is controlling, rather than the health coverage offered to the employee. [I.R.S. Notice 2004-50, Q&A 1, 2004-33 I.R.B. 196]

Q 2:14   Are individuals who are eligible for Medicare but who are not enrolled in Medicare Part A or B eligible to establish HSAs?

Yes. Individuals who are eligible for Medicare but who are not enrolled in Medicare Part A (hospital insurance) or Part B (medical insurance) remain eligible to establish and contribute to an HSA. [I.R.C. § 223(b)(7); I.R.S. Notice 2004-50, Q&A 2, 2004-33 I.R.B. 196] Similarly, an individual who is eligible for but not enrolled in Medicare Part D (or any other Medicare benefit) may establish and contribute to an HSA if otherwise eligible to do so. [I.R.S. Notice 2008-59, Q&A 5 and 6, 2008-29 I.R.B. 123] Medicare Part D is a federal program to subsidize the costs of prescription drugs for Medicare beneficiaries in the United States. It was enacted as part of the Medicare Prescription Drug, Improvement, and Modernization Act of 2003 (MMA) and went into effect on January 1, 2006. All individuals who already have Medicare Part A or Medicare Part B coverage are eligible to enroll in a Medicare Part D prescription drug plan. (See Qs 4:42–4:44 regarding eligibility to make a catch-up contribution.)

Q 2:15 When does eligibility to contribute to an HSA end for a Medicare-eligible individual?

Eligibility for making HSA contributions ends beginning with the month the HSA owner becomes eligible for *and* enrolls in either Medicare Part A or Part B. [I.R.C. § 223(b)(7); I.R.S. Notice 2004-50, Q&A 2, 2004-33 I.R.B. 196] Thus, an otherwise eligible individual who is not actually enrolled in Medicare Part A or Part B may contribute to an HSA until the month that he or she actually enrolls in Medicare Part A or Part B.

Example 1. Yetta, age 66, is covered under her employer's HDHP. Although Yetta is eligible for Medicare, she is not actually entitled to Medicare benefits because she did not apply for benefits under Medicare (i.e., she did not enroll in Medicare Part A or Part B). If Yetta is otherwise an eligible individual, she may contribute to an HSA.

Note. Enrollment in Medicare Part A is automatic if a person begins receiving Social Security retirement benefits.

Example 2. In August 2009, Xavier attains age 65 and applies for and begins receiving Social Security benefits. Xavier is automatically enrolled in Medicare Part A. As of August 1, 2009, Xavier is no longer an eligible individual and may not contribute to an HSA.

Example 3. Evelyn turned age 65 in July 2009 and enrolled in Medicare. Evelyn had self-only coverage under an HDHP with an annual deductible of $1,150. She is eligible for an additional contribution of $1,000 because of the catch-up provisions applicable for 2009. Evelyn's contribution limit for 2009 is $2,000 (the maximum annual contribution limit of $3,000 plus a $1,000 catch-up contribution times 6/12 or 1/2). Evelyn can make contributions for January through June totaling $2,000, but cannot make any contributions for July through December.

Q 2:16 Are individuals who are eligible for medical benefits through the Department of Veterans Affairs (VA) eligible to make contributions to an HSA?

Possibly. Individuals who are eligible for medical benefits through the VA, who are otherwise eligible for an HSA, may contribute to an HSA as long as they have not received medical benefits from the VA at any time during the preceding three months. [I.R.S. Notice 2008-59, Q&A 9, 2008-29 I.R.B. 123, I.R.S. Notice 2004-50, Q&A 5, 2004-33 I.R.B. 196]

Example. Charlie, a military veteran, is eligible for and receives medical benefits (other than disregarded coverage or preventive care) from the VA in October of 2009. Charlie began self-only HDHP coverage on March 1, and continued this coverage until the end of the year. Charlie cannot be treated as an HSA eligible individual for all of 2009 (see Q 4:5) because he received medical benefits from the VA within the three months preceding the first day in December—September through November. However, if otherwise eligible, Charlie may make HSA contributions for seven months—March through September—if he were otherwise an eligible individual (see Qs 2:6, 4:48) for those months during 2009.

Q 2:17   Is a government retiree who is enrolled in Medicare Part B (but not Part A) an eligible individual for HSA purposes?

No. An individual who is enrolled in either Medicare Part A *or* Medicare Part B may not contribute to an HSA. [I.R.C. § 223(b)(7); I.R.S. Notice 2004-50, Q&A 4, 2004-33 I.R.B. 196]

Q 2:18   May an otherwise HSA-eligible individual who is age 65 or older and thus eligible for Medicare, but who is not enrolled in Medicare Part A or Part B, make the additional catch-up contributions for individuals age 55 or older?

Yes. An individual who is eligible for but not enrolled in Medicare Part A or Part B may contribute to an HSA and make additional catch-up contributions if the individual is age 55 or older. [I.R.S. Notice 2004-50, Q&A 3, 2004-33 I.R.B. 196; I.R.S. Notice 2004-2, Q&A 12, 2004-2 I.R.B. 269]

Q 2:19   May active duty or retired service members receiving medical coverage under TRICARE contribute to an HSA?

No. Active duty or retired service members receiving medical coverage under TRICARE are not eligible individuals and may not contribute to an HSA. [I.R.S. Notice 2004-50, Q&A 6, 2004-33 I.R.B. 196] Should TRICARE offer an HSA-qualified HDHP, individuals who select it and are otherwise eligible would be able to make contributions to an HSA. To check the current status of TRICARE plans, visit http://www.tricare.osd.mil/.

Establishment and Effective Dates

Q 2:20   When is an HSA *established*?

An HSA is an exempt trust established through a written governing instrument under state law. [I.R.C. § 223(d)(1)] State trust law determines when an HSA is established. Most state trust laws require that for a trust to exist, an asset must be held in trust; thus, most state trust laws require that a trust must be funded to be established. Whether the HSA owner's signature is required to establish the trust also depends on state law. [I.R.S. Notice 2008-59, Q&A 38, 2008-29 I.R.B. 123]

In general, only qualified medical expenses incurred after an HSA has been established can be reimbursed tax-free through an HSA.

Caution. The applicable law is the law of the state in which the trust is situated (*sitused*), rather than the law of the state in which the HSA owner resides.

Special establishment date rules apply where the funds in the HSA were rolled over or transferred from an Archer MSA or another HSA, or if the owner had previously established an HSA (see Qs 2:25, 2:26).

Q 2:21   Can HSA contributions be made as soon as the HSA is effective?

Although established, an HSA contribution cannot be made before the effective date of the eligible individual's HDHP coverage (see Q 2:23). Nonetheless, in some cases, an individual is treated as being eligible for the entire year (see Q 4:5).

> **Note.** If HDHP coverage begins on any day other than the first day of the month, the HSA account cannot be effective any sooner than the first day of the following month (see Q 2:7).

Q 2:22   Can an HSA be *established* before it becomes effective?

Yes. All of the paperwork to establish an HSA may be completed and the minimum contribution deposited into the HSA before the HDHP coverage becomes effective. However, the account will not become officially effective (see Q 2:7) until HDHP coverage begins.

> **Note.** Once HDHP coverage begins or is treated as having begun (see Q 4:5), expenses for medical care, incurred after the HSA is established, may be paid or reimbursed from the HSA account. Tax-free distribution status does not depend upon the individual who receives distributions being an eligible individual (see Q 2:33). Thus, tax-free distributions may still be made from an HSA to pay or reimburse the qualified medical expenses of an HSA owner, spouse, or dependent within the meaning of Code Section 152, whether or not such individuals are currently *eligible individuals* (see Q 6:11).

> **Practice Pointer.** Completing the necessary steps before HDHP coverage begins will ensure that the HSA will be *established* as early as possible. Establishing the HSA early will prevent potential delays in HSA establishment such as delays that could result when the HDHP becomes effective on a non-business day.

An individual who becomes an eligible individual after January 1 may make the maximum contribution to an HSA on the first day he or she is an eligible individual. [I.R.S. Notice 2004-2, Q&A 21, 2004-2 I.R.B. 269] In that case, the individual's contribution is based on the individual's expected coverage on the first day of the last month of his or her taxable year (subject to testing period rules, see Qs 4:5–4:9, 4:37–4:40). An individual who becomes eligible on January 1 with self-only coverage and who switches to family coverage on or before December 1 may also take advantage of this rule. [I.R.S. Notice 2008-52, 2008-25 I.R.B. 1166]

> **Note.** Expenses incurred before an HSA is established are not qualified medical expenses. Although certain individuals are treated as eligible individuals on the first day of the taxable year in determining the contribution amount (see Qs 4:5–4:9, 4:37–4:39), an HSA is not established before the date that the HSA is actually established. [I.R.S. Notice 2008-52, 2008-25 I.R.B. 1166), modifying I.R.S. Notice 2007-22, 2007-10 I.R.B. 670]

Q 2:23 May a trustee treat an HSA as established before the date of establishment determined under state law, such as the date when HDHP coverage began?

No. Special rules, however, apply in determining the establishment date of an HSA in connection with a rollover, or where a previous HSA was established (see Qs 2:25–2:26). [I.R.S. Notice 2008-59, Q&A 39, 2008-29 I.R.B. 123]

Q 2:24 If an individual sends in paperwork and an initial deposit to the HSA trustee, is the HSA considered established as of the date of mailing?

Possibly. Very little guidance exists on this point. The answer may depend upon when the HSA trustee considers the account to be established in accordance with its own procedures and applicable state law. In the case of the IRS model forms, "an HSA is established after the form is fully executed by both the HSA owner and the trustee" (or custodian). (See *Purpose of Form, General Instructions*, Form 5305-B—*Health Savings Trust Account* and Form 5305-C —*Health Savings Custodial Account*.) However, a trustee is not required to follow these forms and may substitute its own procedures, for example, procedures that are necessary to comply with state law. Special rules apply for determining the date of establishment for an HSA in connection with a rollover, or where a previous HSA was established (see Qs 2:25–2:26).

Q 2:25 When is an HSA established if the funds in the HSA were rolled over or transferred from an Archer MSA or another HSA?

An HSA that is funded by amounts rolled over or transferred from an Archer MSA or another HSA is established as of the date the prior account was established. Qualified HSA distributions (see Q 5:52) or qualified HSA funding distributions (see Q 5:40) do not affect the HSA establishment date. [I.R.S. Notice 2008-59, Q&A 38, 2008-29 I.R.B. 123; see also I.R.S. Notice 2004-2, Q&A 23, 2004-2 I.R.B. 269]

> **Example.** Tanisha established an Archer MSA on October 17, 2000. On May 13, 2004, Tanisha rolled over the entire amount held in the Archer MSA into her HSA. On January 1, 2008, Tanisha has the HSA trustee make a direct transfer of the entire HSA to an HSA with a new trustee in her name. The establishment date of the HSA with the new trustee is October 17, 2000.

Q 2:26   On what date is an HSA established if the owner had previously established an HSA?

If an HSA owner establishes an HSA, and later establishes another HSA, any later HSA is deemed to be established when the first HSA was established if the owner has an HSA with a balance greater than zero at any time during the 18-month period ending on the date the later HSA is established.

> **Example 1.** Juan established an HSA on March 1, 2007. On June 15, 2007, he withdrew all the funds from the HSA, resulting in a zero balance. On November 21, 2008, Juan established a second HSA. Because the second HSA was established within 18 months of June 15, 2007, the second HSA is deemed to be established on March 1, 2007.

> **Example 2.** The same facts as Example 1, except that Juan establishes a third HSA on January 1, 2009. On that date, the second HSA has a balance greater than zero. The third HSA is deemed to be established on March 1, 2007.

[I.R.S. Notice 2008-59, Q&A 41, 2008-29 I.R.B. 123]

Divorced Parents

Q 2:27   Which rules apply to determine whether a child of divorced parents may be covered under a parent's HSA or HDHP on a tax-free basis?

There are different rules that apply to determine whether a child of divorced parents may be covered under an HSA or HDHP on a tax-free basis. These rules are summarized below.

HDHP. A child can receive benefits under his or her divorced parent's health coverage on a tax-free basis—whether or not that parent is the custodial parent—as long as:

1. Both parents, together, provide over half the child's support for the year (other than through multiple support agreements under which a group of contributors provides support for a child); and
2. One or both parents have custody for more than half the calendar year.

> [I.R.C. §§ 105(b), 152(e); see Treas. Reg. § 1.152-4T, Q&A 5]

> There is no corollary rule in Code Section 106 (which allows exclusion of the premium for employer-provided health coverage); however, the IRS has taken the position that the rule described in Code Section 105(b) relating to a child of divorced parents, should apply for purposes of Code Section 106 as well. (See Q 2:44.) [See Rev. Proc. 2008-48, 2008-36 I.R.B. 586]

Note. Code Sections 105(b) and 106 together allow both the benefit and the premium of employer-provided health coverage to be excluded from an employee's income for federal tax purposes.

HSA. Provided that a child receives over half of the child support from his or her parents who are divorced or legally separated, the child will be treated as a tax dependent of both parents for purposes of excluding both the benefit and premium of employer provided dependent coverage from federal income tax. It also means that one or both parents could use his or her HSA to pay for the child's unreimbursed qualified medical expenses.

Qualified Medical Expenses

Q 2:28 Which distributions from an HSA are excludable from gross income?

Distributions from an HSA used exclusively to pay for qualified medical expenses of the HSA owner, or the HSA owner's spouse or dependents, are excludable from gross income (see chapter 6). In general, amounts in an HSA can be used for qualified medical expenses and will continue to be excludable from the HSA owner's gross income even if the individual is not currently eligible to make contributions to the HSA.

Q 2:29 What are qualified medical expenses?

Qualified medical expenses are amounts paid with respect to the HSA owner, or the HSA owner's spouse or dependents, for medical care as defined in Code Section 213(d), provided that compensation for such paid amounts are not received from any other source, including insurance. Qualified medical expenses are more fully discussed in chapter 6.

Q 2:30 What is included in *medical care*?

The term *medical care* includes amounts paid for the diagnosis, cure, mitigation, treatment, or prevention of disease, or for the purpose of affecting any structure or function of the body. [I.R.C. § 213(d)(1); Treas. Reg. § 1.213-1 (e)(1)(ii); see also, Rev. Rul. 2007-72, 2007-50 I.R.B. 1154] An expenditure that is merely beneficial to the general health of an individual, such as an expenditure for a vacation, is not an expenditure for medical care. However, expenditures for "medicines and drugs" are expenditures for medical care. Medical care is more fully discussed in chapter 6.

Q 2:31 Are payments for insurance qualified medical expenses?

Generally, qualified medical expenses do not include payment for insurance. Exceptions to this rule include:

1. Coverage under a health plan during any period of continuation coverage required under federal law (i.e., COBRA);
2. Coverage under a qualified long-term care insurance contract as defined in Code Section 7702B(b) (see Q 6:56);

3. Coverage under a health plan during a period in which the individual is receiving unemployment compensation under any federal or state law [I.R.C. § 223(d)(2)(C)(iii)]; and

4. For individuals over age 65, an HSA can pay for an employee's share of the premiums for Medicare Part A and Part B, Medicare HMO, and for the employee share of the premiums for employer-sponsored health insurance, including premiums for employer-sponsored retiree health insurance (see Q 6:47). However, an HSA cannot pay for Medigap premiums (e.g., in the case of any HSA owner who has attained the age specified in Section 1811 of the Social Security Act, any health insurance other than a Medicare supplemental policy, as defined in Section 1882 of the Social Security Act).

[I.R.S. Notice 2004-2, Q&A 27, 2004-2 I.R.B. 2]

Q 2:32 May qualified medical expenses be incurred before the HSA is established?

No. The qualified medical expenses must be incurred after the HSA has been established. [I.R.S. Notice 2004-2, Q&A 26, 2004-2 I.R.B. 269] The IRS granted transitional relief on this issue for 2004 (see Q 6:22).

Q 2:33 May an HSA be used to pay for an individual's qualified medical expenses on a tax-free basis even if such individual is not covered by an HDHP?

Yes. Distributions from an HSA to pay for qualified medical expenses of the HSA owner, or the HSA owner's spouse or dependents, may be made without regard to their status as eligible individuals. Thus, it is not necessary for an individual to be covered by an HDHP in order to have his or her qualified medical expenses reimbursed by an HSA on a tax-free basis. However, HSA distributions made for expenses reimbursed by another health plan are not excludable from income, regardless of whether the other health plan is an HDHP (see Qs 6:9, 6:23–6:25). [I.R.S. Notice 2004-50, Q&A 36, 2004-33 I.R.B. 196]

Dependents

Q 2:34 What is the significance for HSAs of the Gulf Opportunity Zone Act of 2005?

On December 16, 2005, Congress passed the Gulf Opportunity Zone Act of 2005 (GOZA) (H.R. 4440), which was signed into law by President George W. Bush on December 21, 2005. [Pub. L. No. 109-135, 119 Stat. 2577 (2005)] The act contains tax incentives and other relief to businesses and individuals affected by hurricanes Katrina, Rita, and Wilma. It also includes a package of technical corrections to several tax laws, including the Working Families Tax Relief Act of 2004 ("WFTRA"). [Pub. L. No. 108-311, 118 Stat. 1166 (2004)] The tax technical corrections include a correction to the definition of *dependent* with respect to HSAs and to dependent care flexible spending arrangements ("FSAs"). This change is retroactive to the effective date of WFTRA, January 1, 2005. (See Qs 2:35–2:42.)

Q 2:35   How did WFTRA change the definition of *dependent*?

Section 201 of WFTRA amended the definition of *dependent* in Code Section 152, effective for taxable years beginning after December 31, 2004. In some regards, the new definition is more restrictive. For example, under the new definition, an individual must be either a *qualifying child* or a *qualifying relative* to be a dependent. [I.R.C. § 152; WFTRA § 201, Pub. L. No. 108-311, 118 Stat. 1166 (2004)]

> **Note.** The new definition of "dependent" was intended to provide a uniform definition of *dependent* for purposes of the dependency exemption, the child credit, the earned income credit, the child and dependent care credit, and head-of-household filing status, but not to group health plans, HSAs, or dependent care assistance programs—to which prior law was to apply. Because of an apparent technical oversight, an exception for employer-sponsored group health plans, HSAs, and dependent care assistance programs was not created. In response, with respect to employer-sponsored group health plans, the IRS then issued guidance that essentially restored prior law treatment (the pre-WFTRA definition) to employer-sponsored group health plans. [I.R.S. Notice 2004-79, 2004-49 I.R.B. 898] However, this guidance did not restore the pre-WFTRA definition for HSAs or dependent care assistance programs.

Q 2:36   How did GOZA change the definition of *dependent*?

The technical corrections contained in GOZA extended the same relief to HSAs and dependent care FSAs that the Treasury Department and the IRS extended to health plans through I.R.S. Notice 2004-79, 2004-49 I.R.B. 898, by eliminating the income limitations from the definition of *qualifying relative.* [GOZA § 404(c)] This means that individuals can qualify as dependents for purposes of receiving tax-free HSA or distributions without regard to that individual's gross income. Similarly, individuals can satisfy the definition of *dependent* for purposes of dependent care FSAs without regard to gross income.

The technical correction also specifies that an individual may qualify as a dependent for purposes of an HSA without regard to whether such individual is married and files a joint return with another taxpayer or is a dependent of another taxpayer. [GOZA § 404(c)] Thus, an individual who is treated as a dependent under this rule "is not subject to the general rule that a dependent of a dependent shall be treated as having no dependents. [Joint Committee Report, WFTRA § 404 (J.C.T. Rep. No. JXC-88-05)]

The changes in GOZA with respect to the definition of dependent are retroactive to the WFTRA effective date of January 1, 2005.

Q 2:37   Who is a dependent for HSA purposes?

Beginning January 1, 2005, the term *dependent* for HSA purposes means either a *qualifying child* (see Q 2:39) or a *qualifying relative* (without regard to the gross income limitation under Code Section 152(d)(1)(B) or the requirements of Code Section 152(b)(1)-(2)) (see Qs 2:36, 2:43). [I.R.C. §§ 152(a)]

> **Historical Note.** For years beginning before 2005, under the pre-WFTRA Code Section 152, the term *dependent* generally meant an individual who bears the relationship described in Q 2:38 and who received more than one-half of his or her support for the year from the taxpayer. Thus, prior to the WFTRA amendment, no income or age limitations existed. [I.R.C. § 152, before amendment by WFTRA § 201] GOZA retroactively removed the income limit applicable to HSAs effective on or after January 1, 2005. Thus, beginning in 2005, the income limits that would have applied to a qualifying relative dependent for HSA purposes in 2005 no longer applied. [See I.R.C. § 223(d)(2)(A), as amended by GOZA § 404(c)] A similar change (removing the income limitation) was made to Code Section 21(b)(1)(B), defining the term *qualifying individual* for dependent care services and reimbursement from a dependent care assistance program (e.g., dependent care FSAs).

Q 2:38   What relationship must the individual have to the taxpayer to be treated as a qualifying relative?

To be a qualifying relative dependent, an individual must bear one of the following relationships with respect to the taxpayer:

- Son or daughter (including stepchildren, legally adopted children, and eligible foster children), or a descendent of either;
- Brother, sister, stepbrother, or stepsister;
- Father or mother, or an ancestor of either;
- Stepfather or stepmother;
- Son or daughter of a brother or sister;
- Brother or sister of the father or mother (i.e., uncle or aunt);
- Son-in-law, daughter-in-law, father-in-law, mother-in-law, brother-in-law, or sister-in-law; or
- An individual (other than an individual who at any time during the year was the taxpayer's spouse) who, for the taxable year of the taxpayer, has as his or her principal place of abode the same place as of the taxpayer and is a member of the taxpayer's household.

[I.R.C. §§ 152(a), 152(d), 152(f)]

The terms *brothers* and *sisters* include half-blood relatives. [I.R.C. § 152(f)(4)] The term *child* includes a legally adopted child, a child who is placed in the taxpayer's home by an authorized placement agency for legal adoption, or a foster child. [I.R.C. §§ 152(f)(1)(B)-(C)] Special rules apply to missing children presumed by law enforcement authorities to have been kidnapped. [See I.R.C. § 152(f)(6)]

A *dependent* does not include an individual who is not a citizen or national of the United States unless the individual is a resident of the U.S. or of a country contiguous to the U.S. However, a child who is legally adopted by a U.S. taxpayer does qualify as a dependent. [I.R.C. § 152(b)(3)]

Q 2:39   Who is a qualifying child?

A *qualifying child,* for HSA purposes, is a daughter, son, stepson, stepdaughter, sibling, or stepsibling (or descendant of any of these) who has the same principal place of abode as the taxpayer for more than one-half of the taxable year and who (other than in the case of total disability) has not yet attained the age specified in Code Section 152(c)(3), as amended (see Qs 2:40–2:41). [I.R.C. § 152(c)(1)] For tax years beginning after 2008, a qualifying child:

1. Does not include an individual who files a joint return (other than a claim of refund) with the individual's spouse for the taxable year beginning in the calendar year in which the taxable year of the taxpayer begins. [I.R.C. § 152(c)(1)(D), as amended by the FCSIA of 2008, § 501(b)]

2. Does not include an individual who is older than the taxpayer claiming the individual as a qualifying child. [I.R.C. § 152(c)(3)(A), as amended by the FCSIA of 2008, § 501(a)]

Special rules apply to a child of divorced or legally separated parents (see Q 2:44).

Q 2:40   Does an individual's age affect his or her status as a qualifying child?

Yes. In order to be treated as a qualifying child, an individual must not have attained age 19 (age 24, if a student) before the close of the calendar year in which the HSA owner's taxable year begins. [I.R.C. § 152(c)(3), as amended]

Q 2:41   Does an individual's disability affect his or her status as a qualifying child?

Yes. The age requirement (i.e., that the qualifying child be less than 19 years old, or 24 if a student) (see Q 2:40) does not apply if the child is permanently and totally disabled. Therefore, an individual who is disabled may qualify as a dependent more easily than an individual who is not disabled. *Permanent and total disability* is defined in Code Section 22(e)(3). If an individual experiences the permanent and total disability at any time during the calendar year, he or she will not be required to satisfy the age requirement. [I.R.C. § 152(c)(3)(B), as amended by WFTRA § 201]

Note. Under prior law (before 2004), there was no age requirement. Thus, disability was not an issue.

Q 2:42   When does a child attain a specified age for purposes of the qualifying child definition?

It would appear that a child attains a specific age on the anniversary of the date that the child was born. This uniform definition is used by the IRS for purposes of the dependent care, adoption, child tax, and earned income credits, and it also applies to dependent care assistance programs, foster care payments, adoption assistance programs, and dependency exemptions. [Rev. Rul. 2003-72, 2003-33 I.R.B. 346; I.R.C. §§ 21 (child care credit), 23 (adoption expenses), 24 (child credit), 32 (earned income credit), 129 (dependent care exclusion), 131 (foster care payments), 137 (adoption assistance) & 151 (personal exemptions)]

Note. Code Section 152(c)(3)(A) requires that a child not attain a specified age (19, or 24 if a student) as of the close of the calendar year in which the HSA owner's taxable year begins. Thus, once an individual attains the specified age, the individual will no longer be a qualifying child for the HSA owner for all future taxable years. Further, the individual will not be a qualifying child for the current taxable year if the individual reached the specified age before the end of the calendar year in which the HSA owner's taxable year began.

Q 2:43   Who is a qualifying relative for purposes of an HSA?

For HSA purposes, a *qualifying relative* is a person who satisfies all of the following four requirements:

1. Is not a *qualifying child* of the taxpayer or of any other taxpayer for any taxable year beginning in the calendar year in which the HSA owner's taxable year begins [I.R.C. § 152(d)(1)(D)];
2. Bears a relationship to the taxpayer (see Q 2:38) [I.R.C. §§ 152(d)(1)(A), 152(d)(2)];
3. Receives more than half of his or her support from the taxpayer for the calendar year in which the HSA owner's taxable year begins [I.R.C. §§ 152(d)(1)(C), 152(d)(3), regarding multiple support agreements]; and
4. Does not have gross income for the calendar year in which the HSA owner's taxable year began in excess of the Code Section 151(d) dependency exemption amount ($3,650 for 2009; $3,500 for 2008). It should be noted that this income limit does not apply for purposes of HSAs or HDHPs (see Qs 2:37–2:38).

Example. Frank's taxable year begins on July 1, 2009. His son Sam, a student, will attain age 24 on December 1, 2009. Sam is not a qualifying child for Frank's 2009–2010 taxable year because Sam turned 24 before the calendar year (2009) closed in which Frank's taxable year (2009–2010) began.

Under the prior Code Section 152 definition, the term *dependent* generally meant an individual who bears the relationship described previously and who received more than half of his or her support for the year from the taxpayer (see Q 2:38).

Note. Under Code Section 152, before it was amended, there were no income or age limitations. Aside from this, and the introduction of new terminology, little has changed (confusion aside) from previous law. However, because of the corrections made after Code Section 152 was amended (to remove the income limitation under the *qualifying relative* definition), little has effectively changed since the previous law because an individual that does not satisfy the definition of *qualifying child* can often satisfy the definition of *qualifying relative*.

[I.R.C. §§ 152(d)(1), 223(d), as amended by GOZA § 404(c)]

Q 2:44   Can a child of divorced or separated parents be claimed as a dependent of both parents if the custodial parent has not released the claim to the exemption for a dependent under Code Section 152(e)(2)?

Yes. Revenue Procedure 2008-48 (2008-36 I.R.B. 1) expanded the definition of dependent (see Q 2:39). The IRS will treat a child who meets all of the following requirements as a dependent of both parents under Code Section 223(d) relating to qualified medical expenses, whether or not the custodial parent releases the claim to the exemption under Code Section 152(e)(2).

1. The parents are divorced, legally separated under a decree of divorce or separate maintenance, legally separated under a written separation agreement, or live apart at all times for the last six months of the calendar year; and

2. Are the parents of a child who:
   (a) Receives over one-half of the child support during the calendar year from the child's parents; and
   (b) Is in the custody of one or both parents for more than one-half of the calendar year;

3. Qualifies as a qualifying child (see Q 2:39) or qualifying relative (see Q 2:43) of one of the child's parents.

[I.R.C. §§ 152(e), 223(d); Rev. Proc. 2008-48, § 3 (2008-36 I.R.B. 1). Although effective August 18, 2008, the Rev. Proc. 2008-48 may be applied in any taxable year beginning after 2004, for which the period of limitation on credit or refund (under I.R.C. § 6511) has not expired as of August 18, 2008.]

Historical Note. Under prior Code Section 152(e), children of divorced or separated parents were treated as dependents of both parents under Code Sections 105(b), 132(h)(2)(B), and 213(d)(5) whether or not a parent released the claim to the exemption. The WFTRA (Pub. L. No. 108-311) and the GOZA (Pub. L. No. 109-135) amended Code Section 152(e) for taxable years beginning after December 31, 2004. Section 152(e) now provides that, in the absence of a qualified pre-1985 instrument [I.R.C. § 152(e)(3)], a child may be treated as the dependent of the noncustodial parent only if the custodial parent releases the claim to the exemption. [I.R.C. § 152(e)(2)] If the custodial parent does not release the claim, the right to the exemption is determined under the general rules of Code Section 152 as discussed previously. Consequently, the preamble to Treasury Regulations Section 1.152-4(f) [73 Fed. Reg. 37797 (July 2, 2008)] explains that, if a custodial parent does not release the claim to the exemption, only the taxpayer who is entitled to claim the child as a dependent under Code Sections 152(c) or 152(d) may treat the child as a dependent for purposes of an HSA (among other purposes). Thus, Revenue Procedure 2008-48 provides a limited exception to that conclusion. [Rev. Proc. 2008-48, § 2.07, 2008-36 I.R.B. 1]

Advantages and Disadvantages of HSAs

Q 2:45   What are the potential advantages of an HSA to an individual?

There are many advantages that may accrue from the establishment of an HSA, including the following:

1. *No employer involvement.* Eligible individuals can establish an HSA without employer involvement.

2. *Deductions for contributions.* Except for employer contributions, all HSA after-tax contributions (within limits) are deductible. Employer contributions are excluded from income.

3. *Contributions by family members permitted.* Unlike an FSA or an HRA, family members (among others) may make contributions into an eligible individual's HSA.

4. *Deduction or exclusions from gross income.* Employer contributions are generally excludable from gross income. In other cases, contributions made by or on behalf of an eligible individual are generally deductible from gross income.

   Example. Harry, an eligible individual, has a health plan through his employer with no annual deductible for 2009. The insurer charges an annual premium of $4,000. If Harry switches to an HDHP with a $1,150 annual deductible, the insurer will charge only $3,200 for the same policy. In addition to saving $800 in premiums, Harry will get a federal income tax deduction for his HSA contribution (see Q 4:60). His account will grow tax free, and he will be able to access the funds in the HSA on a tax-free basis when used to pay for qualified medical expenses. Harry may decide, instead, not to use his HSA and allow his funds to grow on a tax-free basis for future medical expenses.

5. *Itemization.* An eligible individual is not required to itemize deductions on Form 1040, Schedule A—*Itemized Deductions* in order to claim a deduction for his or her allowable HSA contribution.

6. *Tax-exempt status.* Distributions from the account of all contributions and earnings are exempt from federal income tax (tax free) if used to pay for qualified medical expenses. In other cases (e.g., when payments are not used for qualified medical expenses), the contributions and earnings are

tax deferred—distribution amounts are considered taxable at the time of distribution rather than at the time of contribution or growth.

7. *One-time transfers permitted.* A direct trustee-to-trustee transfer from an FSA, HRA, and traditional IRA to fund an HSA may be permitted. Special rules apply. See chapter 5, Rollovers and Transfers.

8. *Vesting.* All account balances are fully vested (nonforfeitable). There are no use-it-or-lose-it rules, as is in the case with health FSAs.

9. *Account ownership.* HSAs are owned by the individual HSA owner (even if employer contributions are made into the HSA).

10. *Choice.* The HSA owner chooses: how much to contribute, when to contribute, the type of financial product(s) in which to invest the account assets, which financial institution will hold the account, how much to use for medical expenses, and whether to pay for medical expenses from the HSA or save the account for future use.

11. *Savings.* HSAs encourage HSA owners to save for future medical expenses, such as: long-term care expenses; non-covered services under future health insurance coverage; insurance coverage after retirement, but before Medicare coverage begins; medical expenses after retirement, but before Medicare coverage begins; and out-of-pocket medical expenses incurred after Medicare coverage begins.

12. *Spousal ownership.* Upon the death of the HSA owner, ownership of the account automatically transfers to the HSA owner's spouse.

13. *Portability.* HSA accounts are portable, regardless of: the HSA owner's employment status; the HSA owner's employer; any change in the HSA owner's age or marital status: and any future medical coverage. An HSA can be rolled over or transferred to another HSA (once per 12-month period). Rollovers and transfers from an Archer MSA into an HSA are permitted (once per 12-month period).

14. *No use-it-or-lose-it rules.* Unlike FSAs, unused account balances are not forfeited at any time.

15. *Encourages thrifty spending.* The HSA rules encourage HSA owners to spend their HSA funds wisely and judiciously.

16. *Lower health care premiums.* The premium for a health plan with a higher deductible is likely to be less costly than the same health plan with a lower deductible.

17. *Contributions.* Contributions may be made by the eligible individual, on behalf of an eligible individual, or by the individual's employer (generally through a cafeteria plan).

18. *Higher contribution limits than an Archer MSA.* An Archer MSA limits contributions to 75 percent of the annual deductible amount (65 percent for self-only coverage). For the year 2009, the annual contribution limit for self-only coverage is $3,000, and the annual contribution limit for family coverage is $6,050 (see Q 2:5). [I.R.C. § 220; Rev. Proc. 2008-66, § 3.22, 2008-45 I.R.B. 1]

19. *Catch-up contributions.* Individuals age 55 and older may generally contribute additional "catch-up" amounts ($1,000 for 2009). (See Qs 2:1, 4:42–4:45.)

20. *Dependent treatment.* The HSA owner's spouse and dependents need not be covered by the HDHP to receive benefits from an HSA on a tax-free basis (see Q 2:28).

21. *Consumer choice and flexibility.* HSAs give individuals and employers flexibility and choice regarding the use of health care dollars that have been contributed to the HSA, and the type of HSA-compatible coverage to offer in conjunction with the HSA.

22. *Protection.* When coupled with an HDHP, an HSA protects against catastrophic financial loss due to unforeseen illness or injury.

23. *No gift tax.* The amount that a beneficiary receives from an HSA is not treated as a taxable gift (see Q 6:86).

24. *Long-term care insurance.* Tax-free distributions from an HSA may be used to pay for long-term care insurance premiums (see Q 6:46) as well as for COBRA continuation coverage, and health continuation insurance while the HSA owner is receiving unemployment compensation (see Q 2:26).

25. *Divisibility.* An HSA is divisible upon divorce (see Q 5:34).

26. *Mistake of fact.* A distribution that is made because of a mistake of fact may be returned if the trustee or custodian permits (see Qs 6:78–6:81).

27. *Tax shelter.* High-income individuals are likely to use an HSA as a tax shelter (*i.e.*, for accumulations). These individuals will pay all medical expenses from non-sheltered assets.

28. *Comparability in employer contributions.* Employer contributions (if any are made) to an HSA must be comparable for all comparable participating employees (i.e., individuals in the same category of employees and having the category of HDHP coverage) (see Qs 1:23, 4:70, 4:73, 4:75, 4:113–4:116, 4:118–4:151), unless offered through a cafeteria plan. This requirement does not apply to an HRA or FSA (but highly compensated/non-highly compensated nondiscrimination requirements apply to health care FSAs and HRAs, which are both self-funded health plans). [I.R.C. §§ 105(h), 125, 4980G]

The following examples demonstrate some of the benefits to individuals of having an HSA.

Example 1. The Half-Penny Scale Corporation offers its employees a family health insurance plan with a $5,000 deductible. With its insurance cost savings, Half-Penny contributes $4,000 to each employee's HSA. Newton, an employee, incurs $5,000 of medical expenses during the year. All expenses are qualified medical expenses. If Newton chooses to use his HSA funds to pay for the medical expenses, Newton will only have to pay for $1,000 of the medical expenses. The $1,000 may be paid from the HSA, if sufficient funds are present in the HSA in addition to Half-Penny's $4,000 contribution, or from non-HSA funds.

Example 2. Same facts as in Example 1, except that Newton has a traditional health insurance plan with a 20 percent copayment and a $500 deductible. Newton would be responsible for $1,400 ($500 + (.20 × $4,500)).

Example 3. Same facts as in Example 1, except that Newton incurs no medical expenses for the year. The $4,000 that Half-Penny contributed to his HSA can be carried forward to the next year or can be used in future years when he may no longer have health care coverage.

Q 2:46   What are the potential disadvantages of an HSA for an individual?

Potential disadvantages of an HSA for an individual include:

1. *Increased debt.* HSAs coupled with HDHPs may create a greater risk of accruing medical debts, especially for families with low income levels and few financial resources to draw upon because HSAs are only allowed in conjunction with HDHPs. The deductible must be paid before the insurer will be responsible for any medical expenses. Because the deductibles are high with HDHPs and, unlike health FSA funds, HSA funds can only be used if such funds are present in the account, low income families may find the deductible to be hard to pay.

2. *Increased out-of-pocket costs for less-healthy individuals.* An HDHP may increase out-of-pocket expenses for individuals with high health care consumption. These individuals would probably benefit more from a health plan that has a low deductible or no deductible.

3. *Decreased quality of health.* An HDHP could have an adverse effect on an individual's health if he or she forgoes medication and tests because he or she cannot—or does not want to—pay expenses. Poor personal decision making (e.g., staying at home instead of going to see a doctor in order to save money) can lead to inadequate medical care.

4. *HDHP requirement.* Making contributions to an HSA is dependent on having an HDHP (on the first day of the month).

5. *Excess contribution penalty.* Contributions in excess of annual limits may be subject to a cumulative nondeductible excise tax of 6 percent (see Qs 4:91, 4:96).

6. *Cessation of account.* An account ceases to be an HSA upon the death of the HSA owner unless the spouse is designated as the beneficiary of the HSA (see Qs 5:22, 5:24, 6:83, 7:47, 7:56, 7:67).

7. *Taxation upon death.* Upon the death of the HSA owner, the HSA is taxable unless the beneficiary of the HSA is the HSA owner's spouse (see Q 6:83).

8. *Taxation in estate.* If a decedent's estate is the beneficiary of the HSA, the estate will have to recognize income in respect to a decedent (see Q 6:83).

9. *No deduction for losses.* Because allowable contributions are deductible, a taxpayer cannot claim a loss from declines in the account value.

10. *Insufficient build-up.* An individual establishing a new HSA might not have sufficient funds accumulated in the account to pay for medical expenses below the deductible under the HDHP. But, once the HSA has sufficient funds, the previously incurred medical expenses can be reimbursed with those funds.

11. *Income tax and penalty.* Amounts distributed from an HSA that are not used to pay for qualified medical expenses are subject to federal income tax and, if the individual is under age 65, will be subject to an additional 10 percent penalty, unless another exception applies (see Qs 6:72–6:74).

12. *Individual responsibility.* The HSA owner is responsible for determining that HSA payments are used for qualified medical expenses.

13. *Transfers from FSA, HRA, or an IRA.* If an amount is directly transferred from an FSA, an HRA, or a traditional IRA to an HSA, the individual must remain an eligible individual for a 13-month "testing period" beginning with the month of transfer. Amounts transferred are subject to taxation and an additional 10 percent penalty if the individual does not remain eligible during the entire testing period (except upon disability or death). (See chapter 5.)

14. *IRS reporting.* An HSA owner must generally file Form 8889—*Health Savings Accounts (HSAs),* to report HSA contributions, determine HSA deductions, and report HSA distributions. No reporting forms are required of participants for HRAs and FSAs.

15. *Record retention.* The HSA owner must keep records to demonstrate to the IRS, if audited, that distributions were used to pay for qualifying medical expenses, as defined under Code Section 213(d).

    Note. The insurer may require policyholders to submit claims so that it can track the plan's deductible.

16. *Medicare enrollment.* Eligibility to contribute to an HSA ends in the month in which the HSA owner enrolls in Medicare.

17. *Adverse selection.* Under the theory of adverse selection, healthy people and less-healthy people separate into different insurance arrangements and the cost of insurance for the less-healthy consequently rises. Thus, such individuals may become uninsured or underinsured.

    Note. Employers that provide a choice between comprehensive protection and an HDHP may experience a shift of the healthier employees to the HDHP. Those employees who remain in the comprehensive plan will likely cause the average cost (for that group) to increase. Healthy workers might even abandon employer-based coverage completely and establish HSAs on their own, especially if they are paying a substantial amount of the premium for the HDHP.

Q 2:47   Who is best suited for adopting an HSA?

Those individuals who prefer, or already have, a high deductible on their health insurance policies (especially those individuals who are highly compensated) will gain the most benefits—primarily in terms of tax benefits. Conversely, if an individual has an employer-paid health policy with no (or a low) deductible, such individuals would not be good candidates for an HSA (nor would they qualify).

An HSA can provide a method for contributing a stream of tax-favored savings for those who are healthy enough and who can afford to do so. Simply stated, the higher the tax bracket, the greater the benefit. On the other hand, lower-paid employees—who may find it difficult to save—may have little enthusiasm for an HSA, even if they would benefit from one (see Q 2:46).

Q 2:48   How might an HSA work for an individual?

An individual may be healthy today, or have a condition requiring regular medication, or be faced with an unexpected medical condition. The following examples demonstrate how an HSA could work under specific circumstances. Most people cannot recoup the amount of their premium payment for health insurance unless they have a large, catastrophic-type claim. HDHP policies with an HSA may make sense for some individuals because these types of policies allow the individual to be covered for large health care expenses at a reduced premium, while "self-insuring" themselves for the small ones with tax-free dollars.

Note. In the following examples, if contributions are made through an employer's cafeteria plan, there will be a FICA tax savings for both HDHP premium payments and HSA contributions. If the HSA is established outside of the employer's plan, the individual will have an income tax deduction but will get no FICA tax savings. HSA administrative fees and account earnings are not considered.

Example 1. Sam, who earns $28,000 per year, is young, healthy, and single. Sam was covered by an HDHP (self-only coverage) during the entire 2009 calendar year. The HDHP has a deductible of $1,200 (whereas a typical traditional health plan deductible is $250), but will have a lower premium cost than he would with a traditional health plan.

In January, Sam established an HSA and deposited $650 into an HSA for the year. As a preventive measure, Sam goes to his doctor's office in November and receives a routine annual exam. Sam also uses the dollars in his HSA to reimburse himself on a tax-free basis for the prescription sunglasses he purchased earlier in the year. In this example, Sam will pay over $200 more ($2,090 – $1,870) with an HDHP and an HSA compared to a traditional health plan with a lower deductible. But the $320 ($650 – $330) in his HSA at the end of the year will roll over and remain in Sam's HSA for future use. Thus, overall, Sam paid $100 less with the HSA.

Plan Benefits	Traditional Plan	HDHP Plan with an HSA
Deductible/person	$250	$1,200
Coinsurance (percentages)	80/20	80/20
Out-of-pocket limit[1]	$1,000	$3,000
Office copays	$20	none
Drug copays	$10/$20	none
A. Annual Premium:	**$1,700**	**$1,200**
Medical Expenses:		
Office visit/exam (1 @ $200)	$20	$180
Eyeglasses (1 @ $150)	$150	$150
B. Total Expenses:	**$170**	**$330**
C. HSA Contribution:	**$0**	**$650**
D. Tax Savings on Contribution (assume 28%):	**$0**	**$560** ($650 × .72)
Total Cost:[2]	$1,870	$2,090
Less HSA Account Balance	$0	$320 ($650 – $330)
Net Result:	$1,870	$1,770
Savings ($1,870 – $1,770):		**$100**[3]

---

[1] Includes deductible and coinsurance.
[2] "Total Cost" equals A, plus (greater of B or C), minus D.
[3] The "savings" are only an approximation. Results will vary among individuals depending upon their tax circumstance and actual premium costs.

Example 2. Holly earns $45,000. Holly goes to her doctor twice during 2009 for a back condition ($150/per visit) and takes medication for pain ($90/per month). Holly was covered by an HDHP (self-only coverage) during the entire year and contributed $2,000 into her HSA—the same amount as her deductible under the HDHP—for the 2009 year. In this example, Holly pays an additional $1,000 ($6,200 – $5,200) with an HDHP and an HSA compared to a traditional health plan with a lower deductible, even with the $620 remaining in her HSA at the end of the year for future use.

Plan Benefits	Traditional Plan	HDHP Plan with an HSA
Deductible	$250	$2,000
Coinsurance (percentages)	80/20	80/20
Out-of-pocket limit[1]	$1,000	$3,000
Office copays	$20	none
Drug copays	$10/$20	none

Plan Benefits	Traditional Plan	HDHP Plan with an HSA
A. Annual Premium:	$4,800	$4,000
Medical Expenses:		
Office visit/exam (2 @ $150)	$40	$300
Medication (12 @ $90)	$360	$1,080
B. Total Expenses:	$400	$1,380
C. HSA Contribution:	$0	$2,000
D. Tax Savings on Contribution (assume 28%):	$0	$1,440 ($2,000 × .72)
Total Cost:[2]	$5,200	$6,820
Less HSA Account Balance	$0	$620 ($2,000 − $1,380)
Net Result:	$5,200	$6,200
Additional Cost ($6,200 − $5,200):	$1,000[3]	

[1] Includes deductible and coinsurance.
[2] "Total Cost" equals A, plus (greater of B or C), minus D.
[3] The "savings" are only an approximation. Results will vary among individuals depending upon their tax circumstance and actual premium costs.

Example 3. The same facts as Example 2, except that Holly has an accident and requires surgery on her knee. The surgery costs $7,000. The deductible and coinsurance are applied, and the out-of-pocket maximums are exceeded. In this example, Holly will have to pay an additional $2,640 ($8,440 − $5,800) with an HDHP and an HSA compared to a traditional health plan. Nothing is left in Holly's HSA account.

Example 4. Same facts as in Example 3, except that Holly had $3,000 in her HSA at the start of the calendar year. Holly could use her HSA funds to absorb the $2,640 additional cost. In that case, she would have $360 ($3,000 − $2,640) remaining in her HSA for future use.

Plan Benefits	Traditional Plan	HDHP Plan with an HSA
Deductible	$250	$2,000
Coinsurance (percentages)	80/20	80/20
Out-of-pocket limit[1]	$1,000	$3,000
Office copays	$20	none
Drug copays	$10/$20	none
A. Annual Premium:	$4,800	$4,000
Medical Expenses:		
Office visit/exam (2 @ $150)	$40	$300

Plan Benefits	*Traditional Plan*	*HDHP Plan with an HSA*
Medication (12 @ $90)	$240	$1,080
Surgery	$720	$1,620
B. Total Expenses:	**$1,000**	**$3,000**
C. HSA Contribution:	**$0**	**$2,000**
D. Tax Savings on Contribution (assume 28%):	**$0**	**$1,440** ($2,000 × .72)
Total Cost:[2]	$5,800	$8,440
Less HSA Account Balance	$0	$0 (used $2,000)
Net Result:	$5,800	$8,440
Additional Cost ($8,440 – $5,800):	**$2,640**[3]	

---

[1] Includes deductible and coinsurance.
[2] "Total Cost" equals *A*, plus (greater of *B* or *C*), minus *D*.
[3] The "savings" are only an approximation. Results will vary among individuals depending upon their tax circumstance and actual premium costs.

Practice Pointer. Instead of using the funds in the HSA to pay for the medical expenses in the above examples, the funds could remain in the HSA and accumulate on a tax-free basis for qualified medical expenses incurred in subsequent years. Alternatively, if no deduction was claimed for the current year's qualified medical expenses, the expenses could be reimbursed tax-free in a subsequent year. The taxpayer should be sure to keep proper documentation.

Chapter 3

Medical Coverage and Insurance

Chapter 3 examines medical coverage and insurance for purposes of determining whether the individual is treated as being covered by a high deductible health plan (HDHP) and no other plan that is not a high deductible health plan. Annual deductibles and out-of-pocket expenses are also addressed. Chapter 3 also examines whether certain insurance contracts (policies, riders, and optional benefits) constitute *permitted insurance*, *permitted coverage*, or *preventive care* within the meaning of Code Section 223, so that employees who are covered by the policies, riders, and optional benefits and who are otherwise eligible to contribute to an HSA remain eligible to make HSA contributions. This chapter also explains the transitional rules that may apply in determining whether the HDHP minimum annual deductible requirement is met and whether the HDHP maximum annual out-of-pocket limits are exceeded in a given year. Contributions to HSAs are discussed in chapter 4.

HDHP Requirements 3-2
Plan Deductible 3-6
    Transitional Rule 3-9
    Out-of-Pocket Expenses 3-9
    Transitional Rule 3-11
    Other Out-of-Pocket Issues 3-12
Limitation on Benefits 3-17
Family Coverage vs. Self-Only Coverage 3-20
Other Health Plan Coverage 3-21
    Permitted Insurance 3-23
    Prescription Drug Coverage 3-24
    Preventive Care Safe Harbor 3-24
    Medical Discount Cards 3-38
    Employee Assistance, Disease Management, and Wellness Programs 3-38
    Health Reimbursement Arrangements 3-40
    Long-Term Care Insurance 3-41
    HSAs Under a Code Section 125 Cafeteria Plan 3-41

Retiree Health Coverage 3-44
Miscellaneous Issues 3-44

HDHP Requirements

Q 3:1   What is a high deductible health plan?

Generally, a high deductible health plan (HDHP) is a health plan that satisfies certain requirements with respect to minimum annual deductibles and maximum annual out-of-pocket expenses for self-only coverage and family coverage (see Q 3:17). [I.R.C. § 223(c)(2)] (See appendix F.) For HSA contribution purposes, a health plan must meet two main requirements to be considered an HDHP:

1. *Minimum annual deductible.* The HDHP's annual deductible for the 2009 tax year must be at least $1,150 for self-only coverage (see Q 3:39) and at least $2,300 for family coverage (see Q 3:40). [I.R.C. §§ 223(c)(2)(A)(i)(I), 223(c)(2)(A)(i)(II); Rev. Proc. 2008-29, § 2, 2008-22 I.R.B. 1039] Table 3-1 shows the minimum annual deductibles for 2009 and earlier years.

Table 3-1. Minimum Annual Deductible

Year Coverage	2009	2008	2007	2006	2005	2004
Self-Only	$1,150	$1,100	$1,100	$1,050	$1,000	$1,000
Family	$2,300	$2,200	$2,200	$2,100	$2,000	$2,000

Note. The minimum annual deductible amounts for 2010 are $1,200 (for self-only coverage) and $2,400 (for family coverage). (See Q 3:7.)

2. *Out-of-pocket expenses.* The annual out-of-pocket expenses—including expenses incurred in satisfying the deductible under the HDHP and co-payments required to be paid under the HDHP for covered benefits (other than premiums)—may not exceed specified limits. Special rules apply to deductibles for services performed out-of-network (see Qs 3:11, 3:18). Table 3-2 shows the maximum out-of-pocket expenses (including co-payments) for 2009 and earlier years. [I.R.C. §§ 223(c)(2)(A)(ii)(I), 223(c)(2)(A)(ii)(II); Rev. Proc. 2008-29, § 2, 2008-22 I.R.B. 1039]

Table 3-2. Maximum Out-of-Pocket Expenses

Year Coverage	2009	2008	2007	2006	2005	2004
Self-Only	$ 5,800	$ 5,600	$ 5,500	$ 5,250	$ 5,100	$ 5,000
Family	$11,600	$11,200	$11,000	$10,500	$10,200	$10,000

[See Rev. Proc. 2008-29, § 2, 2008-22 I.R.B. 1039 for 2009; Rev. Proc. 2007-36, § 4, 2007-22 I.R.B. 1335 for 2008; amending Rev. Proc. 2006-53, § 3.24(1), 2006-48 I.R.B. 996 for 2007; Rev. Proc. 2005-70, § 3.22, 2005-47 I.R.B. 979 for 2006; Rev. Proc. 2004-71, § 3.22, 2004-2 C.B. 970 for 2005.]

Note. The maximum out-of-pocket expense limits for 2010 are $5,950 (for self-only coverage) and $11,900 (for family coverage). (See Q 3:7.)

Example 1. A plan provides health coverage for Albert and his family in 2009. The plan provides for the payment of covered medical expenses of any member of Albert's family once the member has incurred covered medical expenses during the year in excess of $1,150 even if the HDHP's minimum annual deductible of $2,300 for family coverage has not been satisfied. If Albert incurred covered medical expenses of $1,500 in a year and no other family member incurred medical expenses during the year, the plan would pay $350. Thus, benefits are potentially available under the plan even if the family's covered medical expenses do not exceed $2,300. Because the plan provides family coverage with an annual deductible of less than $2,300, the plan is not an HDHP for 2009.

Example 2. Same facts as in the preceding example, except that the plan has a $5,950 family deductible and only provides payment for covered medical expenses if any member of Albert's family has incurred covered medical expenses during the year in excess of $2,300. The plan satisfies the requirements for an HDHP with respect to the deductibles for 2009.

Example 3. Perseus has self-coverage under his employer's HDHP for 2009 with a $2,000 annual deductible. This means that Perseus will pay the first $2,000 of any medical expenses incurred during the year before the health plan will pay any benefits. The HDHP then provides that it will pay 80 percent of the next $3,000 in medical expenses incurred by Perseus during the year and Perseus will pay 20 percent of the next $3,000, or $600. The HDHP will then pay 100 percent of the covered medical expenses over $5,000. Perseus's total annual maximum out-of-pocket expenses (not counting any premiums Perseus might have to pay) is $2,600, which is within the 2009 out-of-pocket limit of $5,800 ($5,600 for 2008) for self-coverage and the HDHP deductible of $2,000 is greater than the minimum of $1,150 ($1,100 for 2008) for self-only coverage. Therefore, the plan is an HDHP.

Q 3:2 Can an insured or self-insured medical reimbursement plan sponsored by an employer be an HDHP?

Yes. An HDHP can be an insured or a self-insured plan. [I.R.S. Notice 2004-2, Q&A 7, 2004-2 I.R.B. 269]

Q 3:3 Is a limited coverage plan treated as an HDHP?

No. An HDHP does not include a plan where substantially all of the coverage is for accidents, disability, dental care, vision care, or long-term care (see Qs 3:4, 3:43).

Q 3:4   Must an HDHP provide meaningful medical coverage in order to be considered an HDHP under Code Section 223?

Yes. The fact that Congress clearly specified that a plan that primarily covers "permitted insurance" or accidents, disability, dental care, vision care, or long-term care would not be considered an HDHP for purposes of the HSA rules indicates that the HDHP accompanying the HSA must provide meaningful medical coverage for participants. This is consistent with IRS Notice 2004-50 [2004-33 I.R.B. 196], which allows an HDHP to exclude certain benefits as long as significant benefits remain (see Q 3:32). However, there is no bright line test to determine when HDHP coverage will be considered meaningful and when it will be considered merely a sham. Some employers and insurers may be interested in offering reduced benefits under the HDHP in exchange for lower premiums. However, there is a limit to how much the benefits can be reduced. It would appear that, in order to be considered an HDHP for purposes of the HSA rules, an HDHP must, at a minimum, exhibit risk-shifting and risk distribution characteristics of insurance and cover major medical and hospital benefits. [I.R.S. Notice 2004-50, Q&As 14, 15, 2004-33 I.R.B. 196]

> **Note.** A plan will not be an HDHP if the only coverage it provides is for permitted insurance (see Q 3:44) and/or coverage for accidents, disability, dental care, vision care, or long-term care (see Qs 2:8, 3:32). [I.R.C. § 223(c)(2)(B)]

Q 3:5   Does a state high-risk health plan qualify as an HDHP?

Yes. A state high-risk health plan (high-risk pool) will qualify as an HDHP for 2009 if the plan does not pay benefits below the minimum annual deductible of $1,150 for self-only coverage and $2,300 for family coverage (see Q 3:1). [I.R.S. Notice 2004-50, Q&A 13, 2004-33 I.R.B. 196]

Q 3:6   Would a health plan that negotiates discounted prices for services qualify as an HDHP if an HSA owner receives services at a discount?

Yes. Health plans that negotiate discounted prices for services do not fail to meet the HDHP requirements merely because an HSA owner receives services at the discounted rate before satisfying the plan deductible. [I.R.S. Notice 2004-50, Q&A 25, 2004-33 I.R.B. 196]

Q 3:7   Are the minimum annual deductible and maximum out-of-pocket expense amounts applicable to the HDHP under Code Section 223 adjusted for inflation?

Yes. The annual amounts, as well as the maximum HSA contribution/deduction, are indexed for inflation using annual cost-of-living adjustments. Any increase is rounded to the nearest multiple of $50 (see Table 3-1). [I.R.C.

§ 223(g)(1)-(2); see Rev. Proc. 2008-29, § 2, 2008-22 I.R.B. 1039 for 2009; 2007-36, § 4, 2007-22 I.R.B. 1335 for 2008]

The dollar amounts in Code Section 223(b)(2) (i.e., the $2,250 and $4,500 base limitations) are adjusted to reflect cost-of-living increases relative to the consumer price index (CPI) for 1997. The CPI for a year is the average for the 12-month period ending on March 31 for such year. The $2,250 and $4,500 base amounts used to compute the monthly limitation on deductions for 2009 can be computed as follows (to the nearest multiple of $50):

a. $3,000 = $\dfrac{\$\,2{,}250 \ \times \ \text{Average CPI April 2007 to March 2008}}{\text{Average CPI April 1996 to March 1997}}$

b. $5,950 = $\dfrac{\$\,4{,}500 \ \times \ \text{Average CPI April 2007 to March 2008}}{\text{Average CPI April 1996 to March 1997}}$

For the dollar amounts in Code Section 223(c)(2)(A) (i.e., the $1,000 and $5,000 figures), the adjustment uses 2003 instead of 1997. The $1,000 and $5,000 base amounts used to determine whether a health plan is an HDHP (minimum deductible and maximum out-of-pocket expenses) for 2009 can be computed as follows (to the nearest multiple of $50):

a. $1,150 = $\dfrac{\$\,1{,}000 \ \times \ \text{Average CPI April 2007 to March 2008}}{\text{Average CPI April 2002 to March 2003}}$

b. $5,800 = $\dfrac{\$5{,}000 \ \times \ \text{Average CPI April 2007 to March 2008}}{\text{Average CPI April 2002 to March 2003}}$

Note. For taxable years beginning before 2008, the date for which the CPI is measured is the 12-month period ending on August 31 instead of March 31. The adjusted amounts for any year are required to be published by June 1 of the preceding calendar year. [I.R.C. § 223(g)(1), as amended by the Tax Relief and Health Care Act of 2006; Rev. Proc. 2008-29, 2008-22 I.R.B. 1039]

Q 3:8   Must an HDHP be offered on a calendar year basis?

No. The HDHP need not be offered on a calendar year basis. Code Section 223(c), which defines a high deductible health plan, states only that a high deductible health plan must have a minimum annual deductible. Neither the statute nor any Treasury guidance indicates that the deductible must be based on a calendar year. In fact, Notice 2004-50, Q&A 22 (see example) suggests the opposite by including as part of the facts an HDHP that begins on July 1. [See also I.R.S. Notice 2005-83, 2005-49 I.R.B. 1075]

Q 3:9   How are changes to the deductibles and out-of-pocket expense limits applied?

Any required change to the deductibles and out-of-pocket expense limits may be applied as of the renewal date of the plan in cases where the renewal date occurs after the beginning of the calendar year, but in no event longer than a 12-month period ending on the renewal date. Thus, a fiscal-year plan that satisfies the minimum annual deductible on the first day of the first month of its fiscal year may apply that deductible for the entire fiscal year, even if the minimum annual deductible increases on January 1 of the next calendar year. [I.R.S. Notice 2004-50, Q&A 86, 2004-33 I.R.B. 196; rule also mentioned in Treas. Press Rel. JS-2996 (Nov. 11, 2005)]

> **Example.** An individual obtains self-only coverage under an HDHP on June 1, 2009, the first day of the plan year, with an annual deductible of $1,150—the minimum annual deductible allowed for 2009 for self-only coverage. The cost-of-living adjustment requires the minimum deductible amount to be increased for 2010 to $1,200. The plan's deductible is not increased to comply with the increased minimum deductible amount until the plan's renewal date of June 1, 2010. The plan satisfies the requirements for an HDHP with respect to deductibles through May 30, 2010. The plan must provide disclosure information on cost sharing, deductibles, and limitations on coverage to participants in the plan. The IRS is to determine this disclosure information (see chapter 7).

Plan Deductible

Q 3:10   What is the plan deductible?

The plan deductible is the amount of covered medical expenses that must be paid by the HSA owner before the health plan will begin to cover medical expenses.

Q 3:11   Are plan deductibles for out-of-network services taken into account when determining the HDHP maximum out-of-pocket limitation?

No. In the case of a health plan using a network of providers, such plan's annual deductible for services provided outside of such network is disregarded when determining whether the HDHP maximum out-of-pocket limit ($5,800 for self-only coverage and $11,600 for family coverage for 2009) under an HDHP is satisfied. [I.R.C. §§ 223(c)(2)(D), 223(c)(2)(D)(ii)]

> **Practice Pointer.** Although separate in-network and out-of-network deductibles appear to be permitted, an HDHP is not required to have separate deductibles for in-network and out-of-network services. If there is a separate out-of-network deductible, however, that deductible will be disregarded in determining an HSA owner's maximum annual contribution or deduction for the year pursuant to the Code (see Q 3:18). [I.R.C. § 223(c)(2)(D)(ii)]

Q 3:12   What medical expenses may be taken into account in determining when the HDHP deductible is satisfied for purposes of a post-deductible HRA or post-deductible health FSA?

For purposes of a post-deductible HRA or post-deductible health FSA, only medical expenses described in Code Section 213(d) and covered by the HDHP may be taken into account in determining whether the HDHP maximum annual deductible (see Q 3:10), or the minimum annual deductible (see Q 3:1), has been satisfied. For example, if the HDHP does not cover chiropractic care, expenses incurred for chiropractic care do not count toward satisfying the HDHP deductible or the minimum deductible.

For self-only HDHP coverage, only the covered medical expenses of the covered individual count toward satisfying the HDHP deductible or the minimum deductible. [I.R.S. Notice 2008-59, Q&A 15, 2008-29 I.R.B. 123]

Example. In 2009, Marvin Gail and his spouse and child have family HDHP coverage with a $2,500 deductible. The HDHP does not provide benefits for vision or dental care. The Gails are also covered by a combination limited purpose/post-deductible HRA that pays or reimburses Code Section 223(d) medical expenses incurred by each family member after the family incurs $2,500 in covered medical expenses, and pays or reimburses vision and dental expenses before and after the HDHP deductible is satisfied. On February 15, 2009, the family incurs $2,500 in vision and dental expenses that are reimbursed by the HRA. On March 17, 2009, the family then incurs $400 in expenses covered by the HDHP (but for the deductible). The family must incur an additional $2,100 in covered medical expenses before the HDHP deductible is satisfied. The HRA may not reimburse the family for the $400 of expenses because the family had not incurred $2,500 in covered expenses when the $400 was incurred.

Q 3:13   Can a health plan's deductible period last longer than 12 months?

Yes. However, if the health plan's deductible period is longer than 12 months, the plan's annual deductible limit must be adjusted to determine whether the maximum annual deductible is exceeded. If that limit is exceeded, the plan is not an HDHP.

Q 3:14   How is the plan's annual deductible limit adjusted when the deductible period lasts longer than 12 months?

In the case of self-coverage, the HDHP's annual deductible for the 2009 tax year is $1,150 ($1,100 for 2008). For family coverage, the deductible must be at least $2,300 for 2009 ($2,200 for 2008). For plans that define the deductible period over a period longer than 12 months, the limits must generally be adjusted to determine whether a plan satisfies the HSA requirements (see Q 3:1). [I.R.S. Notice 2004-50, Q&A 24, 2004-33 I.R.B. 196] The limit is adjusted by taking the following steps:

1. Multiply the plan's minimum annual deductible by the number of months allowed to satisfy the deductible.

2. Divide the amount in Step 1 by 12. This is the adjusted deductible for the longer period that is used to test for compliance.

3. Compare the amount in Step 2 to the plan's deductible. If the plan's deductible equals or exceeds the amount in Step 2, the plan satisfies the minimum deductible requirements.

Note. For months before January 1, 2006, a health plan that otherwise would qualify as an HDHP except for an annual deductible that does not satisfy the rules above for periods of more than 12 months may be treated as an HDHP under the transitional rule (see Q 3:15).

Example 1. For 2009, a health plan takes into account medical expenses incurred in the last three months of 2008 to satisfy its deductible for calendar year 2009. The plan's deductible for self-only coverage is $1,500 and covers 15 months (the last three months of 2008 and 12 months of 2009). To determine whether the health plan's deductible satisfies the $1,150 for self-coverage annual deductible limits for 2009, the following calculations are performed:

1. Minimum annual deductible (self-only coverage): $1,150

2. Multiplied by the number of months in which expenses incurred are taken into account to satisfy the deductible: 15 = $17,250

3. Divide the result ($17,250) by 12: = $1,437

The HDHP minimum deductible for self-only coverage for 15 months must be at least $1,437. Because the plan's deductible, $1,500, exceeds $1,437, the plan's self-only coverage satisfies the plan deductible rule. The maximum annual HSA contribution for an eligible individual with self-only coverage for 2009 is $3,000 (the 2009 maximum statutory contribution limit).

Note. For taxable years beginning after 2006, the annual deductible limit no longer applies. As a result, beginning after 2006, contributions up to the annual statutory limit (as indexed for inflation) will be permitted even though the annual deductible under the HDHP is less than the statutory limit (see Q 4:30).

Example 2. Same facts as in the preceding example, except the family deductible for the 15-month period is $3,000. To determine whether the health plan's deductible satisfies the $2,300 for family coverage annual deductible limits for 2009, the following calculations are performed:

1. Minimum annual deductible (family coverage): $2,300

2. Multiplied by the number of months in which expenses incurred are taken into account to satisfy the deductible: 15 = $34,500

3. Divide the result ($34,500) by 12: $2,875

The HDHP minimum deductible for family coverage for 15 months must be at least $2,875. Because the plan's deductible, $3,000, exceeds $2,875, the plan's family coverage satisfies the plan deductible rule. The maximum annual HSA contribution for an eligible individual with family coverage under these facts is $5,950 (the 2009 maximum statutory contribution limit).

Transitional Rule

Q 3:15   Can a health plan that would otherwise qualify as an HDHP but for an annual deductible that does not satisfy the rules for periods of more than 12 months be treated as an HDHP?

Possibly. For months before January 1, 2006, a health plan that would otherwise qualify as an HDHP but for an annual deductible that does not satisfy the rules stated in Q 3:14 for periods of more than 12 months will be treated as an HDHP if the plan was in effect or submitted for approval to state insurance regulators by August 16, 2004 (the date of publication of Notice 2004-50 in the Internal Revenue Bulletin). Individuals covered under these health plans will continue to be eligible to contribute to HSAs before January 1, 2006. [I.R.S. Notice 2004-50, 2004-33 I.R.B. 196, see "Transition Relief" on last page]

Note. The transitional guidance was provided to allow policy providers time to modify HDHP policies to include prescription drug benefits that meet the HDHP requirements.

Out-of-Pocket Expenses

Q 3:16   What are out-of-pocket expenses?

The term *out-of-pocket expenses* includes the plan's annual deductible, co-payments, and any co-insurance payments required by the plan, but does not include premiums for covered benefits. [I.R.C. § 223(c)(2)(A)(ii); I.R.S. Notice 2004-2, Q&A 3, 2004-2 I.R.B. 269; see also I.R.S. Notice 2004-50, Q&A 21, 2004-33 I.R.B. 196]

Q 3:17   What are the limits for out-of-pocket expenses?

The annual out-of-pocket expenses for covered benefits for 2009 may not exceed $5,800 ($5,600 for 2008) for self-only coverage and $11,600 ($11,200 for 2008) for family coverage. [Rev. Proc. 2008-29, 2008-22 I.R.B. 1039 for 2009, Rev. Proc. 2007-36, 2007-22 I.R.B. 1335 for 2008] The annual out-of-pocket expenses for 2010 may not exceed $5,950 for self-only coverage and $11,900 for family coverage. [Rev. Proc. 2009-29, 2009-22 I.R.B. 1050]

Q 3:18   Are amounts paid by the HSA owner toward covered medical expenses for out-of-network services required to be applied toward the out-of-pocket limit?

No. Amounts paid by the HSA owner toward covered medical expenses for out-of-network services are *not* required to be applied toward the out-of-pocket limit. Rather, the annual out-of-pocket limit need only include amounts spent for covered in-network services.

Note. A network plan is a plan that generally provides more favorable benefits for services provided by its network of providers than for services provided outside of the network. In the case of a plan using a network of providers, the plan does not fail to be an HDHP (if it would otherwise meet the requirements of an HDHP) solely because the out-of-pocket expense limits for services provided outside of the network exceed the maximum annual out-of-pocket expense limits allowed for an HDHP (see Q 3:17).

Practice Pointer. The annual out-of-pocket limit need only include amounts spent for covered in-network services. A plan is not required to count out-of-network charges in calculating whether the out-of-pocket limit has been reached. Amounts paid by an HSA owner for covered in-network medical expenses are applied toward the out-of-pocket limit.

Note. In taxable years beginning before 2007, the plan's annual deductible for out-of-network services is not taken into account in determining the annual contribution limit. [I.R.C. § 223(c)(2)(D)(ii)] In other words, if there are two separate deductibles (one for network and one for non-network), only the network deductible would be used to determine the HSA contribution and deduction limit in years beginning before 2007.

Q 3:19 Must a plan specify an out-of-pocket maximum in order to be considered an HDHP?

Generally, a plan that does not specify an out-of-pocket maximum is not an HDHP. However, if a plan is structured in such a way that the HSA owner would never exceed the out-of-pocket limitation, then the plan could be considered an HDHP. [I.R.S. Notice 2004-50, Q&A 17, 2004-33 I.R.B. 196]

Note. The terms *HSA owner, account owner, account holder,* and *account beneficiary* are used interchangeably in IRS publications, notices, and announcements to refer to the person that established the HSA. To avoid confusion, the term *HSA owner* will be used to refer to that person.

Example 1. A plan requires an HSA owner with self-only coverage to satisfy a $2,500 deductible, and then pays 100 percent of covered benefits above the deductible. This plan would never violate the HDHP maximum annual out-of-pocket limitation.

Example 2. A plan provides self-only coverage with a $2,500 deductible. The plan imposes a lifetime limit on reimbursements for covered benefits of $1 million. For expenses for covered benefits incurred above the deductible, the plan reimburses 80 percent of the usual and customary (UCR) costs. Because there is no express limit on out-of-pocket expenses, the plan does not qualify as an HDHP because it is possible that the out-of-pocket maximum limitation will be exceeded.

Example 3. Same facts as in the preceding example, except that after the 20 percent co-insurance paid by the covered individual reaches $3,000, the plan pays 100 percent of the UCR costs until the $1 million limit is reached (see Q 3:32). For the purpose of determining the individual's out-of-pocket expenses, the plan takes into account only the 20 percent of UCR paid by the individual, up to $3,000. This plan satisfies the out-of-pocket maximum limitation even though no express maximum is stated.

Transitional Rule

Although the following transitional relief no longer applies (see Qs 3:20–3:23), it has been retained for historical purposes.

Q 3:20 What transitional relief was granted by the IRS to HDHPs relative to out-of-pocket expenses when the health plan does not provide any maximum on payments above the deductible?

For months before January 1, 2005, a health plan that would qualify as an HDHP but for the lack of an express maximum on payments above the deductible that complies with the out-of-pocket requirement (see Q 3:19) will be treated as an HDHP. Individuals covered under these health plans will continue to be eligible to contribute to HSAs before January 1, 2005. [I.R.S. Notice 2004-50, 2004-33 I.R.B. 196, see "Transitional Rule" of notice on last page]

Q 3:21 What transitional relief was provided for a health plan that complies with state laws that mandate benefits without regard to a deductible or a deductible below the minimum annual deductible?

Several states currently require that health plans provide certain benefits without regard to a deductible that is below the minimum (e.g., first-dollar coverage or coverage with a low deductible). These health plans are not HDHPs. An individual covered under this type of health plan is not eligible to contribute to an HSA. However, because of the short period between the enactment of HSAs and the effective date of Code Section 223, these states did not have sufficient time to modify their laws to conform to the standards of Code Section 223. When a plan is not an HDHP solely because of state-mandated benefits, an otherwise eligible individual covered under this type of plan will be treated as an eligible individual and may contribute to an HSA for months before January 1, 2006 (the transition period) for state-mandated benefits in effect on January 1, 2004. [I.R.S. Notice 2004-43, 2004-27 I.R.B. 10] This transitional rule was extended for certain non-calendar-year health plans (see Q 3:22).

Q 3:22 Why was the transitional relief provided in Notice 2005-83 extended for non-calendar-year health plans?

Generally, a health plan may not reduce existing benefits before the plan's renewal date. Thus, even though a state may amend its laws before January 1,

2006, to authorize HDHPs that comply with Code Section 223(c)(2), non-calendar-year plans may still fail to qualify as HDHPs after January 1, 2006 because existing benefits cannot be changed until the next renewal date.

> **Example.** A state amends its statute effective July 30, 2005 to comply with HDHP requirements under federal law. A fiscal year plan with a year that begins on July 1, 2005 is required to retain the state-mandated low deductible coverage for the plan year July 1, 2005 through June 30, 2006 because the benefits can be modified only on the renewal date. As a result, although the state has amended its statute, the health plan will fail to be an HDHP for months after January 1, 2006 (i.e., for the months of January through June 2006). (See, however, Q 3:23.)

Q 3:23   When did the additional transitional relief for a coverage period of 12 months or less in a non-calendar year health plan expire?

The transition relief in Notice 2004-43 [2004-27 I.R.B. 10] (see Q 3:20) was modified to provide that, for any coverage period of 12 months or less beginning before January 1, 2006, a health plan that otherwise qualifies as an HDHP as defined in Code Section 223(c)(2), except that it complied on its most recent renewal date before January 1, 2006, with state-mandated requirements (in effect on January 1, 2004) to provide certain benefits without regard to a deductible or with a deductible below the minimum annual deductible (see Q 3:1), will be treated as an HDHP. The additional transitional relief does not apply after the earlier of the health plan's next renewal date or December 31, 2006. [I.R.S. Notice 2005-83, 2005-49 I.R.B. 1075]

Other Out-of-Pocket Issues

Q 3:24   Must a penalty payment or flat-dollar charge paid by the covered individual for failure to obtain pre-certification for a specific provider be treated as an out-of-pocket expense?

No. Penalty payments or flat-dollar charges incurred because of a failure to obtain pre-certification for covered expenses are not required to be treated as out-of-pocket expenses. Therefore, an HDHP need not count such amounts toward the $5,800/$11,600 maximum out-of-pocket limits for 2009 (see Q 3:17). [I.R.S. Notice 2004-50, Q&As 18-19, 2004-33 I.R.B. 196]

> **Example.** A health plan that otherwise qualifies as an HDHP generally requires a 10 percent co-insurance payment after a covered individual satisfies the deductible. However, if an individual fails to get pre-certification for a specific provider, the plan requires a 20 percent co-insurance payment. Only the generally applicable 10 percent co-insurance payment is included in computing the maximum out-of-pocket expenses paid. [I.R.S. Notice 2004-50, Q&A 19, 2004-33 I.R.B. 196; see too I.R.S. Notice 2004-2, Q&A 4, 2004-2 I.R.B. 269] The plan satisfies the maximum out-of-pocket limitation requirements for an HDHP. The result in this example would be the same if the plan imposed a higher co-insurance amount for an out-of-network provider.

Q 3:25   **Are cumulative embedded deductibles under family coverage subject to the out-of-pocket maximum?**

Yes. In general, an HDHP must limit the out-of-pocket expenses paid by the covered individuals, either by design or by its express terms (see Qs 3:17, 3:27).

Example. In 2009, a plan that otherwise qualifies as an HDHP provides family coverage with a $2,400 deductible for each family member. The plan pays 100 percent of covered benefits for each family member after that family member satisfies the $2,400 deductible. The plan does not provide any express limit on out-of-pocket expenses. The maximum out-of-pocket expense limit for family coverage is $11,600. The plan is not an HDHP for a family with five or more covered individuals because the amount that these individuals pay in out-of-pocket expenses exceeds the maximum out-of-pocket limitation under Code Section 223 ($2,400 × 5 ($12,000) exceeds $11,600). However, the out-of-pocket expense limit of $11,600 for any family with two to four covered individuals is not exceeded because the amount that these individuals pay in out-of-pocket expenses would not exceed the maximum out-of-pocket threshold under Code Section 223 ($2,400 × 4 ($9,600) does not exceed $11,600 (the 2009 limit)). [I.R.S. Notice 2004-50, Q&A 20 (ex. 1), 2004-33 I.R.B. 196]

Q 3:26   **Are cumulative embedded deductibles under family coverage subject to the out-of-pocket maximum if the plan contains an umbrella deductible of $11,600 or less for 2009?**

No. The plan qualifies as an HDHP for the family, regardless of the number of covered individuals. The out-of-pocket maximum of $11,600 for 2009 cannot be exceeded.

Example. In 2009, a plan that otherwise qualifies as an HDHP provides family coverage with a $3,000 deductible for each family member. The plan pays 100 percent of covered benefits for each family member after that family member satisfies the $3,000 deductible. The plan includes an umbrella deductible of $11,000. The plan reimburses 100 percent of covered benefits if the family satisfies the $11,000 in the aggregate, even if no single family member satisfies the $3,000 embedded deductible. The HDHP out-of-pocket maximum limitation ($11,600 for 2009) is not exceeded and the plan qualifies as an HDHP for the family, regardless of the number of covered individuals. [I.R.S. Notice 2004-50, Q&A 20 (ex. 2), 2004-33 I.R.B. 196]

Q 3:27   **Are amounts incurred by an individual for medical care for noncovered expenses included in computing the plan's out-of-pocket expenses?**

No. Amounts incurred for noncovered benefits (including amounts in excess of UCR and financial penalties) are not counted toward the $1,150/$2,300 HDHP minimum annual deductible or the $5,800/$11,600 out-of-pocket limits for 2009. Note, however, that a health plan's out-of-pocket limit includes the deductible, co-payments, and other amounts (but not premiums). [I.R.S. Notice 2004-2, Q&A 3, 2004-2 I.R.B. 269; I.R.S. Notice 2004-50, Q&A 21, 2004-33 I.R.B. 196]

Note. If a plan does not take co-payments into account in determining whether the deductible is satisfied, the co-payments must still be taken into account in determining whether the out-of-pocket maximum is exceeded.

Example. In 2009, a health plan has a $1,150 deductible for self-only coverage. After the deductible is satisfied, the plan pays 100 percent of UCR for covered benefits. In addition, the plan pays 100 percent for preventive care, minus a $20 co-payment per screening. The plan does not take into account co-payments in determining whether the $1,150 HDHP minimum annual deductible has been satisfied. The co-payments must be included in determining whether the plan meets the HDHP out-of-pocket maximum of $5,800 (the 2009 limit for self-only coverage). Unless the plan includes an express limit on out-of-pocket expenses taking into account the co-payments, or limits the co-payments to $4,650 ($5,800 less $1,150 for 2009), the plan is not an HDHP. If co-payments were limited to $4,650, the $5,800 limit would not be exceeded with a $1,150 deductible.

Q 3:28   If an employer changes health plans midyear, is the minimum annual deductible of $1,150/$2,300 (for 2009) satisfied if the new HDHP provides a credit toward the deductible for expenses incurred during the previous health plan's short plan year?

Yes. If the period during which expenses are incurred for purposes of satisfying the deductible is 12 months or less and the plan satisfies the requirements for an HDHP, the new plan may take into account unreimbursed expenses incurred during the prior plan's short plan year (whether or not the prior plan is an HDHP) without violating the $1,150/$2,300 HDHP annual minimum deductible limits (for 2009). [I.R.S. Notice 2004-50, Q&A 22, 2004-33 I.R.B. 196]

Example. An employer with a calendar-year health plan switches from a non-HDHP plan to a new plan with coverage effective on July 1. The annual deductible under the new plan satisfies the $1,150/$2,300 (for 2009) annual deductible limits for an HDHP. The new plan counts expenses incurred under the prior plan during the first six months of the year in determining whether the new plan's annual deductible is satisfied. The new plan satisfies the HDHP deductible limit.

Q 3:29 If an eligible individual changes coverage during the plan year from self-only HDHP coverage to family HDHP coverage, does the individual fail to be covered by an HDHP merely because the family HDHP coverage takes into account expenses incurred while the individual had self-only coverage?

No. The family plan does not fail to be an HDHP because it takes into account expenses incurred while an individual had self-only coverage under an HDHP. [I.R.S. Notice 2004-50, Q&A 23, 2004-33 I.R.B. 196]

Example. Melody, an eligible individual, has self-only qualifying HDHP coverage from January 1 through April 30, marries in April, and from May 1 through December 31 has family qualifying HDHP coverage. The family coverage plan applies expenses incurred by Melody from January through April toward satisfying the family deductible. Melody's coverage satisfies the HDHP requirements for family coverage.

For taxable years beginning after 2007, an individual who is covered by an HDHP on the first day of the last month of his or her taxable year (generally December 1) may contribute up to the full annual amount ($3,000/$5,950 for 2009) even though he or she was only an eligible individual for part of the taxable year. The individual may have to pay tax on the contribution (plus a 10 percent penalty) if the individual does not remain an eligible individual for a 13-month period beginning with the last month of the taxable year (generally December), except in the case of death or disability. (See Q 4:5.)

Note. For years beginning before 2008, Melody's contribution to an HSA would be based on four months of the HDHP self-only coverage (i.e., 4/12 of the deductible for the self-only coverage) and eight months of HDHP family coverage (8/12 of the deductible for family coverage).

Q 3:30 If an eligible individual changes coverage during the plan year from family HDHP coverage to self-only HDHP coverage, does the individual fail to be covered by an HDHP merely because the self-only HDHP coverage takes into account expenses incurred while the individual had family coverage?

No. An individual who switches from a family HDHP to a self-only HDHP does not fail to be an eligible individual during the period of self-only coverage merely because the self-only HDHP, for the purpose of satisfying the self-only deductible, takes into account expenses incurred while the individual had family HDHP coverage. A self-only HDHP may use any reasonable method to allocate the covered expenses incurred during the period of family coverage for the purpose of satisfying the deductible for self-only coverage. For example, subject to state law requirements, the plan may allocate to the self-only deductible only the expenses incurred by that individual. Alternatively, the plan may allocate the expenses incurred during family HDHP coverage on a per-capita basis according to the number of persons covered by the family HDHP. If the family deductible was satisfied before the change to self-only coverage, the plan may also treat the individual as having satisfied the self-only deductible for that plan year. In all cases, each expense must be allocated on a reasonable and consistent basis and, *except* in the case of COBRA continuation coverage, each expense may be allocated to only one individual, and the plan year must be 12 months.

Note. If COBRA continuation coverage is required to be made available, the HDHP must comply with the requirements of Treasury regulations under Code Section 4980B regarding continuation coverage requirements of group health plans for those individuals receiving COBRA continuation coverage (see Q 4:110). [Treas. Reg. § 54.4980B-5, Q&A 2] Generally, under that section, if the pro rata allocation of expenses are less than the actual expenses incurred, then allocation of only a ratable share of the family expenses would *not* comply with the requirements of the regulations. [I.R.S. Notice 2008-59, Q&A 12, 2008-29 I.R.B. 123]

Example 1. Drake Manufacturing offers its employees a calendar-year health plan otherwise qualifying as an HDHP. Edward, an employee, and his spouse are covered by Drake's family coverage HDHP with a $6,000 deductible. Edward incurs $2,500 in covered expenses and his spouse incurs $2,000 in covered expenses. On July 1, Edward and his spouse each change to self-only HDHP coverage with a $3,000 deductible and Edward's spouse is no longer covered under the plan. For the period from July 1 through December 31, the plan may credit Edward's self-only deductible with either: (1) $2,500 (the actual amount of expenses Edward incurred under family coverage), or (2) $2,250 ($4,500/2), Edward's per capita share of expenses incurred by the two individuals covered by family coverage. In this case the HDHP must credit Edward's spouse with at least $2,500 toward the satisfaction of the deductible.

Note. The HDHP also complies with the requirements of Treasury Regulations Section 54.4980B-5, Q&A 2, regarding the deductible that applies if COBRA continuation coverage is elected by crediting Edward's spouse with $2,250 (the actual expenses incurred) toward the satisfaction of the deductible. See next three examples. [I.R.S. Notice 2008-59, Q&A 12, 2008-29 I.R.B. 123]

Example 2. Assume the same facts as in Example 1, except that Edward's spouse is entitled to elect, and elects, COBRA continuation coverage under the HDHP. In this case, the HDHP must comply with the requirements of Treasury Regulations Section 54.4980B-5, Q&A 2, regarding the deductible that applies if COBRA continuation coverage is elected.

Example 3. Assume the same facts as in Example 2, except that the amounts incurred by Edward and his spouse are reversed: Edward incurred $2,000 of medical expenses and his spouse incurred $2,500. If the HDHP credits Edward's spouse with $2,250 toward the satisfaction of the deductible, this would not satisfy the requirements of Q&A 2. Edward's spouse must be credited with at least $2,500 toward the satisfaction of the deductible to comply with the requirements of Treasury Regulations Section 54.4980B-5,

Q&A 2, regarding the deductible that applies if COBRA continuation coverage is elected.

Example 4. Fizz offers its employees a calendar-year health plan, otherwise qualifying as an HDHP. As of January 1, 2009, George, an employee, and his spouse and child are covered by Fizz's family coverage HDHP with a $6,000 deductible. From January 1 through September 30, 2009, George incurs $2,500 in covered expenses, his spouse incurs $500 in covered expenses, and his child incurs $3,000 in covered expenses. George and his spouse are divorced, effective October 1, 2009. On that date, George changes to self-only HDHP coverage with a $3,000 deductible and the child and ex-spouse elect COBRA continuation coverage in Fizz's family HDHP coverage. The plan may (1) credit George's individual deductible with $2,500 and reduce the expenses allocated to the child and ex-spouse in family coverage by $2,500; (2) credit George's self-only deductible with $2,000 and reduce the expenses allocated to the child and ex-spouse by $2,000 (allocating one-third of the $6,000 in expenses to George's individual deductible and two-thirds of the $6,000 in expenses to the former spouse and child remaining in family coverage); (3) credit George with no expenses and continue to credit the child and ex-spouse with all expenses incurred under family coverage; or (4) treat George as having satisfied the $3,000 individual deductible while treating the former spouse and child as having satisfied the $6,000 family deductible. Coverage of the child and former spouse is COBRA continuation coverage. However, if the pro rata allocation of expenses of the family to the child and former spouse were less than the actual expenses incurred by the child and former spouse ($3,500), then allocation of only the ratable share ($3,000 ($6,000/2)) of the family expenses would not comply with the requirements of Treasury Regulations Section 54.4980B-5, Q&A 2.

Limitation on Benefits

Q 3:31   May an HDHP impose a lifetime limit on benefits?

Yes. An HDHP may impose a reasonable lifetime limit on benefits provided under the plan.

Q 3:32   Are amounts paid by a covered individual above a lifetime limit treated as out-of-pocket expenses?

No. Amounts paid by a covered individual above the lifetime limit are not treated as out-of-pocket expenses in determining the HDHP maximum annual out-of-pocket limit. However, a lifetime limit on benefits designed to circumvent the maximum annual out-of-pocket amount is not reasonable (see Q 3:37). [I.R.S. Notice 2004-50, Q&A 14, 2004-33 I.R.B. 196]

Example. Assume a health plan has an annual deductible that satisfies the $1,150 deductible for self-only coverage and the $2,300 deductible for family coverage for 2009. After satisfying the deductible, the plan pays 100 percent of covered expenses, up to a lifetime limit of $1 million. The lifetime limit of $1 million is reasonable, and the health plan is not disqualified from being an HDHP because of the lifetime limit on benefits.

Q 3:33   If a plan imposes reasonable annual or lifetime limits on specific benefits, are amounts paid by covered individuals beyond these annual or lifetime limits subject to the maximum out-of-pocket limitations?

No. The HDHP out-of-pocket maximum limits ($5,800/$11,600 for 2009) apply to covered benefits only. [I.R.S. Notice 2004-50, Q&A 15, 2004-33 I.R.B. 196]

Q 3:34   May a plan limit covered benefits?

Generally, yes. A plan may be designed with reasonable benefit restrictions limiting the plan's covered benefits.

Q 3:35   If a health plan imposes a separate or higher deductible for specific benefits, are amounts paid by covered individuals to satisfy the separate or higher deductible treated as out-of-pocket expenses?

No. If a health plan imposes a separate or higher deductible for specific benefits (different deductibles), amounts paid by covered individuals to satisfy the separate or higher deductible are not treated as out-of-pocket expenses (see Qs 3:1, 3:19), provided significant other benefits remain available under the plan in addition to the specific benefits subject to the separate or higher deductible. [I.R.S. Notice 2008-59, Q&A 13, 2008-29 I.R.B. 123]

Example. In 2009, a self-only health plan with a $3,000 deductible imposes a lifetime limit of $1,000,000 on reimbursements for covered benefits. The plan pays 100 percent of covered expenses after the $3,000 deductible is satisfied. Although the plan provides benefits for substance abuse treatment, the substance abuse treatment benefits are subject to a separate $5,000 deductible, and these benefits are limited to $10,000, after the separate deductible is satisfied. The plan is an HDHP and no expense incurred by a covered individual other than the $3,000 general deductible is treated as an out-of-pocket expense.

Q 3:36   May a health plan meeting the minimum deductible ($1,150 for self-only coverage and $2,300 for family coverage for 2009) restrict benefits to expenses for hospitalization or in-patient care out-of-pocket expenses?

No. A health plan meeting the minimum deductible ($1,150 for self-only coverage and $2,300 for family coverage for 2009) may not restrict benefits to expenses for hospitalization or in-patient care (see Q 3:4). A plan must provide significant benefits to be an HDHP. A plan may also be designed with reasonable benefit restrictions limiting the plan's covered benefits (see Q 3:34). However, if a plan only provides benefits for expenses of hospitalization or in-patient care, significant other benefits do not remain available under the plan in addition to the benefits subject to exclusion. Therefore, any expenses incurred by a covered individual after satisfying the deductible are treated as out-of-pocket expenses (see Q 3:32). [I.R.S. Notice 2008-59, Q&A 14, 2008-29 I.R.B.123; Notice 2004-50, Q&A 15, 2004-33 I.R.B. 196]

> **Example.** In 2009, a self-only health plan with a $2,000 deductible includes a $3,000,000 lifetime limit on covered benefits. Generally, the plan only provides benefits for medical services provided while a covered individual is admitted to a hospital as an overnight patient or provided at a "same day" surgery facility. A same day surgery facility does not include a hospital emergency room, a trauma center, a physician's office or a clinic. Covered medical services for individuals admitted to a hospital or same day surgery facility include room accommodations, miscellaneous medical services and supplies necessary for treatment, primary surgery, pathology charges and the administration of anesthesia while at the hospital or center, and charges by the primary attending physician for one visit per day while at the hospital. In addition, the plan provides an organ transplant benefit, hospice care benefit, and home health care visits. The home health care benefit is subject to a 60 visit per year limit, and must be in connection with the hospitalization. The plan also pays for certain preventive care screening and ambulance service. The plan does not pay for visits to physician's offices or any other out-patient care other than those noted previously. The maximum dollar amount that the covered individual pays for covered benefits under the plan for 2009 is $5,500. The restriction of benefits to medical services provided while the covered individual is admitted to a hospital or at a same day surgery facility is not reasonable because significant other benefits do not remain available under the plan after application of the restriction. Any expenses incurred by a covered individual for outpatient care or visits to physician's offices are treated as out-of-pocket expenses. Because the plan maximum for amounts paid by a covered individual does not restrict payments for those out-of-pocket expenses, the plan fails to qualify as an HDHP.

Q 3:37   When is a restriction or exclusion on benefits reasonable?

A restriction or exclusion on benefits is reasonable only if significant other benefits remain available under the plan in addition to the benefits subject to the restriction or exclusion. [I.R.S. Notice 2004-50, Q&A 14, 2004-33 I.R.B. 196]

> **Example 1.** In 2009, a self-only health plan with a $2,000 deductible includes a $1 million lifetime limit on covered benefits. The plan provides no benefits for experimental treatments, mental health, or chiropractic care visits. Although the plan provides benefits for substance abuse treatment after the deductible is satisfied, it limits payments to 26 treatments per year. Although the plan provides benefits for fertility treatments, it limits lifetime

reimbursements to $10,000, after the deductible is satisfied. Other than these limits on covered benefits, the plan pays 80 percent of major medical expenses incurred after satisfying the deductible. When the 20 percent co-insurance paid by the covered individuals reaches $4,000, the plan pays 100 percent. Under these facts, the plan is an HDHP and no expenses incurred by a covered individual other than the deductible and the 20 percent co-insurance are treated as out-of-pocket expenses subject to the HDHP maximum out-of-pocket limit.

Example 2. In 2009, a self-only health plan with a $2,000 deductible imposes a lifetime limit on reimbursements for covered benefits of $1 million. Although the plan pays 100 percent of expenses incurred for covered benefits after satisfying the deductible, the plan imposes a $10,000 annual limit on benefits for any single condition. The $10,000 annual limit under these facts is not reasonable because significant other benefits do not remain available under the plan. Under these facts, any expenses incurred by a covered individual after satisfying the $2,000 deductible are treated as out-of-pocket expenses.

Q 3:38   If a plan limits benefits to UCR amounts, are amounts paid by covered individuals in excess of UCR included in determining the out-of-pocket expenses paid for purposes of calculating the maximum out-of-pocket limit?

No. Restricting benefits to UCR is a reasonable restriction on benefits. Thus, amounts paid by covered individuals in excess of UCR that are not paid by an HDHP are not included in determining the HDHP maximum out-of-pocket limit. [I.R.S. Notice 2004-50, Q&A 16, 2004-33 I.R.B. 196]

Family Coverage vs. Self-Only Coverage

Q 3:39   What is self-only coverage under an HDHP?

Self-only coverage under an HDHP means a health plan that covers only one eligible individual. [I.R.S. Notice 2004-50, Q&A 12, 2004-33 I.R.B. 196]

Q 3:40   What is family coverage under an HDHP?

Family coverage under an HDHP is defined as any coverage that is not self-only coverage. [I.R.C. § 223(c)(4)] Thus, family HDHP coverage is a health plan covering one eligible individual and at least one other individual (whether or not the other individual is an eligible individual). [I.R.S. Notice 2004-50, Q&A 12, 2004-33 I.R.B. 196] However, an individual can be eligible to contribute to an HSA if his or her spouse has non-HDHP *family* coverage, provided the spouse's coverage does not cover the individual. [Rev. Rul. 2005-25, 2005-18 I.R.B. 971]

Q 3:41   May a family-coverage HDHP plan cover only the eligible individual?

No. Family coverage under an HDHP is a health plan that covers an eligible individual and at least one other person (see Q 3:40).

Q 3:42   Can benefits under a family-coverage plan be paid before the family incurs annual covered medical expenses in excess of the minimum annual deductible under Code Section 223?

No, except for preventive care. In general, a plan is a family-coverage HDHP only if nothing is payable under the HDHP until the family incurs annual covered medical expenses in excess of the plan's minimum annual deductible. However, an exception applies to expenses for preventive care (see Q 3:49). It does not matter which family member incurs the expenses. [I.R.S. Notice 2004-2, Q&A 3, 2004-2 I.R.B. 269]

Other Health Plan Coverage

Q 3:43   Are there exceptions to the rule requiring that the eligible individual not be covered under any other health plan?

Generally, an eligible individual may not be covered under any other non-HDHP (see Q 2:6). [I.R.C. § 223(c)(1)(A)(ii)] However, there are two exceptions that permit other coverage to be disregarded. [I.R.C. § 223(c)(1)(B)] Disregarded coverage includes:

1. Coverage for any benefit provided by *permitted insurance* (see Q 3:44). [I.R.C. § 223(c)(1)(B)(i)]
2. Coverage, whether through insurance or otherwise, for accidents, disability, dental care, vision care, or long-term care (see Q 2:8). This type of coverage is called *disregarded coverage*. [I.R.C. § 223(c)(1)(B)(ii)]

A health plan is not an HDHP if substantially all of its coverage is for coverage described in (1) or (2) above. [I.R.C. § 223(c)(2)(B)] These rules also apply to employer provided health coverage (see Q 4:20).

An *otherwise* eligible individual who is covered by an HDHP (see Q 3:1), may also be covered by a health plan that is not an HDHP, provided that plan has a deductible equal to or greater than the statutory minimum HDHP deductible (see Example 1). Thus, as long as the deductible of the other coverage equals or exceeds the statutory minimum HDHP deductible ($1,150 for self-only coverage and $2,300 for family coverage for 2009), the individual remains an eligible individual. [I.R.S. Notice 2008-59, Q&A 7, 2008-29 I.R.B. 123]

Example 1. Sasha, an otherwise eligible individual, has self-only HDHP coverage from January 1 through December 31, 2009, with a deductible of $2,500 and a lifetime limit on benefits of $1,000,000. The plan provides no benefits until the $1,000,000 deductible is satisfied. In addition to the HDHP,

Sasha has self-only health plan coverage with a $1,000,000 deductible and a $2,000,000 lifetime limit on benefits. The plan provides no benefits until the $1,000,000 deductible is satisfied. Sasha is an eligible individual (see Q 2:6). [I.R.S. Notice 2008-59, Q&A 7, 2008-29 I.R.B. 123]

Example 2. Barney is covered by an HDHP. In addition, Barney is covered by a "mini-med" plan that provides the following benefits:

1. A fixed amount per day of hospitalization,
2. Coverage for expenses relating to the treatment of a specified list of diseases,
3. A fixed amount per office visit with a physician,
4. A fixed amount per out-patient treatment at a hospital, and
5. A fixed amount per ambulance use.

Although the fixed amount per day of hospitalization benefit and specified disease benefit (items 1 and 2) are allowed in addition to the HDHP as permitted insurance, the other benefits (items 3 through 5) are not disregarded coverage or preventive care and, thus, Barney is not an eligible individual who can contribute to an HSA. [I.R.S. Notice 2008-59, Q&A 3, 2008-29 I.R.B. 123]

Example 3. For 2009, an HDHP with self-only coverage has an annual deductible of $2,500. Gretta, an employee, pays the first $250 of covered medical expenses below the deductible. The employer reimburses the next $1,350 of covered medical expenses below the deductible. Gretta is responsible for the last $900 of covered medical expenses below the deductible. The $1,350 of medical expenses paid or reimbursed by the employer is not a contribution to Gretta's HSA and not disregarded coverage or preventive care. To be an eligible individual, an individual must be covered by an HDHP and no other health plan except disregarded coverage or preventive care. Gretta is not an eligible individual because she has disqualifying coverage from a plan that is not an HDHP. [I.R.S. Notice 2008-59, Q&A 2, 2008-29 I.R.B. 123]

Example 4. For 2009, an HDHP with self-only coverage has an annual deductible of $4,500. Monika, an employee, pays the first $1,150 (the same amount as the minimum annual deductible for 2009 for self-only coverage) of covered medical expenses below the deductible. The employer reimburses Monika the next $3,400 of covered medical expenses below the deductible. The $3,400 of medical expenses paid or reimbursed by the employer is not a contribution to an HSA and not disregarded coverage or preventive care. Monika is an eligible employee, because an employee "covered by this type of plan is an HSA eligible individual because the employee is responsible for the minimum annual deductible." [I.R.S. Notice 2008-59, Q&A 3, 2008-29 I.R.B. 123]

Note. According to a recent IRS guidance, an individual's eligibility is not affected, and an otherwise eligible individual remains an eligible individual, if the individual has family HDHP coverage that covers dependents, and the dependents have other, disqualifying, non-HDHP coverage (see Q 4:20). [I.R.S. Notice 2008-59, Q&A 11, 2008-29 I.R.B. 123]

Permitted Insurance

Q 3:44   What is permitted insurance?

For eligibility purposes, certain types of insurance coverage—referred to as *permitted insurance*—are disregarded in determining if an individual is an eligible individual (see Qs 2:8, 3:43). [I.R.C. § 223(c)(3)]

Q 3:45   What does permitted insurance include?

Permitted insurance includes insurance if substantially all of the coverage provided under such insurance relates to any of the following:

* Liabilities incurred under workers' compensation laws [I.R.C. § 223(c)(3)(A)(i)–(iv)]
* Tort liabilities [I.R.C. § 223(c)(3)(A)(i)–(iv)]
* Liabilities relating to ownership or use of property [I.R.C. § 223 (c)(3)(A)(i)–(iv)]
* Such other similar liabilities as the Secretary of Treasury may specify [I.R.C. § 223(c)(3)(A)(i)–(iv)]
* Insurance for a specified disease or illness [I.R.C. § 223(c)(3)(B)]
* Insurance paying a fixed amount per day (or other period) of hospitalization [I.R.C. § 223(c)(3)(C)]

Note. Medicare supplemental insurance is not included in the types of insurance listed as permitted insurance.

Note. A plan that provides coverage substantially all of which is for a specific disease or illness is not an HDHP.

Q 3:46   May an otherwise eligible individual who is covered by both an HDHP and insurance contracts for one or more specific diseases or illnesses contribute to an HSA if the insurance provides benefits before the deductible of the HDHP is satisfied?

Yes, provided that the principal health coverage is provided by the HDHP. An eligible individual covered under an HDHP may be covered "for any benefit provided by permitted insurance" (see Qs 3:44, 3:45). The term *permitted insurance* includes "insurance for a specified disease or illness." Therefore, an eligible individual may be covered both by an HDHP and by permitted insurance for one or more specific diseases, "such as cancer, diabetes, asthma or congestive heart failure," as long as the HDHP provides principal health coverage. [I.R.S. Notice 2004-50, Q&A 7, 2004-33 I.R.B. 196]

Q 3:47   Must coverage for permitted insurance be provided under an insurance contract?

Generally, yes. Benefits for permitted insurance—liabilities incurred under workers' compensation laws, tort liabilities, liabilities relating to ownership or use of property, insurance for a specified disease or illness, and insurance paying a fixed amount per day (or other period) of hospitalization—must generally be provided through insurance contracts and not on a self-insured basis. However, where benefits (such as workers' compensation benefits) are provided in satisfaction of a statutory requirement and any resulting benefits are secondary or incidental to other benefits, the benefits will qualify as permitted insurance even if self-insured. [I.R.S. Notice 2004-50, Q&A 8, 2004-33 I.R.B. 196]

The IRS has provided additional clarification on how the following affect eligibility for an HSA: prescription drug programs (see Q 3:48), medical discount cards (see Q 3:57), employer-provided employee assistance (see Q 3:58), and wellness and disease management programs (see Q 3:61). Also, the IRS has provided guidance on when other account-based plans (e.g., health FSA, HRA) may be used with an HSA.

Prescription Drug Coverage

Q 3:48   May an individual who is covered by a health plan that provides prescription drug benefits before the deductible of the HDHP is satisfied contribute to an HSA?

No. An individual who is covered by a health plan that provides prescription drug benefits (separately or through a rider) before the HDHP deductible is satisfied cannot normally contribute to an HSA. [Rev. Rul. 2004-38, 2004-15 I.R.B. 717. However, see Rev. Proc. 2004-22, 2004-15 I.R.B. 727 for transitional relief for months before 2006.]

Preventive Care Safe Harbor

Q 3:49   What is the preventive care safe harbor?

The safe harbor for preventive care allows certain benefits to be provided by an HDHP before satisfying the HDHP $1,150/$2,300 minimum annual deductible for 2009. [I.R.S. Notice 2004-23, 2004-15 I.R.B. 725]

In Notice 2004-23 [2004-15 I.R.B. 725], the IRS provides a list of services and benefits that qualify as *preventive care* under Code Section 223(c)(2)(C). That section states, "A plan shall not fail to be treated as a high deductible health plan by reason of failing to have a deductible for preventive care (within the meaning of section 1871 of the Social Security Act, except as otherwise provided by the

Secretary)." [I.R.C. § 223(c)(2)(C)] An HDHP, therefore, may provide preventive care benefits without a deductible or with a deductible below the minimum annual deductible.

Q 3:50 What benefits and services are permitted under the preventive care safe harbor?

The IRS defined the following medical procedures as safe harbor items that could be provided as preventive care before the HDHP deductible is met. The list of allowed preventive care includes, but is not limited to, the following:

- Periodic health evaluations, including tests and diagnostic procedures ordered in connection with routine examinations (e.g., annual physicals)
- Routine prenatal and well-child care
- Child and adult immunizations
- Tobacco cessation programs
- Obesity weight-loss programs
- Screening services specified in Table 3-3

Table 3-3. Preventive Care Safe-Harbor Screening Services

Cancer Screening
    Breast cancer (e.g., mammogram)
    Cervical cancer (e.g., pap smear)
    Colorectal cancer
    Prostate cancer (e.g., PSA test)
    Skin cancer
    Oral cancer
    Ovarian cancer
    Testicular cancer
    Thyroid cancer

Heart and Vascular Diseases Screening
    Abdominal aortic aneurysm
    Carotid artery stenosis
    Coronary heart disease
    Hemoglobinopathies
    Hypertension
    Lipid disorders

Infectious Diseases Screening
    Bacteriuria
    Chlamydial infection

Table 3-3. Preventive Care Safe-Harbor Screening Services (*cont'd*)

> Gonorrhea
>
> Hepatitis B virus infection
>
> Hepatitis C
>
> Human immunodeficiency virus (HIV) infection
>
> Syphilis
>
> Tuberculosis infection

Mental Health Conditions and Substance Abuse Screening

> Dementia
>
> Depression
>
> Drug abuse
>
> Problem drinking
>
> Suicide risk
>
> Family violence

Metabolic, Nutritional, and Endocrine Conditions Screening

> Anemia, iron deficiency
>
> Dental and periodontal disease
>
> Diabetes mellitus
>
> Obesity in adults
>
> Thyroid disease

Musculoskeletal Disorders Screening

> Osteoporosis

Obstetric and Gynecologic Conditions Screening

> Bacterial vaginosis in pregnancy
>
> Gestational diabetes mellitus
>
> Home uterine activity monitoring
>
> Neural tube defects
>
> Preeclampsia
>
> Rh incompatibility
>
> Rubella
>
> Ultrasonography in pregnancy

Pediatric Conditions Screening

> Child developmental delay
>
> Congenital hypothyroidism

Table 3-3. Preventive Care Safe-Harbor Screening Services (*cont'd*)

    Lead levels in childhood and pregnancy

    Phenylketonuria

    Scoliosis, adolescent idiopathic

Vision and Hearing Disorders Screening

    Glaucoma

    Hearing impairment in older adults

    Newborn hearing

[I.R.S. Notice 2004-23, 2004-15 I.R.B. 725]

Q 3:51   Are prescription drugs or medications that are used to prevent a disease or recurrence of a disease from which an HSA owner, spouse, or dependent has recovered eligible for safe-harbor treatment?

Yes. Prescription drugs or medications that are used to prevent a disease or recurrence of a disease from which an HSA owner, spouse, or dependent has recovered are eligible for safe-harbor treatment as preventive care benefits. Thus, coverage for these items may be provided under an HDHP before the annual deductible under the HDHP is satisfied (see Qs 3:49, 3:52). [I.R.S. Notice 2004-50, Q&A 27, 2004-33 I.R.B. 196]

Q 3:52   To what extent do drugs or medications come within the safe harbor for preventive care services as "preventive care?"

I.R.S. Notice 2004-23 [2004-15 I.R.B. 725] sets out a preventive care safe harbor that describes those benefits that can be covered before the HDHP deductible is satisfied (see Q 3:50). [I.R.C. § 223(c)(2)(C)] Solely for this purpose, drugs or medications are preventive care when taken by an individual who has developed risk factors for a disease that has not yet manifested itself or not yet become clinically apparent (i.e., asymptomatic) or to prevent the reoccurrence of a disease from which an individual has recovered.

For example, the treatment of high cholesterol with cholesterol-lowering medications (e.g., statins) to prevent heart disease, or the treatment of recovered heart attack or stroke victims with angiotensin-converting enzyme (ACE) inhibitors to prevent a reoccurrence, constitute preventive care. In addition, drugs or medications used as part of procedures providing preventive care services (see Q 3:50) are eligible for safe-harbor treatment. [I.R.S. Notice 2004-50, Q&A 27, 2004-33 I.R.B. 196]

Q 3:53   Must an HDHP provide preventive care benefits?

No. There is no requirement in the Code that an HDHP provide benefits for preventive care or provide preventive care with a deductible below the minimum annual deductible limit. [I.R.S. Notice 2004-23, 2004-15 I.R.B. 725]

Q 3:54   Does preventive care include the treatment of an existing illness?

Generally, no. Preventive care does not generally include any service or benefit intended to treat an existing illness, injury, or condition (but see Q 3:55). [I.R.S. Notice 2004-50, Q&A 27, 2004-33 I.R.B. 196]

Q 3:55   Does a preventive care service or screening that also includes the treatment of a related condition during that procedure come within the safe harbor for preventive care in I.R.S. Notice 2004-23?

Although Notice 2004-23 [2004-15 I.R.B. 725] states that preventive care generally does not include any service or benefit intended to treat an existing illness, injury, or condition, in situations where it would be unreasonable or impracticable to perform another procedure to treat the condition, any treatment that is incidental or ancillary to a preventive care service or screening as described in Notice 2004-23 also falls within the safe harbor for preventive care. For example, removal of polyps during a diagnostic colonoscopy is preventive care that can be provided before the deductible in an HDHP has been satisfied. [I.R.S. Notice 2004-50, Q&A 26, 2004-33 I.R.B. 196]

Examples of Permitted Insurance, Permitted Coverage, and Preventive Care

The following examples concern whether certain insurance contracts (policies, riders, and optional benefits) constitute *permitted insurance, permitted coverage,* or *preventive care* within the meaning of Code Section 223 so that employees who are covered by the policies, riders, and optional benefits and who are otherwise eligible to contribute to an HSA remain eligible to make HSA contributions. [Ltr. Rul. 200704010 (Oct. 25, 2006)]

Introduction to Examples

In general, eligible individuals for HSAs are individuals who are covered by an HDHP plan and no other health plan that is not an HDHP. Generally, an HDHP may not provide benefits for any year until the deductible for that year is satisfied. An individual with other coverage in addition to an HDHP is still eligible for an HSA if such other coverage is certain permitted insurance (insurance for a specified disease or illness that pays a fixed amount per day (or other period) of hospitalization) [I.R.C. § 223(c)(3)(B)] or permitted coverage

(coverage for accidents, disability, dental care, vision care, or long-term care whether through insurance or otherwise). [I.R.C. § 223(c)(1)(B); see also I.R.S. Notice 2004-2, Q&A 6, 2004-1 C.B. 269; H.R. Conf. Rep. No. 391, 108th Cong., 1st Sess. 841 (2003)]

A safe harbor is also provided for the absence of a preventive care deductible or a preventive care deductible below the minimum annual deductible. [I.R.C. § 223(c)(2)(C)]

An *eligible individual* who is covered by an HDHP may also be covered for any benefit provided by permitted insurance. The term *permitted insurance* includes "insurance for a specified disease or illness." An *eligible individual* may be covered by an HDHP and also by permitted insurance for one or more specific diseases or illnesses, such as cancer, diabetes, asthma, or congestive heart failure, as long as the principal health coverage is provided by the HDHP. [I.R.C. § 223(c)(3)(B); I.R.S. Notice 2004-50, 2004-2 C.B. 196; Rev. Rul. 2004-45, 2004-1 C.B. 971]

> **Example 1.** *Permitted insurance.* Hydrogen Corporation offers its eligible employees health and accident benefits, including an accident and health plan that is intended to qualify as an HDHP. In addition to the coverage under the HDHP, Hydrogen offers its eligible employees the opportunity to purchase a group policy and makes available several optional riders that are available under that policy. Neither the policy nor the riders by themselves qualify as an HDHP. The group policy covers up to specified amounts for comprehensive cancer treatment, including hospital confinement, drugs, diagnostic testing, in-hospital private nursing care, certain surgeries, ambulance transportation, and hospice care. The policy does not cover conditions or illnesses resulting from cancer or any other diseases.
>
> *Rider 1* covers hospitalization in intensive care and ambulance transportation to the intensive care unit for the treatment of cancer.
>
> *Rider 2* provides hospitalization benefits for the treatment of cancer up to a specified amount that increases progressively every year for the first five years the policy and rider are in force.
>
> *Rider 3* provides a return of premium after the policy is in force for five years. The amount to be returned is determined by a formula based on the individual's age, the length of time the policy is in force, and the amount of any claims paid under the policy.
>
> *Rider 4* provides hospital intensive care benefits up to a specified amount and ambulance transportation to the hospital intensive care unit for the treatment of cancer. Benefits are reduced by half when the covered person reaches age 70.
>
> *Rider 5* provides hospital intensive care benefits up to a specified amount and ambulance transportation to the hospital intensive care unit for the treatment of cancer. Benefits are reduced by half when the covered person reaches age 70. No benefits are paid if cancer or a specified disease is diagnosed within the initial 30-day waiting period under the policy.

Analysis. The policy offered by Hydrogen constitutes a specified disease or illness policy (permitted insurance) within the meaning of Code Section 223(c)(3)(B). An individual who is otherwise an eligible individual would remain an *eligible individual* if covered under the policy offered by Hydrogen. All of the riders constitute permitted insurance for a specified disease or illness. An individual who is otherwise an *eligible individual* remains an *eligible individual* if covered under any of the above five riders.

Example 2. *Permitted insurance, specified amount, group policy.* Lava Corporation offers its eligible employees health and accident benefits, including an accident and health plan that is intended to qualify as an HDHP. In addition to the coverage under the HDHP, Lava offers its eligible employees the opportunity to purchase a group policy and makes available several optional riders that are available under that policy. Neither the policy nor the riders by themselves qualify as an HDHP. The policy pays a specified amount upon the first occurrence of most types of cancer. The policy covers certain aspects of cancer treatment including continuous hospital confinement and radiation/chemotherapy, up to specified amounts. The policy does not cover conditions or illnesses resulting from cancer or from any other diseases.

Rider 1 covers hospitalization in intensive care and ambulance transportation to the intensive care unit for the treatment of cancer.

Rider 2 provides a return of premium after the policy is in force for five years. The amount to be returned is determined by a formula based on the individual's age, the length of time the policy is in force, and the amount of any claims paid under the policy.

Rider 3 provides hospital intensive care benefits up to a specified amount and ambulance transportation to the hospital intensive care unit for the treatment of cancer. Benefits are reduced by half when the covered person reaches age 70. No benefits are paid if cancer or a specified disease is diagnosed within the initial 30-day waiting period under the policy.

Analysis. The policy offered by Lava constitutes a specified disease or illness policy (permitted insurance) within the meaning of Code Section 223(c)(3)(B). An individual who is otherwise an eligible individual would remain an "eligible individual" if covered under the policy offered by Lava. All of the riders constitute permitted insurance for a specified disease or illness. An individual who is otherwise an *eligible individual* remains an *eligible individual* if covered under any of the above three riders.

Example 3. *Permitted insurance, specified amount, individual policy.* Neon Corporation offers its eligible employees health and accident benefits, including an accident and health plan that is intended to qualify as an HDHP. In addition to the coverage under the HDHP, Neon offers its eligible employees the opportunity to purchase an individual policy and makes available several optional riders that are available under that policy. Neither the policy nor the riders by themselves qualify as an HDHP. The policy covers treatment up to specified amounts for the treatment of the first occurrence of cancer and certain other specified diseases. The policy's covered treatment benefits include hospital confinement, surgery, in-hospital private duty nursing, ambulance transportation, and radiation/chemotherapy.

Rider 1 pays a specified amount upon the initial diagnosis of cancer.

Rider 2 pays a per diem amount for each day of confinement in the intensive care unit of a hospital up to 45 days, including ambulance transportation to the intensive care unit, for the treatment of one of the specified diseases covered by the policy. Benefits are reduced by half when the covered person reaches age 70.

Rider 3 pays a per diem amount for each day of confinement in the intensive care unit of a hospital up to 45 days, including ambulance transportation to the intensive care unit, for the treatment of a specified disease covered by the policy. Benefits are reduced by half when the covered person reaches age 70. Rider 3 excludes such benefits if the specified disease is diagnosed within the policy's initial 30-day waiting period.

Rider 4 pays up to specified amounts for treatment (such as hospital confinement and surgery) of the specified diseases covered by the policy.

Rider 5 pays a specified amount for the initial diagnosis of cancer. The specified amount increases progressively based on the length of time the rider and policy are in force and pays a surrender value if no cancer diagnosis occurs within the first five years of coverage. The rider terminates after 20 years, at which time the guaranteed value is paid.

Analysis. The policy offered by Neon constitutes a specified disease or illness policy (permitted insurance) within the meaning of Code Section 223(c)(3)(B). An individual who is otherwise an eligible individual would remain an *eligible individual* if covered under the policy offered by Neon. All of the riders constitute permitted insurance for a specified disease or illness. An individual who is otherwise an *eligible individual* remains an *eligible individual* if covered under any of the above five riders.

Example 4. *Permitted insurance, optional benefits.* Spyder Corporation offers its eligible employees health and accident benefits, including an accident and health plan that is intended to qualify as an HDHP. In addition to the coverage under the HDHP, Spyder offers its eligible employees the opportunity to purchase a group policy and makes available several optional benefits that are available under that policy. The policy pays up to a specified amount for the first occurrence of cancer and certain other specified diseases. Policy coverage includes benefits for hospital confinement, surgery, in-hospital private duty nursing, ambulance transportation, anesthesia, and radiation/chemotherapy.

Optional benefit 1 pays a specified amount upon the initial diagnosis of cancer, excluding skin cancer.

Optional benefit 2 pays a per diem amount for each day of confinement in the intensive care unit of a hospital up to 45 days, including a specified amount for ambulance transportation to the intensive care unit for the treatment of one of the specified diseases covered by the policy.

Optional benefit 3 covers up to a specified amount for certain cancer screening services, regardless of whether the covered individual is diagnosed with a specified disease. Covered cancer screening services include colonoscopy, chest X-ray, and bone marrow testing.

Analysis. The policy offered by Spyder constitutes a specified disease or illness policy (permitted insurance) within the meaning of Code Section 223(c)(3)(B). An individual who is otherwise an eligible individual would remain an *eligible individual* if covered under the policy offered by Spyder. Optional benefits 1 and 2 constitute permitted insurance for a specified disease or illness. Optional benefit 3 constitutes preventive care for purposes of Code Section 223(c)(2)(c). An individual who is otherwise an eligible individual remains an *eligible individual* if covered under any of the three optional benefits.

Example 5. *Specified amount.* Board Corporation offers its eligible employees health and accident benefits, including an accident and health plan that is intended to qualify as an HDHP. In addition to the coverage under the HDHP, Board offers its eligible employees the opportunity to purchase a group policy and makes available several optional riders that are available under that policy. Neither the policy nor the riders by themselves qualify as an HDHP. The policy pays a specified amount for treatment of a heart attack, heart disease, or stroke. The policy does not cover any disease, sickness, or incapacity resulting from a heart attack, heart disease, or stroke. Benefits covered under the policy include hospital confinement, drugs, and in hospital private nursing.

Rider 1 pays a specified amount for the initial diagnosis of heart attack, heart disease, or stroke.

Rider 2 pays a per diem amount for confinement in an intensive care unit up to 45 days for the treatment of diseases specified in the policy and ambulance transportation to the intensive care unit for the treatment of such diseases.

Analysis. The policy offered by Board constitutes a specified disease or illness policy (permitted insurance) within the meaning of Code Section 223(c)(3)(B). An individual who is otherwise an *eligible individual* would remain an *eligible individual* if covered under the policy offered by Board. All of the riders constitute permitted insurance for a specified disease or illness. An individual who is otherwise an *eligible individual* remains an *eligible individual* if covered under any of the above two riders.

Example 6. *Specific disease or illness policy.* Lye Corporation offers its eligible employees health and accident benefits, including an accident and health plan that is intended to qualify as an HDHP. In addition to the coverage under the HDHP, Lye offers its eligible employees the opportunity to purchase a non-HDHP group policy and makes available the following optional riders:

Rider 1 pays a per diem amount for every day of hospital confinement for up to one year. Covered confinement may be for the treatment of any sickness or injury that is not a disease specified under the policy.

Rider 2 pays a specified amount for the initial diagnosis of certain types of cancer.

Analysis. The policy offered by Lye constitutes a specific disease or illness policy within the meaning of Code Section 223(c)(3)(B). An individual who is otherwise an *eligible individual* would remain an *eligible individual* if covered under the policy offered by Lye. Rider 1 that pays a per diem amount for every day of hospital confinement for up to one year constitutes insurance paying a fixed amount per day (or other period) within the meaning of Code Section 223(c)(3)(B). Rider 2 constitutes a specific disease or illness policy. An individual who is otherwise an *eligible individual* remains an *eligible individual* if covered under either of the two riders.

Example 7. *Insurance paying a fixed amount per day (or other period).* Valley Corporation offers its eligible employees health and accident benefits, including an accident and health plan that is intended to qualify as an HDHP. In addition to the coverage under the HDHP, Lye offers its eligible employees the opportunity to purchase a non-HDHP group policy and makes available several optional riders under that policy. The policy is a group hospital confinement indemnity policy that pays a specified amount for each day of hospital confinement up to a specified number of days, a specified amount for each day of confinement in an intensive care unit, and a premium waiver during such period of hospital confinement.

Rider 1 pays a specified amount for treatment of a covered individual by a physician outside of a hospital up to a specified number of visits a year.

Rider 2 pays a per diem amount for treatment by a physician in a hospital, other than a surgeon, during hospital confinement.

Rider 3 pays a specified amount for medical or surgical treatment in an emergency room up to twice a year.

Rider 4 pays a specified amount for a surgical operation and anesthesia for surgery performed in a hospital or an ambulatory surgical center.

Rider 5 pays a specified amount for a covered individual's initial confinement to a hospital during a calendar year. This amount is in addition to the per diem amount for hospital confinement paid under the policy.

Rider 6 pays a per diem amount for each day that at-home nursing care is required following a covered hospital confinement. Covered at-home nursing care must be authorized by an attending physician.

Analysis. Valley's policy constitutes insurance paying a fixed amount per day (or other period) of hospitalization within the meaning of Code Section

223(c)(3)(C). An individual who is otherwise an eligible individual remains an eligible individual if covered under this policy. However, Riders 1 through 5 do not constitute permitted coverage, permitted insurance, or preventive care under Code Section 223. An individual who is covered under Valley's policy and who is also covered by any of the riders 1 through 5 is not an eligible individual under Code Section 223.

The Letter Ruling makes clear that the IRS views the hospital indemnity exception as unavailable where the rider provides coverage for a treatment. Further, the Letter Ruling suggests that payment of an initial lump sum upon confinement to a hospital may be outside the definition of a hospital indemnity policy, even if the payment is not contingent upon receiving treatment. Caution should be exercised when offering this type of coverage to an HSA-eligible individual.

Rider 7 pays a specified amount monthly upon receipt of written proof that the covered individual is totally disabled, has been disabled for 30 days, and loses income due to such disability.

Rider 8 pays a specified amount monthly upon receipt of written proof that the covered individual is totally disabled due to cancer, a heart attack, or stroke, has been disabled for 30 days, and loses income due to such disability.

Analysis. Riders 7 and 8 constitute permitted accident or disability coverage within the meaning of Code Section 223(c)(1)(B)(ii). An individual who is otherwise an *eligible individual* remains an *eligible individual* if covered under Rider 7 or 8.

Rider 9 pays a specified amount for ambulance transportation to a hospital or emergency treatment center and, if treatment cannot be obtained locally, a specified amount for non-local transportation.

Analysis. Rider 9 does not constitute permitted coverage, permitted insurance, or preventative care under Code Section 223. An individual who is covered under Valley's policy and also covered by Rider 9 is *not* an *eligible individual* under Code Section 223.

Example 8. *Preventive care.* Ocean Corporation offers its eligible employees health and accident benefits, including an accident and health plan that is intended to qualify as an HDHP. In addition to the coverage under the HDHP, Ocean offers its eligible employees the opportunity to purchase a group hospital confinement indemnity policy that pays a specified amount for each day of hospital confinement up to a specified number of days, a specified amount for each day of confinement in an intensive care unit, a premium waiver during hospital confinement, and a specified amount for initial hospital confinement. Additionally, the policy pays a specified amount for a surgical operation performed in a hospital or ambulatory surgical center, anesthesia for such surgery, inpatient care by a physician other than the surgeon, medical or surgical care in an outpatient emergency treatment center (limited to two visits a year), an outpatient emergency accident benefit, up to five visits a year for any reason for a physician's treatment outside of a hospital, at-home nursing care during the period following hospital confinement, up to three ambulance trips a year to a hospital or emergency treatment center, and non-local transportation required for out-of-area treatment. The policy permits several optional benefits.

Optional benefit 1 pays preventive care up to a specified amount for tests performed for the diagnosis of an injury or sickness suggested by symptoms of an injury or sickness outside of hospital confinement.

Optional benefit 2 pays preventive care up to a specified amount for a routine physical examination or preventive screening services (e.g., bone marrow testing, colonoscopy, chest X-ray) outside of hospital confinement.

Optional benefit 3 covers up to a specified number of prescription drugs.

Analysis. Ocean's policy does *not* constitute permitted coverage, permitted insurance, or preventive care under Code Section 223. An individual covered by Ocean's policy is *not* an *eligible individual* under Code Section 223 (even if none of the optional riders are selected).

Note. Although Optional benefits 1 and 2 constitute preventive care, the individual is also covered by Ocean's policy (which provides coverage that is disqualifying coverage). Thus, the individual is not an *eligible individual* under Code Section 223.

Analysis. Optional benefit 3 does *not* constitute permitted coverage, permitted insurance, or preventive care under Code Section 223. An individual covered by Optional benefit 3 is *not* an *eligible individual* under Code Section 223.

Example 9. *Permitted accident coverage.* Asteroid Corporation offers its eligible employees health and accident benefits, including an accident and health plan that is intended to qualify as an HDHP. In addition to the coverage under the HDHP, Asteroid offers its eligible employees an individual policy that pays a specified amount for covered losses sustained from an off-the-job accident resulting in accidental death or dismemberment within 90 days from the date of the accident. The policy also pays a specified amount for hospital confinement, ambulance transportation, medical expenses, and payment for total disability resulting from the accident. The policy does not cover loss caused by sickness. The policy contains two optional riders.

Rider 1 pays a specified amount per month for total disability resulting from sickness.

Rider 2 pays a specified amount for each day of hospital confinement due to sickness that does not result from an injury, regardless of whether the covered person is disabled as defined in the policy.

Rider 3 pays a specified amount for treatment by a physician outside of a hospital for any reason and regardless of whether the covered individual is disabled as defined in the policy.

Analysis. Asteroid's policy is permitted accident coverage within the meaning of Code Section 223(c)(1)(B)(ii). An individual who is otherwise an *eligible individual* remains an *eligible individual* if covered under the policy. Rider 1 is permitted accident coverage within the meaning of Code Section 223(c)(1)(B)(ii). Rider 2 constitutes insurance paying a fixed amount per day (or other period) of hospitalization within the meaning of Code Section 223(c)(3)(C). An individual who is otherwise an eligible individual remains an eligible individual if covered under Riders 1 or 2. Rider 3 does not constitute permitted coverage, permitted insurance, or preventative care under Code Section 223. An individual who is covered under Asteroid's policy and also covered by Rider 3 is not an *eligible individual* under Code Section 223.

Letter Ruling 200704010 makes clear that the IRS views the hospital indemnity exception as unavailable where the rider provides coverage for a treatment. Further, this Letter Ruling suggests that payment of an initial lump sum upon confinement to a hospital may be outside the definition of a hospital indemnity policy, even if the payment is not contingent upon receiving treatment. Caution should be exercised when offering this type of coverage to an HSA-eligible individual. [Ltr. Rul. 200704010 (Oct. 25, 2006, *rel.* Jan. 26, 2007]

Example 10. *Permitted accident coverage.* Quartz Corporation offers its eligible employees health and accident benefits, including an accident and health plan that is intended to qualify as HDHP. In addition to the coverage under the HDHP, Quartz offers its eligible employees an individual policy that pays a specified amount for covered losses sustained from an on-the-job or off-the-job accident resulting in accidental death or dismemberment within 90 days from the date of the accident. The policy also pays a specified amount for hospital confinement, ambulance transportation, medical expenses, and payment for total disability resulting from the accident. The policy does not cover loss caused by sickness. Several optional riders are available under the policy.

Rider 1 pays a specified amount per month for total disability resulting from sickness.

Rider 2 pays a specified amount for each day of hospital confinement due to sickness that does not result from an injury, regardless of whether the covered person is disabled as defined in the policy.

Rider 3 pays a specified amount for treatment by a physician outside of a hospital for any reason and regardless of whether the covered individual is disabled as defined in the policy.

Analysis. Quartz's policy is permitted accident coverage within the meaning of Code Section 223(c)(1)(B)(ii). An individual who is otherwise an eligible individual as defined by Code Section 223(c)(1) remains an eligible individual if covered under the policy.

Rider 1 is permitted accident coverage within the meaning of Code Section 223(c)(1)(B)(ii). Rider 2 constitutes insurance paying a fixed amount per day (or other period) of hospitalization within the meaning of Code Section 223(c)(3)(C). An individual who is otherwise an eligible individual remains an eligible individual if covered under Riders 1 or 2.

Rider 3 does not constitute permitted coverage, permitted insurance, or preventative care under Code Section 223. An individual who is covered under Quartz's policy and also covered by Rider 3 is not an eligible individual under Code Section 223.

Letter Ruling 200704010 makes clear that the IRS views the hospital indemnity exception as unavailable where the rider provides coverage for a treatment. Further, the Letter Ruling suggests that payment of an initial lump sum upon confinement to a hospital may be outside the definition of a hospital indemnity policy, even if the payment is not contingent upon receiving treatment. Caution should be exercised when offering this type of coverage to an HSA-eligible individual.

Example 11. Circular Corporation offers its eligible employees health and accident benefits, including an accident and health plan that is intended to qualify as an HDHP. In addition to the coverage under the HDHP, Circular offers its eligible employees an individual policy that pays a specified amount for covered losses sustained from an off-the-job accident resulting in accidental death or dismemberment within 90 days from the date of the accident. The policy also pays a specified amount for hospital confinement, ambulance transportation, medical expenses, and payment for total disability resulting from the accident. The policy does not cover loss caused by sickness.

Analysis. Circular's policy is permitted accident coverage within the meaning of Code Section 223(c)(1)(B)(ii). An individual who is otherwise an eligible individual remains an eligible individual if covered under Circular's policy.

Q 3:56   Does the characterization of a benefit required by state law determine whether health care is preventive?

No. The determination of whether health care that is required by state law to be provided by an HDHP without regard to a deductible is "preventive" for purposes of the exception for preventive care is to be based on the standards set forth in Notice 2004-23 [2004-15 I.R.B. 725] and other guidance issued by the IRS, rather than on how that care is characterized by state law.

Note. State insurance laws often require health plans to provide certain health care benefits without regard to a deductible or on terms no less favorable than other benefits provided by the health plan (see Qs 3:21, 8:35).

Note. Code Section 220(c)(2)(B)(ii) allows an HDHP for purposes of an Archer MSA to provide preventive care without a deductible if required by state law. However, that section does not define preventive care for HSA purposes.

Medical Discount Cards

Q 3:57   May an individual who is covered by an HDHP, and also has a discount card that enables the user to obtain discounts for health care services or products, contribute to an HSA?

Yes. Discount cards that entitle the holder to obtain discounts for services or products at managed care market rates will not disqualify an individual from making an HSA contribution as long as the individual is required to pay the discounted cost of health care until the deductible of the HDHP is satisfied. [I.R.S. Notice 2004-50, Q&A 9, 2004-33 I.R.B. 196]

> **Example.** An employer provides its employees with a pharmacy discount card. For a fixed annual fee (paid by the employer) each employee receives a card that entitles the holder to choose any participating pharmacy. During the one-year life of the card, the cardholder receives a 15 to 50 percent discount off the usual and customary fees charged by the pharmacy, with no dollar cap on the amount of discounts received during the year. The cardholder is responsible for paying the discounted costs of any drugs until the deductible of any other health plan covering the individual is satisfied. An employee who is otherwise eligible for an HSA will not become ineligible solely as a result of having this benefit.

Employee Assistance, Disease Management, and Wellness Programs

Q 3:58   Does coverage under an Employee Assistance Program (EAP), disease management program, or wellness program make an individual ineligible to contribute to an HSA?

Coverage under an employer-provided EAP, disease management program, or wellness program does not make an individual ineligible to contribute to an HSA, provided that the program does not provide significant benefits in the nature of medical care or treatment. If it does not, the EAP, disease management program, or wellness program will not be considered a *health plan* for HSA purposes. [I.R.S. Notice 2004-50, Q&A 10, 2004-33 I.R.B. 196]

Q 3:59   Would services provided by a nurse practitioner at an employer's on-site clinic be considered a health plan that makes an individual ineligible to contribute to an HSA?

Probably not. It is likely that a significant component of the services provided by the nurse practitioner will be preventive and can therefore be provided without regard to the deductible under an HDHP (see Q 3:49). Further, to the extent that clinical services are provided, it is likely that such services will be minor in nature (e.g., treatment of minor injuries, illness, or first aid) and not significant benefits in the nature of medical care or treatment.

> **Practice Pointer.** There are exceptions under ERISA (DOL Reg. § 2510.3-1 (c)) and COBRA (Treas. Reg. § 54.4980B-2, Q&A 1(d)) to exempt on-site facilities from the definition of medical care. If the services of a nurse

practitioner are treated as outside of ERISA and not subject to COBRA, that would provide additional support for the conclusion that such services are not a disqualifying "health plan" for purposes of an HSA.

Q 3:60 Does access to free health care or health care at charges below fair market value from an employer's on-site clinic affect an individual's eligibility to contribute to an HSA?

No. An individual will not fail to be an eligible individual merely because the individual has access to free health care or health care at charges below fair market value from an employer's on-site clinic (see Qs 3:59, 3:61), provided the clinic does not provide *significant benefits in the nature of medical care* (in addition to disregarded coverage or preventive care). [I.R.S. Notice 2008-59, Q&A 10, 2008-29 I.R.B. 123]

Example 1. The Surf Manufacturing plant operates an on-site clinic that provides the following free health care for employees:

1. Physicals and immunizations,
2. Injecting antigens provided by employees (e.g., performing allergy injections),
3. A variety of aspirin and other nonprescription pain relievers, and
4. Treatment for injuries caused by accidents at the plant.

The clinic does not provide significant benefits in the nature of medical care in addition to disregarded coverage or preventive care. An employee of Surf will not be ineligible to be an eligible employee because of Surf's on-site clinic.

Example 2. Mercy Hospital permits its employees to receive care at its facilities for all of their medical needs. For employees without health insurance, Mercy provides medical care at no charge. For employees who have health insurance, Mercy waives all deductibles and co-pays. Because Mercy provides significant care in the nature of medical services, its employees are not eligible individuals.

Q 3:61 May the safe-harbor screening and preventive care services be disregarded in determining whether an EAP provides significant benefits for medical care or treatment?

Yes. To determine whether a program provides significant medical benefits, screening and preventive care services described in Notice 2004-23 are disregarded (see Q 3:50).

Example 1. Jupiter Corporation offers a program that provides employees with benefits under an EAP, regardless of enrollment in a health plan. The EAP is specifically designed to assist Jupiter in improving productivity by helping employees identify and resolve personal and work concerns that affect job performance and the work environment. The benefits consist primarily of free or low-cost confidential short-term counseling to identify an employee's problem that may affect job performance and, when appropriate, to provide referrals to an outside organization, facility, or program to assist the employee in resolving the problem. The issues addressed during the short-term counseling include, but are not limited to, substance abuse, alcoholism, mental health or emotional disorders, financial or legal difficulties, and dependent care needs. Jupiter's EAP is not a *health plan* under Code Section 223(c)(1) because it does not provide significant benefits in the nature of medical care or treatment.

Example 2. Saturn Corporation maintains a disease management program that identifies employees and their family members who have, or are at risk for, certain chronic conditions. The disease management program provides evidence-based information, disease-specific support, case monitoring, and coordination of the care and treatment provided by a health plan. Typical interventions include monitoring laboratory or other test results, telephone contacts or Web-based reminders of health care schedules, and providing information to minimize health risks. Saturn's disease management program is not a *health plan* under Code Section 223(c)(1) because it does not provide significant benefits in the nature of medical care or treatment.

Example 3. Venus Corporation offers a wellness program for all employees regardless of whether they participate in a health plan. The wellness program provides a wide range of education and fitness services designed to improve the overall health of the employees and prevent illness. Typical services include education; fitness, sports, and recreation activities; stress management; and health screenings. Any costs charged to the individual for participating in the services are separate from the individual's coverage under the health plan. Venus's wellness program is not a *health plan* under Code Section 223(c)(1) because it does not provide significant benefits in the nature of medical care or treatment.

Practice Pointer. There are exceptions under ERISA [DOL Reg. § 2510.3-1 (c)] and COBRA [Treas. Reg. § 54.4980B-2, Q&A 1(d)] to exempt on-site facilities from the definition of medical care. If the services of a nurse practitioner are treated as being outside of ERISA and therefore not subject to COBRA, that would provide additional support for the conclusion that such services are not a disqualifying *health plan* for HSA purposes.

Health Reimbursement Arrangements

Q 3:62   May an HSA owner who participates in an HDHP and a post-deductible health reimbursement arrangement (HRA) be an eligible individual?

Yes. An HSA owner who participates in an HDHP and a post-deductible HRA may still be an eligible individual. The deductible for the HRA does not need to be the same as the deductible for the HDHP. However, in no event may the HDHP or other health coverage provide benefits before the minimum annual deductible for the HDHP is satisfied (see Q 4:20). [Rev. Rul. 2004-45, 2004-22 I.R.B. 971]

Long-Term Care Insurance

Q 3:63   May an HSA owner pay for long-term care premiums from an HSA?

Yes. An HSA owner may pay for long-term care premiums from an HSA, as long as such premiums are within the limits necessary to be considered qualified medical expenses (see Qs 6:56–6:58). [I.R.S. Notice 2004-50, Q&A 41, 2004-33 I.R.B. 196]

Q 3:64   May an HSA owner pay for long-term care services from an HSA (i.e., services that are provided without regard to insurance)?

Yes. An HSA owner may pay for long-term care services from an HSA, as long as such services are qualified medical expenses (see Q 6:48). [I.R.S. Notice 2004-50, Q&A 42, 2004-33 I.R.B. 196]

Practice Pointer. Although Code Section 106(c) generally prohibits payment of coverage for long-term care benefits under a Code Section 125 plan (cafeteria plan), this prohibition does not apply to distributions from HSAs. [I.R.S. Notice 2004-50, Q&A 42, 2004-33 I.R.B. 196]

HSAs Under a Code Section 125 Cafeteria Plan

Q 3:65   May an HSA be funded by salary reduction contributions through a cafeteria plan?

Yes. An HSA may be funded by salary reduction contributions through a cafeteria plan described in Code Section 125. [I.R.S. Notice 2004-2, Q&A 33, 2004-2 I.R.B. 269] Thus, an employee may elect to have amounts contributed on a pretax basis as employer contributions to an HSA.

Q 3:66   Must a cafeteria plan document be amended to allow employees to fund an HSA with salary reduction contributions?

Yes. A cafeteria plan must be in writing and must, among other things, describe the benefits offered under the plan and the periods during which the benefits are provided. The HSA, therefore, must be described as a benefit in the cafeteria plan. [Prop. Treas. Reg. § 1.125-1(c)(1)] In addition, an employer is required to offer more flexibility to change an HSA salary reduction election than for other cafeteria plan benefits (see Qs 3:65, 3:69). The proposed cafeteria plan regulations contain a new rule regarding salary reduction elections with respect to an HSA. The new rule provides that if a cafeteria plan offers HSA contributions as a qualified benefit, the plan must allow a participant to prospectively make, change, or revoke salary contribution elections for HSA contributions before salary becomes currently available on at least a monthly basis. [Prop.

Treas. Reg. § 1.125-2(c)] Previous IRS guidance allowed an employer to adopt this rule but did not require it.

> **Practice Pointer.** Although the IRS does not review cafeteria plan documents and issue determination letters as it does for Section 401(a) qualified retirement plans, on audit, the IRS would expect an employer to be able to produce a written cafeteria plan that satisfies the requirements specified in the regulations.

Q 3:67   May the employer offer negative elections for an HSA if offered through a cafeteria plan?

Yes. An employer's cafeteria plan may provide for negative elections to enroll employees. Negative elections may be used to enroll employees as described in Revenue Ruling 2002-27 and the new proposed cafeteria plan regulations. [I.R.S. Notice 2004-50, Q&A 61, 2004-33 I.R.B. 196; Rev. Rul. 2002-27, 2002-20 I.R.B. 925; Prop. Treas. Reg. § 1.125-2(b)]

Q 3:68   Which requirements that apply to health flexible spending arrangements (FSAs) under a Code Section 125 cafeteria plan do not apply to HSAs?

1. The following requirements for health FSAs under a Code Section 125 cafeteria plan (which are generally imposed so that health FSAs operate in a manner similar to "insurance-type" accident or health plans under Code Section 105) are not applicable to HSAs: [I.R.S. Notice 2004-50, Q&A 57, 2004-33 I.R.B. 196]. The general prohibition against a benefit that defers compensation by permitting employees to carry over unused elective contributions or plan benefits from one plan year to another plan year. See Q 4:21 regarding the 2½-month-grace-period rules that may affect an individual's eligibility to make HSA contributions. [I.R.C. § 125(d)(2)(D); Prop. Treas. Reg. § 1.125-1(b)(5)];

2. The requirement that the maximum amount of reimbursement must be available at all times during the coverage period [Prop. Treas. Reg. § 1.125-(5)(a)(2)]; and

3. The mandatory 12-month period of coverage. [Prop. Treas. Reg. § 1.125-5(e)]

Note. Health FSA with HSA. The proposed cafeteria plan regulations also retain the rules permitting a "limited purpose" health FSA (reimbursing only those benefits that are permitted with an HSA such as vision or dental only) and a "post deductible" health FSA (reimbursing qualified expenses only after the minimum deductible under Code Section 223 has been incurred). [Prop. Treas. Reg. § 1.125-5(m)] The new proposed regulations also contain a new rule which provides that a health FSA could also be structured as a combination limited-purpose/post-deductible health FSA without impacting HSA eligibility. [Prop. Treas. Reg. § 1.125-5(m)(5)] So, for example, a health FSA could function as a limited-purpose arrangement until the minimum deductible under Code Section 223 is satisfied, and then the FSA could convert to a general purpose FSA. [REG-142695-05; 72 Fed. Reg. 43938–43968 (Aug. 6, 2007)]

Q 3:69 Do the Code Section 125 change-in-status rules apply to elections of HSA contributions through a cafeteria plan?

No. A cafeteria plan may permit an employee to revoke an election during a period of coverage with respect to a qualified benefit and make a new election for the remaining portion of the period only as specified in regulations under Code Section 125. [See Treas. Reg. § 1.125-4; I.R.S. Notice 2004-50, Q&A 58, 2004-33 I.R.B. 196] Because the eligibility requirements and contribution limits for HSAs are determined on a month-by-month basis (see Q 4:30), rather than on an annual basis, an employee who elects to make HSA contributions under a cafeteria plan must be permitted to start or stop the election or increase or decrease the election at any time as long as the change is effective after the request for the change is received (i.e., prospectively).

Q 3:70 Can an employer place additional restrictions on the election of HSA contributions under a cafeteria plan?

Yes. However, if an employer places additional restrictions on the election of HSA contributions under a cafeteria plan, the same restrictions must apply to all employees. [Prop. Treas. Reg. § 1.125-2(c)]

Q 3:71 Can an employer permit employees to elect an HSA midyear if offered as a new benefit under the employer's cafeteria plan?

Yes, provided the election for the HSA is made on a prospective basis. However, the HSA election does not permit a change or revocation of any other coverage under the cafeteria plan unless the change is permitted by regulations under Code Section 125. [See Treas. Reg. § 1.125-4; I.R.S. Notice 2004-50, Q&A 59, 2004-33 I.R.B. 196] This may affect the employees' eligibility to establish an HSA (see Q 3:69).

Q 3:72 When the HSA is offered as a new benefit under the employer's cafeteria plan midyear, are there circumstances that will prevent the employee from being an eligible individual?

Yes. While an HSA may be offered to and elected by an employee midyear, the employee may have other coverage under the cafeteria plan that cannot be changed or limited, (e.g., coverage under a health FSA), which may prevent the employee from being an eligible individual (see, too, Qs 2:6–2:8, 4:20). [See Rev. Rul. 2004-45, 2004-22 I.R.B. 971]

Q 3:73 **If an employee elects to make contributions to an HSA through the employer's cafeteria plan, may the employer contribute amounts to an employee's HSA to cover qualified medical expenses incurred by an employee that exceed the employee's current HSA balance?**

Yes. Where an employee elects to make contributions to an HSA through a cafeteria plan, the employer may, but is not required to, contribute amounts to an employee's HSA up to the maximum amount elected by the employee. While any accelerated contribution made by the employer must be equally available to all participating employees throughout the plan year and must be provided to all participating employees on the same terms, the employee must repay the amount of the accelerated contribution by the end of the plan year. [I.R.S. Notice 2004-50, Q&A 60, 2004-33 I.R.B. 196] An employer may not recoup contributions made to an HSA from an employee's HSA (see Qs 2:1, 6:2). [I.R.S. Notice 2004-50, Q&A 82, 2004-33 I.R.B. 196]

Retiree Health Coverage

Q 3:74 **Are HSA distributions qualified medical expenses if used to pay for the retiree portion of health care coverage once the HSA owner reaches age 65?**

Yes. This exception applies regardless of whether the plan is insured or self-insured (see Q 6:49). [I.R.C. § 223(d)(2)(C)(iv)]

Miscellaneous Issues

Q 3:75 **Is an HSA a group health plan under Code Section 5000(b)(1) for purposes of the 25 percent excise tax on nonconforming group health plans?**

Under Code Section 5000, the term *group health plan* means a plan (including a self-insured plan) of, or contributed to by, an employer (other than a government entity, but including a self-employed person) or employee organization to provide health care (directly or otherwise) to the employees, former employees, the employer, others associated or formerly associated with the employer in a business relationship, or their families. Unless certain participation requirements are satisfied, the plan is treated as a "nonconforming group health plan." Presumably, because HSA distributions may be used for non-medical expenses, an HSA would not be considered a group health plan for purposes of Code Section 5000(b)(1). [I.R.C. § 5000(b)(1), (c)]

Q 3:76 **Do HIPAA privacy and security rules apply to an HSA?**

It depends. This issue is more fully discussed in chapter 8.

Chapter 4

Contributions and Deductions

Contributions and their deductibility or exclusion from gross income, including the repeal of the plan deductible limitation on HSA contributions and full contributions for months preceding high deductible health plan (HDHP) coverage, are discussed in this chapter. The limitations on contributions and special rules for married individuals are explained. This chapter also examines guidance (I.R.S. Notice 2008-59, 2008-29 I.R.B. 123) which covers a wide variety of contribution issues, including limits for individuals with family coverage and dependents with nonpermitted coverage, as well as limits for married couples with different types of HDHP coverage. Chapter 4 also explains the contribution rules and restrictions relating to employer contributions to HSAs either directly or through a cafeteria plan to a health savings account (HSA), including the comparability rules for employer contributions. Moreover, the chapter reviews the tax treatment of contributions, IRS reporting by individuals, and partnership and S corporation considerations. Finally, the chapter discusses what type of coverage an individual is permitted to have with an HSA, and how the grace period (2½ month) FSA rules impact HSA eligibility. Rollover contributions and trustee-to-trustee transfers are more fully discussed in chapter 5; distribution taxation is discussed in chapter 6. See appendix F for a chart containing annual HSA limitations amounts.

On July 31, 2006, the proposed employer contribution comparability requirements were modified and finalized. In August 2007, the IRS issued new proposed regulations providing guidance on cafeteria plans. The new proposed regulations provide more detail than the previous proposed regulations concerning how to determine whether a cafeteria plan complies with these nondiscrimination rules. Chapter 4 also discusses the changes and clarifications that were made under the final employer contribution comparability regulations and their significance (see Qs 4:70, 4:73, 4:74, 4:114–4:151).

Making HSA Contributions 4-2
Eligibility for HSA Contributions 4-12
Other Employee Health Plans 4-13
Cafeteria Plan Grace Period Rules 4-17
Interaction Between HSAs and Health FSAs 4-21
Contribution Limitations 4-23
Catch-Up Contributions 4-35
Computing Annual Contributions 4-38
Special Computation Rules for Married Individuals 4-41
Deductions for Individual Contributions 4-49
Employer Contributions in General 4-52
Employer Responsibility 4-55
Exclusion and Deductibility of Employer Contributions 4-56
Timing of Contributions 4-59
Excess Contributions 4-59
Employer Contributions and ERISA 4-67
Comparability of Employer Contributions 4-69
   Categories of Coverage Relating to Comparability 4-70
   Testing Period for Comparability 4-72
   The Excise Tax and Comparability 4-72
   Employer Contributions 4-73
   Employee for Comparability Testing 4-73
   Comparable Contributions 4-75
   Collectively Bargained Employees 4-75
   Coverage Requirements Under HDHPs 4-76
   Comparability and Former Employees 4-79
   Comparability Rules Relating to Archer MSAs 4-81
   Calculating Comparable Contributions 4-81
   The Comparability Rules in Relation to Full-Time and Part-Time Employees
   4-84
   Notice to Employees Regarding Employer Contributions to HSAs 4-91
   HSA Comparability Rules and Cafeteria Plans 4-95
   Waiver of Excise Tax 4-100
   Tax Treatment of Contributions 4-101
IRS Reporting by Individuals 4-101
Partnership Considerations 4-102
S Corporation Considerations 4-106

Making HSA Contributions

Q 4:1   In what form must contributions be made to an HSA?

Annual contributions to an HSA must be made in cash. Contributions may not be made in the form of stock or other property. [I.R.C. § 223(d)(1)(a)(i); I.R.S. Notice 2004-2, Q&A 16, 2004-2 I.R.B. 269] An exception is made for rollovers and transfers from an Archer MSA, a health reimbursement arrangement (HRA), a flexible spending arrangement (FSA), a traditional individual retirement arrangement (IRA), or another HSA (see Qs 5:6, 5:32). Rollovers and transfers are more fully discussed in chapter 5. A federal income tax refund or Economic Stimulus Payment may be directly deposited to a Roth IRA. [IRS Fact Sheet (FS-2007-5) (Jan. 4, 2007)]

> **Note.** A direct deposit of a 2008 Economic Stimulus Payment may be removed from an IRA or Roth IRA without tax or penalty if removed in a timely manner (see Qs 6:1, 6:73, 6:74). [Information Release (I.R. 2008-68) (Apr. 30, 2008)] A refund to be directly deposited to one account can be done right on the Form 1040. Form 8888, *Direct Deposit of Refund to More Than One Account*, provides direction on how the deposit of a tax refund to an IRA or Roth IRA or other account will work.

For purposes of an HSA, an Archer MSA is a trust or custodial account as described in Code Section 220. [I.R.C. § 223(c)(5)]

Q 4:2 Can a transfer to an HSA be made from an employer's health FSA or HRA?

Yes. The Tax Relief and Health Care Act of 2006 (TRHCA) permits a one-time transfer of the balance remaining in an employee's health FSA or HRA to an HSA to assist individuals in funding these accounts, as long as that balance is no higher than the amount credited to the FSA or HRA on September 21, 2006. [TRHCA § 302 (Pub. L. No. 109-432)] The transfer must be made before January 1, 2012. [I.R.C. §§ 106(e), 223(c)(1)(B)(iii), 408(d)(9), added by TRHCA § 302(a)–(c); for rules in effect for taxable years ending before 2007, see I.R.S. Notice 2004-2, Q&A 23, 2004-2 I.R.B. 269, prohibiting such rollovers and transfers] The amount that is transferred from an FSA or HRA into an HSA is called a qualified HSA distribution, [I.R.C. § 106(e)(2)] and does not count against the HSA annual contribution limit. [I.R.C. § 106(e)(4)(c)] The testing period for such a transfer is the 13-consecutive month period beginning with the month of transfer. [I.R.C. § 106(e)(4)(A)] If, at any time during a testing period the individual ceases to remain an eligible individual, the transferred amounts are includible in income and subject to an additional tax. See chapter 5.

Q 4:3 Can a transfer to an HSA be made from a traditional IRA?

Yes. For taxable years beginning after 2006, an individual may make a qualified HSA funding distribution from an IRA to an HSA. [I.R.C. § 408(d)(9), added by TRHCA § 307(a)] A qualified HSA funding distribution does count against the annual HSA contribution limit. The contribution must be made in a direct trustee-to-trustee transfer and is irrevocable once made. [I.R.C. §§ 408(d)(9)(B), 408(d)(9)(C)(ii)(I)] Only one such distribution is permitted to be made in the individual's lifetime. [I.R.C. § 408(d)(9)(C)(i)(I)] However, if an individual makes a transfer while enrolled in self-only HDHP coverage and later switches to family HDHP coverage, a second qualifying HSA funding distribution representing the difference between the self-only and family limits may be made. Prior to 2007, rollovers or transfers were not permitted to be made to an HSA from an IRA. See chapter 5.

Q 4:4   May an HSA be fully funded in the beginning of a year?

Yes. The maximum annual contribution may be made at the beginning of the year, but not before the start of the year for which the contribution is being made (see Q 4:91 regarding excess contributions). To contribute the maximum annual 2009 contribution, an individual generally must have the same coverage during the entire year or be considered an eligible individual with the same coverage (see Qs 4:5–4:8, and Q 4:140 regarding pre-funding of employer contributions). An ineligible or otherwise eligible individual may be treated as an eligible individual (for the entire year) under the "last-month rule" (see Qs 4:5, 4:6, 4:7, 4:57).

> **Note.** There is no actual "monthly limit" (see Q 4:26). Although the maximum annual HSA contribution limit is the sum of the monthly limits (see Q 4:30), contributions may be made at any time. For example, if an individual has disqualifying coverage and is said to be ineligible for three months ending on March 31, the individual may contribute 9/12ths of the 2009 HSA contribution limit (at any time) during that calendar year, or until the tax filing deadline for that year.

> **Caution.** Absent an exception (see Q 4:5), if an HSA owner's HDHP coverage changes during the year (e.g., to coverage with a lower deductible, or coverage that is not an HDHP), an HSA that was fully funded at the beginning of the year based upon the assumption that the original HDHP would remain in place for the full year may have excess contributions that will have to be withdrawn prior to April 15 of the following year to avoid the 6 percent excise tax.

> **Note.** The terms *HSA owner*, *account owner*, *account holder*, and *account beneficiary* are used interchangeably in IRS publications, notices, and announcements to refer to the person that established the HSA. To avoid confusion, the term *HSA owner* will be used to refer to that person.

Q 4:5   May the full HSA contribution be made for a year for an individual who becomes covered under an HDHP during the year or who increases coverage level during the year?

Yes. In general, an individual must be an eligible individual on the first day of a month to make a contribution for that month. However, for tax years beginning after 2006, it is possible for an individual to be treated as an eligible individual for the entire year (12 months) under the "last-month rule" and contribute the maximum permitted annual contribution amount for the year ($3,000 for self-only coverage and $5,950 for family coverage, plus catch-up contributions of $1,000 for 2009), based on the coverage that the individual has on the first day of the last month of the year (see Qs 4:6, 4:30, 4:42). Thus, an individual who becomes covered under an HDHP after the first month of his or her taxable year (generally January), or an individual who has self-only coverage on the first day of the year but changes to family coverage on or before the first day of the last month of the year, may make the full HSA contribution for the year, based on the coverage that such individual has as of the first day of the last month of the year (see Qs 4:6, 4:7–4:10, 4:48, 4:57). The last month contribution rules also apply to catch-up contributions (see Q 4:42).

> **Caution.** A strict reading of Code Section 223(b)(8), "Increase in limit for individuals becoming eligible <u>after</u> the beginning the year" (emphasis added), implies that a look-back should apply to an individual who is not an eligible individual on the first day of his or her taxable year (generally assume January 1), but who became an eligible individual after January 1 (see Qs 2:6, 2:8). In addition, coverage can only be attributed to previous months of the year during which the individual was not otherwise HSA eligible (under this strict reading). For example, assume an individual has disqualifying other coverage (other than permitted insurance, see Q 3:43) on January 1 that terminated in June. Assume further that beginning on July 1 the individual would have been an eligible individual for the remainder of the year, except that his or her HDHP coverage becomes effective on November 1. Under this strict reading, no contributions can be made for the four months (July through October) the individual could have been an eligible individual (by having HDHP coverage). Thus, under the look-back rule, not more than eight months can be taken into account for computing the limitations on contributions (see Q 4:35). Fortunately, the IRS has a different interpretation—we refer to it as the "last-month rule."

> Code Section 223(b)(8) reads as follows:

> (8) INCREASE IN LIMIT FOR INDIVIDUALS BECOMING ELIGIBLE INDIVIDUALS <u>AFTER THE BEGINNING</u> OF THE YEAR.

> (A) IN GENERAL. For purposes of computing the limitation under paragraph (1) for any taxable year, an individual who is an eligible individual during the *last month* of such taxable year shall be treated.

> (i) as having been an eligible individual during each of the months in such taxable year, and

> (ii) as having been enrolled, during <u>each of the months</u> such individual is treated as an eligible individual solely by reason of clause (i), in the same high deductible health plan in which the individual was enrolled for the last month of such taxable year. [*Emphasis added*]

The IRS has interpreted Code Section 223(b)(8) to permit a calendar-year taxpayer to be treated as an eligible individual with HDHP coverage (for the entire year) if he or she is an eligible individual with HDHP coverage on December 1. The IRS interprets the last-month rule to allow the maximum permitted annual amount to be contributed regardless of whether the individual was an eligible individual on January 1, so long as the individual is an eligible individual with HDHP coverage on December 1. In addition, under the IRS interpretation, in figuring the contribution limit for an individual who changed to a different level of coverage as of December 1 (e.g., from a family HDHP to self-only HDHP or self-only HDHP to family HDHP), the individual's annual HSA contribution limit will be based on the greater of the maximum annual limit ($3,000/$5,950, plus catch up-contributions for 2009), or the monthly limit amount computed as if the last-month rule did not apply (see example in Q 4:6).

Thus, under the IRS's interpretation, if the last-month rule applies (HSA eligible with HDHP coverage on December 1), the monthly limit amounts do not generally have to be separately computed (see Qs 4:30, 4:48). However, if the individual's HDHP coverage level changes during the year, the IRS allows the greater of the coverage limit as of December 1 or the monthly limit to be contributed (see Qs 4:6, 4:37–4:38, 4:51). [See also I.R.S. Notice 2008-52, 2008-25 I.R.B. 1166]

> **Note.** An individual may establish an HSA at any time on or after the date the individual becomes HSA-eligible. Contributions for the taxable year can be made in one or more payments, at any time prior to the time (without extensions) for filing the individual's federal income tax return for the taxable year. An individual who becomes an eligible individual after January 1 may make the maximum contribution to an HSA on the first day he or she is an eligible individual. [I.R.S. Notice 2004-2, Q&A 21, 2004-2 I.R.B. 269] In that case, the individual's contribution is based on the individual's expected coverage on the first day of the last month of his or her taxable year (subject to the testing period rules, see Q 4:8). [I.R.S. Notice 2008-52, 2008-25 I.R.B. 1166, modifying I.R.S. Notice 2004-2, 2004-2 I.R.B. 269 and I.R.S. Notice 2004-50, 2004-33 I.R.B. 196] In addition, an individual who becomes an eligible individual on January 1 with self-only coverage and who switches to family coverage on or before December 1 may also take advantage of this rule. [I.R.S. Notice 2008-52, 2008-25 I.R.B. 1166]

> [See Instructions for Line 3 of Form 8889—*Health Savings Accounts (HSAs)* (2009)] The IRS's liberal interpretation makes sense because the exception is intended to "assist individuals to transfer to HDHPs from other types of health plans" (see Q 4:2). [Joint Committee on Taxation, Technical Analysis of the Tax Relief and Healthcare Act of 2006 (Pub. L. No. 109-432) (JCX-50-06)]

> However, an individual who makes contributions under the exception (12 month rule) must remain an eligible individual during the testing period (see Q 4:10).

> **Caution.** An eligible individual does not include an individual who is enrolled in Medicare or has disqualifying health care coverage at *any time* during that last month (see Qs 2:6, 2:16).

Q 4:6   How is the maximum contribution determined if an individual was, or was considered, an eligible individual for the entire year, and changes their type of coverage during the year?

In general, if an individual was, or was considered, an eligible individual for the entire year, and changes his or her type of coverage during the year, the maximum contribution limit is the *greater of*:

1. One-twelfth (1/12) of the sum of the monthly limits (see Q 4:30), including catch-up contributions if applicable, based on the type of HDHP coverage actually maintained each month during the year; or

2. The maximum permitted contribution amount ($3,000 for self-only coverage and $5,950 for family coverage, plus catch-up contributions of up to $1,000 if applicable for 2009) based on the type of coverage on the first day of the last month of the taxable year (generally December 1).

To remain an eligible individual during the testing period, an individual is not required to keep the same level of HDHP coverage during the testing period. Thus, changing from family HDHP coverage to single HDHP coverage during the testing period does not result in inclusion of amounts in gross income or an additional 10 percent tax (see Q 4:38, Examples 13 and 19).

Example. In 2009, Scott and Myra are both under age 55 and are eligible individuals with family HDHP coverage. On January 24 they divorce. Scott's coverage changes as of February 1 to self-only. Myra continues to have family HDHP coverage and was an eligible individual for the entire year.

Analysis. *No catch-up contribution.* Neither Scott nor Myra qualify for the additional catch-up contribution amount ($1,000 for 2009) because neither had attained age 55 by the end of the taxable year.

Family coverage allocation. The contribution limit for the one month Scott and Myra were considered to have family coverage is $495.83 ($5,950 × 1 ÷ 12). They agree that Scott will claim all of the $495.83 family coverage contribution.

Scott's allocation. Scott's contribution limit for 11 months of self-only coverage is $2,750 ($3,000 × 11 ÷ 12). This amount is not divided between Scott and Myra.

Scott's maximum contribution. The maximum amount that can be contributed for Scott is $3,245.83, computed as follows:

$3,245.83 equals the greater of (a) $3,245.83 ($495.83 family coverage + $2,750 self-only coverage – $0 spousal allocation) or (b) the maximum amount that can be contributed ($3,000 for self-only coverage).

Myra's maximum contribution. The maximum amount that can be contributed for Myra is $5,950, computed as follows:

$5,950 equals the greater of either (a) $5,454.16 ($495.83 family coverage for the one month prior to the divorce + $5,454.16 ($5,950 × 11 ÷ 12) family coverage maintained after the divorce – $495.83 spousal allocation) or (b) the maximum amount that can be contributed ($5,950 for family coverage).

[I.R.C. §§ 223(b)(2), 223(b)(8)]

The rule allowing the full contribution for an eligible individual on December 1 (for calendar year taxpayer) may increase, but not decrease, the contribution limit for an individual (see examples in Q 4:39). [I.R.S. Notice 2008-52, 2008-25 I.R.B. 1166]

Determining annual contribution amounts is more fully discussed in Qs 4:30–4:52; see examples. Preparation of Form 8889—*Health Savings Accounts (HSAs)* is discussed more fully in chapter 7.

Q 4:7   Is an eligible individual on December 1 considered to have self-only or family coverage?

For taxable years beginning after 2006, an individual who is an eligible individual during the last month of a taxable year is treated as having been an eligible individual during every month during the taxable year and considered as having been enrolled in the same HDHP (self-only or family coverage) in which the individual was enrolled during the last month of the taxable year (generally December) (see Qs 4:38–4:40). [I.R.C. § 223(b)(8)(A)(i)] An eligible individual (solely by reason of this exception) is treated as having been enrolled in the same HDHP in which the individual was enrolled during the last month of the taxable year (generally December). However, an eligible individual does not include an individual who is enrolled in Medicare or has disqualifying health care coverage at *any time* during that last month (see Q 2:6, 2:16). [I.R.C. § 223(b)(8)(A)(i)]

However, an individual who makes contributions under the exception must remain an eligible individual during the testing period (see Q 4:10).

Q 4:8   What happens if the individual makes contributions under the exception and does not remain an eligible individual during the testing period?

If an individual makes contributions under the exception and does not remain an eligible individual during the testing period, the amount of the contributions attributable to months preceding the month in which the individual was an eligible individual, which could not have been made but for the provision, is recaptured. Thus, the total contributions made that would not have been made except for the last-month rule are includible in gross income in the taxable year in which the individual first failed (during the testing period) to be an eligible individual. The difference is not required to be distributed (see Q 4:38, Example 14). The amount recaptured may also be subject to an additional 10 percent tax. [I.R.C. § 223(b)(8)(B)] Amounts included in gross income because an individual failed to remain an eligible individual during the testing period are not excess contributions and the 6 percent tax on excess contributions do not apply to such amounts. For this reason, amounts cannot be withdrawn under the excess contribution rules (see Q 4:91).

[I.R.S. Notice 2008-52, 2008-25 I.R.B. 1166, modifying I.R.S. Notice 2004-2, 2004-2 I.R.B. 269 and I.R.S. Notice 2004-50, 2004-33 I.R.B. 196]

Practice Pointer. Unlike the additional 10 percent tax for a distribution not used for qualified medical expenses (see Qs 6:28, 6:72) under Code Section 223(f)(4)(A), the additional 10 percent tax for failing to remain an eligible individual during the testing period (see Qs 4:9, 4:10) under Code Section 223(b)(8)(B)(i)(II) applies regardless of the HSA owner's age (i.e., even after age 65), but the 10 percent tax will not apply if the failure to maintain HDHP coverage is due to death or disability of the HSA owner.

Note. Employers are not responsible for reporting whether an employee remains an eligible individual during the testing period. [I.R.S. Notice 2008-52, 2008-25 I.R.B. 1166, modifying I.R.S. Notice 2004-2, 2004-2 I.R.B. 269 and I.R.S. Notice 2004-50, 2004-33 I.R.B. 196]

Q 4:9 Does the additional 10 percent tax apply if the individual does not remain an eligible individual during the testing period?

Yes. A 10 percent additional tax applies to the amount includible in income. An exception applies if the employee ceases to be an eligible individual by reason of death or disability (see Qs 4:9, 4:39). [I.R.C. § 223(b)(8)(A)(ii)]

Withdrawing the amount includible in income from the HSA will not prevent the inclusion of the amount in income or the additional 10 percent tax for failing to remain an eligible individual during the testing period (following a contribution made under the full contribution rule). However, earnings on the amount are not included in gross income or subject to the 10 percent additional tax, so long as the earnings remain in the HSA or are used for qualified medical expenses. [I.R.S. Notice 2008-52, 2008-25 I.R.B. 1166, modifying I.R.S. Notice 2004-2, 2004-2 I.R.B. 269 and Notice 2004-50, 2004-33 I.R.B. 196]

Q 4:10 What is the testing period during which the individual must remain an eligible individual?

The testing period is the 13-month period beginning with the month of December in the year of the mid-year enrollment and ending at the end of the following December. This exception is more fully discussed in Qs 4:37 and 4:39.

Example. Samantha, age 60, a calendar year taxpayer, is ineligible to contribute to an HSA and make contributions for the 11-month period ending in November 2009 because she participated in a health plan that was not an HDHP in those months. If Samantha establishes an HDHP with self-only coverage effective on December 1, 2009, and does not participate in another health plan which is not an HDHP that provides coverage for any benefit which is covered under the HDHP (other than permitted insurance, permitted coverage, or preventive care), she will be eligible for the month of December. As a result, Samantha will be treated as an eligible individual for all 2009 under the *last-month rule*. She may contribute $4,000 ($3,000, plus a catch-up contribution of $1,000) for 2009. If it were not for the exception, Samantha's contributions would be limited to $333.33 (1/12 of the $4,000 maximum annual contribution limit) for 2009. If Samantha's HDHP were effective on any day after December 1, she would not be an eligible individual for the month of December and the exception treating her as eligible for her entire taxable year would not apply.

Q 4:11　What is the last date for making annual contributions to an HSA?

In general, contributions must be made by the due date of the individual's federal income tax return not including extensions. Thus, a 2009 HSA contribution may generally be made at any time in 2009 and before the due date of the 2009 return (generally April 15 of the following year). [I.R.C. § 223(d)(4)(B)]

> **Note.** Farmers must file their federal income tax returns by March 1 (rather than the general April 15 due date), unless estimated taxes are paid by January 18. Therefore, the contribution date for farmers may vary from that of the general rule.

For 2005 and thereafter, tax-free distributions may be received from the HSA only for qualified medical expenses incurred on or after the date the HSA is established. [I.R.S. Notice 2004-2, 2004-2 I.R.B. 269]

> **Historical Note.** For 2004, if an HSA was established by the due date (generally April 15, 2005), tax-free distributions could have been received from the HSA for qualified medical expenses incurred on or after the first day of the month that the taxpayer became an eligible individual (see chapter 2), under a transitional rule that only applied for calendar year 2004. [I.R.S. Notice 2004-2, Q&A 26, 2004-2 I.R.B. 269, modified by I.R.S. Notice 2004-25, 2004-15 I.R.B. 727 (the "transitional relief")] However, that transitional relief was not extended beyond 2004.

> **Caution.** A contribution postmarked after December 31 will be treated as applying the year that the contribution actually is received by the trustee or custodian unless the taxpayer has designated that the contribution is for the prior year. For example, if an individual is making a contribution in 2010 with respect to the prior year, the contribution form (and preferably the check) should indicate "2009 HSA contribution."

Q 4:12　May an individual who ceases to be an eligible individual during a year still contribute to an HSA with respect to the months of the year when the individual was an eligible individual?

An individual who ceases to be an eligible individual may, until the date for filing the return (without extensions) for the year, make HSA contributions with respect to the months of the year when the individual was an eligible individual (see Qs 4:11, 4:30). [I.R.S. Notice 2008-59, Q&A 19, 2008-29 I.R.B. 123]

> **Example.** Jerome has a self-only HDHP, and is an eligible individual for the first four months of 2009. Jerome has until April 15, 2010 (the date for filing the 2009 return, without extensions) to contribute 4/12 x $3,000 ($1,000) to an HSA.

Q 4:13   May employer contributions to employees' HSAs made between January 1 and the date for filing the employee's return, without extensions, be allocated to the prior year?

An employer contribution to an employee's HSAs made between January 1 and the date for filing the employee's return, without extensions, may be allocated to the prior year. However, the employer must notify the HSA trustee or custodian if the contributions relate to the prior year. The employer must also inform the employee of the designation. However, the contributions designated as made for the prior year are still reported in Box 12 with Code W on the employees' Form W-2 for the year in which the contributions are actually made. [I.R.S. Notice 2008-59, Q&A 21, 2008-29 I.R.B. 123]

> **Example.** In January 2010, Monster contributes $500 to each employee's HSA and notifies the HSA trustee (and provides a statement to the employees) that the contributions are for 2009. Subsequently, in 2010, Monster contributes $250 to each employee's HSA on March 31, June 30, September 30, and December 31. For each employee whose HSA received these contributions, Monster reports a total contribution of $1,500 in Box 12 with Code W on the Form W-2 for 2010. In completing the Form 8889—*Health Savings Accounts (HSAs)* for 2009, to compute Monster's contributions, the employees add the 2009 contribution amount ($500) to any employer contributions reported in Box 12, Code W on the 2009 Form W-2. In completing the Form 8889 for 2010, the employees subtract the $500 from the Box 12, Code W amount ($1,500) on the 2010 Form W-2, and add to the remaining $1,000 ($1,500 - $500) any contributions for 2010 made by Monster between January 1, 2010 and his or her filing date without extensions.

Q 4:14   For contributions to be made on behalf an eligible individual, is the individual required to have compensation?

No. HSA contributions may be made regardless of whether the eligible individual (see Q 2:6) has compensation. However, where an employee funds the HDHP through a pretax cafeteria plan with their employer, compensation or earned income is required. [I.R.C. §§ 223(b)(4)(A), 223(b)(4)(B)]

Practice Pointer. Unlike contributions to Archer MSAs, contributions to an HSA may be made by or on behalf of eligible individuals even if the individuals have no compensation or the contributions exceed their compensation.

Q 4:15   May HSA contributions be made into an individual retirement arrangement (IRA)?

No. Although an HSA is similar to an IRA in many respects, an IRA cannot be used as an HSA, nor can an HSA be combined with an IRA. [See I.R.S. Notice 96-53, A-9, A-10, 1996-2 C.B. 219, regarding Archer MSAs]

Q 4:16   Must contributions be made into an HSA established at the same institution that provides the HDHP?

No. The HSA can be established through a qualified trustee or custodian that is different from the HDHP provider. [I.R.S. Notice 2004-2, Q&A 10, 2004-2 I.R.B. 269]

Eligibility for HSA Contributions

Q 4:17   Who may contribute to an HSA?

Any eligible individual or any other person on an eligible individual's behalf (see Q 2:6) may contribute to an HSA. For example, if the HSA is established by an employee, the employee, the employee's employer, or both may contribute to the HSA. If the HSA is established by a self-employed (or unemployed) individual, the individual may contribute to the HSA. Also, any other individual (e.g., a family member) may make contributions to an HSA on behalf of an individual. [I.R.S. Notice 2004-50, Q&A 28, 2004-33 I.R.B. 196]

Contributions may also be made through a cafeteria plan (see Q 4:18). Further, a partnership may contribute to a partner's HSA (see Q 4:156, and an S corporation may contribute to the HSA of a shareholder-employee (see Q 4:168).

Practice Pointer. The individual who makes the contribution does not qualify for the HSA deduction, however. Rather, the HSA owner may generally take the deduction, or an exclusion from gross income if the contributions are made under a cafeteria plan, for contributions made on his or her behalf (see Qs 4:60, 4:71).

Note. The DOL has approved certain cash bonus incentives paid in connection with the establishment of HSAs and HDHPs by banks and insurance companies to individuals' HSAs (see Q 6:67).

Q 4:18   May contributions to an HSA be made through a cafeteria plan?

Yes. Payments for an HDHP and contributions to an HSA can be made through a cafeteria plan. [I.R.S. Notice 2004-2, Q&As 16 and 33, 2004-2 I.R.B. 269]

Q 4:19   May a state government make an HSA contribution on behalf of an eligible individual?

Yes (see Q 4:17). In addition, a state government's HSA contribution on behalf of an eligible individual for high-risk individuals (state high-risk pool) may qualify as an HDHP if it does not pay benefits below the HDHP minimum annual deductible of $1,150 for self-only coverage and $2,300 for family coverage for 2009 (see Q 3:10). [I.R.S. Notice 2004-50, Q&A 29, 2004-33 I.R.B. 196]

Other Employee Health Plans

Q 4:20   May an employee covered by an HDHP and a health FSA or an HRA make contributions to an HSA?

Generally not. An employee covered by an HDHP and a health FSA or an HRA that pays or reimburses qualified medical expenses generally cannot make contributions to an HSA (see Q 3:72).

Reimbursement by HDHP, HRA, or FSA before minimum HDHP deductible is satisfied. An individual with family HDHP coverage who is covered by a post-deductible HRA or post-deductible health FSA that reimburses the medical expenses (see Qs 6:27–6:58) of any covered individual before the minimum family HDHP deductible ($1,150 for self-only coverage and $2,300 for family coverage for 2009) has been satisfied, that individual is not an eligible individual. [I.R.S. Notice 2008-59, Q&A 8, 2008-29 I.R.B. 123]

> **Example 1.** Murry has family HDHP coverage. His spouse and children (but not Murry) are also covered by non-HDHP family coverage provided by his spouse's employer. In addition, Murry, his spouse, and children are also covered by a post-deductible health FSA. The health FSA pays for unreimbursed medical expenses of the spouse and child without regard to the satisfaction of the deductible of the family HDHP. Because the health FSA covering Murry reimburses medical expenses before the minimum family HDHP deductible is satisfied, he is not an eligible individual. If the health FSA did not cover Murry, he would be an eligible individual.

> **Note.** Only the minimum statutory deductible, not the plan's actual deductible, must be met prior to the post-deductible HRA or FSA beginning payment.

> **Note.** In the authors' opinion, the same logic should apply to post-deductible HRA or FSA where the eligible individual has a self-only HDHP.

Family HDHP coverage and dependents with disqualifying coverage. Q&A 11 of I.R.S. Notice 2008-59 states that an individual's eligibility is not affected, and an otherwise eligible individual remains an eligible individual, if the individual has family HDHP coverage that covers dependents, and the dependents (but not the individual) have "other, disqualifying, non-HDHP coverage." [I.R.S. Notice 2008-59, Q&A 11, 2008-29 I.R.B. 123]

> **Example 2.** Peter has family HDHP coverage for himself and his son Darnell who is mentally and physically disabled. His wife, Georgina, has non-HDHP family coverage with a $500 deductible for herself and Darnell. Nearly all of Darnell's expenses for medical care are covered by Georgina's plan. Peter is an eligible individual with family coverage (whether or not the other individual is an eligible individual, see Q 3:40). Peter will be able to contribute an additional $2,950 for family coverage, that is, $5,950 less the self-only maximum contribution limit of $3,000 (see Q 4:36).

However, an employee can make contributions to an HSA while covered under an HDHP for periods during which the individual is covered under any of the arrangements discussed below.

Limited-purpose health FSA or an HRA. The health FSA and/or an HRA are limited-purpose arrangements if they pay or reimburse only vision and dental expenses (i.e., permitted coverage), or preventive care benefits. An HRA, because it can be used to reimburse premiums, could also reimburse long-term care premiums, premiums for a specified disease or illness, or premiums for a fixed amount per day or other period of hospitalization (i.e., permitted insurance) as well. In certain circumstances (i.e., when an HRA does not satisfy the definition of an FSA under Code Section 106(c)), the HRA may also reimburse long-term care services. If the covered benefits are limited in this manner, it does not matter whether the health FSA and/or HRA pay benefits without imposing a deductible. [I.R.C. § 223(c)(2)(C); see Prop. Treas. Reg. § 1.125-5(m)(3); Rev. Rul. 2004-45, 2004-1 C.B. 971; I.R.S. Notice 2008-59, Q&As 1 and 2, 2008-29 I.R.B. 123]

Example 3. In 2008, Green Corporation provides an HRA that reimburses any Code Section 213(d) medical expense incurred by an employee, employee's spouse, and dependents. For 2009, Green amends the HRA to limit its benefits to expenses for vision care, dental care, and preventive care and to pay the employee's share of the premiums for the employer-sponsored HDHP. During 2009, all employees of Green are otherwise eligible individuals. For 2009, Green's employees are eligible individuals even if covered by the HRA.

Note. Reimbursement of HDHP premiums from an HSA is not disqualifying coverage. [I.R.S. Notice 2008-59, Q&A 1, 2008-29 I.R.B. 123]

The following examples present situations where an individual is covered by an HDHP and a health FSA or an HRA. The individual's eligibility to make HSA contributions is examined.

Example 4. Stuart is covered by an HDHP. The HDHP has an 80/20 percent co-insurance feature above the deductible. Stuart is also covered by a health FSA under a Code Section 125 cafeteria plan and an HRA. The health FSA and the HRA pay or reimburse all of his medical expenses (within the meaning of Code Section 213) that are not covered by the HDHP (e.g., co-payments, co-insurance, expenses not covered due to the deductible, and other medical expenses not covered by the HDHP). The health FSA and the HRA coordinate the payment of benefits under the ordering rules of Notice 2002-45. [2002-28 I.R.B. 93] Stuart is not entitled to benefits under Medicare and may not be claimed as a dependent on another person's tax return.

Here, Stuart is covered by an HDHP and by a health FSA and an HRA that pay or reimburse medical expenses incurred before the minimum annual HSA deductible of $1,150 (the 2009 limit) has been satisfied. The health FSA and the HRA pay or reimburse medical expenses that are not limited to the exceptions for permitted insurance, permitted coverage, or preventive care. As a result, Stuart is not an eligible individual for the purpose of making contributions to an HSA. This result would be the same if Stuart were covered by a health FSA or an HRA sponsored by his spouse's employer. [Rev. Rul. 2004-45, 2004-22 I.R.B. 971; see also Rev. Rul. 2004-38, 2004-15 I.R.B. 717]

Example 5. Same facts as in Example 4, except that the health FSA and the HRA are limited-purpose arrangements that pay or reimburse, pursuant to the written plan document, only vision and dental expenses (whether or not the minimum annual deductible of the HDHP has been satisfied). In addition, the health FSA and the HRA pay or reimburse preventive care benefits as described in Notice 2004-23 [2004-15 I.R.B. 725] (see Q 3:53). Although Stuart is covered by an HDHP and by a health FSA and the HRA that pay or reimburse medical expenses incurred before the HDHP minimum annual deductible ($1,150 for 2009) has been satisfied, the medical expenses paid or reimbursed by the health FSA and the HRA include only vision and dental benefits (which are permitted coverage) and preventive care. All of these benefits may be covered as a separate health plan, as a separate or optional rider, or as part of the HDHP, whether or not the HDHP minimum annual deductible has been satisfied. Stuart is an eligible individual for the purpose of making contributions to an HSA. [Rev. Rul. 2004-45, 2004-22 I.R.B. 971]

Example 6. Same facts as in Example 4, except that Stuart is not covered by a health FSA. Under his employer's HRA, Stuart elects, before the beginning of the HRA coverage period, to forgo the payment or reimbursement of medical expenses incurred during that coverage period. The decision to forgo the payment or reimbursement of medical expenses does not apply to permitted insurance, permitted coverage, and preventive care (referred to as "excepted medical expenses" in Code Section 223) (see Q 3:50; I.R.S. Notice 2004-23, 2004-15 I.R.B. 725). Medical expenses incurred during the suspended HRA coverage period (other than the excepted medical expenses, if otherwise allowed to be paid or reimbursed by an HRA) cannot be paid or reimbursed by the HRA currently or later (i.e., after the HRA suspension ends). However, the employer decides to continue to make employer contributions to Stuart's HRA during the suspension period.

Here, however, Stuart elected to forgo the payment or reimbursement of medical expenses incurred during an HRA coverage period. The suspension of payments and reimbursements by the HRA does not apply to permitted insurance, permitted coverage, and preventive care (if otherwise allowed to be paid or reimbursed by the HRA). Stuart is an eligible individual for the purpose of making contributions to an HSA until the suspension period ends, and he is again entitled to receive, from the HRA, payments or reimbursements of Code Section 213(d) medical expenses incurred after the suspension period.

Example 7. Same facts as in Example 4, except that the health FSA and the HRA are post-deductible arrangements that pay or reimburse only Stuart's medical expenses (including the 20 percent co-insurance responsibility for expenses above the deductible) after the HDHP's minimum annual deductible has been satisfied. Because Stuart's health FSA and the HRA pay or reimburse medical expenses (including the 20 percent co-insurance not otherwise covered by the HDHP) only after the HDHP's minimum annual deductible has been satisfied, he is an eligible individual for the purpose of making contributions to an HSA.

Example 8. Same facts as in Example 4, except that Stuart is not covered by a health FSA. The employer's HRA is a retirement HRA that reimburses only those medical expenses incurred after the individual retires. Stuart is an eligible individual for the purpose of making contributions to an HSA before retirement because the HRA will pay or reimburse only medical expenses incurred after retirement.

Note. In addition, combinations of these arrangements that are consistent with these requirements would not disqualify an individual from being an eligible individual. For example, if an employer offers a combined post-deductible health FSA and a limited-purpose health FSA, this would not disqualify an otherwise eligible individual from contributing to an HSA.

[I.R.C. §§ 125(a), 125(d), 125(f), 223(a), 223(b), 223(c)(1)(A), 223(c)(1)(A)(ii), 223(b)(2)(A), 223(b)(2)(B), 223(c)(1)(B), 223(c)(2)(A), 223(c)(2)(C); Rev. Rul. 2004-45, 2004-22 I.R.B. 971; Rev. Rul. 2004-38, 2004-15 I.R.B. 717; I.R.S. Notices 2005-42, 2005-23 I.R.B. 1204, 2004-23, 2004-15 I.R.B. 725: 2002-45, 2002-2 C.B. 93; see also H.R. Conf. Rep. No. 108-391, at 841 (2003)]

Suspended HRA. A suspended HRA is an HRA that, pursuant to an election made before the beginning of the HRA coverage period, does not pay or reimburse, at any time, any medical expense incurred during the suspension period except preventive care, permitted insurance, and permitted coverage (if otherwise allowed to be paid or reimbursed by the HRA). During the suspension period, the individual participating in the HRA is an eligible individual for the purpose of making contributions to an HSA. When the suspension period ends, the individual is no longer an eligible individual because the individual is again entitled to receive payment or reimbursement of Code Section 213(d) medical expenses from the HRA. An individual who does not forgo the payment or reimbursement of medical expenses incurred during an HRA coverage period is not an eligible individual for HSA purposes during that HRA coverage period.

Caution. If an HSA is funded through salary reduction under a cafeteria plan during the suspension period, the terms of the salary reduction election must indicate that the salary reduction is used only to pay for the HSA offered in conjunction with the HRA, not to pay for the HRA itself. Thus, the mere fact that an individual participates in an HSA funded pursuant to a salary reduction election does not necessarily result in attributing the salary reduction to the HRA.

Post-deductible health FSA or an HRA. A post-deductible health FSA or an HRA does not pay or reimburse any medical expense incurred before the $1,150/$2,300 (for 2009) HDHP minimum annual deductible is satisfied. The participating individual is an eligible individual for the purpose of making contributions to the HSA. The deductible for the HRA or health FSA ("other coverage") need not be the same as the HDHP deductible, but in no event may the HDHP or other coverage provide benefits before the minimum annual deductible has been satisfied. Where the HDHP and the other coverage do not have identical deductibles, contributions to the HSA are limited to the lower of the deductibles. In addition, although the deductibles of the HDHP and the other coverage may be satisfied independently by separate expenses, no benefits may be paid before the minimum annual deductible, $1,150/$2,300 (for 2009) has been satisfied. [I.R.C. §§ 213(d), 223(c)(2)(A)(i); see Prop. Treas. Reg. § 1.125-5 (m)(4); Rev. Rul. 2004-45 (2004-22 I.R.B. 971); I.R.S. Notice 2008-59, Q&A 7, 2008-29 I.R.B. 123]

> **Practice Pointer.** The new proposed cafeteria plan regulations contain a new rule which provides that a health FSA could also be structured as a combination limited-purpose/post-deductible health FSA without impacting HSA eligibility. [Prop. Treas. Reg. § 1.125-5(m)(5)] So, for example, a health FSA could function as a limited purpose arrangement until the minimum deductible under Code Section 223 is satisfied, and then the FSA could convert to a general purpose FSA.

Retirement HRA. A retirement HRA pays or reimburses only those medical expenses incurred after retirement (and no expenses incurred before retirement). In this case, the participating individual is an eligible individual for the purpose of making contributions to the HSA before retirement, but will lose status as an eligible individual at the time the retirement HRA may pay or reimburse Code Section 223(d) medical expenses. Thus, after retirement, the individual is no longer an eligible individual for the purpose of the HSA.

[I.R.C. § 223(c)(3); Rev. Rul. 2004-45, 2004-22 I.R.B. 971]

Cafeteria Plan Grace Period Rules

Q 4:21 May a cafeteria plan permit employees to carry over unused contributions to a subsequent year?

Yes. In Notice 2005-42, the IRS announced that it is permissible for a Code Section 125 plan to provide for a 2½-month "grace period" after the end of a plan year during which a participant with a remaining balance in his or her health FSA (at the end of the plan year) may be reimbursed for eligible expenses incurred up to 2½ months after the plan year's end. This rule also appears in the new cafeteria plan proposed regulations. [Prop. Treas. Reg. § 1.125-1(e)] If a plan is not amended to include a grace period, unused FSA balances are forfeited at the end of the plan year under the so-called "use-it-or-lose-it" rule. The adoption of a grace period might prevent a participant from contributing to an HSA for the period (generally three months) that the employee had disqualifying "other coverage" (see below). Under the Notice, contributions to an HSA generally are not permitted until the first month following the grace period even if a participant's balance in his or her account was zero because of the disqualifying coverage. A transitional rule also is provided for cafeteria plan years ending before June 5, 2006 (see the following).

Practice Pointer. Under the TRHCA, an individual who is HSA-eligible during December (the last month of their taxable year, and not enrolled in Medicare or does not have disqualifying health care coverage in December) as previously discussed, but did not establish an HDHP before December, may be permitted to make the full deductible HSA contribution for the year (see Q 4:5). An individual who is an eligible individual during the last month of a taxable year is treated as having been an eligible individual during every month during the taxable year for purposes of computing the amount that may be contributed to the HSA for the year. Such individual is also treated as having the same HDHP coverage (self-only or family coverage) for the entire taxable year as in the last month of the year. Thus, in such a case, disqualifying coverage during a grace period is disregarded for an individual that established an HDHP after the beginning of a year under the last-month rule (see Q 4:5).

Caution. Because the *annual* limitation for HSA contributions is generally determined on a monthly basis (see Qs 4:30, 4:48), the adoption of a grace period may have an effect upon an individual's eligibility to fully fund his or her HSA. For example, an individual who is participating in a health FSA with a grace period of 2½ months may only be permitted to contribute 9/12 of the full annual contribution amount because such individual may be considered an *ineligible individual* who has non-HDHP health coverage for the first three months of the year. [I.R.S. Notice 2005-86, 2005-49 I.R.B. 1075, amplifying I.R.S. Notice 2005-42, 2005-42 I.R.B. 1204 and Rev. Rul. 2004-45, 2004-22 I.R.B. 971; Treas. Press Release JS-3022 (Nov. 11, 2005)]

Example. Shaquille is a participant in a pretax Code Section 125 cafeteria plan. The plan year is the calendar year. In 2009, Shaquille signs up for an election of $1,500, but only uses $1,000 during the year. He makes no election for 2010 and has no other health coverage. The plan contains a grace period of 2½ months (under Notice 2005-42) in which Shaquille may submit additional claims for expenses that occurred during the 2½-month grace period. Shaquille is not an HSA-eligible individual during 2009 and the months that include the grace period (January through March 2010). The result would be different if the FSA were a limited-purpose health FSA (see above) for all participants during the grace period. Also, depending upon the deductible amount (say $2,500 under the FSA) and how it is applied with respect to 2009 and 2010, if Shaquille was a participant in a post-deductible health FSA, he might not be disqualified from being treated as an eligible individual during the 2½-month period in 2010 (and be permitted to make a contribution).

Note. Although the IRS generally takes the position that allowing cafeteria plan salary reduction contributions to carry over from one plan year to the next is a prohibited deferral of compensation [I.R.C. § 125(d)(2)(A); Prop. Treas. Reg. §§ 1.125-1, 1.125-2], this position was modified by Notice 2005-42, and the new proposed cafeteria plan regulations adopted this modified position. [I.R.S. Notice 2005-42, 2005-23 I.R.B. 1204; Prop. Treas. Reg. § 1.125-1(e)] Under the Notice and the regulations, an employer may adopt a grace period in a cafeteria plan so that the "forfeitures" of unused benefits that might otherwise occur at the end of the plan year under the so-called "use-it-or-lose-it rule" can be avoided.

Q 4:22   How can an employer provide a grace period in a cafeteria plan?

A cafeteria plan document may, at the employer's option, be amended to provide for a grace period immediately following the end of each plan year. For years beginning after 2008, this change must be made prior to the beginning of the applicable plan year. [Prop. Treas. Reg. § 1.125-1(c)] Expenses for qualified benefits incurred during the grace period may be paid or reimbursed from benefits or contributions remaining unused at the end of the immediately preceding plan year. To incorporate this rule, the cafeteria plan document must be amended prior to the end of its plan year (either calendar or fiscal) for which the change will be effective and must identify the benefits under the cafeteria plan to which the extended period will apply. As a practical matter, health and dependent care FSAs are the only benefits for which an extension of this type appears to make sense, and the extension could be limited to just one of these benefits. The new rule cannot be applied retroactively to earlier plan years.

Q 4:23   Is it permissible for a plan to impose a cap on the amount of benefits that are subject to the grace period?

The IRS has indicated informally that it would be permissible for a plan to impose a cap on the amount of benefits that are subject to the grace period as long as the cap is applied uniformly to all plan participants. Further, if an employer has more than one cafeteria plan, the extension can be limited to only one cafeteria plan.

Q 4:24   How long may the grace period last?

The grace period must not extend beyond the 15th day of the third calendar month after the end of the immediately preceding plan year to which it relates (i.e., "the 2½ month rule"). A plan is not required to adopt this rule, or to provide the full 2½ month extension (i.e., a lesser period is acceptable). If a cafeteria plan document is amended to include a grace period, a participant who has unused benefits or contributions relating to a particular qualified benefit from the immediately preceding plan year, and who incurs expenses for that same qualified benefit during the grace period, may be paid or reimbursed for those expenses from the unused benefits or contributions as if the expenses had been incurred in the immediately preceding plan year. The effect of the grace period is that the participant may have as long as 14 months and 15 days (the 12 months in the current cafeteria plan year plus the grace period) to use the benefits or contributions for a plan year before those amounts are "forfeited" under the "use-it-or-lose-it" rule. [I.R.S. Notice 2005-42, 2005-23 I.R.B. 1204]

Q 4:25 May unused benefits be cashed out or converted?

No. During the grace period, a cafeteria plan may not permit unused benefits or contributions to be cashed out or converted to any other taxable or nontaxable benefit. Unused benefits or contributions relating to a particular qualified benefit may be used only to pay or reimburse expenses incurred with respect to that particular qualified benefit. For example, unused amounts elected to pay or reimburse medical expenses in a health FSA may not be used to pay or reimburse dependent care or other expenses incurred during the grace period. To the extent any unused benefits or contributions from the immediately preceding plan year exceed the expenses for the qualified benefit incurred during the grace period, those remaining unused benefits or contributions may not be carried forward to any subsequent period (including any subsequent plan year) and are "forfeited" under the "use-it-or-lose-it" rule.

Practice Pointer. As under current practice, employers may continue to provide a "run-out" period after the end of the grace period, during which expenses for qualified benefits incurred during the cafeteria plan year and the grace period may be paid or reimbursed. [I.R.S. Notice 2005-42, 2005-23 I.R.B. 1204]

Q 4:26 How may an employer adopt a grace period?

An employer may adopt a grace period for the current cafeteria plan year (and subsequent cafeteria plan years) by amending the cafeteria plan document before the end of the current plan year. [I.R.S. Notice 2005-42, 2005-23 I.R.B. 1204]

Example 1. An employer with a cafeteria plan year ending on December 31, 2009, amended the plan document before the end of the plan year to permit a grace period that allows all participants to apply unused benefits or contributions remaining at the end of the plan year to qualified benefits incurred during the grace period immediately following that plan year. The grace period adopted by the employer ends on the fifteenth of the third calendar month after the end of the plan year (March 15, 2010, for the plan year ending December 31, 2009). Benny, an employee, timely elected salary reduction of $1,000 for a health FSA for the plan year ending December 31, 2009. As of December 31, 2009, Benny has $200 remaining unused in his health FSA. Benny timely elected salary reduction for a health FSA of $1,500 for the plan year ending December 31, 2010. During the grace period from January 1 through March 15, 2010, Benny incurs $300 of unreimbursed medical expenses. The unused $200 from the plan year ending December 31, 2009, is applied to pay or reimburse $200 of Benny's $300 of qualified medical expenses incurred during the grace period. Therefore, as of March 16, 2010, Benny has no unused benefits or contributions remaining for the plan year ending December 31, 2009. The remaining $100 of medical expenses incurred between January 1 and March 15, 2010 is paid or reimbursed from Benny's health FSA for the plan year ending December 31,

2010. As of March 16, 2010, Benny has $1,400 remaining in the health FSA for the plan year ending December 31, 2010.

Example 2. Same facts as in the preceding example, except that Benny incurs $150 of qualified medical expenses during the grace period (January 1 through March 15, 2010). As of March 16, 2010, Benny has $50 of unused benefits or contributions remaining for the plan year ending December 31, 2009. The unused $50 cannot be cashed out, converted to any other taxable or nontaxable benefit, or used in any other plan year (including the plan year ending December 31, 2010). The unused $50 is subject to the "use-it-or-lose-it" rule and is "forfeited." As of March 16, 2010, Benny has the entire $1,500 elected in the health FSA for the plan year ending December 31, 2007.

Note. In the above two examples, Benny may have been able to transfer the remaining balance in his health FSA account to an HSA in a one-time transfer provided the FSA plan is amended to allow such transfers. In such case, he would not be treated as an ineligible individual for the months of January through March because of the grace period (see Q 5:52).

Q 4:27   How long does a grace period remain in effect?

If adopted by an employer, the grace period remains in effect for the entire period even though the participant may terminate employment on or before the last day of the grace period. However, an employer may limit the availability of the grace period to certain cafeteria plan benefits and not others. For example, a cafeteria plan offering both a health FSA and a dependent care FSA may limit the grace period to the health FSA. In no event, may the grace period extend beyond the fifth day of the third calendar month after the end of the immediately preceding plan year to which it relates, but it may be adopted for a shorter period. [I.R.S. Notice 2005-42, 2005-23 I.R.B. 1204]

Interaction Between HSAs and Health FSAs

Q 4:28   May an individual who is otherwise eligible for an HSA be covered under certain types of health FSAs and remain eligible to contribute to an HSA?

Yes. An individual who is otherwise eligible for an HSA may be covered under certain types of health FSAs and remain eligible to contribute to an HSA. This result is the same even if the individual is covered by a health FSA sponsored by a spouse's employer.

As discussed in Q 4:20, one HSA-compatible arrangement is a limited-purpose health FSA, which pays or reimburses expenses only for preventive care and "permitted coverage" (e.g., dental care and vision care). Another HSA-compatible arrangement is a post-deductible health FSA, which pays or reimburses preventive care and other qualified medical expenses only if incurred after the minimum annual deductible for the HDHP ($1,150/$2,300 for 2009) is satisfied. Thus, an otherwise HSA-eligible individual will remain eligible if covered under a limited-purpose health FSA, a post-deductible FSA, or a combination of both. A combination arrangement incorporating both of these features is also permissible. [Rev. Rul. 2004-45, 2004-1 C.B. 971; Prop. Treas. Reg. § 1.125-5(m)]

Example. *General purpose health FSA during grace period.* Constellation amends its cafeteria plan document to provide a grace period, but takes no other action with respect to its general purpose health FSA. Because a health FSA that pays or reimburses all qualified medical expenses constitutes impermissible "other coverage" for HSA eligibility purposes, an individual who did not elect a general health FSA or other disqualifying coverage for 2009 is HSA-eligible on April 1, 2009, and may contribute 9/12ths of the 2009 HSA contribution limit. The result is the same even if a participant's health FSA has no unused contributions remaining at the end of the immediately preceding cafeteria plan year.

However, under the TRHCA, if the individual's balance in his or her health FSA is zero as of the end of the preceding year, the individual may nonetheless contribute to an HSA during the grace period (assuming the individual is otherwise an eligible individual in the months that included the grace period). [I.R.S. Notice 2007-22, 2007-10 I.R.B. 670 (Mar. 5, 2007)]

Q 4:29   Who has the responsibility for verifying that the FSA has a zero balance?

It appears that the employer and employee share responsibility for verifying that the FSA has a zero balance. As the plan sponsor, the employer has records of claims submitted and paid and should share this information with the employee. However, the employee has control over whether to submit claims against the amounts in the account, and has responsibility to submit claims so that they can be properly substantiated. If claims are submitted that are not substantiated, an employee may wind up having a balance in the FSA account without intending to. If the employer and employee think that the account has a zero balance as of the end of a particular calendar year but subsequently determine that it did not, the employee will be required to reduce his or her HSA contribution for the calendar year in which the 2½-month grace period was offered (i.e., will only be considered an eligible individual as of the first day of the month following the expiration of the 2½-month grace period). [I.R.S. Notice 2007-22, 2007-10 I.R.B. 670 (Mar. 5, 2007)]

Historical Note. For cafeteria plan years ending before June 5, 2006, an individual participating in a general purpose health FSA that provides coverage during a grace period will be eligible to contribute to an HSA during the grace period if the following requirements are met:

1. If not for the coverage under a general purpose health FSA, the individual would be an *eligible individual* during the grace period (i.e., in general, is covered under an HDHP and is not, while covered under an HDHP, covered under any impermissible other health coverage); and

2. Either the individual's (and the individual's spouse's) general purpose health FSA has no unused contributions or benefits remaining at the end of the immediately preceding cafeteria plan year; or

3. In the case of an individual who is not covered during the grace period under a general purpose health FSA maintained by the employer of the individual's spouse, the individual's employer amends its cafeteria plan document to provide that the grace period does not provide coverage to an individual who elects HDHP coverage (see Q 4:21).

[I.R.S. Notice 2005-86, 2005-49 I.R.B. 1075, amplifying I.R.S. Notice 2005-42, 2005-42 I.R.B. 1204 and Rev. Rul. 2004-45, 2004-22 I.R.B. 971; Treas. Press Release JS-3022 (Nov. 11, 2005)]

Contribution Limitations

Q 4:30   What is the maximum annual contribution that can be made to an HSA?

In general, the maximum annual contribution to an HSA is the sum of the limits determined separately for each month, based on status, eligibility, and health plan coverage as of the first day of the month (see Q 4:46). Although the maximum annual contribution limit is determined on a monthly basis, there is no actual monthly limit on the amount that may be contributed.

Last-month rule. In general, for tax years beginning after 2006, an individual who becomes covered under an HDHP in a month other than January, or is not an eligible individual during every month of their taxable year, may be permitted to make the full HSA contribution for the year (see Qs 4:7, 4:37). [I.R.C. § 223(b)(8)(A)(i)] However, an individual who makes contributions under the exception must remain an eligible individual during the testing period (see Qs 4:10, 4:39). Special rules apply in the case of married individuals (see Q 4:49), ineligible individuals (see Q 4:56), embedded deductibles (see Qs 4:53–4:55), and post-deductible HRA (see Q 4:41). See annual contribution limit chart at Q 4:48.

Self-only coverage (statutory limits). The statutory maximum annual contribution limit for eligible individuals with self-only coverage under an HDHP is $2,250 (base amount, as indexed) (see Q 4:32). [I.R.C. § 223(b); I.R.S. Notice 2004-2, Q&A 12, 2004-2 I.R.B. 269]

For 2009, the maximum annual HSA contribution for an eligible individual with self-only coverage is $3,000. [Rev. Proc. 2008-29, § 2, 2008-22 I.R.B. 1039 for 2009; Rev. Proc. 2007-36, § 4, 2007-22 I.R.B. 1335 for 2008]

Note. The annual contribution limit is reduced by any contribution to an Archer MSA (see Q 4:31). [I.R.C. § 223(b)(5)(B)(i)]

Historical Note. However, in taxable years ending before 2007, the maximum annual contribution could not exceed the annual deductible under the HDHP. The repeal of the annual plan deductible limit is effective for taxable years beginning after 2006. [I.R.C. § 223(b)(2), as amended by TRHCA § 303(a)(1). For the effective date, see TRHCA § 303(c)]

Family coverage (statutory limits). For eligible individuals with family coverage under an HDHP, the statutory maximum annual contribution is $5,150 (base amount, as indexed) (see Q 4:32).

- For 2009, the maximum annual HSA contribution for an eligible individual with family coverage is $5,950. For taxable years beginning before 2007, the annual contribution amount could not exceed the annual deductible under the HDHP. The repeal of the annual plan deductible limit is effective for taxable years beginning after 2006. [I.R.C. § 223(b)(2), as amended by TRHCA § 303(a)(2)] For the effective date, see TRHCA § 303(c). [Rev. Proc. 2008-29, § 2, 2008-22 I.R.B. 1039 for 2009; Rev. Proc. 2007-36, § 4, 2007-22 I.R.B. 1335 for 2008]

Catch-Up Contributions. In addition to the maximum annual contribution amount, catch-up contributions may be made by or on behalf of individuals age 55 or older who are also not enrolled in Medicare (see Qs 2:6, 2:14, 2:15, 4:44–4:49). [I.R.S. Notice 2004-2, Q&A 12, 2004-2 I.R.B. 269, as modified by I.R.S. Notice 2004-50, 2004-33 I.R.B. 196] In general and unless the last-month rule applies, an individual must be an eligible individual for 12 months to contribute the maximum annual catch-up contribution of $1,000 for 2009 (but see Qs 4:7, 4:38).

Note. The base amounts ($2,250/$5,150) are the amounts from which the initial 2004 and subsequent years HSA limits are derived (see Q 4:32). [Rev. Proc. 2008-29, § 2, 2008-22 I.R.B. 1039 for 2009]

Note. *Fiscal year taxpayer.* The maximum annual contribution limit for any taxable year is the annual limit in effect at the beginning of a taxable year. For example, the 2009 self-only maximum annual contribution limit of $3,000 would apply to a fiscal year taxpayer whose taxable year began on July 1, 2009. [I.R.C. § 223(g)(1)(B)]

Historical Note. For taxable years beginning before 2007, the annual contribution amount could not exceed the annual deductible under the HDHP. The repeal of the annual plan deductible limit is effective for taxable years beginning after 2006. [I.R.C. § 223(b)(2), as amended by TRHCA §§ 303(a)(2), 303(c)]

Q 4:31   Are the HSA annual contribution limitations coordinated with contributions made to an Archer MSA?

Yes. The HSA contribution limitations are reduced (but not below zero) by the aggregate amounts contributed by the HSA owner to an Archer MSA. [I.R.C. § 223(b)(4)(A)] The family coverage limit is also reduced further by any contribution to an Archer MSA. [I.R.C. § 223(b)(5)(B)(i)] When completing

Form 8889—*Health Savings Accounts (HSAs)*, amounts contributed to an Archer MSA are entered on Line 4 of Part 1 of that form.

Q 4:32 Are the maximum annual contribution amounts indexed for inflation?

Yes. The dollar amounts specified in Code Section 223(b) are indexed for inflation from 1997. [I.R.C. § 223(g)(1)] Thus, the statutory limit of $2,250 (for self-only coverage) was increased to $3,000, and the $4,500 (for family coverage) statutory limit was increased to $5,950 (for 2009). [I.R.C. § 223(g)(1)-(2); see Rev. Proc. 2008-29, § 2, 2008-22 I.R.B. 1039] The amounts are adjusted to the nearest multiple of $50. [I.R.C. § 223(g)(1), as amended by TRHCA § 304; I.R.C. § 223(g)(2)] The maximum annual HSA contribution amounts (since HSAs were permitted for taxable years beginning in 2004) are shown in Table 4-1. The catch-up contribution limits are adjusted through 2009 (see Q 4:44).

Table 4-1. HSA Maximum Annual Contribution Amounts (Excluding Catch-Up Contributions) for Self-Only and Family Coverage

Coverage	*2004*	*2005*	*2006*	*2007*	*2008*	*2009*
Self-only coverage ($2,250)	$2,600	$2,650	$2,700	$2,850	$2,900	$3,000
Family coverage ($4,500)	$5,150	$5,250	$5,450	$5,650	$5,800	$5,950

[See Rev. Proc. 2008-29, § 2, 2008-22 I.R.B. 1039 for 2009; Rev. Proc. 2007-36, § 4, 2007-22 I.R.B. 1335 for 2008; amending Rev. Proc. 2006-53, § 3.24, 2006-48 I.R.B. 996 for 2007; Rev. Proc. 2005-70, § 3.22, 2005-47 I.R.B. 979 for 2006; Rev. Proc. 2004-71, § 3.22, 2004-2 C.B. 970 for 2005]

For 2010, the maximum HSA annual contribution amounts are increased to $3,050 (for self-only coverage) and $6,150 (for family coverage). [Rev. Proc. 2009-29, § 2, 2009-22 I.R.B. 1050 for 2010] The same annual contribution limit applies whether the contributions are made by an employee, an employer, a self-employed person, or a family member.

Q 4:33 How are the statutory annual contribution limits indexed for inflation?

The $2,250 and $4,500 base amounts used to compute the monthly limitation on deductions for 2009 can be computed as follows (to the nearest multiple of $50):

a. $3,000 = $2,250 × $\dfrac{\text{(Average CPI April 2007 to March 2008)}}{\text{(Average CPI April 1996 to March 1997)}}$

b. $5,950 = $4,500 × $\dfrac{\text{(Average CPI April 2007 to March 2008)}}{\text{(Average CPI April 1996 to March 1997)}}$

Note. The Secretary of the Treasury must publish the adjusted amounts for a year no later that June 1 of the preceding year. [Rev. Proc. 2007-36, 2007-22 I.R.B. 1] Thus, the 2010 statutory maximum annual contribution limit and the dollar amounts for the HDHP requirements (minimum annual deductible and maximum out-of-pocket expenses), as adjusted for cost-of-living increases through March 2009, will be published by June 1, 2009. [I.R.C. § 223(g)(1), [I.R.C. § 223(g)(1), as amended by TRHCA § 304]

Historical Note. For tax years beginning before 2008, the HSA-related inflation adjustment period was the 12-month period ending on August 31 of the calendar year (rather than March 31).

Q 4:34   May an eligible individual have more than one HSA, and do contribution limits apply?

Yes. An eligible individual may establish more than one HSA and may contribute to more than one HSA. The same rules governing HSAs apply (e.g., maximum contribution limit), regardless of the number of HSAs established by an eligible individual. [I.R.S. Notice 2004-50, Q&A 64, 2004-33 I.R.B. 196]

Example. Yuri, an eligible individual, has a maximum annual contribution limit of $3,000 for 2009. Yuri's employer contributes $1,000 to an HSA on behalf of Yuri. Yuri opens a second HSA and contributes $2,000. If additional contributions are made for 2009 to either of the HSAs, those additional contributions will be excess contributions to Yuri's HSAs. An exception is made for a direct transfer from a health FSA or an HRA, which are not subject to the statutory annual contribution limit.

Q 4:35   How are contributions treated if the eligible individual has more than one HSA?

If an individual has more than one HSA, the aggregate annual contributions to all the HSAs are subject to the limit. [I.R.S. Notice 2004-2, Q&A 12, 2004-2 I.R.B. 269]

Q 4:36   How do the maximum annual HSA contribution limits apply to an eligible individual with family HDHP coverage for the entire year if the family HDHP covers spouses or dependent children who also have coverage by a non-HDHP, Medicare, or Medicaid?

An eligible individual with family HDHP coverage for the entire year may contribute the statutory maximum for family coverage ($5,950 for 2009) even if the family HDHP covers spouses or dependent children who also have coverage by a non-HDHP, Medicare, or Medicaid (see Qs 4:30, 4:37, 4:47–4:52). Other coverage of dependent children or spouses does not affect the individual's contribution limit, except that if the spouse is not an otherwise eligible individual, no part of the HSA contribution can be allocated to the spouse (see Q 4:56). [I.R.S. Notice 2008-59, Q&A 16, 2008-29 I.R.B. 123]

Q 4:37   How is the contribution limit computed for an individual who begins coverage under an HDHP midyear and continues to be covered under the HDHP for the rest of the year?

The HSA maximum annual contribution limit is generally based upon the number of months in the year that an individual is covered by a qualifying HDHP. [I.R.S. Notice 2004-2, Q&A 13, 2004-2 I.R.B. 269] An exception is provided for individuals who became eligible after the first month of a taxable year and remain eligible through December 1 of that year (see Q 4:38).

Example. Carmen, an eligible individual, begins HDHP self-only coverage on March 1, 2009 with an annual deductible of $2,000. She remains eligible until May 31. The 2009 HDHP minimum annual deductible limit is $3,000. The monthly contribution limit is $250 ($3,000 divided by 12). The annual contribution limit is $750 (3 × $250).

Note. Although a "monthly limit" is used in calculating the annual HSA contribution, as noted in Qs 4:5 and 4:11, all of an HSA contribution may be contributed on the first day of eligibility, or otherwise as the HSA owner decides, up the due date of the federal income tax return (generally April 15 of the following year). Thus, there is no actual "monthly limit," only a restriction to the annual maximum contribution amount.

Q 4:38   What is the exception for an individual who is an eligible individual on the first day of the last month of his or her taxable year (generally December 1)?

An exception to the monthly limit rules (see Q 4:31) is provided for an individual who is an eligible individual (see Q 2:6) on the first day of the last month of his or her taxable year (generally December 1). In addition to being considered an eligible individual for the entire year (12 months), the individual is treated as having the same coverage for the entire year as the individual had on the first day of the last month of the taxable year. [I.R.C. § 223(b)(8)(A)] The exception is called the "last-month rule." See Qs 4:5 and 4:7. An eligible individual does not include an individual who is enrolled in Medicare or has disqualifying health care coverage at *any time* during that last month (see Qs 2:6, 2:15).

In general, for tax years beginning after 2006, an individual who becomes covered under an HDHP in a month other than January, or is not an eligible individual during every month of their taxable year may be permitted to make the full HSA contribution for the year. An individual who is an eligible individual on the first day of the last month of a taxable year is treated as having been an eligible individual during every month during the taxable year for purposes of computing the amount that may be contributed to the HSA for the year. [I.R.C.

§ 223(b)(8)(A)] As a result, such individual is allowed to make contributions, including catch-up contributions (see Qs 4:44, 4:48) for months before the individual was enrolled in an HDHP. Also see examples in Q 4:6.

The following examples illustrate the application of the rules allowing the full contribution to be made for individual's become eligible after the beginning on the taxable year. It is assumed in the examples that the taxable year of all individuals is the calendar year, and that, for purposes of the 10 percent tax applied, when there is a failure to satisfy, the testing period rules under Code Section 223(b)(8)(B)(ii), no individuals are disabled unless otherwise stated (see Q 4:8). It should be noted that the exceptions from the 10 percent tax under Code Section 223(f)(4) (see Q 6:74), except for death or disability, do not apply to the 10 percent tax under Code Section 223(b)(8)(B)(ii).

Example 1. Gretta, age 25, is an eligible individual with self-only HDHP coverage that began on January 1, 2009. Her coverage was terminated on November 15. The maximum HDHP self-only contribution limit is $3,000 for 2009. Gretta's deductible contribution limit is $2,750 ($3,000 × 11 ÷ 12) for 2009.

Example 2. Same facts as in Example 1, except Gretta was married in November and commenced family HDHP coverage effective December 1, 2009. The maximum HDHP family contribution limit is $5,950 for 2009. An exception permits Gretta and her spouse to contribute the full amount ($5,950) for 2009 (see Q 4:53).

Example 3. Magan, age 40 and a calendar year taxpayer, is an eligible individual with self-only coverage under an HDHP for the months of January and February. As of December 1, she marries Ronan, also age 40, and begins family HDHP coverage. Under the *last-month rule* Magan and Ronan are treated as being eligible for the entire year with family coverage; therefore the maximum permitted contribution limit does not have to be prorated. Magan and Ronan may contribute the maximum family coverage contribution amount ($5,950 for 2009).

Example 4. Marcus, age 35, was an eligible individual with family HDHP for the first 11 months of his taxable year (January through November). Marcus gets divorced on November 25. On December 1, his HDHP coverage changes to self-only coverage. Under the *last-month rule,* Marcus is treated as having self-only coverage for the entire year. However, Marcus may contribute the greater of (a) the maximum self-only coverage contribution amount ($3,000 for 2009) under the *last-month rule* or, (b) his maximum contribution limit based on the type of HDHP coverage he had on the first day of each month.

Example 5. Vanessa, age 30, has HDHP coverage that began on January 1, 2009. Her HDHP coverage was terminated on November 15. For 2009, Vanessa also had coverage under another health plan that is not an HDHP and that provides coverage for the same benefits provided under the HDHP. That policy was terminated on May 15. The maximum HDHP self-only contribution limit is $3,000 for 2009. Vanessa's monthly contribution limit is based on six months. For the first 5 months, Vanessa was ineligible because she had disqualifying other coverage (see Q 2:6). For the next six months (June through November), Vanessa's annual contribution limit is $1,500 ($3,000 × 6 ÷ 12). No amount can be attributable to the last month because she had no HDHP coverage.

Example 6. Albert, age 53, enrolls in family HDHP coverage on December 1, 2009 and he is otherwise an eligible individual on that date. Albert is not an eligible individual in any other month in 2009.

Albert is an eligible individual with family HDHP coverage on December 1, 2009. His full contribution limit under Code Section 223(b)(8) for 2009 is $5,950. The sum of the monthly contribution limits is $495.83 (1/12 × $5,950). Albert's annual contribution limit for 2009 is $5,950, the greater of $5,950 or $495.83.

Example 7. Same facts as in Example 6, except that Albert contributes $5,950 to his HSA on December 1, 2009 and ceases to be an eligible individual in June 2010.

The testing period for 2009 HSA contributions ends on December 31, 2010. In 2010, Albert ceases to be an eligible individual during the testing period. In 2010, Albert must include in gross income $5,454.17, the amount contributed to the HSA for 2009 less the sum of the monthly contribution limits ($5,950 – $495.83). In addition, the 10 percent additional tax ($545.42) in Code Section 223(b)(8)(B)(i) applies to the amount included in gross income.

Example 8. Betty, age 39, enrolls in self-only HDHP coverage on January 1, 2009 and is an eligible individual on that date. Betty's coverage changes to family HDHP coverage on November 1, 2009 and Betty retains family HDHP coverage through December 31, 2009. Betty is an eligible individual from January 1, 2009 through December 31, 2009 and remains an eligible individual through December 31, 2010.

Betty is an eligible individual with family HDHP coverage on December 1, 2009. Betty's full contribution limit under Code Section 223(b)(8) for 2009 is $5,950. The sum Betty's monthly contribution limits is $3,491.66 ((2/12 × $5,950) + (10/12 × $3,000)). Betty's annual contribution limit for 2009 is $5,950, the greater of $5,950 or $3,491.66.

Example 9. In 2008, Casey, age 47, is covered by a general purpose health FSA with a grace period ending March 15, 2009. Casey enrolls in family HDHP coverage on January 1, 2009. Casey becomes an eligible individual on April 1, 2009 and remains an eligible individual through December 31, 2010. On April 2, 2009, Casey contributes $5,950 to his HSA for 2009.

Casey is an eligible individual with family HDHP coverage on December 1, 2009. His full contribution limit under Code Section 223(b)(8) for 2009 is $5,950. The sum of Casey's monthly contribution limits is $4,462.50 (9/12 × $5,950). Casey's annual contribution limit for 2009 is $5,950, the greater of $5,950 or $4,462.50. The testing period for 2009 ends on December 31, 2010. Because he is an eligible individual during the testing period, no amount of the $5,950 contribution is included in Casey's gross income and he is not subject to the 10 percent additional tax under Code Section 223(b)(8)(B)(i)(II).

Example 10. Darleen, age 57, enrolls in family HDHP coverage on December 1, 2009 and is an eligible individual on that date. She was not an eligible individual in any other month in 2009. Darleen contributes $6,615 to her HSA on December 1, 2009 and remains an eligible individual through December 31, 2010.

Darleen is an eligible individual with family HDHP coverage on December 1, 2009 and remains an eligible individual through December 31, 2010. Her full contribution limit under Code Section 223(b)(8) for 2009 is $6,950 ($5,950 family coverage contribution + $1,000 catch-up contribution). The sum of the monthly contribution limits is $579.16 ((1/12 × $5,950) + (1/12 × $1,000)). Darleen's annual contribution limit for 2009 is $6,950, the greater of $6,615 or $579.16.

Example 11. Eugene, age 35, has self-only HDHP coverage and is an eligible individual for the months of May, June, and July 2009.

The full contribution limit under Code Section 223(b)(8) does not apply to Eugene for 2009 because he is not an eligible individual on December 1, 2009. Eugene's contribution limit for 2009 is $750 (3/12 × $3,000).

Example 12. Frank, age 46, enrolls in family HDHP coverage on January 1, 2009 and is an eligible individual on that date. Frank contributes $5,950 to an HSA on January 1, 2009. Frank ceases to be covered by an HDHP on August 1, 2009. On December 15, 2009, Frank withdraws from the HSA $2,479.17 ($5,950 – 3,470.83), plus $45 earnings attributable to the $2,479.17.

Frank ceases to be an eligible individual on August 1, 2009. The full contribution limit does not apply to Frank for 2009 because Frank is not an eligible individual on December 1, 2009, and the testing period in Code Section 223(b)(8)(B)(i) does not apply to Frank. His HSA contribution limit for 2009 is $3,470.83 (7/12 × $5,950). The $2,479.17 is an excess contribution for purposes of Code Section 4973, but is not subject to the 6 percent excise tax under that section because Frank withdrew the excess contribution and earnings attributable to the excess contribution by the due date, with extensions, for filing her 2009 federal income tax return. Frank reports the $45 withdrawn earnings as gross income on his 2009 federal income tax return. The gross income inclusion and 10 percent tax in Code Section 223(f)(3) for distributions not used for qualified medical expenses do not apply because he withdrew an excess contribution.

Example 13. Georgina, age 38, enrolls in family HDHP coverage on January 1, 2009 and is an eligible individual on that date. Georgina's coverage changes to self-only HDHP coverage on September 1, 2009 and she retains that coverage through December 31, 2009. Georgina is an eligible individual for all 12 months in 2009. Georgina contributes $4,966.66

((8/12 × \$5,950) + (4/12 × \$3,000)) to an HSA for 2009. Georgina ceases to be an eligible individual on January 1, 2010.

Georgina is an eligible individual with self-only HDHP coverage on December 1, 2009. Georgina's full contribution limit under Code Section 223(b)(8) for 2009 is \$3,000. Georgina's sum of the monthly contribution limit is \$4,966.66 ((8/12 × \$5,950) + (4/12 × \$3,000)). Georgina's annual contribution limit is \$4,966.66, the greater of \$3,000 or \$4,966.66. The testing period for 2009 HSA contributions ends on December 31, 2010. Georgina ceases to be an eligible individual during the testing period. Because Georgina's contribution of \$4,966.66 is not greater than the sum of the monthly contribution limits, there is no inclusion or additional tax when Georgina ceases to be an eligible individual during the testing period.

Example 14. Hector, age 25, enrolls in self-only HDHP coverage on June 1, 2009 and is an eligible individual on that date. Hector is not an eligible individual prior to June 1, 2009. He contributes \$3,000 to an HSA on July 1, 2009. Hector is an eligible individual on December 1, 2009, and continues to be an eligible individual until February 1, 2010. On February 2, 2010, Hector withdraws \$1,250 from his HSA. The \$1,250 distribution is not used for Hector's qualified medical expenses (see Q 6:28).

Hector is an eligible individual with self-only HDHP coverage on December 1, 2009. Hector's full contribution limit under Code Section 223(b)(8) for 2009 is \$3,000. Hector's sum of the monthly contribution limits is \$1,750 (7/12 × \$3,000). Hector's annual contribution limit is \$3,000, the greater of \$3,000 or \$1,750. The testing period for 2009 HSA contributions ends on December 31, 2010. In 2010, Hector ceases to be an eligible individual during the testing period. In 2010, Hector must include in gross income \$1,250, the amount contributed to the HSA minus the sum of the monthly contribution limits (\$3,000 – \$1,750). In addition, the 10 percent additional tax (\$125) in Code Section 223(b)(8)(B)(i)(II) applies to the amount.

The \$1,250 withdrawn from the HSA is not used for qualified medical expenses and is not a withdrawal of an excess contribution. Therefore, under Code Section 223(f)(2), \$1,250 is also included in Hector's gross income and is also subject to the 10 percent additional tax under Code Section 223(f)(4). As a result, Hector includes \$2,500 (\$1,250 with respect to I.R.C. § 223(f)(4) and \$1,250 with respect to I.R.C. § 223(b)(8)) in gross income in 2010 and an additional tax of \$250 (\$125 with respect to Code Section 223(f)(4) and \$125 with respect to Code Section 223(b)(8)).

Example 15. Joshua, age 27, is eligible for medical benefits through the Department of Veterans Affairs (VA). As a result of medical care (other than disregarded coverage or preventive care) that Joshua received from the VA in January 2009, he is not an eligible individual in January, February, March, or April 2009 (see Q 2:16). Joshua has self-only HDHP coverage and is otherwise an eligible individual from May 1, 2009 through December 31, 2010.

Joshua is an eligible individual with self-only HDHP coverage on December 1, 2009. Joshua's full contribution limit under Code Section

223(b)(8) for 2009 is $3,000. Joshua's sum of the monthly contribution limits is $2,000 (8/12 × $3,000). Joshua's annual contribution limit for 2009 is $3,000, the greater of $3,000 or $2,000.

Example 16. Same facts as in Example 15, except that Joshua also receives medical care (other than disregarded coverage or preventive care) from the VA in October 2009. Joshua is an eligible individual with self-only HDHP coverage in May through September 2009 (see Q 2:16).

The full contribution limit does not apply to Joshua for 2009 because he is not an eligible individual on December 1, 2009. Joshua's 2009 contribution limit is determined under the sum of the monthly contribution limits and is $1,250 (5/12 × $3,000).

Example 17. Karla, age 64, enrolls in family HDHP coverage on April 1, 2009 and is an eligible individual from April 1, 2009 through December 31, 2009. Karla was not an eligible individual prior to April 1, 2009. Karla contributes $6,950 to her HSA for 2009 on April 1, 2009. Karla attains age 65 and enrolls in Medicare on March 24, 2010 and ceases to be an eligible individual.

Karla is an eligible individual with family HDHP coverage on December 1, 2009. Karla's full contribution limit under Code Section 223(b)(8) for 2009 is $6,950 ($5,950 family coverage contribution + $1,000 catch-up contribution). Karla's sum of the monthly contribution limits is $5,212.50 ((9/12 × $5,950) + (9/12 × $1,000)). Karla's annual contribution limit for 2009 is $6,950, the greater of $6,950 or $5,212.50. The testing period for 2009 HSA contributions ends on December 31, 2010. In 2010, Karla ceases to be an eligible individual during the testing period. In 2010, Karla must include $1,737.50, the amount contributed to the HSA minus the sum of the monthly contribution limits ($6,950 − $5,212.50) in gross income. In addition, the 10 percent additional tax ($173.75) in Code Section 223(b)(8)(B)(i) applies to the amount.

Example 18. Same facts as in Example 17, except that *before* enrolling in Medicare, Karla ceases to be an eligible individual during the testing period as a result of becoming disabled. Because Karla ceases to be an eligible individual due to becoming disabled, no amount is required to be included in income in 2010 or is subject to the additional tax under Code Section 223(b)(8).

Example 19. Individuals Larry and Maryanne, both age 40, are a married couple. Larry and Maryanne enroll in family HDHP coverage on December 1, 2009 and are otherwise eligible individuals on that date. Larry and Maryanne are not eligible individuals in any other month in 2009. Larry and Maryanne divide the contribution limit equally between them. On or after December 1, 2009, Larry contributes $3,000 to his HSA and Maryanne contributes $3,000 to her HSA. On June 1, 2010, Maryanne switches to self-only HDHP coverage and remains an eligible individual through December 31, 2010. Larry ceases to be an eligible individual in June 2010.

Larry and Maryanne are eligible individuals with family HDHP coverage on December 1, 2009. Larry and Maryanne's combined full contribution limit for 2009 is $5,950. Larry and Maryanne's combined sum of the monthly contribution limits is $495.84 (1/12 × $5,950), or $247.92 each ((1/12 × $5,950) ÷ 2). Larry and Maryanne's combined annual contribution limit under Code Section 223(b)(8) is $5,950, the greater of $5,950 or $495.84. The testing period for 2009 HSA contributions ends on December 31, 2010. During the testing period for 2009, Maryanne remains an eligible individual but Larry ceases to be an eligible individual. Because Maryanne is an eligible individual during the testing period, no amount of Maryanne's $3,000 contribution is included in Maryanne's gross income and Maryanne is not subject to the 10 percent additional tax. In 2009, Larry must include $2,752.08 in gross income, the amount contributed to the HSA minus the sum of the monthly contribution limits ($3,000 – $247.92). In addition, the 10 percent additional tax ($275.21) in Code Section 223(b)(8)(B)(i)(II) applies to that amount.

Example 20. Same facts as in Example 19, except Maryanne contributes $5,950 to Maryanne's HSA and Larry contributes $0 to Larry's HSA (see Q 4:57). No amount is taxable to either Larry or Maryanne.

[I.R.S. Notice 2008-52, 2008-25 I.R.B. 1166, modifying I.R.S. Notice 2004-2, 2004-2 I.R.B. 269 and Notice 2004-50, 2004-33 I.R.B. 196] (See appendix B.)

Q 4:39   When is the annual contribution made under the last-month rule exception subject to the additional 10 percent tax under Code Section 223(b)(8)(B)?

If an individual makes contributions under the exception and does not remain an eligible individual during the *testing period*, the amount of the contributions attributable to months preceding the month in which the individual was an eligible individual, which could not have been made but for the provision, is includible in gross income. A 10 percent additional tax also applies to the amount includible. An exception applies if the employee ceases to be an eligible individual by reason of death or disability. [I.R.C. § 223(b)(8)(A)–(B)] The additional tax is reported in Part III on Form 8889—*Health Savings Accounts (HSAs)*.

The *testing period* is the period beginning with the last month of the taxable year and ending on the last day of the 12th month following such month. The amount is includible for the taxable year of the first day during the testing period that the individual is not an eligible individual. [I.R.C. § 223(b)(8)(B)]

Example 1. Jose enrolls in an HDHP as of December 1, 2009, and is otherwise an eligible individual in that month. Jose was not an eligible individual in any other month in 2009. Jose may make HSA contributions as if he had been enrolled in the HDHP for all of 2009. If Jose ceases to be an eligible individual (e.g., if he ceases to be covered under the HDHP) in June 2010, an amount equal to the HSA contribution attributable to treating Jose as an eligible individual for January through November 2009 is included in income in 2010. In addition, a 10 percent additional tax applies to the amount includible.

Example 2. Same facts as in Example 1, except Jose turned age 65 and enrolled in Medicare on March 15, 2010. Jose ceases to be an eligible individual (i.e., when he enrolled in Medicare) during the testing period. Therefore, an amount equal to the HSA contribution attributable to treating Jose as an eligible individual from January through November 2009 is included in income in 2010. In addition, a 10 percent additional tax applies to the amount includible.

No distribution of included income. The amount that is included in the individual's gross income is computed by subtracting the sum of the monthly contribution limits that the individual would otherwise have been entitled from the amount actually contributed. It is not necessary to distribute this amount from the HSA, and there may be additional adverse tax consequences from such a distribution (see Q 6:9). Furthermore, withdrawing this amount from the HSA will not prevent the inclusion of the amount in income or the additional 10 percent tax. However, earnings on the amount are not included in gross income or subject to the 10 percent additional tax, so long as the earnings remain in the HSA or are used for qualified medical expenses. [I.R.S. Notice 2008-52, 2008-25 I.R.B. 1166, modifying I.R.S. Notice 2004-2, 2004-2 I.R.B. 269 and Notice 2004-50, 2004-33 I.R.B. 196]

Practice Pointer. Unlike the additional 10 percent tax for a distribution not used for qualified medical expenses (see Q 6:72) under Code Section 223(f)(4)(A), the additional 10 percent tax for failing to remain an eligible individual during the testing period (see Q 4:10) under Code Section 223(b)(8)(B)(ii) applies regardless of the HSA owner's age (i.e., even after age 65).

Q 4:40   In what health plan is the individual treated as having been enrolled in under the exception allowing the full contribution to be made for a year?

For the months preceding the last month of the taxable year that the individual is treated as an eligible individual (solely by reason of this exception), the individual is treated as having been enrolled in the same high deductible health plan in which the individual was enrolled on December 1 of the year of a mid-year enrollment. [I.R.C. § 223(b)(8)(A)(ii)]

Q 4:41   What is the contribution limit for an eligible individual covered by an HDHP and also by a post-deductible HRA or post-deductible health FSA?

A post-deductible HRA that does not pay or reimburse any medical expense incurred before the minimum annual deductible is satisfied is described in Revenue Ruling 2004-45. The ruling states that the HRA deductible need not be the same as the HDHP deductible, but in no event may the HDHP or other coverage provide benefits before the HDHP minimum annual deductible is satisfied ($1,150 for self-only coverage, or $2,300 for family coverage for 2009).

An individual with HDHP coverage who is covered by a post-deductible HRA or post-deductible health FSA that reimburses the medical expenses (see Qs 6:27–6:58) of any covered individual before the minimum HDHP deductible ($1,150 for self-only coverage and $2,300 for family coverage for 2009) has been satisfied is not an eligible individual. [I.R.S. Notice 2008-59, Q&As 7 and 8, 2008-29 I.R.B. 123]

> **Example.** Maury has family HDHP coverage. His spouse and children (but not Maury) are also covered by non-HDHP family coverage provided by his spouse's employer. In addition, Maury, his spouse, and children are also covered by a post-deductible health FSA. The health FSA pays for unreimbursed medical expenses of the spouse and child without regard to the satisfaction of the deductible of the family HDHP. Because the health FSA covering Maury reimburses medical expenses before the minimum family HDHP deductible is satisfied, he is not an eligible individual. If the health FSA did not cover Maury, he would be an eligible individual.

Catch-Up Contributions

Q 4:42   Are catch-up contributions permitted?

Yes. For individuals (and their spouses covered under an HDHP) who have attained age 55 and who are also not enrolled in Medicare, the HSA maximum contribution limit is increased by $1,000 in calendar year 2008. [I.R.S. Notice 2004-2, Q&A 14, 2004-2 I.R.B. 269, as modified by I.R.S. Notice 2004-50, 2004-33 I.R.B. 196] The 2009 catch-up limit is $1,000 (see Q 4:44).

After an individual has enrolled in Medicare (generally, at age 65, the Medicare eligibility age), contributions, including catch-up contributions, are no longer permitted to be made to an HSA (see Q 4:46).

> **Note.** *Fiscal year taxpayer.* The catch-up limit for any taxable year is the annual limit in effect at the beginning of a taxable year. For example, the 2009 catch-up limit of $1,000 would apply to a fiscal-year taxpayer whose taxable year began on July 1, 2009. [I.R.C. § 223(b)(3)(B)]

> **Practice Pointer.** If both spouses are age 55 or older and they both want to make "catch-up" contributions, they must each establish an HSA. Catch-up contributions may not be allocated between spouses. [I.R.C. §§ 223(b)(5)(B), 223(b)(5)(B)(ii); I.R.S. Notice 2008-59, Q&A 22, 2008-29 I.R.B. 123]

An exception is provided for an individual who is an eligible individual with HDHP coverage on the first day of the last month of the individual's taxable year. An individual who is an eligible individual during the last month of a taxable year is treated as having been an eligible individual during every month during the taxable year for purposes of computing the amount that may be contributed to the HSA for the year. See Qs 4:37–4:38.

Q 4:43   May an otherwise HSA-eligible individual who is age 65 or older and thus eligible for Medicare, but is not enrolled in Medicare Part A or Part B, make the additional catch-up contributions for individuals age 55 or older?

Yes. An individual who is 65 or older but who is not enrolled in Medicare (Part A or Part B) may contribute to an HSA and make additional catch-up contributions if age 55 or older. [I.R.S. Notice 2004-50, Q&As 2 and 3, 2004-33 I.R.B. 196; I.R.S. Notice 2004-2, Q&A 14, 2004-2 I.R.B. 269, as corrected by I.R.S. Ann. 2004-67, 2004-36 I.R.B. 459] (See Q 2:26 regarding the payment of Medicare premiums with funds in an HSA.)

> **Note.** An individual who is enrolled in Medicare Part A (hospital insurance) or Medicare Part B (medical insurance) coverage is eligible to enroll in a Medicare Part D prescription drug plan. An individual who is eligible for but not enrolled in Medicare Part D (or any other Medicare benefit) may make additional catch-up contributions to an HSA if otherwise eligible to do so (see Q 2:14). [Rev. Proc. 2008-59, Q&A 5 and 6, 2008-29 I.R.B. 123]

> **Example.** Lilac is an otherwise HSA-eligible individual who is over age 65 and thus eligible for Medicare, but she is not enrolled in Medicare Part A or Part B. Lilac may make the additional catch-up contributions for individuals age 55 or older.

Q 4:44   What are the catch-up contribution limits?

The initial catch-up contribution limit for 2004 ($500) increases in $100 increments annually until it reaches $1,000 in calendar year 2009 and thereafter (see Table 4-2). For 2009, the HSA catch-up limit is $1,000. [I.R.C. § 223(b)(3)(B); I.R.S. Notice 2004-50, Q&A 14, 2004-33 I.R.B. 196]

Table 4-2. Catch-Up Limits for Years 2004 through 2009

For Taxable Years Beginning In	*Catch-Up Limit*
2004	$500
2005	$600
2006	$700
2007	$800
2008	$900
2009 and thereafter (no indexing)	$1,000

Example 1. Mable, an eligible individual for the full year, is single, age 55, and not enrolled in Medicare in 2009. Her HSA maximum annual contribution limit is increased by $1,000. For example, if Mable has self-only coverage, she can contribute up to the amount of her annual contribution limit of $3,000 plus $1,000 for 2009.

Example 2. Same facts as in the preceding example, except that Mable is married to an older individual who is also not enrolled in Medicare. They have family coverage for the entire year. Because both spouses meet the age requirement, the total contribution under family coverage cannot be more than $7,950 ($5,950 + $1,000 + $1,000) for 2009. They each must establish an HSA to make catch-up contributions.

Example 3. For 2009, Mr. Biaggi and his wife both have family coverage under separate HDHPs. Mr. Biaggi is 58 years old, and Mrs. Biaggi is 53. Mr. Biaggi has an HDHP deductible of $3,000, and Mrs. Biaggi has an HDHP deductible of $2,500. Under the TRHCA, Mr. and Mrs. Biaggi both are treated as having an annual HSA contribution limit of $5,950 which they must divide equally or in another manner they agree upon. Each is also permitted to make a catch-up contribution of $1,000 to his or her own HSA.

Historical Note. Prior to TRHCA, for taxable years beginning before 2008, Mr. and Mrs. Biaggi would be treated as being covered under an HDHP with a $2,500 deductible and the contribution amount would be limited to the $2,500 annual deductible under the HDHP. The annual deductible limit has since been repealed (see Q 4:22).

Example 4. Samantha has an HDHP with self-only coverage from January 1, 2009 through June 30, 2009. She attains age 65 and becomes eligible for and enrolls in Medicare in July 2009. Samantha is no longer eligible to make HSA contributions (including catch-up contributions) after June 2009. Samantha's monthly contribution limit can be computed as follows:

($3,000 (annual contribution limit) ÷ 12) + ($1,000 (catch-up contribution for 2009) ÷ 12) = $333.33 (rounded).

Samantha may make contributions for January through June totaling $2,000 (6 × $333.333), but may not make any contributions for July through December 2009. The last-month rule does not apply because Samantha was not an eligible individual on December 1 because she was enrolled in Medicare during the month of December.

Q 4:45   Are the maximum catch-up amounts indexed for inflation?

No. The catch-up limit amount for a calendar year is determined by statute (see Q 4:44). [I.R.C. § 223(b)(3)(B)] There is no indexing of the catch-up limit after that limit reaches the $1,000 statutory limit amount in 2009.

Computing Annual Contributions

Q 4:46 How are catch-up contributions computed?

Unless the last-month rule applies (see Q 4:8), the catch-up contribution limit is computed on a monthly basis in the same manner as the annual contribution limit, taking into account the number of months an individual was an eligible individual covered by an HDHP (see Qs 4:30, 4:44). [I.R.S. Notice 2004-2, Q&A 14, 2004-2 I.R.B. 269]

Q 4:47 How is the annual contribution limit determined for an individual who is an eligible individual, or who is considered an eligible individual under the last-month rule, for the entire year?

If an individual was an eligible individual on the first day of every month during 2009 or the individual is considered an eligible individual for the entire year under the last-month rule (see Qs 4:37–4:38), and he or she did not change the type of coverage during 2009, the HSA annual maximum contribution limit is $3,000 (for self-only coverage) and $5,950 (for family coverage), plus catch-up contributions of $1,000 if age 55 at the end of 2009.

However, if the type of coverage had changed during the year (e.g., from family coverage to self-only coverage, or to no coverage for a month), the maximum contribution limit for an individual that is or was considered an eligible individual for the entire year is the *greater* of:

1. $3,000 (for self-only coverage) or $5,950 (for family coverage), plus catch-up contributions of $1,000 if age 55 at the end of 2009, or
2. The maximum amount that can be contributed based on the type of coverage on the first day of *each* month (the sum of the monthly limits) (see Q 4:48 and examples).

Example 1. Joseph became an eligible individual with self-only coverage on December 1, 2009. He may contribute the greater of $3,000 (the self-only contribution limit) or $250 (the maximum self-only contribution limit pro-rated for the month he was eligible ($3,000 × 1 ÷ 12)).

Historical Note. In taxable years beginning before 2007, the contribution amount could not exceed the annual deductible amount under the HDHP. That limit, the annual deductible limit, has since been repealed (see example below). The following three rules are used for determining the amount of the annual deductible under the HDHP in taxable years beginning before 2007:

1. Use the HSA maximum annual contribution limit for family coverage (e.g., $5,450 for 2006) if the individual and his or her spouse had more than one HDHP and one of the plans provided family coverage. Disregard any plans with self-only coverage.
2. If the individual and his or her spouse had more than one HDHP with family coverage, use the plan with the lowest annual deductible.

3. If the individual had family coverage with both an umbrella deductible and an embedded deductible for each individual covered by the plan, the annual contribution (and annual deduction for individuals making pretax contributions) is the smaller of $5,450 (for 2006) or the:

   a. Umbrella deductible, or

   b. Embedded individual deductible multiplied by the number of family members covered by the plan.

Example 2. In 2009, David and Helen both had HDHP-family coverage and were under age 55 at the end of 2009. The HDHP pays benefits for any family member whose covered expenses exceed $2,300 (the embedded individual deductible) and pays benefits for all family members after the covered expenses exceed $5,000 (the umbrella deductible). The maximum annual contribution is $5,950 for 2009 and David and Helen can divide this amount equally or in any other way they choose. If the embedded individual deductible was less than $2,300 (the minimum annual HDHP deductible limit for 2009), the plan would not qualify as an HDHP and neither David nor Helen would be eligible individuals.

Example 3. Same facts as in Example 2, except David and Helen's taxable year began on January 1, 2006. The annual contribution limit is $4,600 (the smaller of the $5,000 umbrella deductible or the $4,600 ($2,300 × 2) embedded deductibles). David and Helen's HSA maximum contribution is $4,600 (the smaller of $4,600 or the 2006 maximum contribution limit of $5,450).

Q 4:48   **How can the annual contribution limit be computed if the individual did not have the same coverage on the first day of every month during 2009 or was not an eligible individual on December 1, 2009?**

If the individual did not have the same coverage on the first day of every month during 2009, or was not an eligible individual with HDHP coverage on the first day of the last month of the taxable year (generally December 1), the annual contribution limit can be computed by completing the chart in Table 4-3 for each month of 2009. A copy of the chart should be kept with the taxpayer's records. Enter the result on the worksheet next to the corresponding month. The amount entered is used to determine allowable HSA contributions, excess contributions, and deductions for contributions on Form 8889—*Health Savings Accounts (HSAs)*.

Caution. For taxable years beginning after 2006, an individual who has HDHP coverage and no other non-HDHP coverage on December 1 may make a full year HSA contribution (but special testing period requirements apply). See Qs 4:37–4:38.

Practice Pointer. If eligibility and coverage did not change from one month to the next, enter the same number entered for the previous month.

Table 4-3. Annual Contribution Limit Computation

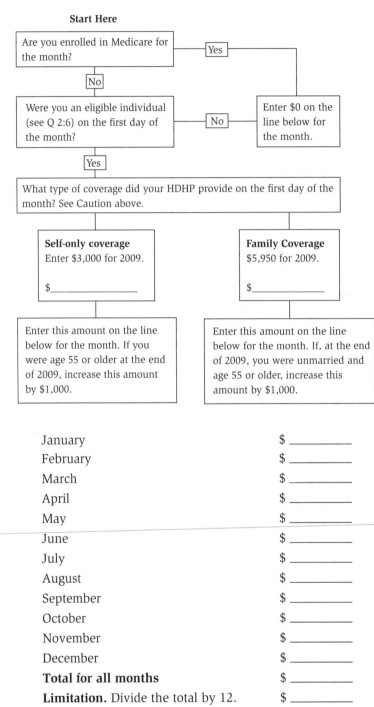

January	$ _____
February	$ _____
March	$ _____
April	$ _____
May	$ _____
June	$ _____
July	$ _____
August	$ _____
September	$ _____
October	$ _____
November	$ _____
December	$ _____
Total for all months	$ _____
Limitation. Divide the total by 12.	$ _____

This amount is the maximum annual contribution limit for the year. The amount is entered on Line 3 of Form 8889—*Health Savings Accounts (HSA) and* is used in computing contribution limits, excess contributions, and deduction amounts. The catch-up contribution limit (up to $1,000 for 2009) for a married individual age 55 or older is entered on Line 7 of Form 8889. If unmarried, the catch-up contribution is taken into account when computing the chart in Table 4-3.

Special Computation Rules for Married Individuals

Q 4:49   If one or both spouses have family coverage, how is the contribution limit computed?

In the case of individuals who are married to each other, if either spouse has family coverage, generally both are treated as having family coverage. [I.R.C. § 223(b)(5)(A)]

Where both spouses have family HDHP coverage, but one spouse has other coverage, the contribution limits for the spouses vary depending on the specific circumstances. See the following examples:

Practice Pointer. A married couple's tax filing status (i.e., joint or separate) does not affect a particular spouse's contribution.

Example. Daniel and Lucy are married. Daniel and Lucy will both turn age 55 by the end of 2009. Daniel has HDHP self-only coverage with a $1,150 deductible and Lucy has separate HDHP family coverage with a $5,000 deductible. Because one spouse has family coverage, they both are treated as having family coverage for purposes of determining the annual maximum contribution limit. Daniel can contribute $3,975 to an HSA (one-half of the deductible of $5,950 family maximum contribution plus $1,000 catch-up contribution) for 2009. Lucy can contribute $3,975 to an HSA (one-half of the $5,950 family maximum contribution plus $1,000 catch-up) for 2009. Daniel and Lucy could agree on a different division of the $5,950.

Note. An individual may be eligible to contribute to an HSA if his or her spouse has non-HDHP *family* coverage, provided the spouse's coverage does not cover the individual (see Q 4:50) . [Rev. Rul. 2005-25, 2005 I.R.B. 18]

Q 4:50   How do the maximum annual HSA contribution limits apply to a married couple if both spouses are eligible individuals and each spouse has family HDHP coverage that does not cover the other spouse?

The maximum annual HSA contribution limit for a married couple if one spouse has family HDHP coverage and the other spouse has self-only HDHP coverage is the statutory maximum for family coverage ($5,950 for 2009). The contribution limit is divided between the spouses by agreement (see Q 4:57). This is the result regardless of whether the family HDHP coverage includes the spouse with self-only HDHP coverage. [I.R.S. Notice 2008-59, Q&A 17, 2008-29 I.R.B. 123]

Example 1. For 2009, Bill and Anne are married. Both are 40 years old. Bill and Anne are otherwise eligible individuals. Bill has self-only HDHP coverage. Anne has an HDHP with family coverage for herself and their two children. The combined contribution limit for Bill and Anne is $5,950, which is the Code Section 223(b)(2)(B) statutory contribution limit for 2009. Bill and Anne divide the $5,950 contribution limit between them by agreement.

Example 2. Andrew and Elaine are married and both are age 40. Throughout 2009, Andrew has HDHP self-only coverage with an annual deductible of $2,000. Andrew has no other health coverage, is not enrolled in Medicare, and may not be claimed as a dependent on another taxpayer's return. Elaine has non-HDHP family coverage for herself and their two dependents, but Andrew is excluded from Elaine's coverage. Although Elaine has non-HDHP family coverage, Andrew is not covered under that health plan. Andrew is, therefore, an eligible individual.

Note. The special rules for married individuals treating both spouses as having family coverage do not apply because Elaine's non-HDHP family coverage does not cover Andrew. Thus, Andrew remains an eligible individual and may contribute up to $3,000 to an HSA (the self-only contribution limit of $3,000 for 2009). Andrew may not make the catch-up contribution because he is not age 55 or older in 2009. Elaine has non-HDHP coverage and therefore is not an eligible individual.

Example 3. The same facts as Example 3, except that Andrew has HDHP family coverage for himself and one of their dependents, with an annual deductible of $5,000. Elaine has non-HDHP family coverage for herself and their other dependent. Andrew is excluded from Elaine's coverage. Because the non-HDHP family coverage does not cover Andrew, the special rules that treat both spouses as having family coverage do not affect Andrew's eligibility to make HSA contributions up to his HSA maximum annual contribution limit. Andrew, therefore, may contribute up to the family HDHP maximum contribution limit of $5,950 for 2009. Elaine has non-HDHP coverage and therefore is not an eligible individual.

Q 4:51   Which plan deductible limit was used before 2007 for computing contributions when each spouse had family coverage under a separate health plan?

For taxable years beginning before 2007, if each spouse has family coverage under a separate health plan, both spouses are treated as covered under the plan with the lowest deductible. For taxable years beginning after 2006, however, an individual with family coverage can contribute up to the maximum annual contribution limit, $5,950 for 2009, without regard to the deductible under the HDHP (see Q 4:30). If the individual is married and the spouse is an eligible individual, they can split the $5,950 equally or agree on a different division.

Example 1. Wally and Georgina are married. Wally is age 55 and Georgina is age 52 at the end of 2009. Wally and Georgina both have family coverage under separate HDHPs. Wally has an HDHP deductible of $3,000 and Georgina has an HDHP deductible of $2,500. Wally can contribute $3,975 to an HSA (one-half of the $5,950 family maximum contribution limit, plus a $1,000 catch-up contribution) and Georgina can contribute $3,000 to an HSA (unless they agree to a different division of the $5,950).

Historical Note. In taxable years beginning before 2007, Wally and Georgina would be treated as covered under the HDHP with the $2,500 deductible (the deductible under the HDHP with the lowest deductible). For 2006, Wally's contribution to an HSA would be limited to $2,050 (one-half of the deductible of $2,500 plus $800 (the 2006 limit) catch-up contribution) and Georgina could have only contributed $1,250 to an HSA (unless they agreed to a different division of the $2,500).

Example 2. Seymour and Darleen are married. Seymour is 40 and Darleen is 33. Seymour and Darleen each have HDHP self-only coverage. Seymour has an HDHP deductible of $2,500 and Darleen has an HDHP deductible of $1,500. For 2009, Seymour can contribute $3,000 to an HSA and Darleen can contribute $3,000 to an HSA.

Q 4:52 What is the contribution limit for spouses?

Both spouses may make the catch-up contributions for individuals age 55 or over without exceeding the family coverage limit. [I.R.C. § 223(b)(3)(A); I.R.S. Notice 2004-50, Q&A 15, 2004-33 I.R.B. 196] Special rules apply if an individual is excluded from his or her spouse's non-HDHP (see Q 4:48).

Example 1. Tom and Jaxx, each age 55, are married. Tom has HDHP family-coverage HDHP with a deductible of $3,500 for 2009. The contribution limit is $2,975 for Tom and $2,975 for Jaxx, unless they agree on a different division. However, if eligible, Tom and Jaxx may each make catch-up contributions (up to $1,000 for 2009) to their HSAs in addition to the $5,950 (as allocated) limit (see Q 4:42).

Note. The annual contribution limit is reduced by any contribution to an Archer MSA (see Q 4:31). [I.R.C. § 223(b)(5)(B)(i)]

The following examples illustrate the contribution limits for a married individual completing Form 8889—*Health Savings Accounts (HSAs)* for 2009.

Caution. The line numbers shown in the following examples are based upon the 2008 version of Form 8889. In the examples below, the individuals are calendar year taxpayers and are not eligible individuals on December 1, and therefore, the maximum annual contribution must be computed for each month.

Example 2. In 2009, Claudia is an eligible individual with HDHP family coverage for the months of July through November. Claudia attains age 55 on September 5, 2009. On the worksheet for Line 3, Claudia would show $5,950 for five months (July through November). She would divide the total of those amounts ($29,750) by 12 to determine her contribution limit ($2,479.17) for 2009. On the worksheet for Line 7, Claudia will enter $416.67, her pro-rata allocation of the $1,000 catch-up limit ($1,000 × 5 ÷ 12).

Example 3. In 2009, Carl is an eligible individual with HDHP self-only coverage for the months of July through November. Carl is under age 55. On the worksheet for Line 3 in the Form 8889 instructions, Carl enters $3,000 for each month (July through November) that he is an eligible individual. Carl divides the total of those amounts ($15,000) by 12 to determine his contribution limit ($1,250) for 2009.

Example 4. For 2009, Daniel is an eligible individual with HDHP self-only coverage. Daniel gets married in March and, beginning April 1, 2009, Daniel and his spouse have HDHP family coverage through the end of November. Both Daniel and his wife Sasha are under age 55. Assume Sasha is not an eligible individual. On the worksheet for Line 3, Daniel would show $3,000 for the first three months and $5,950 for the eight months of family coverage. He would divide the total of those amounts ($56,600) by 12 to determine his contribution limit ($4,716.67) for the year. See Q 4:57 for a division of contributions by spouses.

Q 4:53   What is an umbrella deductible?

The umbrella deductible is the stated maximum amount of expenses that the family could incur before receiving HDHP benefits. [I.R.S. Notice 2004-50, Q&A 30, 2004-33 I.R.B. 196]

Q 4:54   What is an embedded individual deductible?

Although an HDHP may have an umbrella deductible (see Q 4:53), it may also provide payments for covered medical expenses if any individual member of the family incurs medical expenses in excess of the minimum annual deductible ($2,300 for 2009) (see Q 4:51). That limit, which is applied to each family member, is referred to as the *embedded individual deductible.* [I.R.S. Notice 2004-50, Q&A 30, 2004-33 I.R.B. 196]

An individual does not fail to be an eligible individual merely because of an embedded individual deductible that is no less than the minimum family HDHP deductible ($2,300 for 2009). (See Q 3:25.) [I.R.S. Notice 2008-59, Q&A 4(a), 2008-29 I.R.B. 123]

A post-deductible HRA or post-deductible health FSA may pay or reimburse qualified medical expenses of an individual with family HDHP coverage incurred at any time after the minimum annual deductible ($2,300 for 2009) for family HDHP coverage has been satisfied. [I.R.S. Notice 2008-59, Q&A 4(b), 2008-29 I.R.B. 123]

Example. In 2009, a family with family HDHP coverage has an umbrella deductible of $3,500, and an embedded individual deductible of $2,300. A post-deductible HRA reimburses medical expenses (see Qs 6:27–6:58) incurred after $2,300 of medical expenses covered by the HDHP have been incurred. The covered individuals, if otherwise eligible, are eligible individuals. However, a post-deductible HRA or post-deductible FSA that pays or reimburses qualified medical expenses before the minimum family HDHP deductible ($2,300 for 2009) has been satisfied will cause the individual not to be an eligible individual. [I.R.S. Notice 2008-59, Q&A 8, 2008-29 I.R.B. 123]

Q 4:55   How was the maximum annual HSA contribution limit determined before 2007 for an eligible individual with family coverage under an HDHP that included embedded individual deductibles and an umbrella deductible?

Generally, before 2007, the HSA maximum annual contribution limit for an eligible individual with family coverage under an HDHP (without regard to catch-up contributions) is the lesser of:

1. The HDHP annual deductible (see Qs 3:1, 4:30); or

2. The statutory maximum annual contribution limit on family coverage (e.g., $5,450 for 2006) (see Qs 4:30, 4:31).

Note. The embedded individual deductible must satisfy the HDHP minimum annual deductible for family coverage (e.g., $2,100 for 2006; $2,200 for 2007 and 2008; $2,300 for 2009). [I.R.S. Notice 2004-2, Q&A 3, 2004-2 I.R.B. 269]

[I.R.C. §§ 223(b)(2)(B), 223(g); I.R.S. Notice 2004-50, Q&A 30, 2004-33 I.R.B.196]

However, before 2007, the HSA maximum annual contribution limit for an eligible individual who has HDHP family coverage with embedded individual deductibles and an umbrella deductible is the least of the following amounts:

1. The statutory maximum annual contribution limit on family coverage (e.g., $5,450 for 2006);

2. The umbrella deductible (see Q 4:53); or

3. The embedded individual deductible (see Q 4:54) multiplied by the number of family members covered by the plan.

After 2007, it is not necessary to do this calculation to determine the HSA maximum contribution limit. The limit is $5,950 (the 2009 limit) for family coverage regardless of the deductible limit under the HDHP. Spouses who are both eligible individuals must divide this limit equally or can agree on a different division.

Example 1. In 2006, Roger and Shannon, a married couple, have HDHP family coverage for themselves and their two dependent children. The HDHP will pay benefits for any family member whose covered expenses exceed $2,500 (the embedded individual deductible), and will pay benefits for all family members after their covered expenses exceed $7,000. The umbrella deductible is $7,000. The HSA statutory maximum annual contribution limit is $5,450 for 2006. The embedded deductible multiplied by the number of family members covered is $10,000 (4 × $2,500). Accordingly, the maximum annual contribution that Roger and Shannon can make to their HSAs is $5,450 (the least of $7,000, $5,450, or $10,000). The $5,450 limit (for 2006) is divided equally between Roger and Shannon ($2,725 each), unless they agree to a different division.

Example 2. The same facts as the preceding example, except the year is 2009. The HDHP provides family coverage for Roger and Shannon and their two dependent children. The HSA statutory maximum annual contribution limit is $5,950 (the 2009 limit). The maximum annual contribution that Roger and Shannon can make to their HSAs for 2009 is $5,950, and is divided equally unless they agree on a different division.

Q 4:56   How do the maximum annual HSA contribution limits apply to family HDHP coverage that may include an ineligible individual?

If only one spouse is an eligible individual, only that spouse may contribute to an HSA, notwithstanding the special rule for married individuals that generally allows a married couple to divide the maximum HSA contribution between spouses and the treatment of both spouses having family coverage (see Qs 4:46, 4:54).

For 2009, the maximum annual HSA contribution for a married couple with family HDHP coverage is $5,950. [I.R.S. Notice 2004-50, Q&A 31, 2004-33 I.R.B. 196] (See Q 4:56 for an HDHP with embedded individual deductibles.)

Example 1. In 2009, Sandy and Darleen are a married couple, and neither is eligible to make catch-up contributions. Sandy and Darleen have family HDHP coverage with a $5,000 deductible. Sandy is an eligible individual and has no other coverage. Darleen also has self-only coverage with a $200 deductible. Darleen, who has coverage under a low-deductible plan, is not an eligible individual. Sandy may contribute $5,950 to an HSA, while Darleen may not contribute to an HSA for 2009.

Example 2. The same facts as in the preceding example, except that, in addition to the family HDHP with a $5,000 deductible, Darleen has self-only HDHP coverage with a $2,000 deductible rather than self-only coverage with a $200 deductible. Both Sandy and Darleen are eligible individuals. Sandy and Darleen are treated as having only family coverage (see Q 4:49). The maximum combined HSA contribution by Sandy and Darleen is $5,950 (the 2009 limit), to be divided between them by agreement.

Example 3. Cory, a single individual, does not qualify for catch-up contributions. Cory is an eligible individual and has a dependent, Lorri. Cory and his dependent have family HDHP coverage with a $5,000 deductible. The dependent also has self-only coverage with a $200 deductible. Cory may contribute $5,950 to an HSA, while Lorri (an ineligible individual) may not contribute to an HSA for 2009.

Q 4:57   How may spouses agree to divide the annual HSA contribution limit between themselves?

Code Section 223(b)(5) provides special rules for married individuals and states that HSA contributions (without regard to the catch-up contribution) "shall be divided equally between them unless they agree on a different division." Thus, if both spouses are eligible individuals with family HDHP coverage, they can divide the annual HSA family contribution limit any way they want, including allocating nothing to one spouse. [I.R.C. § 223(b)(5); I.R.S. Notice 2004-50, Q&A 32, 2004-33 I.R.B. 196; see also I.R.S. Notice 2004-2, Q&A 15, 2004-2 I.R.B. 269]

Example 1. Amber and Butch, both age 40, are a married couple. They enroll in family HDHP coverage on December 1, 2009, and are otherwise eligible individuals on that date. Amber and Butch are not eligible individuals in any other month in 2009. Under the "last-month rule" Amber and Butch are treated as eligible for the entire year with family HDHP coverage (see Q 4:7). Amber and Butch must divide the maximum annual contribution limit ($5,950 for 2009) equally, unless they agree on another division (see Q 4:38).

Example 2. In 2009, Simon and Gloria are both under age 55 and are eligible individuals with family HDHP coverage for three months—January through March. In March they divorce and the family HDHP is cancelled. Simon's coverage changes as of April 1 to self-only coverage under an HDHP. He continues this coverage for three months—April through June. Simon's self-only HDHP coverage is cancelled effective June 2. Gloria has no medical coverage for the remaining nine months. Because of the divorce, Simon and Gloria file separate income tax returns.

1. *No catch-up contribution.* Neither Simon or Gloria qualify for the additional catch-up contribution amount ($1,000 for 2009) because neither had attained age 55 by the end of the taxable year.
2. The "last-month rule" does not apply because neither Simon or Gloria were covered by a HDHP on December 1, 2009 (see Q 4:7).
3. *Family coverage allocation.* The contribution limit for the three months Simon and Gloria were considered to have family coverage is $1,487.50 ($5,950 × 3 ÷ 12). Instead of splitting the family coverage limit amount equally, they agree that it will be fully allocated to Simon.
4. *Simon's allocation.* Simon's contribution limit for three months of self-only coverage is $2,250 ($3,000 × 9 ÷ 12). This amount is not divided between Simon and Gloria (see Q 4:48).
5. *Simon's maximum contribution.* The maximum amount that can be contributed for Simon is $3,737.50, computed as follows:
    (a) $3,737.50 equals $1,487.50 (for family coverage) + $2,250 (for self-only coverage) – $0 (spousal allocation).
6. *Gloria' maximum contribution.* The maximum amount that can be contributed for Gloria is $0, computed as follows:
    (a) $0 equals $1,487.50 family coverage for the 3 months prior to the divorce minus the spousal allocation of $1,487.50.

Example 3. In 2009, Daniel and Samantha are both under age 55 and are eligible individuals with family HDHP coverage. In March they divorce. Daniel's coverage changes as of April 1 to self-only coverage under an HDHP. Samantha continues to have family HDHP coverage and was an eligible individual for the entire year. Because of the divorce, Daniel and Samantha file separate income tax returns.

1. *No catch-up contribution.* Neither Daniel or Samantha qualify for the additional catch-up contribution amount ($1,000 for 2009) because neither had attained age 55 by the end of the taxable year.

2. *Family coverage allocation.* The contribution limit for the three months Daniel and Samantha were considered to have family coverage is $1,487.50 ($5,950 × 3 ÷ 12). Instead of splitting the family coverage limit amount equally, they agree that it will be fully allocated to Daniel.

3. *Daniel's allocation.* Daniel's contribution limit for nine months of self-only coverage is $2,250 ($3,000 × 9 ÷ 12). This amount is not divided between Daniel and Samantha (see Q 4:57).

4. *Daniel's maximum contribution.* The maximum amount that can be contributed for Daniel is $3,737.50, computed as follows:

   a. $3,737.50 equals the greater of (a) $3,737.50 ($1,487.50 family coverage + $2,250 self-only coverage – $0 (spousal allocation)) or (b) the maximum amount that can be contributed ($3,000 for self-only coverage).

5. *Samantha's maximum contribution.* The maximum amount that can be contributed for Samantha is $5,950, computed as follows:

   a. $5,950 equals the greater of either (a) $4,463.25 ($1,487.50 family coverage for the 3 months prior to the divorce + $4,462.50 ($5,950 × 9 ÷ 12) family coverage maintained for nine months after the divorce – $1,487.50 spousal allocation) or (b) the maximum amount that can be contributed ($5,950 for family coverage).

Example 4. Assume the same facts as in Example 3, except that Daniel and Samantha do not get divorced in 2009. Daniel and Samantha are both treated as having family coverage for the entire year (see Q 4:49). The maximum annual contribution limit ($5,950 for family coverage) for 2009 is divided equally between Daniel and Samantha unless they agree on a different division (see Q 4:57).

[I.R.C. § 223(b)(2), 223(b)(8)] Determining annual contribution amounts is more fully discussed in Qs 4:30–4:52. Preparation of Form 8889—*Health Savings Accounts (HSAs)* is discussed more fully in chapter 7.

Q 4:58   How does an employer report HSA contributions?

Employer contributions to an HSA generally must be reported on the employee's Form W-2—*Wage and Tax Statement.* [I.R.C. § 6051] The IRS has released forms and instructions, similar to those required for Archer MSAs, on how to report HSA contributions, deductions, and distributions. [I.R.S. Notice 2004-2, Q&A 34, 2004-2 I.R.B. 269] Special considerations apply to partners and a more than 2 percent shareholder of an S Corporation (see Qs 4:156, 4:168). The report (Form W-2) must be received by January 31 of the following year.

Q 4:59   How is an employer's contribution to an HSA reflected on Form W-2—*Wage and Tax Statement*?

An employer's contribution to an HSA is entered in Box 12 of Form W-2 with Code W. This applies regardless of whether the contributions are (1) made from employee contributions deducted pursuant to a cafeteria plan election or (b) made by the employer outside of Code Section 125 under the comparability requirements. The amount is entered by the HSA owner on Form 8889—*Health Savings Accounts (HSAs)*. Administration and compliance issues are more fully discussed in chapter 7. [I.R.S. Ann. 2004-2, 2004-2 I.R.B. 322]

For Form W-2 reporting purposes, the amount to enter is determined on a calendar year basis. The HSA trustee would obtain the HSA owner's designation as to the year the contribution is being made for, just like they do for IRA contributions made in the "leeway" period (generally January 1 to April 15).

Practice Pointer. Most trustees and custodians treat all contributions received after the end of a calendar year as being made for the current year unless the contribution is designated as a prior year's contribution. The HSA owner would also complete Form 8889. The instructions for Form 8889 suggest that the employer's contribution for the current year (2009) is computed in the following manner.

a. Employer contributions reported in Box 12 of Form W-2, with Code W $_____

b. Employer contributions made in 2009 for tax year 2008 $_____

c. Employer contributions made in 2010 for tax year 2009 $_____

d. Employer contributions for 2009. Add Lines c and d. The amount is also entered on Form 8889 (Line 9 of the 2008 version of the form) $_____

The reporting of a one-time direct trustee-to-trustee transfer from a health FSA or an HRA to an HSA is discussed in chapter 5.

Deductions for Individual Contributions

Q 4:60   Are an eligible individual's HSA contributions deductible?

Generally, after-tax contributions made to an HSA, within permissible limits, by or on behalf of an HSA owner who is an eligible individual are deductible by the HSA owner. [I.R.C. § 223(a)] The deduction is an adjustment to gross income (that is, an above-the-line deduction) under Code Section 62(a)(19). For an eligible individual, a deduction is permitted for the taxable year equal to an amount that is the aggregate amount paid in cash (or other property in the case of a direct transfer from an IRA in a qualified HSA funding distribution) during such taxable year to an HSA by either the HSA owner or any other person. Employer contributions, including any pretax contributions through the employer's cafeteria plan, are not deductible, but instead are generally excludable from the employee's gross income (see Qs 4:62–4:69).

> **Practice Pointer.** The medical expense deduction is an adjustment to gross income, but only to the extent that medical and dental expenses are more than 7.5 percent of adjusted gross income (Form 1040, Line 37, based on the 2007 version of the form). The HSA contribution deduction is taken above the line (Line 25)—to arrive at gross income—and is not subject to the percentage limitation.

The eligible individual cannot also deduct the HSA contribution as a medical expense under Code Section 213. [I.R.S. Notice 2004-2, Q&A 17, 2004-2 I.R.B. 269]

Q 4:61   Are employer contributions to the HSA of an employee's spouse (who is not an employee of this employer) excluded from the employee's gross income and wages?

No. The exclusion under Code Section 106(d)(1) is limited to contributions by an employer to the HSA of an employee who is an eligible individual. Any contribution by an employer to the HSA of a non-employee (e.g., a spouse of an employee or any other individual), including salary reduction amounts made through a Code Section 125 cafeteria plan, must be included in the gross income and wages of the employee. [I.R.S. Notice 2008-59, Q&A 26, 2008-29 I.R.B. 123]

Q 4:62   How is the deduction taken on the individual's federal income tax return?

Generally, contributions made to an HSA, within permissible limits, by or on behalf of a taxpayer who is an eligible individual are deductible by a taxpayer under Code Section 223(a). The deduction is an adjustment to gross income (i.e., an above-the-line deduction) under Code Section 62(a)(19). [I.R.S. Notice 2004-2, Q&A 17, 2004-2 I.R.B. 269] However, if an employer makes a contribution, within permissible limits, to the HSA on behalf of an employee who is an eligible individual, the contribution is generally excluded from the employee's gross income and wages. [I.R.C. §§ 106(d), 223(a)] Special rules apply to partners and to a 2 percent or more shareholder of an S Corporation (see Qs 4:153–4:176). [See I.R.C. § 1372(b) (defining the term *2 percent shareholder*)]

Q 4:63   Is the deduction for contributions to a self-employed individual's own HSA taken into account in determining net earnings from self-employment under Code Section 1402(a)?

No. The deduction for making the contribution to the self-employed's own HSA is an adjustment to income on his or her personal income tax return.

Because it is not a deduction attributable to a trade or business expense, the deduction is not taken on Form 1040, Schedule C—*Profit or Loss From Business* and is not taken into account when completing Form 1040, Schedule SE—*Self-Employment Tax*. (See Qs 4:156–4:176 regarding the tax treatment of partners and 2 percent shareholders of an S Corporation.) [I.R.S. Notice 2004-50, Q&A 84, 2004-33 I.R.B. 196]

Example. Russ, a self-employed individual, has $10,000 of net earnings from self-employment after all business expenses for 2009. Russ contributes $3,000 into his HSA. Although he will claim a deduction for $3,000 on his Form 1040 (or Form 1040-NR), Russ's income for self-employment tax purposes will be based on $10,000 because the contribution is not treated as a trade or business expense.

Q 4:64 If a C corporation makes a contribution to the HSA of a shareholder who is not an employee of the C corporation, what are the tax consequences to the shareholder and to the C corporation?

If a C corporation makes a contribution to the HSA of a shareholder who is not an employee of the C corporation, the contribution will be treated as a distribution under Code Section 301, regarding distributions of property. The distribution is treated as a dividend to the extent that the C corporation has earnings and profits. The portion of the distribution that is not a dividend is applied against and reduces the adjusted basis of the stock. To the extent that the amount of the distribution exceeds the adjusted basis of the stock, the balance is treated as gain from a sale or exchange of property. [I.R.S. Notice 2004-50, Q&A 88, 2004-33 I.R.B. 196]

Q 4:65 Must an individual itemize deductions in order to claim a deduction for HSA contributions?

No. Allowable contributions are deductible whether or not an eligible individual itemizes deductions. [I.R.S. Notice 2004-2, Q&A 17, 2004-2 I.R.B. 269]

Q 4:66 Can HSA contributions be claimed as an itemized expense on the federal income tax return?

No. The deduction is taken "above the line" (see Q 4:60). The eligible individual cannot also deduct the contribution as a medical expense deduction under Code Section 213. [I.R.S. Notice 2004-2, Q&A 17, 2004-2 I.R.B. 269]

Q 4:67 Are contributions made by a family member or other person on behalf of an eligible individual deductible?

Yes. Contributions made by a family member (or other person) on behalf of an eligible individual to an HSA (which are subject to the limits described in

Qs 4:30–4:45) are deductible by the eligible individual in computing adjusted gross income (whether or not the eligible individual itemizes deductions). [I.R.S. Notice 2004-2, Q&A 18, 2004-2 I.R.B. 269]

Q 4:68   May an individual who may be claimed as a dependent on another person's tax return deduct contributions to an HSA?

No. An individual who may be claimed as a dependent on another person's tax return is not an eligible individual and may not deduct contributions to an HSA. [I.R.C. § 223(b)(6); I.R.S. Notice 2004-2, Q&A 18, 2004-2 I.R.B. 269]

Q 4:69   Do community property rules apply in determining limitations on contributions or their deductibility?

No. HSA limitations are determined without regard to community property rules. [I.R.C. § 223(d)(4)(D)]

Employer Contributions in General

Q 4:70   May employer contributions exceed the maximum allowable amount for the individual?

No. The combined contribution limit to an HSA from all sources (i.e., the HSA owner, a family member or other individual, or an employer) cannot exceed the maximum allowable amount for the eligible individual.

Note. If the employer chooses to make HSA contributions, then the employer is required to make comparable HSA contributions for all participating employees (i.e., eligible employees with comparable coverage) during the same period (see Qs 4:114–4:148) unless contributions are made through a cafeteria plan (see Q 4:149).

Practice Pointer. The IRS final comparability regulations (final rules) governing employer contributions to HSAs were issued on July 31, 2006. [Treas. Reg. § 54.4980G-1 through 5; 71 Fed. Reg. 43056] The final rules clarify the steps employers need to take in order to fall within the "cafeteria plan exception," allowing the employer's HSA contributions to be subject to the cafeteria plan nondiscrimination rules under Code Section 125 rather than the comparability rules. In addition, the final regulations add some important flexibility, such as providing an exception for collectively bargained employees and expanding the categories of HDHP coverage for which employers may vary HSA contributions. However, the final regulations reserved several questions for future determination.

On June 1, 2007, the IRS issued proposed rules (since finalized) on the comparable contribution that govern employer contributions made to HSAs outside of a Code Section 125 cafeteria plan. The proposed rules provide guidance for employers when employees fail to establish an HSA or notify their employers of their HSA prior to December 31 (see Q 4:141). The proposed rules also permit employers to make accelerated calendar-year contributions for employees who incur qualified medical expenses exceeding current HSA contributions (see Q 4:140). [72 Fed. Reg. 30501 (June 1, 2007); Prop. Treas. Reg. § 54.4980G-4, Q&As-14 and 15 (June 1, 2007)] Prior guidance had limited accelerated payments only to those employees who made HSA contributions through a cafeteria plan under Code Section 125 (see Q 4:149).

On April 17, 2008, the IRS issued final regulations that adopted the June 2007 proposed regulations without substantive revision. The final regulations apply to distributions made on or after January 1, 2009, but may be relied on by employers starting on the date of publication of the final regulation on April 17, 2008. [Treas. Reg. § 54.4980G-4, Q&As-14-16, 73 Fed. Reg. 20794 (April 17, 2008)]

Q 4:71   How are employer payments to an HSA treated?

Employer payments to an HSA are generally excluded from an employee's gross income (see Qs 4:59, 4:60). However, to the extent an employer's payments to an HSA exceed the maximum annual contribution limit (that is, the $3,000/$5,950 statutory maximum annual contribution limit for 2009), the payments are not treated as employer-provided coverage for medical expenses under an accident or health plan under Code Section 106(d). Thus, any amount paid by an employer to an HSA that exceeds the statutory limits would be treated as the payment of compensation to the employee and included in the individual's gross income in the tax year for which the amount was contributed. [I.R.C. §§ 106(d)(1), 223(d)(4)(C)] Although a self-employed individual is an employee within the meaning of Code Section 401(c)(1), any contributions over the statutory contribution limit are not treated as compensation because wages are not involved. However, such amounts would be subject to the 6 percent excise tax on excess contributions.

The payment is included in the individual's gross income in the taxable year for which the amount was contributed, whether or not the employee is allowed to deduct the HSA contribution. [I.R.C. §§ 106(d)(1), 223(d)(4)(C)]

Q 4:72   What tax advantages does an employer receive by allowing employees to make HSA contributions through the employer's cafeteria plan?

HSA contributions by an employee through a Section 125 cafeteria plan (provided they are within statutory limits) are not counted as wages for purposes of the Federal Insurance Contributions Act (FICA), the Federal Unemployment Tax Act (FUTA), or the Railroad Retirement Tax Act. Thus, by allowing employees to make HSA contributions through the cafeteria plan, the employer will reduce its liability for these taxes because the employee will have lower wages for purposes of calculating these taxes. [See I.R.S. Notice 2004-2,

Q&A 19, 2004-2 I.R.B. 269] In addition, the employee will not be required to pay his or her share of FICA tax on such contributions.

As a practical matter, the FUTA savings is limited, as the employer pays only 6.2 percent on the first $7,000 of an employee's wages, so unless the HSA contribution reduces the employee's wages below $7,000, it will not have an impact. [I.R.C. § 3306(b)(1)] The FICA savings is more significant: the employer's share for Medicare hospital coverage is 1.45 percent of all of an employee's wages, and the employer's share for Social Security is 6.2 percent on the employee's wages up to $106,800 (the 2009 limit.) [I.R.C. § 3111(a)-(b)] So, any reduction of wages will directly reduce the amount of FICA an employer is required to pay. Similarly, the employee share of FICA is the same as the employer share, so any reduction in wages will also save the employee money in FICA tax. [I.R.C. § 3101(a)-(b)]

Q 4:73   Can an employer make higher contributions to the HSA accounts of participants with chronic health conditions?

Possibly. An employer may make higher contributions to the HSAs of HSA owners with chronic health conditions if the contribution is made "through the cafeteria plan." In that event, the comparable contribution rule under Code Section 4980E does not apply, and the employer has flexibility to vary contributions as long as the Code Section 125 nondiscrimination rules are satisfied. The IRS final comparability regulations for employer contributions to HSAs make clear that an employer's contributions will be considered made through a cafeteria plan if: (1) employees are permitted to make their own contributions to an HSA by salary reduction through a cafeteria plan, and (2) the right to make such contributions is described in a written cafeteria plan document. [Treas. Reg. § 54.4980G-5, Q&A 1-3; 71 Fed. Reg. 43056 (July 31, 2006)] See also I.R.S. Notice 2004-50, which states that the comparable contribution rule does not apply to contributions made through a cafeteria plan. If the contribution is not made through the cafeteria plan and is not the same dollar amount or percentage of deductible for all eligible individuals covered by the employer's HDHP, it would violate the comparable contribution requirements under Code Section 4980G and regulations thereunder. [I.R.S. Notice 2004-50, Q&A 47 through 49, 2004-33 I.R.B. 196]

Q 4:74   Are contributions to an HSA subject to the nonqualified deferred compensation rules under Code Section 409A?

No. An HSA is not subject to the nonqualified deferred compensation plan rules under Code Section 409A, even though all contributions are fully vested and nonforfeitable (see Q 2:1). Code Section 409A provides that all amounts deferred under a nonqualified deferred compensation plan for all taxable years are currently includible in gross income to the extent not subject to a substantial risk of forfeiture and not previously included in gross income, unless certain requirements are met. These rules are not limited to arrangements between an employer and employee. However, there is a specific exemption for HSAs under

IRS guidance, which provides that the term *nonqualified deferred compensation plan* does not include an HSA under Code Section 223. Thus, an HSA is not treated as a nonqualified deferred compensation plan under Code Section 409A(d)(1)(B). [See I.R.S. Notice 2005-1, Q&A 3(c), 2005-2 I.R.B. 274; Treas. Reg. § 1.409A-1(a)(5)]

> **Practice Pointer.** IRS guidance similarly provides that an Archer MSA under Code Section 220 and a medical reimbursement arrangement, including an HRA, that satisfies the requirements of Code Sections 105 and 106 are not treated as a nonqualified deferred compensation plan under Code Section 409A(d)(1)(B).

Employer Responsibility

Q 4:75   Is the employer responsible for determining employee eligibility for an HSA?

To some extent. Apart from the allowable contribution, with respect to specific employee's HSA eligibility, the employer is only responsible for determining:

1. Whether the employee is covered under an HDHP (and the amount of the deductible) or low-deductible health plan or plans (including health FSAs and HRAs) sponsored by that employer; and

2. The employee's age (for catch-up contributions).

[I.R.S. Notice 2004-50, Q&A 81, 2004-33 I.R.B. 196]

> **Note.** If the employer chooses to make HSA contributions, then the employer is required to make comparable HSA contributions for all participating employees (i.e., eligible employees with comparable coverage) during the same period, unless such contributions are made through a cafeteria plan (see Qs 4:113–4:150).

Q 4:76   May the employer rely on an employee's representation of their age?

Yes. The employer may rely on the employee's representation as to his or her date of birth. [I.R.S. Notice 2004-50, Q&A 81, 2004-33 I.R.B. 196]

Q 4:77   Is the employer responsible for determining whether HSA distributions are used exclusively for qualified medical expenses?

No. The individual who establishes the HSA is responsible for determining whether the distributions are used exclusively for the payment of qualified medical expenses—so as to be excludable from gross income (see Q 6:9). [I.R.S. Notice 2004-2, Q&A 30, 2004-2 I.R.B. 269]

Q 4:78   Is an employer permitted to structure cafeteria plan elections for HSAs as negative elections?

Yes. An employer is permitted to structure cafeteria plan elections for all cafeteria plan benefits as negative elections. [See Rev. Rul. 2002-27, 2002-20 I.R.B. 925; Prop. Treas. Reg. § 1.125-2(b)] HSA salary reduction elections should be governed by this revenue ruling.

Example. J Corporation holds an annual open enrollment period and communicates that employees who elected to make salary reduction contributions to the HSA for 2009 through J Corporation's cafeteria plan, and want to keep the same election and contribution for 2010, need not take any action at open enrollment (i.e., their 2009 election carries over to 2010 unless they make a different election). Sally elected to contribute $1,000 to her HSA through J Corporation's cafeteria plan in 2009, and wishes to make this same election for 2010. Sally takes no action at open enrollment, and J Corporation treats Sally as having made a $1,000 cafeteria plan election to the HSA for 2010. J Corporation has satisfied applicable cafeteria plan requirements.

Exclusion and Deductibility of Employer Contributions

Q 4:79   What is the tax treatment of employer contributions on behalf of an eligible individual?

In the case of an employee who is an eligible individual, employer contributions (provided they are within the limits described in Q 4:30) to an employee's HSA are treated as employer-provided coverage for medical expenses under an accident or health plan and are excludable under Code Section 106(d). [I.R.S. Notice 2004-2, Q&A 19, 2004-2 I.R.B. 269]

Example. Gretta has HDHP self-only coverage with a deductible of $1,500 and also has an HSA. Gretta's employer contributes $200 to Gretta's HSA at the end of every quarter in 2009 and at the end of the first quarter in 2010 (March 31, 2010). Gretta can exclude from income in 2009 the employer's total contribution of $1,000 (5 × $200) because Gretta's exclusion for all contributions does not exceed the maximum annual HSA contribution limit of $3,000 for 2009 ($4,000 if age 55 or older in 2009). The trustee or custodian of Gretta's HSA will require that contributions for the prior year be designated as such. Nonetheless, Gretta's employer will only report $800—the amount contributed with Code "W" in Box 12 of Form W-2 for 2009—that it contributed in 2009 (i.e., on a calendar-year basis).

Q 4:80   Are employer contributions on behalf of an eligible individual excluded from the employee's income?

Yes. In the case of an employee who is an eligible individual, employer contributions (provided they are within the limits described in Q 4:30) to an employee's HSA are excludable from the employee's gross income under Code Section 106(d). [I.R.S. Notice 2004-2, Q&A 19, 2004-2 I.R.B. 269]

> **Note.** An employee does not get a deduction for employer contributions to his or her HSA or for amounts the employee contributes on a pretax basis through the employer's cafeteria plan. [I.R.S. Notice 2004-2, Q&A 19, 2004-2 I.R.B. 269]

Q 4:81   Are contributions to an employee's HSA through a cafeteria plan treated as made by the employer or employee?

Contributions to an employee's HSA through a cafeteria plan are treated as employer contributions. However, because pretax salary reductions through cafeteria plans are not part of taxable income reported in Boxes 1, 3, or 5 of Form W-2, an employee does not get a deduction for these contributions when made to his or her HSA. [I.R.S. Notice 2004-2, Q&A 19, 2004-2 I.R.B. 269]

> **Note.** A one-time direct trustee-to-trustee transfer from a health FSA or an HRA to an HSA is treated as a rollover contribution. [I.R.C. § 106(e)(4)(C)] As such, it does not have any effect upon the maximum annual contribution that can be made to the HSA for the year ($3,000/$5,950, plus catch-up contributions of up to $1,000/$2,000 for 2009). Such rollover contributions are excludable from gross income and wages for employment tax purposes. The rollover contributions are not deductible. [Joint Committee on Taxation, Technical Analysis of the Tax Relief and Health Care Act of 2006 (Pub. L. No. 109-432) (JCX-50-06)]

Q 4:82   Are employer contributions subject to Railroad Retirement taxes?

No. Employer contributions are not generally subject to the Railroad Retirement Tax Act. For purposes of the Railroad Retirement Act, the term *compensation* does not include any payment made to or for the benefit of an employee if, at the time of such payment, it is reasonable to believe that the employee will be able to exclude such payment from income under Code Section 106(d), regarding the exclusion of employer contributions to accident and health plans, from an employee's gross income. [I.R.C. §§ 106(b)(2), 106(d), 3231(e)(11); I.R.S. Notice 2004-2, Q&A 19, 2004-2 I.R.B. 269]

Q 4:83   Are employer contributions subject to income withholding from wages?

No. Employer contributions are not subject to withholding from wages for federal income tax purposes if it is reasonable to believe, at the time of payment, that the employee will be able to exclude such payment from income under Code Section 106(d), regarding the exclusion of employer contributions to HSAs, from an employee's gross income. [I.R.C. §§ 3401(a)(21), 3401(a)(22); I.R.S. Notice 2004-2, Q&A 19, 2004-2 I.R.B. 269]

Q 4:84   Are employer contributions subject to FICA taxes?

No. Employer contributions are not subject to FICA taxes. [I.R.S. Notice 2004-2, Q&A 19, 2004-2 I.R.B. 269]

Q 4:85   Are employer contributions made under a cafeteria plan subject to FICA taxes?

No. Employer contributions made under a cafeteria plan are not subject to FICA taxes if (1) such payment would not be treated as wages without regard to such plan and (2) it is reasonable to believe that, if Code Section 125 applied, that section would not treat any wages as constructively received. [I.R.C. § 3121(a)(5)(G); I.R.S. Notice 2004-2, Q&A 19, 2004-2 I.R.B. 269]

Q 4:86   Are employer contributions subject to FUTA taxes?

No. Employer contributions are not subject to FUTA taxes if, at the time of payment, it is reasonable to believe that the employee will be able to exclude such payment from income under Code Section 106(d), regarding the exclusion of employer contributions to accident and health plans, from an employee's gross income. [I.R.C. §§ 106(b)(2), 106(d), 3306(b)(18); I.R.S. Notice 2004-2, Q&A 19, 2004-2 I.R.B. 269]

Q 4:87   May an employee deduct employer contributions made on his or her behalf on his or her federal income tax return?

No. An employee may not deduct employer contributions made on his or her behalf on his or her federal income tax return, either as HSA contributions or as medical expense deductions under Code Section 213. [I.R.S. Notice 2004-2, Q&A 19, 2004-2 I.R.B. 269]

Q 4:88   What is the tax treatment of an HSA?

An HSA is generally exempt from tax (as is an IRA or Archer MSA), unless it has ceased to be an HSA (see Q 6:60). Earnings on amounts in an HSA are not includible in gross income while held an HSA (i.e., inside buildup is not taxable). [I.R.C. § 223(e)(1); I.R.S. Notice 2004-2, Q&A 20, 2004-2 I.R.B. 269] (See Q 6:9 regarding the taxation of distributions from the HSA.)

An HSA is, however, subject to tax on its unrelated business taxable income under Code Section 511. Although there is a specific exemption of $1,000, this tax may apply if the account is used for purposes inconsistent with its exempt purpose (e.g., an HSA engaged in the operation of a grocery store, as opposed to an investment in an unrelated grocery store). [I.R.C. §§ 223(e)(1), 511, 512]

Note. An employer identification number (EIN) is required for an HSA that must file a return to report taxable unrelated business income.

Timing of Contributions

Q 4:89　When may HSA contributions be made?

Contributions for the taxable year can be made in one or more payments, at the convenience of the individual or the employer, at any time prior to the time prescribed by law (without extensions) for filing the eligible individual's federal income tax return for that year, but not before the beginning of that year.

Q 4:90　Is there a deadline for contributions to an HSA for a taxable year?

Yes. Contributions for the taxable year can be made in one or more payments, at the convenience of the individual or the employer, at any time prior to the time prescribed by law (without extensions) for filing the eligible individual's federal income tax return for that year, but not before the beginning of that year. For calendar-year taxpayers, the deadline for contributions to an HSA is generally April 15 following the year for which the contributions are made. Although the annual contribution is determined monthly, the maximum contribution may be made on the first day of the year. [I.R.S. Notice 2004-2, Q&A 21, 2004-2 I.R.B. 269] (See Qs 4:91–4:108 regarding excess contributions.)

> **Example.** Fanny, age 53, has an HDHP with self-only coverage, and she also has an HSA. Fanny's employer contributes $200 to her HSA at the end of every quarter in 2009 and at the end of the first quarter in 2010 (March 31, 2010). Fanny can exclude from income in 2009 the employer's total contribution of $1,000 (5 × $200) because Fanny's exclusion for all contributions does not exceed the maximum annual HSA contribution limit of $3,000. Fanny may make additional contributions of $2,200 ($3,000 – $1,000) to her HSA, assuming the employer's contribution that was made on March 31, 2010, was not designated as being made for the prior year (2009).

Excess Contributions

Q 4:91　How may an excess HSA contribution be created?

In general, an excess contribution results when contributions to all of an individual's HSAs exceed the maximum amount that may be deducted under Code Section 223(a) or excluded from gross income under Code Section 106(d) in a taxable year. [I.R.C. § 223(f)(3)(B)] An excess could also result from a direct transfer or rollover from another HSA that does not qualify to be rolled over or transferred. A one-time transfer from an IRA to an HSA could also create an excess contribution because such transfers are subject to the annual HSA contribution limit for the year, either $3,000 (self-only) or $5,950 (family) (the 2009 limits). Form 8889—*Health Savings Accounts (HSAs)*, which is used to report contributions and distributions, is also used to compute any excess HSA contributions made for a year.

Amounts included in gross income because an individual failed to remain an eligible individual during the testing period (relating to contributions made by individuals that become eligible mid-year or, are eligible on the first day of the year but change coverage during the year (see Q 4:5) and to one-time transfers from an IRA that are not in excess of the annual HSA contribution limits (see Qs 4:29, 5:40)) are not an excess contribution and the 6 percent tax on excess contributions does not apply to such amounts (see Q 5:50, Example 10). For this reason, amounts cannot be withdrawn under the excess contribution rules. [I.R.S. Notice 2008-52, 2008-25 I.R.B. 1166, modifying I.R.S. Notice 2004-2, 2004-2 I.R.B. 269 and I.R.S. Notice 2004-50, 2004-33 I.R.B. 196]

Q 4:92   What is an excess contribution for purposes of the 6 percent excise tax?

For any year, the term *excess contribution* to an HSA means the sum of:

1. The aggregate amount contributed for the taxable year to the accounts (other than rollover contribution and direct transfers) that is neither excludable from gross income under Code Section 106(d), regarding employer-provided coverage, nor allowable as an HSA deduction for such year; and

2. The amount of any excess contribution for the preceding taxable year, reduced by the sum of:

   a. Distributions from accounts that were included in gross income because they were not used for qualified medical expenses [I.R.C. § 223(f)(2)], and

   b. The excess (if any) of:

      – The maximum amount allowable as an HSA deduction without regard to the source of contributions, over

      – The amount contributed to the accounts for the taxable year.

[I.R.C. §§ 220(f)(5), 223(f)(5), 4973(g)(1)-(2)]

Note. A contribution that is distributed from the HSA in a correcting distribution of an excess contribution before the due date (including extensions) of an individual's federal income tax return is not treated as an amount contributed for the current year. [I.R.C. § 4973(g)]

Example. In 2008, Clay made an excess contribution of $500 to his HSA and paid a 6 percent excise tax for the year on Form 5329. The following year, Clay is age 45 and has self-only coverage under a HDHP. He is otherwise an eligible individual for 2009. The following contributions were made to Clay's HSA for 2009:

a. Clay contributes $2,000.

b. Clay's employer contributed $950.

c. During 2009, Clay made a qualifying HSA distribution of $3,000 from his health FSA that was transferred to his HSA (see Q 5:53).

d. Clay rolled over $750 from his HSA to another HSA during the year in a qualifying rollover distribution.

Other than the rollover distribution, the only distribution from Clay's HSA accounts was $100 that was not used for a qualified medical expense. Because Clay does not remove the excess contribution of $450 by the due date of his 2009 tax return he will have to report an excess contribution on Form 5329 of and pay the 6 percent excise tax. The $450 excess amount can be computed as follows:

1. $2,000 (individual contribution)
   + $950 (employer contribution)
   = $2,950 (total contributions)

2. + $500 (excess from prior year)
   –$100 (taxable distribution)
   + 50 (the $3,000 maximum HSA contribution limit less $2,950 of total HSA contributions)
   = $450 excess contribution.

Neither the qualifying HSA distribution of $3,000 nor the $750 rollover contribution is taken into account in computing an excess amount. [I.R.C. § 223(f)(3)(B)] The result would not change even if Clay became ineligible during the testing period following the transfer from his health FSA. If Clay became ineligible during the testing period applicable to the qualifying HSA, the distribution of $3,000 would not be treated as an excess contribution (see Q 4:91), although it would be subject to income tax and a penalty tax.

Q 4:93 Is it permissible for an individual to deduct an HSA contribution that exceeds the maximum amount that may be contributed in a taxable year?

No. Contributions made by an individual, or on behalf of an individual, to an HSA are not deductible to the extent the contributions exceed the limits described in Q 4:30. [I.R.S. Notice 2004-2, Q&A 22, 2004-2 I.R.B. 269]

Q 4:94 How are employer contributions and excess employer contributions reported by the employer?

All employer contributions to an HSA, including excess employer contributions, are reported in Box 12 of Form W-2 with Code W. Employer contributions to an HSA that are not excludable from the employee's income are also reported on Form W-2, in Boxes 1, 3, and 5 (and on Form 940—*Employer's Annual Federal Unemployment (FUTA) Tax Return*).

Note. If an excess HSA contribution is made by an employer and not included in the employee's income, the amount must be reported by the individual as "Other income" on the individual's tax return. An individual may not claim an exclusion of an excess contribution.

Q 4:95　May an employer's HSA contribution to an ineligible individual be deducted by the employee?

No. A contribution by an employer on behalf of an employee who is not an eligible individual (or that exceeds the amount allowed to be contributed to the HSA) is not deductible by the employee (see Qs 4:60, 4:80). [I.R.C. § 223(a); I.R.S. Notice 2004-2, Q&A 22, 2004-2 I.R.B. 269] Unless the excess contribution is corrected by the employee, the employee may be subject to an excess contribution penalty tax (see Qs 4:96–4:107).

Q 4:96　Are excess contributions subject to penalty?

Yes. In general, an excise tax of 6 percent for each taxable year is imposed on the HSA owner for excess individual and employer contributions "made for the year" (see Q 4:92). [I.R.C. § 4973(a)(5); I.R.S. Notice 2004-2, Q&A 22, 2004-2 I.R.B. 269]

Q 4:97　Can the excess contribution penalty be avoided?

Yes. The 6 percent cumulative penalty can be avoided if the excess contributions for a taxable year (and the net income attributable to such excess contributions) are paid to the HSA owner before the last day prescribed by law (including extensions) for filing the HSA owner's federal income tax return for the taxable year (see Q 4:92). [I.R.C. § 223(f)(3)(A)(i))] No deduction or exclusion can be claimed for an excess contribution. If an individual claims a deduction or excludes an excess contribution from income, the 6 percent penalty cannot be avoided (until properly corrected). (See Q 4:99.)

Caution. If the net income is not distributed in a correcting distribution made *before* the tax return due date, the amount distributed, including anything less than the attributable earnings, is treated as a regular distribution and the 6 percent excise tax will apply. [I.R.C. § 223(f)(3)(A)(ii)]

Q 4:98　When is the net income attributable to the excess contribution taxable?

The net income attributable to the excess contribution removed before the tax filing date is included in the HSA owner's gross income for the taxable year in which the distribution is received. However, the 6 percent excise tax is not imposed on the excess contribution, and the distribution of the excess contribution is not taxed. [I.R.C. § 223(f)(3)(A); I.R.S. Notice 2004-2, Q&A 22, 2004-2 I.R.B. 269]

Q 4:99　What is the result if the net income is not distributed in a correcting distribution?

If there is any net income (or loss) on the excess contribution, it must be distributed in a correcting distribution that is made before the tax filing date. If the net income is not distributed, the amount is treated as a regular distribution and the 6 percent tax applies (see Q 4:92). [I.R.C. § 223(f)(3)(A)(ii)]

Q 4:100   Is the excess contribution distributed in a correcting distribution subject to tax?

No. Although the net income in a correcting distribution is taxable in the year withdrawn, the distribution of an excess contribution (timely corrected) is not subject to tax as long as such contribution was made on an after-tax basis by the individual. [I.R.C. § 223(f)(3); I.R.S. Notice 2004-2, Q&A 22, 2004-2 I.R.B. 269]

Q 4:101   How are earnings attributable to the excess HSA contribution calculated?

Earnings attributable to excess HSA contributions are computed in exactly the same manner as excess IRA contributions. [Treas. Reg. § 1.408-11(a); I.R.S. Notice 2004-50, Q&A 34, 2004-33 I.R.B. 196; see also I.R.S. Notice 2004-2, Q&A 22, 2004-2 I.R.B. 269]

Beginning after 2003, the new formula for calculating the net income on a returned excess contribution under the final regulations is:

Net Income[1] = Contribution[2] × (ACB[3] minus AOB[4]) divided by AOB

----

[1] Net Income can be positive or negative.

[2] The amount of the contribution that is being returned.

[3] The adjusted closing balance (see Q 4:102).

[4] The adjusted opening balance (see Q 4:103).

> **Note.** Net earnings may be positive or negative. Thus, any loss in the account is taken into account when calculating the amount to be withdrawn. For example, if the net income attributable to a $500 excess contribution is a negative $30, the correcting distribution would be $470. The amount is not taxable, nor subject to penalty.

Q 4:102   What is the adjusted closing balance used in computing earnings on an excess contribution?

The *adjusted closing balance* (ACB) is the fair market value (FMV) of the HSA at the end of the computation period plus the amount of any distributions or transfers made from the HSA during the computation period (see Q 4:104). Thus, the ACB is the value just before the distribution or recharacterization.

Q 4:103   What is the adjusted opening balance used in computing earnings on an excess contribution?

The *adjusted opening balance* (AOB) is the FMV of the HSA at the beginning of the computation period (see Q 4:104) plus the amount of any contributions (including the contribution that is being returned) or transfers made to the HSA during the computation period.

Where a series of regular contributions was made, the contribution being returned is deemed to be the last contribution made, up to the amount of the contribution identified as the amount to be distributed.

Note. The final regulations do not clarify whether the individual or trustee (or custodian) is responsible for calculating the net income on an excess contribution. Some trustees (and custodians) do not perform this computation.

Q 4:104   What is the computation period used in computing earnings on an excess contribution?

The *computation period* is the period beginning immediately before "the time" that the contribution being returned was made to the HSA and ending immediately before the removal of the contribution.

Q 4:105   How is the account valued when correcting an excess HSA contribution?

The preamble to the final regulations implies that if the account is valued on a daily basis, for purposes of determining the AOB the computation period begins the exact day before the contribution that is being returned was made. If the account is not valued on a daily basis, for purposes of determining the AOB the FMV at the beginning of the computation period is deemed to be the most recent, regularly determined, FMV of the account as of a date that coincides with or precedes the first day of the computation period (that is, the most recent statement value). [Treas. Reg. § 1.408-11, Preamble]

Q 4:106   May an excess contribution be corrected after the extended due date of the individual's federal income tax return?

Yes. After the tax return due date (including any extensions) has passed, an excess contribution may still be corrected by withdrawing the amount of the excess. It is not necessary to remove attributable earnings (gain). Even if the excess amount received in the correcting distribution (not timely completed) is used to pay for qualified medical expenses, the amount distributed will be taxable and, unless an exception applies (e.g., death, disability, or enrolled in Medicare), is subject to a 10 percent additional tax. The 6 percent penalty, however, will no longer apply to the excess contribution after a correcting distribution is made.

In computing the reduction of the taxable portion of HSA distributions in Part II of Form 8889—*Health Savings Accounts,* relating to unreimbursed qualified medical expenses, the return of excess contributions made after the return due date does not reduce the taxable amount. The Instructions for Line 15 (unreimbursed qualified medical expenses) Form 8889 state: "Do not include the distribution of an excess contribution taken out after the due date, including extensions, of your return even if used for qualified medical expenses." The exclusion for the payment or reimbursement of qualified medical expenses from an HSA only applies if the amount is used "exclusively" for such purposes (and not when used to correct an excess contribution). [I.R.C. § 223(f)(2); see also Instructions for Lines 14 and 15 on Form 8889—*Health Savings Accounts (HSAs)*] Thus, the distribution of an excess contribution after the tax return due date (including extensions) will be a taxable event (see exception for timely filers in Q 4:107).

Example 1. Marleen, an eligible individual, made an excess contribution into an HSA of $300 for 2009. She removes $310 (the excess contribution and attributable gain) on February 10, 2010. The gain of $10 is taxable in the year withdrawn (2010). The returned excess of $300 is not subject to income tax or the 10 percent additional tax (see Qs 6:9, 6:72–6:76). The gain ($10), is reported as "Other Income" on Marleen's tax return, but is not subject to the 10 percent additional tax. The 6 percent penalty does not apply for 2009 because the excess amount was withdrawn (with gain) before the due date of Marleen's federal income tax return (including extensions).

Note. An HSA is not subject to the 10 percent tax on premature distributions under Code Section 72(t). That section does not apply to an HSA. [I.R.C. § 72(t)(1), referring to I.R.C. § 4974(c)]

Note. The distribution of gain attributable to the correction of excess contribution (generally *before* the return due date) is not subject to the additional 10 percent tax under Code Section 223(f), referring to distributions from an HSA not used for qualified medical expenses (see Q 6:72). [See Part II of Form 8889—*Health Savings Accounts (HSAs)*] On that form, excess contributions "and the earnings on those excess contributions" are subtracted from the total HSA distributions that could be subject to the additional 10 percent penalty under Code Section 223(f) if not used for qualified medical expenses. In the case of an excess HSA contribution returned before the due date of the individual's federal income tax return, the provisions requiring the inclusion of amounts not used for qualified medical expenses—and subject to the additional 10 percent penalty, unless made after age 65, death or disability—do not apply. Therefore, the 10 percent tax under Code Section 223(f)(4) does not apply to an excess contribution that is returned before the return due date. [See I.R.C. § 223(f)(2), 223(f)(3)(A), 223(f)(4)]

Example 2. Hank, an eligible individual, made an excess contribution into an HSA of $500 for 2009. His federal income tax return is due on April 15, 2010. He does not have a filing extension and filed his return five days late. Assume Hank removes $600 on April 25, 2010. The correcting distribution (made after April 15) was not timely made. Hank did not claim a deduction for his contribution. Hank must pay a 6 percent penalty tax on the $500 excess contribution. The gross income inclusion and 10 percent tax in Code Section 223(f)(3) for distributions not used for qualified medical expenses do not apply because Hank timely withdrew an excess contribution (see Q 6:72) and did not claim a deduction for the contribution.

Even if the amount is used to pay for qualified medical expenses, the amount distributed ($600) will be taxable and, unless an exception applies, also subject to a 10 percent penalty tax (see Qs 6:9, 6:72). The $500 will be treated as a 2010 contribution for penalty purposes. Assuming no excess contributions are made for 2010, the 6 percent excess contribution penalty tax will no longer apply. If Hank had filed his return on April 15, 2010, he might have avoided the 6 percent penalty and taxation of the amount by requesting a six-month extension (see below) that is only available for timely filers to remove excess contribution and attributable gain.

Extension for timely filers. If the tax return was timely filed without withdrawing the excess contributions, the withdrawal can be made no later than six months after the due date of the tax return, excluding extensions. Under the extension, the withdrawal is treated as a before-the-due-date correction (see Q 4:98). If applicable, file an amended return with "Filed pursuant to Section 301.9100-2" written at the top. Report any related earnings for 2009 on the amended return and include an explanation of the withdrawal. Make any other necessary changes on the amended return (e.g., if the contributions were reported as excess contributions on the original return, include an amended Form 5329 reflecting that the withdrawn contributions are no longer treated as having been contributed).

Q 4:107   How are excess HSA contributions corrected after the due date of the owner's return?

Correcting Excess After the Due Date

Unless the timely filer extension previously explained is used, the excess contribution amount will be taxable and, absent an exception, also subject to the 6 percent tax. The 6 percent tax may not exceed the value in the account at the close of the taxable year. [I.R.C. § 4973(a)] If the correction is made before the due date of the return or within the timely filer extension rules, the 6 percent penalty will not apply to the excess contribution. [I.R.C. § 223(f)(3)(A) and (B)] After the due date of the return, the correcting distribution rules do not provide for or require that net earnings (positive or negative) be distributed. [I.R.C. § 223(f)(3)(A)(ii)] Any net income distributed in a correcting distribution (as is required before the tax filing deadline) is included in income in the year in which it is received.

Example 1. Yetta, an eligible individual, made an excess after-tax contribution to an HSA of $300 for 2009. She removes $310, the excess contribution and net income thereon, on February 10, 2010. The net income of $10 is taxable in 2010 and reported as "Other income" on the individual's federal tax return. The net income ($10) distributed is not subject to the 10 percent additional tax (see Q 6:72). The returned excess of $300 is not subject to income tax nor subject to the 10 percent penalty. The 6 percent penalty does not apply for 2009 because the excess amount was withdrawn (with net earnings attributable) before the due date of Yetta's federal income tax return (including extensions) for the year. Excess contributions and gain thereon are returned under Code Section 223(f)(3). [See I.R.C. § 223(f)(4)(A), referring to I.R.C. § 223(f)(2)]

Example 2. Sheldon, an eligible individual, made an excess after-tax contribution to an HSA of $500 for 2009. His federal income tax return is due on April 15, 2010. He does not have a filing extension. Assume Sheldon removes $600 (the excess contribution plus another $100 related to earnings) on April 25, 2010. The correcting distribution (made after April 15) was not timely made. Sheldon must pay a 6 percent penalty tax on the $500 excess contribution. Even if the amount is used to pay for qualified medical expenses, the amount distributed, $600, also will be taxable and, unless an exception applies, also subject to the additional 10 percent penalty tax. Assuming no excess contributions are made for 2010, the 6 percent excess contribution penalty tax no longer will apply in respect to 2009.

Q 4:108   May an individual who has not made excess HSA contributions treat a distribution from an HSA other than for qualified medical expenses as the withdrawal of excess HSA contributions?

No. An individual may not elect to treat a distribution as a correction of an excess contribution unless the individual's contribution limit is exceeded. [I.R.S. Notice 2004-50, Q&A 35, 2004-33 I.R.B. 196] Any such withdrawal is deemed a withdrawal for nonqualified medical expenses and includible in the individual's gross income. The 10 percent additional tax also applies, unless an exception applies (see Q 6:74). [I.R.S. Notice 2004-50, Q&A 35, 2004-33 I.R.B. 196]

Employer Contributions and ERISA

Q 4:109   Is an HSA established in connection with an employment-based group health plan treated as an employee welfare benefit plan under Title I of ERISA?

Generally, no. An employer can make contributions to the HSA of an eligible individual without being considered to have established or maintained the HSA as an ERISA-covered plan, provided that the employer's involvement with the HSA is limited. ERISA issues are more fully discussed in chapter 8.

[Field Assistance Bulletin 2004-01 (Apr. 7, 2004) and Field Assistance Bulletin 2006-02 (Oct. 27, 2006); 29 C.F.R. § 2510.3-1(j)(1)-(4); see also 29 C.F.R. § 2509.99-1 relating to payroll deduction IRAs]

Q 4:110   Is an employer required to make COBRA continuation coverage available with respect to an HSA?

No. An employer's contribution to an HSA is not considered to be part of a group health plan. [I.R.C. §§ 106(b)(5), 106(d)(2); see also Treas. Reg.

§ 54.4980B-2, A-1Q&A 1, regarding Archer MSAs] Thus, an employer is not required to make COBRA continuation coverage under the Consolidated Omnibus Budget Reconciliation Act (COBRA) available with respect to an HSA. [I.R.S. Notice 2004-2, Q&A 35, 2004-2 I.R.B. 269] It should be noted, however, that an ERISA-covered HSA (i.e., an employee welfare benefit plan) may be subject to COBRA (see Qs 8:18, 8:20). [ERISA § 607(i)]

If COBRA continuation coverage is required to be made available, the HDHP must comply with the requirements of Treasury Regulations Section 54.4980B-5 Q&A 2 for those individuals receiving COBRA continuation coverage (see Q 4:110). Generally, under that section, if the pro rata allocation of expenses are less than the actual expenses incurred, then allocation of only a ratable share of the family expenses would *not* comply with the requirements of Q&A 2 of § 54.4980B. [I.R.S. Notice 2008-59, Q&A 12, 2008-29 I.R.B. 123]

Q 4:111   Do the rules under Code Section 419 regarding funded welfare benefit plans affect contributions by an employer to an HSA?

No. Contributions by an employer to an HSA are not subject to the rules under Code Section 419 regarding funded welfare benefit plans. An HSA is a trust or custodial account that is exempt from tax under Code Section 223. Thus, an HSA is not a *fund* under Code Section 419(e)(3) and, therefore, is not a *welfare benefit fund* under Code Section 419(e)(1). [I.R.S. Notice 2004-2, Q&A 36, 2004-2 I.R.B. 269] Neither are contributions subject to the excise tax with respect to funded welfare benefit plans that provide disqualified benefits. [I.R.C. § 4976(a)(1)]

Q 4:112   Do the minimum funding standards under Code Section 412 apply to an HSA?

No. Code Section 412 applies only to certain types of qualified plans under Code Sections 401(a) or 403(a). [I.R.C. § 412(a)] Thus, an employer HSA is not subject to the excise tax relating to minimum funding standards. [I.R.C. §§ 412(a), 4971(a)]

Q 4:113   Are employer contributions to an HSA subject to the 10 percent tax on nondeductible employer contributions?

No. The excise tax under Code Section 4972 on nondeductible employer contributions does not apply to an HSA. [I.R.C. §§ 4972(a), 4972(d)] It should be noted that employer contributions to an HSA are generally excluded from an employee's gross income (see Q 4:60).

Comparability of Employer Contributions

In July 2006, the IRS published final comparability regulations governing employer contributions to HSAs. The final regulations are effective for employer contributions made on or after January 1, 2008. [Treas. Reg. § 54.4980G-1 through 5; 71 Fed. Reg. 43056 (July 31, 2006)] The final regulations reserved several questions for future determination. In June 2008, the IRS issued proposed rules on the comparable contribution rules that govern employer contributions made to HSAs outside of a Code Section 125 cafeteria plan. The proposed rules provide guidance for employers when employees fail to establish an HSA or notify their employers of their HSA prior to December 31 (see Q 4:141). The proposed rules also permit employers to make accelerated calendar-year contributions for employees who incur qualified medical expenses exceeding current HSA contributions (see Q 4:140).

Q 4:114   What are the comparability rules that apply to employer contributions to an HSA?

In general, if an employer chooses to make HSA contributions, then the employer is required to make comparable HSA contributions for all eligible employees with the same category of coverage. If an employer contributes to the HSA of any employee covered under an HDHP provided by the employer, the employer is required to make comparable contributions to all eligible individuals with coverage under any HDHP provided by the employer during a calendar year. An employer that contributes to the HSAs of employees who are covered under the HDHP *provided* by the employer is not required to make comparable contributions to HSAs of employees who are not covered under the HDHP provided by the employer. However, an employer that contributes to the HSA of any eligible individual who are covered under *any* HDHP, even if that coverage is not under an HDHP provided by the employer, must make comparable contributions to all eligible individuals whether or not they are covered under an HDHP provided by the employer. Thus, comparable participating employees must receive comparable contributions if any contributions are made. [I.R.C. §§ 4980E(d), 4980G; Treas. Reg. § 54.4980G-1 through 5]

> **Example.** Meteor Corporation offers its employees three health plans, including HDHP self-only coverage with a $2,000 deductible. For each employee electing the HDHP self-only coverage, Meteor contributes $1,000 per year on behalf of the employee to an HSA. Meteor makes no HSA contributions for employees who do not elect the HDHP coverage. Meteor's HSA contributions satisfy the comparability rule.

Q 4:115   Who are comparable participating employees?

Comparable participating employees are eligible individuals (see Q 2:6) who are in the same category of employees and who have the same category of HDHP coverage (see Q 4:116). [I.R.C. §§ 4980G(b) and 4980E(d)(3); Treas. Reg.

§ 54.4980G-4, Q&A1] (See Qs 4:127, 4:130, 4:131, 4:136–4:138 for the treatment of collectively bargained employees.)

The comparable contribution rules generally preclude an employer from making contributions to HSAs on behalf of non-highly compensated employees (NHCEs) in higher amounts (or higher percentages of deductibles) than to highly compensated employees (HCEs). However, beginning in tax years after 2006, the TRHCA allows employers to make contributions to HSAs on behalf of NHCEs in higher amounts (or higher percentages of deductibles) than to HCEs without violating the comparable contribution rules. [I.R.C. § 4980G(d), added by TRHCA § 306(a)] Under the new provision, employers are permitted to make greater HSA contributions on behalf of NHCEs, but must satisfy the comparability rules with respect to contributions to NHCEs. For these purposes, HCEs are defined under Code Section 414(q), which generally means for 2009, an individual who earned less than $110,000 (the 2009 limit) in the preceding year (2008) and was not a more-than-5-percent owner during that year or the current year.

> **Example.** Glass Corporation makes a $1,000 contribution on behalf of each NHCE in 2009, but does not make any contributions for Kate, an employee who earns in excess of $110,000. Because Kate is an HCE, she is not treated as a comparable participating employee. The comparability rules are not violated.

However, the comparability rules would not be satisfied if the employer contributed a different amount or rate to some, but not all, of the NHCE (even though HCEs received nothing or a lower amount or percentage than NHCEs).

Categories of Coverage Relating to Comparability

Q 4:116   What are the categories of HDHP coverage for purposes of applying the comparability rules?

In general there are only two categories of coverage (a) self-only HDHP coverage and (b) family HDHP coverage.

In general, if an employer makes comparable contributions, the contributions must be comparable for all comparable participating employees. Comparable participating employees are eligible individuals who are in the same category of employees and who have the same category of HDHP coverage. The final regulations allow several categories of HDHPs. HDHP coverage can be divided into the following categories: [I.R.C. § 4980G(b); Treas. Reg. § 54.4980G-1, Q&A 2]

- Self-only;
- Self plus 1;
- Self plus 2;
- Self plus 3; and
- Family HDHP coverage categories.

Example 1. Thread Corporation maintains an HDHP and contributes to the HSAs of eligible employees who elect coverage under the HDHP. The HDHP has self-only coverage and family coverage. Thus, the categories of coverage are self-only and family coverage. Thread contributes $750 to the HSA of each eligible employee with self-only HDHP coverage and $1,000 to the HSA of each eligible employee with family HDHP coverage. Thread's contributions satisfy the comparability rules.

Example 2. Wax Corporation maintains an HDHP and contributes to the HSAs of eligible employees who elect coverage under the HDHP. The HDHP has the following coverage options:

- Self-only;
- Self plus spouse;
- Self plus dependent;
- Self plus spouse plus one dependent;
- Self plus two dependents; and
- Self plus spouse and two or more dependents.

The self plus spouse category and the self plus dependent category constitute the same category of HDHP coverage (self plus one) and Wax must make the same comparable contributions to the HSAs of all eligible individuals who are in either the self plus spouse category of HDHP coverage or the self plus dependent category of HDHP coverage. Likewise, the self plus spouse plus one dependent category and the self plus two dependents category constitute the same category of HDHP coverage (self plus two) and Wax must make the same comparable contributions to the HSAs of all eligible individuals who are in either the self plus spouse plus one dependent category of HDHP coverage or the self plus two dependents category of HDHP coverage.

Example 3. Cream Corporation maintains an HDHP and contributes to the HSAs of eligible employees who elect coverage under the HDHP. The HDHP has the following coverage options:

- Self-only;
- Self plus one;
- Self plus two; and
- Self plus three or more.

Cream contributes $500 to the HSA of each eligible employee with self-only HDHP coverage, $750 to the HSA of each eligible employee with self plus one HDHP coverage, $900 to the HSA of each eligible employee with self plus two HDHP coverage, and $1,000 to the HSA of each eligible employee with self plus three or more HDHP coverage. Cream's contributions satisfy the comparability rules.

Q 4:117   What is family HDHP coverage?

Family HDHP coverage means any coverage other than self-only HDHP coverage. [Treas. Reg. § 54.4980G-1, Q&A 2]

Testing Period for Comparability

Q 4:118   What is the testing period for making comparable contributions to employees' HSAs?

To satisfy the comparability rules, an employer must make comparable contributions (see Q 4:126) for the calendar year to the HSAs of employees who are comparable participating employees. [I.R.C. § 4980G(a)); Treas. Reg. § 54.4980G-1, Q&A 3]

The Excise Tax and Comparability

Q 4:119   What are the consequences of violating the comparability rules?

If the employer violates the comparability rules, then the sum of *all* the contributions that the employer made to HSAs for the year are subject to the 35 percent excise tax. There is no exception for an individual based on different coverage status or employment status. All contributions are subject to the excise tax, even if the failure was limited to one coverage status. Presumably, the employer should still be able to take a deduction for such contributions under Code Section 162, however, as long as such compensation is reasonable. The regulations also state that the excise tax can be waived in situations where the excise tax imposed is excessive relative to the failure involved. [I.R.C. §§ 4980G(b); 4980E(c); Prop. Treas. Reg. § 54.4980G-5, Q&A 5; I.R.S. Notice 2004-2, Q&A 32, 2004-2 I.R.B. 269]

> **Example.** During the 2009 calendar year, Orange Corporation has eight employees who are eligible individuals with self-only coverage under an HDHP provided by Orange. The deductible for the HDHP is $2,000. For the 2009 calendar year, Orange contributes $2,000 each to the HSAs of two employees and $1,000 each to the HSAs of the other six employees, for total HSA contributions of $10,000. Orange's contributions do not satisfy the comparability rules. Therefore, Orange is subject to an excise tax of $3,500 (35% of $10,000) for its failure to make comparable contributions to its employees' HSAs.

> **Note.** If an employer wants to correct a violation of the comparability rules, the employer cannot reduce the contributions already made to an HSA; additional contributions to an HSA must be made to employees who did not receive a comparable contribution. The additional contributions must be made by April 15 of the following year. A reasonable interest factor must be included on these correcting contributions; however, there is no requirement that the contribution be in excess of the maximum annual HSA contribution limit. [I.R.C. § 4980G; Prop. Treas. Reg. § 54.4980G-4, Q&A 12]

Employer Contributions

Q 4:120   Do the comparability rules apply to amounts rolled over from an employee's HSA or Archer Medical Savings Account (Archer MSA)?

No. The comparability rules do not apply to amounts rolled over from an employee's HSA or Archer MSA. [Treas. Reg. § 54.4980G-2, Q&A 1]

Q 4:121   If an employee requests that his or her employer deduct after-tax amounts from the employee's compensation and forward these amounts as employee contributions to the employee's HSA, do the comparability rules apply to these amounts?

No. Amounts contributed by an employer to an eligible employee's HSA are treated as employer-provided coverage for medical expenses and are excludable from the employee's gross income up to the annual contribution limit (see Q 4:30). However, after-tax employee contributions (e.g., by payroll reduction) to an HSA are not subject to the comparability rules because they are not treated as employer contributions. [I.R.C. § 106(d); Treas. Reg. § 54.4980G-2, Q&A 2]

Employee for Comparability Testing

Q 4:122   Do the comparability rules apply to contributions that an employer makes to the HSAs of independent contractors or self-employed individuals?

No. The comparability rules apply only to contributions that an employer makes to the HSAs of employees. [Treas. Reg. § 54.4980G-3, Q&A 1]

Q 4:123   May a sole proprietor who is an eligible individual contribute to his or her own HSA without contributing to the HSAs of his or her employees who are eligible individuals?

Yes. The comparability rules apply only to contributions made by an employer to the HSAs of employees. Because a sole proprietor is not an employee, the comparability rules do not apply to contributions the sole proprietor makes to his or her own HSA. However, if a sole proprietor contributes to any employee's HSA, the sole proprietor must make comparable contributions to the HSAs of all comparable participating employees. In determining whether the comparability rules are satisfied, contributions that a sole proprietor makes to his or her own HSA are not taken into account. [Treas. Reg. § 54.4980G-3, Q&A 2]

> **Example.** Robert, a sole proprietor and an eligible individual for the calendar year, contributes $1,000 to his own HSA. Robert also contributes $500 for the same calendar year to the HSA of each employee who is an eligible individual. The comparability rules are not violated by Robert's $1,000 contribution to his own HSA.

Q 4:124   Do the comparability rules apply to contributions by a partnership to a partner's HSA?

No. Contributions by a partnership to a bona fide partner's HSA are not subject to the comparability rules because the contributions are not contributions by an employer to the HSA of an employee. The contributions are treated as either guaranteed payments under Code Section 707(c) or distributions under Code Section 731 (see Qs 4:156–4:167). However, if a partnership contributes to the HSAs of any employee who is not a partner, the partnership must make comparable contributions to the HSAs of all comparable participating employees. [Treas. Reg. § 54.4980G-3, Q&A 3]

> **Example.** Global Partnership is a limited partnership with three equal individual partners, Alan (a general partner), Ben (a limited partner), and Clyde (a limited partner). Clyde is to be paid $300 annually for services rendered to Global Partnership in his capacity as a partner without regard to partnership income (a Code Section 707(c) guaranteed payment). Dave and Eunice are the only employees of Global Partnership and are not partners in Global Partnership. Dave and Eunice are both comparable participating employees. Alan, Ben, Clyde, Dave, and Eunice are eligible individuals and each has an HSA. During Global Partnership's Year 1 taxable year, which is also a calendar year, Global Partnership makes the following contributions:
>
> - $300 to each of Alan's and Ben's HSAs which are treated as Code Section 731 distributions to Alan and Ben;
> - $300 to Clyde's HSA in lieu of paying Clyde the guaranteed payment directly; and
> - $200 to Dave's and $200 to Eunice's HSAs,
>
> Global's contributions to Alan's and Ben's HSAs are Code Section 731 distributions, which are treated as cash distributions. Global's contribution to Clyde's HSA is treated as a guaranteed payment under Code Section 707(c). The contribution is not excludable from Clyde's gross income under Code Section 106(d) because the contribution is treated as a distributive share of partnership income for purposes of all Code sections (other than Code Sections 61(a) and 162(a)), and a guaranteed payment to a partner is not treated as compensation to an employee. Thus, Global Partnership's contributions to the HSAs of Alan, Ben, and Clyde are not subject to the comparability rules. Global Partnership's contributions to Dave's and Eunice's HSAs are subject to the comparability rules because Dave and Eunice are employees of Global Partnership and are not partners in Global Partnership. Global Partnership's contributions satisfy the comparability rules. [Treas. Reg. § 54.4980G-3, Q&A 3]

Q 4:125   How are members of controlled groups treated when applying the comparability rules?

All persons or entities that are related, controlled, or affiliated are treated as a single employer. [I.R.C. §§ 414 (b), (c), (m), (o); I.R.C. §§ 4980G(b), 4980E(e); Treas. Reg. § 54.4980G-3, Q&A 4]

Comparable Contributions

Q 4:126   What are the categories of employees for comparability testing?

In general, the categories of employees listed below are the exclusive categories for comparability testing. The categories of employees are as follows:

1. Current full-time employees (customarily employed for 30 or more hours per week);

2. Current part-time employees (customarily employed for fewer than 30 hours per week); and

3. Former employees (except for former employees with coverage under the employer's HDHP because of an election under a COBRA continuation provision (see Code Section 9832(d)(1))).

[Treas. Reg. § 54.4980G-3, Q&A 5(a)(1)-(3), (b); I.R.C. §§ 4980G(b), 4980E(d)(4)(A)–(B)]

An employer must make comparable contributions to the HSAs of all comparable participating employees (i.e., eligible individuals who are in the same category of employees with the same category of HDHP coverage) during the calendar year without regard to any classification other than these categories. For example, full-time eligible employees with self-only HDHP coverage and part-time eligible employees with self-only HDHP coverage are separate categories of employees and different amounts can be contributed to the HSAs for each of these categories.

Collectively Bargained Employees

Q 4:127   Do the comparability rules apply to unionized employees or groups of collectively bargained employees?

No. If health benefits were the subject of good faith bargaining between employee representatives and the employer, employees and former employees covered by such collective bargaining agreement are not subject to the comparability rules. Therefore an employer who makes HSA contributions to any of its non-collectively bargained employees may agree to: (1) not make HSA contributions to any of its non-collectively bargained employees; (2) make HSA contributions under some collective bargaining agreements and not others; or (3) provide different levels of HSA contributions under different collective bargaining agreements. [Treas. Reg. § 54.4980G-3, Q&A 6] See also Qs 4:130, 4:136–4:137.

Example 1. Mustard Corporation offers its employees an HDHP with a $1,500 deductible for self-only coverage. Mustard has collectively bargained and non-collectively bargained employees. The collectively bargained employees are covered by a collective bargaining agreement under which health benefits were bargained in good faith. In the 2009 calendar year, Mustard contributes $500 to the HSAs of all eligible non-collectively bargained employees with self-only coverage under Mustard's HDHP. Mustard does not contribute to the HSAs of the collectively bargained employees. Mustard's contributions to the HSAs of non-collectively bargained employees satisfy the comparability rules. The comparability rules do not apply to collectively bargained employees.

Example 2. Spice Corporation offers its employees an HDHP with a $1,500 deductible for self-only coverage. Spice has collectively bargained and non-collectively bargained employees. The collectively bargained employees are covered by a collective bargaining agreement under which health benefits were bargained in good faith. In the 2009 calendar year and in accordance with the terms of the collective bargaining agreement, Spice contributes to the HSAs of all eligible collectively bargained employees. Spice does not contribute to the HSAs of the non-collectively bargained employees. Spice's contributions to the HSAs of collectively bargained employees are not subject to the comparability rules because the comparability rules do not apply to collectively bargained employees. Accordingly, Spice's failure to contribute to the HSAs of the non-collectively bargained employees does not violate the comparability rules.

Example 3. Box Corporation has two units of collectively bargained employees—unit Blue and unit Red—each covered by a collective bargaining agreement under which health benefits were bargained in good faith. In the 2009 calendar year and in accordance with the terms of the collective bargaining agreement, Box contributes to the HSAs of all eligible collectively bargained employees in unit Blue. In accordance with the terms of the collective bargaining agreement, Box makes no HSA contributions for collectively bargained employees in unit Red. Box contributions to the HSAs of collectively bargained employees are not subject to the comparability rules because the comparability rules do not apply to collectively bargained employees.

Example 4. Dalmatian Corporation has a unit of collectively bargained employees that are covered by a collective bargaining agreement under which health benefits were bargained in good faith. In accordance with the terms of the collective bargaining agreement, Dalmatian contributes an amount equal to a specified number of cents per hour for each hour worked to the HSAs of all eligible collectively bargained employees. Dalmatian's contributions to the HSAs of collectively bargained employees are not subject to the comparability rules because the comparability rules do not apply to collectively bargained employees.

Coverage Requirements Under HDHPs

Q 4:128   Is an employer permitted to make comparable contributions only to the HSAs of comparable participating employees who have coverage under the employer's HDHP?

Possibly. If during a calendar year an employer contributes to the HSA of any employee who is an eligible individual covered under an HDHP provided by the employer, the employer is required to make comparable contributions to the

HSAs of all comparable participating employees with coverage under any HDHP provided by the employer. An employer that contributes only to the HSAs of employees who are eligible individuals with coverage under the employer's HDHP is not required to make comparable contributions to HSAs of employees who are eligible individuals but are not covered under the employer's HDHP. However, an employer that contributes to the HSA of any employee who is an eligible individual with coverage under any HDHP, in addition to the HDHPs provided by the employer, must make comparable contributions to the HSAs of all comparable participating employees whether or not covered under the employer's HDHP. [I.R.S. Notice 2004-50, Q&A 53, 2004-33 I.R.B. 196; see also I.R.S. Notice 2004-2, Q&A 32, 2004-2 I.R.B. 269; Treas. Reg. § 54.4980G-3, Q&A 7(a)]

> **Example 1.** In a calendar year, Equinox Corporation offers an HDHP to its full-time employees. Most full-time employees are covered under Equinox's HDHP and Equinox makes comparable contributions only to these employees' HSAs. Henry, a full-time employee of Equinox and an eligible individual, is covered under an HDHP provided by the employer of Henry's spouse and not under Equinox's HDHP. Equinox is not required to make comparable contributions to Henry's HSA.

> **Example 2.** In a calendar year, Falcon Corporation does not offer an HDHP. Several full-time employees of Falcon, who are eligible individuals, have HSAs. Falcon contributes to these employees' HSAs. Falcon must make comparable contributions to the HSAs of all full-time employees who are eligible individuals.

> **Example 3.** In a calendar year, Giant Corporation offers an HDHP to its full-time employees. Most full-time employees are covered under Giant's HDHP and Giant makes comparable contributions to these employees' HSAs and also to the HSAs of full-time employees who are eligible individuals and who are not covered under Giant's HDHP. Sam, a full-time employee of Giant and a comparable participating employee, is covered under an HDHP provided by the employer of Sam's spouse and not under Giant's HDHP. Giant must make comparable contributions to Sam's HSA.

Q 4:129   If an employee and his or her spouse are eligible individuals who work for the same employer and one employee-spouse has family coverage for both employees under the employer's HDHP, must the employer make comparable contributions to the HSAs of both employees?

Possibly. If the employer makes contributions only to the HSAs of employees who are eligible individuals covered under its HDHP, the employer is generally not required to contribute to the HSAs of both employee-spouses. The employer is required to contribute to the HSA of the employee-spouse with coverage under the employer's HDHP, but is not required to contribute to the HSA of the employee-spouse covered under the employer's HDHP by virtue of his or her spouse's coverage. However, if the employer contributes to the HSA of any employee who is an eligible individual with coverage under any HDHP, the employer must make comparable contributions to the HSAs of both employee-spouses if they are both eligible individuals. If an employer is required to contribute to the HSAs of both employee-spouses, the employer is not required to contribute amounts in excess of the annual contribution limits (see Q 4:30). [I.R.C. § 223(b); Treas. Reg. § 54.4980G-3, Q&A 8(a)]

> **Example 1.** In a calendar year, House Corporation offers an HDHP to its full-time employees. Most full-time employees are covered under House's HDHP and House makes comparable contributions only to these employees' HSAs. Thomas and Ulma are married. Thomas, who is a full-time employee of House and an eligible individual, has family coverage under House's HDHP for Thomas and his spouse. Ulma, who is also a full-time employee of House and an eligible individual, does not have coverage under House's HDHP except as the spouse of Thomas. House is required to make comparable contributions to Thomas's HSA, but is not required to make comparable contributions to Ulma's HSA.

> **Example 2.** In a calendar year, Jelly Corporation offers an HDHP to its full-time employees. Most full-time employees are covered under Jelly's HDHP and Jelly makes comparable contributions to these employees' HSAs and to the HSAs of full-time employees who are eligible individuals but are not covered under Jelly HDHP. Richard and Sheila are married. Sheila, who is a full-time employee of Jelly and an eligible individual, has family coverage under Jelly's HDHP for Sheila and her spouse. Richard, who is also a full-time employee of Jelly and an eligible individual, does not have coverage under Jelly's HDHP except as the spouse of Sheila. Jelly must make comparable contributions to Sheila's HSA and to Richard's HSA.

Q 4:130 Does an employer that makes HSA contributions only for one class of non-collectively bargained employees who are eligible individuals but not for another class of non-collectively bargained employees who are eligible individuals (for example, management v. nonmanagement) satisfy the requirement that the employer make comparable contributions?

Possibly. If management employees and nonmanagement employees have HDHP coverage through the employer, the comparability rules are not satisfied unless the employer makes equal contributions or contributes an equal percentage of the HDHP deductibles to the HSAs of these employees. However, if management employees do not have HDHP coverage through the employer, but nonmanagement employees do, nonmanagement employees are comparable participating employees and management employees are not comparable participating employees. In that case, the comparability rules may be satisfied even if the employer makes different contributions to these groups (but see Q 4:149 regarding contributions made through a cafeteria plan). [Treas. Reg. § 54.4980G-3, Q&A 9(a)]

Note. None of the employees in the following examples are covered by a collective bargaining agreement.

Example 1. In a calendar year, Kite Corporation maintains an HDHP covering all management and nonmanagement employees. Kite contributes to the HSAs of nonmanagement employees who are eligible individuals covered under its HDHP. Kite does not contribute to the HSAs of its management employees who are eligible individuals covered under its HDHP. The comparability rules are not satisfied.

Example 2. All of Lock Corporation's employees are located in Indianapolis and Dallas. In a calendar year, Lock maintains an HDHP for all employees working in Indianapolis only. Lock does not maintain an HDHP for its employees working in Dallas. Lock contributes $500 to the HSAs of Indianapolis employees who are eligible individuals with coverage under its HDHP. Lock does not contribute to the HSAs of any of its Dallas employees. The comparability rules are satisfied because none of the employees in Dallas are covered under an HDHP of Lock. However, if any employees in Dallas were covered by an HDHP of Lock, Lock could not fail to contribute to their HSAs merely because they work in a different city.

Example 3. Mighty Corporation has two divisions, division Night and division Day. In a calendar year, Mighty maintains an HDHP for employees working in the Night and Day divisions. Mighty contributes to the HSAs of the Night division employees who are eligible individuals with coverage under its HDHP. Mighty does not contribute to the HSAs of division Day employees who are eligible individuals covered under its HDHP. The comparability rules are not satisfied.

Comparability and Former Employees

Q 4:131   If an employer contributes to the HSAs of former employees who are eligible individuals, do the comparability rules apply to these contributions?

Yes. The comparability rules apply to contributions an employer makes to former employees' HSAs. Therefore, if an employer contributes to any former employee's HSA, it must make comparable contributions to the HSAs of all comparable participating former employees (i.e., former employees who are eligible individuals with the same category of HDHP coverage). However, an employer is not required to make comparable contributions to the HSAs of former employees with coverage under the employer's HDHP because of an election under a COBRA continuation provision. The comparability rules apply separately to former employees because they are a separate category of covered employee (see Q 4:126). Also, former employees who were covered by a collective bargaining agreement immediately before termination of employment are not comparable participating employees (see Q 4:127). [Treas. Reg. § 54.4980G-3, Q&A 10(a)]

Note. None of the employees in the following examples are covered by a collective bargaining agreement.

Example 1. In a calendar year, Sunshine Corporation contributes $1,000 to the HSA of each current employee who is an eligible individual with coverage under any HDHP. Sunshine does not contribute to the HSA of any former employee who is an eligible individual. Sunshine's contributions satisfy the comparability rules.

Example 2. In a calendar year, Opal Corporation contributes to the HSAs of current employees and former employees who are eligible individuals covered under any HDHP. Opal contributes $750 to the HSA of each current employee with self-only HDHP coverage and $1,000 to the HSA of each current employee with family HDHP coverage. Opal also contributes $300 to the HSA of each former employee with self-only HDHP coverage and $400 to the HSA of each former employee with family HDHP coverage. Opal's contributions satisfy the comparability rules.

Q 4:132   What action must an employer take to locate former employees?

Where the employer is required to make comparable contributions to former employees, the employer must take "reasonable actions" to locate such eligible former employees. Reasonable actions include the use of certified mail, the Internal Revenue Service Letter Forwarding Program, or the Social Security Administration's Letter Forwarding Service. [Treas. Reg. § 54.4980G-3, Q&A 10(b)]

Caution. As a practical matter, the final regulations do not provide guidance regarding how an employer would go about determining whether any former employees might be covered under an HDHP other than one sponsored by that employer. The administrative burden of locating former employees and making this determination may result in employers limiting or eliminating HSA contributions to former employees. [Treas. Reg. § 54.4980G-3, Q&A 10(b)]

Q 4:133   Is an employer permitted to make comparable contributions only to the HSAs of comparable participating former employees who have coverage under the employer's HDHP?

Possibly. If, during a calendar year, an employer contributes to the HSA of any former employee who is an eligible individual covered under an HDHP provided by the employer, the employer is required to make comparable contributions to the HSAs of all former employees who are comparable participating former employees with coverage under any HDHP provided by the employer. An employer that contributes only to the HSAs of former employees who are eligible individuals with coverage under the employer's HDHP is not required to make comparable contributions to the HSAs of former employees who are eligible individuals and who are not covered under the employer's

HDHP. However, an employer that contributes to the HSA of any former employee who is an eligible individual with coverage under any HDHP, even if that coverage is not the employer's HDHP, must make comparable contributions to the HSAs of all former employees who are eligible individuals whether or not covered under an HDHP of the employer. [Treas. Reg. § 54.4980G-3, Q&A 11]

Q 4:134 If an employer contributes only to the HSAs of former employees who are eligible individuals with coverage under the employer's HDHP, must the employer make comparable contributions to the HSAs of former employees who are eligible individuals with coverage under the employer's HDHP because of an election under a COBRA continuation provision (as defined in Code Section 9832(d)(1))?

No. An employer that contributes only to the HSAs of former employees who are eligible individuals with coverage under the employer's HDHP is not required to make comparable contributions to the HSAs of former employees who are eligible individuals with coverage under the employer's HDHP because of an election under a COBRA continuation provision (as defined in Code Section 9832(d)(1)). [Treas. Reg. § 54.4980G-3, Q&A 12]

Comparability Rules Relating to Archer MSAs

Q 4:135 How do the comparability rules apply if some employees have HSAs and other employees have Archer MSAs?

The comparability rules apply separately to employees who have HSAs and employees who have Archer MSAs. However, if an employee has both an HSA and an Archer MSA, the employer may contribute to either the HSA or the Archer MSA, but not to both. [Treas. Reg. § 54.4980G-3, Q&A 13]

Example. In a calendar year, Pasta Corporation contributes $600 to the Archer MSA of each employee who is an eligible individual and who has an Archer MSA. Pasta contributes $500 for the calendar year to the HSA of each employee who is an eligible individual and who has an HSA. If an employee has an Archer MSA and an HSA, Pasta contributes to the employee's Archer MSA and not to the employee's HSA. Xavier, an employee of Pasta, has an Archer MSA and an HSA. Pasta contributes $600 for the calendar year to Xavier's Archer MSA but does not contribute to Xavier's HSA. Pasta's contributions satisfy the comparability rules.

Calculating Comparable Contributions

Q 4:136 What are comparable contributions under Code Section 4980G?

Contributions are comparable if, for each month in a calendar year, the contributions are either the same amount or the same percentage of the deductible under the HDHP for employees who are eligible individuals with the same category of coverage on the first day of that month. Employees with self-only HDHP coverage are tested separately from employees with family HDHP coverage. Similarly, employees with different categories of family HDHP coverage may be tested separately (see Q 4:116). An employer is not required to contribute the same amount or the same percentage of the deductible for employees who are eligible individuals with one category of HDHP coverage that it contributes for employees who are eligible individuals with a different category of HDHP coverage. For example, an employer that satisfies the comparability rules by contributing the same amount to the HSAs of all employees who are eligible individuals with family HDHP coverage is not required to contribute any amount to the HSAs of employees who are eligible individuals with self-only HDHP coverage, or to contribute the same percentage of the self-only HDHP deductible as the amount contributed with respect to family HDHP coverage. However, the contribution with respect to the self plus two category may not be less than the contribution with respect to the self plus one category and the contribution with respect to the self plus three or more category may not be less than the contribution with respect to the self plus two category. [Treas. Reg. § 54.4980G-4, Q&A 1]

Note. None of the employees in the following examples are covered by a collective bargaining agreement.

Example 1. In the 2009 calendar year, Rock Corporation offers its full-time employees three health plans, including an HDHP with self-only coverage and a $2,000 deductible. Rock contributes $1,000 for the calendar year to the HSA of each employee who is an eligible individual electing the self-only HDHP coverage. Rock makes no HSA contributions for employees with family HDHP coverage or for employees who do not elect the employer's self-only HDHP. Rock's HSA contributions satisfy the comparability rules.

Example 2. In the 2009 calendar year, Stone Corporation offers its employees an HDHP with a $3,000 deductible for self-only coverage and a $4,000 deductible for family coverage. Stone contributes $1,000 for the calendar year to the HSA of each employee who is an eligible individual electing the self-only HDHP coverage. Stone contributes $2,000 for the calendar year to the HSA of each employee who is an eligible individual electing the family HDHP coverage. Stone's HSA contributions satisfy the comparability rules.

Example 3. In the 2009 calendar year, Cobalt Corporation offers its employees an HDHP with a $1,500 deductible for self-only coverage and a $3,000 deductible for family coverage. Cobalt contributes $1,000 for the calendar year to the HSA of each employee who is an eligible individual electing the self-only HDHP coverage. Cobalt contributes $1,000 for the calendar year to the HSA of each employee who is an eligible individual electing the family HDHP coverage. Cobalt's HSA contributions satisfy the comparability rules.

Example 4. In the 2009 calendar year, Density Corporation offers its employees an HDHP with a $1,500 deductible for self-only coverage and a $3,000 deductible for family coverage. Density contributes $1,500 for the calendar year to the HSA of each employee who is an eligible individual electing the self-only HDHP coverage. Density contributes $1,000 for the calendar year to the HSA of each employee who is an eligible individual electing the family HDHP coverage. Density's HSA contributions satisfy the comparability rules.

Example 5. In the 2009 calendar year, Emerald Corporation maintains two HDHPs. Plan A has a $2,000 deductible for self-only coverage and a $4,000 deductible for family coverage. Plan B has a $2,500 deductible for self-only coverage and a $4,500 deductible for family coverage. For the calendar year, Emerald makes contributions to the HSA of each full-time employee who is an eligible individual covered under Plan A of $600 for self-only coverage and $1,000 for family coverage. Emerald satisfies the comparability rules if it makes either of the following contributions for the 2009 calendar year to the HSA of each full-time employee who is an eligible individual covered under Plan B—

• $600 for each full-time employee with self-only coverage and $1,000 for each full-time employee with family coverage; or

• $750 for each employee with self-only coverage and $1,125 for each employee with family coverage (the same percentage of the deductible Emerald contributes for full-time employees covered under Plan A, 30 percent of the deductible for self-only coverage and 25 percent of the deductible for family coverage).

Emerald also makes contributions to the HSA of each part-time employee who is an eligible individual covered under Plan A of $300 for self-only coverage and $500 for family coverage. Emerald satisfies the comparability rules, if it makes either of the following contributions for the 2009 calendar year to the HSA of each part-time employee who is an eligible individual covered under Plan B—

• $300 for each part-time employee with self-only coverage and $500 for each part-time employee with family coverage; or

• $375 for each part-time employee with self-only coverage and $563 for each part-time employee with family coverage (the same percentage of the deductible Emerald contributes for part-time employees covered under Plan A, 15 percent of the deductible for self-only coverage and 12.5 percent of the deductible for family coverage).

Example 6. In the 2009 calendar year, Freedom Corporation maintains an HDHP. The HDHP has the following coverage options—

• A $2,500 deductible for self-only coverage;

• A $3,500 deductible for self plus one dependent (self plus one);

• A $3,500 deductible for self plus spouse (self plus one);

• A $3,500 deductible for self plus spouse and one dependent (self plus two); and

• A $3,500 deductible for self plus spouse and two or more dependents (self plus three or more).

Freedom makes the following contributions for the calendar year to the HSA of each full-time employee who is an eligible individual covered under the HDHP—

- $750 for self-only coverage;
- $1,000 for self plus one dependent;
- $1,000 for self plus spouse;
- $1,500 for self plus spouse and one dependent; and
- $2,000 for self plus spouse and two or more dependents.

Freedom's HSA contributions satisfy the comparability rules.

Example 7. In a calendar year, Galina Corporation offers its employees an HDHP and a health flexible spending arrangement (health FSA). The health FSA reimburses employees for qualified medical expenses. Some of Galina's employees have coverage under the HDHP and the health FSA; some have coverage under the HDHP and their spouse's FSA; and some have coverage under the HDHP and are enrolled in Medicare. For the calendar year, Galina contributes $500 to the HSA of each employee who is an eligible individual. No contributions are made to the HSAs of employees who have coverage under Galina's health FSA or under a spouse's health FSA or who are enrolled in Medicare.

The employees who have coverage under a health FSA (whether Galina's or their spouse's FSA) or who are covered under Medicare are not eligible individuals. Specifically, the employees who have coverage under the health FSA or under a spouse's health FSA are not comparable participating employees because they are not eligible individuals (see Q 2:6). Similarly, the employees who are enrolled in Medicare are not comparable participating employees because they are not eligible individuals. [I.R.C. §§ 223(b)(7), 223(c)(1)] Therefore, employees who have coverage under the health FSA or under a spouse's health FSA and employees who are enrolled in Medicare are excluded from comparability testing. [I.R.C. §§ 4980G(b), 4980E] Galina's contributions satisfy the comparability rules.

The Comparability Rules in Relation to Full-Time and Part-Time Employees

Q 4:137   How does an employer comply with the comparability rules when some non-collectively bargained employees who are eligible individuals do not work for the employer during the entire calendar year?

In general, in determining whether the comparability rules are satisfied, an employer must take into account all full-time and part-time employees who were employees and eligible individuals for any month during the calendar year. Full-time and part-time employees are tested separately. [Treas. Reg. § 54.4980G-4, Q&A 2(a)] There are two methods used to comply with the comparability rules when some employees who are eligible individuals do not work for the employer during the entire calendar year; contributions may be made on a pay-as-you-go basis or on a look-back basis. (See Q 4:126 regarding comparable contributions to the HSAs of former employees.)

Contributions on a pay-as-you-go basis. An employer may comply with the comparability rules by contributing amounts at one or more times for the calendar year to the HSAs of employees who are eligible individuals, if contributions are the same amount or the same percentage of the HDHP deductible for employees who are eligible individuals as of the first day of the month with the same category of coverage and are made at the same time. Contributions made at the employer's usual payroll interval for different groups of employees are considered to be made at the same time. For example, if salaried employees are paid monthly and hourly employees are paid biweekly, an employer may contribute to the HSAs of hourly employees on a biweekly basis and to the HSAs of salaried employees on a monthly basis. An employer may change the amount that it contributes to the HSAs of employees at any point. However, the changed contribution amounts must satisfy the comparability rules. [Treas. Reg. § 54.4980G-4, Q&A 2(b)]

Example 1. Beginning on January 1, Sandstone Corporation contributes $50 per month on the first day of each month to the HSA of each employee who is an eligible individual on that date. Sandstone does not contribute to the HSAs of former employees. In mid-March of the same year, Joe, an employee and an eligible individual, terminates employment after Sandstone has contributed $150 to Joe's HSA. After Joe terminates employment, Sandstone does not contribute additional amounts to Joe's HSA. In mid-April of the same year, Sandstone hires Yetta, an eligible individual, and contributes $50 to Yetta's HSA in May and $50 in June. Effective in July of the same year, Sandstone stops contributing to the HSAs of all employees and makes no contributions to the HSA of any employee for the months of July through December. In August, Sandstone hires Employee Zeb, an eligible individual. Sandstone does not contribute to Zeb's HSA. After Zeb is hired, Sandstone does not hire additional employees. As of the end of the calendar year, Sandstone has made the following HSA contributions to its employees' HSAs—

- Sandstone contributed $150 to Joe's HSA;
- Sandstone contributed $100 to Yetta's HSA;
- Sandstone did not contribute to Zeb's HSA; and
- Sandstone contributed $300 to the HSA of each employee who was an eligible individual and employed by Sandstone from January through June.

Sandstone's contributions satisfy the comparability rules.

Example 2. In a calendar year, Justice Corporation offers its employees an HDHP and contributes on a monthly pay-as-you-go basis to the HSAs of employees who are eligible individuals with coverage under Justice's HDHP. In the calendar year, Justice contributes $50 per month to the HSA of each of employee with self-only HDHP coverage and $100 per month to the HSA of each employee with family HDHP coverage. From January 1 through

March 31 of the calendar year, Barbara, an employee, is an eligible individual with self-only HDHP coverage. From April 1 through December 31 of the calendar year, Barbara is an eligible individual with family HDHP coverage. For the months of January, February, and March of the calendar year, Justice contributes $50 per month to Barbara's HSA. For the remaining months of the calendar year, Justice contributes $100 per month to Barbara's HSA. Justice's contributions to Barbara's HSA satisfy the comparability rules.

Contributions on a look-back basis. An employer may also satisfy the comparability rules by determining comparable contributions for the calendar year at the end of the calendar year, taking into account all employees who were eligible individuals for any month during the calendar year and contributing the correct amount (i.e., a percentage of the HDHP deductible or a specified dollar amount for the same categories of coverage) to the employees' HSAs.

Example 3. In a calendar year, Kryptonite Corporation offers its employees an HDHP and contributes on a look-back basis to the HSAs of employees who are eligible individuals with coverage under Kryptonite's HDHP. Kryptonite contributes $600 ($50 per month) for the calendar year to the HSA of each employee with self-only HDHP coverage and $1,200 ($100 per month) for the calendar year to the HSA of each employee with family HDHP coverage. From January 1 through June 30 of the calendar year Joanne, an employee, is an eligible individual with family HDHP coverage. From July 1 through December 31, Joanne is an eligible individual with self-only HDHP coverage. Kryptonite contributes $900 on a look-back basis for the calendar year to Joanne's HSA ($100 per month for the months of January through June and $50 per month for the months of July through December). Kryptonite's contributions to Joanne's HSA satisfy the comparability rules.

Example 4. On December 31, Lucite Corporation contributes $50 per month on a look-back basis to each employee's HSA for each month in the calendar year that the employee was an eligible individual. In mid-March of the same year, Darla, an employee and an eligible individual, terminated employment. In mid-April of the same year, Lucite hired Ester, who becomes an eligible individual as of May 1 and works for Lucite through December 31. On December 31, Lucite contributes $150 to Darla's HSA and $400 to Ester's HSA. Lucite's contributions satisfy the comparability rules.

Note. *Periods and dates for making contributions.* With both the pay-as-you go method and the look-back method, an employer may establish, on a reasonable and consistent basis, periods for which contributions will be made (for example, a quarterly period covering three consecutive months in a calendar year) and the dates on which such contributions will be made for that designated period (for example, the first day of the quarter or the last day of the quarter in the case of an employer who has established a quarterly period for making contributions). An employer that makes contributions on a pay-as-you-go basis for a period covering more than one month will not fail to satisfy the comparability rules because an employee who terminates employment prior to the end of the period for which contributions were made has received more contributions on a monthly basis than employees who have worked the entire period. In addition, an employer that makes contributions on a pay-as-you-go basis for a period covering more than one month must make HSA contributions for any comparable participating employees hired after the date of initial funding for that period. [Treas. Reg. § 54.4980G-4, Q&A 2(f)]

Example 5. Mercury Corporation has established, on a reasonable and consistent basis, a quarterly period for making contributions to the HSAs of eligible employees on a pay-as-you-go basis. Beginning on January 1, Mercury contributes $150 for the first three months of the calendar year to the HSA of each employee who is an eligible individual on that date. On January 15, Virginia, an employee and an eligible individual, terminated employment after Mercury has contributed $150 to her HSA. On January 15, Mercury hired Wally, who becomes an eligible individual as of February 1. On April 1, Mercury has contributed $100 to Wally's HSA for the two months (February and March) in the quarter period that Wally was an eligible employee. Mercury's contributions satisfy the comparability rules.

Q 4:138 How do the comparability rules apply to employer contributions to employees' HSAs if some non-collectively bargained employees work full-time during the entire calendar year, and other non-collectively bargained employees work full-time for less than the entire calendar year?

An employer's contributions to the HSAs of employees who work full-time for less than 12 months satisfy the comparability rules if the contribution amount is comparable when determined on a month-to-month basis. For example, if the employer contributes $240 to the HSA of each full-time employee who works the entire calendar year, the employer must contribute $60 to the HSA of each full-time employee who works on the first day of each three months of the calendar year. [Treas. Reg. § 54.4980G-4, Q&A 3]

Note. The final regulations retain and expand on the rules in the proposed regulations concerning the timing of employer contributions for employees who do not work for the employer during the entire calendar year. As described above, under the proposed regulations, employers could use either the pay-as-you-go or look-back method of contributions to satisfy the comparability requirements for employees who work for less than a full year. The final regulations retain this rule but clarify that for the pay-as-you-go and look-back methods, an employer may establish, on a reasonable and consistent basis, periods for which contributions will be made, such as quarterly, as well as a specific date, such as the first day of the quarter. Presumably, these rules are intended to clarify that employers are not required to deviate from their scheduled funding of HSA accounts to accommodate employees who begin work after the start of the year (as long as the contributions attributable to that employee are made as part of the next scheduled funding) or who terminate employment before the end of the year.

Q 4:139   May an employer make contributions for the entire year to the HSAs of its employees who are eligible individuals at the beginning of the calendar year (on a pre-funded basis) instead of contributing on a pay-as-you-go or on a look-back basis?

Yes. An employer may make contributions for the entire year to the HSAs of its employees who are eligible individuals at the beginning of the calendar year. An employer that pre-funds the HSAs of its employees will not fail to satisfy the comparability rules because an employee who terminates employment prior to the end of the calendar year has received more contributions on a monthly basis than employees who work the entire calendar year. An owner's interest (i.e., the employee's interest) in an HSA is nonforfeitable. An employer must make comparable contributions for all employees who are comparable participating employees for any month during the calendar year, including employees who are eligible individuals hired after the date of initial funding. An employer that makes HSA contributions on a pre-funded basis may also contribute on a pre-funded basis to the HSAs of employees who are eligible individuals hired after the date of initial funding. Alternatively, an employer that has pre-funded the HSAs of comparable participating employees may contribute to the HSAs of employees who are eligible individuals hired after the date of initial funding on a pay-as-you-go basis or on a look-back basis. An employer that makes HSA contributions on a pre-funded basis must use the same contribution method for all employees who are eligible individuals hired after the date of initial funding. [Treas. Reg. § 54.4980G-4, Q&A 4]

> **Example.** On January 1, Nitrogen Corporation contributes $1,200 for the calendar year on a pre-funded basis to the HSA of each employee who is an eligible individual. In mid-May, Nitrogen hires Lynn, who becomes an eligible individual as of June 1. Therefore, Nitrogen is required to make comparable contributions to Lynn's HSA beginning in June. Nitrogen satisfies the comparability rules with respect to contributions to Lynn's HSA if it makes HSA contributions in any one of the following ways—
>
> - Pre-funding Lynn's HSA by contributing $700 to Lynn's HSA;
> - Contributing $100 per month on a pay-as-you-go basis to Lynn's HSA; or
> - Contributing to Lynn's HSA at the end of the calendar year taking into account each month that Lynn was an eligible individual and employed by Nitrogen.
>
> If Nitrogen hires additional employees who are eligible individuals after initial funding, it must use the same contribution method for these employees that it used to contribute to Lynn's HSA.

Q 4:140   Must an employer use the same contribution method for all employees who were comparable participating employees for any month during the calendar year?

Yes. If an employer makes comparable HSA contributions on a pay-as-you-go basis, it must do so for each employee who is a comparable participating employee as of the first day of the month. If an employer makes comparable contributions on a look-back basis, it must do so for each employee who is a comparable participating employee for any month during the calendar year. If an employer makes HSA contributions on a pre-funded basis, it must do so for all employees who are comparable participating employees at the beginning of the calendar year and must make comparable HSA contributions for all employees who are comparable participating employees for any month during the calendar year, including employees who are eligible individuals hired after the date of initial funding. (See Qs 4:137, 4:138 for rules regarding contributions for employees hired after initial funding.) [Treas. Reg. § 54.4980G-4, Q&A 5]

Accelerated Employer Contributions. In June 2007, the IRS issued proposed rules that allow an employer to accelerate HSA contributions for all HSA eligible employees who have incurred qualified medical expenses that exceed the employer's current calendar year contributions (REG-143797-06). [See 26 C.F.R. § 54 (June 1, 2007)] Prior guidance had limited accelerated payments only to those employees who made HSA contributions through a Code Section 125 cafeteria plan. [See I.R.S. Notice 2004-50, 2004-33 I.R.B. 10, Q&A 60 (July 6, 2004)] On April 17, 2008, the IRS finalized the proposed regulations without substantive revision. [Treas. Reg. § 54.4980G-4, Q&A 15, 73 Fed. Reg. 20795 (April 17, 2008)]

Under the new rules, if an employer elects to accelerate contributions, such contributions must be available on an equal and uniform basis to all eligible employees throughout the calendar year. The employer is required to establish reasonable uniform methods and requirements for determining acceleration eligibility and procedures for providing accelerated contributions. An employer that accelerates contributions to the HSAs of its employees will not fail to satisfy the comparability rules because employees who incur qualifying medical expenses exceeding the employer's cumulative HSA contributions at that time have received more contributions in a given period than comparable employees who do not incur such expenses, provided that all comparable employees receive the same amount or the same percentage for the calendar year. Also, an employer that accelerates contributions to the HSAs of its employees will not fail to satisfy the comparability rules because an employee who terminates employment prior to the end of the calendar year has received more contributions on a monthly basis than employees who work the entire calendar year. An employer is not required to contribute reasonable interest on either accelerated or non-accelerated HSA contributions. [Treas. Reg. § 54.4980G-4, Q&A 15] This proposed rule offers additional flexibility for employers who are interested in accommodating employee needs as they arise. Because of the additional administrative effort involved, however, it remains to be seen whether this new rule will be broadly utilized. Reliance on the proposed regulations was permitted. The final regulations are effective for contributions made for calendar years beginning on or after January 1, 2009, but may be relied upon by employers beginning on April 17, 2008, the date of publication in the Federal Register. [Treas. Reg. § 54.4980G-4, Q&A 16]

Q 4:141　How can an employer comply with the comparability rules if an employee has not established an HSA at the time the employer contributes to its employees' HSAs?

If an employee has not established an HSA at the time the employer funds its employees' HSAs, the employer satisfies the comparability rules by contributing comparable amounts plus reasonable interest (see Q 4:140) to the employee's HSA when the employee establishes the HSA, taking into account each month that the employee was a comparable participating employee.

> **Note.** The original proposed regulations on comparable contribution provided that, if an employee had not established an HSA at the time that the employer funded its employees' HSAs, the employer was required to contribute comparable amounts plus reasonable interest to each employee's HSA when the employee did establish the HSA, taking into account each month that the employee was a comparable participating employee. The proposed regulations contained an exception to this rule for employees who did not establish an HSA by December 31, which provided that the employer was not required to make contributions for such employees for that year. [Treas. Reg. § 54.4980G-4, Q&A 6] The final regulations retained the rule regarding retroactive contributions, but did not adopt the December 31 exception. Instead, the final regulations contained a new reserved subsection under the heading "Employee has not established an HSA by the end of the calendar year." On April 17, 2008, the IRS finalized the proposed regulations (discussed below) without substantive revision. [Treas. Reg. § 54.4980G-4, Q&A 15, 73 Fed. Reg. 20795 (April 17, 2008)]

Employee Fails to Notify Employer of HSA or to Establish HSA by December 31. In June 2007, the IRS issued proposed rules (finalized in 2008, see below) that added a new requirement for employers in complying with the comparability rules when employees fail to establish an HSA prior to the end of the calendar year or to notify their employer that an HSA has been established. [See 26 C.F.R. § 54 [72 Fed. Reg. 30501 (June 1, 2007)]; Prop. Treas. Reg. § 54.4980G-4, Q&A 14] The previous final comparability rules required an employer to make a comparable contribution (calculating interest and months of eligibility) to an employee who opened an HSA after January 1, but reserved the question of whether contributions are required for employees who fail to establish an HSA during the calendar year. [See Treas. Reg. § 54.4980G-4, Q&A 6]

Under the rules proposed in 2007 and finalized in 2008, when employees fail to establish an HSA prior to the end of the calendar year, an employer must provide these employees with a written notice by January 15 of the following calendar year notifying the employees that if they both establish an HSA and notify their employer or notify their employer of an existing HSA prior to the end of February, the employee will receive a comparable contribution to the HSA. The notice may be provided as early as 90 days prior to the first employer contribution for that year and no later than January 15 of the following year. If required, the employer must make a contribution to the employee's HSA by April 15. The contribution must take into account the number of months that the employee was eligible for contributions and add reasonable interest in factoring the contribution amount. The notice may be provided electronically. The regulations also provide a model notice that employers may use for this purpose (see below for an example). If, after receiving the notice, an employee still fails to open an HSA, the employer is not required to make a contribution to the employee's HSA. This rule places new administrative burdens on employers. Under the prior rules, if an employee failed to open an HSA before the end of the calendar year, no contribution was required. Employers will now need to track employee HSAs and draft and deliver notices according to the timeline, in addition to calculating interest on the delayed contributions. [Treas. Reg., § 54.4980G-4, Q&A 14(a); Prop. Treas. Reg. § 54.4980G-4, Q&A 14(a)] The final regulations are effective for contributions made for calendar years beginning on or after January 1, 2009, but may be relied upon by employers beginning on April 17, 2008, the date of publication in the Federal Register. [Treas. Reg. § 54.4980G-4, Q&A 16]

> **Caution.** The majority of employers do not have to comply with these comparable contribution rules because such employers make HSA contributions through their cafeteria plans.

Employers may use the following sample language as a basis for preparing their own notices. [Prop. Treas. Reg. § 54.4980G-4, Q&A 14(b)] The notice may be provided electronically. [Prop. Treas. Reg. § 54.4980G-4, Q&A 14(a) and 14(e)]

Notice to Employees Regarding Employer Contributions to HSAs

This notice explains how you may be eligible to receive contributions from [employer] if you are covered by a High Deductible Health Plan (HDHP). [Employer] provides contributions to the Health Savings Account (HSA) of each employee who is [insert employer's eligibility requirements for HSA contributions] ("eligible employee"). If you are an eligible employee, you must do the following in order to receive an employer contribution:

1. Establish an HSA on or before the last day in February of [insert year after the year for which the contribution is being made]; and
2. Notify [insert name and contact information for appropriate person to be contacted] of your HSA account information on or before the last day in February of [insert year after year for which the contribution is being made]. [Specify the HSA account information that the employee must provide (e.g., account number, name and address of trustee or custodian, etc.) and the method by which the employee must provide this account information (e.g., in writing, on a certain form, etc.)].

If you establish your HSA on or before the last day of February in [insert year after year for which the contribution is being made] and notify [employer] of your HSA account information, you will receive your HSA contributions, plus reasonable interest, for [insert year for which contribution is being made] by April 15 of [insert year after year for which the contribution is being made]. If, however, you do not establish your HSA or you do not notify us of your HSA account information by the deadline, then we are not required to make any contributions to your HSA for [insert applicable year]. You may notify us that you have established an HSA by sending an [e-mail or] a written notice to [insert name, title and, if applicable, e-mail address]. If you have any questions about this notice, you can contact [insert name and title] at [insert telephone number or other contact information].

Example 1. In a calendar year, Heart Partnership contributes to the HSAs of current employees who are eligible individuals covered under any HDHP. For the 2010 calendar year, Heart contributes $50 per month on the first day of each month, beginning January 1, to the HSA of each employee who is an eligible employee on that date. For the 2010 calendar year, Heart provides written notice satisfying the content requirements on October 16, 2009 to all employees regarding the availability of HSA contributions for eligible employees. For eligible employees who are hired after October 16, 2009, Heart provides such a notice no later than January 15, 2011. Heart's notice satisfies the comparability rule notice requirements.

Example 2. Orange Corporation's written cafeteria plan permits employees to elect to make pretax salary reduction contributions to their HSAs. Employees making this election have the right to receive cash or other taxable benefits in lieu of their HSA pretax contribution. Orange automatically contributes a non-elective matching contribution to the HSA of each employee who makes a pretax HSA contribution. Because Orange's HSA contributions are made through the cafeteria plan, the comparability requirements do not apply to the HSA contributions made by Orange (see Q 4:149). Consequently, Orange is not required to provide written notice to its employees regarding the availability of this matching HSA contribution.

Example 3. In a calendar year, Steel Corporation maintains an HDHP and only contributes to the HSAs of eligible employees who elect coverage under its HDHP. For the 2010 calendar year, Steel employs 10 eligible employees. For the 2010 calendar year, all 10 employees have elected coverage under Steel's HDHP and have established HSAs. For the 2010 calendar year, Steel makes comparable contributions to the HSAs of all 10 employees. Steel satisfies the comparability rules. Thus, Steel is not required to provide written notice to its employees regarding the availability of HSA contributions for eligible employees.

Example 4. In a calendar year, Tibor Corporation contributes to the HSAs of current full-time employees with family coverage under any HDHP. For the 2010 calendar year, Tibor provides timely written notice satisfying the content requirements to all employees regardless of HDHP coverage. Tibor makes identical monthly contributions to all eligible employees (meaning full-time employees with family HDHP coverage) that establish HSAs. Tibor contributes comparable amounts (taking into account each month that the employee was a comparable participating employee) plus reasonable interest to the HSAs of the eligible employees that establish HSAs and provides the necessary information after the end of the year but on or before the last day of February 2011. Tibor makes no contribution to the HSAs of employees that do not establish an HSA and provides the necessary information on or before the last day of February 2009. Tibor satisfies the comparability requirements.

Example 5. For 2009, Tulip Corporation contributes to the HSAs of current full-time employees with family coverage under any HDHP. Tulip has 500 current full-time employees. As of the date for Tulip's first HSA contribution for the 2009 calendar year, 450 employees have established HSAs. Tulip provides timely written notice satisfying the content requirements only to those 50 current full-time employees who have not established HSAs. Tulip makes identical quarterly contributions to the 450 employees who established HSAs. Tulip contributes comparable amounts to the eligible employees who establish HSAs and provides the necessary information after the end of the year but on or before the last day of February 2010. Tulip makes no contribution to the HSAs of employees that do not establish an HSA and provides the necessary information on or before the last day of February 2009. Tulip satisfies the comparability rules.

Example 6. Beginning on January 1, Ozone Corporation contributes $500 per calendar year on a pay-as-you-go basis to the HSA of each employee who is an eligible individual. Employee C is an eligible individual during the entire calendar year but does not establish an HSA until March. Notwithstanding C's delay in establishing an HSA, Ozone must make up the missed HSA contributions plus reasonable interest for January and February by April 15 of the following calendar year.

Q 4:142   If an employer bases its contributions on a percentage of the HDHP deductible, how is the correct percentage or dollar amount computed?

The correct percentage is determined by rounding to the nearest 1/100th of a percentage point and the dollar amount is determined by rounding to the nearest whole dollar. [Treas. Reg. § 54.4980G-4, Q&A 7]

Example. Assume that each HDHP provided by Density Corporation satisfies the definition of an HDHP for the 2009 calendar year. In the 2009 calendar year, Density maintains two HDHPs. Plan A has a deductible of $3,000 for self-only coverage. Density contributes $1,000 for the calendar year to the HSA of each employee covered under Plan A. Plan B has a deductible of $3,500 for self-only coverage. Density satisfies the comparability rules if it makes either of the following contributions for the 2009 calendar year to the HSA of each employee who is an eligible individual with self-only coverage under Plan B—

- $1,000; or
- $1,167 (33.33% of the deductible rounded to the nearest whole dollar amount).

Q 4:143 **Does an employer that contributes to the HSA of each comparable participating employee in an amount equal to the employee's HSA contribution or a percentage of the employee's HSA contribution (matching contributions) satisfy the rule that all comparable participating employees receive comparable contributions?**

No. If all comparable participating employees do not contribute the same amount to their HSAs and, consequently, do not receive comparable contributions to their HSAs, the comparability rules are not satisfied, notwithstanding that the employer offers to make available the same contribution amount to each comparable participating employee. (But see Q 4:149 regarding contributions to HSAs made through a cafeteria plan.) [Treas. Reg. § 54.4980G-4, Q&A 8]

Q 4:144 **If an employer conditions contributions by the employer to an employee's HSA on an employee's participation in health assessments, disease management programs, or wellness programs and makes the same contributions available to all employees who participate in the programs, do the contributions satisfy the comparability rules?**

No. If all comparable participating employees do not elect to participate in all the programs and consequently, all comparable participating employees do not receive comparable contributions to their HSAs, the employer contributions fail to satisfy the comparability rules. (But see Q 4:149 regarding contributions to HSAs made through a cafeteria plan.) [Treas. Reg. § 54.4980G-4, Q&A 9]

Q 4:145 **If an employer makes additional contributions to the HSAs of all comparable participating employees who have attained a specified age or who have worked for the employer for a specified number of years, do the contributions satisfy the comparability rules?**

No. If all comparable participating employees do not meet the age or length of service requirement, all comparable participating employees do not receive comparable contributions to their HSAs and the employer contributions fail to satisfy the comparability rules. [Treas. Reg. § 54.4980G-4, Q&A 10]

Q 4:146 **If an employer makes additional contributions to the HSAs of all comparable participating employees who are eligible to make the additional contributions (HSA catch-up contributions), do the contributions satisfy the comparability rules?**

No. If all comparable participating employees are not eligible to make the additional HSA contributions under Code Section 223(b)(3), all comparable participating employees do not receive comparable contributions to their HSAs, and the employer contributions fail to satisfy the comparability rules. [Treas. Reg. § 54.4980G-4, Q&A 11]

Q 4:147   If an employer's contributions to an employee's HSA result in noncomparable contributions, may the employer recoup the excess amount from the employee's HSA?

Generally no. An employer normally may not recoup from an employee's HSA any portion of the employer's contribution to the employee's HSA (see Q 6:2). An employee's interest in his or her HSA is nonforfeitable. However, an employer may make additional HSA contributions to satisfy the comparability rules. An employer may make a contribution up until April 15 following the calendar year in which the noncomparable contributions were made. An employer that makes additional HSA contributions to correct noncomparable contributions must also contribute reasonable interest (see Q 4:148). However, an employer is not required to contribute amounts in excess of the annual HSA contribution limits (see Q 4:30). [Treas. Reg. § 54.4980G-4, Q&A 12]

Q 4:148   What constitutes a reasonable interest rate for purposes of making comparable contributions?

The determination of whether a rate of interest used by an employer is reasonable will be based on all of the facts and circumstances. If an employer calculates interest using the federal short-term rate as determined by the Secretary in accordance with Code Section 1274(d), the employer is deemed to use a reasonable interest rate. [Treas. Reg. § 54.4980G-4, Q&A 13]

HSA Comparability Rules and Cafeteria Plans

Q 4:149   If an employer makes contributions through a cafeteria plan to the HSA of each employee who is an eligible individual, are the contributions subject to the comparability rules?

Generally no. The comparability rules do not apply to HSA contributions that an employer makes through a Code Section 125 cafeteria plan. [Medicare Prescription Drug, Improvement, and Modernization Act of 2003, Conf. Rep. No. 391, 108th Cong., 1st Sess. 840 (2003); I.R.S. Notice 2004-2, Q&A 32, 2004-2 I.R.B. 269; Treas. Reg. § 54.4980G-5, Q&A 1] However, contributions to an HSA made through a cafeteria plan are subject to the Code Section 125 nondiscrimination rules regarding eligibility, contributions and benefits tests, and key employee concentration tests. [See I.R.C. §§ 125(b), (c), and (g)] Employer contributions to employees' HSAs made through a Code Section 125 cafeteria plan are subject to the Code Section 125 cafeteria plan nondiscrimination rules and not the comparability rules if under the written cafeteria plan, the employees have the right to elect to receive cash or other taxable benefits in lieu of all or a portion of an HSA contribution (meaning that all or a portion of the HSA contributions are available as pretax salary reduction amounts), regardless of whether an employee actually elects to contribute any amount to the HSA by salary reduction. [Treas. Reg. § 54.4980G-5, Q&A 1; Prop. Treas. Reg. § 1.125-7(n)]

Practice Pointer. The significance of this rule is that contributions made through a cafeteria plan are subject to the nondiscrimination requirements of Code Section 125 rather than the comparable contribution requirements of Code Section 4980G. This means that an employer is prohibited from favoring HCEs or key employees with respect to cafeteria plan eligibility or benefits, including HSA contributions, but the employer is not required to contribute similar amounts to employees' HSAs. This should allow employers more flexibility and creativity in benefit design structures. For example, by using a cafeteria plan, employers can provide matching contributions to match employees' contributions to their HSAs (i.e., employer contributions that are equal to or a percentage of the employee's contribution). Employers also can make HSA contributions contingent upon participation in health risk assessments, disease management programs, or wellness programs. None of these contribution structures would pass the Code Section 4980G comparable contribution requirement without this exception because all employees will not elect to make the same HSA contribution or to participate in the same program, and therefore, will receive different amounts of employer contributions.

Under Code Section 125, if a cafeteria plan discriminates in favor of highly compensated individuals, the highly compensated participants must include in income an amount equal to the highest value of benefits he or she could have elected to receive under the discriminatory cafeteria plan. Similarly, if key employees elect more than 25 percent of the aggregate benefits elected by all employees under a cafeteria plan, key employees must include in income amounts that could have been elected.

In August 2007, the IRS issued new proposed regulations providing guidance on cafeteria plans. The new proposed regulations provide more detail than the previous proposed regulations concerning how to determine whether a cafeteria plan complies with these nondiscrimination rules. However, more specific guidance and examples are critical in order to fully understand these requirements, particularly with respect to HSA contributions. The following is a summary of the new proposed cafeteria plan nondiscrimination rules:

Highly Compensated Individuals. For purposes of applying the nondiscrimination rules for cafeteria plans, highly compensated individuals are those who in the current year are (i) an officer, (ii) a 5 percent shareholder, or (iii) a highly compensated employee. [Prop. Treas. Reg. § 1.125-7(a)(3) and (a)(8)] While similar to the rules used for determining who is a highly compensated employee under the tax-qualified plan nondiscrimination rules, the definitions under the cafeteria plan rules are not the same. This will require employers to separately track who constitutes a highly compensated employee for different nondiscrimination testing purposes.

An employee is an "officer" for purposes of these nondiscrimination tests based on the duties and responsibilities of the individual, requiring an analysis of what an individual's job position entails. [Prop. Treas. Reg. § 1.125-7(a)(7)] There is no minimum compensation requirement for being considered an officer or no overall limit on how many employees can be counted as officers.

An employee is a "highly compensated employee" for purposes of these nondiscrimination tests if the employee's compensation is over $110,000 (for 2009) in the preceding plan year (2008, or the current year in the case of the first year of employment). [Prop. Treas. Reg. § 1.125-7(a)(9), referring to I.R.C. § 414(q)(1)(B)] In contrast, the qualified plan rules do not include someone as highly compensated in their first year of employment. The alternate rule in qualified plan nondiscrimination testing for determining whether someone is highly compensated—limiting the group to the top 20 percent of employees in terms of compensation during the year—may also be used to determine who is highly compensated under the cafeteria plan nondiscrimination testing rules.

Caution. The definition of highly compensated individual for purposes of the new proposed cafeteria plan nondiscrimination rules is not the same as the definition that applies for purposes of the qualified retirement plan rules under Code Section 414(s).

Nondiscrimination in Eligibility. A cafeteria plan cannot discriminate in favor of highly compensated employees with regard to eligibility to participate in the cafeteria plan or with respect to the contributions and benefits provided in a cafeteria plan. [Prop. Treas. Reg. § 1.125-7(b)(1) and (c)(1)] The new proposed regulations provide some detail as to how the various nondiscrimination tests are to be applied but the requirements are still not entirely clear.

The nondiscrimination rules regarding eligibility to participate follow the reasonable classification test provided for in the tax-qualified plan nondiscrimination rules. This rule consists of a two-part test. First, an employer can only limit eligibility to certain "reasonable classifications" of employees, such as those based on job categories, salaried or hourly job categories, geographic location, and other bona fide business classifications. Second, the percentage of non-highly compensated employees who are able to participate in the cafeteria plan as a percentage of the entire employee population must meet or exceed various safe harbor percentages. In making this determination, employers who do not allow employees to participate in the cafeteria plan until they have completed three years of employment can disregard such employees in determining whether eligibility for the plan discriminates in favor of highly compensated employees. [Prop. Treas. Reg. § 1.125-7(b)(1) and (3)] Also excluded from this determination are employees covered by a collective bargaining agreement (except key employees), nonresident aliens with no earned income in the U.S. from the employer, and those employees who are participating in the cafeteria plan due to COBRA. Of course, a cafeteria plan that allows every employee to participate will not be considered discriminatory with respect to eligibility. [Prop. Treas. Reg. § 1.125-7(b)(3)(ii)]

Note. The proposed regulations do not include much needed examples to illustrate how the reasonable classification test should be applied in the cafeteria plan context.

Nondiscrimination in Contributions and Benefits. A cafeteria plan also must not discriminate with regard to benefit availability and the benefits elected. The new proposed regulations provide that each similarly situated employee must have the same opportunity to elect qualified cafeteria plan benefits and those benefits must not be disproportionately elected by highly compensated participants. [Prop. Treas. Reg. § 1.125-7(c)(1) and (2)]

In this regard, the new proposed regulations state that the dollar amount of benefits elected by all highly compensated participants in the plan divided by the aggregate compensation of those employees (expressed as a percentage) cannot exceed the dollar amount of benefits elected by all non-highly compensated participants divided by the aggregate compensation of those employees (also expressed as a percentage). Regarding contributions to the cafeteria plan, similarly situated participants must also be given the same opportunity to elect employer contributions under the cafeteria plan. In addition, highly compensated participants cannot disproportionately utilize the cafeteria plan contributions for qualified benefits; whether this has occurred is determined in a manner similar to that used to determine whether benefit election disproportionately benefited highly compensated participants. [Prop. Treas. Reg. § 1.125-7(c)(2)]

> **Note.** Examples are needed in the final regulations to illustrate how the contribution and benefits test should be applied in the cafeteria plan context, and with respect to contributions to an HSA.

Key Employee Concentration Test. A cafeteria plan is also considered to be discriminatory if more than 25 percent of the aggregate benefits provided under a cafeteria plan go to key employees. Generally this will not affect cafeteria plans of larger employers, since the number of key employees is limited to 50 employees and shareholders of 5 percent or more and 1 percent of shareholders who have compensation in excess of $145,000. However, it is not clear how to measure benefits for purposes of this test, particularly with respect to HSAs. [Prop. Treas. Reg. § 1.125-7(d)(1)]

> **Note.** Examples are needed to illustrate how the key employee test should be applied in the cafeteria plan context, including with respect to contributions to an HSA.

Safe Harbors. The new proposed regulations provide two safe harbors from the nondiscrimination rules. [Prop. Treas. Reg. § 1.125-7(e)] One safe harbor, which is provided in the statute itself, states that contributions on behalf of each participant are at least equal to (i) 100 percent of the cost of the health plan coverage of the plan that benefits the majority of highly compensated participants; or (ii) 75 percent of the cost of the highest cost health benefit in the plan, and any contributions in excess of the 100 percent or 75 percent amount must bear a uniform relationship to compensation. It is not clear how to apply this safe harbor, and the new proposed regulations do not provide any clarification or helpful examples. The second safe harbor, which is new, provides that premium only plans are also considered a safe harbor design if they pass the nondiscrimination test regarding eligibility.

> **Note.** Examples are needed to show how the safe harbors should be applied, including with respect to contributions to an HSA.

Other Rules. The new proposed regulations state that the actual operation of the plan must not discriminate in favor of highly compensated participants in operation. [Prop. Treas. Reg. § 1.125-7(k)] However, there are no helpful illustrations of how this requirement would apply. In addition, the new proposed regulations provide rules for aggregating and disaggregating cafeteria plans for purposes of determining whether the plan is discriminatory, but again, contain no illustrations of these rules. [Prop. Treas. Reg. § 1.125-7(g) and (h)]

The new proposed regulations provide that the nondiscrimination tests must be conducted annually as of the last day of the plan year and must include any non-excludable employees who were employees at any time during the year. There is much less flexibility in the timing and manner of the nondiscrimination testing of cafeteria plans than is permitted for qualified plans. [Prop. Treas. Reg. § 1.125-7(j)]

Note. The timing and manner of nondiscrimination testing for purposes of these rules are not the same as the timing and manner of nondiscrimination testing that applies for purposes of the qualified retirement plan rules.

Q 4:150   If an employer makes contributions through a cafeteria plan to the HSA of each employee who is an eligible individual in an amount equal to the amount of the employee's HSA contribution or a percentage of the amount of the employee's HSA contribution (matching contributions), are the contributions subject to the Code Section 4980G comparability rules?

No. The comparability rules do not apply to HSA contributions that an employer makes through a Code Section 125 cafeteria plan. Thus, where matching contributions are made by an employer through a cafeteria plan, the contributions are not subject to the comparability rules of Code Section 4980G. However, contributions, including matching contributions, to an HSA made under a cafeteria plan are subject to the Code Section 125 nondiscrimination rules (eligibility rules, contributions and benefits tests, and key employee concentration tests). [Treas. Reg. § 4980G-5, Q&A 2]

Q 4:151   If under the employer's cafeteria plan, employees who are eligible individuals and who participate in health assessments, disease management programs, or wellness programs receive an employer contribution to an HSA and the employees have the right to elect to make pretax salary reduction contributions to their HSAs, are the contributions subject to the comparability rules?

Generally no. The comparability rules do not apply to employer contributions to an HSA made through a cafeteria plan (see Q 4:149). [Treas. Reg. § 54.4980G-5, Q&A 3]

Example 1. Agate Corporation's written cafeteria plan permits employees to elect to make pretax salary reduction contributions to their HSAs. Employees making this election have the right to receive cash or other taxable benefits in lieu of their HSA pretax contribution. The Code Section 125 cafeteria plan nondiscrimination rules and not the comparability rules apply because the HSA contributions are made through the cafeteria plan.

Example 2. Battery Corporation's written cafeteria plan permits employees to elect to make pretax salary reduction contributions to their HSAs. Employees making this election have the right to receive cash or other taxable benefits in lieu of their HSA pretax contribution. Battery automatically contributes a nonelective matching contribution or seed money to the HSA of each employee who makes a pretax HSA contribution. The Code Section 125 cafeteria plan nondiscrimination rules and not the comparability rules apply to Battery's HSA contributions because the HSA contributions are made through the cafeteria plan.

Example 3. Cable Corporation's written cafeteria plan permits employees to elect to make pretax salary reduction contributions to their HSAs. Employees making this election have the right to receive cash or other taxable benefits in lieu of their HSA pretax contribution. Cable makes a nonelective contribution to the HSAs of all employees who complete a health risk assessment and participate in Cable's wellness program. Employees do not have the right to receive cash or other taxable benefits in lieu of Cable's nonelective contribution. The Code Section 125 cafeteria plan nondiscrimination rules and not the comparability rules apply to Cable's HSA contributions because the HSA contributions are made through the cafeteria plan.

Example 4. Gallery Corporation's written cafeteria plan permits employees to elect to make pretax salary reduction contributions to their HSAs. Employees making this election have the right to receive cash or other taxable benefits in lieu of their HSA pretax contribution. Employees participating in the plan who are eligible individuals receive automatic employer contributions to their HSAs. Employees make no election with respect to Gallery's contribution and do not have the right to receive cash or other taxable benefits in lieu of Gallery's contribution, but are permitted to make their own pretax salary reduction contributions to fund their HSAs. The Code Section 125 cafeteria plan nondiscrimination rules and not the comparability rules apply to Gallery's HSA contributions because the HSA contributions are made through the cafeteria plan.

Waiver of Excise Tax

Q 4:152 May all or part of the excise tax imposed under Code Section 4980G be waived?

Yes. In the case of a failure that is due to reasonable cause and not to willful neglect, all or a portion of the excise tax imposed under Code Section 4980G may be waived to the extent that the payment of the tax would be excessive relative to the failure involved. [I.R.C. §§ 4980G(b) and 4980E(c); Treas. Reg. § 54.4980G-5, Q&A 4; I.R.S. Notice 2004-2, Q&A 32, 2004-2 I.R.B. 269]

Tax Treatment of Contributions

Q 4:153 What are the main areas to consider relative to taxation of contributions?

There are three general areas of consideration for taxation of contributions:

1. Tax reporting by individuals (see Qs 4:154, 4:155);
2. Partnership considerations (see Qs 4:156–4:167); and
3. S corporation considerations (see Qs 4:168–4:176).

IRS Reporting by Individuals

Q 4:154 How are HSA contributions reported to the IRS by the taxpayer?

Form 8889—*Health Savings Accounts (HSAs)* is used to report HSA contributions (including those made on the HSA owner's behalf and employer contributions) and distributions. Form 8889 is also used to report distributions from an HSA. The taxpayer's deduction for contributions to an HSA is claimed on Form 1040, Line 25, or Form 1040-NR, Line 28 (based on the 2008 version of those forms).

Note. The maximum HSA contribution is reduced on Form 8889 for employer contributions to an HSA that are excluded from the employee's gross income and for a direct trustee-to-trustee transfer of an amount in a tradition a IRA (other than a SEP-IRA or SIMPLE IRS) to an HSA (see chapter 5).

Form 8889 is filed as an attachment to the taxpayer's federal income tax return, Form 1040. All contributions, including cafeteria plan pretax contributions, made for the year (including those made after the end of the year designated as made for the prior year) must be included on Form 8889. Contributions made by an employer, although generally excluded from an employee's gross income, must also be reflected on the form.

Note. The amount contributed during the year will be reflected on Form 5498-SA—*HSA, Archer MSA, or Medicare Advantage MSA Information*, which is received from the trustee or custodian of the HSA. An employer's contribution (if any) will be shown in Box 12 of Form W-2—*Wage and Tax Statement* and coded W.

Q 4:155 Who must file Form 8889—*Health Savings Accounts (HSAs)*?

Form 8889—*Health Savings Accounts (HSAs)* must be filed by an individual if any of the following circumstances apply:

1. The individual made contributions to an HSA for the year, including a direct trustee-to-trustee transfer from a traditional IRA (not including a SEP-IRA or a SIMPLE IRA).

2. The individual's employer made contributions (even if through a cafeteria plan or a health FSA on a pretax basis).

3. Someone on the individual's behalf (including an employer) made contributions for the year.

4. The individual received distributions from an HSA during the year.

5. The individual acquired an interest in an HSA because of the death of the HSA owner (the account holder).

6. The individual must include certain amounts in income because they failed to be an eligible individual during the testing period.

Partnership Considerations

Q 4:156   May a partnership make HSA contributions on behalf of a partner or guaranteed payment partner?

Yes. A partnership may make contributions to an HSA on behalf of a partner or guaranteed payment partner (see example in Q 4:167).

Note. A partner is not an employee and therefore the comparable contribution rules do not apply to contributions made by a partnership to a bona fide partner's HSA (see Q 4:124). Instead, the contributions either are treated as distributions under Code Section 731 or guaranteed payments under Code Section 707(c), as described below. [Treas. Reg. § 54.4980G-3, Q&A 3]

Q 4:157   Are contributions by a partnership that are treated as distributions to the partner under Code Section 731 treated as a contribution to an HSA?

No. Generally, when an employer makes a contribution, within permissible limits, to the HSA on behalf of an employee who is an eligible individual, the contribution is excluded from the employee's gross income and wages. [I.R.C. § 106(d)] However, contributions by a partnership to a bona fide partner's HSA are not treated as contributions by an employer to the HSA of an employee. [Rev. Rul. 69-184, 1969-1 C.B. 256]

Q 4:158   What is the tax treatment of contributions to an HSA by a partnership that are considered distributions to the partner under Code Section 731?

Contributions by a partnership to a partner's HSA that are treated as distributions to the partner under Code Section 731 (regarding the extent of recognition or gain or loss on partnership distributions) are not deductible by the partnership and do not affect the distributive shares of partnership income and deductions. [Rev. Rul. 91-26, 1991-1 C.B. 184 (analysis of situation 1, last paragraph)]

Q 4:159 **How are contributions by a partnership that are treated as distributions to the partner under Code Section 731 reported to the partner?**

Contributions by a partnership that are treated as distributions to the partner under Code Section 731 are reported by the partnership as distributions of money on Form 1065, Schedule K-1—*Partner's Share of Income, Credits, Deductions, etc.*

Q 4:160 **Are contributions by a partnership that are treated as distributions to the partner under Code Section 731 included in a partner's net earnings from self-employment (NESE)?**

No. Contributions by a partnership that are treated as distributions to the partner under Code Section 731 are not included in the partner's NESE under Code Section 1402(a) because the distributions under Code Section 731 do not affect a partner's distributive share of partnership income or loss under Code Section 702(a)(8).

Q 4:161 **Are contributions by a partnership that are treated as distributions to the partner under Code Section 731 deductible by the partner?**

Yes. The partner, if an eligible individual (see Q 2:6), may deduct the amount of the allowable contributions made to the partner's HSA during the taxable year as an adjustment to gross income on his or her federal income tax return. [I.R.C. §§ 62(a)(19), 223(a)]

Q 4:162 **Are contributions by a partnership that are treated as guaranteed payments under Code Section 707(c), are derived from the partnership's trade or business, and are for services rendered to the partnership treated as contributions to an HSA?**

No. Contributions by a partnership to a bona fide partner's HSA are not contributions by an employer to the HSA of an employee. [Rev. Rul. 69-184, 1969-1 C.B. 256]

Q 4:163 **Are contributions by a partnership that are treated as guaranteed payments under Code Section 707(c) deductible by the partnership?**

Yes. Contributions by a partnership to a partner's HSA for services rendered to the partnership that are treated as guaranteed payments under Code Section 707(c) are deductible by the partnership under Code Section 162 regarding trade or business expenses, provided the requirements of that section are satisfied, taking into account the rules of Code Section 263 (regarding capital expenditures). [I.R.C. §§ 162(a), 707(c); I.R.S. Notice 2005-8, Q&A 2, 2005-4 I.R.B. 368]

Q 4:164   Are contributions by a partnership that are treated as guaranteed payments under Code Section 707(c), are derived from the partnership's trade or business, and are for services rendered to the partnership included in a partner's gross income?

Yes. Contributions by a partnership that are treated as guaranteed payments under Code Section 707(c) are included in a partner's gross income. The contributions are not excludable from the partner's gross income under Code Section 106(d) because the contributions are treated as a distributive share of partnership income under Treasury Regulations Section 1.707-1(c) for purposes of all Code Sections other than Code Sections 61(a) and 162(a). [I.R.C. §§ 106(d), 707(c); see Rev. Rul. 91-26, 1991-1 C.B. 184; I.R.S. Notice 2005-8, Q&A 2, 2005-4 I.R.B. 368]

Q 4:165   How are contributions by a partnership to a partner's HSA that are treated as guaranteed payments under Code Section 707(c) reported by the partnership to the partner?

Contributions by a partnership to a partner's HSA that are treated as guaranteed payments under Code Section 707(c) are reported as guaranteed payments on Form 1065, Schedule K-1—*Partner's Share of Income, Credits, Deductions, etc.* [I.R.S. Notice 2005-8, Q&A 1, 2005-4 I.R.B. 368]

Q 4:166   Are contributions by a partnership that are treated as guaranteed payments under Code Section 707(c), are derived from the partnership's trade or business, and are for services rendered to the partnership treated as net earnings from self-employment?

Yes. Because the contributions are guaranteed payments that are derived from the partnership's trade or business, and are for services rendered to the partnership, the contributions are included in the partner's net earnings from self-employment under Code Section 1402(a) on the partner's Schedule SE (Form 1040). [I.R.S. Notice 2005-8, Q&A 2, 2005-4 I.R.B. 368]

Q 4:167   How are contributions by a partnership that are treated as guaranteed payments under Code Section 707(c), are derived from the partnership's trade or business, and are for services rendered to the partnership included in a partner's gross income?

The partner, if an eligible individual (see Q 2:6), is entitled to deduct the amount of the allowable contributions made to the partner's HSA during the taxable year as an adjustment to gross income on his or her federal income tax return. [I.R.C. §§ 62(a)(19), 223(a), 223(c)(1); I.R.S. Notice 2005-8, Q&A 2, 2005-4 I.R.B. 368]

The following example illustrates the answers in Qs 4:156 through 4:166.

Example. ABC Partnership is a limited partnership with three equal individual partners: Garry (a general partner), Lorrin (a limited partner), and Lezlie (a limited partner). Lezlie is to be paid $500 annually for services rendered to ABC Partnership in his capacity as a partner and without regard to ABC Partnership income (a guaranteed payment under Code Section 707(c)). The $500 payment to Lezlie is derived from ABC Partnership's trade or business. ABC Partnership has no employees. Garry, Lorrin, and Lezlie are eligible individuals (as defined in Code Section 223(c)(1)), and each has an HSA. During ABC Partnership's Year 1 taxable year, ABC Partnership makes the following contributions: a $300 contribution to Garry's HSA and a $300 contribution to Lorrin's HSAs, which are treated by ABC Partnership as Code Section 731 distributions to Garry and Lorrin; and a $500 contribution to Lezlie's HSA in lieu of paying Lezlie the guaranteed payment directly.

ABC Partnership's contributions to Garry's and Lorrin's HSAs are not deductible by ABC Partnership and, therefore, do not affect ABC Partnership's calculation of its taxable income or loss. [Rev. Rul. 91-26, 1991-1 C.B. 184] Garry and Lorrin are entitled to an above-the-line deduction, under Code Sections 223(a) and 62(a)(19), for the amount of the contributions made to their HSAs. The Code Section 731 distributions to Garry's and Lorrin's individual HSAs are reported as cash distributions to Garry and Lorrin on Garry's and Lorrin's Schedule K-1 (Form 1065). The distributions to Garry's and Lorrin's HSAs are not includible in Garry's and Lorrin's net earnings from self-employment under Code Section 1402(a), because distributions under Code Section 1402(a) do not affect a partner's distributive share of the partnership's income or loss under Code Section 702(a)(8).

ABC Partnership's contribution to Lezlie's HSA, which is treated as a guaranteed payment under Code Section 707(c) for services rendered to the partnership, is deductible by ABC Partnership under Code Section 162 (if the requirements of that section are satisfied, taking into account the rules of Code Section 263) and is includible in Lezlie's gross income. The contribution is not excludable from Lezlie's gross income under Code Section 106(d) because (1) the contribution is treated as a distributive share of partnership income for purposes of all Code Sections other than Code Sections 61(a) and 162(a), and (2) a guaranteed payment to a partner is not treated as compensation to an employee. [Rev. Rul. 91-26, 1991-1 C.B. 184] The payment to Lezlie's HSA should be reported as a guaranteed payment on Schedule K-1 (Form 1065). Because the contribution is a guaranteed payment that is derived from the partnership's trade or business and is for services rendered to the partnership, the contribution constitutes net earnings from self-employment to Lezlie under Code Section 1402(a), which should be reported on Schedule SE (Form 1040). Lezlie is entitled, under Code Sections 223(a) and 62(a)(19), to deduct as an adjustment to gross income the amount of the contribution made to his HSA.

S Corporation Considerations

Q 4:168 **How is an S corporation treated with respect to contributions made by the S corporation to the HSA of a 2 percent shareholder, who is also an employee (2 percent shareholder-employee) in consideration for services rendered to the S corporation?**

Under Code Section 1372, for purposes of applying the provisions of Subtitle A that relate to fringe benefits, an S corporation is treated as a partnership. [I.R.C. §§ 1372(a)(1), 1372(b)]

Q 4:169 **How is a 2 percent shareholder treated with respect to contributions made by the S corporation to the HSA of a 2 percent shareholder, who is also an employee (2 percent shareholder-employee) in consideration of services rendered to the S corporation?**

Under Code Section 1372, for purposes of applying the provisions of Subtitle A that relate to fringe benefits, a 2 percent shareholder of the S corporation is treated as a partner of such partnership. [I.R.C. §§ 1372(a)(2), 1372(b); I.R.S. Notice 2005-8, Q&A 3, 2005-4 I.R.B. 368]

Practice Pointer. The term *2 percent shareholder* means any person who owns, or is considered to own through attribution, on any day during the taxable year of the S corporation, more than 2 percent of the outstanding stock of such corporation or stock possessing more than 2 percent of the total combined voting power of all stock of such corporation. [I.R.C. § 1372(b)] The attribution rules of Code Section 318 are used for the purpose of determining ownership.

Q 4:170 **What is the tax treatment of an S corporation's contributions to an HSA of a 2 percent shareholder who is also an employee (2 percent shareholder-employee)?**

When an S corporation, which is treated as a partnership (see Q 4:169), makes contributions to an HSA of a 2 percent shareholder-employee in consideration for services rendered, such contributions are treated as guaranteed payments under Code Section 707(c). [I.R.C. §§ 707(c), 1372(a)]

Q 4:171 **Are contributions by an S corporation to an HSA of a 2 percent shareholder-employee in consideration for services rendered deductible by the S corporation?**

Yes. Contributions by an S corporation, which is treated as a partnership (see Q 4:168), to an HSA of a 2 percent shareholder-employee in consideration for services rendered are deductible by the S corporation under Code Section 162, provided the requirements of that section are satisfied, taking into account the rules of Code Section 263 (regarding capital expenditures). [I.R.C. §§ 162(a), 707(c); I.R.S. Notice 2005-8, Q&A 3, 2005-4 I.R.B. 368]

Q 4:172 Are contributions by an S corporation to an HSA of a 2 percent shareholder-employee in consideration of services rendered excluded from a 2 percent shareholder-employee's gross income?

No. Contributions by an S corporation, which is treated as a partnership (see Q 4:168), to an HSA of a 2 percent shareholder-employee in consideration of services rendered are includible in the 2 percent shareholder-employee's gross income. A 2 percent shareholder-employee is not entitled to exclude these contributions from gross income under Code Section 106(d). [Rev. Rul. 91-26, 1991-1 C.B. 184]

Q 4:173 Are contributions made by an S corporation to an HSA of a 2 percent shareholder-employee subject to FICA tax?

Maybe. For employment tax purposes, when contributions are made by an S corporation to an HSA of a 2 percent shareholder-employee, the 2 percent shareholder-employee generally is treated as an employee subject to FICA tax (see Q 4:174). [I.R.S. Notice 2005-8, Q&A 3, 2005-4 I.R.B. 368]

Q 4:174 Is there an exception relative to FICA taxes for a contribution made by an S corporation to an HSA of a 2 percent shareholder-employee?

Yes. If the requirements for the exclusion under Code Section 3121(a)(2)(B) are satisfied, the S corporation's contributions to an HSA of a 2 percent shareholder-employee are not wages subject to FICA tax, even though the amounts must be included in wages for income tax withholding purposes on the 2 percent shareholder-employee's Form W-2—*Wage and Tax Statement.* [I.R.S. Notice 2005-8, Q&A 3, 2005-4 I.R.B. 368]

Practice Pointer. Code Section 3121 does not generally include as *wages* payments for "medical or hospitalization expenses in connection with sickness or accident disability." [I.R.C. § 3121(a)(2)(B)]

Q 4:175 Are contributions made by an S corporation to an HSA of a 2 percent shareholder-employee subject to SECA taxes?

No. Contributions made by an S corporation to an HSA of a 2 percent shareholder-employee are not subject to the SECA tax. [See I.R.S. Ann. 92-16, 1992-5 I.R.B. 53, clarifying the FICA (Social Security and Medicare) tax treatment of accident and health premiums paid by an S corporation on behalf of a 2 percent shareholder-employee.]

Q 4:176   May a 2 percent shareholder-employee who is an eligible individual deduct the amount of the contributions made to an HSA by his or her employer during the taxable year as an adjustment to gross income on his or her federal income tax?

Yes. The 2 percent shareholder-employee, if an eligible individual (see Q 2:6), is entitled under Code Sections 223(a) and 62(a)(19) to deduct the amount of the employer's contributions to the 2 percent shareholder-employee's HSA during the taxable year as an adjustment to gross income on his or her federal income tax return. [I.R.S. Notice 2005-8, Q&A 3, 2005-4 I.R.B. 368; see I.R.S. Notice 2004-2, Q&A 19, 2004-2 I.R.B. 269, for employment tax rules concerning employer contributions to HSAs of employees other than 2 percent shareholder-employees (see Q 4:71)]

Chapter 5

HSA Rollovers and Transfers

This chapter examines rollovers and trustee-to-trustee transfers, which generally are permitted to be made between health savings accounts (HSAs) of an HSA owner or between HSAs of a designated surviving spouse beneficiary. Likewise, the rules relating to rollovers and direct transfers between trustees and custodians from an Archer Medical Savings Account (Archer MSA) to an HSA also are examined.

In addition, the modifications made by Tax Relief and Health Care Act of 2006 (TRHCA) [Pub. L. No. 109-432] that allow an individual to transfer the balance remaining in his or her flexible spending arrangement (FSA) or health reimbursement account (HRA) to an HSA (qualified HSA distribution) and to make a one-time rollover from a traditional IRA to fund an HSA (qualified HSA funding distribution) are also discussed in this chapter.

Rollovers and Transfers from IRAs and HSAs 5-2
    General Rules 5-2
    Inherited HSAs 5-7
    HSA Transfers 5-8
    Transfer Incident to Divorce 5-9
    Other Issues 5-11
Qualified HSA Funding Distributions (IRA to HSA) 5-11
    Tax Treatment 5-12
    No Pro-Rata Recovery 5-14
    Maximum Lifetime Distribution Rules 5-15
    Testing Period 5-16
    Examples of Qualified HSA Funding Distributions 5-17
Qualified HSA Distributions (One-Time HRA and FSA Transfers to an HSA) 5-21
    In General 5-21
    Plan Amendment Required 5-23
    Other Rules 5-24
    Treatment of Qualified HSA Distributions 5-25
    Comparability Rule 5-25
    Transfer Amount 5-26
    Minimum Transfer Amount 5-26

Timing Issues 5-27
Testing Period 5-27
Access to Funds 5-29
Disregarded FSA Coverage 5-29
Permanent Rule Under I.R.S. Notice 2007-22 (after March 15, 2007) 5-33
HRA/FSA-Compatible Coverage Rules 5-40
Treatment of Qualified HSA Distributions 5-41
Reporting FSA/HRA Transfers 5-41

Rollovers and Transfers from IRAs and HSAs

General Rules

Q 5:1   Are rollovers permitted between HSA accounts?

Yes. If the HSA owner receives a distribution from an HSA account, he or she may generally roll over the distribution to an HSA (see Q 5:22). The HSA used to receive the distribution may be the same HSA that made the distribution, or a different HSA may be used. [I.R.C. § 223(f)(5); I.R.S. Notice 2004-2, Q&A 23, 2004-2 I.R.B. 269; I.R.S. Notice 2004-50, Q&A 77, 2004-33 I.R.B. 196] A distribution from an Archer MSA may generally be rolled over to an HSA (see Q 5:2). Trustee-to-trustee transfers between HSAs are also permitted (see Qs 5:30– 5:33).

An individual who is not an eligible individual may make a rollover contribution from his or her existing HSA to a new HSA. (Compare with Q 5:40 regarding qualified funding distributions from an IRA). [I.R.S. Notice 2008-59, Q&A 20, 2008-29 I.R.B. 123]

Note. The terms *HSA owner*, *account owner*, *account holder*, and *account beneficiary* are used interchangeably in IRS publications, notices, and announcements to refer to the person that established the HSA. To avoid confusion, the term *HSA owner* will be used to refer to that person.

Q 5:2   Are rollovers permitted from an Archer MSA to an HSA?

Yes. If a taxpayer receives a distribution from an Archer MSA, he or she may generally roll over the distribution into an HSA for his or her own benefit. [I.R.C. § 223(f)(5); I.R.S. Notice 2004-2, Q&A 23, 2004-2 I.R.B. 269] A non-spouse beneficiary may not roll over a distribution from an Archer MSA. [I.R.C. §§ 220(f)(5), 220(f)(8)]

Q 5:3   May distributions from an individual retirement account (IRA), a health reimbursement arrangement (HRA), or a health care flexible spending account (FSA) be rolled over into an HSA?

In taxable years beginning after 2006, a one-time rollover by direct transfer from a traditional IRA or a Roth IRA to an HSA is generally permitted subject to the maximum contribution limits. [I.R.C. §§ 223(b)(4)(C), 408(d)(9), added by TRHCA § 307(a)-(c) (Pub. L. No. 109-432); for rules in effect for tax years prior to 2007, see I.R.S. Notice 2004-2, Q&A 23, 2004-2 I.R.B. 269, prohibiting such rollovers and transfers] The special rules that apply to one-time transfers are discussed in Qs 5:40– 5:51.

After December 20, 2006, a qualified distribution from an HRA or an FSA may generally be rolled over, by direct transfer, to an HSA. [I.R.C. §§ 223(b)(4)(C), 408(d)(9), added by TRHCA § 307(a)-(c); for rules in effect for taxable years ending before 2007, see I.R.S. Notice 2004-2, Q&A 23, 2004-2 I.R.B. 269, prohibiting such rollovers and transfers] The special rules that apply to transfers from an HRA or FSA are discussed in Qs 5:53–5:90.

Q 5:4   May an individual claim a deduction for the amount rolled over?

No. Although the amount rolled over is generally not included in gross income, an individual may not claim a deduction for an amount that is rolled over. [I.R.C. §§ 219(d)(2), 223(d)(4)(A)]

Q 5:5   Must rollover contributions be made in cash?

No. Rollover contributions need not be in cash. [I.R.C. § 223(d)(1)(A); I.R.S. Notice 2004-50, Q&A 73, 2004-33 I.R.B. 196]

Q 5:6   Must the same property received in a distribution from an HSA or Archer MSA be rolled over?

Yes. The same property distributed from the HSA or Archer MSA must be rolled over. Proceeds from the sale of the property distributed may not be rolled over. [I.R.C. §§ 220(f)(5)(A), 223(f)(5)(A)]

Q 5:7   Must all of the cash or property received in a distribution from an HSA or Archer MSA be rolled over?

No. There is no requirement that the entire amount of cash or other property distributed from an HSA (or Archer MSA) to an HSA owner be rolled over (see Q 5:8). (See Q 5:23 regarding spouses.) Form 8889—*Health Savings Accounts (HSAs)* is used to calculate the taxable portion of an HSA distribution and any penalties that may apply. (For more information, see chapter 6.)

Q 5:8   Is an HSA trustee or custodian required to accept rollover contributions?

No. An HSA trustee or custodian is not required to accept rollover contributions. [I.R.S. Notice 2004-50, Q&A 78, 2004-33 I.R.B. 196]

Q 5:9   What are the tax consequences with respect to the portion of an HSA distribution that is not rolled over to an HSA?

The portion of a distribution that is not rolled over to an HSA may be subject to tax and penalty if not used to pay for qualified medical expenses. (For more information, see chapter 6.)

Q 5:10   Are rollovers from an Archer MSA or another HSA subject to the annual contribution limits?

No. Rollovers from an Archer MSA or another HSA are not subject to the maximum annual contribution limit (see Q 4:91). [I.R.S. Notice 2004-2, Q&A 23, 2004-2 I.R.B. 269]

> **Note.** In taxable years beginning after 2006, a one-time rollover from a traditional IRA or a Roth IRA to an HSA is generally permitted subject to the maximum annual contribution limit ($3,000 for self-only coverage or $5,950 for family coverage for 2009) (see Q 5:40).

After December 20, 2006, a qualified HSA distribution from an HRA or an FSA may generally be rolled over, by direct transfer, to an HSA and is not subject to the HSA maximum annual contribution limit (see Q 5:53).

Q 5:11   May an HSA holder make a rollover contribution more than once during a one-year period?

No. In general, an HSA owner may make only one rollover contribution to an HSA during a one-year period. [I.R.C. § 223(f)(5)(B); I.R.S. Notice 2004-23, Q&A 55, 2004 I.R.B. 725] The one-year period begins on the date that an amount distributed from an HSA, not included in income by reason of a prior rollover, was received. Thus, if a rollover is made from one HSA to another HSA, another rollover cannot be made from either of those HSAs until 12 months have passed from the date the individual received the distribution that was rolled over. [I.R.S. Notice 2004-50, Q&A 55, 2004-33 I.R.B. 196]

> **Practice Pointer.** The one-year rule applicable to an HSA is more restrictive than the one-year rule applicable to a traditional IRA (see examples below). The traditional IRA rules limit the number of distributions from the same IRA that may be rolled over. The IRA rules are based on proposed regulations issued in 1984. [Prop. Treas. Reg. § 1.408-4(b)(4)(ii)]
>
> **Example 1.** Kayla established two traditional IRAs in 2006, IRA-A and IRA-B. She has never received a distribution from either IRA. On January 5, 2009, she rolls IRA-A to IRA-C. On February 5, 2009, she rolls IRA-B to IRA-C. The one-year rule has not been violated because the rule applies separately to each IRA. IRA-C may not be rolled over until the 12-month period has elapsed.
>
> **Example 2.** Same facts as in the preceding example, except Kayla established two HSAs instead of traditional IRAs. The rollover of HSA-B to HSA-C violates the one-year rule, because only one rollover may be made to an HSA

by an owner during the one-year period beginning on the date that an amount distributed from an HSA, not included in income by reason of a prior rollover, was received.

Q 5:12   How is a second rollover from an HSA treated if it is made before the one-year period has expired?

If a second rollover is made from an HSA before the one-year period has expired, such subsequent rollover cannot be treated as a tax-free rollover and may be subject to tax and penalty if not used to pay for qualified medical expenses in the year the distribution occurred. [I.R.C. § 223(f)(5)] (For more information, see chapter 6.)

> **Example.** Wanda received a distribution from HSA-1 on January 15, 2009, and rolled it over to HSA-2 within the 60-day period (see Q 5:15). On January 14, 2010, Wanda received another distribution from HSA-1 (or HSA-2) and rolled over the entire amount distributed into HSA-3. Wanda may have to include the amount she received on January 14, 2010, in income because it was received within the one-year period that began on the date the amount initially rolled over was received (January 15, 2009). An excess contribution to the HSA has been made (see Q 4:91).

Q 5:13   Does a rollover of a distribution from an Archer MSA into another Archer MSA affect eligibility to roll over a distribution from an HSA?

No. Although rollovers between Archer MSAs are also subject to a one-year rule, the rule applies separately to rollovers between Archer MSAs. [I.R.C. § 220(f)(5)(B)]

> **Example 1.** Radcliff received distributions from an HSA and an Archer MSA during the same year. Subject to the 60-day rules, both the HSA and the Archer MSA may be rolled over into an HSA. [I.R.C. §§ 220(f)(5), 223(f)(5)] The same HSA may be used to receive both rollovers.

> **Example 2.** Jill received a rollover eligible distribution from an Archer MSA (MSA-1) and promptly rolled it over to an HSA (HSA-1). Because the one-year rule applies separately to HSAs and Archer MSAs, she may roll over the resulting amount from HSA-1 to another HSA (or back into HSA-1). The one-year period will commence when amounts are distributed from or rolled over from HSA-1.

Q 5:14   If an Archer MSA is rolled over into an HSA, when does the one-year rule pertaining to HSAs apply?

The one-year period applicable to an HSA begins when an amount in the HSA that is subsequently rolled over is withdrawn from the HSA.

Example 1. Gloria has only one HSA from which no distributions have been made. She receives a distribution from an Archer MSA and promptly rolls it over into the HSA. Three weeks later, she withdraws the balance in her HSA and promptly rolls the amount into another HSA. The one-year period applicable to rollovers between HSAs has not been violated because the first rollover from the Archer MSA to the HSA is not counted (see Q 5:11).

Example 2. Same facts as in the preceding example, except Gloria subsequently received another distribution from her Archer MSA within the one-year period. She may not roll over any portion of this distribution into either an HSA or another Archer MSA because the one-year period applicable to Archer MSAs has not expired. [I.R.C. § 220(f)(5)]

Q 5:15   Must the rollover be completed within 60 days?

Yes. To qualify as a rollover, any amount paid or distributed to the HSA owner from an Archer MSA or another HSA must be paid to an HSA within 60 days after the date of receipt of the payment or distribution. [I.R.C. § 223(f)(5)(A); I.R.S. Notice 2004-23, Q&A 55, 2004 I.R.B. 725] This requirement also applies to a spouse beneficiary who inherits an HSA (see Q 5:24). Similar rules apply to the rollover of an Archer MSA into an HSA. [I.R.C. § 220(f)(5)(A)]

Q 5:16   Must the total amount be distributed in order to roll over an HSA to another HSA?

No. A total distribution is not required from the distributing HSA or MSA in order to make a rollover contribution into another HSA. [I.R.C. § 223(f)(5)(A)]

Q 5:17   Must the same property received in a distribution from an Archer MSA be rolled over?

Yes. The property itself received in a distribution from an Archer MSA must be rolled over. There is no provision that permits property distributed from the HSA to be sold and the proceeds rolled over in its place. [I.R.C. § 223(f)(5)(B); see also I.R.C. § 408(d)(3)(A)]

Q 5:18   May an HSA trust or custodial agreement restrict the HSA owner's ability to roll over amounts from that HSA?

No. The HSA rules under Code Section 223 permit the rollover of amounts in an HSA to another HSA, and transfers from one trustee to another trustee. Thus, the trust or custodial agreement may not contain restrictions on the right to transfer from one HSA to another HSA. [I.R.C. § 223(f)(5); I.R.S. Notice 2004-50, Q&A 77, 2004-33 I.R.B. 196]

Note. An HSA trustee is not, however, required to accept a rollover contribution. [I.R.S. Notice 2004-50, Q&A 78, 2004-33 I.R.B. 196]

Q 5:19   How does a taxpayer report a rollover contribution from an Archer MSA or another HSA?

The total of all distributions, including rollover contributions, from an Archer MSA or another HSA is reported in Part II, Line 14a, of Form 8889—*Health Savings Accounts (HSAs)*. Any distributions received during a year are to be included on that year's version of Form 8889. These amounts should be shown in Box 1 of Form 1099-SA that is received from the HSA trustee or custodian. Form 8889 should be attached to Form 1040—*U.S. Individual Income Tax Return, or Form 1040NR—U.S. Nonresident Alien Income Tax Return.* Reporting issues are more fully discussed in chapter 7.

Practice Pointer. It may be necessary to complete Form 8853—*Archer MSAs and Long-Term Care Insurance Contracts*, if required, before completing Form 8889.

Practice Pointer. A separate Part II must be completed when a joint return is filed and each spouse has a "separate HSA." [See Form 8889—*Health Savings Accounts (HSAs)*, Part II.] It does not appear that separate forms are required when a spouse, as designated beneficiary, is treated as the HSA owner.

Q 5:20   How are rollover contributions reported by the trustee or custodian of the distributing HSA on Form 1099-SA?

A trustee or custodian that distributes a rollover contribution will report the contribution to the IRS on Form 1099-SA—*Distributions From an HSA, Archer MSA, or Medicare Advantage MSA* in Box 1 by May 31. A code identifying the distribution is to be entered in Box 3. Reporting issues are more fully discussed in chapter 7.

Q 5:21   When must Form 5498-SA be provided to participants?

If a trustee or custodian is required to file Form 5498-SA—*HSA, Archer MSA, or Medicare Advantage MSA Information*, a statement (generally Copy B) must be provided to the participant by May 31, 2010. This form may also be used to report the December 31, 2009, fair market value of the HSA if provided by January 31, 2010.

Inherited HSAs

Q 5:22   How is an HSA treated when the HSA owner dies?

If the spouse is a designated beneficiary of the HSA, the spouse is automatically treated as the HSA owner thereafter. [I.R.C. § 223(f)(8)(A)] The rollover rules now apply to that spouse as the HSA owner.

Practice Pointer. If a surviving spouse who is the sole designated beneficiary of an HSA remarries and designates his or her new spouse as the HSA's sole designated beneficiary, it appears that the new spouse could become the HSA owner in the same manner. However, the issue is not specifically addressed by the HSA statute, legislative history, or IRS guidance.

Q 5:23   May an inherited HSA be rolled over?

Maybe. If an HSA is inherited due to the death of the HSA owner, no rollover of that HSA is permitted unless the spouse of the decedent is the sole designated beneficiary. [I.R.C. § 223(f)(8)(A)]

Q 5:24   How is an HSA treated when the surviving spouse is not the sole designated beneficiary?

If a person other than the surviving spouse acquires an interest in an HSA, the account ceases to be an HSA as of the date of death (see Q 6:82). The fair market value of the HSA becomes taxable to the beneficiary. However, if any portion of the HSA passes to a nonspouse beneficiary, the entire distribution becomes taxable to the beneficiaries. Reporting issues are more fully discussed in chapter 7.

> **Example.** Paul and Paula are married. Paul has an HSA designating his wife, Paula, and daughter, Sarah, as equal-share beneficiaries of his HSA. Paul dies. Neither Paula nor Sarah may roll over their shares into an HSA. Paula and Sarah must include the value of Paul's HSA in their respective gross incomes.

Q 5:25   How is the value of an HSA reported if the HSA owner's estate is the beneficiary?

If the HSA owner's estate is the beneficiary, the value of the HSA as of the date of death is included on the HSA owner's final income tax return.

Q 5:26   How are earnings after the date of death treated?

Earnings on the account after the date of death are reported as income by the holder of the account (unless the spouse is the sole designated beneficiary; see Q 5:24).

Q 5:27   Are earnings after death subject to the additional 10 percent tax?

No. Earnings on the account after death are not subject to the 10 percent additional tax (see Q 6:74).

HSA Transfers

Q 5:28   Is there a limit on the number of trustee-to-trustee transfers permitted between HSAs?

No. The rules under Code Section 223(f)(5) limiting the number of rollover contributions to one a year do not apply to trustee-to-trustee transfers. Thus, there is no limit on the number of trustee-to-trustee transfers allowed during a year. [I.R.S. Notice 2004-50, Q&As 56 and 77, 2004-33 I.R.B. 196]

Q 5:29   How are trustee-to-trustee transfers between HSAs treated?

Trustee-to-trustee transfers between HSAs are not treated as distributions so long as there is no payment to the HSA owner or to any medical services provider. The amount transferred directly from one trustee or custodian to another trustee or custodian is not included in income, nor is it deducted as a contribution or included as a contribution on Line 14a of Form 8889—*Health Savings Accounts (HSAs)*.

Q 5:30   Are HSA trustees or custodians required to accept trustee-to-trustee transfers?

No. HSA trustees are not required to accept trustee-to-trustee transfers from an HSA (or an Archer MSA). [I.R.S. Notice 2004-50, Q&A 78, 2004-2 I.R.B. 196]

Q 5:31   May the trust or custodial agreement contain restrictions concerning transfers from one HSA to another?

No. The HSA rules under Code Section 223 permit trustee-to-trustee transfers from one HSA to another HSA. Thus, the trust or custodial agreement may not contain restrictions on the right to transfer from one HSA to another HSA. [I.R.C. § 223(f)(5); I.R.S. Notice 2004-50, Q&A 77, 2004-33 I.R.B. 196]

Q 5:32   Must trustee-to-trustee transfers be made in cash?

No. Trustee-to-trustee transfers need not be made in cash. [I.R.C. § 223(d)(1)(A); I.R.S. Notice 2004-50, Q&A 73, 2004-33 I.R.B. 196]

Transfer Incident to Divorce

Q 5:33   May an HSA be transferred to a spouse or former spouse?

Yes. A transfer incident to divorce or separation agreement can occur between HSA accounts in a manner similar to IRAs. The transfer must take the form of a trustee-to-trustee transfer. [I.R.C. § 223(f)(7)]

Q 5:34   Is a transfer incident to divorce or a separation agreement treated as a taxable distribution?

No. Code Section 223(f)(7) provides that the transfer of all or a portion of the HSA holder's interest in an HSA to his or her spouse or former spouse under a divorce or separation instrument (see Qs 5:35, 5:36) is not considered a taxable distribution. [I.R.C. §§ 223(f)(7), 408A(a)]

Q 5:35   What is a divorce or separation instrument?

For HSA purposes, a divorce or separation instrument must be:

- A decree of divorce or separate maintenance or a written instrument incident to such a decree;
- A written separation agreement; or
- A decree requiring a spouse to make payments for the support or maintenance of the other spouse.

Consequently, if an individual divides his or her HSA under a private separation agreement that is not incident to either a divorce or a legal separation, the individual will be taxed pursuant to the general rule under Code Section 223(f). [I.R.C. §§ 71(b)(2)(A), 223(f)(7)]

Q 5:36   Is a transfer incident to divorce or a separation agreement treated as a taxable transfer?

No. The transfer of an individual's interest in an HSA to an individual's spouse or former spouse under a divorce or separation instrument described in Code Section 71(b)(2)(A) will not be considered a taxable transfer. The transfer must be a direct trustee-to-trustee or custodian-to-custodian transfer. A rollover of a distribution does not qualify "as a transfer incident. . . ." Thus, it is not possible for a spouse or former spouse to retain a portion of any cash or property that is directly transferred. [I.R.C. § 223(f)(7)] Direct transfers between custodians and trustees, and vice versa, are also permitted.

Q 5:37   How is an HSA treated after a transfer incident to divorce?

After a transfer incident to divorce, the HSA is treated as an HSA with respect to which the spouse to whom the HSA was transferred is the HSA owner. [I.R.C. § 223(f)(7)]

Note. If such transfer is done properly (e.g., not transferred by rollover), it is not treated as a taxable distribution and the transferee spouse becomes the HSA owner of the HSA account with respect to the portion transferred pursuant to the divorce.

Q 5:38   May a trustee-to-trustee transfer be made to an HSA from an IRA, an HRA, or a health care FSA?

Possibly. In general, direct transfers to an HSA from a traditional IRA, Roth IRA, HRA, or health care FSA to an HSA are not permitted. [I.R.S. Notice 2004-2, Q&A 23, 2004-2 I.R.B. 269] Although there are two exceptions, only distributions from an HSA or an Archer MSA may be directly transferred into an HSA.

1. *Transfer of IRA or Roth IRA to HSA (qualified funding distributions).* In taxable years beginning after 2006, a one-time rollover by direct transfer from a traditional IRA or a Roth IRA to an HSA is generally permitted subject to the maximum contribution limits. The special rules that apply to one-time transfers are discussed in Qs 5:40–5:51.

2. *Transfer of HRA or FSA to HSA (qualified HSA distribution).* After December 20, 2006, a qualified HSA distribution from an HRA or an FSA may generally be rolled over, by direct transfer, to an HSA. The special rules that apply to transfers from an HRA or FSA are discussed in Qs 5:53–5:90.

[I.R.C. §§ 223(b)(4)(C), 408(d)(9), added by TRHCA § 307(a)–(c) (Pub. L. No. 109-432); for rules in effect for taxable years ending before 2007, see I.R.S. Notice 2004-2, Q&A 23, 2004-2 I.R.B. 269, prohibiting such rollovers and transfers]

Other Issues

Q 5:39   May the health coverage tax credit be claimed for premiums paid with tax-free distributions from an HSA?

No. The health coverage tax credit under Code Section 35 regarding health insurance costs of eligible individuals is not available for premiums paid with tax-free distributions from an HSA. [I.R.C. § 35(g)(3); Rev. Proc. 2004-12, 2004-9 I.R.B. 528]

The health coverage tax credit is available to certain individuals who receive a pension benefit from the Pension Benefit Guaranty Corporation (PBGC) or are eligible to receive certain Trade Adjustment Assistance (TAA) or who are eligible for the Alternate Trade Adjustment Assistance (ATAA) program. (See Pub. 502—*Medical and Dental Expenses (Including the Health Coverage Tax Credit)*.)

Qualified HSA Funding Distributions (IRA to HSA)

Q 5:40   May an individual rollover or transfer an amount from a traditional IRA to an HSA?

Yes, in a qualified HSA funding distribution. For taxable years beginning after 2006, an individual may make a qualified HSA funding distribution from an IRA to an HSA. [I.R.C. § 408(d)(9), added by TRHCA § 307(a)] As a result, an HSA may be more attractive to individuals previously unable to fund them because HSA withdrawals for qualified medical expenses are (unlike IRAs generally) not considered taxable income.

An individual must be an eligible individual at the time of a qualified funding distribution. [I.R.S. Notice 2008-51, 2008-25 I.R.B. 1163]. The contribution must be made in a direct trustee-to-trustee transfer and is irrevocable once made. [I.R.C. §§ 408(d)(9)(B), 408(d)(9)(C)(ii)(I)] In general, only one such distribution is permitted to be made in the individual's lifetime (see Q 5:49). Prior to 2007, rollovers or transfers were not permitted to be made to an HSA from an IRA. For example, if a check from an IRA or Roth IRA is made payable to an HSA trustee or custodian and delivered by the IRA or Roth IRA HSA owner to the HSA trustee or custodian, the payment to the HSA will be considered a direct payment by the IRA or Roth IRA trustee, custodian or issuer to the HSA. [I.R.S. Notice 2008-51, 2008-25 I.R.B. 1163; I.R.C. § 408(d)(9)].

Caution. If the individual who makes an IRA transfer to an HSA does not remain an eligible individual during the testing period, the amount of the distribution and contribution is includible in gross income of the individual. The amount will also be subject to an additional 10 percent tax (see Q 5:46).

After the death of an IRA or Roth IRA HSA owner, a qualified HSA funding distribution may be made from an IRA or Roth IRA maintained for the benefit of an IRA or Roth IRA beneficiary. In such case, this distribution is taken into account in determining whether the required minimum distribution requirements have been satisfied. [I.R.C. §§ 408(a)(6), 408(b)(3), and 408A(c)(5); I.R.S. Notice 2008-51, 2008-25 I.R.B. 1163]

Note. There are no special reporting rules applicable to qualified HSA funding distributions which are transferred to an HSA.

Q 5:41   Do the qualified HSA funding distribution rules apply to a Roth IRA?

No. The qualified HSA funding distribution rules only apply to a traditional IRA, other than an "ongoing" SEP IRA or SIMPLE IRA (which are also traditional IRAs). (See Q 5:42.)

Q 5:42   May a qualified funding distribution be made from a SEP IRA or SIMPLE IRA?

Maybe a qualified HSA funding distribution cannot be made from an IRA that is used in connection with a SEP or SIMPLE IRA plan if such plan is "ongoing." [I.R.C. § 408(d)(9)(B); but see, I.R.S. Notice 2008-51, 2008-25 I.R.B. 1163] For this purpose, a SEP IRA or SIMPLE IRA is treated as *ongoing* if an employer contribution is made for the plan year ending with or within the IRA owner's taxable year in which the qualified HSA funding distribution would be made.

In any event, an individual may rollover or transfer funds in a SEP to a separate traditional IRA and then make a qualified HSA funding distribution from that IRA into an HSA.

Tax Treatment

Q 5:43   Can a deduction be taken for the amount distributed from an IRA and transferred to an HSA in a qualified HSA funding distribution?

No. A deduction is not allowed for the amount transferred from an IRA to an HSA in a qualified HSA funding distribution. [Joint Committee on Taxation, Technical Analysis of the Tax Relief and Healthcare Act of 2006, page 79 (Pub. L. No. 109-432) (JCX-50-06); I.R.S. Notice 2008-51, 2008-25 I.R.B. 1163]

Q 5:44   To what extent are the amounts transferred in a qualified HSA funding distribution not included in the IRA owner's gross income?

The amounts distributed from an IRA are not includible in income to the extent that the distribution would otherwise be includible in income under a special rule (see Q 5:46). However, the HSA owner must remain an eligible individual during a testing period (see Q 5:50). In addition, such distributions are not subject to the 10 percent additional tax on early distributions. [I.R.C. § 72; see also I.R.C. § 408(9)(9)(A)]

> **Note.** A qualified HSA funding distribution will likely affect the basis of any assets remaining in the IRA after the qualified funding distribution is made under the pro-rata recovery rules which would generally apply.

Q 5:45   Does a qualified HSA funding distribution count towards the maximum annual contribution limit?

Yes. A qualified HSA funding distribution counts toward the individual's HSA contribution limit for the year ($3,000 for self-only coverage and $5,950 for family coverage for 2009) (see Q 4:30). [I.R.C. § 408(d)(9)(C)(i)] For example, in 2009, an IRA owner who is an eligible individual with family HDHP coverage at the time of the distribution and who is age 55 or over by the end of the year is allowed a qualified HSA funding distribution of $5,950, plus the $1,000 catch-up contribution. An IRA or Roth IRA owner who is an eligible individual with self-only HDHP coverage, and who is under age 55 as of the end of the taxable year, is allowed a qualified HSA funding distribution of $3,000 for 2009.

A qualified HSA funding distribution relates to the taxable year in which the distribution is actually made. The rules that allow contributions made before the deadline for filing the individual's federal income tax return to be treated as made on the last day of the preceding taxable year do not apply to qualified HSA funding distributions. [I.R.S. Notice 2008-51, 2008-25 I.R.B. 1163]

Q 5:46   What happens if the individual does not remain an eligible individual during the testing period?

If the individual does not remain an eligible individual during the testing period (see Q 5:50), the amount of the distribution and contribution is includible in gross income of the individual (see Q 5:47). The amount is includible for the taxable year that includes the first day during the testing period that the individual is not an eligible individual. A 10 percent additional tax also applies to the amount includible. [I.R.C. § 408(d)(9)(D)]

Amounts included in gross income because an individual failed to remain an eligible individual during the testing period is not an excess contribution and the 6 percent tax on excess contributions do not apply to such amounts. For this reason, amounts cannot be withdrawn under the excess contribution rules (see Qs 4:86, 6:4). [I.R.S. Notice 2008-51, 2008-25 I.R.B. 1163]

Note. Eligible individuals for HSAs are generally individuals who are covered by a high deductible health plan (HDHP) and no other health plan that is not an HDHP that provides coverage for any benefit which is covered under the HDHP (see Q 2:6).

No Pro-Rata Recovery

Q 5:47   Do the pro-rata recovery rules apply in determining how much of the qualified HSA funding distribution would otherwise have been includible in income?

No. In determining the extent to which amounts distributed from the IRA in a qualified HSA funding distribution would otherwise be includible in income, the aggregate amount distributed from the IRA is treated as includible in income to the extent of the aggregate amount which would have been includible if all amounts were distributed from all IRAs of the same type (i.e., in the case of a traditional IRA, there is no pro-rata distribution of basis). [I.R.C. § 408(d)(9)(E)] Thus, the amount transferred is treated as coming first from the taxable portion of the IRA. This is another exception to the normal pro-rata recovery rules that generally apply to IRAs. For example, suppose an individual who has $200 of basis in an IRA with a fair market value of $2,000 makes a qualified HSA funding distribution of $1,500 from the IRA. Immediately after the qualified HSA funding distribution, the individual retains $200 of basis in an IRA that has a fair market value of $500 (see examples below).

As under present law, this rule is applied separately to Roth IRAs and other IRAs.

> **Practice Pointer.** If an IRA contains any basis, a qualified HSA funding distribution will likely reduce the taxable portion of amounts subsequently distributed from an IRA under the pro-rata recovery rules that would generally apply.

> **Example 1.** Henry, age 60, has two traditional IRAs. Over the past few years, Henry contributed, but did not deduct, $6,000 in contributions he made to IRA-1 which is now worth $6,900. He also contributed and deducted a $3,000 contribution he made to IRA-2, which is now worth $3,100. No other contributions were made to any IRA or Roth IRA. If Henry removes $1,000 from an IRA he will not have to pay tax on $600 which is treated as a return of basis. [$1,000 times ($6,000 of nondeductible contributions (basis) divided by $10,000 ($6,900 + $3,100))] Henry's remaining basis in the IRA is $5,400 ($6,000 − $600). Henry will have to include $400 in his gross income for the year of the distribution.

> **Example 2.** Same facts as in the preceding example, except Henry's IRA trustee (or custodian) transfers the $1,000 to Henry's HSA in a qualified funding distribution instead. If Henry removed all assets from all IRAs he would pay tax on $4,000 ($10,000 of FMV minus $6,000 of basis). Although no amount of the qualified funding distribution is included in income, the amount transferred is treated as coming first from the taxable portion of the

IRA. Thus, his remaining basis after the qualified funding distribution remains at $6,000. Having a larger basis (compared to $5,400 in Example 1), will reduce the taxable portion (under the pro-rata recovery rule) of subsequent distributions made from the IRA.

If a qualified HSA funding distribution from an individual's IRA or Roth IRA exceeds the aggregate amount which would have been included in gross income if there were a total distribution from that individual's IRA or Roth IRA accounts, the individual's basis in the excess amount (i.e., the amount that would have been excluded from gross income in a distribution to which I.R.C. § 408(d)(9) did not apply) does not carry over to the HSA.

Maximum Lifetime Distribution Rules

Q 5:48   Is there a limit on the amount that can be transferred to an HSA in a qualified HSA funding distribution?

Yes. The amount that can be distributed from the IRA and contributed to an HSA is limited to the otherwise maximum annual contribution limit ($3,000 for self-only coverage or $5,950 for family coverage for 2009). The amount that could otherwise be contributed to the HSA for that year is reduced by the amount contributed from the IRA in a qualified HSA funding distribution. [I.R.C. § 408(d)(9)(C)(i)]

Q 5:49   May an individual make more than one qualified HSA funding distribution?

Generally, no. In general, only one distribution and contribution may be made during the lifetime of the individual. However, if a distribution and contribution are made during a month in which an individual has self-only coverage as of the first day of the month, an additional distribution and contribution may be made during a subsequent month within any taxable year in which the individual has family coverage. The limit applies to the combination of both contributions. [I.R.C. § 408(d)(9)(C)(i)(I)]

The distributions must be from an IRA or Roth IRA to an HSA owned by the individual who owns the IRA or Roth IRA or, in the case of an inherited IRA, for whom the IRA or Roth IRA is maintained. Thus, a qualified HSA funding distribution cannot be made to an HSA owned by any other person, including the individual's spouse. An IRA or Roth IRA owner is not required to make the maximum qualified HSA funding distribution or to make any qualified HSA funding distribution. [I.R.S. Notice 2008-51, 2008-25 I.R.B. 1163]

Note. If an individual owns two or more IRAs, and wants to use amounts in multiple IRAs to make a qualified HSA funding distribution, the individual must first make an IRA-to-IRA transfer of the amounts to be distributed into a single IRA, and then make the one-time qualified HSA funding distribution from that IRA.

Testing Period

Q 5:50   What is the testing period for an IRA transfer to an HSA?

If the individual who makes an IRA transfer to an HSA does not remain an eligible individual during the testing period, the amount of the distribution and contribution is includible in gross income of the individual. This rule is nearly identical to the 13-month rules described later in this chapter for transfers from an HRA or FSA to an HSA. An exception applies if the employee ceases to be an eligible individual by reason of death or disability. [I.R.C. §§ 72(m)(7), 408(d)(9)] The testing period is the period beginning with the first day of the month of the HSA contribution and ending on the last day of the 12th month following such month. If the testing period requirement is not satisfied, the transferred amount is includible for the taxable year that includes the first day during the testing period that the individual is not an eligible individual. A 10 percent additional tax also applies to the amount includible. [I.R.C. § 408(d)(9)(D)(i)-(iii)] Thus, if an individual remains an eligible individual during the entire 13-month testing period, then no amount of the qualified HSA funding distribution is included in income and no amount is subject to the 10 percent additional tax.

Earnings on the amount of the qualified HSA funding distribution are not included in gross income. Amounts included in the IRA or Roth IRA owner's gross income under the 13-month rules are not also included in gross income under the general rules regarding the taxation of distributions under Code Sections 408(d)(1) or 408(d)(2), nor subject to penalty under Code Section 72. [I.R.S. Notice 2008-51, 2008-25 I.R.B. 1163]

Application of the separate testing period rules. If an HSA owner's contributions to his or her HSA in a taxable year include *both* a qualified HSA funding distribution (or distributions) and contributions for individuals that become eligible after the beginning of the year, the testing period rules in Q 5:55 apply to qualified HSA funding distribution (or distributions) and the testing period rules in Q 4:10 apply to the other contributions. If the individual fails to remain an eligible individual during the 13-month testing period applicable to the increased limit for individuals that become eligible after the beginning of the year (see Q 4:10), but does remain a qualified individual during the 13-month testing period applicable to qualified HSA funding distributions discussed in this question, then the amount included in the individual's gross income is the lesser of:

(1) the amount that would otherwise be included under the 13-month testing period rules applicable to the increased limit for individuals that become eligible after the beginning of the year (see Q 4:10), or

(2) The amount of contributions to the HSA for the taxable year other than the amount contributed through qualified HSA funding distributions.

Examples of Qualified HSA Funding Distributions

The following examples illustrate the qualified HSA funding distribution rules discussed in Qs 5:40 through 5:51. The examples assume the following:

- No previous qualified HSA funding distributions have been made by the individual.
- All distributions are from IRAs and are otherwise included in the IRA owner's gross income.
- None of the IRAs are "ongoing" SEP IRAs or ongoing SIMPLE IRAs (see Q 4:46).
- None of the IRA owners or HSA account beneficiaries is disabled.
- None of the exceptions to the 10 percent tax under Code Section 72(t) apply.

Example 1. Rhonda, age 45, enrolls in family HDHP coverage on January 1, 2009, is otherwise an eligible individual as of that date and through December 31, 2010. Rhonda's maximum annual HSA contribution for 2009 is $5,950. Rhonda owns an IRA with a balance of $2,000. A direct trustee-to-trustee transfer of $2,000 is made from Rhonda's IRA trustee to her HSA trustee on April 2, 2009.

The $2,000 distribution is a qualified HSA funding distribution, and accordingly is not included in Rhonda's gross income and is not subject to the additional 10 percent tax under Code Section 72(t). Rhonda's testing period with respect to the qualified HSA funding distribution begins in April 2009 and ends on April 30, 2010.

After the qualified HSA funding distribution of $2,000, $3,950 of Rhonda's 2009 HSA maximum annual contribution remains.

Example 2. Same facts as Example 1, except that Rhonda ceases to be an eligible individual on January 1, 2010. In 2010, Rhonda must include $2,000 in gross income, the amount of the qualified HSA funding distribution, plus an additional tax of $200 (10 percent of the amount included in her income). [I.R.C. § 408(d)(9)(D)(II)] The additional 10 percent penalty under Code Section 408(d)(9)(D) would not apply if Rhonda died or was disabled.

Example 3. Victoria, age 57, enrolls in self-only HDHP coverage effective January 1, 2009, is otherwise an eligible individual as of that date and through December 31, 2010. Victoria's maximum annual HSA contribution for 2009 is $4,000 ($3,000 plus the $1,000 catch-up contribution). Victoria owns an IRA with a balance of $13,550. A direct trustee-to-trustee transfer of $4,000 is made from Victoria's IRA trustee to her HSA trustee on June 4, 2009.

The $4,000 distribution is a qualified HSA funding distribution. The distribution from Victoria's IRA is not included in her gross income and is not subject to the 10 percent additional tax under Code Section 72(t). The qualified HSA funding distribution of $4,000 equals her 2009 maximum annual HSA contribution. Victoria's testing period with respect to the qualified HSA funding distribution begins in June 2009 and ends on June 30, 2010.

Example 4. Happy, age 38, enrolls in self-only HDHP coverage on January 1, 2009, is otherwise an eligible individual on January 1, and remains an eligible individual through December 31, 2010. Happy owns an IRA with a balance of $12,550. A qualified HSA funding distribution of $2,950 is made from Happy's IRA trustee directly to her HSA trustee on June 4, 2009.

On August 1, Happy enrolls in family HDHP coverage. A transfer of $3,000 is made from her IRA trustee directly to her trustee on August 15, 2009.

The $2,950 and $3,000 distributions are qualified HSA funding distributions. The distributions from the IRA are not included in Happy's gross income and are not subject to the additional 10 percent tax under Code Section 72(t). The qualified HSA funding distributions of $5,950 ($2,950 + $3,000) equal Happy's 2009 maximum annual HSA contribution. Happy's testing period for the first qualified HSA funding distribution begins in June 2009 and ends on June 30, 2010 and the testing period for the second qualified HSA funding distribution begins in August 2009 and ends on August 31, 2010.

Example 5. Emily, age 43, enrolls in family HDHP coverage on January 1, 2009, is otherwise an eligible individual on January 1, and remains an eligible individual through December 31, 2010. Emily owns an IRA with a balance of $17,500. A qualified HSA funding distribution of $5,950 is made from Emily's IRA trustee directly to her HSA trustee on March 18, 2009. On June 1, Emily changes from family HDHP coverage to self-only HDHP coverage. The $5,950 distribution from the IRA is not included in Emily's gross income and is not subject to the 10 percent additional tax under Code Section 72(t). The qualified HSA funding distribution of $5,950 equals her maximum annual HSA contribution at the time the transfer occurred. Emily's testing period begins in March 2009 and ends on March 31, 2010.

Example 6. Individual Shawn, age 50, begins family HDHP coverage and is first an eligible individual on June 1, 2009. Shawn owns an IRA with a balance of $20,000. A direct trustee-to-trustee transfer of $3,500 is made from Shawn's IRA trustee to his HSA trustee on June 4, 2009. Shawn also contributes $2,450 in cash to his HSA on June 4, 2009, for a total contribution of $5,950. On July 1, 2010, he ceases to be an eligible individual.

The $3,500 distribution from the IRA is a qualified HSA funding distribution, is not included in Shawn's gross income, and is not subject to the additional tax under Code Section 72(t). Shawn's testing period with respect to the qualified HSA funding distribution begins in June 2009 and ends on June 30, 2010. Shawn remains an eligible individual during the qualified HSA funding distribution testing period. No amount of the $3,500 distribution is included in Shawn's gross income.

The testing period for the $2,450 contribution begins in December 2009 and ends on December 31, 2010 (see Q 4:9). Shawn's full contribution limit for 2009 is $5,950. Shawn's sum of the monthly contribution limits is $3,470.83 (7/12 × $5,950). Shawn's maximum annual contribution for 2009 is $5,950, the greater of $5,950 or $3,470.83 (see Q 4:6).

The amount included in Shawn's gross income and subject to the 10 percent additional tax under Code Section 223(b)(8)(B) in 2010 is $2,479.17 ($5,950 ($3,500 + $2,450) less the allowable pro-rata contribution limit of $3,470.83) (see Q 4:7). [I.R.C. § 223(b)(8)(B) regarding failure to remain an eligible individual during the testing period] The cash contribution to Shawn's HSA is $2,450. The amount included in Shawn's gross income and subject to additional tax is $2,450, the lesser of $2,479.17 (the amount that he would otherwise be entitled to contribute) or $2,450 (the amount of the contribution to the HSA for the taxable year other than amounts funded through qualified HSA funding distributions (see *application of the separate testing period rules* in Q 5:50).

Example 7. Same facts as Example 6, except that the distribution from Shawn's IRA to Shawn's HSA is $1,000 and Shawn contributes $4,950 in cash for a total HSA contribution of $5,950 in 2009.

Shawn remains an eligible individual during the qualified HSA funding distribution testing period. No amount of the $1,000 distribution is included in Shawn's gross income.

Shawn's full contribution limit for 2009 is $5,950. Shawn's sum of the monthly contribution limits is $3,470.83 (7/12 × $5,950). Shawn's maximum annual contribution limit for 2009 is $5,950, the greater of $5,950 or $3,470.83. The amount included in Shawn's gross income and subject to the 10 percent additional tax under Code Section 223(b)(8)(B) is $2,479.17 ($5,950 – $3,470.83). The cash contribution to Shawn's HSA is $4,950. The amount included in Shawn's gross income and subject to the additional tax in 2010 is $2,470.83, the lesser of $2.470.83 (the amount that he would otherwise be entitled to contribute) or $4,950 (the amount of the contribution to the HSA for the taxable year other than amounts funded through qualified HSA funding distributions) (see *application of the separate testing period rules* in Q 5:50).

Example 8. Same facts as Example 6, except that Shawn ceases to be an eligible individual on May 1, 2010.

The $3,500 distribution (from the IRA) is a qualified HSA funding distribution, is not included in Shawn's gross income in the year of the distribution, and is not subject to the additional tax under Code Section 72(t). Shawn's testing period with respect to the qualified HSA funding distribution begins in June 2009 and ends on June 30, 2010. Shawn ceases to be an eligible individual during the qualified HSA funding distribution testing period. The $3,500 distribution is included in Shawn's gross income. In addition, the 10 percent additional tax ($350) under Code Section

408(d)(9)(D)(II) regarding the failure to maintain high deductible health coverage applies to the amount.

The testing period for the $2,450 contribution begins in December 2009 and ends on December 31, 2010. Shawn's full contribution limit for 2009 is $5,950. Shawn's sum of the monthly contribution limits is $3,470.83 (7/12 × $5,950). Shawn's maximum annual contribution limit for 2009 is $5,950, the greater of $5,950 or $3,470.83.

The amount included in Shawn's gross income and subject to the 10 percent additional tax in 2010, under Code Section 223(b)(8) regarding the increased contribution limit for individuals becoming eligible after the beginning of the taxable year is $2,479.17 ($5,950 − $3,470.83) (see Q 4:6). The cash contribution to Shawn's HSA is $2,495. The amount included in Shawn's gross income and subject to additional tax is $2,479.17, the lesser of $2,479.17 (the amount that he would otherwise be entitled to contribute) or $2,495 (the amount of the contribution to the HSA for the taxable year other than amounts funded through qualified HSA funding distributions) (see *application of the separate testing period rules* in Q 5:50).

Example 9. Morgan, age 47, has family HDHP coverage and is first an eligible individual on January 1, 2009. Morgan's maximum annual HSA contribution for 2009 is $5,950. Morgan owns an IRA with a balance of $10,000. A direct trustee-to-trustee transfer of $10,000 is made from his IRA trustee to his HSA trustee on September 26, 2009.

The $10,000 contribution exceeds Morgan's $5,950 contribution limit. In 2009, $4,050 ($10,000 − $5,950) is included in his gross income under Code Section 408(d) as a taxable IRA distribution. [I.R.C. § 408] The $4,050 is also subject to an additional 10 percent tax under Code Section 72, as well as a 6 percent excise tax on excess HSA contributions unless timely corrected (see Q 4:92).

Example 10. Garvin, age 32, has self-only HDHP coverage and is first an eligible individual on January 1, 2008. Garvin remains an eligible individual through December 31, 2010. Garvin's maximum annual HSA contribution for 2008 is $2,900 and $3,000 for 2009. Garvin owns an IRA with a balance of $4,500. A direct trustee-to-trustee transfer of $1,000 from his IRA trustee to his HSA trustee is made on September 6, 2008.

Another direct trustee-to-trustee transfer of $1,500 from Garvin's IRA trustee to his HSA trustee is made on April 28, 2009. He makes no other contributions to his HSA for 2009.

The $1,000 contribution to Garvin's HSA in September 2008 is a qualified HSA funding distribution, is not included in Garvin's gross income, and is not subject to the additional tax under Code Section 72(t). Garvin's testing period with respect to this contribution begins in September 2008 and ends on September 30, 2009. The $1,500 contribution to Garvin's HSA in April 2009 is not a qualified HSA funding distribution because he does not satisfy the exception to the one-time transfer rule (see Q 5:49 and Examples 4 and 5 above), is included in Garvin's gross income for 2009 under Code Section 408 as a taxable IRA distribution. The amount is subject to the additional 10 percent tax under Code Section 72(t). However, the $1,500 contribution to Garvin's HSA is allowed as a deduction in 2009, because he remains an eligible individual in 2009 and has not otherwise made contributions to the HSA or had contributions on his behalf made to an HSA in excess of $3,000 for 2009 (see Q 4:6). No testing period applies to the "annual" $1,500 contribution.

Q 5:51 Must an individual that fails to remain an eligible individual during the testing period have to remove the amount transferred in the qualified HSA funding distribution?

No. Failing to remain an eligible individual after making a qualified HSA funding distribution from an IRA does not require the withdrawal of the qualified HSA funding distribution, and the amount is not an excess contribution. [See I.R.S. Notice 2007-22, 2007-10 I.R.B. 670 (Mar. 5, 2007), as modified by I.R.S. Notice 2008-51, 2008-25 I.R.B. 1163]

Caution. An HSA withdrawal not used for qualified medical expenses is included in income and subject to an additional 10 percent tax (with certain exceptions) under Code Section 223(f)(1), regardless of whether the HSA received a qualified HSA funding distribution that was previously included in the HSA owner's income and subject to the additional 10 percent tax (see Qs 6:72-6:77). [I.R.C. § 223(f)(4)(B)]

Qualified HSA Distributions (One-Time HRA and FSA Transfers to an HSA)

In General

Q 5:52 What is a qualified HSA distribution?

In general, a qualified HSA distribution is a one-time transfer of the balance remaining in an employee's health care FSA or HRA account to an HSA to assist individuals in funding HSA accounts. Qualified HSA distributions can be made after December 20, 2006. [TRHCA § 302(c)] Under prior law, no transfer from an FSA or an HRA to any other type of account, including an HSA, was permitted. The changes in the law resulted in a potential source for funding HSAs. Allowing employees to make qualified HSA distributions will also help transition employees to HDHP coverage.

Q 5:53　What are the steps an employer and employee must follow to transfer amounts from a health care FSA or HRA to an HSA on a tax-free basis?

On February 15, 2007, the IRS issued much-anticipated guidance, Notice 2007-22 [I.R.S. Notice 2007-22, 45 I.R.B. 670 (Mar. 5, 2007)], describing the steps that an employer and employee must follow to transfer amounts from a health care FSA or HRA to an HSA on a tax-free basis. Although the statute [TRHCA § 302(a) amended I.R.C. § 106 by creating a new subsection (e), which allows for a tax-free transfer from an FSA or HRA to an HSA] that created the transfer rights is relatively straightforward, the Notice imposes detailed timing and account balance requirements that must be followed to avoid adverse tax consequences for the HSA owner. The new proposed cafeteria plan regulations implement the changes made in the Tax Relief and Health Care Act of 2006, and adopt the administratively cumbersome requirements for tax-free rollovers described in Notice 2007-22. [Prop. Treas. Reg. § 1.125-5(n)]

In general, the transfer must be made before January 1, 2012, and the amount transferred cannot exceed the balance credited on September 21, 2006 (see Q 5:68). Thus, the rules are of no use to an individual that did not have a balance on that date. [I.R.C. §§ 106(e), 223(c)(1)(B)(iii), 408(d)(9), added by TRHCA § 302(a)–(c); for rules in effect for taxable years ending before 2007, see I.R.S. Notice 2004-2, Q&A 23, 2004-2 I.R.B. 269, prohibiting such rollovers and transfers]

If, at any time during a testing period the individual ceases to remain an eligible individual, the transferred amounts are includible in income and subject to a 10 percent additional tax under Code Section 106(e)(3). The distributions that are transferred into the HSA are called qualifying HSA distributions. [I.R.C. § 106(e)(1)]

Note. Eligible individuals for HSAs are generally individuals who are covered by an HDHP and not covered by any other health plan that is not an HDHP that provides coverage for any benefit which is covered under the HDHP (see Q 2:6).

Caution. If, at any time during the 13-month period beginning with the month of the transfer, the individual is covered by a non-HDHP, or the individual is no longer an eligible individual (e.g., is no longer covered by an HDHP, is enrolled in Medicare, or can be clamed as a dependent on another person's tax return), the transferred amounts are generally includible in income and subject to a 10 percent additional tax (see Q 5:74). [I.R.C. § 106(e)(3)(a)–(b)]

Q 5:54　May a qualified HSA distribution be made from limited purpose or post-deductible FSA/HRA arrangements?

Yes. The TRHCA, which refers to Code Sections 106 and 105, does not carve out or otherwise distinguish limited purpose or post-deductible FSA/HRA arrangements from general purpose arrangements. Accordingly, transfers from limited purpose or post-deductible FSA/HRA arrangements should also be permitted. Similarly, the transfer rule should also apply to variations of the HRA, such as an HRA that is limited to retirees, or an HRA that may only be used to pay premiums.

Q 5:55 May a qualified HSA distribution be made from a dependent care FSA?

No. The qualifying HSA distribution transfer provisions do not apply to a dependent care FSA, which is subject to Code Section 129. The transfer rules are limited to a health care FSA or HRA, which are subject to Code Sections 106 and 105.

Q 5:56 May an employer unilaterally decide to make a qualified HSA distribution?

No. The employer is not required to offer the option. However, an employer may not unilaterally decide to make qualified HSA distributions. An employee must "elect" to do a tax-free transfer in such a manner. [I.R.S. Notice 2007-22, 2007-10 I.R.B. 670 (Mar. 5, 2007)]

Q 5:57 Must the option to make a qualified HSA distribution be offered to all employees?

No. The employer is not required to offer the option. However, an employer allowing any employee to make qualifying HSA distributions must make the option available to all eligible individuals covered by an HDHP of the employer. [I.R.C. § 106(e)(5)(b)]

Q 5:58 May an individual request more than one qualified HSA distribution?

No. The transfer provisions are limited to one distribution with respect to each health FSA or HRA of the individual. The employer determines if and when a qualified HSA distribution may be made from an HRA or an FSA to an HSA. [I.R.C. §§ 106(e)(1), 106(e)(2)]

Plan Amendment Required

Q 5:59 Must an employer offer a qualified HSA distribution option?

No. An employer is not required to allow employees to transfer amounts from an HRA or an FSA. However, if the employer wants to add this design feature to the plan, the employer may do so (see Q 5:60). [I.R.C. § 106(e)(1)]

Q 5:60 Must the FSA or HRA contain provisions allowing qualified HSA distributions?

Yes. The plan must contain provisions providing for the election to make a qualified HSA distribution. For an existing FSA or HRA, this would require a plan amendment to the FSA and/or HRA plan document. [See I.R.C. § 106(e)(1)]

Other Rules

Q 5:61 May the opportunity to make a qualified HSA distribution be provided on a one-time basis?

Yes. The employer could offer the transfer opportunity on a one-time basis, and there would be no obligation to offer it again in future years.

Q 5:62 Must an employer with an FSA and an HRA who wishes to allow for qualified HSA distributions do so for both the FSAs and the HRA?

No. The HSA legislation does not require an employer who wishes to allow for qualified HSA distributions do so for both an FSA and an HRA. The legislation merely provides that a plan shall not fail to be treated as an FSA or HRA under Code Sections 106 (which allows employer contributions to be excluded from income) or 105 (which allows reimbursements from health plans to be excluded from income) if the employer makes a distribution from an FSA or an HRA to an HSA, subject to balance restrictions (see below), and prior to January 1, 2012. [I.R.C. § 106(e)(1)] Accordingly, the employer can choose to allow a transfer from just the FSA or HRA, to allow a transfer from both arrangements, or to allow no transfer at all.

> **Practice Pointer.** The employer could amend the FSA for a plan year (prior to 2012) if that FSA has a grace period to allow FSA participants to transfer the amount credited to their FSA on a future date, or if less, the amount that was credited to their FSA as of September 21, 2006. For example, an employer could choose to allow a one-time FSA transfer of the amount credited to the account as of the last day of any plan year prior to 2012, and it thereby allows FSA participants to not lose all of the amounts credited to the FSA.

> **Note.** If there are any amounts credited to the FSA on the last day of the plan year that exceed the balance on September 21, 2006, it would be impossible to satisfy the requirement in Notice 2007-22 that the transfer result in a zero balance in the FSA. Thus, in that circumstance, a tax-free transfer could not be made. However, the TRHCA added an exception for a "zero balance" FSA and for a qualified HSA distribution of the remaining year-end balance. If such a transfer is made, the disqualifying coverage under that FSA would be disregarded (see Qs 5:80–5:84).

Q 5:63   May a qualified HSA distribution be made in property?

Yes. A qualified HSA distribution does not have to be made in cash, and may be made in property acceptable to the trustee or custodian. [I.R.C. § 223(d)(1)(A); I.R.S. Notice 2004-50, Q&A 73, 2004-33 I.R.B. 196]

Treatment of Qualified HSA Distributions

Q 5:64   How are qualified HSA distributions treated?

A qualified HSA distribution is treated as an employer contribution and as a rollover contribution. Thus, it is excludable from gross income and wages for employment tax purposes. [I.R.C. § 106(e)(4)(C); Joint Committee on Taxation, Technical Analysis of the Tax Relief and Healthcare Act of 2006 (Pub. L. No. 109-432) (JCX-50-06)]

Q 5:65   Is a qualified HSA distribution taken into account for purposes of determining the HSA annual contribution limitation?

No. A qualified HSA distribution is not taken into account for purposes of determining the HSA annual contribution limitation (i.e., $3,000 for self-only coverage and $5,950 for family coverage for 2009). [I.R.C. § 223(b)(4)(C)]

Q 5:66   May an individual who makes a qualified HSA distribution claim a deduction for the amount transferred to the HSA?

No. The individual may not claim a deduction for the qualified HSA distribution that is transferred to an HSA. [I.R.C. § 223(b)(4)(C)]

Comparability Rule

Q 5:67   Must an employer that allows any employee to make a transfer from an HRA or FSA to an HSA offer the same right to all eligible individuals?

Yes. An employer that allows any employee to make a transfer from an HRA or FSA to an HSA, must offer the same right to all eligible individuals covered under an HDHP offered by the employer. If not, the failure is treated as a violation of the comparability rules and subject to a 35 percent excise tax. [I.R.C. § 106(e)(5)(B)(ii); I.R.S. Notice 2007-22, 2007-10 I.R.B. 670 (Mar. 5, 2007)] Qualified HSA distributions are not otherwise subject to the comparability rules. [I.R.C. § 106(e)(5)(B)(i)] An employer would not be required to offer a transfer to any employees who have HDHP coverage that the employer does not sponsor.

Transfer Amount

Q 5:68 Is there a limit to the amount that may be transferred to an HSA in a qualified HSA distribution?

Yes. For an HRA, the amount that can be transferred is the actual dollar amount (balance) that was credited to the account as of September 21, 2006 or, if less, the balance in the account on the date of the transfer. The legislative history indicates that the balance as of any date is determined on a cash basis (i.e., expenses incurred that have not been reimbursed as of the date the determination is made are not taken into account). [Joint Committee on Taxation, Technical Analysis of the Tax Relief and Healthcare Act of 2006, page 75 (Pub. L. No. 109-432) (JCX-50-06)] Thus, pending and unsubmitted claims are not taken into account, regardless of when the expense was incurred. [I.R.S. Notice 2007-22, 2007-10 I.R.B. 670 (Mar. 5, 2007)]

For an FSA, the amount that could be transferred to an HSA is the actual dollar amount that was credited to the account as of September 21, 2006, or if less, the balance in the FSA account on the last day of the plan year for which the transfer is elected.

Caution. The transfer rules only apply to existing FSAs and HRAs on September 21, 2006, and only to those which are amended or contain provisions for such transfers. [I.R.C. § 223(b)(2)(A)] An FSA or HRA established after that date would have had a *zero* balance on September 21, 2006.

Note. Congress intended to apply the FSA transfer rule not only to FSA elections made in 2006, but to future FSA elections through 2011. So, as long as an individual had an FSA with a balance on September 21, 2006, it appears that individual can make a future FSA election and transfer a portion of that future FSA into an HSA (capped at the Sept. 21, 2006 account balance).

Q 5:69 May the September 21, 2006 balance be based on the balance in the FSA or HRA account of a former employer?

No. The Treasury has confirmed that the September 21, 2006 balance may not be determined based on the balance in the FSA or HRA account of a former employer. [I.R.S. Notice 2007-22, 2007-10 I.R.B. 670 (Mar. 5, 2007)]

Minimum Transfer Amount

Q 5:70 What is the minimum amount that must be transferred in a qualified HSA distribution?

Generally, the full account balance under the FSA or HRA on the last day of the plan year must be transferred in a qualified HSA distribution in order for the transfer to be tax-free. However, see Q 5:72 regarding a limited purpose FSA or other arrangement described in Revenue Ruling 2004-45. [2004-1 C.B. 971]

Timing Issues

Q 5:71   Is it possible for an employee to do a tax-free transfer during the year?

Generally, no. In determining what requirements an employer must satisfy to comply with new Code Section 106(e), the IRS has taken a surprisingly narrow reading of the statute that results in several complex and restrictive rules. For example, the IRS has determined that it is generally not possible for an employee to do a tax-free transfer during the year, but rather, that the transfer must take place during the 2½–month period following the close of the year and the employer must "freeze" the balance that is left in the account as of the last day of the plan year. For an FSA, this means that the employer must adopt a grace period extension in order to make a tax-free transfer (so that the disqualifying coverage under the FSA or HRA during the grace is disregarded). The IRS further determined that any transfer must result in a zero balance in a general purpose health FSA or HRA in order to be tax-free to the HSA owner. As a result, the amount that must be transferred from a general purpose health FSA or HRA cannot be less than the amount in the account on the date of distribution. Thus, any individual with a balance in his or her general purpose health FSA or HRA account on the date of the transfer that exceeds the balance on September 21, 2006 cannot do a tax-free transfer. However, see Q 5:54 regarding a limited purpose or other arrangement described in Revenue Ruling 2004-45. [2004-1 C.B. 971]

Q 5:72   Is it possible to make a mid-year transfer from a limited purpose FSA or HRA? Must the transfer result in a zero balance?

Yes. If the FSA or HRA arrangement is a limited purpose or other arrangement described in Revenue Ruling 2004-45 [2004-1 C.B. 971], it appears that the transfer could be made at any time during the plan year, and need not result in a zero balance. The IRS is expected to issue further guidance addressing this. Unfortunately, the Notice indicates that an employer may not convert a general purpose HRA or FSA to an HSA-compatible arrangement only for HSA-eligible individuals who elect transfers. Rather, such arrangement would have to be converted for all employees.

Note. If future guidance were to allow conversions to an HSA-compatible arrangement for just those employees who elect transfers, the qualified HSA distribution rules would be much easier to administer.

Testing Period

Q 5:73   What is the testing period for a qualified HSA distribution?

The testing period is the period beginning with the first day of the month the qualified HSA distribution is contributed to the HSA and ends on the last day of the 12th month following such month. [I.R.C. § 106(e)(4)(A)] If applicable, income tax applies for the taxable year that includes the first month of the testing period in which the owner ceased to be an eligible individual.

Example 1. Karla intends to enroll in Medicare when she attains age 65 in December 2010. In December 2009, Karla's employer makes a qualified HSA distribution from her HRA (which has a fiscal year ending on October 31, 2009) that is transferred to her HSA. Karla enrolls in Medicare in December 2010. As a result, Karla did not remain eligible for the entire testing period—the 12-month period following the month the qualified HSA distribution was made. Karla must include the qualified HSA distribution in her income in 2010 (the taxable year that included the month she became ineligible). Had Karla made the qualified HSA distribution in November 2009, she could enroll in Medicare as she planned in December (the month following the end of the testing period of November 2009 to November 2010) because she remained an HSA eligible individual for the entire testing period. Alternatively, if Karla waits one month and enrolls in Medicare in January 2011, the testing period rules would be satisfied.

Q 5:74 What happens if the individual does not remain an eligible individual during the testing period following a qualified HSA distribution?

If, at any time during the 13-month period beginning with the month of the transfer, an individual is no longer an eligible individual (e.g., is no longer covered by an HDHP, is enrolled in Medicare, or can be clamed as a dependent on another person's tax return), the transferred amounts are includible in income and subject to a 10 percent additional tax. The rule does not apply if the individual ceases to be an eligible individual by reason of death or disability. [I.R.C. § 106(e)(3)(B)] For this purpose, the Code Section 72(m)(7) definition of disability is used. Except for these two circumstances, the decision to take a qualified HSA distribution effectively locks the individual into maintaining an HDHP for the following 12 months.

Q 5:75 Is withdrawal of the transferred amount required if an individual fails to remain an eligible individual during the testing period?

Failing to remain an eligible individual during the testing period does not require the withdrawal of the transferred amount, and the amount is not an excess contribution and does not need to be withdrawn in order to avoid incurring the 6 percent excise tax that generally applies to excess contributions made to an HSA. [I.R.S. Notice 2007-22, 2007-10 I.R.B. 640 (Mar. 5, 2007), Example 11, 2007-10 I.R.B. 670. A qualified HSA distribution "is treated as a rollover contribution" under I.R.C. § 223(f)(5). The definition of *excess contribution* (to an HSA) does not include a rollover contribution described in I.R.C. § 223(f)(5). See I.R.C. §§ 223(f)(3)(B), 106(e)(4)(C) referencing I.R.C. § 223(f)(5); see also I.R.C. § 4973 regarding the 6 percent tax]

Q 5:76 Is an employer responsible for reporting whether an employee who makes an FSA or HRA transfer remains an eligible individual during the testing period?

Employers are not responsible for reporting whether an employee who makes an FSA or HRA transfer remains an eligible individual during the testing period. It is not required that an employee be an eligible individual with HDHP coverage in order to have a transfer made on the employee's behalf. However, as a practical matter, the employer should verify eligible individual status before making the transfer, because otherwise the transfer will be taxable to the employee and subject to a 10 percent additional tax.

Practice Pointer. Employers do not have any obligation to monitor an employee's coverage during the testing period following a transfer. However, it appears that if the requirements of Notice 2007-22 are not satisfied at the time of transfer, the employer may be required to report the transferred amount as wages on the employee's Form W-2. It would be helpful if the IRS clarified this point, however.

Note. A qualified HSA funding distribution is not subject to withholding under Code Section 3405 because an IRA or Roth IRA owner that requests such a distribution is deemed to have elected out of withholding under section 3405(a)(2). For purposes of determining whether a distribution requested by an IRA or Roth IRA owner is a qualified HSA funding distribution, the IRA or Roth IRA trustee may rely upon reasonable representations made by the HSA owner. [I.R.S. Notice 2008-51, 2008-25 I.R.B. 1163]

Access to Funds

Q 5:77 Does an employee have immediate ability to access the HSA funds that are transferred in a qualified HSA distribution?

Yes. Subject to any reasonable restrictions imposed by the HSA custodian or trustee, the employee should have immediate ability to access the HSA funds that are transferred. This is true whether or not the employee is enrolled in a qualified HDHP at the time of the qualified HSA distribution. Of course, if the employee is not enrolled in an HDHP at the time of the transfer or during the 13-month period beginning with the month of the distribution, there would be income tax and a 10 percent additional tax imposed on the HSA owner.

Disregarded FSA Coverage

Q 5:78 Is there an exception to the zero balance requirement following a qualified HSA distribution?

Yes. The TRHCA added an exception for a "zero balance" FSA and for a qualified HSA distribution of the remaining year-end balance (see Qs 5:80–5:84). If such a transfer is made, the disqualifying coverage under that FSA would be disregarded.

Prior to the TRHCA an individual that participated in a health FSA with a grace period was not treated as an eligible individual even if the individual's health FSA had no unused benefits as of the end of the prior year (i.e., the balance in the health FSA was zero as of the last day of the plan year). Notice 2005-86 provided transitional "grace period" relief that applied before March 15, 2007, and allowed an employer to amend its cafeteria plan health FSA to provide that disqualifying coverage during the grace period does not apply (would not be provided) to an individual that elected HDHP coverage. The transitional relief also applied to an individual who had no unused benefits or contributions remaining at the end of the prior year. [I.R.S. Notice 2005-86, 2005-2 C.B. 1075] Thus, an otherwise eligible individual would not be treated as having disqualifying coverage under the FSA.

Note. Coverage by an HSA-compatible health FSA or HRA (limited-purpose health FSA or HRA, post-deductible health FSA or HRA, retirement HRA, or suspended HRA) does not affect an employee's eligibility to make a qualified HSA distribution, or affect an individual's eligibility to contribute to an HSA, including coverage during a health FSA grace period. [I.R.S. Notice 2005-86, 2005-2 C.B. 1075]

Q 5:79   What were the steps an employer had to take under the transitional relief that applied before March 15, 2007?

Under the transitional relief, which applied before March 15, 2007, and only to general purpose HRA plans or calendar year health FSA plans that already have a grace period, an employer must have:

- Amended the FSA and HRA written plan document by March 15, 2007, to allow a qualified HSA distribution prior to March 15, 2007.
- Provided employees an election form to request a transfer any time from January 1, 2007, through March 15, 2007, if they:
  - Had established an HSA and were or would be eligible individuals by the first day of the month of the transfer due to coverage under the employer's HDHP;
  - Had an FSA or HRA on September 21, 2006, with a positive balance; and
  - Currently had an FSA or HRA with funds credited to it.
- Provided information to employees regarding the requirements of making a transfer:
  - Explaining how transfer amount is calculated (i.e., on cash basis).
  - Explaining that the maximum amount that can be transferred is the lesser of the balance that was in the account on September 21, 2006, or the date of the transfer.
  - Explaining that if the balance in an FSA or HRA at time of transfer is greater than the balance on September 21, 2006, a tax-free transfer cannot be made because the transfer would not result in a zero balance as required by IRS guidelines.

- Explaining that the employee may make only one transfer from a particular FSA or HRA.
- Providing an overview of the testing period requirements to ensure employees have a basic understanding of the risk of failing to maintain status as an eligible individual (although the employer is not required to report this information to the HSA trustee/custodian or the IRS).

- Made the transfer for employees who returned election forms on or before March 15, 2007, by transferring funds from the FSA or HRA directly to the HSA trustee/custodian by March 15, 2007, but after the employee is an eligible individual.

- Informed the HSA trustee/custodian that the amounts are intended to be a qualified HSA distribution.

[See I.R.S. Notice 2007-22, 2007-10 I.R.B. 640 (Mar. 5, 2007). There may be additional flexibility for HSA-compatible health FSAs or HRAs that satisfy the requirements of Rev. Rul. 2004-45 (2004-1 C.B. 971).]

Transition Rule Examples

The following examples illustrate the transitional rules for qualifying HSA distributions made before March 15, 2007. All references to balances in the following examples are determined on a cash basis. All grace periods satisfy the requirements of Notice 2005-42. None of the employees in the examples are disabled.

Example 1. For 2006, Salmon Corporation has a calendar year general purpose health FSA with a grace period ending on March 15, 2007. Salmon offers employees the option of electing HDHP coverage for the plan year beginning January 1, 2007.

Salmon amends the health FSA to allow for qualified HSA distributions. The amended plan allows an employee electing HDHP coverage to also elect to have any health FSA balance at year-end, determined on a cash basis, contributed directly to an HSA trustee for the employee. For this purpose, the year-end balance is the balance of the health FSA without regard to any expenses incurred but not paid. During the period from January 1, 2007 to March 15, 2007, an employee electing HDHP coverage for 2007 may elect a qualified HSA distribution of the health FSA balance. The amount of the qualified HSA distribution is determined on a cash basis on the date of the distribution.

A. Marvin, an employee of Salmon, has a balance of $850 remaining in the general purpose health FSA on December 31, 2006. On or before December 31, 2006, he elects HDHP coverage beginning January 1, 2007. Marvin does not elect to have a qualified HSA distribution of the $850 remaining in the health FSA on December 31, 2006. Marvin incurred $850 of qualified medical expenses after January 1 and the health FSA reimbursed Marvin for that amount. Marvin's health FSA balance is zero on January 22, 2007. Marvin is otherwise an eligible individual as of January 1, 2007.

Marvin has disqualifying coverage by the health FSA until April 1, 2007 because he neither had a zero balance in the FSA on December 31, 2006 nor did he have a zero balance following a qualified HSA distribution on or before March 15, 2007.

B. Nancy, an employee of Salmon, has a balance of $800 in the general purpose health FSA on September 21, 2006, and a balance of $200 on December 31, 2006. On or before December 31, 2006, Nancy elects HDHP coverage beginning January 1, 2007. During January 2007, the health FSA reimburses her for $50 in qualified medical expenses. On February 12, 2007, Nancy elects to have a qualified HSA distribution of the remaining health FSA balance of $150. Salmon contributes $150 to an HSA on behalf of Nancy on or before March 15, 2007. Nancy is otherwise an eligible individual as of January 1, 2007.

Nancy is an eligible individual as of January 1, 2007 because after the qualified HSA distribution Nancy has a zero balance in a health FSA.

C. Otto, an employee of Salmon, has a balance of $300 in a health FSA on September 21, 2006, and a balance of $175 on December 31, 2006. On or before December 31, 2006, Otto elects HDHP coverage for 2007. On or before March 15, 2007, Otto also elects to have a qualified HSA distribution of the $175 remaining in the health FSA on December 31, 2006. Salmon contributes $175 to an HSA on behalf of Otto on or before March 15, 2007. Otto is otherwise an eligible individual as of January 1, 2007.

Otto is an eligible individual as of January 1, 2007 because after the qualified HSA distribution Otto has a zero balance in a health FSA.

Example 2. The same facts as Example 1, except Marvin and Nancy incurred their respective $850 and $50 in qualified medical expenses in December 2006. Marvin and Nancy submitted the expenses and were reimbursed from the health FSA for the expenses after January 1, 2007 and before February 1, 2007. On February 12, 2007, Nancy elects to have a qualified HSA distribution of the remaining health FSA balance of $150. Salmon contributes $150 to an HSA on behalf of Nancy on or before March 15, 2007. Nancy is otherwise an eligible individual as of January 1, 2007. Marvin does not make an election to have an HSA qualified distribution because he has no funds remaining in his account in January 2007.

Marvin has disqualifying coverage by the health FSA until April 1, 2007 because Marvin neither had a zero balance in the FSA on December 31, 2006 nor did Marvin have a zero balance following a qualified HSA distribution on or before March 15, 2007. Nancy is an eligible individual as of January 1, 2007 because after the qualified HSA distribution Nancy has a zero balance in a health FSA.

Permanent Rule Under I.R.S. Notice 2007-22 (after March 15, 2007)

Q 5:80   **Must an employer adopt a grace period extension and must the qualified HSA distribution result in a zero balance?**

Probably yes. In general, it is not possible for an employee to do a tax-free transfer during the year, but rather, the transfer must take place during the 2½ month period following the close of the year and the employer must "freeze" the balance that is left in the account as of the last day of the plan year (see Qs 5:81, 5:82). For an FSA, this means that the employer must adopt a grace period extension in order to make a tax-free transfer. [I.R.S. Notice 2007-22, 2007-10 I.R.B. 640 (Mar. 5, 2007)]

Q 5:81   **Must the participant have a zero balance after a qualified HSA distribution is made?**

In general, any transfer must result in a zero balance in the FSA or HRA in order to be tax-free to the HSA owner. Thus, any individual with a balance in his or her FSA or HRA account on the date of the transfer that exceeds the balance on September 21, 2006, cannot do a tax-free transfer (but see Q 5:54). [I.R.S. Notice 2007-22, 2007-10 I.R.B. 640 (Mar. 5, 2007)]

Q 5:82   **Is a participant with a zero balance treated as having coverage during the grace period?**

A participant in a general purpose heath FSA with a grace period who has a zero balance on the last day of the plan year does not fail to be an eligible individual as of the first day of the immediately following health FSA plan year because of coverage during a grace period. [I.R.S. Notice 2007-22, 2007-10 I.R.B. 640 (Mar. 5, 2007)]

Q 5:83   **What happens if the steps identified in I.R.S. Notice 2007-22 are not followed?**

If the steps identified in I.R.S. Notice 2007-22 are not followed, the transfer will be includible in the employee's income and subject to a 10 percent additional tax. The circumstances that may cause an HSA transfer to be taxable to the HSA owner and subject to an additional 10 percent tax include the following:

- Failure to transfer entire balance from a general purpose health FSA or HRA.
- Transfer before or after the 2½ month period following the end of FSA or HRA plan year.
- A transfer that occurs during a month in which the individual does not have HDHP coverage as of the first of the month.

- Disqualifying coverage under HRA or FSA after the transfer, which includes reimbursing expenses out of the account after the end of the plan year.
- Failure to remain an eligible individual during the 13-month testing period following the transfer.

[I.R.S. Notice 2007-22, 2007-10 I.R.B. 640 (Mar. 5, 2007)]

Q 5:84   What must an employer do under the permanent rule of I.R.S. Notice 2007-22 to allow qualified HSA distributions?

Under the permanent rule that starts on March 16, 2007 and ends on December 31, 2011, an employer, before the end of a plan year, must:

- Amend the FSA and HRA written plan document to allow a qualified HSA distribution.
- For an FSA, amend the plan to include a grace period so that participants are not required to forfeit account balances on the last day of the plan year.
- Provide employees an election form to elect a transfer if they:
  - Have established an HSA that plan year and are or will be eligible individuals by the first day of the month of the transfer due to coverage under the employer's HDHP;
  - Had an FSA or HRA on September 21, 2006, with a positive balance; and
  - Have an FSA or HRA with funds credited to it (or may have such account prior to the end of the plan year).
- Provide the following information to employees regarding the requirements of making a transfer:
  - Explain how transfer amount is calculated (i.e., on cash basis based upon account balance on last day of plan year).
  - Explain that the maximum amount that can be transferred is the lesser of the balance that was in the account on September 21, 2006, or on the date of the transfer.
  - Explain that if the balance in the FSA or HRA at the time of transfer is greater than the balance on September 21, 2006, a tax-free transfer cannot be made because the transfer would not result in a zero balance as required by IRS guidelines.
  - Provide an overview of the testing period requirements to ensure employees have a basic understanding of the risk of failing to maintain status as an eligible individual (although the employer is not required to report this information to the HSA trustee/custodian or the IRS).
- Collect election forms from employees on or before the last day of the plan year.

- Freeze the FSA/HRA account balances for employees who elect the transfer, effective on the last day of the plan year (i.e., for calendar-year plan, 12/31). Do not process any claims after the freeze date.

- Make the transfer for employees who return election forms on or before the last day of the plan year by transferring funds from the FSA or HRA directly to the HSA trustee/custodian by the 15th day of the third month following the end of that plan year but after the employee is an eligible individual. Inform the HSA trustee/custodian that the amounts are intended to be qualified HSA distributions.

[I.R.S. Notice 2007-22, 2007-10 I.R.B. 640 (Mar. 5, 2007)]

Permanent Rule Examples

The following examples illustrate the permanent rule for qualifying HSA distributions (i.e., those made after March 15, 2007). All references to balances in the following examples are determined on a cash basis. All grace periods satisfy the requirements of Notice 2005-42. None of the employees in the examples are disabled.

Example 1. For 2009, Dust Corporation maintains a calendar year general purpose health FSA with a grace period ending March 15, 2010. For 2009, Patrick, an employee, timely elects salary reduction of $500 for the general purpose health FSA. Dust offers employees the option of electing HDHP coverage for the plan year beginning January 1, 2010. On or before December 31, 2009, Patrick elects HDHP coverage beginning January 1, 2010. On December 31, 2009, Patrick has a zero balance in the health FSA. Patrick is otherwise an eligible individual on January 1, 2010.

Patrick does not fail to be an eligible individual on January 1, 2010, merely because of the health FSA grace period.

Example 2. For 2009, Touchstone Corporation has a calendar year general purpose health FSA with a grace period ending on March 15, 2010. Touchstone offers employees the option of electing HDHP coverage for the plan year beginning January 1, 2010. Before January 1, 2010, Touchstone amends the health FSA to allow for qualified HSA distributions. The amended plan allows an employee electing HDHP coverage to also elect to have any health FSA balance at year end, determined on a cash basis, contributed directly to an HSA trustee for the employee. For this purpose, the year-end balance is the balance of the health FSA without regard to any expenses incurred but not paid. Under the amendment, if an employee elects the qualified HSA distribution, the employee cannot submit any additional claims after December 31, 2009, regardless of when the underlying expense was incurred nor are any claims paid after December 31, 2009, even if submitted prior to December 31, 2009.

A. Betty, an employee of Touchstone, has a balance of $950 in the health FSA on September 21, 2006, and a balance of $700 on December 31, 2009. On or before December 31, 2009, Betty elects HDHP coverage beginning January 1,

2010. Betty also elects to have a qualified HSA distribution of the $700 remaining in the health FSA on December 31, 2009. Touchstone contributes $700 to an HSA on behalf of Betty on or before March 15, 2010. Betty is otherwise an eligible individual as of January 1, 2010. Betty does not fail to be an eligible individual as of January 1, 2010 because after the qualified HSA distribution, she has a zero balance in the health FSA.

B. Harry, an employee of Touchstone, has a balance of $850 on December 31, 2009. On or before December 31, 2009, Harry elects HDHP coverage for 2010. Harry does not elect to have a qualified HSA distribution of the $850 remaining in the health FSA on December 31, 2009. Harry is otherwise an eligible individual. Harry is an eligible individual on April 1, 2010. His coverage during the grace period makes him ineligible during the months of January, February, and March.

Example 3. For 2009, Grape Corporation has a calendar year general purpose HRA. Grape offers employees the option of electing HDHP coverage for the plan year beginning January 1, 2010. Before January 1, 2010, Grape amends the HRA to allow for qualified HSA distributions. The amended HRA allows an employee electing HDHP coverage for the plan year to also elect to have the lesser of the balance in the HRA on September 21, 2006 or the HRA balance at year-end, determined on a cash basis, contributed directly to an HSA trustee for the employee. For this purpose, the year-end balance is the balance of the HRA without regard to any expenses incurred but not paid. Under the amendment, if an employee elects the qualified HSA distribution, the employee cannot submit any additional claims after December 31, 2009, regardless of when the underlying expense was incurred, nor will the HRA reimburse any claim submitted but unpaid as of December 31, 2009. The amendment also provides that an employee who elects a qualified HSA distribution may also elect to waive participation in the HRA.

A. Marla, an employee of Grape, has a balance of $300 in the HRA on September 21, 2006, and a balance of $175 on December 31, 2009. On or before December 31, 2009, Marla elects HDHP coverage for 2010. Marla also elects to have a qualified HSA distribution of the $175 remaining in the HRA on December 31, 2009, and to waive participation in the HRA effective after December 31, 2009. Grape contributes $175 to an HSA on behalf of Marla on or before March 15, 2010. Marla is otherwise an eligible individual as of January 1, 2010.

Marla does not fail to be an eligible individual as of January 1, 2010 because after the qualified HSA distribution she has a zero balance in the HRA and does not participate in any non-HSA compatible HRA.

B. Roberta, an employee of Grape, has a balance of $300 in the HRA on September 21, 2006, and a balance of $550 on December 31, 2009. On or before December 31, 2009, Roberta elects HDHP coverage for 2010. Roberta also elects to have a qualified HSA distribution of the $300 that was in the HRA on September 21, 2006. Grape contributes $300 to an HSA on behalf of

Roberta on March 15, 2010. Roberta is otherwise an eligible individual as of January 1, 2010.

Roberta fails to be an eligible individual after the qualified HSA distribution, because she has a balance exceeding zero in the HRA after the distribution. Roberta must include $300 in gross income in 2010, as well as pay an additional 10 percent tax.

C. Herbert, an employee of Grape, has a balance of $400 in the HRA on September 21, 2006. On or before December 31, 2009, Herbert elects HDHP coverage for 2010. On June 15, 2010, Herbert has a balance of $275 in the HRA, and elects to have a qualified HSA distribution of the $275. Grape contributes $275 to an HSA on behalf of Herbert on August 20, 2010. Herbert is otherwise an eligible individual as of January 1, 2010.

Herbert fails to be an eligible individual after the qualified HSA distribution, because Herbert remains a participant in an HRA that is not HSA-compatible until the end of the HRA plan year. The result is the same regardless of whether Herbert waived participation in the HRA after June 15, 2010. Thus, Herbert must include $275 in gross income in 2010, as well as pay an additional 10 percent tax.

Example 4. The same facts as Example 3, except Grape converted the general purpose HRA to an HSA-compatible retirement HRA for all employees effective January 1, 2010.

Shelly, an employee of Grape, has a balance of $275 in the HRA on September 21, 2006, and a balance of $700 on December 31, 2009. On or before December 31, 2009, Shelly elects HDHP coverage beginning January 1, 2010. Shelly is otherwise an eligible individual as of January 1, 2010. Shelly also elects to have a qualified HSA distribution of the $275 that was his HRA on September 21, 2006. Grape treats Shelly's remaining $425 HRA balance as part of a retirement HRA.

Shelly is an eligible individual as of January 1, 2010 because the HRA he participates in is HSA-compatible.

Example 5. Denise Corporation has a fiscal year general purpose health FSA with a grace period. The fiscal year of the health FSA is October 1–September 30. The grace period ends on December 15. For the plan year beginning October 1, 2009, Denise offers employees the option of electing HDHP coverage.

On September 1, 2009, Denise amends the health FSA to allow for qualified HSA distributions. The amended plan allows an employee electing HDHP coverage for the plan year to also elect to have any health FSA balance at the end of the plan year, determined on a cash basis, contributed directly to an HSA trustee for the employee. For this purpose, the plan year-end balance is the balance of the health FSA without regard to any expenses incurred but not paid. If an employee elects the qualified HSA distribution, the employee cannot submit any additional claims after September 30, 2009, regardless of when the underlying expense was incurred. The health FSA does not reimburse claims submitted but unpaid as of September 30, 2009.

Horace, an employee of Grape, has a balance of $600 in the health FSA on September 21, 2006, and a balance of $500 on September 30, 2009. On or before September 30, 2009, Horace elects HDHP coverage for the plan year beginning October 1, 2009. Horace also elects to have a qualified HSA distribution of the $500 remaining in the health FSA on September 30, 2009. Denise contributes $500 to an HSA on behalf of Horace on or before December 15, 2009. Horace is otherwise an eligible individual as of October 1, 2009.

Horace does not fail to be an eligible individual as of October 1, 2009 because after the qualified HSA distribution he has a zero balance in the health FSA.

Example 6. The same facts as Example 5, except Denise has a limited purpose health FSA. Helen, an employee of Denise, has a balance of $2,000 in the limited purpose health FSA on September 21, 2006, and a balance of $3,000 on September 30, 2009. On or before September 30, 2009, Helen elects HDHP coverage for the plan year beginning October 1, 2009. Helen also elects to have a qualified HSA distribution of $2,000 that was in the health FSA on September 21, 2006. Denise contributes $2,000 to an HSA on behalf of Helen on or before December 15, 2009. Helen has a balance of $1,000 in a limited purpose health FSA. Helen is otherwise an eligible individual as of October 1, 2009.

Helen does not fail to be an eligible individual because she participates in an HSA-compatible health FSA.

Example 7. For 2009, Joint Corporation has a calendar year general purpose health FSA with a grace period ending on March 15, 2010. Joint has a fiscal year health plan that begins July 1, 2009. For the plan year beginning July 1, 2009, Joint offers employees the option of electing HDHP coverage.

Before January 1, 2010, Joint amends the health FSA to allow for qualified HSA distributions. The amended plan allows an employee electing HDHP coverage to also elect to have any health FSA balance at year end, determined on a cash basis, contributed directly to an HSA trustee for the employee. For this purpose, the year-end balance is the balance of the health FSA without regard to any expenses incurred but not paid. Under the amendment, if an employee elects the qualified HSA distribution, the employee cannot submit any additional claims after December 31, 2009, regardless of when the underlying expense was incurred. The health FSA does not pay claims submitted but unpaid as of December 31, 2009.

Juan, an employee of Joint, has a balance of $500 in a health FSA on September 21, 2006, and a balance of $400 on June 30, 2009. On or before June 30, 2009, Juan elects HDHP coverage for the immediately following health plan year. Juan also elects to have a qualified HSA distribution of $400 that was in his health FSA on June 30, 2009. Joint contributes $400 to an HSA on behalf of Juan on or before September 15, 2009. Juan is an otherwise eligible individual as of July 1, 2009.

Juan fails to be an eligible individual after the distribution because Juan's participation in a health FSA is not disregarded coverage until January 1, 2010, even though the qualified HSA distribution reduces the balance of the health FSA to zero. Juan must include $400 in his gross income for 2009, and pay an additional 10 percent tax. Juan is an eligible individual on January 1, 2010.

Example 8. For 2009, Tarpon Corporation has a calendar year general purpose health FSA with a grace period ending on March 15, 2010. Tarpon offers employees the option of electing HDHP coverage for the plan year beginning January 15, 2010.

Before January 1, 2010, Tarpon amends the health FSA to allow for qualified HSA distributions. The amended plan allows an employee electing HDHP coverage to also elect to have any health FSA balance at year end, determined on a cash basis, contributed directly to an HSA trustee for the employee. For this purpose, the year-end balance is the balance of the health FSA without regard to any expenses incurred but not paid. Under the amendment, if an employee elects the qualified HSA distribution, the employee cannot submit any additional claims after December 31, 2009, regardless of when the underlying expense was incurred. The health FSA does not pay claims submitted but unpaid as of December 31, 2009.

A. Darleen, an employee of Tarpon, has a balance of $1,000 in a health FSA on September 21, 2006, and a balance of $700 on December 31, 2009. On or before December 31, 2009, Darleen elects HDHP coverage for the plan year beginning January 15, 2010. Darleen also elects to have a qualified HSA distribution of the $700 remaining in her health FSA on December 31, 2009. Tarpon contributes $700 to an HSA on behalf of Darleen after February 1, 2010, but before March 15, 2010. Darleen is otherwise an eligible individual as of January 15, 2010.

Darleen does not fail to be an eligible individual because she has a zero balance in the health FSA after the qualified HSA distribution. Darleen is eligible to contribute to the HSA as of February 1, 2010.

B. Terry, an employee of Tarpon, has a balance of $175 in a health FSA on September 21, 2006, and a balance of $150 on December 31, 2009. On or before December 31, 2009, Terry elects HDHP coverage for the plan year beginning January 15, 2010. Terry also elects to have a qualified HSA distribution of the $150 remaining in the health FSA on December 31, 2009. Tarpon contributes $150 to an HSA on behalf of Terry on January 25, 2010.

Terry is not an eligible individual at the time of the distribution because he does not have HDHP coverage on the first day of January. Terry must include $150 in gross income in 2010, and pay an additional 10 percent tax. As of February 1, 2010, Terry is an eligible individual because Terry has HDHP coverage and no other health plan coverage that is not an HDHP, is not enrolled in Medicare, and cannot be claimed as a dependent on another person's tax return.

Examples of Additional 10 Percent Tax

The following examples illustrate the application of the 10 percent additional tax. All references to balances in the following examples are determined on a cash basis. None of the employees in the examples are disabled.

Example 9. Josephine, who is 32 years old, has HDHP coverage as of January 1, 2010. Josephine elects to have a qualified HSA distribution on or before December 31, 2009. On or before March 15, 2010, Josephine's employer contributes $250 from a general purpose health FSA to an HSA on behalf of Josephine in a qualified HSA distribution. Following the qualified HSA distribution, Josephine has a balance of zero in the general purpose health FSA.

In July 2010, Josephine terminates employment with the employer maintaining the HDHP and begins employment with a new employer that does not offer an HDHP. Josephine obtains health coverage under a low deductible health plan, and ceases to be an eligible individual for HSA purposes. Josephine must include the $250 qualified HSA distribution in her gross income for 2010, and pay an additional 10 percent tax on that amount under Code Section 106(e)(3). Josephine does not have to withdraw the $250 from her HSA, and the amounts in the HSA may grow tax-free.

Note. The additional tax in Example 9 is for the failure to maintain HDHP coverage. In the following example the additional tax is for a distribution not used for qualified medical expenses.

Example 10. The same facts as Example 9, except in February 2011, Josephine uses $200 from her HSA for a nonqualified medical expense. The $200 is included in Josephine's gross income for 2011 and is subject to an additional 10 percent tax under Code Section 223(f)(4).

Example 11. The same facts as Example 10, except Josephine uses $200 from her HSA for a qualified medical expense. The $200 distributed from the HSA is not included in Josephine's gross income, and there is no additional tax.

HRA/FSA-Compatible Coverage Rules

Q 5:85　May an employer convert a general purpose HRA or FSA to an HSA-compatible arrangement only for HSA-eligible individuals who elect to make qualified HSA distributions?

No. The rules described in Q 5:53 presume that the FSA or HRA is a "general purpose arrangement," which would be disqualifying coverage for an HSA-eligible individual. If the FSA or HRA arrangement presumably is a limited purpose or other arrangement described in Revenue Ruling 2004-45 [2004-1 C.B.

971], the transfer could be made at any time during the plan year, and need not result in a zero balance (see Q 5:54).

Q 5:86   May an employer convert a general purpose HRA or FSA to an HSA-compatible arrangement?

Yes and no. I.R.S. Notice 2007-22 indicates that an employer may not convert a general purpose HRA or FSA to an HSA-compatible arrangement only for HSA-eligible individuals who elect transfers. Rather, such arrangement would have to be converted for all employees.

Practice Pointer. It is not clear why the IRS has adopted this rule for HRAs. There is no statutory basis for the rule and this notice is the only IRS guidance that contains this prohibition.

Treatment of Qualified HSA Distributions

Q 5:87   Are qualified HSA distributions taken into account in computing the maximum HSA contribution limit?

No. A qualified HSA distribution is not taken into account for purposes of determining the HSA annual contribution limitation (i.e., $3,000 for self-only coverage and $5,950 for family coverage for 2009). [I.R.C. § 223(b)(4)(C); I.R.S. Notice 2007-22, 2007-10 I.R.B. 640 (Mar. 5, 2007)]

Q 5:88   May a participant deduct qualified HSA distributions on their federal income tax return?

No. A qualified HSA distribution that is transferred to an HSA is excludable from income and wages for FICA tax purposes. In addition, a transfer is not deductible as an HSA contribution on an individual's Form 1040. The amount of the qualified HSA distribution must be reported to the employee (see Q 5:90). [I.R.C. §§ 106(e)(4)(C), 223(b)(4)(C); I.R.S. Notice 2007-22, 2007-10 I.R.B. 640 (Mar. 5, 2007)]

Reporting FSA/HRA Transfers

Q 5:89   How does an employer report a qualifying HSA distribution to the trustee or custodian of the HSA?

An employer must report a transfer of a qualified HSA distribution as rollover contributions to the HSA trustee/custodian, who, in turn, is required to report this information to the IRS on Form 5498-SA. [I.R.S. Notice 2007-22, 2007-10 I.R.B. 640 (Mar. 5, 2007)] Accordingly, this is an area that the IRS has some ability to monitor. Plan sponsors should therefore exercise caution in determining that all requirements described in Notice 2007-22 have been satisfied before making the transfer. Reporting issues are more fully discussed in chapter 7.

Q 5:90   Does an employer report a qualifying HSA distribution to the participant?

No. A qualified HSA distribution is treated as a rollover contribution (see Q 5:89). The amount transferred in a qualified HSA distribution is not reported in Box 12 of Form W-2. Box 12 of Form W-2 is used to report all contributions an employer makes to an employee's HSA. To the extent employer contributions (other than contributions treated as rollover contributions) to an HSA do not exceed the maximum annual contribution limit ($3,000 for self-only coverage and $5,950 for family coverage for 2009), they are not reported in other boxes on Form W-2. Reporting issues are more fully discussed in chapter 7.

Chapter 6

Distributions

Chapter 6 examines distributions made from an HSA and the taxation of those distributions. The treatment of the account and distributions from the account to the spouse, estate, or other beneficiary after death are discussed, as well as the income tax withholding rules. This chapter also discusses the return of contributions mistakenly made and the coordination of HSAs with the medical expense deduction. This chapter discusses distributions resulting from prohibited transactions or upon the account's ceasing to be an HSA due to a pledge of security for a loan. Prohibited transaction issues include borrowing from an HSA, loans from a trustee to an HSA, pledging HSA assets as security for a loan, and the consequences for entering into a prohibited transaction.

The final Department of Labor (DOL) regulations and a proposed class exemption relating to the provision of fee-level or computer model investment advice arrangements that were published on August 22, 2008, are also discussed in this chapter.

Taxation of HSA Distributions 6-2
    Responsibility 6-6
Restrictions on Distributions 6-7
Medical Care Paid from an HSA 6-11
Medicine and Drugs 6-20
Distributions Used for Long-Term Care Insurance Premiums 6-22
Deemed Distributions Due to Prohibited Transactions 6-23
    Personalized Investment Advice 6-26
Transactions with Service Providers 6-35
Other Prohibited Transaction Exemptions 6-36
The 10 Percent Additional Tax 6-40
Returning Distributions Mistakenly Made 6-44
Death Distributions to Designated Beneficiaries 6-45
Income Tax Withholding on HSA Distributions 6-47

Taxation of HSA Distributions

Q 6:1 When is an individual permitted to receive distributions from an HSA?

An individual is permitted to receive distributions from an HSA at any time. [I.R.S. Notice 2004-2, Q&A 24, 2004-2 I.R.B. 269]

Note. A direct deposit of a 2008 Economic Stimulus Payment to an IRA or Roth IRA may be removed without tax or penalty if removed in a timely manner (see Qs 4:1, 6:73, 6:74).

Q 6:2 May an employer request a distribution from an employee's HSA?

Generally no. Because the HSA owner's interest in an HSA is nonforfeitable, an employer generally may not request a distribution from an employee's HSA, even to recoup a portion of a contribution that the employer made to the employee's HSA in error or when the employee terminates employment or ceases to be an eligible individual during the year (see Q 6:5). [I.R.C. § 223(d)(1)(E); I.R.S. Notice 2008-59, Q&A 25, 2008-29 I.R.B. 123, I.R.S. Notice 2004-50, Q&A 82, 2004-33 I.R.B. 196] Contributions to individuals who were never eligible individuals and those that exceed the maximum annual contribution limits are treated differently (see Qs 6:3, 6:4).

Note. The terms *HSA owner*, *account owner*, *account holder*, and *account beneficiary* are used interchangeably in IRS publications, notices, and announcements to refer to the person that established the HSA. To avoid confusion, the term *HSA owner* will be used to refer to that person.

Example 1. On January 2, 2009, Starship Corporation makes the maximum annual contribution to the HSA of Edward, its only employee, with the expectation that Edward will work for the entire 2009 calendar year. On February 1, 2009, Edward terminates employment. The employer may not recoup from Edward's HSA any portion of the contribution it previously made.

Example 2. Western held an open enrollment period in fall of 2008 for plan year 2009 during which time employees were given the opportunity to elect either an HDHP/HSA option or, alternatively, an indemnity option, both of which could be paid for on a pretax basis, under Western's Code Section 125 cafeteria plan. On January 1, 2009, the effective date of HDHP coverage, Western Corporation made $500 contributions to the HSAs of all employees who had elected the HDHP option during open enrollment and completed the HSA paperwork timely. On January 2, 2009, Steve, a Western employee, notified the human resources department that he had "changed his mind" and wanted to switch to the indemnity option. Under these facts, Western may not permit Steve to change his election for HDHP coverage, because the election was made on a pretax basis through Western's cafeteria plan and none of the mid-year change events in Treasury Regulations Section 1.125-4 have occurred ("changing one's mind" about an election is not a permissible mid-year change event). Further, even if Western were able to allow Steve to change to the indemnity option on a pretax basis, Western could not withdraw the $500 contribution made to Steve's HSA because such contribution is nonforfeitable.

Note. If Steve had alleged that a "mistake" was made in electing the HDHP/HSA coverage, there is still no direct authority that would allow Western to recover the $500 contribution. However, see Qs 6:78–6:79 regarding mistaken distributions.

Q 6:3 If an employer contributes to the account of an employee who was never an eligible individual, can the employer recoup the amounts?

If an employer contributes to the account of an employee who was never an eligible individual, the employer may recoup the amounts. If the employee was never an eligible individual (see Q 2:6), "then no HSA ever existed and the employer may correct the error. At the employer's option, the employer may request that the financial institution return the amounts to the employer. However, if the employer does not recover the amounts by the end of the taxable year, then the amounts must be included as gross income and wages on the employee's Form W-2 for the year during which the employer made the contributions." In other situations, except for errors resulting in excess contributions described below, an employer may not generally recoup contributions once made (see Qs 3:73, 4:71, 4:147, 6:2, 6:4). [I.R.S. Notice 2008-59, Q&A 25, 2008-29 I.R.B. 123]

Example 1. In February 2009, Skylark Computing contributed $500 to an account of Mildred, reasonably believing the account to be an HSA. In July 2009, Skylark first learned that Mildred's account is not an HSA because Mildred has never been an eligible individual under Code Section 223(c) (see Q 2:6). Skylark may request that the financial institution holding Mildred's account return the balance of the account ($500 plus earnings less administration fees directly paid from the account) to Skylark. If Skylark does not receive the balance of the account, it must include the amounts in Mildred's gross income and wages on her Form W-2 for 2009.

Example 2. The same facts as in Example 1, except Skylark first discovers the mistake in July 2010. Skylark issues a corrected 2009 Form W-2 for Mildred, and Mildred files an amended income tax return for 2009.

Q 6:4 May an employer recover amounts contributed in excess of the maximum annual contribution limit?

Yes. If the employer contributes amounts to an employee's HSA that exceed the maximum annual contribution allowed ($3,000 for self-only coverage and $6,000 for family coverage for 2009) due to an error, the employer may correct the error. In that case, at the employer's option, the employer may request that the financial institution return the excess amounts to the employer. Alternatively, if the employer does not recover the amounts, then the amounts must be included as gross income and wages on the employee's Form W-2 for the year during which the employer made contributions. If, however, amounts contributed are less than or equal to the maximum annual contribution allowed, the employer may not recoup any amount from the employee's HSA. [I.R.S. Notice 2008-59, Q&A 24, 2008-29 I.R.B. 123]

Q 6:5   If an employer contributes to the HSA of an employee who ceases to be an eligible individual during a year, can the employer recoup amounts that the employer contributed after the employee ceased to be an eligible individual?

An employer that contributes to the HSA of an employee who ceases to be an eligible individual during a year cannot recoup amounts that the employer contributed after the employee ceased to be an eligible individual (see Qs 3:73, 4:71, 6:2–6:4). [I.R.S. Notice 2008-59, Q&A 25, 2008-29 I.R.B. 123]

> **Example.** Nanette was an eligible individual on January 1, 2008. On April 1, 2008, Nanette is no longer an eligible individual because Nanette's spouse enrolled in a general purpose health FSA that covers all family members. Nanette first realizes that she is no longer eligible on July 17, 2008, at which time Nanette informs Optics, her employer, to cease HSA contributions. Optic's contributions into Nanette's HSA between April 1, 2008, and July 17, 2008, cannot be recouped by Optics because Nanette has a nonforfeitable interest in her HSA (see Q 6:2). Nanette is responsible for determining if the contributions exceed the maximum annual contribution limit, and for withdrawing the excess contribution and the income attributable to the excess contribution and including both in gross income.

Q 6:6   May an HSA be administered through a debit card that restricts payments and reimbursements to health care?

Yes. An HSA may be administered through a debit card that restricts payments and reimbursements to health care, provided the funds are otherwise readily available (see Q 8:13). For example, in addition to the restricted debit card, the HSA owner must also be able to access the funds other than by purchasing health care with the debit card, such as through online transfers, withdrawals from automatic teller machines, or check writing. Employers must notify employees that other access to the funds is available. [I.R.S. Notice 2008-59, Q&A 27, 2008-29 I.R.B. 123; see also I.R.S. Notice 2004-50, Q&A 77 and Q&A 79, 2004-33 I.R.B. 196.]

Q 6:7   Must HSA distributions commence when the HSA owner attains a specified age?

No. An HSA is not subject to any required minimum distributions when the HSA owner reaches a stated age (e.g., age 70).

Q 6:8   May an HSA owner authorize someone else to withdraw funds from his or her HSA?

Yes. An HSA owner may authorize someone else (third-party authorization) to withdraw funds from his or her HSA. Although an HSA is an individual account, an HSA owner can designate other individuals to withdraw funds pursuant to the procedures of the trustee or custodian of the HSA. Distributions are subject to tax if they are not used to pay for qualified medical expenses for the HSA owner, the HSA owner's spouse, or dependents. [I.R.S. Notice 2008-59, Q&A 28, 2008-29 I.R.B. 123; I.R.S. Notice 2004-2, Q&A 25, 2004-2 I.R.B. 269]

Caution. Notwithstanding the previously stated, a third-party authorization is subject to the prohibited transaction rules that include prohibitions against borrowing and making loans from an HSA (see Qs 6:59–6:71).

Q 6:9   How are distributions from an HSA taxed?

Distributions from an HSA used exclusively to pay for qualified medical expenses of the HSA owner, his or her spouse, or dependents generally are excludable from gross income (see Qs 6:9, 6:28). [I.R.C. § 223(f)(1)] Distributions used for other purposes are includible in the HSA owner's gross income and may also be subject to a 10 percent additional tax (see Qs 6:72; 6:74).

Caution. Distributions from an HSA for expenses that have been previously paid or otherwise reimbursed from another source or that have been taken as an itemized deduction must be included in the HSA owner's gross income and may be subject to a 10 percent additional tax. [I.R.S. Notice 2004-50, Q&A 39, 2004-33 I.R.B. 196]

Practice Pointer. The taxation of reimbursements from an HSA are governed by Code Section 223, and not by Code Section 105 (regarding amounts received under employer-sponsored accident and health plans) or Code Section 106 (regarding contributions by employers to accident and health plans). Thus, it is not necessary to rely on Code Section 105(b) to exclude from income an HSA distribution for medical care.

An HSA distribution not used for qualified medical expenses is subject to the additional 10 percent tax (with certain exceptions) under Code Section 223(f)(4), regardless of whether the amount contributed to the HSA under the full contribution limit for individuals eligible after the beginning of the year (see Qs 4:6, 5:50) is included in the HSA owner's income and subject to the additional tax under Code Section 223(b)(8)(B)(i) (see Q 4:38, Example 14). [I.R.S. Notice 2007-22, 2007-10 I.R.B. 670 regarding consequences of distributions from HSAs; as modified by I.R.S. Notice 2008-52, 2008-25 I.R.B. 1166]

Note. Expenses incurred before an HSA is established are not qualified medical expenses. [I.R.S. Notice 2004-2, Q&A 26] Although certain individuals are treated as eligible individuals on the first day of the taxable year in determining the contribution amount, an HSA is not established before the date that the HSA is actually established. [I.R.S. Notice 2008-52, 2008-25 I.R.B. 1166, modifying I.R.S. Notice 2007-22, 2007-10 I.R.B. 670]

Q 6:10   May an HSA owner claim an investment loss if his or her HSA declines in value?

No. The HSA owner is entitled to a deduction (or exclusion in the case of an HSA funded through a cafeteria plan) for the allowable HSA contributions when made; therefore, no claim for loss on investments is permitted (even if the account is closed). The basis in an HSA is zero. It could also be argued that amounts when distributed would not necessarily have been taxable and, therefore, that no tax loss would have resulted and none can be recognized. [I.R.C. § 212; Treas. Reg. § 1.212-1]

> **Example.** Jo-Ann establishes an HSA on January 1, 2009, and invests her HSA contribution of $3,000 in one of the riskier investment options. Before Jo-Ann withdraws any of the funds in her HSA, her investment is declared worthless and her HSA account reflects a zero balance. Jo-Ann terminates her HSA. Jo-Ann may not claim an investment loss; she has already received a tax benefit in the form of a deduction for the contributions previously made.

Q 6:11   Can tax-free distributions be received by an individual who is not an HSA eligible individual (e.g., an individual who does not have HDHP coverage)?

Yes. Tax-free distribution status does not depend upon the individual who receives distributions being an eligible individual (see Q 2:33). Thus, tax-free distributions may still be made from an HSA to pay or reimburse the qualified medical expenses of an HSA owner, spouse, or dependent within the meaning of Code Section 152, whether or not such individuals are currently *eligible individuals*. For example, an individual over age 65 and entitled to Medicare benefits or who no longer has a high deductible health plan (HDHP) still can receive tax-free distribution treatment as long as the distributions are used to pay qualified medical expenses. [I.R.S. Notice 2004-2, Q&A 25, 2004-2 I.R.B. 269] Amounts not used for qualified medical expenses may be subject to a 10 percent additional tax unless an exception applies, such as when the HSA owner reaches age 65 (see Q 6:72).

Responsibility

Q 6:12   Is the trustee responsible for determining whether HSA distributions are used exclusively for qualified medical expenses?

No. Trustees are not responsible for determining whether the distributions are used exclusively for the payment of qualified medical expenses and thus are excludable from gross income (see Q 6:13). [I.R.S. Notice 2004-2, Q&A 29, 2004-2 I.R.B. 269]

Q 6:13   Who is responsible for determining whether HSA distributions are used exclusively for qualified medical expenses?

The individual who establishes the HSA is responsible. Individuals who establish HSAs make that determination and should maintain records of their medical expenses sufficient to show that the distributions have been made exclusively for qualified medical expenses and are, therefore, excludable from gross income. [I.R.S. Notice 2004-2, Q&A 29, 2004-2 I.R.B. 269] It should be noted that employers are not responsible for making medical expense determinations, either.

Practice Pointer. HSA trustees or custodians are not required to determine whether HSA distributions are used for qualified medical expenses.

Restrictions on Distributions

Q 6:14   May a trustee or custodian place reasonable restrictions on withdrawals from an HSA?

Yes. As a general rule, an HSA owner must have the ability to request a withdrawal from the HSA at any time and for any reason (see Q 6:1). However, a trustee or custodian may place reasonable restrictions on both the frequency and the minimum amount of distributions from an HSA (see Q 8:13). For example, the trustee may prohibit distributions for amounts of less than $50 or allow only a certain number of distributions per month. Generally, the terms regarding the frequency or minimum amount of distributions from an HSA are matters of contract between the trustee and the HSA owner and should be specified in the Trust/Custodial agreement. [I.R.S. Notice 2004-50, Q&A 80, 2004-33 I.R.B. 196]

Q 6:15   May an HSA trust or custodial agreement restrict HSA distributions to pay or reimburse only the HSA owner's qualified medical expenses?

No. An HSA trust or custodial agreement may not contain a provision that restricts HSA distributions to pay or reimburse only the HSA owner's qualified medical expenses (or the qualified medical expenses of a spouse or dependent). Thus, the HSA owner is entitled to distributions for any purpose and distributions can be used to pay or reimburse qualified medical expenses or other, nonmedical expenditures. Only the HSA owner can determine how the HSA distributions will be used. (See Q 6:14 regarding reasonable restrictions on the frequency or minimum amount of HSA distributions.)

Q 6:16   Must distributions from an HSA that are not used exclusively for qualified medical expenses be included in the HSA owner's gross income?

Yes. Any amounts distributed from an HSA account that are not used to pay exclusively the qualified medical expenses of the HSA owner, spouse, and dependent (within the meaning of Code Section 152) are included in the gross income of the HSA owner and may be subject to an additional 10 percent tax (see Q 6:72). [I.R.S. Notice 2004-50, Q&A 25, 2004-33 I.R.B. 196]

Q 6:17   How are distributions from an HSA that are not used exclusively for qualified medical expenses reported by the HSA owner to the IRS?

The HSA owner must report all distributions from an HSA on Form 8889—*Health Savings Accounts (HSAs)*. The taxable portion is to be included in the total on Line 21 of Form 1040 or Form 1040NR, Line 21 (based on the 2008 version of the forms). The completion of Form 8889 is more fully discussed in chapter 7.

Q 6:18   How are distributions from an HSA that are subject to the 10 percent additional tax reported to the IRS by the HSA owner?

The 10 percent additional tax is computed on Form 8889—*Health Savings Accounts (HSAs)* and reported on Line 17b of that form. Form 8889 is filed with Form 1040 (or Form 1040 NR). The additional tax is reported on Line 61, of Form 1040 (Line 57 of Form 1040 NR) with "HSA" entered on the dotted line next to Line 61 or Line 57, respectively. (*Note.* Line numbers are from the 2008 version of those forms.)

Q 6:19   Are amounts distributed to an individual not currently eligible to make contributions excluded from gross income if used exclusively for qualified medical expenses?

Yes. In general, amounts in an HSA can be used for qualified medical expenses of the HSA owner, his or her spouse, or a dependent and will be excludable from gross income even if the individual receiving the payment is not currently eligible for contributions to the HSA (e.g., the individual is over age 65 and entitled to Medicare benefits or no longer has an HDHP). [I.R.S. Notice 2004-2, Q&A 25, 2004-2 I.R.B. 269] Amounts not used for qualified medical expenses may be subject to a 10 percent additional tax (see Q 6:72).

Q 6:20 Will tax-free treatment apply to a distribution made directly from the HSA to a third party if the distribution is used exclusively to pay for qualified medical expenses incurred by the HSA owner, spouse, or dependent?

Yes. This tax-free treatment applies to payments made directly from the HSA to the medical service provider, to payments from the HSA to the HSA owner as reimbursement for qualified medical expenses incurred, or to payments that the HSA owner uses to pay the service provider. [I.R.C. § 223(f)(1)]

Q 6:21 May qualified medical expenses incurred before establishment of an HSA be reimbursed from an HSA?

In general, qualified medical expenses may be paid or reimbursed by an HSA only if they were incurred after the HSA was established. [I.R.S. Notice 2004-2, Q&A 26, 2004-2 I.R.B. 269] A transitional rule was established for 2004 (see Q 6:22).

Example. Fenway, an eligible individual, establishes and contributes $1,000 to an HSA on January 1, 2009. Shortly thereafter, on February 1, 2009, Fenway incurs a $1,500 qualified medical expense and has a balance in his HSA of $1,025, but does not take a distribution. On January 3, 2010, he contributes another $1,000 to his HSA, bringing the balance in the HSA to $2,025. In June 2010, Fenway receives a distribution from his HSA of $1,500 as reimbursement for the $1,500 medical expense incurred in the prior year (2009). If Fenway can show that the $1,500 HSA distribution in 2010 is a reimbursement for a qualified medical expense that has not been previously paid for by a health insurance plan or otherwise reimbursed and has not been taken as an itemized deduction, the distribution is excludable from Fenway's gross income.

Q 6:22 Why was transitional relief provided in 2004?

Because of the short time period between the enactment of HSAs and the effective date of Code Section 223 (see Q 2:4), many taxpayers who otherwise would be eligible to establish and contribute to HSAs (i.e., generally, individuals covered by an HDHP) were unable to do so early in 2004 because they were unable to locate trustees or custodians that were willing and able to open HSAs at that time. The IRS provided transitional relief, which expired on April 15, 2005. [I.R.S. Notice 2004-25, 2004-15 I.R.B. 727, modifying I.R.S. Notice 2004-2, Q&A 26, 2004-2 I.R.B. 269]

Example 1. Same facts as in Q 6:21, example, except that Fenway established the HSA on November 15, 2004. The expense was incurred before the HSA was established. Assuming Fenway had no other qualified medical expenses during 2004, the $1,500 distributed to Fenway in 2005 is includable in Fenway's gross income and may be subject to a 10 percent additional tax (see Q 6:72).

Example 2. Quark, an eligible individual, establishes and contributes $1,000 for 2004 to an HSA on April 10, 2005. On February 1, 2004, Quark incurred a $500 qualified medical expense. In November 2005, Quark receives a distribution from his HSA of $500 as reimbursement for the $500 medical expense incurred in 2004 (see Q 6:25). If Quark can show that the $500 HSA distribution in 2005 is a reimbursement for a qualified medical expense that has not been previously paid for by a health insurance plan or otherwise reimbursed and has not been taken as an itemized deduction, the distribution is excludable from Quark's gross income because of the transitional relief that applied in 2004 (see below).

Transitional relief. For calendar year 2004, qualified medical expenses incurred on or after the later of January 1, 2004, or the first day of the month the individual became eligible for an HSA (i.e., covered under the HDHP) may be reimbursed from the HSA on a tax-free basis, as long as the HSA is established on or before April 15, 2005. In all other cases, qualified medical expenses may be paid or reimbursed by an HSA only if incurred after the HSA has been established (see Q 6:21).

Q 6:23   Are distributions from an HSA for expenses that were already reimbursed by another health plan excludable from gross income?

No. Distributions from an HSA made for expenses reimbursed by another health plan are not excludable from gross income, whether or not the other health plan is an HDHP. [I.R.S. Notice 2004-50, Q&A 36, 2004-33 I.R.B. 196; see also I.R.S. Notice 2004-2, Q&A 26, 2002-2 I.R.B. 269]

Q 6:24   In cases where both spouses have an HSA and one spouse (i.e., the HSA owner) uses distributions from his or her HSA to pay or reimburse the qualified medical expenses of the other spouse, are the distributions excluded from the HSA owner's gross income?

Yes. In the case of married account beneficiaries, each spouse owns his or her own HSA (no joint HSA between a married couple is possible), and qualified medical expenses of either spouse may be paid from either HSA. However, both HSAs may not reimburse the same expenses. [I.R.S. Notice 2004-50, Q&A 38, 2004-50, 2004-33 I.R.B. 196]

Q 6:25   What is the time limit for taking a distribution from an HSA to pay for a qualified medical expense incurred during the current year?

There is no time limit for taking a distribution from an HSA to pay for a qualified medical expense incurred during any year subsequent to the date the HSA is established. In other words, a qualified medical expense incurred in Year 1 could provide the basis for a tax-free HSA distribution in Year 10.

However, the HSA owner must keep sufficient documentation to later show that amounts distributed were used for qualified medical expenses and were not previously paid or reimbursed from another source or claimed as an itemized deduction in a prior year. [I.R.S. Notice 2004-50, Q&A 39, 2004-33 I.R.B. 196]

Q 6:26   Do the Code Section 105(h) discrimination rules, which apply to self-insured plans, apply to a distribution from an HSA?

No. A self-insured medical reimbursement plan must satisfy the requirements of Code Section 105(h). That section is not satisfied if the plan discriminates in favor of highly compensated individuals (generally, the top-paid 25 percent of the workforce) as to eligibility to participate or to receive benefits. Because the exclusion from gross income for amounts distributed from an HSA is not determined by Code Section 105(b) but by Code Section 223(b), Section 105(h) does not apply to HSAs. [I.R.C. §§ 105(h), 223(b); I.R.S. Notice 2004-50, Q&A 83, 2004-33 I.R.B. 196]

Medical Care Paid from an HSA

Q 6:27   Who must incur the expense in order to qualify for tax-free distributions from the HSA?

Medical expenses incurred by the HSA owner, the HSA owner's spouse, or dependents (as defined in Code Section 152; see Q 2:37) qualify for tax-free distributions from the HSA, but only to the extent that such amounts are not compensated for by insurance or otherwise. [I.R.C. § 223(d)(2)(A)]

Q 6:28   What are qualified medical expenses for purposes of an HSA under Code Section 223?

Qualified medical expenses for purposes of an HSA are those expenses—incurred by the HSA owner, his or her spouse, and dependents—that would generally qualify for the medical and dental expenses deduction under Code Section 213(a) (except for premiums for health coverage, which only are considered qualified medical expenses in limited circumstances (see Q 6:42)). (See IRS Publication 969, *Health Savings Accounts and Other Tax-Favored Plans*, p. 7 (2008); IRS Publication 502, *Medical and Dental Expenses*.) Examples include amounts paid for doctors' fees, prescription medicines, and necessary hospital services not paid for by insurance. In addition, nonprescription medicines are also qualified medical expenses (notwithstanding that such amounts are not deductible). [See I.R.S. Notice 2004-2, Q&A 26, 2004-2 I.R.B. 269]

Caution. Not all expenses listed as deductible in Publication 502 (e.g., general-purpose health insurance premiums) are reimbursable from the HSA on a tax-free basis. In addition, not all expenses that are reimbursable from an HSA (e.g., nonprescription medicines) on a tax-free basis are deductible. Qualified medical expenses and the deduction for medical expenses are more fully discussed in Qs 6:29 through 6:58.

Q 6:29   What types of expenses are deductible under Code Section 213(a) as medical expenses?

Code Section 213(a) allows a deduction for uncompensated expenses for medical care of an individual, the individual's spouse, or a dependent, to the extent that the expenses exceed 7.5 percent of adjusted gross income. *Medical care* means amounts paid for the diagnosis, cure, mitigation, treatment, or prevention of disease, or for the purpose of affecting any structure or function of the body, and includes related transportation, lodging, and premium expenses. [I.R.C. §§ 213(a), 213(d), 213(d)(1)]

Practice Pointer. If an expense is not deductible under Code Section 213(a) because the 7.5 percent threshold is not satisfied, that expense may still be considered a qualified medical expense for HSA purposes.

Caution. Even though premiums for health coverage are deductible under Code Section 213, such amounts are generally not qualified medical expenses for HSA purposes (except for limited exceptions, see Q 6:42).

Q 6:30   Are HSA distributions coordinated with the medical expense deduction?

Yes. Any distribution for qualified medical expenses from an HSA that is not includible in the HSA owner's income will not be permitted to be used for purposes of determining whether the taxpayer has a deduction for medical expenses in excess of 7.5 percent of adjusted gross income (AGI) under Code Section 213 (see Q 6:29). Thus, "double dipping" is not permitted.

Q 6:31   May a payment or distribution from an HSA for a qualified medical expense also be deducted as an expense for medical care under Code Section 213(a)?

No. For purposes of determining the amount of the deduction for medical expenses under Code Section 213, any payment or distribution from an HSA for qualified medical expenses is not treated as an expense paid for medical care. [I.R.C. § 223(f)(6)]

Q 6:32   What requirements must medical care expenses satisfy to be deductible?

The deduction for medical care expenses will be confined strictly to expenses incurred primarily for the prevention or alleviation of a physical or mental defect or illness. Whether an expenditure is "primarily for" medical care is a question of fact. An expense that is merely beneficial to the general health of an individual is not an expense for medical care. [Treas. Reg. § 1.213-1(e)(1)(ii)]

Medical care includes X-rays and laboratory and other diagnostic services. Amounts paid for obstetrical services are deemed to be for the purpose of affecting a structure or function of the body and therefore are paid for medical care. [Treas. Reg. § 1.213-1(e)(1)(ii)]

Diagnosis is the determination of a medical condition, such as a disease, by physical examination or study of symptoms. [Black's Law Dictionary (8th ed. 2004)] A diagnosis may encompass a determination that disease is absent. The determination of a medical condition may include testing for changes in the functions of the body, such as those resulting from pregnancy, that are unrelated to disease.

In determining whether an expense is for either medical or personal reasons, the recommendation of a physician is important. [Havey v. Comm'r, 12 T.C. 409, 412 (1949)] However, this determination is unnecessary in the case of expenses for items that are wholly medical in nature and serve no other function in everyday life. [Stringham v. Comm'r, 12 T.C. 580, 584 (court reviewed), *aff'd,* 183 F.2d 579 (6th Cir. 1950)]

The deduction amount under Code Section 213 is not limited by a ceiling and, although additional costs for personal convenience are not allowable, Code Section 213 does not limit the deduction to amounts paid for the least expensive form of medical care available. [Ferris v. Commissioner, 582 F.2d 1112, 1116 (7th Cir. 1978)]

> **Note.** Code Section 262 provides that, except as otherwise expressly provided by the Code, no deduction is allowed for personal, living, or family expenses (see Q 6:38).

Medical care expenses that are deductible and can therefore be paid from an HSA include:

Amounts paid for the diagnosis, cure, mitigation, treatment, or prevention of disease, or for the purpose of affecting any structure or function of the body (see Q 6:29). For example, the following are deductible expenditures for medical care:

- An annual physical exam, even though an individual may not be experiencing any symptoms of an illness.
- A full body scan, even though the individual does not experience specific symptoms of an illness or procure a physician's recommendation for the scan.
- The purchase of a pregnancy kit qualifies as medical care because it relates to testing of a change in body function.

[I.R.C. § 213(d)(1)(A); Rev. Rul. 2007-72, 2007-50 I.R.B. 1154]

- Expenses for transportation primarily for and essential to medical care referred to above (see Q 6:37)
- Amounts paid for certain lodging while away from home primarily for and essential to medical care (see Q 6:38)

(See Q 6:39, Example 2.)

Q 6:33　Are Medicare Part D premiums qualified medical expenses?

Yes and no. If the HSA owner has attained age 65, Medicare Part D premiums are qualified medical expenses. In addition, if an HSA owner has attained age 65, premiums for Medicare Part D for the HSA owner, the HSA owner's spouse, or the HSA owner's dependents are qualified medical expenses (see Q 6:28). [I.R.S. Notice 2008-59, Q&A 29, 2008-29 I.R.B. 123] Conversely, if the HSA owner has not attained age 65, Medicare premiums for coverage of an HSA owner's spouse (who has attained age 65) are not generally qualified medical expenses. [I.R.S. Notice 2008-59, Q&A 30, 2008-29 I.R.B. 123]

Q 6:34　Are premiums for continuation coverage required under federal law for the spouse or dependent of an HSA owner qualified medical expenses?

Yes. Premiums for continuation coverage required under federal law for the spouse or dependent of an HSA owner are qualified medical expenses. Although qualified medical expenses generally exclude payments for insurance, there is an exception for the expense of coverage under a health plan during any period of continuation coverage (see Q 2:26). [I.R.S. Notice 2008-59, Q&A 31. 2008-29 I.R.B. 123]

Q 6:35　Are premiums for health coverage for a spouse or dependent during a period when the spouse or dependent is receiving unemployment compensation under any federal or state law qualified medical expenses?

Yes. Premiums for health coverage for a spouse or dependent during a period when the spouse or dependent is receiving unemployment compensation under any federal or state law are qualified medical expenses. Although qualified medical expenses generally exclude payments for insurance, there is an exception for the expense of coverage under a health plan during a period in which an individual is receiving unemployment compensation under any federal or state law (see Q 2:26). [I.R.S. Notice 2008-59, Q&A 32, 2008-29 I.R.B. 123]

Q 6:36　Do qualified medical expenses for HSA purposes include the Code Section 213(d) medical expenses incurred by an HSA owner's child who is claimed as a dependent by the HSA owner's former spouse?

Yes. Qualified medical expenses for HSA purposes include the medical expenses incurred by an HSA owner's child who is claimed as a dependent by the HSA owner's former spouse (see Q 2:24). [I.R.C. §§ 152(e), 213(d)(5); I.R.S. Notice 2008-59, Q&A 33. 2008-29 I.R.B. 123]

Q 6:37   Are transportation expenses related to medical care deductible?

Maybe. The term *medical care* also includes transportation that is "primarily for and essential to" medical care referred to in Code Section 213.

Example 1. Mandy, for purely personal reasons, travels to another locality to obtain an operation and other medical care prescribed by a doctor. Because the travel expenses were not "primarily for and essential to" medical care, Mandy may not deduct the costs of transportation as a medical expense. [I.R.C. § 213(d)(1); Treas. Reg. § 1.213-1(e)(1)(iv)]

Example 2. Sybil lives away from home at a psychiatric center. Her parents incur transportation costs to visit Sybil at regular intervals on the advice of the child's doctors and as an essential part of the child's therapy. The transportation costs are primarily for and essential to medical care and are deductible. (See Q 6:39, Example 2.) [I.R.C. § 213; Rev. Rul. 58-533, 1958-2 C.B. 108]

Q 6:38   Are lodging expenses related to medical care deductible?

Possibly. The cost of lodging (up to $50 per night) while away from home that is primarily for and essential to medical care is deductible if:

- The medical care is provided by a physician in a licensed hospital or a related or equivalent facility; and
- There is no significant element of personal pleasure, recreation, or vacation in the travel away from home.

(See Q 6:39, Example 2.) [I.R.C. §§ 213(d), 213(d)(1)(A)]

Q 6:39   Are meal expenses related to medical care deductible?

Meal expenses are deductible as expenses for medical care if they are provided at a hospital or similar institution at which the taxpayer, the taxpayer's spouse, or dependent is receiving medical care. [Treas. Reg. §§ 1.213-1(e)(1)(iv), 1.213-1(e)(1)(v)]

Diet foods, meal replacements, and dietary supplements to help people reduce their weight do not qualify as medical care expenses under Code Section 213(d). Instead they are substitutes for the food that individuals normally consume to satisfy their nutritional requirements and are nondeductible personal expenses. [IRS Information Letter 20070037 (Aug. 9, 2007)]

The following examples illustrate Qs 6:32 through 6:39.

Example 1. Upon the recommendation of a physician, Fluffy takes a cruise to relax. She incurs transportation expenses to get to the cruise and pays for the cost of the cruise. On the cruise, doctors provide both instructional seminars relating to nutrition, exercise, and adequate sleep, and certain medical services such as counseling. The seminars are to preserve Fluffy's general health only, and the medical services are available in Fluffy's hometown. The transportation costs and costs of the cruise are not primarily for and essential to medical care; thus they are not deductible. [Rev. Rul. 76-79, 1976-1 C.B. 70]

Example 2. Earl, a taxpayer, resides in City Q and is the parent of Dorothy, who is Earl's dependent. Dorothy suffers from a chronic disease and is being treated by physician C. At C's recommendation and for the purpose of obtaining medical information that may be useful in making decisions concerning Dorothy's treatment or in providing care to Dorothy, Earl travels to City W to attend a conference sponsored by an association that supports research and education concerning the disease. The conference is attended by medical practitioners and by individuals with the disease and their families. Earl spends the majority of his time at the conference attending sessions that disseminate medical information concerning Dorothy's disease. Other sessions at the conference involve presentations or discussions of legal issues, family finances, and other matters commonly arising in families in which a member has the disease. While in City W, Earl's social and recreational activities outside of the conference are secondary to Earl's attendance at the conference.

Earl pays the following expenses in connection with the conference:

- Transportation to City W
- Local transportation to the conference site
- A registration fee
- Meals while attending the conference
- Lodging at a hotel while attending the conference

Under these facts, the registration fee paid by Earl to attend the conference is primarily for medical care, and Earl's travel is primarily for and essential to medical care. Accordingly, Earl may deduct the registration fee and transportation expenses under Code Section 213 (subject to the limitations of that section). Earl may not deduct the cost of meals and lodging while attending the conference because neither Earl, Earl's spouse, nor a dependent is receiving medical care from a physician at a licensed hospital or similar institution. [I.R.C. § 213(d)(2); Treas. Reg. § 1.213-1(e)(1)(iv)] The result would be the same if Earl, and not Earl's dependent, were the individual with the disease. Thus, amounts paid by an individual for expenses of admission and transportation to a medical conference relating to the chronic disease of the individual's dependent are deductible as medical expenses under Code Section 213 (subject to the limitations of that section) if the costs are primarily for and essential to the medical care of the dependent. The costs of meals and lodging while attending the conference are not deductible as medical expenses under Code Section 213. [Rev. Rul. 2000-24, 2000-1 C.B. 963; Rev. Rul. 76-79, 1976-1 C.B. 70 is distinguished]

Q 6:40   Is cosmetic surgery deductible?

Generally, no. The term *medical care* generally does not include cosmetic surgery unless the surgery is necessary to ameliorate a deformity arising from, or directly related to, a congenital abnormality, a personal injury resulting from an accident or trauma, or a disfiguring disease.

In Letter Ruling 200344010, the IRS ruled that the costs of an individual's repeated cosmetic surgeries, performed to reduce a facial deformity arising out of earlier surgeries to treat several congenital abnormalities, are deductible medical expenses. [I.R.C. §§ 213(a), 213(d)(1)(A), 213(d)(9)(A), 213(d)(9)(B); Ltr. Rul. 200344010 (Mar. 27, 2003)]

Q 6:41   Are expenses for nonprescription drugs qualified medical expenses for purposes of an HSA?

Yes, the term *qualified medical expenses* includes nonprescription drug expenses for medical care (see Q 6:28) paid by the HSA owner, or his or her spouse or dependents (as defined in Code Section 152). [I.R.S. Notice 2004-2, Q&A 26, 2004-2 I.R.B. 269] The definition of "nonprescription drugs" for this purpose is contained in Revenue Ruling 2003-102 and includes only those drugs used to alleviate an injury or medical condition, and not merely to improve general health. Such expenses are only qualified medical expenses to the extent that the expenses are not covered by insurance or otherwise (see Q 6:28). [I.R.S. Notice 2004-2, Q&A 26, 2004-2 I.R.B. 269; Rev. Rul. 2003-102, 2003-38 I.R.B. 559]

Example. Gretta established an HSA. She buys a nonprescription antacid, allergy medicine, pain reliever, and cold medicine from a pharmacy. The items are either for personal use or use by Gretta's spouse or dependents to alleviate or treat personal injuries or sickness. Gretta also buys dietary supplements—vitamins—without a prescription to maintain general health. Gretta is not compensated for the expenses by insurance or other sources. Gretta's expenses for everything but the vitamins were for medical care and are qualified medical expenses. The vitamins were merely beneficial to the HSA owner's general health and not an expense for medical care (see Q 6:54). [Rev. Rul. 2003-102, 2003-38 I.R.B. 559; see also Rev. Rul. 2003-58, 2003-22 I.R.B. 959, regarding expenses for certain nonprescription equipment, supplies, or diagnostic devices]

Q 6:42   Are health insurance premiums qualified medical expenses for purposes of an HSA?

Generally, no. Amounts in the HSA may generally not be used to pay health insurance premiums on a tax-free basis. The HSA owner would be subject to income tax and a 10 percent penalty for doing so. The four exceptions to this rule are as follows (see Q 2:26):

1. For HSA owners who are age 65 and over;
2. For COBRA beneficiaries;

3. For individuals receiving unemployment compensation; and

4. For long-term care premiums (see Q 6:56).

[I.R.C. §§ 223(d)(2)(B), 223(d)(2)(C)]

Q 6:43   Are Medicare premiums that are deducted from a retiree Medicare beneficiary's Social Security benefits considered qualified medical expenses for purposes of an HSA?

Yes. HSA distributions used to reimburse a retiree Medicare beneficiary for premiums deducted from his or her Social Security benefits are qualified medical expenses. [I.R.S. Notice 2004-50, Q&A 45, 2004-33 I.R.B. 196]

Q 6:44   Can medical expenses paid or reimbursed by distributions from an HSA be treated as expenses paid for medical care for purposes of taking an itemized deduction under Code Section 213(a)?

No. For purposes of determining the itemized deduction for medical expenses, medical expenses paid or reimbursed by distributions from an HSA are not treated as expenses paid for medical care under Code Section 213. [I.R.S. Notice 2004-2, Q&A 26, 2004-2 I.R.B. 269]

Q 6:45   What are Medigap policies?

Medigap policies are Medicare supplement insurance policies sold by private insurance companies to fill "gaps" in the Original Medicare Plan coverage. Except in Massachusetts, Minnesota, and Wisconsin, there are 10 standardized plans, labeled Plan A through Plan J. Medigap policies work only with the Original Medicare Plan. [http://www.medicare.gov/glossary/search.asp (search Medigap Policy)]

Q 6:46   Are premiums for Medigap policies treated as qualified medical expenses?

No. Premiums for Medigap policies are not qualified medical expenses. [I.R.S. Notice 2004-2, Q&A 27, 2004-2 I.R.B. 269]

Q 6:47   Can accident or disability insurance premiums be paid out of an HSA?

No. Accident or disability insurance premiums generally cannot be paid out of an HSA (see Q 3:43). For example, even for an HSA owner who is age 65 or older the tax-free reimbursement of insurance premiums from HSA funds is limited to insurance that covers "medical care" as defined in Code Section 213(d)(1)(D) (i.e., due to insurance premiums that can be deducted). The regulations under Code Section 213 make clear that an insurance policy providing an indemnity for loss of income (i.e., due to disability) or for loss of life, limb, or sight (i.e., due to accident) shall not be treated as covering expenses for medical care, unless such insurance contains a separate medical care component that is separately stated in the contract or furnished to the policy-holder in a separate statement. [Treas. Reg. § 1.213-1(e)(4)]

Q 6:48   Are distributions from an HSA for long-term care services considered qualified medical expenses that are excluded from the HSA owner's income?

Yes. Code Section 213(d) provides that amounts paid for qualified long-term care services are considered medical care. These amounts are, therefore, *qualified medical expenses* for purposes of an HSA. Amounts paid or distributed from an HSA and used to pay for qualified medical expenses are not includible in gross income. [I.R.C. §§ 213(d)(1)(C), 223(f)(1); I.R.S. Notice 2004-2, Q&A 27, 2004-2 I.R.B. 2; I.R.S. Notice 2004-50, Q&A 42, 2004-33 I.R.B. 196]

> **Note.** Employer-provided coverage for long-term care services provided through a flexible spending or similar arrangement is included in an employee's gross income under Code Section 106. [I.R.C. § 106(c)] Although that section applies to benefits provided by a flexible spending or similar arrangement, it does not apply to distributions from an HSA (which is a personal health care savings vehicle used to pay for qualified medical expenses through a trust or custodial account) whether or not the HSA is funded by salary-reduction contributions through a Section 125 cafeteria plan. [I.R.C. § 223(f)(1)]

Q 6:49   May a retiree who is age 65 or older receive tax-free distributions from an HSA to pay the retiree's contributions to an employer's self-insured retiree health coverage?

Yes. Although the purchase of health insurance is generally not a qualified medical expense that can be paid or reimbursed by an HSA, there is an exception for coverage for health insurance once an HSA owner has attained age 65. [I.R.C. §§ 223(d)(2)(B), 223(d)(2)(C)(iv); see I.R.S. Notice 2004-2, Q&A 27, 2004-2 I.R.B. 269] The exception applies to both insured and self-insured plans, but not to Medigap coverage (see Qs 6:45–6:46). [I.R.S. Notice 2004-50, Q&A 43, 2004-33 I.R.B. 196] In addition, even if an HSA owner is not age 65, he or she (or his or her spouse and/or dependents) can receive tax-free HSA distributions for health insurance premiums if he or she is a COBRA beneficiary or an individual receiving unemployment compensation (see Q 6:42). Further, long-term care premiums may be purchased with HSA funds on a tax-free basis at any time, to the extent that they constitute deductible medical expense (see Q 6:56).

Q 6:50   **May an individual who is under age 65 and has end stage renal disease or is disabled receive tax-free distributions from an HSA to pay for health insurance premiums?**

Maybe. An HSA may not be used to pay for health insurance premiums on a tax-free basis unless the HSA owner has attained the age specified in Section 1811 of the Social Security Act (i.e., age 65), is a COBRA beneficiary, or is an individual receiving unemployment compensation (see Q 6:42). [I.R.C. §§ 223(d)(2)(B), 223(d)(2)(C)(iv); I.R.S. Notice 2004-50, Q&A 44, 2004-33 I.R.B. 196]

Q 6:51   **Are amounts paid by an individual for equipment, supplies, and diagnostic devices that may be purchased without a prescription from a physician qualified medical expenses for purposes of an HSA?**

Yes, they are.

Example. Larry, who is a diabetic with an injured leg, uses crutches, bandages, and a blood sugar test kit and takes aspirin on the recommendation of his doctor. Code Section 213(b) allows deductions only for prescribed drugs and insulin. That section, however, applies only to medicines and drugs; other expenses, such as crutches, are deductible if they otherwise meet the definition of expenses for medical care (see Qs 2:25; 6:29). In addition, expenses for *medical care* includes amounts paid for the diagnosis, cure, mitigation, treatment, or prevention of disease or for the purpose of affecting any structure or function of the body. [I.R.C. § 213(d)(1)]

Because aspirin is a drug and does not require a physician's prescription, its cost is not deductible as a medical expense, even if a physician recommends its use to a patient. However, the cost of the aspirin may be paid from the HSA on a tax-free basis (see Q 6:54). In this case, the crutches and bandages mitigate the effect of Larry's injured leg, and the blood sugar test kit monitors and assists in treating Larry's diabetes. Therefore, the costs of these items are deductible as amounts paid for medical care and are qualified medical expenses. [Rev. Rul. 2003-58, 2003-22 I.R.B. 959, distinguished by Rev. Rul. 2003-102, 2003-38 I.R.B. 559]

Medicine and Drugs

Q 6:52   **What does the term *medicine and drugs* include?**

The term *medicine and drugs* includes only items that are legally procured and generally accepted as falling within the category of medicine and drugs. Toiletries (e.g., toothpaste), cosmetics (e.g., face creams), and sundry items are not medicines and drugs, and amounts expended for these items are not expenditures for medical care. [Treas. Reg. § 1.213-1(e)(2)]

Q 6:53 Can an HSA reimburse the cost of prescription drugs imported from Canada (or other countries)?

Generally, no. Medicines and drugs qualify as medical care under Code Section 213(d) only if they are "legally procured" and meet other IRS restrictions. Beginning with the 2004 version of IRS Publication 502—*Medical and Dental Expenses*, the IRS added the following item entitled "Medicines and Drugs from Other Countries":

> In general, you cannot include in your medical expenses the cost of a pre-scribed drug brought in (or ordered shipped) from another country, be-cause you can only include the cost of a drug that was imported legally.

Exceptions. IRS Publication 502 contains two exceptions from the general prohibition; they are:

1. Prescribed drugs that the Food and Drug Administration (FDA) an-nounces can be legally imported by individuals; and
2. Prescribed drugs purchased and consumed in another country, if the drugs are legal in both the United States and the other country. Conse-quently, whether an HSA can reimburse claims for prescription drugs imported from Canada generally will depend upon whether the FDA has declared importation of that particular drug to be legal.

[Pub. 502 (for 2008), p. 16]

The FDA takes the position that "virtually all shipments of prescription drugs imported from a Canadian pharmacy will run afoul of the [Federal Food, Drug, and Cosmetic] Act." [See FDA Position on Foreign Drug Imports available at http://www.fda.gov/ora/import/] The Secretary of Health and Human Services and the Secretary of Commerce indicate that there are very significant safety and economic issues that must be addressed before importation of prescription drugs is permitted. [See *HHS Report on Prescription Drug Importation*, available at http://www.hhs.gov/importtaskforce/]

Q 6:54 Are amounts paid by an individual for medicines that may be purchased without a prescription of a physician qualified medical expenses for purposes of an HSA?

Yes; amounts paid by an individual for medicines that may be purchased without a prescription of a physician are qualified medical expenses for HSA purposes as long as the medicine or drug is for medical care (e.g., pain reliever, antacid, allergy medicine, aspirin, or cold medicine) and not merely to improve general health (e.g., vitamins) (see Q 6:41). [Rev. Rul. 2003-102, 2003-38 I.R.B. 559; I.R.S. Notice 2004-2, Q&A 26, 2004-2 I.R.B. 269]

Example. Zebert's doctor recommends that he take aspirin. Because aspirin is a drug that does not require a physician's prescription, he cannot include its cost in his medical expenses for federal income tax deduction purposes. In general, only prescribed drugs and insulin are treated as medical expenses. However, the cost of the aspirin may be paid from the HSA on a tax-free basis.

Q 6:55 What is meant by the term *prescribed drug*?

A *prescribed drug* is a drug or biological that requires a prescription from a physician for its use by an individual. [I.R.C. § 213(d)(3)]

Distributions Used for Long-Term Care Insurance Premiums

Q 6:56 May an HSA owner pay qualified long-term care insurance premiums with a tax-free distribution from an HSA?

Yes, within limits. For HSA purposes, the payment for coverage under a qualified long-term care insurance contract by any HSA owner, spouse, or dependent is a qualified medical expense. [I.R.C. § 223(d)(2)(C)(ii)] However, the amount that is permitted to be distributed from an HSA on a tax-free basis is subject to an age-based limit set forth in Code Section 213(d)(10) (see Q 6:49). [I.R.C. § 213(d)(10); I.R.S. Notice 2004-50, Q&A 40 and 41, 2004-33 I.R.B. 196]

The term *qualified long-term care insurance contract* is defined in Code Section 7702B(2).

Q 6:57 May an HSA owner pay qualified long-term care insurance premiums with tax-free distributions from an HSA if contributions to the HSA are made by salary reduction through a Code Section 125 cafeteria plan?

Yes. Code Section 125(f) provides that the term *qualified benefit* under a Code Section 125 cafeteria plan does not include any product that is advertised, marketed, or offered as long-term care insurance. However, for HSA purposes, the payment for coverage under a qualified long-term care insurance contract is a qualified medical expense (see Q 6:56). [I.R.S. Notice 2004-50, Q&A 40, 2004-33 I.R.B. 196]

Note. Where an HSA that is offered under a cafeteria plan pays or reimburses individuals for qualified long-term care insurance premiums, the cafeteria plan rules are not applicable. This is because it is the HSA, not the long-term care insurance, that is offered under the cafeteria plan.

Q 6:58 Are tax-free distributions from an HSA for long-term care insurance premiums limited in amount?

Yes. Code Section 213(d)(10) limits the deduction for long-term care insurance premiums; thus, the amount of distributions for qualified medical expenses that may be excluded from an HSA owner's income under an HSA may be less than the actual premium paid (see example below). [I.R.C. § 213(d)(10); I.R.S. Notice 2004-50, Q&A 41, 2004-33 I.R.B. 196]

Note. Although eligible long-term care insurance premiums are deductible medical expenses under Code Section 213, the deduction is limited to the annually adjusted amounts in Code Section 213(d)(10), which are based on age. Table 6-1 shows the deductible limits for 2009 and 2008. Thus, HSA distributions to pay or reimburse qualified long-term care insurance premiums are qualified medical expenses, but the exclusion from gross income (tax-free distribution) is limited to the adjusted amounts.

Any excess premium reimbursements are includible in gross income and may also be subject to the 10 percent additional tax (see Q 6:72).

Table 6-1. Eligible Long-Term Care Premiums

Attained Age on Last Day of Taxable Year	Limitation on Premiums 2009	Limitation on Premiums 2008
40 or below	$ 320	$ 310
41–50	$ 600	$ 580
51–60	$1,190	$1,150
61–70	$3,180	$3,080
71 and above	$3,980	$3,850

[Rev. Proc. 2008-66, § 3.21, 2008-45 I.R.B. 1 for 2009. See Rev. Proc. 2007-66, § 3.21, 2007-45 I.R.B. 956 for 2008]

Example. In 2009, Candace, age 41, pays premiums of $775 for a qualified long-term care insurance contract. The Code Section 213(d)(10) limit in calendar year 2009 for deductions for person's ages 41 through 50 is $600. Candace's HSA may reimburse Candace up to $600 on a tax-free basis for the long-term care premiums. The remaining $175 ($775 – $600), if reimbursed from the HSA, is not for qualified medical expenses and is includible in gross income. It may also be subject to an additional 10 percent tax (see Q 6:72).

Deemed Distributions Due to Prohibited Transactions

Q 6:59 Are account beneficiaries prohibited from engaging in any transactions involving an HSA?

Yes. The HSA owner (and his or her HSA owner) may not enter into activities that are termed *prohibited transactions* involving an HSA (see Q 6:62). [I.R.C. §§ 223(e)(2), 408(e)(2)]

Q 6:60 What are the results if an individual engages in a prohibited transaction?

If an HSA owner (or his or her HSA owner) engages in a prohibited transaction during a taxable year involving the HSA, the HSA account ceases to be an HSA as of the first day of the taxable year and is deemed distributed at that time. The deemed distribution will be treated as not being used for qualified medical expenses. Therefore, the taxpayer will be subject to income taxes and to the 10 percent additional tax applicable to HSA distributions that are not used for qualified medical expenses (see Q 6:72). [I.R.C. § 223(f)(2); I.R.S. Notice 2004-2, Q&A 25, 2004-2 I.R.B. 269]

The prohibited transaction penalty tax does not apply (see Q 6:67).

Q 6:61 May an HSA owner pledge his or her HSA as security for a loan?

No. If an HSA owner pledges any portion of an HSA as security for a loan, the portion so pledged is treated as a deemed distribution as of the first day of the taxable year and is subject to income tax and the 10 percent additional tax on HSA distributions that are not used for qualified medical expenses. [I.R.C. §§ 223(e)(2), 408(e)(4)] The prohibited transaction penalty tax does not apply (see Q 6:67).

Note. Any amount treated as distributed as the result of pledging the amount as security for a loan will not be treated as used to pay for qualified medical expenses. The HSA owner must, therefore, include the distribution in gross income and generally will be subject to the additional 10 percent tax on distributions not used for qualified medical expenses. [I.R.C. § 223(f)(2); I.R.S. Notice 2004-2, Q&A 25, 2004-2 I.R.B. 269]

Q 6:62 Is an HSA subject to the prohibited transaction provisions of the Code?

Yes. Notwithstanding whether an HSA is a plan within the meaning of Title I of ERISA (see Qs 8:1, 8:2), the prohibited transaction provisions of Code Section 4975 apply to an HSA. [I.R.C. §§ 223(e)(2), 408(e), 4975(e)(1)] However, if the account ceases be an HSA as of the first day of the year because the HSA owner engages in a prohibited transaction, the 15 percent prohibited transaction penalty tax does not apply. Neither will the tax apply if the account, or a portion thereof, is treated as distributed on the first day of the year because of the HSA owner's pledging the account, or a portion thereof, as security for a loan. [I.R.C. § 4975(c)(6)]

ERISA Section 406 generally prohibits "transactions" between the plan and a fiduciary. Therefore, unless there is an exemption, a fiduciary is prohibited from rendering investment advice to a plan participant that results in the payment of additional advisory or other fees to the fiduciary or any of its affiliates. [DOL Field Assistance Bulletin 2007-1 (Feb. 2, 2007)]. The fiduciary would also be prohibited from engaging in any other type of "transaction" in connection with the provision of investment advice—including those transactions that fall within the broadly-constructed category of dealing with the plan assets in his or her own interest or for his or her own account.

ERISA Section 408(b)(14) provides a statutory exemption for any transaction in connection with the rendering of investment advice by a fiduciary to a participant or beneficiary which permits the participant or beneficiary to direct the investment of their individual account if the requirements of the exemption are satisfied. The statutory exemption, ERISA Section 408(g), allows a fiduciary adviser to provide advice under an "eligible investment advice arrangement." On August 22, 2008, the EBSA and the DOL issued a proposed class exemption for the provision of certain investment advice (see Q 6:63).

Q 6:63   What is a prohibited transaction?

A prohibited transaction includes any direct or indirect:

- Sale, exchange, or lease of any property between a plan (defined in Code Section 4975(e)(1) to include an HSA account) and a disqualified person (defined in Code Section 4975(e)(2)) (see Q 6:69);
- Loan of money or other extension of credit between a plan and a disqualified person; [I.R.S. Notice 2008-59, Q&A 34, 2008-29 I.R.B. 123]
- Provision of goods, services, or facilities between a plan and a disqualified person;
- Transfer to, or use by or for the benefit of, a disqualified person of the income or assets of a plan;
- Act by a disqualified person who is a fiduciary (defined in Code Section 4975(e)(3)) whereby he or she deals with the income or assets of the plan in his or her own interest or for his or her own account; or
- Receipt of any consideration for his or her own personal account by any disqualified person who is a fiduciary from any party dealing with the plan in connection with a transaction involving the income or assets of the plan.

[I.R.C. § 4975(c); ERISA § 406; see DOL Interp. Bull. 94-3, 59 Fed. Reg. 66,735 (1994) (in-kind contributions to satisfy statutory or contractual funding obligations); Marshall v. Snyder, 430 F. Supp. 1224 (E.D.N.Y. 1977), *aff'd in part and remanded in part*, 572 F.2d 894 (2d Cir. 1978) (furnishing of goods, services, or facilities); Leigh v. Engle, 727 F.2d 113 (7th Cir. 1984) (self-dealing); New York State Teamsters Council Health & Hosp. Fund v. Estate of De Perno, 816 F. Supp. 138 (N.D.N.Y. 1993), *aff'd in part and remanded*, 18 F.3d 179 (2d Cir. 1994) (self-dealing, financial loss to trust fund not necessary); see also DOL Adv. Ops. 86-01A, 88-03A, 89-089A, 93-06A (direct expenses of salary and related cost of employees that work on plans)]

Loan from trustee to HSA. A prohibited transaction results if an HSA trustee lends money to the HSA. An HSA trustee is a disqualified person (see Q 6:62). A loan or extension of credit between a plan and a disqualified person is a prohibited transaction (see Q 6:63). Thus, any direct or indirect extension of credit between the HSA trustee and the HSA is a prohibited transaction. [I.R.S. Notice 2008-59, Q&As 34 through 36, 2008-29 I.R.B. 123]

Example 1. Greentree Bank is the trustee of an HSA. Greentree extends a line of credit to the HSA. The line of credit is a prohibited transaction.

Example 2. Moola Bank is the trustee of an HSA. The HSA owner accesses the funds in the HSA through a debit card. In addition, Moola extends a line of credit to the HSA owner that is not secured by the HSA owner's HSA, and amounts in the HSA cannot be used to repay the line of credit. The line of credit is not a prohibited transaction.

Pledging HSA as security for a loan. A prohibited transaction occurs when an HSA owner pledges his or her HSA as security for a loan. Any direct or indirect extension of credit between the HSA owner and his or her HSA is a prohibited transaction. [I.R.S. Notice 2008-59, Q&A 36, 2008-29 I.R.B. 123]

Example 3. Paolo is an HSA owner of an HSA. Marine Bank is the trustee of the HSA. Marine extends to Paolo a line of credit secured by the HSA. The pledge securing the line of credit is a prohibited transaction.

Q 6:64   What are the consequences if an HSA owner or other disqualified persons enter into a prohibited transaction with an HSA?

Code Section 223(e)(2) provides that rules similar to the rules of Code Sections 408(e)(2) and (4) apply to HSAs. Therefore, HSA owners may not enter into "prohibited transactions" with an HSA (e.g., the HSA owner may not sell, exchange, or lease property; borrow or lend money; pledge the HSA; furnish goods, services or facilities; transfer to or use by or for the benefit of himself/herself any assets of the HSA; etc.). (See Qs 6:59–6:69.) If an HSA owner engages in a prohibited transaction with his or her HSA, the sanction, in general, is a disqualification of the account (see Q 6:57). Thus, the HSA stops being an HSA as of the first day of the taxable year of the prohibited transaction. The assets of the beneficiary's account are deemed distributed, and the appropriate taxes, including the 10 percent additional tax for distributions not used for qualified medical expenses, apply (see Q 6:72).

Note. If the employer sponsoring the account (or other disqualified person) is the party engaging in a prohibited transaction, then the employer (or other party) is liable for the excise tax, but the HSA owner is not (the "innocent owner rule"). [I.R.S. Notice 2008-59, Q&A 37, 2008-29 I.R.B. 123]

Personalized Investment Advice

The prohibited transaction provisions of ERISA and the Code prohibit an investment advice fiduciary from using the authority, control, or responsibility that makes it a fiduciary to cause itself, or a party in which it has an interest that may affect its best judgment as a fiduciary, to receive additional fees. As a result, in the absence of a statutory or administrative exemption, fiduciaries are prohibited from rendering investment advice to plan participants regarding investments that result in the payment of additional advisory or other fees to the fiduciaries or their affiliates.

Q 6:65 Is the provision of investment advice through an "eligible investment advice arrangement" a prohibited transaction?

No. The Pension Protection Act of 2006 (PPA) (Pub. L. No. 109-280, 120 Stat. 780) adds a new category of prohibited transaction exemption—under ERISA Section 408(b)(14) and Code Section 4975(d)—applicable to the provision of investment advice through an "eligible investment advice arrangement" to beneficiaries of HSA accounts who direct the investment of their accounts under the plan. [See DOL Reg. § 2550.408g-1(c)(4) defining the term "IRA" to include an HSA.] The statutory exemption permits investment advice to be given either on a level-fee basis or via a computer model certified as unbiased by a fiduciary adviser. If the requirements of the exemption are met, the restrictions under ERISA Sections 406(a) and (b), relating to prohibited transactions, and the sanctions resulting from the application of the prohibited transaction rules under Code Sections 4975(c)(1)(A) through (F), do not apply, and the following are exempt from prohibited transaction treatment:

1. The provision of investment advice;
2. An investment transaction (i.e., a sale, acquisition, or holding of a security or other property) pursuant to the advice; and
3. The direct or indirect receipt of fees or other compensation in connection with the provision of the advice or an investment transaction pursuant to the advice.

[PPA § 601, adding ERISA §§ 408(b)(14) and 408(g) and I.R.C. §§ 4975(d)(17), 4975(f)(8)]

Note 1. The prohibited transaction exemptions described above does not in any manner alter existing individual or class exemptions provided by statute or administrative action.

Note 2. Generally, an affiliate of a person affiliated with funds offered under a plan may not give investment advice under the prohibited transaction rules. Although the DOL had carved out administrative exceptions, the PPA's exemption added a "flat-fee" rule where any fees for the advice do not vary depending upon the option selected (see example in Q 6:66), and for model-driven advice similar to the DOL's administrative exception (but now also applicable to IRAs and HSAs). The PPA's statutory exemption and proposed class exemption for eligible investment advice arrangements apply to parties affiliated with the funds offered under the plan.

Note 3. The PPA also directs the Secretary of Labor, in consultation with the Secretary of the Treasury, to determine, based on certain information to be solicited by the Secretary of Labor, whether there is any computer model investment advice program that meets certain statutory requirements of the exemption and may be used by an HSA (or IRA). [Compare DOL Advisory Opinion 2001-09A (Dec. 14, 2001) available at https://www.dol.gov/ebsa/regs/AOs/ao2001-09a.html]

The determination regarding a computer model was to be made by December 31, 2007. If the Secretary of Labor determines that there is such a program (which it has), the statutory exemption described above applies to the use of the program with respect to HSA beneficiaries. The DOL and Treasury Department concluded that there are computer model investment advice programs that meet the PPA criteria. As a result, the PPA restriction on the availability of the statutory exemption was lifted as of August 21, 2008, the date the DOL submitted its report to Congress. [See U.S. DOL Report to Congress (August 21, 2008), available at http://www.dol.gov/ebsa/publications/reporttocongress.html]

On August 21, 2008, the DOL also released a proposed regulation (which has since been finalized) implementing the statutory exemption under the PPA for the provision of investment advice to participants in participant-directed individual account plans and IRAs (including an HSA), and also providing for the provision of investment advice through a computer model. [RIN 1210-AB13, 73 Fed. Reg. 164, 49896–49923 (Aug. 22, 2008); Prop. DOL Reg. § 2550.408g-1 (j)(2)] The proposed DOL regulations (as do the final regulations) adopt mostly procedural standards for the certification of computer models under the PPA's exemptive relief and the obligations of providers. [Prop. DOL Reg. § 2550.408g-1 and 2550.408g-2] In addition, a proposed class exemption from the prohibited transaction rules was issued for the provision of individualized investment advice to individuals following the furnishing of recommendations generated by a computer model (or, in the case of an IRA (or HSA) with respect to which modeling is not feasible, the furnishing of certain investment educational material). Additional conditions apply. [See Proposed PTE (RIN 1210-ZA14), 73 Fed. Reg. 164, 49924 (Aug. 22, 2008)]

Note. Unlike the statutory exemption and DOL regulations, the class exemption provides relief for individualized investment advice to individuals following the furnishing of recommendations generated by a computer model or, in the case of an IRA or HSA with respect to which modeling is not feasible, the furnishing of certain investment education material. The computer generated advice recommendations and investment education materials are intended to provide individual account plan participants and beneficiaries and IRA beneficiaries with a context for assessing and evaluating the individualized investment advice contemplated by the exemption.

On January 21, 2009, the DOL finalized the investment advice regulations. [74 Fed. Reg. 3822-3851 (Jan. 21, 2009)] The final regulations make clear that:

1. A plan or plan sponsor is not under any obligation to provide investment advice. [DOL Reg. § 2550.408g-1(a)(2)]

2. Neither the statutory exemption under ERISA Section 408(g)(1) nor the regulations issued thereunder invalidate or otherwise affect prior guidance concerning the circumstances under which the provision of investment advice would not constitute a prohibited transaction. [DOL Reg. § 2550.408g-1(a)(3)]

3. Investment advice provided to plan sponsors is not covered by the exemption.

4. ERISA Section 404(c) does not limit the liability of fiduciary advisers that, pursuant to the exemptions, specifically assume and acknowledge fiduciary responsibility for the provision of investment advice. This is because the investment advice (and related transactions) covered by the exemption and furnished to participants and beneficiaries are not the result of a participant's or beneficiary's exercise of control and, accordingly, the fiduciary adviser would not be relieved of liability for such advice.

5. A fiduciary adviser may provide advice to its own employees (or employees of an affiliate) pursuant to an arrangement, provided that the fiduciary adviser or affiliate offers the same arrangement to participants and beneficiaries of unaffiliated plans in the ordinary course of its business. [DOL Reg. § 2550.498g-1(b)(5)(ii) and (d)(5)(ii)]

Note. Neither the statutory exemption nor the class exemption provides relief for the selection of the fiduciary adviser or the arrangement pursuant to which advice will be provided. Accordingly, plan fiduciaries must nonetheless be prudent in their selection and may not, in contravention of ERISA Section 406(b), use their position to benefit themselves. If a fiduciary provides services to a plan without the receipt of compensation or other consideration (other than reimbursement of direct expenses properly and actually incurred in the performance of such services), the provision of such services does not, in and of itself, constitute a prohibited act. [Preamble, DOL Reg. § 2550.408g-1 (Jan. 21, 2009), 74 Fed. Reg. 3828; see also DOL Reg. § 2550.408b-2(e)(3)]

Q 6:66 What is an "eligible investment advice arrangement?"

The exemptions discussed in Q 6:65 apply in connection with the provision of investment advice by a fiduciary adviser under an "eligible investment advice arrangement." An *eligible investment advice arrangement* is an arrangement:

1. That meets certain requirements (discussed below), and

2. Which either

   (a) Provides that any fees (including any commission or compensation) received by the fiduciary adviser for investment advice or with respect to an investment transaction involving plan assets do not vary depending on the basis of any investment option selected (sometimes referred to as fee-leveling), or

   Note. Unlike the statutory exemption and final regulations, the class exemption [RIN 1210-AB13] applies the fee-leveling limits solely to the compensation received by the employee, agent, or registered representative providing the advice on behalf of the fiduciary adviser. The fee-leveling limits under the class exemption do not consider compensation received by the fiduciary adviser on whose behalf the employee, agent or registered representative is providing such advice. [See also DOL Field Assistance Bulletin (Feb. 2, 2007) providing preliminary advice on the PPA's advice rules.]

Example. The Fine Family of Funds (a money management company) has an affiliate, Fine Advisers and Distributors, which provides advice to John, the owner of an HSA. Sarah, a registered representative with Fine Advisers and Distributors, suggests that John exchange his fund shares in Fund Y for shares in Fund Z which have higher expense ratios than Fund Y. Under the proposed regulations, the additional compensation that is received by the Fine Family of Funds because of Sarah's redemption of Fund Y and exchange into Fund Z does not violate the flat fee rule.

    (b) Uses a computer model under an investment advice program as described below in connection with the provision of investment advice to a participant or beneficiary.

In the case of an eligible investment advice arrangement, the arrangement must be expressly authorized by a plan fiduciary other than the person offering the investment advice program, or any person providing investment options under the plan, including an affiliate of either person. [Prop. DOL Reg. § 2550.408g-1 (e)] An eligible investment advice arrangement does not include "brokerage windows," "self-directed brokerage accounts," or similar plan arrangements that enable participants and beneficiaries to select investments beyond those designated by the plan. [Preamble, DOL Reg. § 2550.408g-1, 74 Fed. Reg. 3826 (Jan. 21, 2009)]

Investment advice program using computer model. In general, if an eligible investment advice arrangement provides investment advice pursuant to a computer model, the model must satisfy all of the following requirements:

1. Applies generally accepted investment theories that takes into account the historic returns of different asset classes over defined periods of time. The regulations do not preclude investment advice under a computer model from also taking into account generally accepted investment theories that take into account additional considerations. [DOL Reg. §§ 2550.408g-1(b)(4)(i)(A), 2550.408g-1(b)(4)(i)(C); Prop. DOL Reg. § 2550.408g-1(c)(1)(i)]

2. Uses relevant information about the participant or beneficiary, such as age, time horizons (such as life expectancy and retirement age), risk tolerance, current investments in designated investment options, other assets or sources of income, and investment preferences. A computer model may take into account additional information that a plan or a participant or beneficiary may provide. [DOL Reg. § 2550.408g-1(b) (4)(i)(C); Prop. DOL Reg. § 2550.408g-1(d)(1)(ii)]

3. Uses prescribed objective criteria to provide asset allocation portfolios comprised of investment options under the plan. [DOL Reg. § 2550.408g-1(B)(4)(i)(D); Prop. DOL Reg. § 2550.408g-1(d)(1)(iii)]

4. Operates in a manner that is not biased in favor of any investment options offered by the fiduciary adviser or related person. [DOL Reg. § 2550.408g-1(b)(4)(i)(E); Prop. DOL Reg. § 2550.408g-1(d)(iv)(B)]

5. Takes into account all the investment options under the plan in specifying how a participant's or beneficiary's account should be invested without the inappropriate weighting of any investment option. Investment options that constitute an investment in primarily employer securities or retirement annuities do not have to be included under the computer model. [DOL Reg. § 2550.408g-1(b)(4)(i)(F)(1) and (2); Prop. DOL Reg. § 2550.408g-1(d)(1)(v)] Where an investment fund, product, or service is itself designed to maintain a particular asset allocation taking into account the time horizons (retirement age, life expectancy) or risk level of a participant, such fund is not required to be included in the computer modeled investment advice. [Preamble, DOL Reg. § 2550.408g-1, 74 Fed. Reg. 12, 3826]

6. An eligible investment expert must certify in writing, before the model is used and in accordance with rules prescribed by the Secretary of Labor, that the model meets these requirements. The certification must be renewed if there are material changes to the model as determined under regulations. For this purpose, an eligible investment expert is a person that, through employees or otherwise, has the appropriate technical training or experience and proficiency to analyze, determine, and certify, in a manner consistent with the DOL regulations, whether a computer model meets the requirements of the regulations. However, the term "eligible investment expert" does not include any person that has any material affiliation or material contractual relationship with the fiduciary adviser, with a person with a material affiliation or material contractual relationship with the fiduciary adviser, or with any employee, agent, or registered representative of the foregoing. [DOL Reg. § 2550.408g-1 (b)(4)(ii) through (iv); Prop. DOL Reg. § 2550.408g-1(d)(2) through 2550.408g-1(d)(4)]

The fiduciary adviser (and not, for example, the plan sponsor) is responsible for determining whether a person meets these criteria. [DOL Reg. § 2550.408g-1 (b)(5); Prop. DOL Reg. § 2550.408g-1(a), 2550.408g-1(e)] A fiduciary adviser may not be the person (or organization) that offers the arrangement, provides designated investment options under the plan, or any affiliate of either (other than an IRA beneficiary who is an employee of such person or organization).

Note. In the case of an IRA or HSA, the beneficiary (owner) of the HSA owner is the fiduciary adviser. [DOL Reg. § 2550.408g-1(b)(5); Prop. DOL Reg. § 2550.408g-1(e)]

The certification must be signed by the eligible investment expert and contain the following:

(a) An identification of the methodology or methodologies applied in determining whether the computer model meets applicable requirements

(b) An explanation of how the applied methodology or methodologies demonstrated that the computer model met those requirements

(c) A description of any limitations that were imposed by any person on the eligible investment expert's selection or application of methodologies

(d) A representation that the methodology or methodologies were applied by a person or persons with appropriate educational background, technical training, or experience

In the event that the report of the auditor identifies noncompliance, the DOL regulations require that the fiduciary adviser forward a copy of the report to the DOL within 30 days following the receipt of the report from the auditor. [DOL Reg. § 2550.408g-1(b)(6)(ii)(A); Prop. DOL Reg. § 2550.408g-1(f)(2)]

In addition, if a computer model is used, the only investment advice that may be provided under the arrangement is the advice generated by the computer model, and any investment transaction pursuant to the advice must occur solely at the direction of the participant or beneficiary. This requirement does not preclude the participant or beneficiary from requesting other investment advice, but only if the request has not been solicited by any person connected with carrying out the investment advice arrangement.

Audit requirements. In the case of an eligible investment advice arrangement with respect to an IRA-based plan, an audit is required at such times and in the manner prescribed by the Secretary of Labor. The regulations require the fiduciary adviser to, at least annually, engage an independent auditor, who has appropriate technical training or experience and proficiency. [DOL Reg. § 2550. 408g-1(b)(6)(i); Prop. DOL Reg. § 2550.408g-1(f)]

Notice requirements. Before the initial provision of investment advice, the fiduciary adviser must provide written notice (which may be in electronic form) containing various information to the recipient of the advice, including information relating to:

- The role of any party affiliated with the fiduciary adviser in the development of the investment advice program

- The past performance and historical rates of return of the designated investment options available under the plan (if not otherwise provided)

- All fees or other compensation relating to the advice that the fiduciary adviser or any affiliate is to receive

- Any material affiliation or material contractual relationship of the fiduciary adviser or affiliates in the security or other property as to which advice is provided

- The manner, and under what circumstances, any participant information provided under the arrangement will be used or disclosed

- The types of services provided by the fiduciary adviser in connection with the provision of investment advice (and for computer models, any limitations on the ability of the model to take into account an investment primarily in qualifying employer securities)
- That the adviser is acting as a fiduciary of the plan in connection with the provision of the advice
- That a recipient of the advice may separately arrange for the provision of advice by another adviser that could have no material affiliation with and receive no fees or other compensation in connection with the security or other property as to which advice is provided.

This information must be maintained in accurate form and must be provided to the recipient of the investment advice, without charge, on an annual basis, upon request, or in the case of any material change.

[DOL Reg. § 2550.408g-1(b)(7); Prop. DOL Reg. § 2550.408g-1(d)(3), 2550. 408g-1(g)]Any notification must be written in a clear and conspicuous manner, calculated to be understood by the average plan participant, and sufficiently accurate and comprehensive so as to reasonably apprise participants and beneficiaries of the required information. [DOL Reg. § 2550.408g-1(b)(7)(ii); Prop. DOL Reg. § 2550.408g-1(g)(2)] The Secretary of Labor has issued a model form for the disclosure of fees and other compensation as required by the PPA. [DOL Reg. § 2550.408g-1, Appendix; Prop. DOL Reg. § 2550.408g-1, Appendix] The fiduciary adviser must maintain for at least six years any records necessary for determining whether the requirements for the prohibited transaction exemption were met. A prohibited transaction will not be considered to have occurred solely because records were lost or destroyed before the end of six years due to circumstances beyond the adviser's control. [DOL Reg. § 2550.408g-1(e); Prop. DOL Reg. § 2550.408g-1(g)(2)]

Additional requirements. In order for the exemption to apply, the following additional requirements must be satisfied: [DOL Reg. § 2550.408g-1(b)(8); Prop. DOL Reg. § 2550.408g-1(h)]

1. The fiduciary adviser must provide disclosures applicable under securities laws;
2. An investment transaction must occur solely at the direction of the recipient of the advice;
3. Compensation received by the fiduciary adviser or affiliates in connection with an investment transaction must be reasonable; and
4. The terms of the investment transaction must be at least as favorable to the plan as an arm's length transaction would be.

Fiduciary adviser. For purposes of the exemption, a *fiduciary adviser* is defined as a person who is a fiduciary of the plan by reason of the provision of investment advice to a participant or beneficiary and who is also (1) a registered investment adviser under the Investment Advisers Act of 1940 or under state laws; (2) a bank, a similar financial institution supervised by the United States or a state, or a savings association (as defined under the Federal Deposit

Insurance Act), but only if the advice is provided through a trust department that is subject to periodic examination and review by federal or state banking authorities; (3) an insurance company qualified to do business under state law; (4) a registered broker or dealer under the Securities Exchange Act of 1934; (5) an affiliate of any of the preceding; or (6) an employee, agent or registered representative of any of the preceding who satisfies the requirements of applicable insurance, banking, and securities laws relating to the provision of advice. A person who develops the computer model or markets the investment advice program or computer model is treated as a person who is a plan fiduciary by reason of the provision of investment advice and is treated as a fiduciary adviser, except that the Secretary of Labor may prescribe rules under which only one fiduciary adviser may elect treatment as a plan fiduciary. *Affiliate* means an affiliated person as defined under Section 2(a)(3) of the Investment Company Act of 1940. *Registered representative* means a person described in Section 3(a)(18) of the Securities Exchange Act of 1934 or a person described in Section 202(a)(17) of the Investment Advisers Act of 1940. [DOL Reg. § 2550.408g-1 (c)(2)(i); Prop. DOL Reg. § 2550.408g-1(j)(2)]

Fiduciary rules. Subject to certain requirements, an employer or other person who is a plan fiduciary, other than a fiduciary adviser, is not treated as failing to meet the fiduciary requirements of ERISA, solely by reason of the provision of investment advice as permitted under this exemption or of contracting for or otherwise arranging for the provision of the advice. This rule applies if (1) the advice is provided under an arrangement—between the employer or plan fiduciary and the fiduciary adviser—whereby the fiduciary adviser provides investment advice as permitted under the exemption; (2) the terms of the arrangement require compliance by the fiduciary adviser with the requirements of the exemption; and (3) the terms of the arrangement include a written acknowledgement by the fiduciary adviser that the fiduciary adviser is a plan fiduciary with respect to the provision of the advice.[DOL Reg. § 2550.408g-2; Prop. DOL Reg. § 2550.408g-1(d)(4), 2550.408g-1(e), § 2550.408g-2(b)(2)(C)]

Practice Pointer. The employer or a plan fiduciary retains responsibility under ERISA for the prudent selection and periodic review of a fiduciary adviser with whom the employer or plan fiduciary has arranged for the provision of investment advice. However, the employer or plan fiduciary does not have the duty to monitor the specific investment advice given by a fiduciary adviser. The exemption also provides that nothing in the fiduciary responsibility provisions of ERISA is to be construed to preclude the use of plan assets to pay for reasonable expenses in providing investment advice.

Practice Pointer. The person who develops a computer model or who markets a computer model or investment advice program used in an "eligible investment advice arrangement" shall be treated as a fiduciary of a plan by reason of the provision of investment advice referred to in ERISA Section 3(21)(A)(ii) to the plan participant or beneficiary, and shall be treated as a "fiduciary adviser" for purposes of ERISA Section 408(b)(14) and (g). [ERISA § 408(g)(11)(A)] Code Section 4975(f)(8) contains a parallel provision to ERISA Section 408(g)(11). This section sets forth requirements that must be satisfied in order for one such fiduciary adviser to elect to be treated as a fiduciary with respect to a plan under an eligible investment advice arrangement. In general, that identified person is the sole fiduciary adviser to be treated as a fiduciary by reason of developing or marketing the computer model, or marketing the investment advice program, used in an eligible investment advice arrangement. An eligible investment expert, in performing the computer model certification described previously, would neither be acting as a fiduciary under ERISA, nor be "handling" plan assets such that the bonding requirements would be applicable to the eligible investment expert. [Preamble, DOL Reg. § 2550.408g-1, 74 Fed. Reg. 3827-3828 (Jan. 21, 2009)]

Note. Any person may request the Secretary of Labor to make a determination with respect to any computer model investment advice program as to whether it can be used by IRAs and HSAs, and the Secretary must make such determination within 90 days of the request.

Effective date. The investment adviser provisions are effective with respect to investment advice provided on or after January 1, 2007. The provision relating to the study by the Secretary of Labor is effective on the date of enactment. [ERISA §§ 408(b)(14), 408(g), 4975(d)(17), 4975(f)(8), as amended by PPA § 601] The proposed DOL regulations became effective on October 21, 2008 (which date is 60 days after the publication of the proposed regulations in the Federal Register). The proposed class exemption is effective on November 20, 2008 (which date is 90 days after the publication of the proposed regulations in the Federal Register). The final regulations which were issued on January 21, 2009, are applicable to transactions occurring on or after March 23, 2009. [DOL Reg. § 2550.408g-1(g)] However on January 20, 2009, Rahm Emanual, Chief of Staff for President Obama, issued a memorandum that stopped all federal agencies from issuing new regulations before they were first approved by the Obama Administration. This memo requires the DOL to consider delaying the March 29, 2009, effective date and reopen the regulations to public comment. On February 4, 2009, the DOL reopened the comment period until February 18, 2009. On May 22, 2009, the DOL announced its decision to further delay the effective date of the regulations until November 19, 2009. [RIN 1210–AB13, 74 FR 98, 23951 (May 22, 2009)]

Transactions with Service Providers

The PPA offers relief in that a transaction between a plan and a disqualified person, who is not a fiduciary, is not a prohibited transaction (i.e., sale, exchange, lease, loan, or use of plan assets) under ERISA Section 406 as long as the plan receives no less than adequate consideration, or pays no more than adequate consideration for the transaction. [I.R.C. § 4975(d)(20); ERISA §§ 406(a)(1)(A), (B) and (D); 408(b) (17). See PPA § 611.]

Other Prohibited Transaction Exemptions

Prohibited transaction exemptions include:

- *Block trades.* Additional relief is provided for "block trades" (any trade of at least 10,000 shares or a fair market value of at least $200,000), between a plan and a disqualified person, which will be allocated among two or more client accounts of a fiduciary. At the time of the transaction, the interest of the plan (together with the interests of any other plans maintained by the same plan sponsor) may not exceed 10 percent of the aggregate size of the block trade. [PPA § 611(a); ERISA § 408(b)(15); I.R.C. §§ 4975(d)(18), 4975(f)(9)]

- *Electronic communication networks.* An exemption is provided for certain transactions on electronic communication networks. [PPA § 611(c); ERISA § 408(b)(16); I.R.C. § 4975(d)(18)]

- *Foreign exchange transactions.* An exemption is provided for certain foreign exchange transactions. [PPA § 611(e); ERISA § 408(b)(18); I.R.C. § 4975(d)(21)]

- *Cross-trading.* An exemption for certain cross-trading transactions that allows cross-trades between accounts managed by the same investment manager is provided. [PPA § 611(g); ERISA § 408(b)(19); I.R.C. § 4975(d)(22); DOL Reg. § C.F.R. 2550.408(b)-19, 73 Fed. Reg. 58, 450 (Oct. 7, 2008)]

- *Special correction period.* A prohibited transaction involving securities or commodities would be exempt if the correction is completed within 14 days after the fiduciary discovers (or should have discovered) that the transaction was prohibited. This prohibited transaction exemption does not apply to transactions involving employer securities. It also does not apply if, at the time of the transaction, the fiduciary or other party-in-interest (or any person knowingly participating in the transaction) knew (or should have known) that the transaction was prohibited. [PPA § 612]

Effective date. The new exemptions would be effective for transactions occurring after the PPA's enactment date, August 17, 2006. The correction period exemption applies to prohibited transactions that the fiduciary discovers (or should have discovered) after the date of enactment.

Q 6:67　What is the prohibited transaction penalty tax rate?

The penalty for initial violations is 15 percent of the amount involved for prohibited transactions occurring after August 5, 1997. If the transaction is not corrected, there is a second-tier excise tax of 100 percent of the amount involved. [I.R.C. § 4975(a); SBJA § 1453(a); TRA '97 § 1074(a)] The penalty tax does not apply, however, if the account ceased to be an HSA as of the first day of the year because the HSA owner engaged in a prohibited transaction or pledged the HSA as security for a loan. [I.R.C. § 4975(c)(6)] Excise taxes are not deductible.

Q 6:68   May the prohibited transaction rules be waived?

Yes. The Secretary of Labor has established a procedure under which a conditional or unconditional exemption from all or part of the prohibited transaction rules may be granted to any disqualified person or transaction or to any class of disqualified persons or transactions. [29 C.F.R. §§ 2570. 30–2570.52] The Secretary of Labor generally may not grant an exemption unless he or she finds that such an exemption is:

1. Administratively feasible;
2. In the interests of the plan and its participants and beneficiaries; and
3. Protective of the rights of participants and beneficiaries of the plan.

[I.R.C. § 4975(c)(2); Reorganization Plan No. 4 of 1978, 43 Fed. Reg. 47,713 (Oct. 17, 1978) (transferring the authority of the Secretary of the Treasury to issue rulings under Code Section 4975 to the Secretary of Labor)] The Secretary of Labor has delegated this authority, along with most other responsibilities under ERISA, to the Assistant Secretary for the EBSA. [Sec'y of Labor's Order 1-87, 52 Fed. Reg. 13,139 (Apr. 28, 1987)]

Q 6:69   What is meant by a disqualified person under the Code and by a party in interest under ERISA?

For purposes of the Code, the term *disqualified person* refers to any of the following:

1. A fiduciary (see Q 6:70);
2. A person providing services to a plan;
3. An employer, any of whose employees are covered by a plan;
4. An employee organization, any of whose members are covered by a plan;
5. An owner, direct or indirect, of 50 percent or more of the combined voting power of all classes of stock entitled to vote or the total value of shares of all classes of stock of a corporation, the capital interest or the profits interest of a partnership, or the beneficial interest of a trust or unincorporated enterprise that is an employer or an employee organization described in item 3 or 4;
6. A member of the family (spouse, ancestor, lineal descendant, or any spouse of a lineal descendant) of a person described in item 1, 2, 3, or 5;
7. A corporation, partnership, or trust or estate of which (or in which) 50 percent or more of the combined voting power of all classes of stock entitled to vote or the total value of shares of all classes of stock of such corporation, the capital interest or profits interest of such partnership, or the beneficial interest of such trust or estate is owned directly or indirectly or held by a person described in item 1, 2, 3, 4, or 5;
8. An officer or director (or an individual having powers or responsibilities similar to those of an officer or a director), a 10 percent or more shareholder, or a highly compensated employee (earning 10 percent or

more of the yearly wages of an employer) of a person described in item 3, 4, 5, or 7; or

9. A 10 percent or more (in capital or profits) partner or joint venturer of a person described in item 3, 4, 5, or 7.

Note. ERISA prohibits certain transactions between a plan and a party in interest. Under the Code, the term *disqualified person* is used instead of *party in interest,* and is defined slightly differently.

[I.R.C. § 4975(e)(2)]

For purposes of ERISA, the term *party in interest* refers to the following:

1. Any fiduciary (including, but not limited to, any administrator, officer, trustee, or custodian), counsel, or employee of an employee benefit plan;

2. A person providing services to a plan; [*See* Harris Trust and Savings Bank v. Solomon Smith Barney, 530 U.S. 238 (2000) (broker-dealer providing nondiscretionary equity trades to a plan automatically classified as a party in interest)]

3. An employer, any of whose employees are covered by a plan;

4. An employee organization, any of whose members are covered by a plan;

5. An owner, direct or indirect, of 50 percent or more of the combined voting power of all classes of stock entitled to vote or the total value of shares of all classes of stock of a corporation, the capital interest or the profits interest of a partnership, or the beneficial interest of a trust or unincorporated enterprise that is an employer or an employee organization described in item 3 or 4;

6. A relative (spouse, ancestor, lineal descendant, or any spouse of a lineal descendant) of any person described in item 1, 2, 3, or 5;

7. A corporation, partnership, or trust or estate of which (or in which) 50 percent or more of the combined voting power of all classes of stock entitled to vote or the total value of shares of all classes of stock of such corporation, the capital interest or profits interest of such partnership, or the beneficial interest of such trust or estate is owned directly or indirectly or held by persons described in item 1, 2, 3, 4, or 5;

8. An employee, an officer or director (or an individual having powers or responsibilities similar to those of an officer or a director), a 10 percent or more shareholder, or a highly compensated employee (earning 10 percent or more of the yearly wages of an employer) of a person described in item 2, 3, 4, 5, or 7; or

9. A 10 percent or more (in capital or profits) partner or joint venturer of a person described in item 2, 3, 4, 5, or 7.

[ERISA § 3(14)]

Q 6:70 What is meant by the term *fiduciary* for purposes of ERISA?

The term *fiduciary* refers to any person who:

1. Exercises any discretionary authority or discretionary control respecting management of a plan or exercises any authority or control respecting management or disposition of its assets;

2. Renders investment advice for a fee or other compensation, direct or indirect, with respect to any monies or other property of a plan, or has any authority or responsibility to do so; or

3. Has any discretionary authority or discretionary responsibility in the administration of a plan. Because the administration of a plan is the responsibility of the plan administrator, under ERISA the plan administrator is a fiduciary and thus is subject to the fiduciary duties imposed by ERISA.

Note. A person designated by a named fiduciary to carry out fiduciary responsibilities (other than trustee responsibilities under the plan) is treated as a fiduciary.

Accountants, attorneys, actuaries, insurance agents, and consultants who provide services to a plan are not considered fiduciaries unless they exercise discretionary authority or control over the management or administration of the plan or the assets of the plan, even if such activities are unauthorized. [ERISA § 3(21)(A); PWBA Interpretive Bulletin 75-5, Q&A D-1; 29 C.F.R. § 2509.75-5, Q&A D-1; John Hancock Mut. Life Ins. Co. v. Harris Trust & Sav. Bank, 510 U.S. 86 (1993); Kaniewski v. Equitable Life Assurance Soc'y, 1993 W.L. 88200 (6th Cir. Mar. 26, 1993) (unpublished opinion); Kyle Rys Inc. v. Pacific Admin. Servs. Inc., 990 F.2d 513 (9th Cir. 1993) (third-party administrator); Nieto v. Ecker, 845 F.2d 868 (9th Cir. 1988) (attorneys); Olson v. EF Hutton & Co., 957 F.2d 622 (8th Cir. 1992); Procacci v. Drexel Burnham Lambert, Inc., 1989 U.S. Dist. LEXIS 12208 (E.D. Pa. 1989); Painters of Phila. Dist. Council No. 21 Welfare Fund v. Price Waterhouse, 879 F.2d 1146 (3d Cir. 1989) (accountants); Pappas v. Buck Consultants Inc., 923 F.2d 531 (7th Cir. 1991) (actuaries); Schloegel v. Boswell, 994 F.2d 266 (5th Cir. 1993) (insurance agent)]. Fiduciary status is more fully discussed in chapter 23 of *The 2009 Pension Answer Book* (Aspen Publishers, 2009).

Note. Since an HSA owner likely exercises discretionary authority or discretionary control with respect to management or disposition of its assets, the HSA owner will likely be a fiduciary. In addition, although accountants, attorneys, actuaries, insurance agents, and consultants may not be considered fiduciaries, such individuals may be liable to a plan under traditional theories of malpractice.

Q 6:71 May an insurer offer a cash incentive to establish an HSA and an HDHP without violating the prohibited transaction rules?

Yes. The Department of Labor approved an insurer's program that awarded a $100 bonus payment to anyone who signed up for an HSA and an HDHP with the insurer. The DOL also approved a similar situation involving a bank that had a contractual relationship with an insurer. In that instance, the bank offered a $100 cash bonus if an individual established an HSA with the bank and an HDHP with the insurer. In both cases, (1) the individual was not required to make a contribution to receive the $100 bonus payment; (2) the payment, which could not be diverted, was made directly into the individual's HSA; and (3) neither the HDHP premiums nor the HSA account charges would vary (increase or decrease) as a result of the cash bonus payment. Thus, in those situations, the $100 cash bonus payment program was not a prohibited transaction. [I.R.C. §§ 4975(c)(2), 4975(e)(1)(E); DOL Adv. Op. 2004-09A (Dec. 22, 2004). See appendix C.]

If the cash bonus payment were to be made to the individual (or other disqualified person), rather than to the HSA, the payment would have constituted a prohibited transaction. Similarly, if the cash bonus payment were conditioned on the investment in products of the bank or insurer, the cash bonus program would likely have constituted a prohibited transaction. The controlled group rules under Code Section 414(b), (c), and (m) would also have to be considered in some situations in determining the identity of all disqualified persons (see Q 6:69). [DOL Adv. Op. 2004-09A (Dec. 22, 2004) footnotes 2 and 4]

The 10 Percent Additional Tax

Q 6:72   When is a distribution from an HSA subject to the 10 percent additional tax under Code Section 223(f)(4)?

Unless an exception applies, all HSA distributions that are not used exclusively to pay or reimburse qualified medical expenses of the HSA owner, his or her spouse, or a dependent are subject to a 10 percent additional tax (see Q 6:74). [I.R.C. § 223(f)(4)(A); I.R.S. Notice 2004-2, Q&A 25, 2004-2 I.R.B. 269]

Note. The distribution of gain attributable to the correction of excess contribution (generally before the return due date) is not subject to the additional 10 percent tax under Code Section 223(f)(4)(A) referring to distributions from an HSA not used for qualified medical expenses. [See Part II of Form 8889—*Health Savings Accounts (HSAs)*. On that form, excess contributions "and the earnings on those excess contributions" reflected on Line 14(b) are subtracted from the total distributions (shown on Line 14(b) that could be subject to additional 10 percent penalty (line 17(b)) if not used for qualified medical expenses.] In the case of an excess HSA contribution returned before the due date of the individual's federal income tax return, the provisions requiring the inclusion of amounts not used for qualified medical expenses—which are subject to the additional 10 percent penalty, unless made after age 65, death or disability—do not apply. Therefore, the additional 10 percent tax under Code Section 223(f)(4) applicable to distributions not used for qualified medical expenses does not apply to an excess contribution that is returned before the return due date of the return. [See I.R.C. §§ 223(f)(2), 223(f)(3)(A), 223(f)(4)]

Note. HSA distributions are not subject to the 10 percent tax on premature distributions under Code Section 72(t). That section does not apply to an HSA. [I.R.C. § 72(t)(1), referring to I.R.C. § 4974(c)]

Q 6:73 May a distribution that does not violate the contribution limit be treated as a distribution of an excess amount?

No. Except as noted below, an individual may not elect to treat a distribution as a correction of an excess contribution unless the contribution exceeds the contribution limits discussed in chapter 4. [I.R.S. Notice 2004-50, Q&A 35, 2004-33 I.R.B. 196] Any distribution from the account that is not a correction of a true excess is generally subject to the additional 10 percent tax to the extent it is not used for qualified medical expenses, unless another exception applies.

Note. An individual may withdraw from a tax-favored account, such as a Roth IRA, an amount less than or equal to the amount of a 2008 Economic Stimulus Payment directly deposited into such account, notwithstanding any restrictions in the Code (see Q 4:1) To the extent that the withdrawal is made no later than the time for filing the taxpayer's income tax return for 2009, plus extensions (or in the case of a Coverdell ESA (CESA), the later of May 31, 2010, or the time for filing the taxpayer's income tax return for 2009, plus extensions), the amount withdrawn is treated as neither contributed to nor distributed from the account. Thus, the amount withdrawn will not be subject to regular federal income tax nor to any additional tax or penalty under the Code. The IRS recognizes that financial institutions may not be able to distinguish these contributions and distributions from others that may occur. Therefore, the financial institution receiving the direct deposit of the Economic Stimulus Payment and making the distribution should report the deposit and distribution in the usual manner. Taxpayers who choose to withdraw their 2008 Economic Stimulus Payments received instructions in their Form 1040 package that will allow them to report the distribution on their individual income tax return in a manner that shows that the amount withdrawn is not subject to taxes or penalties. [I.R.S. Ann. 2008-44 (2008-20 I.R.B. 982 (May 19, 2008)]

Q 6:74 What are the exceptions to the 10 percent additional tax on distributions not used exclusively to pay or reimburse qualified medical expenses of the HSA owner, his or her spouse, or a dependent?

The four general exceptions to the 10 percent additional tax are as follows:

1. *Disability.* Distributions made after the HSA owner becomes disabled [I.R.C. § 223(f)(4)(B)];

2. *Death.* Distributions made to the designated beneficiary (or beneficiaries) upon the death of the HSA owner [I.R.C. § 223(f)(4)(B)];

3. *Age (currently 65).* Distributions made to an HSA owner after he or she becomes eligible for Medicare (i.e., the age specified in Section 1811 of the Social Security Act, currently age 65) [I.R.C. § 223(f)(4)(C)];

4. *Rollovers and transfers.* Distributions from an HSA that are rolled over to another HSA within 60 days after the day of receipt of the distribution or transferred directly from one HSA to another HSA (see chapter 5).

There are several additional exceptions that avoid the 10 percent additional tax, including the following:

- A distribution made by a mistake of fact due to reasonable cause that is timely repaid into an HSA (see Q 6:78)
- An eligible rollover distribution that is deposited into another HSA within 60 days of the receipt of the distribution (see Q 5:1) [I.R.C. §§ 223(f)(2), 223(f)(5)]
- A direct transfer (trustee-to-trustee) of an HSA account from one spouse to another spouse, or former spouse, under a divorce or separation instrument (see Q 5:29) [I.R.C. § 223(f)(7)]
- An amount less than or equal to the amount of the Economic Stimulus Payment directly deposited into such account (see Qs 4:1, 6:73) in 2008. [Information Release (I.R. 2008-68) (Apr. 30, 2008); see also Ann. 2008-44 (2008-20 I.R.B. 982 (May 19, 2008)]

Rollovers and transfers are more fully discussed in chapter 5.

Q 6:75 When is an individual disabled?

An individual is disabled if all three of the following conditions are satisfied:

1. The individual is unable to engage in any substantial gainful activity due to a medically determinable physical or mental impairment;
2. The disability is expected to result in death or to be of a long-continued and indefinite duration; and
3. The individual furnishes proof of the disability in the form and manner required by the IRS.

[I.R.C. § 72(m)(7)]

Whether or not the impairment in a particular case constitutes a disability will be determined with reference to all the facts in the case. The following are examples of impairments that would ordinarily be considered as preventing substantial gainful activity:

- Cancer that is inoperable or progressive;
- Loss of use of two limbs;
- Certain progressive diseases that have resulted in the physical loss or atrophy of a limb (e.g., diabetes, multiple sclerosis, or Buerger's disease);
- Diseases of the heart, lungs, or blood vessels that have resulted in major loss of heart or lung reserve as evidenced by X-ray, electrocardiogram, or

other objective findings, so that, despite medical treatment, breathless-ness, pain, or fatigue is produced on slight exertion (e.g., walking several blocks, using public transportation, or doing small chores);

- Damage to the brain or a brain abnormality that has resulted in severe loss of judgment, intellect, orientation, or memory;

- Mental diseases (e.g., psychosis or severe psychoneurosis) requiring continued institutionalization or constant supervision of the individual;

- Loss or diminution of vision to the extent that the affected individual has a central visual acuity of no better than 20/200 in the better eye after best correction, or has a limitation in the fields of vision such that the widest diameter of the visual fields subtends an angle no greater than 20 degrees;

- Permanent and total loss of speech; and

- Total deafness uncorrectable by a hearing aid.

It should be noted that the existence of one or more of the impairments described above (or of an impairment of greater severity) will not, in and of itself, always permit a finding that an individual is disabled. Any impairment, whether of lesser or greater severity, must be evaluated in terms of whether it does, in fact, prevent the individual from engaging in the individual's customary or any comparable substantial gainful activity. [Treas. Reg. § 1.72-17A(f)(2)]

Q 6:76 What is a substantial gainful activity for purposes of the disability exception?

The term *substantial gainful activity* means an activity or any comparable activity in which an individual customarily engaged prior to the advent of the disability. [Treas. Reg. § 1.72-17A(f)(1)]

In determining whether an individual's impairment renders the individual unable to engage in any substantial gainful activity, primary consideration is given to the nature and severity of the impairment. Consideration is also given to other factors (e.g., the individual's education, training, and work experience). Substantial gainful activity is the activity, or a comparable activity, in which the individual customarily engaged prior to the advent of the disability or prior to retirement if the individual was retired at the time the disability arose. [Treas. Reg. § 1.72-17A(f)(1)]

An impairment that is remediable does not constitute a disability. An individual will not be deemed disabled if, with reasonable effort and safety, the impairment can be diminished to the extent that the individual will not be prevented by the impairment from engaging in the customary or any compa-rable substantial gainful activity. [Treas. Reg. § 1.72-17A(f)(4)]

Q 6:77   What is an indefinite duration for purposes of the disability exception?

The term *indefinite duration* means that the individual is unable to reasonably anticipate that the disability will, in the foreseeable future, be so diminished as no longer to prevent any substantial gainful activity. For example, an individual who suffers a broken bone that prevents him or her from working cannot be considered disabled if his or her recovery can be expected in the foreseeable future. [Treas. Reg. § 1.72-17A(f)(3)]

The term *indefinite* is used in the sense that it cannot reasonably be anticipated that the impairment will, in the foreseeable future, be so diminished as no longer to prevent substantial gainful activity. For example, an individual who suffers a bone fracture that prevents the individual from working for an extended period of time will not be considered disabled, if recovery can be expected in the foreseeable future; however, if the fracture persistently fails to knit, the individual would ordinarily be considered disabled. [Treas. Reg. § 1.72-17A(f)(3); Williams v. Comm., T.C. Summ. Op. 2004-57 (May 13, 2004); Meyer v. Comm., T.C. Memo 2003-12 (Jan. 13, 2003)]

Returning Distributions Mistakenly Made

Q 6:78   May a distribution made erroneously be redeposited into an HSA?

Possibly. If there is clear and convincing evidence that amounts were distributed from an HSA because of a mistake of fact due to reasonable cause, the HSA owner can repay the mistaken distribution no later than April 15 following the first year the HSA owner knew or should have known that the distribution was a mistake (provided the trustee allows this; see Q 6:80). [I.R.S. Notice 2004-50, Q&A 37, 2004-33 I.R.B. 196]

Q 6:79   What is reasonable cause that would permit a mistake-of-fact distribution from an HSA to be redeposited into an HSA?

In general, reasonable cause exists when there is "clear and convincing evidence" that the HSA owner reasonably, but mistakenly, believed that an expense was a qualified medical expense and was reimbursed for that expense from the HSA. [I.R.S. Notice 2004-50, Q&A 37, 2004-33 I.R.B. 196]

Q 6:80   Are trustees and custodians required to accept the return of mistaken distributions?

No. A trustee or custodian is not obligated to accept a return of a mistaken distribution. If the trustee agrees to accept a return due to a mistake of fact, the trustee may rely upon the HSA owner's representation that the contribution is a repayment of a mistake-of-fact distribution and not subject to the contribution limit. [I.R.S. Notice 2004-50, Q&A 76, 2004-33 I.R.B. 196]

Q 6:81   What is the tax treatment of a mistake-of-fact HSA distribution that is properly and timely repaid into an HSA?

A mistake-of-fact HSA distribution that is properly and timely redeposited into an HSA is treated as follows:

1. The distribution is not included in gross income.
2. The distribution is not subject to the 10 percent additional tax (see Q 6:72).
3. The repayment is not subject to the 6 percent excise tax on excess contributions (see Q 4:92).

[I.R.S. Notice 2004-50, Q&A 37, 2004-33 I.R.B. 196] (See also Q 7:31.)

Death Distributions to Designated Beneficiaries

Q 6:82   What happens to an HSA upon the death of the HSA owner?

The answer depends upon who is designated—the spouse or another beneficiary—as the HSA owner. A beneficiary may be selected when the HSA account is selected.

Q 6:83   What are the federal income tax consequences of the HSA owner's death?

General rules upon the death of the HSA owner (account owner) depend upon the identity of the designated beneficiary, and are as follows:

1. *Spouse beneficiary.* If the taxpayer designated his or her spouse as the designated beneficiary, the surviving spouse is automatically treated as the HSA owner of the HSA after the taxpayer's death. Thus, if the surviving spouse is the designated beneficiary when the HSA owner dies, then the HSA is assumed automatically by the surviving spouse. [I.R.C. § 223(f)(8)(A)]

2. *Non-spouse beneficiary.* If a non-spouse beneficiary (other than the estate) is the designated beneficiary, the HSA ceases to be an HSA on the date of death and the fair-market value of the HSA account on the date of death is treated as taxable to the non-spouse beneficiary in the tax year that included the date of death. [I.R.C. §§ 223(f)(8)(B)(i)(I), 223(f)(8)(B)(i)(II); I.R.S. Notice 2004-2, Q&A 31, 2004-2 I.R.B. 269]

    Practice Pointer. A non-spouse designated beneficiary is entitled to the Income in Respect to a Decedent deduction under Code Section 691. [I.R.C. §§ 223(f)(8)(B)(i), 691(c)]

Note. In the case of a non-spouse beneficiary, any earnings on the account after the date of death (Box 1 minus Box 4 of Form 1099-SA) are taxable. In the case of an HSA, the amount included on the federal income tax return (other than an estate) is first reduced by any payments from the HSA made for the decedent's qualified medical expenses incurred before the decedent's death and paid within one year after the date of death. (See Q 7:56.)

3. *Estate beneficiary.* If the taxpayer's estate is the designated beneficiary, the fair market value of the HSA on the date of death is includible on the decedent's final return.

Distributions made to a designated beneficiary are not taxable to the extent that the decedent incurred qualified medical expenses prior to death and the designated beneficiary pays such amounts within one year of the date of death. [I.R.C. § 223(f)(8)(B)(ii)(I)]

If the designated beneficiary is the estate, and the decedent's gross income for the last taxable year is increased by the amount of the distribution, then the estate taxes are reduced by that amount. [I.R.C. § 223(f)(8)(B)(ii)(II)]

Q 6:84   Is a surviving spouse who assumes ownership of an HSA upon the death of his or her spouse (and former HSA owner) subject to income tax upon transfer of the HSA?

No; the surviving spouse who assumes ownership of an HSA is subject to income taxes only to the extent that HSA distributions are not used to pay for qualified medical expenses. [I.R.S. Notice 2004-2, Q&A 31, 2004-2 I.R.B. 269]

Q 6:85   How is an HSA treated for federal estate tax purposes?

Generally, there is no specific exclusion for HSAs under the federal estate tax rules. Therefore, in the event of death, the HSA balance will be includible in the HSA owner's gross estate for federal estate tax purposes. However, if the surviving spouse is the beneficiary of the HSA, the amount in the HSA may qualify for the marital deduction available under Code Section 2056.

Q 6:86   How is an HSA treated for federal gift tax purposes?

The amount that a beneficiary receives from an HSA plan is not treated as a transfer of property for federal gift tax purposes. [I.R.C. §§ 2503(e)(1), 2503(e)(2)(A)]

Income Tax Withholding on HSA Distributions

Q 6:87   Is a distribution from an HSA subject to federal income tax withholding?

No. Code Section 3405 does not apply, because an HSA would not be considered a pension plan. Since distributions used to pay for qualified medical expenses are not subject to income tax, no withholding of federal income tax would apply. However, in cases where the HSA distribution is not used for medical expenses, or the HSA owner dies and the designated beneficiary is either a non-spouse or the HSA owner's estate, the value of the distribution would become taxable.

Q 6:88   Are payers required to withhold income taxes on distributions that are not used for qualified medical expenses?

No. Although certain distributions may be taxable, the payer of the HSA distribution is not required to withhold income taxes from the HSA distribution. The HSA owner is responsible for determining the taxability or nontaxability of any distribution from an HSA (see Q 6:13).

Chapter 7

Administration and Compliance

This chapter examines the administrative and compliance issues relating to trustees and custodians with respect to IRS reporting and participant information reporting. The sponsor's use of model documents for establishing Health Savings Accounts (HSAs) is also discussed in this chapter, as well as restrictions on investments and distributions. Finally, the specific requirements for filing IRS forms are addressed in this chapter.

HSA Documents 7-2
Permissible Investments 7-5
Account Fees 7-6
Trustees and Custodians 7-7
Reports 7-10
Form Filing Requirements 7-10
   Reporting HSA Contributions on Form 5498-SA 7-11
   Reporting HSA Distributions on Form 1099-SA 7-13
   Form 5329: Reporting Additional Taxes on Excess HSA Contributions 7-17
   Reporting Excise Tax on Prohibited Transactions 7-19
   Form 8889: Health Savings Accounts (HSAs) 7-20
   Reporting Deemed Distributions 7-26
   Reporting Employer Contributions on Form W-2 7-28

Note. Line numbers are based on the 2009 version of Form W-2—*Wage and Tax Statement*; Form 5330—*Return on Excise Taxes Related to Employee Benefit Plans*; Form 1099-SA—*Distributions from an HSA, Archer MSA, or Medicare Advantage MSA*; and Form 5498-SA—*HSA, Archer MSA, or Medicare Advantage MSA Information*. Line numbers of other forms mentioned in this chapter are based on the 2008 version of those forms.

HSA Documents

Q 7:1   Must an HSA be offered in the form of a trust?

No. HSAs may be offered in the form of a trust or a custodial account. [I.R.C. §§223(d)(1), 223(d)(4)(E)]

Q 7:2   What is the difference between an HSA trustee and an HSA custodian?

The differences between an HSA *trustee* and an HSA *custodian* are minor. A trust is a legal entity under which assets are actually owned and held on behalf of a beneficiary. As the legal owner, a trustee has some level of discretionary fiduciary authority over the assets of the fund. The trustee must exercise that authority in the best interests of the beneficial owner (i.e., the HSA owner).

Note. The terms *HSA owner*, *account owner*, *account holder*, and *account beneficiary* are used interchangeably in IRS publications, notices, and announcements to refer to the person that established the HSA. To avoid confusion, the term *HSA owner* will be used to refer to that person.

A custodial arrangement is similar to a trust, but the custodian simply holds the assets on behalf of the owner of the assets. Other than holding the assets and doing as the owner orders, the custodian has no fiduciary obligations to the owner.

Q 7:3   Does federal or state law determine whether an arrangement is a trust or custodial account?

Whether an arrangement constitutes a trust or custodial arrangement is determined under state law.

Q 7:4   Has the IRS issued any documents that an individual may use to establish an HSA?

Yes. In August 2004, the IRS issued Model Form 5305-B—*Health Savings Trust Account* (rev. Aug. 2004) and Model Form 5305-C—*Health Savings Custodial Account* (rev. Aug. 2004), which allow individuals to create HSA trust accounts and HSA custodial accounts, respectively. [I.R.S. Notice 2004-50, Q&A 62, 2004-33 I.R.B. 196] On November 27, 2007, the IRS released new model forms for establishing an HSA. The new forms have been updated to incorporate changes from the Health Opportunity Patient Empowerment (HOPE) Act of 2006. The changes address increased contribution limits (see Q 4:5), as well as new methods for funding an HSA using dollars from an IRA, a health care flexible spending arrangement or a health reimbursement arrangement. The model forms now include the following legislative changes that became effective in 2007:

- Qualified HSA distributions from a health care flexible spending arrangement or health reimbursement arrangement are permitted to be transferred, in a trustee-to-trustee transfer, to an HSA (see Q 5:52). Such transfers are not subject to the maximum annual contribution limit.

- Qualified HSA funding distributions from an individual retirement account are permitted to be transferred, in a trustee-to-trustee transfer, to an HSA (see Q 5:40). Such transfers from an IRA are subject to the maximum annual contribution limits for the year ($3,000 for self-only coverage and $5,950 for family coverage for 2009).

Caution. The IRS has not issued any guidance regarding whether an HSA trustee or custodian is required to notify an existing user of the 2004 version of the model trust account (Form 5305-B) or model custodial account (Form 5305-C) of the changes made in the 2007 version of the forms and whether an individual adopting a 2004 model HSA is required to adopt the 2007 version of the form. Article X of the model forms provides that "[t]his agreement will be amended from time to time to comply with the provisions of the Code or IRS published guidance. Other amendments may be made with the consent of the persons whose signatures appear below." [See Form 5305-B, Art. X (Nov. 2007); Form 5305-C, Art. X (Nov. 2007).] Although it does not appear that the 2007 versions of the model HSA forms are required to be adopted by users of the 2004 versions of the forms, trustees and custodians should use the 2007 versions of the forms to establish new HSAs.

Note. The sponsor may include optional provisions regarding amendments to the agreement (see Qs 7:7, 7:8).

Q 7:5   Should Model Form 5305-B or Model Form 5305-C be filed with the IRS?

No. The model forms are pre-approved by the IRS (see Q 7:8). The model forms are not to be filed with the IRS, but rather should be kept with the HSA owner's permanent tax records.

Q 7:6   May a sponsor of a Model Form 5305-B or Model Form 5305-C add provisions to the model forms?

Yes. In both model forms, a sponsor may add provisions to or incorporate provision into Article XI and any article that follows it, as long as the HSA owner and trustee/custodian agree to the additional provisions.

Q 7:7   What type of additional provisions can be added to Model Form 5305-B and Model Form 5305-C?

The model forms contain specific instructions that list numerous examples of provisions that may be added to or incorporated into the model forms. The sponsor may attach additional pages if necessary. Among the additional provisions that may be included are: definitions; restrictions on rollover contributions from HSAs or Archer MSAs (e.g., requiring a rollover within 60 days after receipt of a distribution and limiting rollovers to one per year); investment powers; voting rights; exculpatory provisions; amendment and termination; removal of trustee/custodian; trustee/custodian's fees; state law requirements; treatment of excess contributions; distribution procedures (e.g., frequency and minimum dollar amount); use of debit, credit, or stored-value cards; return of mistaken distributions; and descriptions of prohibited transactions.

Q 7:8   What happens if the additional provisions are inconsistent with Code Section 223 or published IRS guidance?

The model forms treat any provision that is added to or incorporated into the model forms as being void if it is inconsistent with Code Section 223 or IRS published guidance. [Form 5305-B, Art. IX; Form 5305-C, Art. IX]

Q 7:9   When are the model forms deemed established?

Model Form 5305-B and Model Form 5305-C are considered established when the HSA owner and the HSA trustee or custodian have fully executed the model form. The model forms can be completed at any time during the tax year. However, an HSA account cannot be effective before the effective date of the eligible individual's High-Deductible Health Plan (HDHP) coverage (see Qs 2:6, 2:20–2:26), unless it is used solely to make a rollover contribution.

Q 7:10   Must the HSA be created in the United States?

Yes. HSA trust or custodial accounts must be created in the United States for the exclusive benefit of the HSA owner.

Q 7:11   What is the HSA owner's "identifying number" for use in establishing an HSA using Model Form 5305-B or Model Form 5305-C?

When an HSA owner completes the model forms, he or she should use his or her Social Security number as the identifying number.

Q 7:12   What documents should an HSA trustee or custodian provide to the HSA owner when an HSA is established?

The HSA trustee or custodian should provide a trust document or custodial agreement, respectively; a disclosure statement; and an adoption agreement for the HSA owner to complete and sign. Organizations that offer an HSA may also use certain administrative forms to facilitate such items as beneficiary designations, contributions, and distribution requests.

Q 7:13   May a plan sponsor design an IRS-approved prototype HSA?

Yes. The IRS has not announced a procedure for an HSA trustee or custodian to obtain IRS approval as a plan sponsor on a prototype HSA trust or HSA custodial account. Nonetheless, the IRS issued draft forms in June 2004 "to allow HSA trustees and custodians to use some or all of the language from the draft forms in their own trust or custodial agreements."

Note. The draft forms were not intended to be used as stand-alone trust or custodial agreements until they became finalized. [Treasury Press Release, Office of Public Affairs, June 25, 2004 (JS-1748)]

Permissible Investments

Q 7:14   How may HSA funds be invested?

HSA funds may be invested in any investments approved for IRAs (e.g., bank accounts, annuities, certificates of deposit, stocks, mutual funds, or bonds). [I.R.S. Notice 2004-50, Q&A 65, 2004-33 I.R.B. 196] HSAs may not invest in life insurance contracts or in collectibles (i.e., any work of art, antique, metal, gem, stamp, coin, alcoholic beverage, or other tangible personal property specified in IRS guidance under Code Section 408(m)(3)). HSAs may invest in certain types of bullion or coins, as described in Code Section 408(m)(3).

Q 7:15   May an HSA trust or custodial agreement restrict investments to certain types of permissible investments?

The HSA trust or custodial agreement may restrict investments to certain types of permissible investments (e.g., particular investment funds). [I.R.S. Notice 2004-50, Q&A 65, 2004-33 I.R.B. 196]

Q 7:16   May HSA funds be commingled in a common trust fund or common investment fund?

Yes. Code Section 223(d)(1)(D) states that the HSA trust assets may not be commingled except in a common trust fund or common investment fund. Thus, individual accounts maintained on behalf of individual HSA account beneficiaries may be held in a common trust fund or common investment fund. [I.R.C. §223(d)(1)(D)] A common trust fund is defined in Treasury Regulations Section 1.408-2(b)(5)(ii). A common investment fund is defined in Code Section 584(a)(1).

Note. An employer identification number (EIN) is required for a common trust fund created for HSAs.

Q 7:17   Are HSA trustees and custodians also subject to the rules against prohibited transactions?

Yes. The same rules that apply to account beneficiaries apply to trustees and custodians. [I.R.S. Notice 2004-50, Q&A 68, 2004-33 I.R.B. 196]

Account Fees

Q 7:18   If HSA administration and account maintenance fees are withdrawn from the HSA, are the withdrawn amounts treated as taxable distributions to the HSA owner?

No. Amounts withdrawn from an HSA for administration and account maintenance fees (e.g., flat administrative fees) will not be treated as a taxable distribution and will not be included in the HSA owner's gross income (see Q 7:19). [I.R.S. Notice 2004-50, Q&A 69, 2004-33 I.R.B. 196]

Q 7:19   How do HSA trustees report amounts withdrawn from the HSA to pay for HSA administration and account maintenance fees?

An HSA trustee reports amounts withdrawn from the HSA to pay HSA administration and account maintenance fees on Form 5498-SA in the fair market value (FMV) of the HSA at the end of the taxable year. These fees are not reported as distributions from the HSA. [I.R.S. Notice 2008-59, Q&A 41, 2008-29 I.R.B. 123]

Q 7:20   If HSA administration and account maintenance fees are withdrawn from the HSA, does the withdrawn amount increase the maximum annual HSA contribution limit?

No. For example, if the maximum annual contribution limit is $3,000, and a $25 administration fee is withdrawn from the HSA, the annual contribution limit is still $3,000, not $3,025. [I.R.S. Notice 2004-50, Q&A 70, 2004-33 I.R.B. 196]

Q 7:21   If HSA administration and account maintenance fees are paid by the HSA owner or employer directly to the HSA trustee or HSA custodian, do these payments count toward the annual maximum contribution limit for the HSA?

No. Administration and account maintenance fees paid directly by the HSA owner or employer will not be considered contributions to the HSA.

Example. An individual, Eric, contributes the maximum annual amount of $3,000 (the 2009 limit for self-only coverage) to his HSA. Eric pays an annual administration fee of $25 directly to the trustee. Eric's maximum annual contribution limit is not affected by the payment of the administration fee. [I.R.S. Notice 2004-50, Q&A 71, 2004-33 I.R.B. 196]

Trustees and Custodians

Q 7:22   Is any insurance company a qualified HSA trustee or HSA custodian?

Yes. Any insurance company or any bank (including a similar financial institution as defined in Code Section 408(n)) can be an HSA trustee or HSA custodian. Insured banks and credit unions are automatically qualified to handle HSAs. Any bank, credit union, or any other entity that currently meets the IRS standards for being an HSA trustee or HSA custodian for an IRA or Archer Medical Savings Account (MSA) can be an HSA trustee or HSA custodian.

In addition, any other person already approved by the IRS to be an HSA trustee or HSA custodian of an IRA or Archer MSA is automatically approved to be an HSA trustee or HSA custodian. Other persons may request approval to be an HSA trustee or HSA custodian in accordance with the procedures set forth in Treasury Regulations Section 1.408-2(e) (relating to IRA nonbank trustees). [I.R.S. Notice 2004-50, Q&A 72, 2004-33 I.R.B. 196]

Q 7:23   Can an individual qualify to be an HSA trustee or custodian?

No. An individual cannot qualify to be an HSA trustee or custodian (see Q 7:22). An individual would not satisfy many of the requirements to be a non-bank HSA trustee or custodian (e.g., continuity of existence).

Q 7:24   Is there a limit on the annual HSA contribution which the HSA trustee or custodian may accept?

Yes. Except in the case of rollover contributions or trustee-to-trustee transfers (see Q 5:30), the HSA trustee or custodian may not accept annual contributions to any HSA that exceed the annual contribution limit for family coverage (see Q 4:30) and catch-up contribution amount (see Q 4:44). [I.R.S. Notice 2004-50, Q&A 73, 2004-33 I.R.B. 196]

Q 7:25   May an HSA trustee or custodian accept contributions of property?

All contributions to an HSA must be in cash, other than rollover contributions or trustee-to-trustee transfers. [I.R.C. §223(d)(1)(A); I.R.S. Notice 2004-50, Q&A 73, 2004-33 I.R.B. 196]

Q 7:26   Who is responsible for determining whether contributions to an HSA exceed the maximum annual contribution limit for a particular HSA owner?

The HSA owner is responsible for determining whether contributions to an HSA exceed the maximum annual contribution limit for each particular account. [I.R.S. Notice 2004-50, Q&A 74, 2004-33 I.R.B. 196]

Q 7:27   **Who is responsible for notifying the HSA trustee or custodian of any excess contribution and requesting a withdrawal of the excess contribution?**

The HSA owner is responsible for notifying the HSA trustee or HSA custodian of any excess contribution and requesting a withdrawal of the excess contribution together with any net income attributable to the excess contribution. [I.R.S. Notice 2004-50, Q&A 74, 2004-33 I.R.B. 196]

Q 7:28   **Is the HSA trustee or custodian responsible for accepting cash contributions?**

Yes. The HSA trustee or custodian is responsible for accepting cash contributions within the limits up to the maximum annual contribution limit (see Q 7:24). [I.R.S. Notice 2004-50, Q&A 74, 2004-33 I.R.B. 196]

Q 7:29   **Is the HSA trustee or custodian responsible for filing required information returns with the IRS?**

Yes. The HSA trustee or custodian is responsible for filing required information returns with the IRS (Form 5498-SA and Form 1099-SA). [I.R.C. §223(h); I.R.S. Notice 2004-50, Q&A 74, 2004-33 I.R.B. 196]

Q 7:30   **Is the HSA trustee or custodian responsible for tracking the HSA owner's age?**

Yes. The HSA trustee or custodian is responsible for tracking the HSA owner's age, but the trustee or custodian may rely on the HSA owner's representation as to his or her date of birth. [I.R.S. Notice 2004-50, Q&A 75, 2004-33 I.R.B. 196]

Q 7:31   **Must the HSA trustee or custodian allow account beneficiaries to return mistaken distributions to the HSA?**

No. The HSA trustee or custodian is not required to permit account beneficiaries to return mistaken distributions to the HSA. If the HSA trust or custodial agreement allows the return of mistaken distributions (see Q 6:78), the HSA trustee or HSA custodian may rely on the HSA owner's representation that the distribution was, in fact, a mistake. [I.R.S. Notice 2004-50, Q&A 76, 2004-33 I.R.B. 196] The HSA trustee or custodian is required to correct with the IRS and HSA owner any filed Form 1099-SA that reflected the mistaken distributions. This must be done because such repayments are not included in gross income or subject to the 10 percent additional tax, and the payment is not subject to the excise tax on excess contributions. The repayment also is not treated as a contribution on Form 5498-SA.

Q 7:32   May an HSA trust or custodial agreement restrict the HSA owner's ability to roll over amounts from that HSA?

No (see Q 5:18). [I.R.S. Notice 2004-50, Q&A 77, 2004-33 I.R.B. 196]

Q 7:33   Are HSA trustees or custodians required to accept rollover contributions or trustee-to-trustee transfers?

No. Rollover contributions or trustee-to-trustee transfers from other HSAs or from Archer MSAs are allowed, but HSA trustees or custodians are not required to accept them. [I.R.S. Notice 2004-50, Q&A 78, 2004-33 I.R.B. 196; I.R.S. Notice 2004-2, Q&A 23, 2004-2 I.R.B. 269] Similarly, qualified HSA distributions from an employer's Flexible Spending Arrangement (FSA) or a Health Reimbursement Arrangement (HRA) that are transferred to an HSA (see Q 5:52), or as of 2007, a direct transfer from an IRA to an HSA in a qualified HSA funding distribution (see Q 5:40), are allowed but trustees and custodians are not required to accept them. [The qualified HSA distribution rules apply to distributions made after December 20, 2006. The qualified HSA funding distribution rules are effective for taxable years beginning after 2006. See Tax Relief and Health Care Act of 2006 (TRHCA). (Pub. L. No. 109-432), §§302(c)(1), 307(c)]

Q 7:34   May an HSA trust or custodial agreement restrict HSA distributions to pay or reimburse only the HSA owner's qualified medical expenses?

No. The HSA trust or custodial agreement may not contain a provision that restricts HSA distributions to pay or reimburse only the HSA owner's qualified medical expenses (see Q 6:15). [I.R.S. Notice 2004-50, Q&A 79, 2004-33 I.R.B. 196]

Q 7:35   May an HSA trustee or custodian restrict the frequency or minimum amount of distributions from an HSA?

Yes. HSA trustees or custodians may place reasonable restrictions on both the frequency and the minimum amount of distributions from an HSA (see Q 6:14). [I.R.S. Notice 2004-50, Q&A 80, 2004-33 I.R.B. 196]

Q 7:36   May an HSA trustee or custodian that does not sponsor the HDHP require proof or certification that the HSA owner is an eligible individual?

Where an HSA trustee or custodian does not sponsor the HDHP, the trustee or custodian may require proof or certification that the HSA owner is an eligible individual. [I.R.S. Notice 2004-2, Q&A 10, 2004-2 I.R.B. 269]

Q 7:37   May an HSA trustee or custodian that does not sponsor the HDHP require proof or certification that the HSA owner is covered by an HDHP?

Where an HSA trustee or custodian does not sponsor the HDHP, the HSA trustee or HSA custodian may require proof or certification that the health plan that covers the HSA owner meets all of the requirements of an HDHP. [I.R.S. Notice 2004-2, Q&A 10, 2004-2 I.R.B. 269]

Reports

Q 7:38   What reports may the IRS require in connection with an HSA?

There are two types of reports that the IRS may require in connection with an HSA: (see Qs 7:42, 7:49, 7:57) [I.R.C. §223(h)]

1. The trustee or custodian of an HSA to make such reports regarding such account to the IRS and to the HSA owner with respect to contributions, distributions, the return of excess contributions, and such other matters as the Secretary determines to be appropriate. [I.R.C. §223(h)(1)]

2. Any organization that provides an individual with an HDHP to make such reports to the Secretary and to the HSA owner with respect to such plan as the IRS determines to be appropriate. [I.R.C. §223(h)(2)]

Q 7:39   When must reports regarding HSA accounts be provided?

The reports required by the IRS, are to be filed at such time and in such manner and furnished to such individuals at the time and in the manner that the Secretary may require (see Qs 7:45, 7:46, 7:53, 7:60, 7:63). [I.R.C. §223(f)]

Q 7:40   What is the penalty if an HSA trustee, custodian, or employer fails to file a required report with the IRS?

Generally, if a trustee, custodian, or an employer fails to file a required report (other than an information return or a payee statement) with the IRS, there is a penalty of $50 for each failure unless it is shown that such failure is due to reasonable cause. [I.R.C. §§223(h), 6693(a)(1), 6693(a)(2)(c), 6724(d)(1)(C)(i) (concerning information returns), 6724(d)(2)(W) (concerning payee statements)]

Form Filing Requirements

Q 7:41   Is an employer required to provide participants in an HSA or an HDHP with an SPD?

No. An employer is not required to provide a participant with an SPD for the HSA or the HDHP, unless either constitutes an employee welfare benefit plan under ERISA (see chapter 8).

Reporting HSA Contributions on Form 5498-SA

Q 7:42   What is the purpose of Form 5498-SA—HSA, Archer MSA, or Medicare Advantage MSA Information?

Form 5498-SA is used to report contributions to an HSA, an Archer MSA, or a Medicare Advantage MSA (MA-MSA). A separate Form 5498-SA must be filed for each type of account.

Generally, HSA contributions made by the HSA owner or by someone other than the HSA owner's employer are deductible by the HSA owner, while HSA contributions made by the HSA owner's employer are excludable from the HSA owner's income but are not deductible by the HSA owner. Also, the HSA owner and his or her employer may contribute to the HSA owner's HSA for the same tax year (in contrast, an Archer MSA HSA owner and his or her employer may not contribute to the HSA owner's Archer MSA for the same tax year).

> **Note.** An individual may withdraw from a tax-favored account, such as a Roth IRA, an amount less than or equal to the amount of a 2008 Economic Stimulus Payment directly deposited into such account, notwithstanding any restrictions in the Code (see Qs 4:1, 6:73, 6:74). The amount timely withdrawn will not be subject to regular federal income tax nor to any additional tax or penalty under the Code. The IRS recognizes that financial institutions may not be able to distinguish these contributions and distributions from others that may occur. Therefore, the financial institution receiving the direct deposit of the Economic Stimulus Payment and making the distribution should report the deposit and distribution in the usual manner. Taxpayers who choose to withdraw their Economic Stimulus Payments will receive instructions in their Form 1040 package that will allow them to report the distribution on their individual income tax return in a manner that shows that the amount withdrawn is not subject to taxes or penalties. [I.R.S. Ann. 2008-44 (2008-20 I.R.B. 982 (May 19, 2008)]

Q 7:43   For whom is Form 5498-SA required to be filed?

An HSA trustee or custodian must file Form 5498-SA—*HSA, Archer MSA, or Medicare Advantage MSA Information*, with the IRS and to each person for whom it maintained an HSA (or Archer MSA, or MA-MSA) during the year.

Rollovers. The receipt of a rollover from an Archer MSA or an HSA to an HSA (and receipt of a rollover from one Archer MSA to another Archer MSA) are reported in Box 4.

Transfers. A trustee-to-trustee transfer from an Archer MSA to an HSA, or from one HSA to another HSA (or one Archer MSA or MA-MSA to another Archer MSA or MA-MSA) are not required to be reported. For reporting purposes, contributions and rollovers do not include these transfers. On the other hand, a qualified HSA distribution from an employer's FSA or an HRA is to be reported in Box 4 on Form 5498-SA as a rollover contribution. A qualified HSA distribution is also reported by the employer in Box 12 of Form W-2.

As of 2007, a qualified funding distribution which is transferred from an IRA to an HSA will be treated as a contribution to the HSA by the HSA trustee or custodian on Form 5498-SA. A qualified funding distribution is subject to the maximum annual contribution limit ($3,000 for self-only coverage or $5,950 for family coverage for 2009). Qualified HSA funding distributions (trustee-to-trustee transfers from an IRA to an HSA) are reported in Box 2 on Form 5498-SA.

Q 7:44 Is Form 5498-SA required if no contributions were made and there was a total distribution made from the HSA?

Generally, if a total distribution was made from an HSA during the year and no contributions were made for that year, Form 5498-SA is not required to be filed, nor must a statement be furnished to the participant to reflect that the FMV on December 31 was zero.

Q 7:45 When must Form 5498-SA be filed with the IRS?

If required to be filed, the 2009 version of Form 5498-SA must be filed with the IRS by June 1, 2010.

Q 7:46 When must Form 5498-SA be provided to the recipient?

If the 2009 version of Form 5498-SA is required to be filed with the IRS, a statement must be provided to the recipient (generally Copy B) by June 1, 2010. The participant may be, but is not required to be, provided with a statement of the December 31, 2009, FMV of the participant's account by Monday, February 1, 2010. [*Instructions for Forms 1099-SA and 5498-SA*]

Q 7:47 Must Form 5498-SA be filed if the owner of an HSA dies?

Generally, for the year in which an HSA owner dies, a Form 5498-SA must be filed with the IRS and a December 31 statement of FMV must be provided for the decedent.

Note. If the designated HSA beneficiary is the HSA owner's spouse, the spouse becomes the owner of the HSA and the spouse (if an eligible individual) may make contributions into the HSA. If the designated HSA beneficiary is not the HSA owner's spouse or there is no designated HSA beneficiary, the account ceases to be an HSA, an Archer MSA, or an MA-MSA (see Qs 5:24, 6:83, 7:47, 7:56, 7:67).

Q 7:48 How are the boxes on Form 5498-SA completed for an HSA?

For 2009, purposes of Form 5498-SA, the HSA distribution reporting codes are as follows:

Box 1: Enter Archer MSA contributions made in 2009. Do not enter HSA contributions.

Box 2: *Total Contributions Made in 2009.* Enter the total amount of HSA (or Archer MSA) contributions made in 2009, including any contributions made in 2010 that are designated for 2009. Include any qualified HSA funding distributions (trustee-to-trustee transfers) from an IRA to fund an HSA received during 2009.

Note. For contributions made between January 1 and April 15, 2010, the HSA trustee or HSA custodian should obtain the participant's designation of the year for which the contributions are made.

Box 3: *Total HSA (or Archer MSA contributions) made in 2010 for 2009.* Enter the total amount of HSA contributions made in 2010 for 2009. Do not include repayments of mistaken distributions. The HSA trustee or HSA custodian may have to file a corrected Form 1099-SA (see Q 7:31).

Box 4: *Rollover Contributions and Direct Transfers.* Enter any rollover contribution amounts to an HSA (or Archer MSA) received during 2009, including any qualified HSA distributions (direct transfers of employer contributions) from a health FSA or HRA to fund an HSA. The amount on Line 4 is not included in Box 1, 2, or 3.

Note. See Form 8889 and its instructions for information on reporting distributions and rollovers.

A *rollover* means that the HSA owner takes a distribution from one account and redeposits the distribution into another account within a 60-day period (aka "a rollover").

Box 5: *Fair Market Value.*

The HSA trustee or custodian may include other information about an account (e.g., the FMV as of December 31, 2009) in Box 5 of this form.

Note. HSA administration and maintenance fees withdrawn by the trustee are reflected on Form 5498-SA in the FMV market value of the HSA at the end of the taxable year. These fees are not reported as distributions from the HSA. [I.R.S. Notice 2008-59, Q&A 42, 2008-29 I.R.B. 123]

Box 6: *Checkbox.* Check the "HSA" box.

Reporting HSA Distributions on Form 1099-SA

Q 7:49   What is the purpose of Form 1099-SA?

Form 1099-SA—*Distributions from an HSA, Archer MSA, or Medicare Advantage MSA* is used to report distributions made from an HSA, Archer MSA, or MA-MSA. A separate return must be filed for each plan type. If no distributions have been made from the account for that year, an HSA trustee or custodian is not required to file a Form 1099-SA.

Note. An individual may withdraw from a tax-favored account, such as a Roth IRA, an amount less than or equal to the amount of a 2008 Economic Stimulus Payment directly deposited into such account, notwithstanding any restrictions in the Code (see Qs 4:1, 6:73, 6:74). The amount timely withdrawn will be subject to neither the regular federal income tax nor any additional tax or penalty under the Code. The IRS recognizes that financial institutions may not be able to distinguish these contributions and distributions from others that may occur. Therefore, the financial institution receiving the direct deposit and making the distribution of an Economic Stimulus Payment should report the deposit and distribution in the usual manner. Taxpayers who choose to withdraw their Economic Stimulus Payments will receive instructions in their Form 1040 package that will allow them to report the distribution on their individual income tax return in a manner that shows that the amount withdrawn is not subject to taxes or penalties. [I.R.S. Ann. 2008-44 (2008-20 I.R.B. 982 (May 19, 2008)]

Q 7:50 In what year are distributions from an HSA required to be reported?

The year in which a distribution is made from an HSA is the year that the distribution should be reported.

Q 7:51 Must Form 1099-SA be provided to the HSA owner and/or account beneficiaries?

If Form 1099-SA is required to be filed with the IRS, the payor must also furnish a statement to recipients containing the information furnished to the IRS.

Q 7:52 When is Form 1099-SA required to be provided to the recipient?

If Form 1099-SA must be filed with the IRS, the 2009 version of Copy B of Form 1099-SA or a substitute statement must be provided to the recipient by February 1, 2010.

Q 7:53 When is Form 1099-SA required to be filed with the IRS?

If Form 1099-SA must be filed with the IRS, the 2009 version of Form 1099-SA must be filed with the IRS by March 1, 2010, or by March 31, 2010, if filed electronically. The electronic and magnetic media filing requirements for 2008 are contained in Revenue Procedure 2008-30. [2008-23 I.R.B. 1056]

Q 7:54 What is a substitute statement for Form 1099-SA?

Generally, a substitute statement for Form 1099-SA is any statement other than Copy B (and C in some cases) of the official form. Substitute statements may be developed or purchased from a private printer. However, the substitutes must comply with the format and content requirements specified in IRS Publication 1179, *General Rules and Specifications for Substitute Forms 1096, 1098, 1099, 5498, and W-2G (and 1042-S).*

Q 7:55   How are transfers between trustees and/or custodians treated for purposes of Form 1099-SA?

For Form 1099-SA reporting purposes, contributions and rollovers do not include direct transfers from an Archer MSA to an HSA or from one HSA to another HSA.

However, a qualified HSA distribution from an employer's FSA or an HRA are to be reported in Box 4 on Form 5498-SA as a rollover contribution. A qualified HSA distribution is also reported by the employer in Box 12 of Form W-2. Beginning in 2007, a qualified HSA funding distribution which is transferred from an IRA to an HSA will be treated as a contribution to the HSA by the HSA trustee or custodian and reported in Box 2 on Form 5498-SA. A qualified HSA funding distribution is subject to the maximum annual contribution limit ($3,000 for self-only coverage or $5,950 for family coverage for 2009). (See Qs 5:52 and Q 7:43.)

Q 7:56   How is Form 1099-SA completed for an HSA?

The rules and coding for Form 1099-SA depend upon when the distribution is made (i.e., in the year of death or in the year after the year of death). If the HSA owner dies and the designated HSA beneficiary is the HSA owner's spouse, the spouse becomes the HSA owner. If the designated HSA beneficiary is not the spouse, or if there is no designated HSA beneficiary, the account ceases to be an HSA on the date of the HSA owner's death. If there is no designated HSA beneficiary, or the beneficiary becomes the person's estate, the FMV of the HSA as of the date of the HSA owner's death must be reported in Box 4 of Form 1099-SA.

Note. It is the responsibility of the HSA beneficiary to determine whether a distribution is used for qualified medical expenses and to determine any taxes or penalties due (see chapter 6).

For 2009, the numbered boxes on Form 1099-SA (2009) are completed as follows:

Box 1: Gross Distribution. Box 1 shows the amount distributed from the HSA for the year. Enter the gross amount of the distribution, including any earnings on excess contributions reported in Box 2. Do not report a negative amount in Box 1. The payer is not responsible for determining the taxable amount of a distribution. The distribution may have been paid directly to a medical service provider or the HSA owner. If the payment was made directly to a medical service provider, show the HSA owner as the recipient.

Death. The gross distribution is also reported when a final distribution is made to the HSA beneficiary in the year of the HSA owner's death or in a year after the year of death.

Box 2: Earnings on Excess Contributions. Enter only the earnings attributable to an excess contribution made to an HSA or Archer MSA that was returned to the HSA owner by the due date of the HSA owner's tax return.

This amount is also included in Box 1. However, earnings on other distributions are reported only in Box 1.

Note. In the case of a non-spouse HSA beneficiary, any earnings on the account after the date of death (Box 1 minus Box 4 of Form 1099-SA) are taxable. In the case of an HSA, the amount included on the federal income tax return (other than the tax return for the HSA owner's estate) is first reduced by any payments from the HSA made for the decedent's qualified medical expenses incurred before the decedent's death and paid within one year after the date of death.

Box 3: Distribution Code. Enter one of the following distribution codes. (If more than one code applies to multiple distributions from the same account, separate Forms 1099-SA must be filed showing the proper code for that distribution):

Code 1: *Normal Distributions.* Use Code 1 for normal distributions to the HSA owner and any direct payments to a medical service provider. Use this code if no other code applies.

Death. If a final distribution is made to a surviving spouse beneficiary after the year of death, use Code 1.

Code 2: *Excess Contributions.* Use Code 2 for distributions of excess HSA contributions that include any earnings.

Code 3: *Disability.* Use Code 3 if distributions are made after the HSA owner was disabled (see Q 6:77).

Code 4: *Death Distribution (Other Than Code 6).* Use Code 4 for payments to a decedent HSA owner's estate in the year of death. Also use Code 4 for payments to an HSA owner's estate after the year of death. Do not use with Code 6.

Note. If the HSA beneficiary is the estate, enter the estate's name and taxpayer identification number (TIN) in place of the recipient's on the form.

Code 5: *Prohibited Transaction.* Use Code 5 for amounts treated as distributed if the HSA account loses its exemption from taxation when the HSA owner or HSA owner's beneficiary engages in a prohibited transaction. [I.R.C. §223(e)(2)]

Pledge of Account. To the extent that assets in an HSA are pledged as security for a loan and treated as distributed, use Code 5. [I.R.C. §223(e)(2)]

Code 6: *Death Distribution After Year of Death to a Non-Spouse HSA Beneficiary.* Use Code 6 for payments to a non-spouse HSA beneficiary, other than an estate, after the year of death. Do not use with Code 4. (See Codes 1 and 4.)

Box 4: FMV on Date of Death. Enter the FMV of the account on the decedent HSA owner's date of death in Box 4.

Note. If a non-spouse beneficiary inherits an HSA, the FMV on the date of death is reported on the beneficiary's tax return for the year the HSA owner died, even if the distribution is received in a later year.

Box 5: Checkbox. Box 5 shows the type of account that is being reported. Check the appropriate box (e.g., HSA, Archer MSA, or MA-MSA).

Form 5329: Reporting Additional Taxes on Excess HSA Contributions

Q 7:57   What is the purpose of Form 5329?

Form 5329—*Additional Taxes on Qualified Plans (Including IRAs) and Other Tax-Favored Accounts* is used by individuals to report additional taxes on many different types of retirement, education, and health arrangements. Part VII of Form 5329 addresses the tax on excess contributions to an HSA under Code Section 4973 (see Q 7:27).

Q 7:58   Under what circumstances must Form 5329 be filed with respect to an HSA?

An individual must file Form 5329 for 2009 only if contributions in respect to 2009 exceed the maximum contribution limit.

Note. An individual must also file Form 5329 if there was a tax due from an excess contribution on Lines 17 (regarding traditional IRAs), 25 (regarding Roth IRAs), 33 (regarding Coverdell Education Savings Accounts [ESAs]), 41 (regarding Archer MSAs), or 49 (regarding HSAs) of the prior year's (2008) Form 5329. Excess contributions to an HSA for the current year are addressed on Form 8889 (discussed in Q 7:68), but reported on Form 5329.

Q 7:59   If applicable, can a married couple who are filing a joint tax return file one Form 5329?

No. In the case of a married couple who are filing a joint tax return, if both spouses must file Form 5329, then each spouse must complete and file a separate form. The combined tax, however, is reported on Form 1040 (Line 59) or Form 1040NR (Line 54).

Amended return. If filing an amended 2009 Form 5329, check the box at the top of page 1 of the form. Do not use the 2009 Form 5329 to amend a return for any other year (see Q 7:60).

Q 7:60   When must Form 5329 be filed?

Form 5329 must be filed as an attachment to Form 1040 or Form 1040NR by the due date, including extensions, of Form 1040 or Form 1040NR. If filing Form 1040 or Form 1040NR is not required, complete and file Form 5329 by itself at the time and place Form 1040 or Form 1040NR must be filed (if required).

Note. Be sure to include address information and signature. Enclose, but do not attach, a check or money order payable to "United States Treasury" for any taxes due. Write the taxpayer's SSN and "2009 Form 5329" on the check.

Prior tax years. If filing Form 5329 for a prior year, use that year's version of the form. Form 5329 can be filed by itself. Therefore, unless that year's tax return must also be amended (by filing Form 1040X—*Amended U.S. Individual Income Tax Return*) that year's Form 5329 can be filed alone.

Q 7:61   How is Part VII of Form 5329 completed for an HSA?

If the contributions to an individual's HSA exceed the contribution limit for 2009 and were not timely removed (see Qs 4:30, 4:91), complete Form 5329 as follows:

Line 42: Enter the excess contributions from Line 48 of the prior year (2008).

Line 43: Enter the difference between what could have been contributed to the HSA for 2009 (from Form 8889, Line 12) and the amount that was contributed for 2009 (from Form 8889, Line 2). Otherwise enter zero.

Note. Also enter on Form 8889, Line 13, the smaller of Form 5329, Line 43, or the excess (if any) of Form 5329 Line 42 over Line 44.

Line 44: Enter 2009 distributions from HSA (from Form 8889, Line 16).

Line 45: Enter the sum of Lines 43 and 44.

Line 46: Enter the difference between Lines 45 and 42 (i.e., subtract Line 45 from Line 42). If the difference is zero or less, enter zero.

Line 47: Enter the contributions made for 2009, unless withdrawn (see below) that exceed the contribution limit. The instructions for Form 8889 (see Qs 7:65–7:70) explain how to figure excess contributions. Some or all of the excess contributions for 2009 may be withdrawn, and they will not be treated as having been contributed if:

- The withdrawal is made by the due date, including extensions, of the 2009 return;
- No exclusion from income is claimed for the amount of the withdrawn contributions; and
- Any earnings on the withdrawn contributions are also withdrawn and included in gross income.

Note. Include the withdrawn contributions and related earnings on Form 8889, Lines 14a and 14b.

Line 48: Enter the sum of Lines 46 and 47.

Line 49: Enter 6 percent tax, or the FMV of account if it is less. The tax will need to be calculated. Also enter the amount of tax on Form 1040 (Line 59) or Form 1040NR (Line 54).

Extension for timely filers. If the tax return was timely filed without withdrawing the excess contributions, the withdrawal can be made no later than six months after the due date of the tax return, excluding extensions. If applicable, file an amended return with "Filed pursuant to Section 301.9100-2" written at the top. Report any related earnings for 2009 on the amended return and include an explanation of the withdrawal. Make any other necessary changes on the amended return (e.g., if the contributions were reported as excess contributions on the original return, include an amended Form 5329 reflecting that the withdrawn contributions are no longer treated as having been contributed).

Reporting Excise Tax on Prohibited Transactions

Q 7:62   What is the purpose of Form 5330?

Form 5330—*Return on Excise Taxes Related to Employee Benefit Plans* is used to report any tax on a prohibited transaction (see Q 6:63). Code Section 4975 generally imposes an excise tax on a disqualified person that engages in a prohibited transaction with an HSA (as well as other types of health, education, and retirement plans). Form 5330 was redesigned in January 2008 and now groups the various excise taxes by due date.

Note. If the HSA owner engages in a prohibited transaction with respect to an HSA, the account ceases to be an HSA (see Q 6:60) and the prohibited transaction tax does *not* apply. Other individuals that are disqualified individuals (e.g., the employer), however, may have participated in the prohibited transaction and are required to file Form 5330.

Caution. Regardless of whether an HSA is an ERISA plan (see Qs 1:9, 6:62), an HSA remains subject to the excise tax on prohibited transactions under Code Section 4975.

[I.R.C. §4975. See also I.R.C. §§4975(d), 4975(f)(6)(B)(ii), and 4975(f)(6)(B)(iii) for specific exemptions to prohibited transactions. Also see I.R.C. §4975(c)(2) for certain other transactions or classes of transactions that may be exempt.]

Q 7:63   When must Form 5330 be filed?

If a prohibited transaction is subject to the prohibited transaction excise tax, Form 5330 must be filed by the last day of the seventh month (generally July 31) after the end of the tax year of the employer or other person who must file the return.

Q 7:64   How is Form 5330 completed when a disqualified person participates in a prohibited transaction involving an HSA?

When a disqualified person participates in a prohibited transaction involving an HSA (other than his or her own HSA [see Q 6:60]), the disqualified person must complete Form 5330. If all prohibited transactions have not been corrected by the end of the tax year, an explanation must be attached indicating when the correction has been or will be made. Then, all prohibited transactions must be entered on Schedule C of Form 5330. The tax determined must be entered on Schedule C (Line 3) on Line 3a of the Form 5330 on page 1. If the prohibited transaction is not corrected within the taxable period, a 100 percent tax on the amount involved in the prohibited transaction is reported on Line 3b. The total tax due must be shown in Part II, Tax Due, on Line 19. "Form 5330, Section(s) 4975, _____ (include other applicable Code Sections) _____" should be shown in the space provided on the Form 5330 by Line 19 and on the payment along with the taxpayer's name and tax identifying number.

Form 8889: Health Savings Accounts (HSAs)

Q 7:65   What is the purpose of Form 8889?

Form 8889—*Health Savings Accounts (HSAs)* is used to:

- Report HSA contributions (including those made on behalf of the HSA owner and by the HSA owner's employer);
- Figure the HSA deduction; and
- Report distributions from HSAs.

Note. Line numbers shown are from the 2008 version of Form 8889.

Q 7:66   Who must file Form 8889?

The HSA owner must file Form 8889 with the IRS as an attachment to Form 1040 (or 1040NR) only if any of the following apply:

- Contributions were made to the HSA, including contributions made on behalf the HSA owner and by the HSA owner's employer, in 2009;
- The HSA owner received distributions from his or her HSA in 2009; or
- A beneficiary (including an estate) acquired an interest in an HSA because of the death of the HSA owner.

Note. Forms 1040EZ or 1040A are designed to be filed without attachments, so a taxpayer (who is otherwise qualified to use either form) would be unable to report contributions and distributions if filing Forms 1040EZ or 1040A. Form 8889 must be attached to Form 1040 (or Form 1040NR).

Q 7:67   How is Form 8889 completed upon the death of the owner?

If the HSA owner's surviving spouse is the designated beneficiary, the HSA is treated as if the surviving spouse were the HSA owner. The surviving spouse completes Form 8889 as though the HSA belonged to him or her.

If the designated beneficiary is not the HSA owner's surviving spouse, or there is no designated beneficiary, the account ceases to be an HSA as of the date of the HSA owner's death. The beneficiary completes Form 8889 as follows:

1. "Death of HSA owner" is entered across the top of Form 8889.

2. The name(s) and the SSN(s) shown on the designated beneficiary's tax return are entered in the spaces provided at the top of the form; skip Part I, regarding contributions and deductions.

3. The FMV of the HSA as of the date of the HSA owner's death is entered on Line 14a.

4. For a beneficiary other than the estate, qualified medical expenses incurred by the HSA owner before the date of the HSA owner's death that are paid within one year of that date are entered on Line 15.

5. The rest of Part II is completed.

If the HSA owner's estate is the beneficiary, the value of the HSA as of the date of the HSA owner's death is included on the HSA owner's final income tax return. Complete Form 8889 as described above, except that Part I should be completed if applicable.

Note. The distribution is not subject to the additional 10 percent tax (see Q 6:72). Report any earnings on the account after the date of the HSA owner's death as income on the designated beneficiary's tax return.

Q 7:68 How are contributions, excess contributions, and deductions reported on Form 8889?

Generally, the HSA owner can deduct from his gross income any HSA contributions he or she made or someone other than the HSA owner's employer made. HSA contributions made by the HSA owner's employer are excludable from the HSA owner's income but the HSA owner cannot deduct them from his gross income.

Note. Also, the HSA owner and his or her employer may contribute to the HSA owner's HSA for the same tax year (in contrast, an Archer MSA HSA owner and his or her employer may not contribute to the HSA owner's Archer MSA for the same tax year). Part I of Form 8889 is used to determine the amount of the HSA deduction an HSA owner may take, any excess contributions made to the HSA (including those made on behalf of the HSA owner), and any excess contributions made to the HSA by an employer.

Caution. If spouses are filing jointly and they have an HDHP with family coverage, but each spouse has a separate HSA, each spouse must complete and file a separate Form 8889, specifying the portion of the family coverage contribution limit allocated to the other spouse. The amounts on Line 13 of both Forms 8889 are combined and entered on Form 1040 (Line 25), or Form 1040NR (Line 25). Both Forms 8889 should be attached to the tax return.

Practice Pointer. Before completing Part I of Form 8889, it may be necessary to complete Form 8853—*Archer MSAs and Long-Term Care Insurance Contracts* (see Line 4).

For 2009, complete Part I of Form 8889—*HSA Contributions and Deductions* as follows:

Line 1: If the HSA owner is covered, or considered covered, by a self-only HDHP and a family HDHP at different times during the year, the box for the plan that was in effect for a longer period. If the HSA owner is covered by both a self-only HDHP and a family HDHP at the same time, the HSA owner is treated as having family coverage during that period. If, on the first day of the last month of the HSA owner's tax year (generally December 1), the HSA owner had family coverage, the "family" box will be checked.

Line 2: On Line 2 include only those amounts the HSA owner, or others on behalf of the HSA owner, contributed to the HSA. Be sure to include those contributions made from January 1, 2010 through April 15, 2010 that were made for 2009. Do not include any employer contributions (see Line 9), any amounts rolled over from another HSA or Archer MSA, any qualified HSA distributions, or any qualified HSA funding distributions (see Line 10).

Note. Contributions to an employee's account through a cafeteria plan are treated as employer contributions and are not included on Line 2.

Line 3: Use the following rules to figure out the amount to enter on Line 3 (see examples in Qs 4:37, 4:46, 4:47, 4:49):

a. Use the family coverage amount if the HSA owner or his or her spouse had an HDHP with family coverage. Disregard any plan with self-only coverage.

b. If the last-month rule (see Qs 4:5, 4:6) applies, the HSA owner is considered an eligible individual for the entire year. The HSA owner is treated as having the same HDHP coverage for the entire year as he or she had on the first day of the last month of his or her tax year.

c. If the HSA owner was, or was considered, an eligible individual for the entire year and he or she did not change his or her type of coverage, $3,000 for self-only HDHP coverage or $5,950 for a family HDHP coverage will be entered on Line 3. (See f below.)

d. If the HSA owner was, or was considered, an eligible individual for the entire year and he or she changed his or her type of coverage during the year, the amount entered will be (see f below) the greater of:

  • The limitation shown on the last line of the chart at Q 4:48 (also in the instructions for Form 8889), or

  • The maximum amount that can be contributed based on the type of HDHP coverage the HSA owner had on the first day of the last month of the HSA owner's tax year.

Practice Pointer. If the HSA owner had family coverage on the first day of the last month, the worksheet does not need to be used and $5,950 is to be entered on Line 3.

e. If the HSA owner was not an eligible individual on the first day of the last month of his or her tax year, the chart at Q 4:48 (also in the instructions for Form 8889) is used to determine the amount to enter. (See f below.)

f. If, at the end of 2009, the HSA owner was unmarried and age 55 or older, the amount determined in items c or d above can be increased by $1,000 (the additional contribution amount). The additional contribution amount is taken into account for each month the HSA owner is an eligible individual.

Note. If the HSA owner is married, the additional contribution amount is figured on Line 7 (discussed later) and is not included on Line 3.

Practice Pointer. If the chart (see Q 4:48) must be completed, and the HSA owner's eligibility and coverage did not change from one month to the next, the same number you entered for the previous month is entered.

Line 4: Enter the amount contributed to the HSA owner's Archer MSA for 2009 (including employer contributions) from Form 8853, Lines 3 and 4. If the HSA owner or his or her spouse had family coverage under an HDHP at any time during 2009, the amount contributed to his or her spouse's Archer MSA must be included.

Line 5: Enter the difference between Lines 4 and 3 (i.e., subtract Line 4 from Line 3). If the difference is zero or less, enter zero.

Line 6: Generally, enter the amount on Line 5. However, spouses who have separate HSAs and had family coverage under an HDHP at any time during 2009 must use the following rules to figure the amount to be entered on Line 6:

• If the HSA owner is treated as having family coverage for each month, the amount on Line 5 is divided equally between the HSA owner and his or her spouse, unless they both agree on a different allocation (such as allocating nothing to one spouse). Enter the allocable share on Line 6.

Example 1. In 2009, an HSA owner is an eligible individual and has self-only HDHP coverage. In March the HSA owner marries, and as of April 1, he or she has family HDHP coverage. Neither the HSA owner nor his or her spouse qualifies for the additional contribution amount. The spouse of the HSA owner has a separate HSA and is an eligible individual from April 1 to December 31, 2009. Because the HSA owner and his or her spouse are considered to have family coverage on December 1, the HSA owner's contribution limit is $5,950 (the family coverage maximum). The HSA owner and his or her spouse can divide this amount in any allocation to which they agree (such as allocating nothing to one spouse).

• If the HSA owner is not treated as having family coverage for each month, the following steps will determine the amount to enter on Line 6:
  – Step 1. The contribution limit that would have been entered on Line 5 is refigured as if the HSA owner had entered on Line 3 the total of the worksheet amounts only for the months he or she was treated as having family coverage. When refiguring Line 5, the same amount previously entered on Line 4 is used.
  – Step 2. The refigured contribution limit from Step 1 is divided equally between the HSA owner and his or her spouse, unless they both agree on a different allocation (such as allocating nothing to one spouse).

- Step 3. The part of the contribution limit allocated to the HSA owner's spouse in Step 2 is subtracted from the amount determined in Step 1.
- Step 4. Add any other contribution limits that apply for the tax year to the result in Step 3 and enter the total on Line 6.

Example 2. In 2009, an HSA owner is an eligible individual and has family HDHP coverage that also covers their children. In March the HSA owner divorces and changes his or her coverage as of April 1 to self-only. Neither the HSA owner nor his or her spouse qualifies for the additional contribution amount. The HSA owner's former spouse continued to have family HDHP coverage and was an eligible individual for the entire year. The contribution limit for the three months the HSA owner and his or her spouse both were considered to have family coverage is $1,487.50 ($5,950 × 3 ÷ 12). The HSA owner and his or her former spouse divide the family coverage contribution equally. The HSA owner's contribution limit for nine months of self-only coverage is $2,250 ($3,000 × 9 ÷ 12). This amount is not divided between the HSA owner and his or her spouse.

Because the HSA owner is covered under a self-only policy on December 1, he or she will show $3,000 on Line 6—the greater of either (a) $2,993.75 ($1,487.50 family coverage + $2,250 self-only coverage – $743.75 spousal allocation) or (b) the maximum amount that can be contributed ($3,000 for self-only coverage). The HSA owner's ex-spouse who continues to have family coverage would show $5,950 on Line 6—the greater of either (a) $5,206.25 ($1,487.50 family coverage for the three months prior to the divorce + $4,462.50 ($5,950 × 9 ÷ 12) family coverage maintained after the divorce – $743.75 spousal allocation) or (b) the maximum amount that can be contributed ($5,950 for family coverage).

Line 7: If, at the end of 2009, the HSA owner is age 55 or older and married, the number of months eligible will be multiplied by $1,000 and that amount will be divided by 12, with the result entered on Line 7 if both of the following apply:

1. The HSA owner and his or her spouse had family coverage under an HDHP, or were considered to be, eligible individuals on the first day of the month.
2. The HSA owner was not enrolled in Medicare for the month.

Example 3. At the end of 2009, the HSA owner was age 55 and married. The HSA owner had family coverage under an HDHP from January 1 through June 30, 2009 (6 months). The HSA owner was not enrolled in Medicare in 2009. An additional contribution amount of $500 would be entered on Line 7 ($1,000 × 6 ÷ 12).

Line 8: Enter the sum of Lines 6 and 7.

Line 9: Enter employer contributions (including contributions through a cafeteria plan), including any amount an employer contributes to any HSA for the HSA owner for 2009. These contributions should be shown in Box 12 of Form W-2 with Code W. If either of the following apply, complete the Employer Contribution Worksheet below.

- Employer contributions for 2008 are included in the amount reported in Box 12 of Form W-2 with Code W (but not in Boxes 1, 3, and 5) for 2009. If an employer made excess contributions, the excess may have to be reported as income. The excess employer contributions are the excess, if any, of the employer's contribution over the taxpayer's limitation shown on Line 13 of Form 8889. If the excess was not included in income on Form W-2, it is to be reported as "Other income" on Form 1040 (unless corrected, see Q 4:94).

- Employer contributions for 2009 are made in 2010.

If the HSA owner's employer made excess contributions, the excess may have to be reported for tax year 2009.

1. Enter the employer contributions reported in Box 12 of Form W-2, with Code W $_____

2. Enter employer contributions made in 2009 for tax year 2008 $_____

3. Subtract Line 2 from Line 1 $_____

4. Enter employer contributions made in 2010 for tax year 2009 $_____

5. Employer contributions for 2009. Enter the sum of Lines 3 and 4 here and on Form 8889, Line 9 $_____

Line 10: Enter any qualified HSA funding distributions from an IRA (see Q 5:40). This distribution is not included in income, is not deductible, and reduces the amount that can be contributed to the HSA.

The maximum amount that can be excluded from income is based on the HSA owner's HDHP coverage (self-only or family). Only one qualified HSA funding distribution can be made during an HSA owner's lifetime. However, if the HSA owner makes the distribution during a month when he or she has self-only HDHP coverage, then the HSA owner can make another qualified HSA funding distribution in a later month in that tax year if the HSA owner changes to family HDHP coverage (see Q 5:49).

Line 11: Enter the sum of Lines 9 and 10.

Line 12: Enter the difference between Lines 11 and 8 (i.e., subtract Line 11 from Line 8). If the result is zero or less, enter zero.

Line 13: Deductible Amount: The allowable HSA deduction (taking into account employer contributions that were excluded from income) is shown on Line 13 of Form 8889. Enter the lesser of Lines 2 and 12. This is the amount of HSA contributions that are deductible. The amount on Line 13 is entered on Form 1040 (Line 25) or Form 1040NR (Line 25).

Practice Pointer. If Line 2 (actual contributions) is more than Line 13 (deductible contributions), the individual made an excess contribution and has to pay an additional tax. See prior discussion of Form 5329 for methods of correction to avoid the 6 percent tax on excess contributions.

Reporting Deemed Distributions

Q 7:69 How are deemed distributions from an HSA reported on Form 8889?

The following situations result in deemed distributions from an HSA. These distributions are reported on Form 8889 in the following manner:

1. *The owner participated in a prohibited transaction with respect to an HSA, at any time in 2009.* The account ceases to be an HSA as of January 1, 2009, and the FMV of all assets in the account of January 1, 2009, must be included on Line 14a.

2. *Any portion of an HSA was used as security for a loan at any time in 2009.* The FMV of the assets used as security for the loan must be included as income on Form 1040, Line 21. On the dotted line next to Line 21, enter "HSA" and the amount used as security.

Q 7:70 How is Form 8889 completed if a distribution is made from the account?

If a distribution is made from an HSA, Part II, *HSA Distributions*, of Form 8889 must be completed as follows:

Line 14a: Enter the total distributions received in 2009 from all HSAs. Include amounts paid with a debit card that restricts payments to health care and amounts withdrawn by other designated individuals.

Line 14b: Enter any distributions included on Line 14a that were received in 2009 qualified as a rollover contribution to another HSA. Also any excess contributions (and the earnings on those excess contributions) included on Line 14a that were withdrawn by the due date, including extensions, of the return are entered in Line 14b.

Line 15: In general, enter the total amount of distributions from all HSAs in 2009 that were used for the qualified medical expenses of the HSA owner and his or her spouse or dependents that were incurred on or after the first day of the first month during which the HSA owner became an eligible individual.

Caution. No deduction may be claimed on Schedule A (Form 1040) for any amount included on Line 15.

Line 16: Enter the taxable HSA distribution.

Line 17a and 17b: Additional 10 percent Tax: HSA distributions included in income (Line 16) are subject to an additional 10 percent tax unless an exception applies (see Q 6:74). The additional 10 percent tax does not apply to distributions made after the HSA owner dies, becomes disabled, or turns age 65. If any of these exceptions applies to any of the distributions included on Line 16, check the box on Line 17a. Enter on Line 17b only 10 percent (.10) of any amount included on Line 16 that does not meet any of the exceptions.

Example 1. An HSA owner turned age 63 in 2009 and received a distribution from an HSA that is included in income. The box on Line 17a should not be checked because the HSA owner did not meet the age exception for the distribution. Ten percent of the amount from Line 16 is entered on Line 17b.

Example 2. An HSA owner turned age 65 in 2009 and received distributions that are included in income both before and after the HSA owner turned age 65. The box on Line 17a should be checked because the additional 10 percent tax does not apply to the distributions made after the date the HSA owner turned age 65. However, the additional 10 percent tax does apply to the distributions made on or before the date the HSA owner turned age 65. Consequently, 10 percent of the amount of these distributions included in Line 16 should be entered on Line 17b.

Q 7:71   How is Form 8889 completed if HDHP coverage is not maintained during the testing period?

Part III of Form 8889 is used to determine any income and additional tax that must be reported on Form 1040 or Form 1040NR for failure to be an eligible individual during the testing period for:

- A qualified HSA distribution from a health care FSA or HRA to an IRA (see Qs 5:52, 5:74),
- Part-year coverage (see last-month rule in Qs 4:5, 4:10), or
- A qualified HSA funding distribution (see Qs 5:40, 5:46).

The amount is included in income in the year in which the HSA owner failed to be an eligible individual. Form 8889 must be completed to compute the additional tax for failure to maintain HDHP coverage as follows:

Line 18: Enter the total of any qualified HSA distribution.

Line 19: Last month rule. The limitation chart in the Instructions for Form 8889 (Q 4:48) for the year the contribution was made is used to determine the contribution that could have been made if the last-month rule did not apply. Enter the excess of the amount contributed over the redetermined amount on line 13.

Line 20: Enter the total of any qualified HSA funding distribution.

Line 21: Enter the sum of Lines 18, 19, and 20. Include this amount on Form 1040, Line 21, or Form 1040NR, Line 21. On the dotted line next to Line 21 of Form 1040 or 1040NR, enter "HSA" and the amount.

Line 22: The amount on Line 21 is multiplied by 10 percent and included on Form 1040, Line 61, or Form 1040NR, Line 57. On the dotted line next to Line 61 of Form 1040 or Line 57 of Form 1040NR, enter "HDHP" and the amount.

Reporting Employer Contributions on Form W-2

Q 7:72   How is Form W-2, Wage and Tax Statement, completed if an employer makes contributions to an HSA?

Employer contributions to an HSA are reported in Box 12 of Form W-2, using Code W. Generally, employer contributions to an employee's HSA are not subject to income, Social Security/Medicare, or Railroad Retirement taxes and will not affect amounts otherwise reported in Boxes 1, 3, and 5 of Form W-2. The amount shown as an HSA contribution in Box 12 of Form W-2 that is marked with Code W should be entered on Line 9 of Form 8889 (see Q 7:68).

Q 7:73   How should pretax contributions made to an HSA through an employer's cafeteria plan be reported?

An employer should report pretax contributions of employees made through a cafeteria plan on Form W-2 in Box 12 (but not in Boxes 1, 3, and 5). Pretax salary reduction contributions are treated as employer contributions for purposes of the Tax Code (see Q 7:72). It makes sense to report these contributions on Form W-2, because when an employee is completing Form 8889—*Health Savings Accounts (HSAs)*, these contributions will be designated as amounts that are not deductible. This applies regardless of whether the contributions are (1) made from employee contributions deducted pursuant to a cafeteria plan election, or (2) made by the employer outside of Code Section 125 under the comparability requirements. The HSA owner enters the amount on Form 8889.

Q 7:74   How does an employer report contributions on Form W-2 that are recouped because the employee was never an eligible individual or that exceeded the maximum annual contributions limit?

If an employer contributes to the account of an employee who was never an eligible individual, the employer may recoup the amounts (see Qs 6:2, 6:3). At the employer's option, the employer may request that the financial institution return the amounts to the employer. However, if the employer does not recover the amounts by the end of the taxable year, then the amounts must be included as gross income and wages on the employee's Form W-2 for the year during which the employer made the contributions. In other situations, except for errors resulting in excess contributions described below, an employer may not generally recoup contributions once made (see Qs 3:73, 4:71, 4:147, 6:2–6:5). [I.R.S. Notice 2008-59, Q&A 25, 2008-29 I.R.B. 123]

If the employer contributes amounts to an employee's HSA that exceed the maximum annual contribution allowed ($3,000 for self-only coverage and $5,950 for family coverage for 2009) due to an error, the employer may correct the error (see Qs 6:2, 6:4). In that case, at the employer's option, the employer may request that the financial institution return the excess amounts to the employer. However, if the employer does not recover the amounts by the end of the taxable year, then the amounts must be included as gross income and wages on the employee's Form W-2 for the year during which the employer made contributions. If, however, amounts contributed are less than or equal to the maximum annual contribution allowed, the employer may not recoup any amount from the employee's HSA. [I.R.S. Notice 2008-59, Q&A 24, 2008-29 I.R.B. 123]

Q 7:75 How are employer contributions to the HSA of an employee's spouse (who is not an employee of this employer) treated?

Employer contributions to an HSA of an employee's spouse (who is not an employee of this employer) are included in the employee's gross income and wages. Under Code Section 106(d)(1), employer contributions are excluded from an employee's gross income and wages only when the contributions are made by the employer to the HSA of an employee who is an eligible individual (see Qs 4:62, 4:80). Any contribution by an employer to the HSA of a non-employee (e.g., a spouse of an employee or any other individual), including salary reduction amounts made through a Code Section 125 cafeteria plan, must be included in the gross income and wages of the employee. [I.R.S. Notice 2008-59, Q&A 26, 2008-29 I.R.B. 123] However, the contributions will be deducted on the employee's tax return if the employee and his or her spouse file a joint return.

Chapter 8

Federal and State Laws Affecting HSAs

Although most of the requirements of HSAs are set forth in the Internal Revenue Code and IRS guidance, another federal law that could affect HSAs is the Employee Retirement Income Security Act of 1974 (ERISA). In addition, certain state laws may affect HSA administration or influence whether an HDHP can be offered in a particular state. Finally, because an HSA is an investment vehicle, federal laws that regulate securities may also apply. This chapter begins by examining both the Department of Labor (DOL) guidance that sets the parameters regarding ERISA plan status and the consequences of such status. It then discusses the effect that state law may have on HSAs and their accompanying HDHPs. Finally, the chapter discusses the potential effect of other federal laws, including the securities laws on HSAs.

ERISA 8-1
HIPAA Privacy 8-18
Medicare Part D 8-19
State Benefit Mandates 8-20
State Tax Consequences 8-22
Davis-Bacon Act 8-24
USA Patriot Act 8-25
Securities Law 8-26
Use of Electronic Media 8-27
Creditor Protection 8-27

ERISA

Q 8:1   What guidance did the DOL issue regarding HSAs and ERISA?

In April 2004 and October 2006, the DOL issued guidance that should allow most HSAs to be outside the scope of ERISA, as long as specific requirements are satisfied. The guidance was issued in the form of two Field Assistance Bulletins (FAB 2004-01 and FAB 2006-02) which provide that, although an HDHP sponsored by an employer will be considered an ERISA plan, the HSA itself will generally not be considered an ERISA plan as long as certain conditions are satisfied even if the employer makes contributions to the HSA and selects only one HSA provider to which it forwards employer and employee contributions. See appendix E.

Q 8:2   What conditions must be satisfied in order for an HSA to be exempt from ERISA?

There are six conditions that the employer must satisfy in order for an HSA to be exempt from ERISA. In order to be exempt, the employer may *not* do any of the following:

- Require employees to establish an HSA (i.e., an employee's establishment of an HSA must be completely voluntary);
- Limit the ability of participants to roll funds over to another HSA, if such rollovers are allowed by the Code;
- Impose conditions on the use of HSA funds (e.g., state that HSA distributions may be used only for medical expenses);
- Make or influence the employee's investment decisions with respect to funds contributed to an HSA;
- Represent that the HSA is an employee welfare benefit plan established and maintained by the employer; and
- Receive any payment or compensation in connection with an HSA.

Q 8:3   How does the guidance issued in FAB 2006-02 differ from earlier DOL guidance with respect to other arrangements?

On October 27, 2006, the DOL issued FAB 2006-02 addressing frequently asked questions that the DOL has received concerning the application of ERISA to HSAs since the release of FAB 2004-01 in April 2004. The guidance is helpful to employers because it identifies several ways in which an employer can assist employees with setting up an HSA without causing the HSA to become subject to ERISA. Particularly significant is that the DOL has clarified that the prohibition on employer "endorsement" that applies under other DOL safe harbor guidance relating to group or group-type insurance does not apply to an HSA as long as the employer satisfies the specific requirements of FAB 2004-01.

FAB 2006-02 clarifies that an employer can take the following actions and still satisfy the above requirements of FAB 2004-01, allowing employee HSAs to be outside the scope of ERISA:

- Open an account for employees and make contributions on behalf of employees. The DOL states that this would not violate the "voluntary" requirement of FAB 2004-01, as long as employees could decide whether or not to make salary reduction contributions, and could move funds to a different HSA provider.

- Select an HSA provider that also offers some or all of the investment options made available to employees in the employer-sponsored 401(k) plan. The DOL states that this would not violate the prohibition against making investment decisions as long as employees have a reasonable choice of investment options and employees are not limited in moving their funds to another HSA. However, the DOL states that the selection of a single HSA provider that offers a single investment option would not afford employees a reasonable choice of investment options. Given this guidance, it is not clear whether an HSA provider could require an HSA owner to accumulate a threshold HSA account balance before offering additional investment options and still satisfy the "reasonable choice of investment options" requirement.

  Note. The terms *HSA owner*, *account owner*, *account holder*, and *account beneficiary* are used interchangeably in IRS publications, notices, and announcements to refer to the person that established the HSA. To avoid confusion, the term *HSA owner* will be used to refer to that person.

- Pay HSA fees that the employees otherwise would have to pay. The DOL states that because employers are allowed to contribute to an HSA without causing it to be subject to ERISA, employers should be able to pay fees as well.

- Limit the HSA providers that an employer allows to market their HSA products in the workplace or select a single HSA provider to which it will forward contributions. The DOL also provided this information in FAB 2004-01. This guidance makes clear that such actions will not be considered prohibited "endorsement" by the employer.

- Allow employees to contribute to HSAs through the employer's cafeteria plan. The DOL states that the FICA and FUTA tax savings that an employer achieves by allowing employees to make HSA contributions through the employer's cafeteria plan should not be viewed as violating the prohibition in FAB 2004-01 that an employer not pay or receive compensation in connection with an HSA.

An HSA provider may offer an HSA product that it offers to the public to its own employees without the employee HSAs being considered ERISA plans (see Q 8:15).

Q 8:4   What are the safe harbor rules that apply to determine whether Title I coverage under ERISA applies to a group or group-type insurance program offered to employees by an employer?

Under the group insurance safe harbor rules, Title I of ERISA, relating to the protection of employee benefit rights, does not apply to a group or group-type insurance program offered by an insurer to employees or to members of an employee organization, under which:

1. No contributions are made by an employer or employee organization (but see Qs 8:1 and 8:3, describing that an employer may contribute to an HSA);

2. Participation in the program is completely voluntary for employees or members;

3. The sole functions of the employer or employee organization with respect to the program are, without endorsing the program, to permit the insurer to publicize the program to employees or members, to collect premiums through payroll deductions or dues check-offs, and to remit them to the insurer; and

4. The employer or employee organization receives no consideration in the form of cash or otherwise in connection with the program, other than reasonable compensation, excluding any profit, for administrative services actually rendered in connection with payroll deductions or dues check-offs.

[29 C.F.R. Reg. § 2510.3-1(j); see also 29 C.F.R. Reg. §§ 2509.99-1 and 2510.3-2 (d) for similar rules relating to payroll deduction IRAs; see DOL Adv. Opn. 94-26A (July 11, 1994); DOL Adv. Opn. 80-21A (April 17, 1980); DOL Adv. Opn. 75-06 (November 3, 1975); Nicholas v. Standard Ins. Co., 29 EBC 1570 (6th Cir. 2002); Adams v. Unum Life Ins. Co. of Am., 200 F. Supp. 2d 796 (N.D. Ohio 2002).]

Q 8:5   What weight would a court give to a FAB?

A FAB is guidance that the DOL issues to its enforcement staff to follow in conducting an audit. Although the guidance is not directly binding on employers like a statute or administrative regulation [see Chevron U.S.A., Inc. v. Natural Resources Defense Council, 467 U.S. 837 (1984)], a court would likely defer to the position taken by the DOL in a FAB since FABs are considered views of the agency responsible for interpreting and issuing guidance with respect to ERISA. [See In re WorldCom, Inc., 2005 WL 221263 (S.D.N.Y. Feb. 1, 2005) (Court relied heavily on a DOL FAB in ruling that Merrill Lynch had no liability as a directed trustee in connection with losses suffered by the WorldCom 401(k) plan resulting from its holdings in WorldCom stock.)]

Q 8:6   What types of employer actions would not be viewed by the DOL as "representing that an HSA is an employee welfare plan established and maintained by the employer?"

Under the new standard the DOL articulated in FAB 2006-02, an employer should be able to take the following actions with respect to the HSA without representing that the HSA is an employee welfare benefit plan established and maintained by the employer:

- Distribute materials prepared by the HSA vendor, including providing cover letters;

- Allow the HSA vendor directly to send HSA materials to employees;

- Use materials describing the HSA that contain both the employer's and HSA vendor's logos and names (co-branding);
- Put the HSA vendor's information on the employer's own Web site (However, a cautious approach would be for the employer to include a statement to the effect that HSA participation is voluntary, the employer's HSA involvement is limited, and that the HSA is not part of an employer-maintained ERISA-covered plan); and
- Make some positive statements about the HSA, such as explaining how the HSA works, how the HSA relates to the HDHP, the advantages and benefits of enrolling in an HSA, the prudence of savings for medical expenses, and a statement to the effect that it is advisable to enroll and contribute to the HSA if you enroll in the HDHP option offered under the Plan.

The employer should avoid taking the following actions with respect to the HSA in order to reduce the likelihood that it could be viewed as representing that the HSAs are an employee welfare benefit plan established and maintained by the employer:

- Make statements that are very promotional and biased in favor of HSAs; and
- State that either the HSA is an ERISA plan or part of the employer's ERISA plan.

Q 8:7 Is FAB 2004-01 more flexible than the group insurance safe harbor with respect to "endorsement?"

Yes. It appears that FAB 2004-01 is more flexible than the group insurance safe harbor with respect to "endorsement" and that the HSA safe harbor may be met if: (1) the establishment of the HSA is voluntary, and (2) the employer is "neutral" with regard to the HSA's establishment. FAB 2006-02 appears to define *neutrality* as only prohibiting employers from:

- Limiting the ability of participants to roll over funds to another HSA, if allowed by the Code;
- Imposing conditions on the use of HSA funds (e.g., stating that HSA distributions may only be used for medical expenses);
- Making or influencing the investment decisions with respect to funds contributed to an HSA;
- Representing that the HSAs are an employee welfare benefit plan established and maintained by the employer; and
- Receiving any payment or compensation in connection with an HSA.

As such, the FAB may permit other actions by employers that could have constituted "endorsement" under the group insurer regulation, as described in Q 8:4. [See DOL Adv. Opn. 94-26A (July 11, 1994); DOL Adv. Opn. 80-21A (Apr. 17, 1980); DOL Adv. Opn. 75-06 (Nov. 3, 1975); Nicholas v. Standard Ins. Co., 29 EBC 1570 (6th Cir. 2002); Adams v. Unum Life Ins. Co. of Am., 200 F. Supp. 2d 796 (N.D. Ohio 2002).]

The following examples illustrate the types of actions that the employer may take or should avoid, to increase the likelihood that the HSA will not be considered an ERISA plan if the employer is relying on the group insurance safe harbor with respect to the HSA.

Example 1. Employer A wishes to make HSAs available to employees who participate in the HDHP that Employer A sponsors. Employer A contacts potential HSA trustees and selects one HSA trustee to provide trust services to its employees. Employer A signs a contract with the HSA trustee that identifies the specific services that the HSA trustee will provide to Employer A's employees, including accepting pretax salary reduction contributions from Employer A's payroll system. Employer A also signs a trust agreement with the HSA trustee on behalf of all employees (employees do not execute their own individual trust agreements with the HSA trustee). Employer A distributes enrollment materials bearing only the Employer's logo to employees with instructions that employees may establish an HSA by completing and returning such materials to Employer A during the open enrollment period. Employer A distributes an HSA SPD bearing only Employer A's logo to each employee who enrolls in the HSA option. The SPD indicates that Employer A is the plan administrator of the HSA, and that all questions about the HSA should be directed to Employer A. Under this fact pattern, it would appear that the employer has represented that it is establishing and maintaining the HSA. Thus, the HSA would likely be subject to ERISA.

Example 2. Same facts as above, except that Employer B:

1. Does not sign a trust agreement with the HSA trustee. Rather, Employer B specifies in the contract with the HSA trustee that the trustee must execute separate trust agreements with each of Employer B's employees who decide to enroll in the HSA.

2. Distributes enrollment materials that clearly identify the HSA trustee and indicate that the employer is merely facilitating enrollment in the HSA but is not the sponsor of the HSA. The enrollment materials advise employees to direct questions about the operation of the HSA directly to the HSA trustee. A contact name and phone number of the HSA trustee is provided.

3. Distributes an SPD that briefly describes the HSA but also clearly identifies the HSA trustee, states that Employer B is not the plan administrator of the HSA, and states that the HSA is not intended to be subject to ERISA.

Under this fact pattern, it would not appear that Employer B has represented that it is establishing and maintaining the HSA. Thus, in the absence of other circumstances prohibited in the DOL FAB 2006-02, the HSA would likely not be subject to ERISA.

Q 8:8   If an employer offering an HSA to employees asks the HSA provider for specific investment options, will the HSA be subject to ERISA?

Probably. If an employer requests that specific investment options be offered in connection with an HSA, there is a risk that the DOL will consider the HSA to be subject to ERISA. Under FAB 2004-01, an employer is permitted to contribute to an HSA and select one HSA trustee to which it will forward salary reduction contributions without causing the HSA to be subject to ERISA (see Q 8:1). (See appendix E.) [FAB 2004-01 (Apr. 7, 2004)] However, for the HSA to be outside the scope of ERISA, the employer must, among other things, limit its involvement in the design of the HSA and refrain from making or influencing investment decisions with respect to funds contributed to an HSA (see Q 8:2). Thus, if the employer requests that the HSA trustee/custodian modify one of its standard offerings to accommodate the employer's unique preferences for its workforce, such as a particular investment option, such action could be viewed as violating both of these prohibitions, making the HSA subject to ERISA.

Q 8:9   May an employer select an HSA provider that also offers some or all of its investment options made available to employees in the employer-sponsored 401(k) plan?

Yes. An employer may select an HSA provider that also offers some or all of the investment options made available to employees in the employer-sponsored 401(k) plan. The DOL states that this would not violate the prohibition against making investment decisions as long as there are reasonable investment options available and employees are not limited in moving their funds to another HSA. However, the DOL states that the selection of a single HSA provider that offers a single investment option would not afford employees a reasonable choice of investment options (see Q 8:10). Given this guidance, it is not clear whether an HSA provider could require an HSA owner to accumulate a threshold HSA account balance before offering additional investment options and still satisfy the "reasonable choice of investment options" requirement. [FAB 2006-02 (Oct. 27, 2006)]

Q 8:10   Can an employer select a single HSA trustee that offers a limited range of investment options to provide HSA services to its employees without violating the FAB prohibition against making or selecting investment options?

Yes. The FAB 2006-02 expressly provides that an employer is permitted to select a single HSA provider to which it will forward employer and employee contributions. By choosing one HSA provider over another, an employer is, to a certain extent, limiting an employee's HSA investment options. However, as long as the employer does not request that the HSA provider change its standard offerings the mere act of selecting a single HSA trustee, even one with limited investment options, should not be viewed by the DOL as a violation of the prohibition against making or selecting investment options.

Practice Pointer. No matter which HSA provider the employer selects, the employee may establish a second HSA with any trustee or custodian and transfer or roll over amounts from the employer HSA into the second HSA (see Qs 5:1, 5:29).

Q 8:11   May an employer encourage participation in the HSA program?

To a certain extent an employer may encourage participation by employees by providing general information on the HSA program and other educational materials that explain the prudence of savings for medical expenses, including the advantages of contributing to an HSA, without thereby converting the program to an ERISA-covered plan.

Q 8:12   May an employer that makes an HSA program available to employees pay the fees imposed by the HSA provider without causing the HSA to be subject to ERISA, or without generating adverse tax consequences for employees?

Yes. FAB 2006-02 specifically states that the employer should be permitted to pay any fee that the HSA provider imposes on HSA owners for services the provider performs in connection with establishing and maintaining the contribution deduction process itself without causing the HSA to be subject to ERISA. The FAB provides that an employer is permitted to make contributions to an HSA without causing the HSA to be subject to ERISA, and therefore, administrative fees also should not cause the HSA to be subject to ERISA. Similarly, the employer should also be permitted to assume the internal costs (e.g., for overhead, bookkeeping, and so on) of implementing and maintaining the contribution deduction program without causing the HSA to be subject to ERISA. [See 29 C.F.R. § 2509.99-1(e), relating to payroll deduction IRAs.]

In addition, these fees should be excludable from the employees' gross income and not counted as wages for FICA and FUTA purposes. Although there is no authority directly on point, this is generally how administrative fees are treated with respect to individual retirement arrangements (IRAs) and employer-sponsored group health arrangements, and the tax treatment of HSA administrative fees should be analogous. In the IRA context, the IRS has ruled that expenses charged by an insurance company under an annuity contract, including a flat annual charge per participant account, could be paid directly to the employer and still be excludable from the employees' income and wages for FICA and FUTA purposes. [See, e.g., Priv. Ltr. Ruls. 7948017, 7951122.] Similarly, for health plans subject to Code Section 106(a), it generally is accepted that the employer's payment of administrative fees associated with such coverage should be excludable from the employee's income (even though not technically a "health benefit"). For example, fees that an employer pays to a health insurer that are part of the insurance premium are not required to be segregated from the premium and imputed as taxable income.

Q 8:13 **If an employer makes arrangements with an HSA trustee to offer an HSA with a debit card to employees, can the employer specify that the debit card be used only for medical expenses without violating the FAB prohibition against imposing conditions on the use of HSA funds?**

A debit, credit, or stored value card may be used with an HSA to receive distributions for qualified medical expenses (see Q 6:6). However, it is not clear what impact, if any, the use of a debit card will have on the ERISA status of an HSA. For example, if an employer makes arrangements with an HSA trustee to offer an HSA with a debit card to employees, but the employer chooses a restricted debit card that can only be used for medical expenses, it is possible that the DOL could take the position that the employer has impermissibly restricted the use of the HSA by limiting the debit card to use for medical expenses.

Although the DOL has not issued any direct guidance on this point, as long as an HSA owner has the ability to make withdrawals from the HSA in some reasonable manner (e.g., a checkbook or withdrawal request form), it would appear that a debit card accompanying the HSA could be limited to use for medical expenses without violating the prohibition in the FABs against imposing conditions on the use of HSA funds. Also, this should not violate the IRS prohibition that the use of the HSA not be limited to medical expenses. [See I.R.S. Notice 2004-50, Q&A 79, 2004-33 I.R.B. 196.] It should be noted, however, that the answer may differ if the employer customizes the debit card to suit its particular needs. For example, if an employer requested that the HSA trustee offer a debit card that only could be used in a certain store or to purchase a particular product, the employer may be found to have imposed conditions on the use of HSA funds, resulting in impermissible employer involvement and ERISA status. To the extent possible, to avoid ERISA status, the employer should seek an "off the shelf" HSA with debit card to offer to employees.

Note. Regulation E, a federal banking regulation issued by the Board of Governors of the Federal Reserve System, which is designed to limit the liability of consumers engaged in electronics fund transfers, does not apply to an HSA. The Federal Reserve System has stated that "cards used solely for health related expenses—such as cards linked to flexible spending accounts, health savings accounts, or health reimbursement arrangements—are not governed by the regulation, whether funded by the employer or employee." [12 C.F.R. Part 205, 71 Fed. Reg. 51,437 (Aug. 30, 2006). Copy available at http://edocket.access.gpo.gov/2006/pdf/06-7223.pdf.] When a credit card is used, as opposed to a debit card, other issues may arise, such as Truth-in-Lending Act (Regulation Z) requirements. [See 12 C.F.R. § 226.]

Q 8:14   May an HSA owner direct the payment of HSA funds to a credit line vendor to reimburse the vendor for HSA expenses paid with a credit card?

Yes. An HSA owner may direct the payment of HSA funds to a credit line vendor to reimburse the vendor for HSA expenses paid with a credit card, but certain other transactions involving a line of credit associated with an HSA could raise prohibited transaction issues.

Q 8:15   If an employer is in the business of providing HSAs, can it offer HSAs to its employees on the same terms as offered to the public without causing the HSA to be subject to ERISA?

The DOL specifically stated in FAB 2006-02 that offering HSA products that the employer offers to the public in the regular course of business would not mean that an HSA provider has established or is maintaining the HSA as an employer. This position is consistent with the DOL guidance for IRA providers. In the IRA guidance, the DOL indicated that a financial institution may select itself to be the exclusive provider for payroll deduction IRAs offered to its own employees without creating an ERISA-covered IRA. [29 C.F.R. § 2509.99-1(g)]

   Practice Pointer. Because an employer is permitted to make contributions to the HSAs of employees, it would seem that an employer who is in the business of providing HSAs could waive administrative fees normally charged to the public for its own employees without causing the HSA to be subject to ERISA. However, the DOL has not issued guidance on this issue.

An HSA provider may offer an HSA product that it offers to the public to its own employees without the employee HSA being considered an ERISA-covered plan. The DOL states that offering HSA products that the employer offers to the public in the regular course of business would not mean that an HSA provider has established or is maintaining the HSA as an employer. [FAB 2006-02 (Oct. 27, 2006)]

Q 8:16   Can an employer offer the HDHP and HSA as a single option without making the HSA subject to ERISA?

Probably. As long as an employee is not required to make salary reduction contributions to the HSA, this arrangement should not be viewed by the DOL as violating the rule that HSA participation must be voluntary. If the other requirements of FAB 2004-01 are satisfied, the HDHP/HSA options should not be viewed as subject to ERISA (see appendix E). [FAB 2004-01 (Apr. 7, 2004)]

Q 8:17   Can an employer limit an employee's HSA contributions without causing the HSA to be subject to ERISA?

Probably not. If the employer imposes restrictions on the amount that an employee is permitted to contribute to the HSA linked to the employer's HDHP, such contribution cap could be viewed as impermissible employer involvement under FAB 2004-01, causing the HSA to be subject to ERISA. The statute itself [I.R.C. § 223] already contains contribution limits, and the DOL could easily take the position that an employer that restricts an employee from fully funding a particular HSA up to this limit has imposed restrictions that cause the HSA to be an ERISA plan.

Q 8:18   What are the consequences if an HSA is not subject to ERISA?

If the HSA is not subject to ERISA, there is no obligation to file a Form 5500 [ERISA § 103], provide a summary plan description (SPD) [ERISA § 102], adopt a claims procedure [ERISA § 503], offer COBRA coverage [ERISA Title I, Part 6], or comply with portability or nondiscrimination rules under the Health Insurance Portability and Accountability Act (HIPAA) [ERISA Title I, Part 7] with respect to the HSA. In addition, the fiduciary responsibility requirements of Part 4 of Title I of ERISA will not apply. Similarly, ERISA Section 502 and the legal actions available under Part 5 of Title I ERISA will not apply. If an employer or insurer is sued in connection with an HSA, state law, rather than ERISA, will control, since ERISA preemption [ERISA § 514] would not apply. Note that the prohibited transaction rules in Code Section 4975 will continue to apply (see Q 6:62).

Q 8:19   What are the employer's legal obligations and consequences if the HSA is subject to ERISA?

Although there is no DOL guidance on this point, if the HSA is subject to ERISA, presumably the employer is required to treat the HSA as it would any other group health plan that is subject to ERISA. This would include complying with applicable Form 5500 filing requirements, maintaining a plan document, and providing an SPD to participants. In addition, as described below (see Qs 8:20–8:22), the employer will have to determine how, if at all, to comply with the federal mandates that apply to group health plans, including COBRA rules, HIPAA portability/nondiscrimination rules, and claims procedure requirements for group health plans, notwithstanding that, from a practical standpoint, these rules may not make sense in the HSA context. Finally, the ERISA fiduciary rules will apply (see Q 8:24), and, if an employer or insurer is sued in connection with an HSA, ERISA, rather than state law, will generally control because of ERISA preemption.

Q 8:20   If an HSA is subject to ERISA, would an employer be required to distribute a COBRA General Notice?

Probably not. IRS Notice 2004-2, Q&A 35 [2004-2 I.R.B. 269] provides that HSAs are not subject to COBRA continuation coverage under Code Section 4980B. However, the IRS left open the question of whether HSAs are subject to COBRA continuation coverage under ERISA Part 6. The DOL has not addressed this issue, and it is possible that if the DOL considers an HSA sponsored by an employer to be a *group health plan* under ERISA Part 6, an employer would have to satisfy all applicable COBRA notice and disclosure requirements, including providing a COBRA General Notice within 90 days of enrollment in the HSA.

However, the IRS and the DOL jointly administer COBRA, with the IRS responsible for interpreting the substantive rules and the DOL responsible for interpreting the notice and disclosure rules. [Treas. Reg. §§ 54.4980B-1–54.4980B-10; 29 C.F.R. §§ 2590.606-1–2590.606-4] It is, therefore, unlikely that the DOL would unilaterally enforce a COBRA obligation where the IRS has stated in guidance that COBRA does not apply for purposes of the Code. Further, because the HSA account must be nonforfeitable to satisfy requirements under Code Section 223 (see Qs 2:1, 6:2), an HSA owner should never lose HSA coverage. Thus, there would generally not be a qualifying event with respect to an HSA for purposes of COBRA. [ERISA § 603]

Q 8:21 If an HSA is subject to ERISA, is an employer required to distribute a HIPAA certificate of creditable coverage and comply with the HIPAA nondiscrimination rules?

Possibly. The DOL has not addressed this issue, but if the DOL considers an HSA sponsored by an employer to be a *group health plan* for purposes of ERISA Part 7, an employer would technically be required to comply with the HIPAA portability and nondiscrimination rules, including providing a HIPAA certificate of creditable coverage upon request and not discriminating between HSA participants on the basis of a health factor (but see note below regarding preexisting conditions and special enrollment). ERISA Section 733(a) provides that the term *group health plan* means an employee welfare benefit plan that provides medical care to employees or their dependents (as defined under the terms of the plan) directly or through insurance, reimbursement, or otherwise. The term *medical care* for this purpose means amounts paid for:

1. The diagnosis, cure, mitigation, treatment, or prevention of disease, or amounts paid for the purpose of affecting any structure or function of the body;
2. Amounts paid for transportation primarily for and essential to medical care referred to in item 1;
3. Amounts paid for insurance covering medical care referred to in items 1 and 2.

Because an HSA is primarily designed to provide funds for medical care, the HIPAA portability and nondiscrimination rules will technically apply to an HSA, requiring an employer with two or more active employees [ERISA § 732(a)] enrolled in an HSA to comply with the HIPAA portability and nondiscrimination requirements of Part 7 of Title I of ERISA. These rules would, among other things, require an employer to issue a certificate of creditable coverage with respect to the HSA upon request of the HSA owner in order to comply with ERISA Section 701(e)(1)(A) and 29 C.F.R. Section 2590.701-5(a)(2)(iii). Although a certificate of coverage is also required upon loss of coverage, an HSA owner generally will not lose HSA coverage (as noted in Q 8:20). In addition, the HIPAA nondiscrimination rules (described in ERISA Section 702 and 29 C.F.R. Section 2590.702) prohibit an employer that sponsors a group health plan from discriminating on the basis of any health factor. These rules could be relevant in the HSA context if, for example, the employer wished to contribute an additional amount to the HSAs of employees who were willing to participate in a wellness program, for which the DOL sets forth specific requirements. [ERISA § 702(b)(2)(B); 29 C.F.R. § 2590.702(c)(3)]

> **Note.** The final HIPAA portability regulations note in the preamble that, as a practical matter, the rules pertaining to preexisting conditions and special enrollment will generally not apply to HSAs. [69 Fed. Reg. 78,720, 78,734 (Dec. 30, 2004); 29 C.F.R. Part 2590; 26 C.F.R. Parts 54 and 602; 45 C.F.R. Parts 144 and 146]

Q 8:22   If an HSA is subject to ERISA, is an employer required to comply with the DOL claims procedure rules that apply to group health plans?

Possibly. The DOL has not addressed this issue, but if the DOL should consider an HSA sponsored by an employer to be a welfare plan for purposes of ERISA generally, an employer would be required to implement a claims procedure that satisfies certain requirements. [ERISA § 503; 29 C.F.R. § 2560.503-1] Presumably, that claims procedure would have to comply with the requirements applicable to group health plans. An employee welfare benefit plan is defined in ERISA Section 3(1) as any plan, fund, or program established or maintained by an employer or by an employee organization, or by both, for the purpose of providing benefits for its participants or their beneficiaries that include medical, surgical, or hospital care or benefits, or benefits in the event of sickness. Because an HSA is primarily designed to provide funds for medical care, in the absence of further DOL guidance, it appears that the claims procedure rules would apply. These rules would, for example, require an employer to provide a notice of adverse determination and appeal rights within a certain time frame when an employee requests a withdrawal from an HSA that contains insufficient funds.

However, the claims procedures, if required by the DOL, will have limited applicability. IRS Notice 2004-2, Q&A 29 and 30 [2004-2 I.R.B. 269] provides that an HSA owner is not required to submit receipts for medical expenses to trustees, custodians, or employers. Rather, a self-substantiation rule is in place (i.e., an HSA owner is responsible for determining on his or her own whether an item is a medical expense). Thus, there will be few circumstances in which the employee makes a "claim" with the employer for HSA funds. However, as noted above, if an employee attempts to withdraw amounts from an HSA with insufficient funds, the employer would presumably be required to provide a notice of adverse determination and appeal rights. In addition, for urgent care claims and pre-service claims, the DOL claims procedures require that claimants be apprised of the plan's benefit determination, whether the determination is adverse or a complete grant, in accordance with the time frames generally applicable to urgent care and pre-service claims. [See 29 C.F.R. § 2560.503-1 (f)(2)(i) and (iii)] Such notices must contain sufficient information to fully apprise the claimant of the plan's decision to approve the requested benefits. Accordingly, it appears that there may be situations in which an employer is technically required to provide a notice of approval when an employee withdraws an amount from his or her HSA. However, this rule will be difficult to administer in practice, given the fact that the employer may not know the reason that an employee requests an HSA distribution.

Q 8:23   If an HSA is subject to ERISA, could its funds be held in a custodial account rather than a trust?

Probably not. Although there is an IRA exception to the ERISA Section 403 trust requirement in ERISA Section 403(b)(3)(B) that permits plan assets for ERISA-covered IRAs to be held in custodial accounts, this rule does not, on its face, extend to HSAs.

Practice Pointer. If an HSA is subject to ERISA, but an entity that would normally act as trustee (e.g., a bank) wishes to limit liability, the employer could be the trustee and the bank could continue in a custodial role. Alternatively, the bank could be a directed trustee, which would limit its liability more than if it were a regular trustee (but the liability would be greater than if the bank were a custodian).

Q 8:24   If an HSA is subject to ERISA, what fiduciary standards would apply to the HSA trustee or custodian?

If an HSA is subject to ERISA, the following fiduciary standards, set forth in ERISA Title I, Part 4, would have to be satisfied:

1. *Written plan document.* The HSA written plan document would have to describe the funding policy, procedure for allocation of responsibilities under plan, procedure for amending the plan, and basis on which payments are made to and from the plan. A fiduciary must follow the written plan document. [ERISA §§ 402, 404(a)(1)(D)]

2. *Trust/custodial account.* HSA plan assets would be required to be held in a trust or custodial account (but see Q 8:23). [ERISA § 403] This is also a requirement for purposes of Code Section 223 (Q 7:1).

3. *Prudent man standard.* The "prudent man" standard of care requires a fiduciary to discharge its duties with the care, skill, prudence, and diligence under the circumstances then prevailing that a prudent man

acting in a like capacity and familiar with such matters would use in the conduct of an enterprise of like character and with like aims. [ERISA § 404(a)(1)(B)] The fiduciary of an HSA would have to comply with this standard. Although ERISA Section 404(c) is available to protect fiduciaries who oversee participant-directed pension plans, this section would not apply to HSAs. Thus, the fiduciary could be exposed to liability for loss on participant-directed investments in an HSA.

4. *Diversification.* The duty to diversify plan investments would require an HSA fiduciary to diversify the investments of the HSA so as to minimize the risk of large losses, unless under the circumstances it is clearly prudent not to do so. [ERISA § 404(a)(1)(C)]

5. *Exclusive benefit rule.* The exclusive benefit rule requires that plan money must be spent only on benefits or expenses of plan administration. [ERISA § 404(a)(1)(A)] The exclusive benefit rule would prohibit a fiduciary from using HSA assets for any purpose other than to benefit the HSA owner or to pay HSA plan expenses.

Q 8:25 Does an entity incur additional risk and responsibilities as an HSA trustee as compared to an HSA custodian?

Yes. A trustee has fiduciary responsibilities and potential liabilities that a custodian does not have. A custodian simply holds the assets on behalf of the owner of the assets. Other than holding the assets and doing as the owner orders, the custodian has no fiduciary obligations to the owner. A trustee may also have custody of the assets, but, in addition, a trustee is also a fiduciary under ERISA (and common law as well). This means that a trustee's duties to take care of the assets may extend beyond what the trustee has agreed to do under contract. The trustee's duties include following the terms of the written plan document, adhering to a "prudent man" standard of care in discharging fiduciary duties, diversifying plan investments to minimize the risk of large losses if prudent to do so, and limiting the use of plan assets for any purpose other than to benefit the beneficiary or to pay plan expenses. In addition, the trustee could be found to have a duty to disclose certain relevant information to beneficiaries under principles of common law. This duty would generally not apply to the custodian. The trustee is subject to liability for failure to satisfy any of these duties.

Q 8:26 Is it possible to designate one entity as the trustee of an HSA and another entity as the custodian of an HSA?

Yes. The custodian and trustee do not have to be the same entity. So, for example, if an HSA is subject to ERISA (e.g., because of a high level of employer involvement), it would be possible to designate the bank as custodian of the HSA and some other party, such as the employer, as trustee of the HSA. Alternatively, a trustee can contract to be a "directed trustee." In this regard, ERISA Section 403(a) specifically recognizes that, where a plan expressly provides that the trustee is subject to the direction of a named fiduciary who is not a trustee (e.g., an HSA owner), such trustee will have limited authority or discretion. This limited authority or discretion, in turn, limits a trustee's fiduciary liabilities (although a directed trustee would still have more fiduciary liability than a custodian). [FAB 2004-03 (Dec. 17, 2004)]

Q 8:27   What are the potential consequences when a fiduciary violates ERISA?

The potential consequences of a fiduciary violation of ERISA are as follows:

1. The fiduciary is personally liable to make good any losses suffered by the plan on account of the fiduciary's violation and to restore to the plan any profits that the fiduciary made by use of plan assets in violation of its fiduciary duties. [ERISA §§ 409, 502(a)(2)]

2. Plan participants and beneficiaries, and other fiduciaries can sue and, in the discretion of the court, can be awarded reasonable attorneys' fees and court costs in addition to the cost of making up losses and restoring any improper profits. [ERISA § 502(g)(1)]

3. In any action or settlement involving the DOL, the DOL must assess a penalty of 20 percent of the "applicable recovery amount" in a case of a breach of fiduciary duty or co-fiduciary liability. The DOL may waive or reduce the penalty only if it concludes that (1) the fiduciary acted reasonably and in good faith, or (2) the fiduciary could not be expected to make the plan whole without severe hardship unless a waiver is granted. [ERISA § 502(l)]

4. A court can order the fiduciary removed from its position as a fiduciary, can enjoin further breaches by the fiduciary or other party in interest, and can order other equitable relief. [ERISA §§ 409, 502(a) (3), 502(a)(5)]

5. In the case of a criminal, willful violation of the reporting and disclosure rules of ERISA Title I, Part 1, an individual may be subject to fines of up to $100,000 and imprisonment for up to 10 years, and a corporation may be subject to fines of up to $500,000. [ERISA § 501]

6. In the case of a prohibited transaction by a party in interest (which is generally the same as a "disqualified person" (see Q 6:69)), the IRS may assess a penalty of 15 percent of the "amount involved" (defined under Code Section 4975(f)(4) and accompanying regulations) in each transaction for each year or part thereof during which the prohibited transaction continues. If the transaction is not corrected within the taxable period, such penalty may be in an amount not more than 100 percent of the amount involved. [I.R.C. § 4975]

Q 8:28   If an HSA is not subject to ERISA, what fiduciary standards would apply to the HSA trustee or custodian?

If an HSA is not subject to ERISA, state law fiduciary trust requirements (which may be similar to the ERISA requirements described in Q 8:24), will apply. The following is an illustration of such requirements under Minnesota and Connecticut law:

Trust document. A trustee is required to administer the trust in accordance with the terms of its underlying trust documents. This is particularly relevant with regard to investment strategy and the allocation of receipts to and disbursements from the trust. To the extent the trust documents are silent, state law may impose different duties on the trustee. [See, e.g., Minn. Trust Companies § 48A.07 (where no written instruction, bank or trust company must use best judgment in selection of authorized securities and is responsible for the validity, regularity, quality and value of them at the time made, and for their safekeeping); Conn. Principal and Income Act § 45a–542b; § 45a–542c (if unable to comply with written terms of trust, a trustee shall consider all factors relevant to the trust and its beneficiaries, including the needs for liquidity, regularity of income and preservation and appreciation of capital)]

Best judgment/prudent investor rules. A trustee must invest the trust assets with reasonable care and must diversify the trust assets unless contrary to the purposes of the trust. [Minn. Trust Companies § 48A.07; Conn. Uniform Prudent Investor Act § 45a–541b]

Loyalty. A trustee must administer the trust solely in the interest of the trust's beneficiaries. [Minn. Uniform Custodial Trust Act § 529.06; Conn. Uniform Prudent Investor Act § 45-541e]

Records. The trustee must maintain adequate records supporting all transactions with the trust and the records must be made reasonably available to the trust beneficiaries. The trustee must also separately account for each beneficiary under the trust. [Minn. Uniform Custodial Trust Act §§ 529.05, 529.06]

Q 8:29   Has the DOL issued any guidance regarding incentive payments made into an HSA other than FAB 2004-01 relating to HSAs?

Yes. The DOL issued Advisory Opinion 2004-09A [Dec. 22, 2004], which held that an incentive payment deposited by an HSA trustee to an account holder's HSA would not violate the prohibited transaction rules of Code Section 4975 or ERISA Section 406. (See Q 6:63 for further discussion; see appendix E.) FAB 2006-02 also clarifies that an HSA provider may offer cash incentives that are put directly into accounts without violating the prohibited transaction rules.

Q 8:30   Do the prohibited transaction rules under Code Section 4975 apply if an HSA is not subject to ERISA?

Yes. The prohibited transaction rules are located in both the Internal Revenue Code [I.R.C. § 4975] and ERISA [ERISA § 406]. Even if an HSA is not subject to ERISA, the prohibited transaction rules of Code Section 4975 will apply. [I.R.C. § 4975(e)(1)(E)]

Note. Certain ERISA prohibited transaction class exemptions that apply to IRA owners do not apply to HSA owners.

HIPAA Privacy

Q 8:31   Is an HSA subject to the HIPAA privacy regulations?

Possibly. The Centers for Medicare and Medicaid Services (CMS) has not yet issued any guidance concerning whether an HSA is subject to the HIPAA privacy regulations. However, the regulations apply to health plans, which are broadly defined to include "any other individual or group plan or combination of individual, or group plans, that provides or pays for the cost of medical care." [45 C.F.R. § 160.103] It would seem that this definition would be broad enough to encompass an HSA arrangement, whether provided by the employer or individually, since it is an arrangement primarily intended to pay for medical care. Whether an HSA is subject to ERISA is not relevant to this determination. As a practical matter, health information may not actually be used or disclosed, since HSA owners are not required to submit receipts for medical care in order to obtain reimbursement. Accordingly, there may be little need for safeguards. Nevertheless, the privacy notice and business associate requirements may technically apply.

> **Practice Pointer.** The fact that someone is a participant in a plan can be considered protected health information. Accordingly, the HSA (e.g., trustee/administrator) must not disclose a list of participants for purposes other than administering the plan (e.g., it is not permitted to sell or provide a list of participants for marketing purposes). The trustee or administrator should consider providing a privacy notice when an employee enrolls in the HSA, including language explaining that HSA funds used for medical expenses are self-substantiated, and so, generally, the HSA has no access to health information. However, to the extent it does, the notice would apply. If the employer is involved in assisting employees with establishing an HSA with a particular trustee or custodian, the employer should enter into a business associate contract with the administrator or trustee or custodian.

Q 8:32   Would the HIPAA Electronic Standards Regulations apply to HSAs?

They may, depending on how payments from the HSA are structured. The HIPAA Electronic Standards Regulations require that a *covered entity* that conducts certain transactions electronically with another covered entity must conduct those transactions under the standards set by the Secretary of the Department of Health and Human Services (HHS). [45 C.F.R. § 162.923(a)] In addition, if any party requests that a health plan conduct one of the listed transactions as a standard transaction, the health plan must do so. [45 C.F.R. § 162.925(a)]

A *covered entity* is defined as a health plan, provider, or clearinghouse. For example, if a provider submits a claim to a health plan electronically, the claim must be submitted and received using the standard transactions. When the health plan sends a payment to the provider electronically, this transmission also must be conducted in accordance with the standard transactions. The regulations do not apply to a transmission involving a noncovered entity, including an individual. So, if an individual submits a claim to a plan and the plan sends payment to the individual, these transmissions would fall outside the regulations because they would not be between two covered entities.

If the HSA is considered a *health plan* for HIPAA purposes (see Q 8:31), the HIPAA Electronic Standard Regulations may apply. Note that CMS has not issued guidance on this question. However, if this is the case and if the party submitting the request for payment and receiving the payment is the individual, the transmission would not involve two covered entities and would fall outside the regulations. CMS addressed a similar fact pattern as in Q 8:13, discussing the use of a debit card under an FSA or HRA, and stated that this transmission would be between an individual and a plan, and so would fall outside of the regulations. [See https://questions.cms.hhs.gov Answer ID 2352 (search on "FSA")]

However, if the HSA is considered a *health plan* for HIPAA purposes and the HSA is structured so that a provider can directly submit claims to and receive payment from the HSA, and these transmissions are conducted electronically, CMS may consider these transmissions to be covered under the Electronic Standards Regulations. Note that the regulations also state that any party may request a health plan to conduct a transaction as a standard transaction. So, if an individual or other party did request an HSA to receive claims or make payments using the standard transactions, the HSA would have to do so. However, this seems very unlikely.

Medicare Part D

Q 8:33   Is an HSA a plan for which an employer must issue a certificate of creditable coverage for purposes of Medicare Part D?

No. CMS issued final regulations [42 C.F.R. § 423] implementing the new Voluntary Medicare Part D prescription drug benefit that took effect in January 2006 pursuant to the Medicare Prescription Drug, Improvement, and Modernization Act of 2003. Under the CMS final regulations [42 C.F.R. § 423.56], all group health plan sponsors that offer prescription drug coverage are required to provide a notice to all Medicare-eligible participants that states whether prescription drug coverage under its plan is "creditable" when compared to the prescription drug coverage under Medicare Part D. CMS believes that this information will help participants decide whether to enroll in Part D. In addition, a participant who has a certificate of creditable coverage has the ability to stay in the employer-sponsored health plan and enroll in Medicare Part D at a later date without incurring a late enrollment penalty. Coverage is considered "creditable" if its actuarial value equals or exceeds the value of Medicare Part D coverage. With respect to HSAs, however, CMS subsequently issued guidance on account-based plans which indicates that HSAs are not retiree plans for purposes of the creditable coverage rules due to the fact that no contributions can be made to HSAs once the retiree becomes entitled to Medicare. The guidance is available at: http://www.cms.hhs.gov/EmployerRetireeDrug Subsid/downloads/AccountbasedPlansGuidanceRev1.pdf.

> **Practice Pointer.** Even though an employer is not required to provide a notice of creditable coverage with respect to the HSA, such notice will still be required for Medicare-eligible individuals participating in the HDHP.

Q 8:34   Is an HSA a plan for which an employer may apply for the employer subsidy under Medicare Part D?

No. Beginning in 2006, employer and union sponsors of qualified retiree prescription drug plans have the ability to receive tax-free retiree drug subsidy payments for a portion of their plan's prescription drug costs. For each qualifying covered retiree, the sponsor is eligible to receive payments of 28 percent of the allowable drug costs attributable to gross prescription drug costs between the cost threshold ($295 in 2009) and the cost limit ($6,000 in 2009). [Social Security Act § 1860D-22, 42 C.F.R. Part 423] With respect to HSAs, however, CMS issued guidance on account-based plans which indicates that HSAs are not retiree plans for purposes of the employer subsidy because no contributions can be made to HSAs once the retiree becomes entitled to Medicare. Accordingly, employers and unions cannot receive retiree drug subsidy payments with respect to HSAs. The guidance is available at: http://www.cms.hhs.gov/EmployerRetireeDrug Subsid/downloads/AccountbasedPlansGuidanceRev1.pdf.

> **Note.** The cost threshold is adjusted in the same manner as the annual Medicare Part D deductible and the annual Medicare Part D out-of-pocket threshold and is adjusted annually as defined in 42 C.F.R. § 423.104(d)(1)(ii) and (d)(5)(iii)(B), respectively.

> **Note.** The cost limit is adjusted in the same manner as the annual Medicare Part D deductible and the annual Medicare Part D out-of-pocket limit and is adjusted annually as defined in 42 C.F.R. § 423.104(d)(1)(ii) and (d)(5)(iii)(B), respectively.

State Benefit Mandates

Q 8:35   What state laws could affect the HDHP that accompanies the HSA?

A state could have laws that regulate insured HDHPs. These laws may, for example, require certain benefits to be covered under an HDHP without regard to whether the deductible is satisfied. Unless a state's mandated benefits satisfy the definition of preventive care for federal purposes, this would cause the HDHP to fail to satisfy the federal requirements under Code Section 223. Thus, an individual in a state with those laws could not contribute to an HSA. Other state laws may require an insurer or HMO to comply with limits on deductibles, which could also conflict with federal requirements.

Q 8:36   What transition relief has the IRS issued with respect to HDHPs that are subject to state mandates?

The IRS addressed the fact that, in certain states, it is not possible to issue an HDHP that satisfies both state and federal requirements by issuing transition relief for months prior to January 1, 2006, with respect to state requirements in effect on January 1, 2004 (see Q 3:21). [I.R.S. Notice 2004-43, 2004-27 I.R.B. 10] This guidance states that, during this time, an HDHP will not be considered to violate federal requirements if the sole reason it does not comply with federal requirements is that it is complying with state benefit mandates. However, after January 1, 2006, individuals who are covered by calendar-year insured HDHPs or HMOs subject to state laws that conflict with Code Section 223 requirements will not be considered *eligible individuals* who are permitted to contribute to HSAs.

In Notice 2005-83 [I.R.S. Notice 2005-83, 2005-49 I.R.B. 1075], the IRS extended the expiration date of the transition guidance provided in Notice 2004-43 for non-calendar-year HDHPs to the earlier of (1) the health plan's next renewal date, or (2) December 31, 2006 (see Q 3:22). The reason for this extension is that, generally, a health plan may not reduce existing benefits before the plan's renewal date. Thus, even though a state may amend its laws before January 1, 2006, to authorize HDHPs that comply with Code Section 223(c)(2), non-calendar-year plans may still fail to qualify as HDHPs after January 1, 2006, because existing benefits cannot be changed until the next renewal date. Accordingly, the IRS concluded in Notice 2005-83 that additional transitional relief is appropriate for non-calendar-year health plans. Under this additional transition relief, for any coverage period of 12 months or less beginning before January 1, 2006, a health plan that otherwise qualifies as an HDHP as defined in Code Section 223(c)(2), except that it complied on its most recent renewal date before January 1, 2006, with state-mandated requirements (in effect on January 1, 2004) to provide certain benefits without regard to a deductible or with a deductible below the minimum annual deductible specified in Code Section 223(c)(2), will be treated as an HDHP.

Example. A state amends its laws to authorize HDHPs, effective November 1, 2005. A health plan with a renewal date of July 1, 2005, is required to retain the state-mandated low-deductible coverage for the plan year July 1, 2005, through June 30, 2006, because under state law, the benefits can only be modified on the renewal date. Under the transition relief provided in Notice 2005-83 [2005-49 I.R.B. 1075], the health plan may be treated as an HDHP until the renewal date of the policy, when it can be amended to comply with federal requirements (i.e., for the months of January through June 2006).

Q 8:37   Can an employer make the same HDHP/HSA available to its employees in Hawaii as is available in other states?

Generally, no. The state of Hawaii has a unique exception from the preemption provision of ERISA that allows it to regulate directly the terms of ERISA health plans, including self-funded plans. [ERISA § 514(b)(5)] Hawaii's Prepaid Health Care Act (PHCA) requires employers to provide health benefits to

Hawaii-based employees who are employed at least 20 hours per week for four consecutive weeks. [Haw. Rev. Stat. §§ 393-3(8), 393-4, 393-11] In addition, the PHCA also sets forth various requirements concerning plan benefits and cost-sharing. [Haw. Rev. Stat. § 393] Accordingly, an HDHP offered by an employer in Hawaii, whether self-insured or insured, must satisfy the requirements of the PHCA.

An employer in Hawaii essentially has three options in deciding how to satisfy the PHCA's benefit requirements:

1. The employer may buy health insurance coverage that has been preapproved by Hawaii Department of Labor and Industrial Relations (DLIR);

2. The employer may seek DLIR approval for a health insurance policy not yet approved by DLIR; or

3. The employer may seek DLIR approval for self-funded plan coverage.

There are not yet any preapproved HDHP/HSA products available on the Hawaii insurance market. If an employer offers a plan that has not been preapproved by the DLIR, it must submit an application to the state and request approval. It appears, based on informal comments from the DLIR, that in order to view the HDHP as satisfying the requirements of the PHCA, the DLIR may require significant employer HSA contributions to ensure that most of the high deductible is covered by the employer, not the employee.

State Tax Consequences

Q 8:38 If an HSA satisfies applicable federal requirements, will a participant have the same favorable tax consequences under state law as under federal law?

Not necessarily. Although most states follow the federal tax law with respect to determination of taxable income, some states do not provide tax benefits for HSA participation. There are currently four states in which the state tax consequences of HSA participation differ from the federal tax consequences (e.g., where HSA employer contributions that are excludable for federal tax purposes are required to be included in income, where interest earned on the HSA is taxed, or where deduction for state tax purposes is not available). These states are Alabama, California, New Jersey, and Wisconsin. (See Qs 6:41, 8:39, 8:40, 8:41, and 8:42.) In addition, it is possible that in certain states, the 2007 TRHCA provisions that apply to HSAs (e.g., increased contribution limits) do not apply for purposes of state tax law.

Q 8:39 Is it possible to have an HDHP in New Jersey that satisfies federal requirements?

Currently, New Jersey does not conform to Code Section 223. As a result, New Jersey does not exclude HSA contributions by employers or by employees through an employer's cafeteria plan from an individual's income. Also, it appears that earnings on these contributions will be subject to state income tax. It is unclear whether distributions are taxable, as such distribution amounts already have been taxed under state law. Like Alabama (see Q 4:45), New Jersey does not appear to have amended individual income tax forms or instructions to inform HSA participants of their obligation to report these amounts as income.

New Jersey statute A4543, [Pub. L. No. 2005, Ch. 248 (Dec. 21, 2005)] makes it possible for insurers and HMOs to offer HDHPs that satisfy federal requirements in that state. New Jersey requires insurers and HMOs for groups with more than 50 persons to provide coverage below the deductible to pay for lead poisoning screening, medical evaluation, and necessary medical follow up and treatment for children with lead poisoning. This caused a problem for HDHPs, because the rule under Code Section 223 is that the only benefits that can be provided below the deductible are those that satisfy the definition of "preventive care." (See Q 3:49.) Since New Jersey law requires treatment, which is not preventive care, it would not have been possible to offer an insured or HMO member an HDHP in New Jersey without statutory change. (The IRS did have limited transition guidance in place under Notice 2004-43 [2004-27 I.R.B. 10], but that only covered months before January 1, 2006, for calendar year plans.) This law creates an exception to this rule for HDHPs that are intended to be used with an HSA. Under the exception, a deductible for lead poisoning benefits can be imposed under the HDHP, unless such services satisfy the definition of preventive care under federal law.

Q 8:40   Is it possible to have an HDHP in Wisconsin that satisfies federal requirements?

In general, Wisconsin law conforms to the Internal Revenue Code as of December 31, 2002. As a result, Wisconsin has not conformed to the tax treatment of HSAs, and therefore, Wisconsin does not exclude HSA contributions by employers or by employees through an employer's cafeteria plan from an individual's income. Also, earnings on HSA amounts are taxable. HSA distributions, however, may be included in the computation of the Wisconsin itemized deduction credit (see Instructions for Schedule I and News for Tax Practitioners, August 24, 2005, http://www.revenue.wi.gov/taxpro/news/080212.html).

The Wisconsin state legislature passed legislation conforming to the federal tax treatment of HSAs in 2004 and 2006. However, the Wisconsin governor vetoed these measures.

Q 8:41   What impact did California's Assembly Bill 115 have on HSAs?

California's Assembly Bill 115 [Stat. 2005, Ch. 691 (Oct. 17, 2005)] conforms California income tax law to federal tax law as of April 15, 2005, but specifically excludes HSAs. Under A.B. 115, HSA contributions may not be made on a pretax basis, no deduction is available for after-tax contributions, and earnings are taxed.

Q 8:42   Does Alabama conform to Code Section 223?

No. Currently, Alabama does not conform to Code Section 223, and there-fore, it does not afford the favorable tax treatment for individuals under Code Section 223 for state individual income tax purposes. Therefore, employer HSA contributions are not excludable from income for state income tax purposes, unless such contributions are made through a cafeteria plan, as described below. Also, it appears that earnings on these contributions will be subject to state income tax. It is unclear whether distributions are taxable, as such distribution amounts have already been taxed under state law when contributed. Interestingly, Alabama has not amended its tax forms and instruc-tions to inform HSA participants of their obligation to report this income, so it is unclear whether Alabama intends to enforce the taxation of HSAs for state income tax purposes.

Alabama conforms to Code Section 125. Therefore, HSA contributions that are made through a cafeteria plan are free from state income tax. It appears, however, that earnings will continue to be subject to state income tax.

Q 8:43   What impact did the Health Savings Account Act in Pennsylvania have on HSAs?

The Health Savings Account Act (S.B. 300) was enacted into law on July 6, 2006. The bill exempts contributions to an HSA from the state's 3.07 percent personal income tax. Before the S.B. 300 was enacted, interest income earned by an HSA and distributions used to pay for eligible medical or dental expenses were exempt from Pennsylvania state personal income tax, but Pennsylvania did not exclude HSA contributions by employers or by employees through an employer's cafeteria plan from an individual's income. Now, HSA contributions by employers and by employees through an employer's cafeteria plan are excludable from an individual's income for state income tax purposes. Similarly, earnings on these amounts are tax-free.

Davis-Bacon Act

Q 8:44   Do employer contributions to an HSA count as fringe benefits under the Davis-Bacon Act?

Employer contributions to an HSA most likely count as fringe benefits under the Davis-Bacon Act. The Act requires contractors and subcontractors working on federally-funded construction projects in excess of $2,000 to pay their laborers and mechanics a wage that is not less than the prevailing wage for similarly-situated employees in the locality. [40 U.S.C. §§ 3141–3144, 3146 and 3147.] Included in the prevailing wage are two components: (1) basic hourly wages, and (2) fringe benefits. Although the basic hourly wages must be paid in cash, fringe benefit obligations may be satisfied by paying fringe benefits in cash as additional wages, contributing payments to a bona fide plan, or both. [*See* 40 U.S.C. § 1341; 29 C.F.R. § 5.31]

Employer contributions to HSAs likely are to count as fringe benefits under the Act because HSAs are designed to pay for medical expenses, which are a benefit listed under the Act. Also, HSAs are funded and non-forfeitable, and therefore, appear to satisfy the funded plans requirements under 29 C.F.R. Section 5.26. Although the HSA funds could be used for nonmedical purposes if a participant is willing to incur income tax and a 10 percent additional tax, a contractor is permitted to substitute cash for the fringe benefits. Accordingly, it is likely that the DOL would consider employer contributions to an HSA to satisfy the fringe benefits requirements under the Act.

USA Patriot Act

Q 8:45   Do the Customer Identification Procedures of the USA Patriot Act apply to HSAs for which a bank is trustee or custodian?

Yes. The USA Patriot Act, Title III, "International Money Laundering Abatement and Anti-terrorist Financing Act of 2001," adds several new provisions to the Bank Secrecy Act (BSA) [31 U.S.C. § 5311 *et seq.*] that are designed to facilitate the prevention, detection, and prosecution of international money laundering and the financing of terrorism. [USA Patriot Act (Pub. L. No. 107-56)]

Section 326 of the Act adds a new subsection (1) to 31 U.S.C. Section 5318 of the BSA, which directs the Secretary of the Treasury to draft regulations establishing minimum standards that apply in connection with the opening of an account at a financial institution regarding the identity of the customer. The regulation under 31 C.F.R. Section 103.121 entitled "Customer Identification Programs for banks, savings associations, credit unions, and certain non-federally regulated banks" (CIP regulation) sets forth minimum information that a bank must obtain from a customer before opening an account.

These rules generally require that a bank implement a written Customer Identification Program appropriate for its size and type of business that includes obtaining the name, date of birth, address, and taxpayer identification number of a customer prior to opening an account. After obtaining this information, the bank must verify the identity of the customer within a reasonable time after the account is opened (e.g., by reviewing a customer's unexpired government-issued identification, such as a driver's license or passport). If the bank cannot form a reasonable belief that it knows the true identity of a customer, the bank must follow procedures that it has describing (1) when the bank should not open an account; (2) when a customer may use an account while the bank attempts to verify the customer's identity; (3) when the bank should close an account (after attempts to verify a customer's identity have failed); and (4) when the bank should file a Suspicious Activity Report in accordance with applicable law and regulation. The CIP regulation also requires that the bank keep records of identifying information about a customer, including any document that was relied on to verify the identity of the customer. These records must be retained for five years after the date the account is closed. Finally, the bank must adopt procedures for determining whether the customer appears on any list of known or suspected terrorists or terrorist organizations issued by any federal government agency. Bank customers must also be given notice that the bank is requesting information to verify their identities. A sample notice is provided in the regulation for this purpose.

Securities Law

Q 8:46   Is an HSA subject to regulation by the Securities and Exchange Commission?

Possibly, although the Securities and Exchange Commission (SEC) has not issued any guidance on this issue. The threshold question is whether HSAs are *securities*. If HSAs are securities, then persons in the business of selling HSAs would have to register as brokers or dealers. In addition, if HSAs are securities, it is likely that interests in HSAs would have to be registered as securities under the Securities Act of 1933 and that the issuer of the HSA may have to register as an investment company under the Investment Company Act of 1940.

Q 8:47   Under what circumstances would an HSA be considered a security for purposes of the federal securities laws?

The federal securities laws define the term *security* as including an *investment contract* (e.g., Securities Exchange Act of 1934 Section 3(10)). Therefore, an HSA will be a security if it qualifies as an investment contract. An investment contract involves a contract, transaction, or scheme whereby (1) a person invests his or her money, (2) in a common enterprise, (3) with an expectation of profit, (4) solely from the efforts of a promoter or other third party. [SEC v. W.J. Howey Co., 328 U.S. 293 (1946)]

Q 8:48   Is guidance relating to IRAs relevant for purposes of determining whether an HSA is a security?

Possibly. Because HSAs have many of the same features as IRAs, and because Code Section 223 refers to IRA rules with respect to certain issues (e.g., identity of trustee), SEC guidance regarding IRAs may be helpful in determining the status of HSAs under federal securities laws.

Q 8:49   What is the SEC's position regarding IRAs?

The SEC has taken the position that most IRAs are investment contracts. [SEC Release 33-6188, 1980 WL 2942, at *13 (Feb. 1, 1980) (Rel. No. 6188)] However, the SEC has also opined that certain types of IRAs do not constitute securities separate from the underlying investment by the IRA. Thus, IRAs invested in the following manner generally need not be registered under federal securities laws:

- IRAs involving direct investment by an individual in an exempt security (e.g., government-issued securities or certain securities issued by a bank);
- IRAs involving direct investment by an individual in an underlying investment that is not a security (e.g., a traditional fixed annuity); and
- IRAs funded solely by mutual fund shares registered under the Securities Act of 1933.

If the SEC were to take a similar position with respect to HSAs, HSAs invested in the same manner would not be required to be registered.

Use of Electronic Media

Q 8:50   To what extent can an employer use electronic technologies for providing employee benefit notices and transmitting employee benefit elections and consents?

The Treasury Department and the IRS have issued final regulations regarding the use of electronic media to provide notices to employee benefit plan participants and beneficiaries and to transmit elections or consents from participants and beneficiaries to employee benefit plans. The standards set forth in these final regulations apply to "any notice, election, or similar communication" made to or by a participant or beneficiary under an HSA. [Treas. Reg. § 35.3405-1, Q&A D-35; TD 9294, 71 Fed. Reg. 61877, 61880 (Oct. 20, 2006)]

Creditor Protection

Q 8:51   Are HSAs subject to the claims of creditors?

Most likely yes. Under federal bankruptcy law, a debtor's bankruptcy estate includes, among other things, "all legal or equitable interests of the debtor in property." [11 U.S.C. § 541(a)(1)] Once an item is included in the bankruptcy estate, an exemption may apply to exclude the item. No protection (exemption) is provided for an HSA account under the Federal Bankruptcy Code.

Even if an HSA were subject to Title I of ERISA (see Qs 8:1–8:30), the prohibition against the alienation of benefits would not apply to an HSA because an HSA is not treated as an employee pension benefit plan under Part 2 of Title I of ERISA, which contains the restrictions on the alienation of benefits. [See ERISA §§ 3(1), 3(2), 206(c)]

In a non-bankruptcy situation, state and local law may provide some protection. The authors are not aware of any state that currently grants creditor protection for an owner's interest in an HSA account.

Appendix A

Extracts from Relevant Code Sections

Appendix A reflects all changes made to the Internal Revenue Code through December 31, 2009, including additions, amendments, and technical corrections made by the Worker, Retiree, and Employer Recovery Act of 2008 (Pub. L. No. 110-458), the Fostering Connections to Success and Increasing Adoptions Act of 2008 (Pub. L. No. 110-351), the Tax Relief and Health Care Act of 2006 (TRHCA) (Pub. L. No. 109-432), and the Pension Protection Act of 2006 (PPA) (Pub. L. No. 109-280).

A Code section can be divided into several parts. The §symbol is frequently used to abbreviate the word *section*. For example, the parts to the citation § 223(d)(1)(A)(i)(I) are as follows:

§ 223 (d) (1) (A) (i) (I)

223 Section

    (d) Subsection

        (1) Paragraph

            (A) Subparagraph

                (i) Clause

                    (I) Subclause

Code Section 62	A-2
Code Section 106	A-2
Code Section 152	A-4
Code Section 213	A-8
Code Section 219	A-12
Code Section 220	A-13
Code Section 223	A-13
Code Section 408	A-23
Code Section 4973	A-25
Code Section 4975	A-27
Code Section 4980G	A-45

Code Section 6693 . . . . A-46
Code Section 7702B A-46

Code Section 62—Adjusted Gross Income Defined

(a) GENERAL RULE.—For purposes of this subtitle, the term "adjusted gross income" means, in the case of an individual, gross income minus the following deductions:

***

(16) ARCHER MSAs.—The deduction allowed by section 220.

***

(19) HEALTH SAVINGS ACCOUNTS.—The deduction allowed by section 223.

***

Code Section 106—Contributions by Employer to Accident and Health Plans

(a) GENERAL RULE.—Except as otherwise provided in this section, gross income of an employee does not include employer-provided coverage under an accident or health plan.

***

Note. Code Section 106(d) is effective for tax years beginning after 2003.

(d) CONTRIBUTIONS TO HEALTH SAVINGS ACCOUNTS.

(1) IN GENERAL.—In the case of an employee who is an eligible individual (as defined in section 223(c)(1)), amounts contributed by such employee's employer to any health savings account (as defined in section 223(d)) of such employee shall be treated as employer-provided coverage for medical expenses under an accident or health plan to the extent such amounts do not exceed the limitation under section 223(b) (determined without regard to this subsection) which is applicable to such employee for such taxable year.

(2) SPECIAL RULES.—Rules similar to the rules of paragraphs (2), (3), (4), and (5) of subsection (b) shall apply for purposes of this subsection.

(3) CROSS REFERENCE.—For penalty on failure by employer to make comparable contributions to the health savings accounts of comparable employees, see section 4980G.

Note. Code Section 106(e) is effective for distributions on or after December 20, 2006.

(e) FSA AND HRA TERMINATIONS TO FUND HSAS.—

(1) IN GENERAL.—A plan shall not fail to be treated as a health flexible spending arrangement or health reimbursement arrangement under this section or section 105 merely because such plan provides for a qualified HSA distribution.

(2) QUALIFIED HSA DISTRIBUTION.—The term "qualified HSA distribution" means a distribution from a health flexible spending arrangement or health reimbursement arrangement to the extent that such distribution—

(A) does not exceed the lesser of the balance in such arrangement on September 21, 2006, or as of the date of such distribution, and

(B) is contributed by the employer directly to the health savings account of the employee before January 1, 2012.

Such term shall not include more than 1 distribution with respect to any arrangement.

(3) ADDITIONAL TAX FOR FAILURE TO MAINTAIN HIGH DEDUCTIBLE HEALTH PLAN COVERAGE.—

(A) IN GENERAL.—If, at any time during the testing period, the employee is not an eligible individual, then the amount of the qualified HSA distribution—

(i) shall be includible in the gross income of the employee for the taxable year in which occurs the first month in the testing period for which such employee is not an eligible individual, and

(ii) the tax imposed by this chapter for such taxable year on the employee shall be increased by 10 percent of the amount which is so includible.

(B) EXCEPTION FOR DISABILITY OR DEATH.—Clauses (i) and (ii) of subparagraph (A) shall not apply if the employee ceases to be an eligible individual by reason of the death of the employee or the employee becoming disabled (within the meaning of section 72(m)(7)).

(4) DEFINITIONS AND SPECIAL RULES.—For purposes of this subsection—

(A) TESTING PERIOD.—The term "testing period" means the period beginning with the month in which the qualified HSA distribution is contributed to the health savings account and ending on the last day of the 12th month following such month.

(B) ELIGIBLE INDIVIDUAL.—The term "eligible individual" has the meaning given such term by section 223(c)(1).

(C) TREATMENT AS ROLLOVER CONTRIBUTION.—A qualified HSA distribution shall be treated as a rollover contribution described in section 223(f)(5).

(5) TAX TREATMENT RELATING TO DISTRIBUTIONS.—For purposes of this title—

(A) IN GENERAL.—A qualified HSA distribution shall be treated as a payment described in subsection (d).

(B) COMPARABILITY EXCISE TAX.—

(i) IN GENERAL.—Except as provided in clause (ii), section 4980G shall not apply to qualified HSA distributions.

(ii) FAILURE TO OFFER TO ALL EMPLOYEES.—In the case of a qualified HSA distribution to any employee, the failure to offer such distribution to any eligible individual covered under a high deductible health plan of the employer shall (notwithstanding section 4980G(d)) be treated for purposes of section 4980G as a failure to meet the requirements of section 4980G(b).

Code Section 152—Dependent Defined (Effective 01/01/05)

(a) IN GENERAL.—For purposes of this subtitle, the term "dependent" means—

(1) a qualifying child, or

(2) a qualifying relative.

(b) EXCEPTIONS.—For purposes of this section—

(1) DEPENDENTS INELIGIBLE.—If an individual is a dependent of a taxpayer for any taxable year of such taxpayer beginning in a calendar year, such individual shall be treated as having no dependents for any taxable year of such individual beginning in such calendar year.

Note. For HSA purposes, the term *qualified medical expenses* is determined without regard to subsection (1) above or subsection (2) below for tax years beginning after 2004. [See I.R.C. § 223(d)(2)(A)]

(2) MARRIED DEPENDENTS.—An individual shall not be treated as a dependent of a taxpayer under subsection (a) if such individual has made a joint return with the individual's spouse under section 6013 for the taxable year beginning in the calendar year in which the taxable year of the taxpayer begins.

(3) CITIZENS OR NATIONALS OF OTHER COUNTRIES—

(A) IN GENERAL.—The term "dependent" does not include an individual who is not a citizen or national of the United States unless such individual is a resident of the United States or a country contiguous to the United States.

(B) EXCEPTION FOR ADOPTED CHILD.—Subparagraph (A) shall not exclude any child of a taxpayer (within the meaning of subsection (f)(1)(B)) from the definition of "dependent" if—

(i) for the taxable year of the taxpayer, the child has the same principal place of abode as the taxpayer and is a member of the taxpayer's household, and

(ii) the taxpayer is a citizen or national of the United States.

(c) QUALIFYING CHILD.—For purposes of this section—

(1) IN GENERAL.—The term "qualifying child" means, with respect to any taxpayer for any taxable year, an individual—

(A) who bears a relationship to the taxpayer described in paragraph (2),

(B) who has the same principal place of abode as the taxpayer for more than one-half of such taxable year,

(C) who meets the age requirements of paragraph (3),

(D) who has not provided over one-half of such individual's own support for the calendar year in which the taxable year of the taxpayer begins, and

Note. Code Section 152(c)(1)(E), below, as added by the Fostering Connections to Success and Increasing Adoptions Act of 2008 (Pub. L. No. 110-351, § 501(b)), applies to tax years beginning after December 31, 2008.

(E) who has not filed a joint return (other than only for a claim of refund) with the individual's spouse under section 6013 for the taxable year beginning in the calendar year in which the taxable year of the taxpayer begins.

(2) RELATIONSHIP.—For purposes of paragraph (1)(A), an individual bears a relationship to the taxpayer described in this paragraph if such individual is—

(A) a child of the taxpayer or a descendant of such a child, or

(B) a brother, sister, stepbrother, or stepsister of the taxpayer or a descendant of any such relative.

(3) AGE REQUIREMENTS.—

Note. Code Section 152(c)(3)(A), below, as amended by the Fostering Connections to Success and Increasing Adoptions Act of 2008 (Pub. L. No. 110-351, § 501(a)), added "is younger than the taxpayer claiming such individual as a qualifying child . . . " and applies to tax years beginning after December 31, 2008.

(A) IN GENERAL.—For purposes of paragraph (1)(C), an individual meets the requirements of this paragraph if such individual is younger than the taxpayer claiming such individual as a qualifying child and—

(i) has not attained the age of 19 as of the close of the calendar year in which the taxable year of the taxpayer begins, or

(ii) is a student who has not attained the age of 24 as of the close of such calendar year.

(B) SPECIAL RULE FOR DISABLED.—In the case of an individual who is permanently and totally disabled (as defined in section 22(e)(3)) at any time during such calendar year, the requirements of subparagraph (A) shall be treated as met with respect to such individual.

(4) SPECIAL RULE RELATING TO 2 OR MORE CLAIMING QUALIFYING CHILD. ***

(d) QUALIFYING CHILD.—For purposes of this section—

(1) IN GENERAL.—The term "qualifying child" means, with respect to any taxpayer for any taxable year, an individual—

(A) who bears a relationship to the taxpayer described in paragraph (2),

Note. For HSA purposes, the term *"qualified medical expenses"* is determined without regard to subparagraph (B) below for tax years beginning after 2004. [See I.R.C. § 223(d)(2)(A)]

(B) whose gross income for the calendar year in which such taxable year begins is less than the exemption amount (as defined in section 151(d)),

Note. For 2009, the exemption amount is $3,650 ($3,500 for 2008). [See Rev. Proc. 2008-66, § 3.19, 2008-45 I.R.B. 1]

(C) with respect to whom the taxpayer provides over one-half of the individual's support for the calendar year in which such taxable year begins, and

(D) who is not a qualifying child of such taxpayer or of any other taxpayer for any taxable year beginning in the calendar year in which such taxable year begins.

(2) RELATIONSHIP.—For purposes of paragraph (1)(A), an individual bears a relationship to the taxpayer described in this paragraph if the individual is any of the following with respect to the taxpayer:

(A) A child or a descendant of a child.

(B) A brother, sister, stepbrother, or stepsister.

(C) The father or mother, or an ancestor of either.

(D) A stepfather or stepmother.

(E) A son or daughter of a brother or sister of the taxpayer.

(F) A brother or sister of the father or mother of the taxpayer.

(G) A son-in-law, daughter-in-law, father-in-law, mother-in-law, brother-in-law, or sister-in-law.

(H) An individual (other than an individual who at any time during the taxable year was the spouse, determined without regard to section 7703, of the taxpayer) who, for the taxable year of the taxpayer, has the same principal place of abode as the taxpayer and is a member of the taxpayer's household.

(3) SPECIAL RULE RELATING TO MULTIPLE SUPPORT AGREEMENTS. ***

(4) SPECIAL RULE RELATING TO INCOME OF HANDICAPPED DEPENDENTS.***

(e) SPECIAL RULE FOR DIVORCED PARENTS, ETC.—

(1) IN GENERAL.—Notwithstanding subsection (c)(1)(B), (c)(4), or (d)(1)(C), if—

(A) a child receives over one-half of the child's support during the calendar year from the child's parents—

(i) who are divorced or legally separated under a decree of divorce or separate maintenance,

(ii) who are separated under a written separation agreement, or

(iii) who live apart at all times during the last 6 months of the calendar year, and

Caution. Code Section 152(e)(1)(B), below, as amended by the Gulf Opportunity Zone Act of 2005 (H.R. 4440 § 404(a)) conforms the definition of dependent for HSAs to that which is applicable to other health plans and MSAs. The amendment is effective for taxable years beginning after 2004.

(B) such child is in the custody of 1 or both of the child's parents for more than one-half of the calendar year, such child shall be treated as being the qualifying child or qualifying relative of the noncustodial parent for a calendar year if the requirements described in paragraph (2) or (3) are met.

(2) REQUIREMENTS. ***

(3) CUSTODIAL PARENT AND NONCUSTODIAL PARENT. ***

(4) EXCEPTION FOR MULTIPLE-SUPPORT AGREEMENTS. ***

(f) SPECIAL RULE FOR DIVORCED PARENTS, ETC.—

(1) CHILD DEFINED.—

(A) IN GENERAL.—The term "child" means an individual who is—

(i) a son, daughter, stepson, or stepdaughter of the taxpayer, or

(ii) an eligible foster child of the taxpayer.

(B) ADOPTED CHILD.—In determining whether any of the relationships specified in subparagraph (A)(i) or paragraph (4) exists, a legally adopted individual of the taxpayer, or an individual who is lawfully placed with the taxpayer for legal adoption by the taxpayer, shall be treated as a child of such individual by blood.

(C) ELIGIBLE FOSTER CHILD.—For purposes of subparagraph (A)(ii), the term "eligible foster child" means an individual who is placed with the taxpayer by an authorized placement agency or by judgment, decree, or other order of any court of competent jurisdiction.

(2) STUDENT DEFINED.—The term "student" means an individual who during each of 5 calendar months during the calendar year in which the taxable year of the taxpayer begins—

(A) is a full-time student at an educational organization described in section 170(b)(1)(A)(ii), or

(B) is pursuing a full-time course of institutional on-farm training under the supervision of an accredited agent of an educational organization described in section 170(b)(1)(A)(ii) or of a State or political subdivision of a State.

(3) DETERMINATION OF HOUSEHOLD STATUS.—An individual shall not be treated as a member of the taxpayer's household if at any time during the taxable year of the taxpayer the relationship between such individual and the taxpayer is in violation of local law.

(4) BROTHER AND SISTER.—The terms "brother" and "sister" include a brother or sister by the half blood.

(5) SPECIAL SUPPORT TEST IN CASE OF STUDENTS.—For purposes of subsections (c)(1)(D) and (d)(1)(C), in the case of an individual who is—

(A) a child of the taxpayer, and

(B) a student, amounts received as scholarships for study at an educational organization described in section 170(b)(1)(A)(ii) shall not be taken into account.

(6) TREATMENT OF MISSING CHILDREN. ***

(7) CROSS REFERENCES.—For provision treating child as dependent of both parents for purposes of certain provisions, see sections 105(b) and 213(d)(5).

Code Section 213—Medical, Dental, Etc., Expenses

(a) ALLOWANCE OF DEDUCTION.—There shall be allowed as a deduction the expenses paid during the taxable year, not compensated for by insurance or otherwise, for medical care of the taxpayer, his spouse, or a dependent (as defined in section 152, determined without regard to subsections (b)(1), (b)(2), and (d)(1)(B) thereof), to the extent that such expenses exceed 7.5 percent of adjusted gross income.

> **Note.** Code Section 213(a), above, as amended by the Working Families Tax Relief Act of 2004 (P.L. 108–311), added ", determined without regard to subsections (b)(1), (b)(2), and (d)(1)(B) thereof" after "section 152", for tax years beginning after December 31, 2004.

(b) LIMITATION WITH RESPECT TO MEDICINE AND DRUGS.—An amount paid during the taxable year for medicine or a drug shall be taken into account under subsection (a) only if such medicine or drug is a prescribed drug or is insulin.

(c) SPECIAL RULE FOR DECEDENTS.—

(1) TREATMENT OF EXPENSES PAID AFTER DEATH.—For purposes of subsection (a), expenses for the medical care of the taxpayer which are paid out of his estate during the 1-year period beginning with the day after the date of his death shall be treated as paid by the taxpayer at the time incurred.

(2) LIMITATION.—Paragraph (1) shall not apply if the amount paid is allowable under section 2053 as a deduction in computing the taxable estate of the decedent, but this paragraph shall not apply if (within the time and in the manner and form prescribed by the Secretary) there is filed—

(A) a statement that such amount has not been allowed as a deduction under section 2053, and

(B) a waiver of the right to have such amount allowed at any time as a deduction under section 2053.

(d) DEFINITIONS.—For purposes of this section—

(1) THE TERM "MEDICAL CARE" MEANS AMOUNTS PAID—

(A) for the diagnosis, cure, mitigation, treatment, or prevention of disease, or for the purpose of affecting any structure or function of the body,

(B) for transportation primarily for and essential to medical care referred to in subparagraph (A),

(C) for qualified long-term care services (as defined in section 7702B(c)), or

(D) for insurance (including amounts paid as premiums under part B of title XVIII of the Social Security Act, relating to supplementary medical insurance for the aged) covering medical care referred to in subparagraphs (A) and (B) or for any qualified long-term care insurance contract (as defined in section 7702B(b)).

In the case of a qualified long-term care insurance contract (as defined in section 7702B(b)), only eligible long-term care premiums (as defined in paragraph (10)) shall be taken into account under subparagraph (D).

(2) AMOUNTS PAID FOR CERTAIN LODGING AWAY FROM HOME TREATED AS PAID FOR MEDICAL CARE.—Amounts paid for lodging (not lavish or extravagant under the circumstances) while away from home primarily for and essential to medical care referred to in paragraph (1)(A) shall be treated as amounts paid for medical care if—

(A) the medical care referred to in paragraph (1)(A) is provided by a physician in a licensed hospital (or in a medical care facility which is related to, or the equivalent of, a licensed hospital), and

(B) there is no significant element of personal pleasure, recreation, or vacation in the travel away from home.

The amount taken into account under the preceding sentence shall not exceed $50 for each night for each individual.

(3) PRESCRIBED DRUG.—The term "prescribed drug" means a drug or biological which requires a prescription of a physician for its use by an individual.

(4) PHYSICIAN.—The term "physician" has the meaning given to such term by section 1861(r) of the Social Security Act (42 U.S.C. 1395x(r)).

(5) SPECIAL RULE IN THE CASE OF CHILD OF DIVORCED PARENTS, ETC.—Any child to whom section 152(e) applies shall be treated as a dependent of both parents for purposes of this section.

(6) In the case of an insurance contract under which amounts are payable for other than medical care referred to in subparagraphs (A), (B) and (C) of paragraph (1)—

(A) no amount shall be treated as paid for insurance to which paragraph (1)(D) applies unless the charge for such insurance is either separately stated in the contract, or furnished to the policyholder by the insurance company in a separate statement,

(B) the amount taken into account as the amount paid for such insurance shall not exceed such charge, and

(C) no amount shall be treated as paid for such insurance if the amount specified in the contract (or furnished to the policyholder by the insurance company in a separate statement) as the charge for such insurance is unreasonably large in relation to the total charges under the contract.

(7) Subject to the limitations of paragraph (6), premiums paid during the taxable year by a taxpayer before he attains the age of 65 for insurance covering medical care (within the meaning of subparagraphs (A), (B), and (C) of paragraph (1)) for the taxpayer, his spouse, or a dependent after the taxpayer attains the age of 65 shall be treated as expenses paid during the taxable year for insurance which constitutes medical care if premiums for such insurance are payable (on a level payment basis) under the contract for a period of 10 years or more or until the year in which the taxpayer attains the age of 65 (but in no case for a period of less than 5 years).

(8) The determination of whether an individual is married at any time during the taxable year shall be made in accordance with the provisions of section 6013(d) (relating to determination of status as husband and wife).

(9) COSMETIC SURGERY.—

(A) IN GENERAL.—The term "medical care" does not include cosmetic surgery or other similar procedures, unless the surgery or procedure is necessary to ameliorate a deformity arising from, or directly related to, a congenital abnormality, a personal injury resulting from an accident or trauma, or disfiguring disease.

(B) COSMETIC SURGERY DEFINED.—For purposes of this paragraph, the term "cosmetic surgery" means any procedure which is directed at improving the patient's appearance and does not meaningfully promote the proper function of the body or prevent or treat illness or disease.

(10) ELIGIBLE LONG-TERM CARE PREMIUMS.—

(A) IN GENERAL.—For purposes of this section, the term "eligible long-term care premiums" means the amount paid during a taxable year for any qualified long-term care insurance contract (as defined in section 7702B(b)) covering an individual, to the extent such amount does not exceed the limitation determined under the following table:

In the case of an individual with an attained age before the close of the taxable of:

	The limitation is:
40 or less	$ 200
More than 40 but not more than 50	375
More than 50 but not more than 60	750
More than 60 but not more than 70	2,000
More than 70	2,500

Note. For taxable years beginning after 2006, the limitations under Code Section 213(d)(10) (regarding eligible long-term care premiums includible in the term *medical care*) have been indexed as follows: [See Rev. Proc. 2008-66, § 3.21; Rev. Proc. 2007-66, § 3.21, 2007-45 I.R.B. 956; Rev. Proc. 2007-66, § 3.19, 2007-45 I.R.B. 970; Rev. Proc. 2006-53, § 3.20, 2006-48 I.R.B. 996]

Attained Age Before the Close of the Taxable Year	*Limitation on Premiums*		
	2007	*2008*	*2009*
40 or less	$ 290	$ 310	$ 320
More than 40 but not more than 50	$ 550	$ 580	$ 600
More than 50 but not more than 60	$1,110	$1,050	$1,190
More than 60 but not more than 70	$2,950	$3,080	$3,180
More than 70	$3,680	$3,850	$3,980

(B) INDEXING.—

(i) IN GENERAL.—In the case of any taxable year beginning in a calendar year after 1997, each dollar amount contained in subparagraph (A) shall be increased by the medical care cost adjustment of such amount for such calendar year. If any increase determined under the preceding sentence is not a multiple of $10, such increase shall be rounded to the nearest multiple of $10.

(ii) MEDICAL CARE COST ADJUSTMENT.—For purposes of clause (i), the medical care cost adjustment for any calendar year is the percentage (if any) by which—

(I) the medical care component of the Consumer Price Index (as defined in section 1(f)(5) for August of the preceding calendar year, exceeds

(II) such component for August of 1996.

The Secretary shall, in consultation with the Secretary of Health and Human Services, prescribe an adjustment which the Secretary determines is more appropriate for purposes of this paragraph than the adjustment described in the preceding sentence, and the adjustment so prescribed shall apply in lieu of the adjustment described in the preceding sentence.

(11) CERTAIN PAYMENTS TO RELATIVES TREATED AS NOT PAID FOR MEDICAL CARE.—An amount paid for a qualified long-term care service (as defined in section 7702B(c)) provided to an individual shall be treated as not paid for medical care if such service is provided—

(A) by the spouse of the individual or by a relative (directly or through a partnership, corporation, or other entity) unless the service is provided by a licensed professional with respect to such service, or

(B) by a corporation or partnership which is related (within the meaning of section 267(b) or 707(b)) to the individual.

For purposes of this paragraph, the term "relative" means an individual bearing a relationship to the individual which is described in any of subparagraphs (A) through (G) of section 152(d)(2). This paragraph shall not apply for purposes of section 105(b) with respect to reimbursements through insurance.

Caution. Code section 213(d)(11), above, as amended by the Working Families Tax Relief Act of 2004 (P.L. 108-311), inserted "subparagraphs (A) through (G) of section 152(d)(2)" and removed "paragraphs (1) through (8) of section 152(a)" from the second sentence, for tax years beginning after December 31, 2004.

(e) EXCLUSION OF AMOUNTS ALLOWED FOR CARE OF CERTAIN DEPENDENTS.—Any expense allowed as a credit under section 21 shall not be treated as an expense paid for medical care.

Code Section 219—Retirement Savings

(a) ALLOWANCE OF DEDUCTION. ***

***

(d) OTHER LIMITATIONS AND RESTRICTIONS.—

(2) RECONTRIBUTED AMOUNTS.—No deduction shall be allowed under this section with respect to a rollover contribution described in section 402(c), 403(a)(4), 403(b)(8), 408(d)(3), or 457(e)(16).
***

(f) OTHER DEFINITIONS AND SPECIAL RULES
***

(3) TIME WHEN CONTRIBUTIONS DEEMED MADE.—For purposes of this section, a taxpayer shall be deemed to have made a contribution to an individual retirement plan on the last day of the preceding taxable year if the contribution is made on account of such taxable year and is made not later than the time prescribed by law for filing the return for such taxable year (not including extensions thereof).
***

(5) EMPLOYER PAYMENTS.—For purposes of this title, any amount paid by an employer to an individual retirement plan shall be treated as payment of compensation to the employee (other than a self-employed individual who is an employee within the meaning of section 401(c)(1)) includible in his gross income in the taxable year for which the amount was contributed, whether or not a deduction for such payment is allowable under this section to the employee.
***

Code Section 220—Archer MSAs

(a) DEDUCTION ALLOWED.—***

***

(f) TAX TREATMENT OF DISTRIBUTIONS.—

(5) ROLLOVER CONTRIBUTION.—An amount is described in this paragraph as a rollover contribution if it meets the requirements of subparagraphs (A) and (B).

(A) IN GENERAL.—Paragraph (2) shall not apply to any amount paid or distributed from an Archer MSA to the account holder to the extent the amount received is paid into an Archer MSA or a health savings account (as defined in section 223(d)) for the benefit of such holder not later than the 60th day after the day on which the holder receives the payment or distribution.

(B) LIMITATION.—This paragraph shall not apply to any amount described in subparagraph (A) received by an individual from an Archer MSA if, at any time during the 1-year period ending on the day of such receipt, such individual received any other amount described in subparagraph (A) from an Archer MSA which was not includible in the individual's gross income because of the application of this paragraph.

(6) COORDINATION WITH MEDICAL EXPENSE DEDUCTION.—For purposes of determining the amount of the deduction under section 213, any payment or distribution out of an Archer MSA for qualified medical expenses shall not be treated as an expense paid for medical care.

Code Section 223—Health Savings Accounts

(a) DEDUCTION ALLOWED.—In the case of an individual who is an eligible individual for any month during the taxable year, there shall be allowed as a deduction for the taxable year an amount equal to the aggregate amount paid in cash during such taxable year by or on behalf of such individual to a health savings account of such individual.

(b) LIMITATIONS.—

(1) IN GENERAL.—The amount allowable as a deduction under subsection (a) to an individual for the taxable year shall not exceed the sum of the monthly limitations for months during such taxable year that the individual is an eligible individual.

(2) MONTHLY LIMITATION.—The monthly limitation for any month is of—

(A) in the case of an eligible individual who has self-only coverage under a high deductible health plan as of the first day of such month, $2,250.

Note. For calendar years beginning before 2007, the monthly limitation on deductions under Code Section 223(b)(2)(A) for an individual with self-only coverage under a high deductible plan as of the first day of such month is 1/12 of the lesser of (1) the annual deductible under the HDHP, or (2) the maximum contribution limit for the year (see Q 4:20). For 2009, the maximum contribution limit is $3,000 for an individual with self-only coverage under an HDHP ($2,900 for 2008). [Rev. Proc. 2008-29, § 2, 2008-22 I.R.B. 1039; Rev. Proc. 2007-36, § 4, 2007-22 I.R.B. 1335 for 2008; Rev. Proc. 2007-36, § 3, 2007-22 I.R.B. 1, modifying Rev. Proc. 2006-53, § 3.24(1), 2006-48 I.R.B. 996 for 2007] See appendix F.

(B) in the case of an eligible individual who has family coverage under a high deductible health plan as of the first day of such month, $4,500.

Note. For calendar years beginning before 2007, the monthly limitation on deductions under Code Section 223(b)(2)(B) for an individual with family coverage under a high deductible plan as of the first day of such month is 1/12 of the lesser of (1) the annual deductible, or (2) the maximum contribution limit for the year (see Q 4:20). For 2009, the maximum contribution limit is $5,950 for an individual with family coverage under an HDHP ($5,800 for 2008). [Rev. Proc. 2008-29, § 2, 2008-22 I.R.B. 1039; Rev. Proc. 2007-36, § 4, 2007-22 I.R.B. 1335 for 2008; Rev. Proc. 2007-36, § 3, 2007-22 I.R.B. 1, modifying Rev. Proc. 2006-53, § 3.24(1), 2006-48 I.R.B. 996 for 2007] See appendix F.

(3) ADDITIONAL CONTRIBUTIONS FOR INDIVIDUALS 55 OR OLDER.—

(A) IN GENERAL.—In the case of an individual who has attained age 55 before the close of the taxable year, the applicable limitation under subparagraphs (A) and (B) of paragraph (2) shall be increased by the additional contribution amount.

(B) ADDITIONAL CONTRIBUTION AMOUNT.—For purposes of this section, the additional contribution amount is the amount determined in accordance with the following table:

For taxable years beginning in:	The additional contribution amount is:
2004	$500
2005	$600

For taxable years beginning in:	The additional contribution amount is:
2006	$ 700
2007	$ 800
2008	$ 900
2009 and thereafter	$1,000

(4) COORDINATION WITH OTHER CONTRIBUTIONS.—The limitation which would (but for this paragraph) apply under this subsection to an individual for any taxable year shall be reduced (but not below zero) by the sum of—

(A) the aggregate amount paid for such taxable year to Archer MSAs of such individual, and

(B) the aggregate amount contributed to health savings accounts of such individual which is excludable from the taxpayer's gross income for such taxable year under section 106(d) (and such amount shall not be allowed as a deduction under subsection (a)), and

Note. Code Section 223(b)(4)(C) is effective for taxable years beginning after 2006.

(C) the aggregate amount contributed to health savings accounts of such individual for such taxable year under section 408(d)(9) (and such amount shall not be allowed as a deduction under subsection (a)).

Subparagraph (A) shall not apply with respect to any individual to whom paragraph (5) applies.

(5) SPECIAL RULE FOR MARRIED INDIVIDUALS.—In the case of individuals who are married to each other, if either spouse has family coverage—

(A) both spouses shall be treated as having only such family coverage (and if such spouses each have family coverage under different plans, as having the family coverage with the lowest annual deductible), and

(B) the limitation under paragraph (1) (after the application of subparagraph (A) and without regard to any additional contribution amount under paragraph (3))—

(i) shall be reduced by the aggregate amount paid to Archer MSAs of such spouses for the taxable year, and

(ii) after such reduction, shall be divided equally between them unless they agree on a different division.

(6) DENIAL OF DEDUCTION TO DEPENDENTS.—No deduction shall be allowed under this section to any individual with respect to whom a deduction under section 151 is allowable to another taxpayer for a taxable year beginning in the calendar year in which such individual's taxable year begins.

(7) MEDICARE ELIGIBLE INDIVIDUALS.—The limitation under this subsection for any month with respect to an individual shall be zero for the first month such individual is entitled to benefits under title XVIII of the Social Security Act and for each month thereafter.

Note. Code Section 223(b)(8) is effective for taxable years beginning 2006.

(8) INCREASE IN LIMIT FOR INDIVIDUALS BECOMING ELIGIBLE INDIVIDUALS AFTER THE BEGINNING OF THE YEAR.—

(A) IN GENERAL.—For purposes of computing the limitation under paragraph (1) for any taxable year, an individual who is an eligible individual during the last month of such taxable year shall be treated—

(i) as having been an eligible individual during each of the months in such taxable year, and

(ii) as having been enrolled, during each of the months such individual is treated as an eligible individual solely by reason of clause (i), in the same high deductible health plan in which the individual was enrolled for the last month of such taxable year.

(B) FAILURE TO MAINTAIN HIGH DEDUCTIBLE HEALTH PLAN COVERAGE.—

(i) IN GENERAL.—If, at any time during the testing period, the individual is not an eligible individual, then—

(I) gross income of the individual for the taxable year in which occurs the first month in the testing period for which such individual is not an eligible individual is increased by the aggregate amount of all contributions to the health savings account of the individual which could not have been made but for subparagraph (A), and

(II) the tax imposed by this chapter for any taxable year on the individual shall be increased by 10 percent of the amount of such increase.

(ii) EXCEPTION FOR DISABILITY OR DEATH.—Subclauses (I) and (II) of clause (i) shall not apply if the individual ceased to be an eligible individual by reason of the death of the individual or the individual becoming disabled (within the meaning of section 72(m)(7)).

(iii) TESTING PERIOD.—The term "testing period" means the period beginning with the last month of the taxable year referred to in subparagraph (A) and ending on the last day of the 12th month following such month.

(C) DEFINITIONS AND SPECIAL RULES.—For purposes of this section—

(1) ELIGIBLE INDIVIDUAL.—

(A) IN GENERAL.—The term "eligible individual" means, with respect to any month, any individual if—

(i) such individual is covered under a high deductible health plan as of the 1st day of such month, and

(ii) such individual is not, while covered under a high deductible health plan, covered under any health plan—

(I) which is not a high deductible health plan, and

(II) which provides coverage for any benefit which is covered under the high deductible health plan.

(B) CERTAIN COVERAGE DISREGARDED.—Subparagraph (A)(ii) shall be applied without regard to—

(i) coverage for any benefit provided by permitted insurance, and

(ii) coverage (whether through insurance or otherwise) for accidents, disability, dental care, vision care, or long-term care, and

(iii) for taxable years beginning after December 31, 2006, coverage under a health flexible spending arrangement during any period immediately following the end of a plan year of such arrangement during which unused benefits or contributions remaining at the end of such plan year may be paid or reimbursed to plan participants for qualified benefit expenses incurred during such period if—

(I) the balance in such arrangement at the end of such plan year is zero, or

(II) the individual is making a qualified HSA distribution (as defined in section 106(e)) in an amount equal to the remaining balance in such arrangement as of the end of such plan year, in accordance with rules prescribed by the Secretary.

(2) HIGH DEDUCTIBLE HEALTH PLAN.—

(A) IN GENERAL.—The term "high deductible health plan" means a health plan—

(i) which has an annual deductible which is not less than—

(I) $1,000 for self-only coverage, and

(II) twice the dollar amount in subclause (I) for family coverage, and

(ii) the sum of the annual deductible and the other annual out-of-pocket expenses required to be paid under the plan (other than for premiums) for covered benefits does not exceed—

(I) $5,000 for self-only coverage, and

(II) twice the dollar amount in subclause (I) for family coverage.

Note. For calendar year 2009, a high deductible health plan is defined under Code Section 223(c)(2)(A) as a health plan with an annual deductible that is not less than $1,150 for self-only coverage or $2,300 for family coverage, and the annual out-of-pocket expenses (deductibles, co-payments, and other amounts, but not premiums) do not exceed $5,800 for self-only coverage or $11,600 for family coverage (see Q 3:1). See appendix F for dollar limitation for other years. [Rev. Proc. 2008-29, § 2, 2008-22 I.R.B. 1039; Rev. Proc. 2007-36, § 4, 2007-22 I.R.B. 1335 for 2008; Rev. Proc. 2007-36, § 3, 2007-22 I.R.B. 1, modifying Rev. Proc. 2006-53, § 3.24(1), 2006-48 I.R.B. 996 and Rev. Proc. 2006-53, § 3.24(2), 2006-48 I.R.B. 996 for 2007]

(B) EXCLUSION OF CERTAIN PLANS.—Such term does not include a health plan if substantially all of its coverage is coverage described in paragraph (1)(B).

(C) SAFE HARBOR FOR ABSENCE OF PREVENTIVE CARE DEDUCTIBLE.—A plan shall not fail to be treated as a high deductible health plan by reason of failing to have a deductible for preventive care (within the meaning of section 1871 of the Social Security Act, except as otherwise provided by the Secretary).

(D) SPECIAL RULES FOR NETWORK PLANS.—In the case of a plan using a network of providers—

(i) ANNUAL OUT-OF-POCKET LIMITATION.—Such plan shall not fail to be treated as a high deductible health plan by reason of having an out-of-pocket limitation for services provided outside of such network which exceeds the applicable limitation under subparagraph (A)(ii).

(ii) ANNUAL DEDUCTIBLE.—Such plan's annual deductible for services provided outside of such network shall not be taken into account for purposes of subsection (b)(2).

(3) PERMITTED INSURANCE.—The term "permitted insurance" means—

(A) insurance if substantially all of the coverage provided under such insurance relates to—

(i) liabilities incurred under workers' compensation laws,

(ii) tort liabilities,

(iii) liabilities relating to ownership or use of property, or

(iv) such other similar liabilities as the Secretary may specify by regulations,

(B) insurance for a specified disease or illness, and

(C) insurance paying a fixed amount per day (or other period) of hospitalization.

(4) FAMILY COVERAGE.—The term "family coverage" means any coverage other than self-only coverage.

(5) ARCHER MSA.—The term "Archer MSA" has the meaning given such term in section 220(d).

(d) HEALTH SAVINGS ACCOUNT.—For purposes of this section—

(1) IN GENERAL.—The term "health savings account" means a trust created or organized in the United States as a health savings account exclusively for the purpose of paying the qualified medical expenses of the account beneficiary, but only if the written governing instrument creating the trust meets the following requirements:

(A) Except in the case of a rollover contribution described in subsection (f)(5) or section 220(f)(5), no contribution will be accepted—

(i) unless it is in cash, or

(ii) to the extent such contribution, when added to previous contributions to the trust for the calendar year, exceeds the sum of—

(I) the dollar amount in effect under subsection (b)(2)(B), and

(II) the dollar amount in effect under subsection (b)(3)(B).

(B) The trustee is a bank (as defined in section 408(n)), an insurance company (as defined in section 816), or another person who demonstrates to the satisfaction of the Secretary that the manner in which such person will administer the trust will be consistent with the requirements of this section.

(C) No part of the trust assets will be invested in life insurance contracts.

(D) The assets of the trust will not be commingled with other property except in a common trust fund or common investment fund.

(E) The interest of an individual in the balance in his account is nonforfeitable.

(2) QUALIFIED MEDICAL EXPENSES.—

Caution. Code Section 223(d)(2)(A), below, as amended by the Gulf Opportunity Zone Act of 2005 (H.R. 4440, § 404(c)) conforms the definition of dependent for HSAs to that which is applicable to other health plans and MSAs. The amendment is effective for taxable years beginning after 2004 (H.R. 4440, § 404(d)).

(A) IN GENERAL.—The term "qualified medical expenses" means, with respect to an account beneficiary, amounts paid by such beneficiary for medical care (as defined in section 213(d) for such individual, the spouse of such individual, and any dependent (as defined in section 152, determined without regard to subsections (b)(1), (b)(2), and (d)(1)(B) thereof) of such individual, but only to the extent such amounts are not compensated for by insurance or otherwise.

(B) HEALTH INSURANCE MAY NOT BE PURCHASED FROM ACCOUNT.—Subparagraph (A) shall not apply to any payment for insurance.

(C) EXCEPTIONS.—Subparagraph (B) shall not apply to any expense for coverage under—

(i) a health plan during any period of continuation coverage required under any Federal law,

(ii) a qualified long-term care insurance contract (as defined in section 7702B(b)),

(iii) a health plan during a period in which the individual is receiving unemployment compensation under any Federal or State law, or

(iv) in the case of an account beneficiary who has attained the age specified in section 1811 of the Social Security Act, any health insurance other than a Medicare supplemental policy (as defined in section 1882 of the Social Security Act).

(3) ACCOUNT BENEFICIARY.—The term "account beneficiary" means the individual on whose behalf the health savings account was established.

(4) CERTAIN RULES TO APPLY.—Rules similar to the following rules shall apply for purposes of this section:

(A) Action 219(d)(2) (relating to no deduction for rollovers).

(B) section 219(f)(3) (relating to time when contributions deemed made).

(C) Except as provided in section 106(d), section 219(f)(5) (relating to employer payments).

(D) section 408(g) (relating to community property laws).

(E) section 408(h) (relating to custodial accounts).

(e) TAX TREATMENT OF ACCOUNTS.—

(1) IN GENERAL.—A health savings account is exempt from taxation under this subtitle unless such account has ceased to be a health savings account. Notwithstanding the preceding sentence, any such account is subject to the taxes imposed by section 511 (relating to imposition of tax on unrelated business income of charitable, etc. organizations).

(2) ACCOUNT TERMINATIONS.—Rules similar to the rules of paragraphs (2) and (4) of section 408(e) shall apply to health savings accounts, and any amount treated as distributed under such rules shall be treated as not used to pay qualified medical expenses.

(f) TAX TREATMENT OF DISTRIBUTIONS.—

(1) AMOUNTS USED FOR QUALIFIED MEDICAL EXPENSES.—Any amount paid or distributed out of a health savings account which is used exclusively to pay qualified medical expenses of any account beneficiary shall not be includible in gross income.

(2) INCLUSION OF AMOUNTS NOT USED FOR QUALIFIED MEDICAL EXPENSES.—Any amount paid or distributed out of a health savings account which is not used exclusively to pay the qualified medical expenses of the account beneficiary shall be included in the gross income of such beneficiary.

(3) EXCESS CONTRIBUTIONS RETURNED BEFORE DUE DATE OF RETURN.—

(A) IN GENERAL.—If any excess contribution is contributed for a taxable year to any health savings account of an individual, paragraph (2) shall not apply to distributions from the health savings accounts of such individual (to the extent such distributions do not exceed the aggregate excess contributions to all such accounts of such individual for such year) if—

(i) such distribution is received by the individual on or before the last day prescribed by law (including extensions of time) for filing such individual's return for such taxable year, and

(ii) such distribution is accompanied by the amount of net income attributable to such excess contribution.

Any net income described in clause (ii) shall be included in the gross income of the individual for the taxable year in which it is received.

(B) EXCESS CONTRIBUTION.—For purposes of subparagraph (A), the term "excess contribution" means any contribution (other than a rollover contribution described in paragraph (5) or section 220(f)(5)) which is neither excludable from gross income under section 106(d) nor deductible under this section.

(4) ADDITIONAL TAX ON DISTRIBUTIONS NOT USED FOR QUALIFIED MEDICAL EXPENSES.—

(A) IN GENERAL.—The tax imposed by this chapter on the account beneficiary for any taxable year in which there is a payment or distribution from a health savings account of such beneficiary which is includible in gross income under paragraph (2) shall be increased by 10 percent of the amount which is so includible.

(B) EXCEPTION FOR DISABILITY OR DEATH.—Subparagraph (A) shall not apply if the payment or distribution is made after the account beneficiary becomes disabled within the meaning of section 72(m)(7) or dies.

(C) EXCEPTION FOR DISTRIBUTIONS AFTER MEDICARE ELIGIBILITY. —Subparagraph (A) shall not apply to any payment or distribution after the date on which the account beneficiary attains the age specified in section 1811 of the Social Security Act.

(5) ROLLOVER CONTRIBUTION.—An amount is described in this paragraph as a rollover contribution if it meets the requirements of subparagraphs (A) and (B).

(A) IN GENERAL.—Paragraph (2) shall not apply to any amount paid or distributed from a health savings account to the account beneficiary to the extent the amount received is paid into a health savings account for the benefit of such beneficiary not later than the 60th day after the day on which the beneficiary receives the payment or distribution.

(B) LIMITATION.—This paragraph shall not apply to any amount described in subparagraph (A) received by an individual from a health savings account if, at any time during the 1-year period ending on the day of such receipt, such individual received any other amount described in subparagraph (A) from a health savings account which was not includible in the individual's gross income because of the application of this paragraph.

(6) COORDINATION WITH MEDICAL EXPENSE DEDUCTION.—For purposes of determining the amount of the deduction under section 213, any payment or distribution out of a health savings account for qualified medical expenses shall not be treated as an expense paid for medical care.

(7) TRANSFER OF ACCOUNT INCIDENT TO DIVORCE.—The transfer of an individual's interest in a health savings account to an individual's spouse or former spouse under a divorce or separation instrument described in subparagraph (A) of section 71(b)(2) shall not be considered a taxable transfer made by such individual notwithstanding any other provision of this subtitle, and such interest shall, after such transfer, be treated as a health savings account with respect to which such spouse is the account beneficiary.

(8) TREATMENT AFTER DEATH OF ACCOUNT BENEFICIARY.—

(A) TREATMENT IF DESIGNATED BENEFICIARY IS SPOUSE.—If the account beneficiary's surviving spouse acquires such beneficiary's interest in a health savings account by reason of being the designated beneficiary of such account at the death of the account beneficiary, such health savings account shall be treated as if the spouse were the account beneficiary.

(B) OTHER CASES.—

(i) IN GENERAL.—If, by reason of the death of the account beneficiary, any person acquires the account beneficiary's interest in a health savings account in a case to which subparagraph (A) does not apply—

(I) such account shall cease to be a health savings account as of the date of death, and

(II) an amount equal to the fair market value of the assets in such account on such date shall be includible if such person is not the estate of such beneficiary, in such person's gross income for the taxable year which includes such date, or if such person is the estate of such beneficiary, in such beneficiary's gross income for the last taxable year of such beneficiary.

(ii) SPECIAL RULES.—

(I) REDUCTION OF INCLUSION FOR PREDEATH EXPENSES.— The amount includible in gross income under clause (i) by any person (other than the estate) shall be reduced by the amount of qualified medical expenses which were incurred by the decedent before the date of the decedent's death and paid by such person within 1 year after such date.

(II) DEDUCTION FOR ESTATE TAXES.—An appropriate deduction shall be allowed under section 691(c) to any person (other than the decedent or the decedent's spouse) with respect to amounts included in gross income under clause (i) by such person.

(g) COST-OF-LIVING ADJUSTMENT.—

(1) IN GENERAL.—Each dollar amount in subsections (b)(2) and (c)(2)(A) shall be increased by an amount equal to—

(A) such dollar amount, multiplied by

(B) the cost-of-living adjustment determined under section 1(f)(3) for the calendar year in which such taxable year begins determined by substituting for "calendar year 1992" in subparagraph (B) thereof—

(i) except as provided in clause (ii), "calendar year 1997", and

(ii) in the case of each dollar amount in subsection (c)(2)(A), "calendar year 2003". In the case of adjustments made for any taxable year beginning after 2007, section 1(f)(4) shall be applied for purposes of this paragraph by substituting "March 31" for "August 31", and the Secretary shall publish the adjusted amounts under subsections (b)(2) and (c)(2)(A) for taxable years beginning in any calendar year no later than June 1 of the preceding calendar year.

(2) ROUNDING.—If any increase under paragraph (1) is not a multiple of $50, such increase shall be rounded to the nearest multiple of $50.

(h) REPORTS.—The Secretary may require—

(1) the trustee of a health savings account to make such reports regarding such account to the Secretary and to the account beneficiary with respect to contributions, distributions, the return of excess contributions, and such other matters as the Secretary determines appropriate, and

(2) any person who provides an individual with a high deductible health plan to make such reports to the Secretary and to the account beneficiary with respect to such plan as the Secretary determines appropriate.

The reports required by this subsection shall be filed at such time and in such manner and furnished to such individuals at such time and in such manner as may be required by the Secretary.

Code Section 408—Individual Retirement Accounts

(a) INDIVIDUAL RETIREMENT ACCOUNT.—***

***

Note. Code Section 408(d)(9) is effective for taxable years beginning after 2006.

(d) TAX TREATMENT OF DISTRIBUTIONS

***

(9) DISTRIBUTION FOR HEALTH SAVINGS ACCOUNT FUNDING.—

(A) IN GENERAL.—In the case of an individual who is an eligible individual (as defined in section 223(c)) and who elects the application of this paragraph for a taxable year, gross income of the individual for the taxable year does not include a qualified HSA funding distribution to the extent such distribution is otherwise includible in gross income.

(B) QUALIFIED HSA FUNDING DISTRIBUTION.—For purposes of this paragraph, the term "qualified HSA funding distribution" means a distribution from an individual retirement plan (other than a plan described in subsection (k) or (p)) of the employee to the extent that such distribution is contributed to the health savings account of the individual in a direct trustee-to-trustee transfer.

(C) LIMITATIONS.—

(i) MAXIMUM DOLLAR LIMITATION.—The amount excluded from gross income by subparagraph (A) shall not exceed the excess of —

(I) the annual limitation under section 223(b) computed on the basis of the type of coverage under the high deductible health plan covering the individual at the time of the qualified HSA funding distribution, over

(II) in the case of a distribution described in clause (ii)(II), the amount of the earlier qualified HSA funding distribution.

(ii) ONE-TIME TRANSFER.—

(I) IN GENERAL.—Except as provided in subclause (II), an individual may make an election under subparagraph (A) only for one qualified HSA funding distribution during the lifetime of the individual. Such an election, once made, shall be irrevocable.

(II) CONVERSION FROM SELF-ONLY TO FAMILY COVERAGE.—If a qualified HSA funding distribution is made during a month in a taxable year during which an individual has self-only coverage under a high deductible health plan as of the first day of the month, the individual may elect to make an additional qualified HSA funding distribution during a subsequent month in such taxable year during which the individual has family coverage under a high deductible health plan as of the first day of the subsequent month.

(D) FAILURE TO MAINTAIN HIGH DEDUCTIBLE HEALTH PLAN COVERAGE.—

(i) IN GENERAL.—If, at any time during the testing period, the individual is not an eligible individual, then the aggregate amount of all contributions to the health savings account of the individual made under subparagraph (A)—

(I) shall be includible in the gross income of the individual for the taxable year in which occurs the first month in the testing period for which such individual is not an eligible individual, and

(II) the tax imposed by this chapter for any taxable year on the individual shall be increased by 10 percent of the amount which is so includible.

(ii) EXCEPTION FOR DISABILITY OR DEATH.—Subclauses (I) and (II) of clause (i) shall not apply if the individual ceased to be an eligible individual by reason of the death of the individual or the individual becoming disabled (within the meaning of section 72(m)(7)).

(iii) TESTING PERIOD.—The term "testing period" means the period beginning with the month in which the qualified HSA funding distribution is contributed to a health savings account and ending on the last day of the 12th month following such month.

(E) APPLICATION OF SECTION 72.—Notwithstanding section 72, in determining the extent to which an amount is treated as otherwise includible in gross income for purposes of subparagraph (A), the aggregate amount distributed from an individual retirement plan shall be treated as includible in gross income to the extent that such amount does not exceed the aggregate amount which would have been so includible if all amounts from all individual retirement plans were distributed. Proper adjustments shall be made in applying section 72 to other distributions in such taxable year and subsequent taxable years.

* * *

(g) COMMUNITY PROPERTY LAWS.—This section shall be applied without regard to any community property laws.

(h) CUSTODIAL ACCOUNTS.—For purposes of this section, a custodial account shall be treated as a trust if the assets of such account are held by a bank (as defined in subsection (n)) or another person who demonstrates, to the satisfaction of the Secretary, that the manner in which he will administer the account will be consistent with the requirements of this section, and if the custodial account would, except for the fact that it is not a trust, constitute an individual retirement account described in subsection (a). For purposes of this title, in the case of a custodial account treated as a trust by reason of the preceding sentence, the custodian of such account shall be treated as the trustee thereof.

* * *

Code Section 4973—Tax on Excess Contributions to Certain Tax-Favored Accounts and Annuities

(a) TAX IMPOSED.—In the case of—

(1) an individual retirement account (within the meaning of section 408(a)),

(2) an Archer MSA (within the meaning of section 220(d)),

(3) an individual retirement annuity (within the meaning of section 408(b)), a custodial account treated as an annuity contract under section 403(b)(7)(A) (relating to custodial accounts for regulated investment company stock),

(4) a Coverdell education savings account (as defined in section 530, or

(5) a health savings account (within the meaning of section 223(d)),

there is imposed for each taxable year a tax in an amount equal to 6 percent of the amount of the excess contributions to such individual's accounts or annuities (determined as of the close of the taxable year). The amount of such tax for any taxable year shall not exceed 6 percent of the value of the account or annuity (determined as of the close of the taxable year). In the case of an endowment contract described in section 408(b), the tax imposed by this section does not apply to any amount allocable to life, health, accident, or other insurance under such contract. The tax imposed by this subsection shall be paid by such individual.

(b) EXCESS CONTRIBUTIONS.—For purposes of this section, in the case of individual retirement accounts or individual retirement annuities, the term "excess contributions" means the sum of—

(1) the excess (if any) of—

    (A) the amount contributed for the taxable year to the accounts or for the annuities (other than a contribution to a Roth IRA or a rollover contribution described in section 402(c), 403(a)(4), 403(b)(8), 408(d)(3), or 457(e)(16)), over

    (B) the amount allowable as a deduction under section 219 for such contributions, and

(2) the amount determined under this subsection for the preceding taxable year reduced by the sum of—

    (A) the distributions out of the account for the taxable year which were included in the gross income of the payee under section 408(d)(1),

    (B) the distributions out of the account for the taxable year to which section 408(d)(5) applies, and

    (C) the excess (if any) of the maximum amount allowable as a deduction under section 219 for the taxable year over the amount contributed (determined without regard to section 219(f)(6)) to the accounts or for the annuities (including the amount contributed to a Roth IRA) for the taxable year.

For purposes of this subsection, any contribution which is distributed from the individual retirement account or the individual retirement annuity in a distribution to which section 408(d)(4) applies shall be treated as an amount not contributed. For purposes of paragraphs (1)(B) and (2)(C), the amount allowable as a deduction under section 219 shall be computed without regard to section 219(g).

    ***

    (g) EXCESS CONTRIBUTIONS TO HEALTH SAVINGS ACCOUNTS.—For purposes of this section, in the case of health savings accounts (within the meaning of section 223(d)), the term "excess contributions" means the sum of—

(1) the aggregate amount contributed for the taxable year to the accounts (other than a rollover contribution described in section 220(f)(5) or 223(f)(5)) which is neither excludable from gross income under section 106(d) nor allowable as a deduction under section 223 for such year, and

(2) the amount determined under this subsection for the preceding taxable year, reduced by the sum of—

    (A) the distributions out of the accounts which were included in gross income under section 223(f)(2), and

    (B) the excess (if any) of—

        (i) the maximum amount allowable as a deduction under section 223(b) (determined without regard to section 106(d)) for the taxable year, over

        (ii) the amount contributed to the accounts for the taxable year.

For purposes of this subsection, any contribution which is distributed out of the health savings account in a distribution to which section 223(f)(3) applies shall be treated as an amount not contributed.

Code Section 4975—Tax on Prohibited Transactions

(a) INITIAL TAXES ON DISQUALIFIED PERSON.—There is hereby imposed a tax on each prohibited transaction. The rate of tax shall be equal to 15 percent of the amount involved with respect to the prohibited transaction for each year (or part thereof) in the taxable period. The tax imposed by this subsection shall be paid by any disqualified person who participates in the prohibited transaction (other than a fiduciary acting only as such).

(b) ADDITIONAL TAXES ON DISQUALIFIED PERSON.—In any case in which an initial tax is imposed by subsection (a) on a prohibited transaction and the transaction is not corrected within the taxable period, there is hereby imposed a tax equal to 100 percent of the amount involved. The tax imposed by this subsection shall be paid by any disqualified person who participated in the prohibited transaction (other than a fiduciary acting only as such).

(c) PROHIBITED TRANSACTION.—

(1) GENERAL RULE.—For purposes of this section, the term "prohibited transaction" means any direct or indirect—

(A) sale or exchange, or leasing, of any property between a plan and a disqualified person;

(B) lending of money or other extension of credit between a plan and a disqualified person;

(C) furnishing of goods, services, or facilities between a plan and a disqualified person;

(D) transfer to, or use by or for the benefit of, a disqualified person of the income or assets of a plan;

(E) act by a disqualified person who is a fiduciary whereby he deals with the income or assets of a plan in his own interest or for his own account; or

(F) receipt of any consideration for his own personal account by any disqualified person who is a fiduciary from any party dealing with the plan in connection with a transaction involving the income or assets of the plan.

(2) SPECIAL EXEMPTION.—The Secretary shall establish an exemption procedure for purposes of this subsection. Pursuant to such procedure, he may grant a conditional or unconditional exemption of any disqualified person or transaction, or class of disqualified persons or transactions, from all or part of the restrictions imposed by paragraph (1) of this subsection. Action under this subparagraph may be taken only after consultation and coordination with the Secretary of Labor. The Secretary may not grant an exemption under this paragraph unless he finds that such exemption is—

(A) administratively feasible,

(B) in the interests of the plan and of its participants and beneficiaries, and

(C) protective of the rights of participants and beneficiaries of the plan.

Before granting an exemption under this paragraph, the Secretary shall require adequate notice to be given to interested persons and shall publish notice in the Federal Register of the pendency of such exemption and shall afford interested persons an opportunity to present views. No exemption may be granted under this paragraph with respect to a transaction described in subparagraph (E) or (F) of paragraph (1) unless the Secretary affords an opportunity for a hearing and makes a determination on the record with respect to the findings required under subparagraphs (A), (B), and (C) of this paragraph, except that in lieu of such hearing the Secretary may accept any record made by the Secretary of Labor with respect to an application for exemption under section 408(a) of title I of the Employee Retirement Income Security Act of 1974.

(3) SPECIAL RULE FOR INDIVIDUAL RETIREMENT ACCOUNTS. * * *

(4) SPECIAL RULE FOR ARCHER MSAs. * * *

(5) SPECIAL RULE FOR COVERDELL EDUCATION SAVINGS ACCOUNTS. * * *

(6) SPECIAL RULE FOR HEALTH SAVINGS ACCOUNTS.—An individual for whose benefit a health savings account (within the meaning of section 223(d)) is established shall be exempt from the tax imposed by this section with respect to any transaction concerning such account (which would otherwise be taxable under this section) if, with respect to such transaction, the account ceases to be a health savings account by reason of the application of section 223(e)(2) to such account.

(d) EXEMPTIONS.—Except as provided in subsection (f)(6), the prohibitions provided in subsection (c) shall not apply to—

(1) any loan made by the plan to a disqualified person who is a participant or beneficiary of the plan if such loan—

(A) is available to all such participants or beneficiaries on a reasonably equivalent basis,

(B) is not made available to highly compensated employees (within the meaning of section 414(q)) in an amount greater than the amount made available to other employees,

(C) is made in accordance with specific provisions regarding such loans set forth in the plan,

(D) bears a reasonable rate of interest, and

(E) is adequately secured;

(2) any contract, or reasonable arrangement, made with a disqualified person for office space, or legal, accounting, or other services necessary for the establishment or operation of the plan, if no more than reasonable compensation is paid therefore;

(3) any loan to a leveraged employee stock ownership plan (as defined in subsection (e)(7)), if—

(A) such loan is primarily for the benefit of participants and beneficiaries of the plan, and

(B) such loan is at a reasonable rate of interest, and any collateral which is given to a disqualified person by the plan consists only of qualifying employer securities (as defined in subsection (e)(8));

(4) the investment of all or part of a plan's assets in deposits which bear a reasonable interest rate in a bank or similar financial institution supervised by the United States or a State, if such bank or other institution is a fiduciary of such plan and if—

(A) the plan covers only employees of such bank or other institution and employees of affiliates of such bank or other institution, or

(B) such investment is expressly authorized by a provision of the plan or by a fiduciary (other than such bank or institution or affiliates thereof) who is expressly empowered by the plan to so instruct the trustee with respect to such investment;

(5) any contract for life insurance, health insurance, or annuities with one or more insurers which are qualified to do business in a State if the plan pays no more than adequate consideration, and if each such insurer or insurers is—

(A) the employer maintaining the plan, or

(B) a disqualified person which is wholly owned (directly or indirectly) by the employer establishing the plan, or by any person which is a disqualified person with respect to the plan, but only if the total premiums and annuity considerations written by such insurers for life insurance, health insurance, or annuities for all plans (and their employers) with respect to which such insurers are disqualified persons (not including premiums or annuity considerations written by the employer maintaining the plan) do not exceed 5 percent of the total premiums and annuity considerations written for all lines of insurance in that year by such insurers (not including premiums or annuity considerations written by the employer maintaining the plan);

(6) the provision of any ancillary service by a bank or similar financial institution supervised by the United States or a State, if such service is provided at not more than reasonable compensation, if such bank or other institution is a fiduciary of such plan, and if—

(A) such bank or similar financial institution has adopted adequate internal safeguards which assure that the provision of such ancillary service is consistent with sound banking and financial practice, as determined by Federal or State supervisory authority, and

(B) the extent to which such ancillary service is provided is subject to specific guidelines issued by such bank or similar financial institution (as determined by the Secretary after consultation with Federal and State supervisory authority), and under such guidelines the bank or similar financial institution does not provide such ancillary service—

(i) in an excessive or unreasonable manner, and

(ii) in a manner that would be inconsistent with the best interests of participants and beneficiaries of employee benefit plans;

(7) the exercise of a privilege to convert securities, to the extent provided in regulations of the Secretary but only if the plan receives no less than adequate consideration pursuant to such conversion;

(8) any transaction between a plan and a common or collective trust fund or pooled investment fund maintained by a disqualified person which is a bank or trust company supervised by a State or Federal agency or between a plan and a pooled investment fund of an insurance company qualified to do business in a State if—

(A) the transaction is a sale or purchase of an interest in the fund,

(B) the bank, trust company, or insurance company receives not more than reasonable compensation, and

(C) such transaction is expressly permitted by the instrument under which the plan is maintained, or by a fiduciary (other than the bank, trust company, or insurance company, or an affiliate thereof) who has authority to manage and control the assets of the plan;

(9) receipt by a disqualified person of any benefit to which he may be entitled as a participant or beneficiary in the plan, so long as the benefit is computed and paid on a basis which is consistent with the terms of the plan as applied to all other participants and beneficiaries;

(10) receipt by a disqualified person of any reasonable compensation for services rendered, or for the reimbursement of expenses properly and actually incurred, in the performance of his duties with the plan, but no person so serving who already receives full-time pay from an employer or an association of employers, whose employees are participants in the plan or from an employee organization whose members are participants in such plan shall receive compensation from such fund, except for reimbursement of expenses properly and actually incurred;

(11) service by a disqualified person as a fiduciary in addition to being an officer, employee, agent, or other representative of a disqualified person;

(12) the making by a fiduciary of a distribution of the assets of the trust in accordance with the terms of the plan if such assets are distributed in the same manner as provided under section 4044 of title IV of the Employee Retirement Income Security Act of 1974 (relating to allocation of assets);

(13) any transaction which is exempt from section 406 of such Act by reason of section 408(e) of such Act (or which would be so exempt if such section 406 applied to such transaction) or which is exempt from section 406 of such Act by reason of section 408(b)(12) of such Act;

(14) any transaction required or permitted under part 1 of subtitle E of title IV or section 4223 of the Employee Retirement Income Security Act of 1974, but this paragraph shall not apply with respect to the application of subsection (c)(1) (E) or (F);

(15) a merger of multiemployer plans, or the transfer of assets or liabilities between multiemployer plans, determined by the Pension Benefit Guaranty Corporation to meet the requirements of section 4231 of such Act, but this paragraph shall not apply with respect to the application of subsection (c)(1)(E) or (F);

Caution. Code Section 4975(d)(16), as added by American Jobs Creation Act of 2004 (Pub. L. No. 108-357), is effective October 22, 2004.

(16) a sale of stock held by a trust which constitutes an individual retirement account under section 408(a) to the individual for whose benefit such account is established if—

(A) such stock is in a bank (as defined in section 581),

(B) such stock is held by such trust as of the date of the enactment of this paragraph,

(C) such sale is pursuant to an election under section 1362(a) by such bank,

(D) such sale is for fair market value at the time of sale (as established by an independent appraiser) and the terms of the sale are otherwise at least as favorable to such trust as the terms that would apply on a sale to an unrelated party,

(E) such trust does not pay any commissions, costs, or other expenses in connection with the sale, and

(F) the stock is sold in a single transaction for cash not later than 120 days after the S corporation election is made;

Note. Code Section 4975(d)(17) applies with respect to advice referred to in Code Section 4975(e)(3)(B) provided after 2006.

(17) Any transaction in connection with the provision of investment advice described in subsection (e)(3)(B) to a participant or beneficiary in a plan that permits such participant or beneficiary to direct the investment of plan assets in an individual account, if—

(A) the transaction is—

(i) the provision of the investment advice to the participant or beneficiary of the plan with respect to a security or other property available as an investment under the plan,

(ii) the acquisition, holding, or sale of a security or other property available as an investment under the plan pursuant to the investment advice, or

(iii) the direct or indirect receipt of fees or other compensation by the fiduciary adviser or an affiliate thereof (or any employee, agent, or registered representative of the fiduciary adviser or affiliate) in connection with the provision of the advice or in connection with an acquisition, holding, or sale of a security or other property available as an investment under the plan pursuant to the investment advice; and

(B) the requirements of subsection (f)(8) are met,

(18) any transaction involving the purchase or sale of securities, or other property (as determined by the Secretary of Labor), between a plan and a disqualified person (other than a fiduciary described in subsection (e)(3)) with respect to a plan if—

(A) the transaction involves a block trade,

(B) at the time of the transaction, the interest of the plan (together with the interests of any other plans maintained by the same plan sponsor), does not exceed 10 percent of the aggregate size of the block trade,

(C) the terms of the transaction, including the price, are at least as favorable to the plan as an arm's length transaction, and

(D) the compensation associated with the purchase and sale is not greater than the compensation associated with an arm's length transaction with an unrelated party,

(19) any transaction involving the purchase or sale of securities, or other property (as determined by the Secretary of Labor), between a plan and a disqualified person if—

(A) the transaction is executed through an electronic communication network, alternative trading system, or similar execution system or trading venue subject to regulation and oversight by—

(i) the applicable Federal regulating entity, or

(ii) such foreign regulatory entity as the Secretary of Labor may determine by regulation,

(B) either—

(i) the transaction is effected pursuant to rules designed to match purchases and sales at the best price available through the execution system in accordance with applicable rules of the Securities and Exchange Commission or other relevant governmental authority, or

(ii) neither the execution system nor the parties to the transaction take into account the identity of the parties in the execution of trades,

(C) the price and compensation associated with the purchase and sale are not greater than the price and compensation associated with an arm's length transaction with an unrelated party,

(D) if the disqualified person has an ownership interest in the system or venue described in subparagraph (A), the system or venue has been authorized by the plan sponsor or other independent fiduciary for transactions described in this paragraph, and

(E) not less than 30 days prior to the initial transaction described in this paragraph executed through any system or venue described in subparagraph (A), a plan fiduciary is provided written or electronic notice of the execution of such transaction through such system or venue,

(20) transactions described in subparagraphs (A), (B), and (D) of subsection (c)(1) between a plan and a person that is a disqualified person other than a fiduciary (or an affiliate) who has or exercises any discretionary authority or control with respect to the investment of the plan assets involved

in the transaction or renders investment advice (within the meaning of subsection (e)(3)(B)) with respect to those assets, solely by reason of providing services to the plan or solely by reason of a relationship to such a service provider described in subparagraph (F), (G), (H), or (I) of subsection (e)(2), or both, but only if in connection with such transaction the plan receives no less, nor pays no more, than adequate consideration,

(21) any foreign exchange transactions, between a bank or broker-dealer (or any affiliate of either) and a plan (as defined in this section) with respect to which such bank or broker-dealer (or affiliate) is a trustee, custodian, fiduciary, or other party in interest person, if—

> (A) the transaction is in connection with the purchase, holding, or sale of securities or other investment assets (other than a foreign exchange transaction unrelated to any other investment in securities or other investment assets),

> (B) at the time the foreign exchange transaction is entered into, the terms of the transaction are not less favorable to the plan than the terms generally available in comparable arm's length foreign exchange transactions between unrelated parties, or the terms afforded by the bank or broker-dealer (or any affiliate of either) in comparable arm's-length foreign exchange transactions involving unrelated parties,

> (C) the exchange rate used by such bank or broker-dealer (or affiliate) for a particular foreign exchange transaction does not deviate by more than 3 percent from the interbank bid and asked rates for transactions of comparable size and maturity at the time of the transaction as displayed on an independent service that reports rates of exchange in the foreign currency market for such currency, and

> (D) the bank or broker-dealer (or any affiliate of either) does not have investment discretion, or provide investment advice, with respect to the transaction,

(22) any transaction described in subsection (c)(1)(A) involving the purchase and sale of a security between a plan and any other account managed by the same investment manager, if—

> (A) the transaction is a purchase or sale, for no consideration other than cash payment against prompt delivery of a security for which market quotations are readily available,

> (B) the transaction is effected at the independent current market price of the security (within the meaning of section 270.17a-7(b) of title 17, Code of Federal Regulations),

> (C) no brokerage commission, fee (except for customary transfer fees, the fact of which is disclosed pursuant to subparagraph (D)), or other remuneration is paid in connection with the transaction,

> (D) a fiduciary (other than the investment manager engaging in the cross-trades or any affiliate) for each plan participating in the transaction authorizes in advance of any cross-trades (in a document that is separate from any other written agreement of the parties) the investment manager to

engage in cross trades at the investment manager's discretion, after such fiduciary has received disclosure regarding the conditions under which cross trades may take place (but only if such disclosure is separate from any other agreement or disclosure involving the asset management relationship), including the written policies and procedures of the investment manager described in subparagraph (H),

(E) each plan participating in the transaction has assets of at least $100,000,000, except that if the assets of a plan are invested in a master trust containing the assets of plans maintained by employers in the same controlled group (as defined in section 407(d)(7) of the Employee Retirement Income Security Act of 1974), the master trust has assets of at least $100,000,000,

(F) the investment manager provides to the plan fiduciary who authorized cross trading under subparagraph (D) a quarterly report detailing all cross trades executed by the investment manager in which the plan participated during such quarter, including the following information, as applicable: (i) the identity of each security bought or sold; (ii) the number of shares or units traded; (iii) the parties involved in the cross-trade; and (iv) trade price and the method used to establish the trade price,

(G) the investment manager does not base its fee schedule on the plan's consent to cross trading, and no other service (other than the investment opportunities and cost savings available through a cross trade) is conditioned on the plan's consent to cross trading,

(H) the investment manager has adopted, and cross-trades are effected in accordance with, written cross-trading policies and procedures that are fair and equitable to all accounts participating in the cross-trading program, and that include a description of the manager's pricing policies and procedures, and the manager's policies and procedures for allocating cross trades in an objective manner among accounts participating in the cross-trading program, and

(I) the investment manager has designated an individual responsible for periodically reviewing such purchases and sales to ensure compliance with the written policies and procedures described in subparagraph (H), and following such review, the individual shall issue an annual written report no later than 90 days following the period to which it relates signed under penalty of perjury to the plan fiduciary who authorized cross trading under subparagraph (D) describing the steps performed during the course of the review, the level of compliance, and any specific instances of non-compliance.

The written report shall also notify the plan fiduciary of the plan's right to terminate participation in the investment manager's cross-trading program at any time, or

(23) except as provided in subsection (f)(11), a transaction described in subparagraph (A), (B), (C), or (D) of subsection (c)(1) in connection with the acquisition, holding, or disposition of any security or commodity, if the transaction is corrected before the end of the correction period.

(e) DEFINITIONS.—

    (1) PLAN.—For purposes of this section, the term "plan" means—

        (A) a trust described in section 401(a) which forms a part of a plan, or a plan described in section 403(a), which trust or plan is exempt from tax under section 501(a),

        (B) an individual retirement account described in section 408(a),

        (C) an individual retirement annuity described in section 408(b),

        (D) an Archer MSA described in section 220(d),

        (E) a health savings account described in section 223(d),

        (F) a Coverdell education savings account described in section 530, or

        (G) a trust, plan, account, or annuity which, at any time, has been determined by the Secretary to be described in any preceding subparagraph of this paragraph.

    (2) DISQUALIFIED PERSON.—For purposes of this section, the term "disqualified person" means a person who is—

        (A) a fiduciary;

        (B) a person providing services to the plan;

        (C) an employer any of whose employees are covered by the plan;

        (D) an employee organization any of whose members are covered by the plan;

        (E) an owner, direct or indirect, of 50 percent or more of—

            (i) the combined voting power of all classes of stock entitled to vote or the total value of shares of all classes of stock of a corporation,

            (ii) the capital interest or the profits interest of a partnership, or

            (iii) the beneficial interest of a trust or unincorporated enterprise,

which is an employer or an employee organization described in subparagraph (C) or (D);

an owner, direct or indirect, of 50 percent or more of—

        (F) a member of the family (as defined in paragraph (6)) of any individual described in subparagraph (A), (B), (C), or (E);

        (G) a corporation, partnership, or trust or estate of which (or in which) 50 percent or more of—

            (i) the combined voting power of all classes of stock entitled to vote or the total value of shares of all classes of stock of such corporation,

            (ii) the capital interest or profits interest of such partnership, or

            (iii) the beneficial interest of such trust or estate,

        is owned directly or indirectly, or held by persons described in subparagraph (A), (B), (C), (D), or (E);

        (H) an officer, director (or an individual having powers or responsibilities similar to those of officers or directors), a 10 percent or more shareholder, or a highly compensated employee (earning 10 percent or more of the yearly wages of an employer) of a person described in subparagraph (C), (D), (E), or (G); or

(I) a 10 percent or more (in capital or profits) partner or joint venturer of a person described in subparagraph (C), (D), (E), or (G).

The Secretary, after consultation and coordination with the Secretary of Labor or his delegate, may by regulation prescribe a percentage lower than 50 percent for subparagraphs (E) and (G) and lower than 10 percent for subparagraphs (H) and (I).

(3) FIDUCIARY.—For purposes of this section, the term "fiduciary" means any person who—

(A) exercises any discretionary authority or discretionary control respecting management of such plan or exercises any authority or control respecting management or disposition of its assets,

(B) renders investment advice for a fee or other compensation, direct or indirect, with respect to any moneys or other property of such plan, or has any authority or responsibility to do so, or

(C) has any discretionary authority or discretionary responsibility in the administration of such plan.

Such term includes any person designated under section 405(c)(1)(B) of the Employee Retirement Income Security Act of 1974.

(4) STOCKHOLDINGS.—For purposes of paragraphs (2)(E)(i) and (G)(i) there shall be taken into account indirect stockholdings which would be taken into account under section 267(c), except that, for purposes of this paragraph, section 267(c)(4) shall be treated as providing that the members of the family of an individual are the members within the meaning of paragraph (6).

(5) PARTNERSHIPS; TRUSTS.—For purposes of paragraphs (2)(E)(ii) and (iii), (G)(ii) and (iii), and (I) the ownership of profits or beneficial interests shall be determined in accordance with the rules for constructive ownership of stock provided in section 267(c) (other than paragraph (3) thereof), except that section 267(c)(4) shall be treated as providing that the members of the family of an individual are the members within the meaning of paragraph (6).

(6) MEMBER OF FAMILY.—For purposes of paragraph (2)(F), the family of any individual shall include his spouse, ancestor, lineal descendant, and any spouse of a lineal descendant.

(7) EMPLOYEE STOCK OWNERSHIP PLAN.—The term "employee stock ownership plan" means a defined contribution plan—

(A) which is a stock bonus plan which is qualified, or a stock bonus and a money purchase plan both of which are qualified under section 401(a), and which are designed to invest primarily in qualifying employer securities; and

(B) which is otherwise defined in regulations prescribed by the Secretary.

Caution. Code Section 4975(e)(7), closing paragraph, below, as amended by Economic Growth & Tax Relief Reconciliation Act of 2001 (Pub. L. No. 107-16), generally applies to plan years beginning after December 31, 2004.

A plan shall not be treated as an employee stock ownership plan unless it meets the requirements of section 409(h), section 409(o), and, if applicable, section 409(n), 409(p), and section 664(g) and, if the employer has a registration-type class of securities (as defined in section 409(e)(4)), it meets the requirements of section 409(e).

(8) QUALIFYING EMPLOYER SECURITY.—The term "qualifying employer security" means any employer security within the meaning of section 409(l). If any moneys or other property of a plan are invested in shares of an investment company registered under the Investment Company Act of 1940, the investment shall not cause that investment company or that investment company's investment adviser or principal underwriter to be treated as a fiduciary or a disqualified person for purposes of this section, except when an investment company or its investment adviser or principal underwriter acts in connection with a plan covering employees of the investment company, its investment adviser, or its principal underwriter.

(9) SECTION MADE APPLICABLE TO WITHDRAWAL LIABILITY PAYMENT FUNDS.—For purposes of this section—

(A) IN GENERAL.—The term "plan" includes a trust described in section 501(c)(22). ***

(B) DISQUALIFIED PERSON.—***

(f) OTHER DEFINITIONS AND SPECIAL RULES.—For purposes of this section—

(1) JOINT AND SEVERAL LIABILITY.—If more than one person is liable under subsection (a) or (b) with respect to any one prohibited transaction, all such persons shall be jointly and severally liable under such subsection with respect to such transaction.

(2) TAXABLE PERIOD.—The term "taxable period" means, with respect to any prohibited transaction, the period beginning with the date on which the prohibited transaction occurs and ending on the earliest of—

(A) the date of mailing a notice of deficiency with respect to the tax imposed by subsection (a) under section 6212,

(B) the date on which the tax imposed by subsection (a) is assessed, or

(C) the date on which correction of the prohibited transaction is completed.

(3) SALE OR EXCHANGE; ENCUMBERED PROPERTY.—A transfer of real or personal property by a disqualified person to a plan shall be treated as a sale or exchange if the property is subject to a mortgage or similar lien which the plan assumes or if it is subject to a mortgage or similar lien which a disqualified person placed on the property within the 10-year period ending on the date of the transfer.

(4) AMOUNT INVOLVED.—The term "amount involved" means, with respect to a prohibited transaction, the greater of the amount of money and the fair market value of the other property given or the amount of money and the fair market value of the other property received; except that, in the case of services described in paragraphs (2) and (10) of subsection (d) the amount involved shall be only the excess compensation. For purposes of the preceding sentence, the fair market value—

(A) in the case of the tax imposed by subsection (a), shall be determined as of the date on which the prohibited transaction occurs; and

(B) in the case of the tax imposed by subsection (b), shall be the highest fair market value during the taxable period.

(5) CORRECTION.—The terms "correction" and "correct" mean, with respect to a prohibited transaction, undoing the transaction to the extent possible, but in any case placing the plan in a financial position not worse than that in which it would be if the disqualified person were acting under the highest fiduciary standards.

(6) EXEMPTIONS NOT TO APPLY TO CERTAIN TRANSACTIONS.—

(A) IN GENERAL.—In the case of a trust described in section 401(a) which is part of a plan providing contributions or benefits for employees some or all of whom are owner-employees (as defined in section 401(c)(3), the exemptions provided by subsection (d) (other than paragraphs (9) and (12)) shall not apply to a transaction in which the plan directly or indirectly—***

(7) S CORPORATION REPAYMENT OF LOANS FOR QUALIFYING EMPLOYER SECURITIES. ***

(8) PROVISION OF INVESTMENT ADVICE TO PARTICIPANT AND BENEFICIARIES.—

(A) IN GENERAL.—The prohibitions provided in subsection (c) shall not apply to transactions described in subsection (d)(17) if the investment advice provided by a fiduciary adviser is provided under an eligible investment advice arrangement.

(B) ELIGIBLE INVESTMENT ADVICE ARRANGEMENT.—For purposes of this paragraph, the term "eligible investment advice arrangement" means an arrangement—

(i) which either—

(I) provides that any fees (including any commission or other compensation) received by the fiduciary adviser for investment advice or with respect to the sale, holding, or acquisition of any security or other property for purposes of investment of plan assets do not vary depending on the basis of any investment option selected, or

(II) uses a computer model under an investment advice program meeting the requirements of subparagraph (C) in connection with the provision of investment advice by a fiduciary adviser to a participant or beneficiary, and

(ii) with respect to which the requirements of subparagraphs (D), (E), (F), (G), (H), and (I) are met.

(C) INVESTMENT ADVICE PROGRAM USING COMPUTER MODEL.—

(i) IN GENERAL.—An investment advice program meets the requirements of this subparagraph if the requirements of clauses (ii), (iii), and (iv) are met.

(ii) COMPUTER MODEL.—The requirements of this clause are met if the investment advice provided under the investment advice program is provided pursuant to a computer model that—

(I) applies generally accepted investment theories that take into account the historic returns of different asset classes over defined periods of time,

(II) utilizes relevant information about the participant, which may include age, life expectancy, retirement age, risk tolerance, other assets or sources of income, and preferences as to certain types of investments,

(III) utilizes prescribed objective criteria to provide asset allocation portfolios comprised of investment options available under the plan,

(IV) operates in a manner that is not biased in favor of investments offered by the fiduciary adviser or a person with a material affiliation or contractual relationship with the fiduciary adviser, and

(V) takes into account all investment options under the plan in specifying how a participant's account balance should be invested and is not inappropriately weighted with respect to any investment option.

(iii) CERTIFICATION.—

(I) IN GENERAL.—The requirements of this clause are met with respect to any investment advice program if an eligible investment expert certifies, prior to the utilization of the computer model and in accordance with rules prescribed by the Secretary of Labor, that the computer model meets the requirements of clause (ii).

(II) RENEWAL OF CERTIFICATIONS.—If, as determined under regulations prescribed by the Secretary of Labor, there are material modifications to a computer model, the requirements of this clause are met only if a certification described in subclause (I) is obtained with respect to the computer model as so modified.

(III) ELIGIBLE INVESTMENT EXPERT.—The term "eligible investment expert" means any person which meets such requirements as the Secretary of Labor may provide and which does not bear any material affiliation or contractual relationship with any investment adviser or a related person thereof (or any employee, agent, or registered representative of the investment adviser or related person).

(iv) EXCLUSIVITY OF RECOMMENDATION.—The requirements of this clause are met with respect to any investment advice program if—

(I) the only investment advice provided under the program is the advice generated by the computer model described in clause (ii), and

(II) any transaction described in (d)(17)(A)(ii) occurs solely at the direction of the participant or beneficiary.

Nothing in the preceding sentence shall preclude the participant or beneficiary from requesting investment advice other than that described in clause (i), but only if such request has not been solicited by any person connected with carrying out the arrangement.

(D) EXPRESS AUTHORIZATION BY SEPARATE FIDUCIARY.—The requirements of this subparagraph are met with respect to an arrangement if the arrangement is expressly authorized by a plan fiduciary other than the person offering the investment advice program, any person providing investment options under the plan, or any affiliate of either.

(E) AUDITS.—

(i) IN GENERAL.—The requirements of this subparagraph are met if an independent auditor, who has appropriate technical training or experience and proficiency and so represents in writing—

(I) conducts an annual audit of the arrangement for compliance with the requirements of this paragraph, and

(II) following completion of the annual audit, issues a written report to the fiduciary who authorized use of the arrangement which presents its specific findings regarding compliance of the arrangement with the requirements of this paragraph.

(ii) SPECIAL RULE FOR INDIVIDUAL RETIREMENT AND SIMILAR PLANS.—In the case of a plan described in subparagraphs (B) through (F) (and so much of subparagraph (G) as relates to such subparagraphs) of subsection (e)(1), in lieu of the requirements of clause (i), audits of the arrangement shall be conducted at such times and in such manner as the Secretary of Labor may prescribe.

(iii) INDEPENDENT AUDITOR.—For purposes of this subparagraph, an auditor is considered independent if it is not related to the person offering the arrangement to the plan and is not related to any person providing investment options under the plan.

(F) DISCLOSURE.—The requirements of this subparagraph are met if—

(i) the fiduciary adviser provides to a participant or a beneficiary before the initial provision of the investment advice with regard to any security or other property offered as an investment option, a written notification (which may consist of notification by means of electronic communication)—

(I) of the role of any party that has a material affiliation or contractual relationship with the fiduciary adviser in the development of the investment advice program and in the selection of investment options available under the plan,

(II) of the past performance and historical rates of return of the investment options available under the plan,

(III) of all fees or other compensation relating to the advice that the fiduciary adviser or any affiliate thereof is to receive (including compensation provided by any third party) in connection with the provision of the advice or in connection with the sale, acquisition, or holding of the security or other property,

(IV) of any material affiliation or contractual relationship of the fiduciary adviser or affiliates thereof in the security or other property,

(V) the manner, and under what circumstances, any participant or beneficiary information provided under the arrangement will be used or disclosed,

(VI) of the types of services provided by the fiduciary adviser in connection with the provision of investment advice by the fiduciary adviser,

(VII) that the adviser is acting as a fiduciary of the plan in connection with the provision of the advice, and

(VIII) that a recipient of the advice may separately arrange for the provision of advice by another adviser, that could have no material affiliation with and receive no fees or other compensation in connection with the security or other property, and

(ii) at all times during the provision of advisory services to the participant or beneficiary, the fiduciary adviser—

(I) maintains the information described in clause (i) in accurate form and in the manner described in subparagraph (H),

(II) provides, without charge, accurate information to the recipient of the advice no less frequently than annually,

(III) provides, without charge, accurate information to the recipient of the advice upon request of the recipient, and

(IV) provides, without charge, accurate information to the recipient of the advice concerning any material change to the information required to be provided to the recipient of the advice at a time reasonably contemporaneous to the change in information.

(G) OTHER CONDITIONS.—The requirements of this subparagraph are met if—

(i) the fiduciary adviser provides appropriate disclosure, in connection with the sale, acquisition, or holding of the security or other property, in accordance with all applicable securities laws,

(ii) the sale, acquisition, or holding occurs solely at the direction of the recipient of the advice,

(iii) the compensation received by the fiduciary adviser and affiliates thereof in connection with the sale, acquisition, or holding of the security or other property is reasonable, and

(iv) the terms of the sale, acquisition, or holding of the security or other property are at least as favorable to the plan as an arm's length transaction would be.

(H) STANDARDS FOR PRESENTATION OF INFORMATION.—

(i) IN GENERAL.—The requirements of this subparagraph are met if the notification required to be provided to participants and beneficiaries under subparagraph (F)(i) is written in a clear and conspicuous manner and in a manner calculated to be understood by the average plan participant and is sufficiently accurate and comprehensive to reasonably apprise such participants and beneficiaries of the information required to be provided in the notification.

(ii) MODEL FORM FOR DISCLOSURE OF FEES AND OTHER COMPENSATION.—The Secretary of Labor shall issue a model form for the disclosure of fees and other compensation required in subparagraph (F)(i)(III) which meets the requirements of clause (i).

(I) MAINTENANCE FOR 6 YEARS OF EVIDENCE OF COMPLIANCE.— The requirements of this subparagraph are met if a fiduciary adviser who has provided advice referred to in subparagraph (A) maintains, for a period of not less than 6 years after the provision of the advice, any records necessary for determining whether the requirements of the preceding provisions of this paragraph and of subsection (d)(17) have been met. A transaction prohibited under subsection (c) shall not be considered to have occurred solely because the records are lost or destroyed prior to the end of the 6-year period due to circumstances beyond the control of the fiduciary adviser.

(J) DEFINITIONS.—For purposes of this paragraph and subsection (d)(17)—

(i) FIDUCIARY ADVISER.—The term "fiduciary adviser" means, with respect to a plan, a person who is a fiduciary of the plan by reason of the provision of investment advice referred to in subsection (e)(3)(B) by the person to a participant or beneficiary of the plan and who is—

(I) registered as an investment adviser under the Investment Advisers Act of 1940 (15 U.S.C. 80b-1 et seq.) or under the laws of the State in which the fiduciary maintains its principal office and place of business,

(II) a bank or similar financial institution referred to in subsection (d)(4) or a savings association (as defined in section 3(b)(1) of the Federal Deposit Insurance Act (12 U.S.C. 1813(b)(1)), but only if the advice is provided through a trust department of the bank or similar financial institution or savings association which is subject to periodic examination and review by Federal or State banking authorities,

(III) an insurance company qualified to do business under the laws of a State,

(IV) a person registered as a broker or dealer under the Securities Exchange Act of 1934 (15 U.S.C. 78a et seq.),

(V) an affiliate of a person described in any of subclauses (I) through (IV), or

(VI) an employee, agent, or registered representative of a person described in subclauses (I) through (V) who satisfies the requirements of applicable insurance, banking, and securities laws relating to the provision of the advice.

For purposes of this title, a person who develops the computer model described in subparagraph (C)(ii) or markets the investment advice program or computer model shall be treated as a person who is a fiduciary of the plan by reason of the provision of investment advice referred to in subsection (e)(3)(B) to a participant or beneficiary and shall be treated as a fiduciary adviser for purposes of this paragraph and subsection (d)(17), except that the Secretary of Labor may prescribe rules under which only 1 fiduciary adviser may elect to be treated as a fiduciary with respect to the plan.

(ii) AFFILIATE.—The term "affiliate" of another entity means an affiliated person of the entity (as defined in section 2(a)(3) of the Investment Company Act of 1940 (15 U.S.C. 80a-2(a)(3))).

(iii) REGISTERED REPRESENTATIVE.—The term "registered representative" of another entity means a person described in section 3(a)(18) of the Securities Exchange Act of 1934 (15 U.S.C. 78c(a)(18)) (substituting the entity for the broker or dealer referred to in such section) or a person described in section 202(a)(17) of the Investment Advisers Act of 1940 (15 U.S.C. 80b-2(a)(17)) (substituting the entity for the investment adviser referred to in such section).

(9) BLOCK TRADE.—The term "block trade" means any trade of at least 10,000 shares or with a market value of at least $200,000 which will be allocated across two or more unrelated client accounts of a fiduciary.

(10) ADEQUATE CONSIDERATION.—The term "adequate consideration" means—

(A) in the case of a security for which there is a generally recognized market—

(i) the price of the security prevailing on a national securities exchange which is registered under section 6 of the Securities Exchange Act of 1934, taking into account factors such as the size of the transaction and marketability of the security, or

(ii) if the security is not traded on such a national securities exchange, a price not less favorable to the plan than the offering price for the security as established by the current bid and asked prices quoted by persons independent of the issuer and of the party in interest, taking into account factors such as the size of the transaction and marketability of the security, and

(B) in the case of an asset other than a security for which there is a generally recognized market, the fair market value of the asset as determined in good faith by a fiduciary or fiduciaries in accordance with regulations prescribed by the Secretary of Labor.

(11) CORRECTION PERIOD.—

(A) IN GENERAL.—For purposes of subsection (d)(23), the term "correction period" means the 14-day period beginning on the date on which the disqualified person discovers, or reasonably should have discovered, that the transaction would (without regard to this paragraph and subsection (d)(23)) constitute a prohibited transaction.

(B) EXCEPTIONS.—-

(i) EMPLOYER SECURITIES.—Subsection (d)(23) does not apply to any transaction between a plan and a plan sponsor or its affiliates that involves the acquisition or sale of an employer security (as defined in section 407(d)(1) of the Employee Retirement Income Security Act of 1974) or the acquisition, sale, or lease of employer real property (as defined in section 407(d)(2) of such Act).

(ii) KNOWING PROHIBITED TRANSACTION.—In the case of any disqualified person, subsection (d)(23) does not apply to a transaction if, at the time the transaction is entered into, the disqualified person knew (or reasonably should have known) that the transaction would (without regard to this paragraph) constitute a prohibited transaction.

(C) ABATEMENT OF TAX WHERE THERE IS A CORRECTION.—If a transaction is not treated as a prohibited transaction by reason of subsection (d)(23), then no tax under subsection (a) and (b) shall be assessed with respect to such transaction, and if assessed the assessment shall be abated, and if collected shall be credited or refunded as an overpayment.

(D) DEFINITIONS.—For purposes of this paragraph and subsection (d)(23)—

(i) SECURITY.—The term "security" has the meaning given such term by section 475(c)(2) (without regard to subparagraph (F)(iii) and the last sentence thereof).

(ii) COMMODITY.—The term "commodity" has the meaning given such term by section 475(e)(2) (without regard to subparagraph (D)(iii) thereof).

(iii) CORRECT.—The term "correct" means, with respect to a transaction—

(I) to undo the transaction to the extent possible and in any case to make good to the plan or affected account any losses resulting from the transaction, and

(II) to restore to the plan or affected account any profits made through the use of assets of the plan.

(g) APPLICATION OF SECTION.—This section shall not apply—

(1) in the case of a plan to which a guaranteed benefit policy (as defined in section 401(b)(2)(B) of the Employee Retirement Income Security Act of 1974) is issued, to any assets of the insurance company, insurance service, or insurance organization merely because of its issuance of such policy;

(2) to a governmental plan (within the meaning of section 414(d)); or

(3) to a church plan (within the meaning of section 414(e)) with respect to which the election provided by section 410(d) has not been made.

In the case of a plan which invests in any security issued by an investment company registered under the Investment Company Act of 1940, the assets of such plan shall be deemed to include such security but shall not, by reason of such investment, be deemed to include any assets of such company.

(h) NOTIFICATION OF SECRETARY OF LABOR.—Before sending a notice of deficiency with respect to the tax imposed by subsection (a) or (b), the Secretary shall notify the Secretary of Labor and provide him a reasonable opportunity to obtain a correction of the prohibited transaction or to comment on the imposition of such tax.

(i) CROSS REFERENCE.—For provisions concerning coordination procedures between Secretary of Labor and Secretary of the Treasury with respect to application of tax imposed by this section and for authority to waive imposition of the tax imposed by subsection (b), see section 3003 of the Employee Retirement Income Security Act of 1974.

Code Section 4980G—Failure of Employer to Make Comparable Health Savings Account Contributions

(a) GENERAL RULE.—In the case of an employer who makes a contribution to the health savings account of any employee during a calendar year, there is hereby imposed a tax on the failure of such employer to meet the requirements of subsection (b) for such calendar year.

(b) RULES AND REQUIREMENTS.—Rules and requirements similar to the rules and requirements of section 4980E shall apply for purposes of this section.

(c) REGULATIONS.—The Secretary shall issue regulations to carry out the purposes of this section, including regulations providing special rules for employers who make contributions to Archer MSAs and health savings accounts during the calendar year.

(d) EXCEPTION.—For purposes of applying section 4980E to a contribution to a health savings account of an employee who is not a highly compensated employee (as defined in section 414(q)), highly compensated employees shall not be treated as comparable participating employees.

Code Section 6693—Failure to Provide Reports on Certain Tax-Favored Accounts or Annuities; Penalties Relating to Designated Nondeductible Contributions

(a) REPORTS.—

(1) IN GENERAL.—If a person required to file a report under a provision referred to in paragraph (2) fails to file such report at the time and in the manner required by such provision, such person shall pay a penalty of $50 for each failure unless it is shown that such failure is due to reasonable cause.

(2) PROVISIONS.—The provisions referred to in this paragraph are—

(A) subsections (i) and (l) of section 408 (relating to individual retirement plans),

(B) section 220(h) (relating to Archer MSAs),

(C) section 223(h) (relating to health savings accounts),

(D) section 529(d) (relating to qualified tuition programs), and

(E) section 530(h) (relating to Coverdell education savings accounts).

This subsection shall not apply to any report which is an information return described in section 6724(d)(1)(C)(i) or a payee statement described in section 6724(d)(2)(W). This subsection shall not apply to any report which is an information return described in section 6724(d)(1)(C)(i) or a payee statement described in section 6724(d)(2)(X).

Code Section 7702B—Treatment of Qualified Long-Term Care Insurance

(a) IN GENERAL.—For purposes of this title—

(1) a qualified long-term care insurance contract shall be treated as an accident and health insurance contract,

* * *

(b) QUALIFIED LONG-TERM CARE INSURANCE CONTRACT.—For purposes of this title—

(1) IN GENERAL.—The term "qualified long-term care insurance contract" means any insurance contract if—

(A) the only insurance protection provided under such contract is coverage of qualified long-term care services,

(B) such contract does not pay or reimburse expenses incurred for services or items to the extent that such expenses are reimbursable under title XVIII of the Social Security Act or would be so reimbursable but for the application of a deductible or coinsurance amount,

(C) such contract is guaranteed renewable,

(D) such contract does not provide for a cash surrender value or other money that can be—

(i) paid, assigned, or pledged as collateral for a loan, or

(ii) borrowed,

other than as provided in subparagraph (E) or paragraph (2)(C),

(E) all refunds of premiums, and all policyholder dividends or similar amounts, under such contract are to be applied as a reduction in future premiums or to increase future benefits, and

(F) such contract meets the requirements of subsection (g).

SPECIAL RULES.—

(A) PER DIEM, ETC. PAYMENTS PERMITTED.—A contract shall not fail to be described in subparagraph (A) or (B) of paragraph (1) by reason of payments being made on a per diem or other periodic basis without regard to the expenses incurred during the period to which the payments relate.

(B) SPECIAL RULES RELATING TO MEDICARE.—(i) Paragraph (1)(B) shall not apply to expenses which are reimbursable under title XVIII of the Social Security Act only as a secondary payor.

(i) No provision of law shall be construed or applied so as to prohibit the offering of a qualified long-term care insurance contract on the basis that the contract coordinates its benefits with those provided under such title.

(C) REFUNDS OF PREMIUMS.—Paragraph (1)(E) shall not apply to any refund on the death of the insured, or on a complete surrender or cancellation of the contract, which cannot exceed the aggregate premiums paid under the contract. Any refund on a complete surrender or cancellation of the contract shall be includible in gross income to the extent that any deduction or exclusion was allowable with respect to the premiums.

***

Appendix B

IRS Notices

Notice 2008-59 .... B-1
Notice 2008-52 .... B-20
Notice 2008-51 .... B-28
Notice 2007-22 .... B-37
Notice 2005-86 .... B-44
Notice 2005-83 .... B-47
Notice 2005-8 .... B-49
Notice 2004-79 .... B-52
Notice 2004-50 .... B-54
Notice 2004-43 .... B-85
Notice 2004-25 .... B-86
Notice 2004-23 .... B-88
Notice 2004-2 .... B-91

Notice 2008-59, 2008-29 I.R.B. 123

[**Summary:** The new guidance includes several topic areas, amplifying prior guidance including:

- *Who is an eligible individual.* Guidance topics regarding eligibility mostly center on the effect of other insurance or benefits. Some of these issues examined include the payment of HDHP premiums by a Health Reimbursement Account, disqualifying benefits paid or reimbursed before the HDHP minimum deductible is satisfied, Medicare benefits, Department of Veterans Affairs benefits, access to employer-provided free or low-cost health care, and family HDHP coverage for dependents with disqualifying coverage.

- *High-Deductible Health Plans (HDHPs).* The HDHP issues relate mostly to permitted deductibles and required coverage. The guidance examines the transition from family HDHP coverage to self-only HDHP coverage, and it discusses plans with higher deductibles for specific benefits, plans that restrict benefits to hospitalization or in-patient care, and expenses that apply toward meeting the deductible.

- *Contributions to HSAs.* The guidance discusses a wide variety of contribution issues including limits for individuals with family coverage and dependents with nonpermitted coverage, as well as limits for married couples with different types of HDHP coverage. It also examines rollovers, catch-up contributions for spouses, excess contributions due to errors, employer contributions to an HSA of the employee's spouse.
- *Distributions from HSAs.* Guidance topics for HSA distributions include debit cards, third-party authorization, payment of Medicare Part D premiums, Medicare premiums for a spouse, continuation coverage premiums, premiums for a dependent receiving unemployment benefits, and expenses for a child claimed as a dependent by another.
- *Prohibited transactions.* Prohibited transaction issues include borrowing from an HSA, loans from a trustee to an HSA, pledging HSA assets as security for a loan, and the consequences for entering into a prohibited transaction.
- *Establishing an HSA.* Topics related to establishing an HSA include determining when an HSA is established, and the establishment date for rollovers and for successive HSAs.]

PURPOSE

This notice provides guidance on Health Savings Accounts.

BACKGROUND

Section 1201 of the Medicare Prescription Drug, Improvement, and Modernization Act of 2003, Pub. L. No. 108-173, added § 223 to the Internal Revenue Code to permit eligible individuals to establish Health Savings Accounts (HSAs) for taxable years beginning after December 31, 2003. The Health Opportunity Patient Empowerment Act of 2006, Pub. L. No. 109-432 (HOPE Act), amended § 223 of the Code effective generally for taxable years after December 31, 2006.

Notice 2004-2, 2004-1 C.B. 269, and Notice 2004-50, 2004-2 C.B. 196, provide guidance on HSAs in question and answer format. This notice addresses additional questions relating to HSAs.

TABLE OF CONTENTS

The following is an outline of the questions and answers covered in this Notice.

DEFINITIONS

I. Eligible Individuals

Q&A-1. Payment of HDHP premiums by an HRA not disqualifying coverage

Q&A-2. Disqualifying benefits before HDHP minimum deductible satisfied

Q&A-3. Employer reimbursement of medical expenses before HDHP minimum deductible satisfied

Q&A-4. HDHP and HSA-compatible HRA or health FSA

Q&A-5. Eligible for Medicare Part D and contributions to HSA

Q&A-6. Enrolled in Medicare Part D and contributions to HSA

Q&A-7. HDHP and other high deductible coverage

Q&A-8. HDHP and HRA or health FSA that reimburses family members before minimum HDHP deductible satisfied

Q&A-9. Disregarded coverage or preventive care through Department of Veterans Affairs

Q&A-10. Access to health care that is free or at charges below fair market value

Q&A-11. Family HDHP coverage and dependents with disqualifying coverage

II. High Deductible Health PLANS

Q&A-12. Changing from family HDHP to self-only HDHP

Q&A-13. Different deductibles for specific benefits

Q&A-14. Benefits limited to hospitalization or in-patient care

Q&A-15. Expenses that apply towards meeting deductible

III. Contributions

Q&A-16. Contribution limits for individuals with family coverage and dependents with non-permitted coverage

Q&A-17. Contribution limits for married couples with different types of HDHP coverage

Q&A-18. Contributions for married couples who each have family HDHP coverage

Q&A-19. Contributions for months when covered by an HDHP

Q&A-20. Rollovers from an existing HSA to a new HSA

Q&A-21. Employer contributions for prior year

Q&A-22. Catch-up contributions for spouses

Q&A-23. Contributions to an employee who was never an eligible individual

Q&A-24. Error resulting in excess contributions

Q&A-25. Contributions to an employee who ceases to be an eligible individual

Q&A-26. Employer contributions to HSA of employee's spouse

IV. Distributions

Q&A-27. Debit cards

Q&A-28. Third party authorization

Q&A-29. Payment of Medicare Part D premiums

Q&A-30. Medicare premiums for spouse

Q&A-31. Continuation coverage premiums

Q&A-32. Premiums for a dependent receiving unemployment benefits

Q&A-33. Expenses for a child claimed as a dependent by another

V. Prohibited Transactions

Q&A-34. Borrowing from HSA

Q&A-35. Loan from trustee to HSA

Q&A-36. Pledging HSA as security for a loan

Q&A-37. Consequences for entering into a prohibited transaction

VI. Establishing an HSA

Q&A-38. When an HSA is established

Q&A-39. Not treating as established before state law considers HSA established

Q&A-40. Establishment date for rollovers

Q&A-41. Establishment date for successive HSAs

VII. Administration

Q&A-42. Reporting HSA administration and maintenance fees withdrawn by the trustee from an HSA

DEFINITIONS

The following definitions apply for purposes of this Notice.

Eligible individual means an individual who: (1) is covered by a high deductible health plan (HDHP); (2) is not also covered by any other health plan that is not an HDHP (with certain exceptions for plans providing certain types of limited coverage); (3) is not enrolled in Medicare; and (4) may not be claimed as a dependent on another person's tax return. See § 223(c)(1).

Limited-purpose health flexible spending arrangement (FSA) means a health FSA described in a cafeteria plan that only pays or reimburses permitted coverage benefits (as defined in § 223(c)(2)(C)), such as vision care, dental care or preventive care (as defined for purposes of § 223(c)(2)(C)). See Prop. Treas. Reg. § 1.125- 5(m)(3).

Limited-purpose health reimbursement arrangement (HRA) means an HRA that only pays or reimburses permitted coverage benefits (as defined in § 223(c)(2)(C)), such as vision care, dental care or preventive care. See Rev. Rul. 2004-45, 2004-1 C.B. 971.

Post-deductible health FSA means a health FSA in a cafeteria plan that only pays or reimburses medical expenses (as defined in § 213(d)) for preventive care or medical expenses incurred after the minimum annual HDHP deductible under § 223(c)(2)(A)(i) is satisfied. No medical expenses incurred before the annual HDHP deductible is satisfied may be reimbursed by a post-deductible FSA, regardless of whether the HDHP covers the expense or whether the deductible is later satisfied. See Prop. Treas. Reg. § 1.125-5(m)(4).

Post-deductible HRA means an HRA that only pays or reimburses medical expenses (as defined in § 213(d)) for preventive care or medical expenses incurred after the minimum annual HDHP deductible under § 223(c)(2)(A)(i) is satisfied. No medical expenses incurred before the annual HDHP deductible is satisfied may be reimbursed by a post-deductible HRA, regardless of whether the HDHP covers the expense or whether the deductible is later satisfied. See Rev. Rul. 2004-45.

QUESTIONS AND ANSWERS

I. Eligible Individuals

Q-1. Does an individual fail to be an eligible individual, as defined in § 223(c)(1), merely because the individual is covered by an HRA which, in addition to paying and reimbursing expenses for vision, dental and preventive care, pays and reimburses premiums for coverage by an accident and health plan?

A-1. No. An individual who is otherwise an eligible individual does not fail to be an eligible individual merely because the individual is covered by an HRA which, in addition to paying and reimbursing expenses for vision, dental and preventive care, pays and reimburses premiums for coverage by an accident and health plan. See Notice 2002-45, 2002-2 C.B. 93, and Rev. Rul. 2002-41, 2002-2 C.B. 75, for guidance on HRAs.

Example. In 2008, Employer A provides an HRA which reimburses any § 213(d) medical expense incurred by an employee, employee's spouse and dependents. For 2009, Employer A amends the HRA to limit its benefits to expenses for vision care, dental care, and preventive care and to pay the employee's share of the premiums for the employer-sponsored HDHP. During 2009, A's employees are otherwise eligible individuals.

For 2009, Employer A's employees are eligible individuals even if covered by the HRA.

Q-2. If an individual is covered under a plan that pays for medical expenses incurred before the minimum HDHP deductible is satisfied and the coverage is not permitted insurance under § 223(c)(3), disregarded coverage under § 223(c)(1)(B)(ii) or preventive care under § 223(c)(2)(C), is that individual an eligible individual as defined in § 223(c)(1)?

A-2. No. To be an eligible individual, an individual must be covered by an HDHP and by no other health plan that provides coverage other than disregarded coverage under § 223(c)(1)(B) or preventive care under § 223(c)(2)(C). See Rev. Rul. 2004-45.

Example. Individual B is covered by an HDHP. In addition, Individual B is covered by a "mini-med" plan that provides the following benefits: a fixed amount per day of hospitalization; a fixed amount per office visit with a physician; a fixed amount per out-patient treatment at a hospital; a fixed amount per ambulance use; and coverage for expenses relating to the treatment of a specified list of diseases.

Although the fixed amount per day of hospitalization benefit and specified disease benefit are allowed in addition to the HDHP as permitted insurance, the other benefits are not disregarded coverage or preventive care and, thus, Individual B is not an eligible individual who can contribute to an HSA.

Q-3. If an employee is covered by an HDHP and the employer pays or reimburses some or all of the employee's medical expenses incurred before the minimum HDHP deductible is satisfied (other than disregarded coverage under § 223(c)(1)(B) or preventive care under § 223(c)(2)(C)), is the employee an eligible individual under § 223(c)(1)?

A-3. No. To be an eligible individual, an individual must be covered by an HDHP and no other health plan except disregarded coverage or preventive care. If at any time, an employer pays or reimburses, directly or indirectly, all or part of employees' medical expenses below the minimum HDHP deductible under § 223(c)(2)(A) (other than for disregarded coverage or preventive care) the employees are not eligible to contribute to an HSA.

Example 1. For 2008, an HDHP with self-only coverage has an annual deductible of $2,500. The employee pays the first $250 of covered medical expenses below the deductible. The employer reimburses the next $1,350 of covered medical expenses below the deductible. The employee is responsible for the last $900 of covered medical expenses below the deductible. The $1,350 of medical expenses paid or reimbursed by the employer is not a contribution to an HSA and not disregarded coverage or preventive care.

An employee covered by this type of plan is not an eligible individual under § 223(c)(1) because the employee has disqualifying coverage from a plan that is not an HDHP.

Example 2. For 2008, an HDHP with self-only coverage has an annual deductible of $4,500. The employee pays the first $1,100 of covered medical expenses below the deductible. The employer reimburses the next $3,400 of covered medical expenses below the deductible. The $3,400 of medical expenses paid or reimbursed by the employer is not a contribution to an HSA and not disregarded coverage or preventive care.

An employee covered by this type of plan is an eligible individual under § 223(c)(1) because the employee is responsible for the minimum annual deductible under § 223(c)(2)(A).

Q-4(a). If an individual has family HDHP coverage under which benefits are paid once the entire family incurs a minimum amount of covered expenses (an umbrella deductible), but which also provides benefits to each individual if that individual incurs expenses in excess of the minimum family HDHP deductible in § 223(c)(2)(A)(i)(II) (the embedded individual deductible), does the individual fail to be an eligible individual merely because of the embedded individual deductible?

A-4(a). No, the individual does not fail to be an eligible individual merely because of an embedded individual deductible that is no less than the minimum family HDHP deductible in § 223(c)(2)(A)(i)(II).

Q-4(b). May a post-deductible HRA or post-deductible health FSA pay or reimburse qualified medical expenses of an individual with family HDHP coverage once the minimum annual deductible in § 223(c)(2)(A)(i)(II) for family HDHP coverage has been satisfied?

A-4(b). Yes, a post-deductible HRA or post-deductible health FSA may pay or reimburse qualified medical expenses of an individual with family HDHP coverage incurred at any time after the minimum annual deductible in § 223(c)(2)(A)(i)(II) for family HDHP coverage has been satisfied.

Example. In 2008, a family with family HDHP coverage has an umbrella deductible of $3,500, and an embedded individual deductible of $2,200. A post- deductible HRA reimburses § 213(d) medical expenses incurred after $2,200 of medical expenses covered by the HDHP have been incurred.

The covered individuals, if otherwise eligible, are eligible individuals.

Q-5. Does an individual fail to be an eligible individual merely because the individual is eligible for, but not enrolled in, Medicare Part D (or any other Medicare benefit)?

A-5. No. However, an individual is not an eligible individual under § 223(c)(1) in any month during which such individual is both eligible for benefits under Medicare and enrolled to receive benefits under Medicare. See also Notice 2004-50, Q&A-2 and 3, regarding Medicare Parts A and B.

Q-6. Does an individual fail to be an eligible individual merely because the individual is enrolled in Medicare Part D, or any other Medicare benefit?

A-6. Yes. Under § 223(b)(7), an individual who is enrolled in Medicare is not an eligible individual in any month during which the individual is enrolled in Medicare.

See also Q&A-29 of this Notice regarding paying Medicare premiums with funds in an HSA.

Q-7. May an otherwise eligible individual covered by an HDHP as defined in § 223(c)(2) also be covered by a health plan that is not an HDHP with a deductible equal to or greater than the statutory minimum HDHP deductible?

A-7. Yes, as long as the deductible of the other coverage equals or exceeds the statutory minimum HDHP deductible, the individual remains an eligible individual.

Example. An otherwise eligible individual has self-only HDHP coverage from January 1 through December 31, 2008, with a deductible of $2,500 and a lifetime limit on benefits of $1,000,000. In addition to the HDHP, the individual has self-only health plan coverage with a $1,000,000 deductible and a $2,000,000 life-time limit on benefits.

The individual is an eligible individual.

Q-8. Is an individual with family HDHP coverage who is also covered by a post-deductible HRA or post-deductible health FSA an eligible individual under § 223(c)(1) if the post-deductible HRA or post-deductible health FSA reimburses § 213(d) medical expenses of a spouse or dependent incurred before the minimum family HDHP deductible under § 223(c)(2)(A)(i)(II) has been satisfied?

A-8. No. If an individual with family HDHP coverage is covered by a post-deductible HRA or post-deductible health FSA that reimburses the § 213(d) medical expenses of any covered individual before the minimum family HDHP deductible under § 223(c)(2)(A)(i)(II) has been satisfied, that individual is not an eligible individual under § 223(c)(1).

Example 1. Carl, an employee, has family HDHP coverage. Carl's spouse and children (but not Carl) are also covered by non-HDHP family coverage provided by the spouse's employer. Carl, his spouse, and his children are also covered by a post-deductible health FSA. The health FSA pays for unreimbursed medical expenses of the spouse and child without regard to the satisfaction of the deductible of the family HDHP.

Because the health FSA covering Carl reimburses medical expenses before the minimum family HDHP deductible is satisfied, Carl is not an eligible individual.

Example 2. Same facts as Example 1, except the health FSA does not cover Carl. Carl is an eligible individual.

Q-9. Is an individual an eligible individual if he or she is eligible for medical benefits through the Department of Veterans Affairs (VA) but only receives medical care that is disregarded coverage or preventive care from the VA and is otherwise an eligible individual?

A-9. Yes. Although an individual actually receiving medical benefits from the VA at any time in the previous three months is generally not an eligible individual, this rule does not apply if the medical benefits consist solely of disregarded coverage or preventive care.

Q-10. Is an otherwise eligible individual who has access to free health care or health care at charges below fair market value from a clinic on an employer's premises an eligible individual under § 223(c)(1)?

A-10. An individual will not fail to be an eligible individual under § 223(c)(1)(A) merely because the individual has access to free health care or health care at charges below fair market value from an employer's on-site clinic if the clinic does not provide significant benefits in the nature of medical care (in addition to disregarded coverage or preventive care).

Example 1. A manufacturing plant operates an on-site clinic that provides the following free health care for employees: (1) physicals and immunizations; (2) injecting antigens provided by employees (e.g., performing allergy injections); (3) a variety of aspirin and other nonprescription pain relievers; and (4) treatment for injuries caused by accidents at the plant.

The clinic does not provide significant benefits in the nature of medical care in addition to disregarded coverage or preventive care.

Example 2. A hospital permits its employees to receive care at its facilities for all of their medical needs. For employees without health insurance, the hospital provides medical care at no charge. For employees who have health insurance, the hospital waives all deductibles and co-pays.

Because the hospital provides significant care in the nature of medical services, the hospital's employees are not eligible individuals under § 223(c)(1)(A).

Q-11. If an otherwise eligible individual under § 223(d)(1) has family HDHP coverage that covers dependents, and the dependents have other, disqualifying, non HDHP coverage, is the individual an eligible individual?

A-11. Yes. See also Rev. Rul. 2005-25. See Q&A-16 of this Notice regarding the contribution limit.

II. High Deductible Health Plans

Q-12. If an individual switches from a family HDHP to a self-only HDHP, does the individual fail to be an eligible individual during the period of self-only coverage merely because the self-only HDHP, for the purpose of satisfying the self-only deductible, takes into account expenses incurred while the individual had family HDHP coverage?

A-12. A self-only HDHP may use any reasonable method to allocate the covered expenses incurred during the period of family coverage for the purpose of satisfying the deductible for self-only coverage. For example, subject to state law requirements, the plan may allocate to the self-only deductible only the expenses incurred by that individual. Alternatively, the plan may allocate the expenses incurred during family HDHP coverage on a per-capita basis according to the number of persons covered by the family HDHP. If the family deductible was satisfied before the change to self-only coverage, the plan may also treat the individual as having satisfied the self-only deductible for that plan year. In all cases, each expense must be allocated on a reasonable and consistent basis and, except in the case of COBRA continuation coverage, each expense may be allocated to only one individual, and the plan year must be 12 months. For individuals switching from self-only HDHP coverage to family HDHP coverage, see Notice 2004-50, Q&A-23. If COBRA continuation coverage is required to be made available, the HDHP must comply with the requirements of Q&A-2 of § 54.4980B-5 for those individuals receiving COBRA continuation coverage.

Example 1. Employer D offers its employees a calendar year health plan otherwise qualifying as an HDHP. Employee E and E's spouse are covered by Employer D's family coverage HDHP with a $6,000 deductible. Employee E incurs $2,500 in covered expenses; Employee E's spouse incurs $2,000 in covered expenses. On July 1, Employee E and Employee E's spouse each change to self-only HDHP coverage with a $3,000 deductible and Employee E's spouse is no longer covered under the plan.

For the period from July 1 through December 31, the plan may credit Employee E's self-only deductible with either: (1) $2,500 (the actual amount of expenses Employee E incurred under family coverage), or (2) $2,250 ($4,500/2), Employee E's per-capita share of expenses incurred by the two individuals covered by family coverage. In this case the HDHP must credit Employee E's spouse with at least $2,000 toward the satisfaction of the deductible; the HDHP also complies with the requirements of Q&A-2 of § 54.4980B-5 by crediting Employee E's spouse with $2,250 toward the satisfaction of the deductible.

Example 2. The same facts as Example 1, except that Employee E's spouse is entitled to elect, and elects, COBRA continuation coverage under the HDHP. In this case, the HDHP must comply with the requirements of Q&A-2 of § 54.4980B-5.

Example 3. The same facts as Example 2, except that the amounts incurred by Employee E and Employee E's spouse are reversed: Employee E incurred $2,000 of medical expenses and Employee E's spouse incurred $2,500.

If the HDHP credits Employee E's spouse with $2,250 toward the satisfaction of the deductible, this would not satisfy the requirements of Q&A-2 of § 54.4980B-5. Employee E's spouse must be credited with at least $2,500 toward the satisfaction of the deductible to comply with the requirements of Q&A-2 of § 54.4980B-5.

Example 4. Employer F offers its employees a calendar year health plan, otherwise qualifying as an HDHP. As of January 1, 2008, Employee G, and Employee G's spouse and child are covered by Employer F's family coverage HDHP with a $6,000 deductible. From January 1 through September 30, 2008, Employee G incurs $2,500 in covered expenses; Employee G's spouse incurs

$500 in covered expenses, and Employee G's child incurs $3,000 in covered expenses. Employee G and spouse are divorced, effective October 1, 2008. On that date, Employee G changes to self-only HDHP coverage with a $3,000 deductible and the child and ex-spouse elect COBRA continuation coverage in Employer F's family HDHP coverage.

The plan may (1) credit Employee G's individual deductible with $2,500 and reduce the expenses allocated to the child and ex-spouse in family coverage by $2,500; or (2) credit Employee G's self-only deductible with $2,000 and reduce the expenses allocated to the child and ex-spouse by $2,000 (allocating one-third of the $6,000 in expenses to Employee G's individual deductible and two-thirds of the $6,000 in expenses to the former spouse and child remaining in family coverage). Coverage of the child and former spouse is COBRA continuation coverage. However, if the pro rata allocation of expenses of the family to the child and former spouse were less than the actual expenses incurred by the child and former spouse, then allocation of only the ratable share of the family expenses would not comply with the requirements of Q&A-2 of § 54.4980B-5; (3) credit Employee G with no expenses and continue to credit the child and ex-spouse with all expenses incurred under family coverage; or (4) treat Employee G as having satisfied the $3,000 individual deductible while treating the former spouse and child as having satisfied the $6,000 family deductible.

Q-13. If a health plan imposes a separate or higher deductible for specific benefits, are amounts paid by covered individuals to satisfy the separate or higher deductible treated as out-of-pocket expenses under § 223(c)(2)(A)?

A-13. If significant other benefits remain available under the plan in addition to the specific benefits subject to the separate or higher deductible, amounts paid to satisfy the separate or higher deductible are not treated as out-of-pocket expenses under § 223(c)(2)(A).

Example. In 2008, a self-only health plan with a $3,000 deductible imposes a lifetime limit of $1,000,000 on reimbursements for covered benefits. The plan pays 100 percent of covered expenses after the $3,000 deductible is satisfied. Although the plan provides benefits for substance abuse treatment, the substance abuse treatment benefits are subject to a separate $5,000 deductible, and these benefits are limited to $10,000, after the separate deductible is satisfied.

The plan is an HDHP and no expense incurred by a covered individual other than the $3,000 general deductible is treated as an out-of-pocket expense under § 223(c)(2)(A).

Q-14. If a health plan meeting the minimum deductible of § 223(c)(2)(A) restricts benefits to expenses for hospitalization or in-patient care, is the plan an HDHP?

A-14. No. A plan must provide significant benefits to be an HDHP. A plan may also be designed with reasonable benefit restrictions limiting the plan's covered benefits. See Notice 2004-50, Q&A-15. However, if a plan only provides benefits for expenses of hospitalization or in-patient care, significant other benefits do not remain available under the plan in addition to the benefits subject to exclusion. Therefore, any expenses incurred by a covered individual after satisfying the deductible are treated as out-of-pocket expenses under § 223(c)(2)(A).

Example. In 2008, a self-only health plan with a $2,000 deductible includes a $3,000,000 lifetime limit on covered benefits. Generally, the plan only provides benefits for medical services provided while a covered individual is admitted to a hospital as an overnight patient or provided at a "same day" surgery facility. A same day surgery facility does not include a hospital emergency room, a trauma center, a physician's office or a clinic. Covered medical services for individuals admitted to a hospital or same day surgery facility include room accommodations, miscellaneous medical services and supplies necessary for treatment, primary surgery, pathology charges and the administration of anesthesia while at the hospital or center, and charges by the primary attending physician for one visit per day while at the hospital. In addition, the plan provides: an organ transplant benefit, a hospice care benefit, and home health care visits. The home health care benefit is subject to a 60 visit per year limit, and must be in connection with the hospitalization. The plan also pays for certain preventive care screening and ambulance service. The plan pays for no visits to physician's offices nor any other outpatient care other than those noted above. The maximum dollar amount that the covered individual pays for covered benefits under the plan for 2008 is $5,500.

The restriction of benefits to medical services provided while the covered individual is admitted to a hospital or at a same day surgery facility is not reasonable because significant other benefits do not remain available under the plan after application of the restriction. Any expenses incurred by a covered individual for outpatient care or visits to physician's offices are treated as out-of-pocket expenses under § 223(c)(2)(A). Because the plan maximum for amounts paid by a covered individual does not restrict payments for those out-of-pocket expenses, the plan fails to qualify as an HDHP.

Q-15. What medical expenses may be taken into account in determining when the HDHP deductible is satisfied for purposes of a post-deductible HRA or post- deductible health FSA?

A-15. Only medical expenses described in § 213(d) and covered by the HDHP may be taken into account in determining whether the HDHP deductible, or the minimum deductible in § 223(c)(2)(A)(i), has been satisfied. For example, if the HDHP does not cover chiropractic care, expenses incurred for chiropractic care do not count toward satisfying the HDHP deductible or the minimum deductible in § 223(c)(2)(A)(i). For self-only HDHP coverage, only the covered medical expenses of the covered individual count toward satisfying the HDHP deductible or the minimum deductible in § 223(c)(2)(A)(i)(I).

Example. In 2008, an individual, spouse and child have family HDHP coverage with a $2,500 deductible. The HDHP does not provide benefits for vision or dental care. They are also covered by a combination limited purpose/post-deductible HRA that pays or reimburses § 213(d) medical expenses incurred by each family member after the family incurs $2,500 in covered medical expenses, and pays or reimburses vision and dental expenses before and after the HDHP deductible is satisfied. On February 15, 2008, the family incurs $2,500 in vision and dental expenses that are reimbursed by the HRA. On March 17, 2008, the family then incurs $400 in expenses covered by the HDHP (but for the deductible). The family must incur an additional $2,100 in covered medical expenses before the HDHP deductible is satisfied.

The HRA may not reimburse the family for the $400 of expenses because the family had not incurred $2,500 in covered expenses when the $400 was incurred.

III. Contributions

Q-16. How do the maximum annual HSA contribution limits apply to an eligible individual with family HDHP coverage for the entire year if the family HDHP covers spouses or dependent children who also have coverage by a non-HDHP, Medicare, or Medicaid?

A-16. The eligible individual may contribute the § 223(b)(2)(B) statutory maximum for family coverage. Other coverage of dependent children or spouses does not affect the individual's contribution limit, except that if the spouse is not an otherwise eligible individual, no part of the HSA contribution can be allocated to the spouse.

Q-17. How do the maximum annual HSA contribution limits apply to a married couple if both spouses are eligible individuals and one spouse has self-only HDHP coverage and the other spouse has family HDHP coverage?

A-17. The maximum annual HSA contribution limit for a married couple if one spouse has family HDHP coverage and the other spouse has self-only HDHP coverage is the § 223(b)(2)(B) statutory maximum for family coverage. The contribution limit is divided between the spouses by agreement. See § 223(b)(5) and Notice 2004-50, Q&A-32. This is the result regardless of whether the family HDHP coverage includes the spouse with self-only HDHP coverage. See Notice 2004-2, Q&A-15. If only one spouse is an eligible individual, see Rev. Rul. 2005-25.

Example. For 2008, H and W are married. Both are 40 years old. H and W are otherwise eligible individuals. H has self-only HDHP coverage. W has an HDHP with family coverage for W and their two children.

The combined contribution limit for H and W is $5,800, which is the § 223(b)(2)(B) statutory contribution limit for 2008. H and W divide the $5,800 contribution limit between them by agreement.

Q-18. How do the maximum annual HSA contribution limits apply to a married couple if both spouses are eligible individuals and each spouse has family HDHP coverage that does not cover the other spouse?

A-18. The maximum HSA contribution limit for a married couple where both spouses have family HDHP coverage is the § 223(b)(2)(B) statutory maximum. This rule applies regardless of whether each spouse's family coverage covers the other spouse. The contribution limit is divided between the spouses by agreement.

Example. In 2008, H, who is 37, and W, who is 32, are married with two dependent children. H has HDHP family coverage for H and their two children with an annual deductible of $3,000. W has HDHP family coverage for W and their two children with a deductible of $3,500.

The combined contribution limit for H and W is $5,800, the maximum annual contribution limit. H and W divide the $5,800 contribution limit between them by agreement.

Q-19. May an individual who ceases to be an eligible individual during a year still contribute to an HSA with respect to the months of the year when the individual was an eligible individual?

A-19. Yes. An individual who ceases to be an eligible individual may, until the date for filing the return (without extensions) for the year, make HSA contributions with respect to the months of the year when the individual was an eligible individual.

Example. J has a self-only HDHP, and is an eligible individual for the first four months of 2008. J has until April 15, 2009 (the date for filing the 2008 return, without extensions) to contribute 4/12 x $2,900 ($967) to an HSA.

Q-20. May an individual who is not an eligible individual make a rollover contribution from his or her existing HSA to a new HSA?

A-20. Yes.

Q-21. May employer contributions to employees' HSAs made between January 1 and the date for filing the employee's return, without extensions, be allocated to the prior year?

A-21. Yes. For employer contributions (including salary reduction contributions) made between January 1 and the date for filing the employees' returns without extension, the employer must notify the HSA trustee or custodian if the contributions relate to the prior year. The employer must also inform the employee of the designation. However, the contributions designated as made for the prior year are still reported in box 12 with code W on the employees' Form W-2 for the year in which the contributions are actually made.

Example. In January 2009, Employer K contributes $500 to each employee's HSA and notifies the HSA trustee (and provides a statement to the employees) that the contributions are for 2008. Subsequently, in 2009, Employer K contributes $250 to each employee's HSA on March 31, June 30, September 30 and December 31. For each employee whose HSA received these contributions, Employer K reports a total contribution of $1,500 in box 12 with code W on the Form W-2 for 2009.

In completing the Form 8889 for 2008, to compute Employer K's contributions, the employees add the $500 to any employer contributions reported in box 12, code W on the 2008 Form W-2. In completing the Form 8889 for 2009, the employees subtract the $500 from the box 12 code W amount on the 2009 Form W-2 and add to the remaining $1,000 any contributions for 2009 made by Employer K between January 1, 2009 and his or her filing date without extensions. See Instructions to Form 8889.

Q-22. If a husband and wife are each eligible to make catch-up contributions under § 223(b)(3), must each spouse contribute their catch-up contributions to their own HSA?

A-22. Yes. An individual who is eligible to make catch-up contributions may only make such contributions to his or her own HSA. See also Notice 2004-50, Q&A-32. If both spouses are eligible for the catch-up contribution, each spouse must make catch-up contributions to his or her own HSA.

Q-23. If an employer contributes to the account of an employee who was never an eligible individual, can the employer recoup the amounts?

A-23. If the employee was never an eligible individual under § 223(c), then no HSA ever existed and the employer may correct the error. At the employer's option, the employer may request that the financial institution return the amounts to the employer. However, if the employer does not recover the amounts by the end of the taxable year, then the amounts must be included as gross income and wages on the employee's Form W-2 for the year during which the employer made the contributions.

Example 1. In February 2008, Employer L contributed $500 to an account of Employee M, reasonably believing the account to be an HSA. In July 2008, Employer L first learned that Employee M's account is not an HSA because Employee M has never been an eligible individual under § 223(c).

Employer L may either request that the financial institution holding Employee M's account return the balance of the account ($500 plus earnings less administration fees directly paid from the account) to Employer L. If Employer L does not receive the balance of the account, Employer L must include the amounts in Employee M's gross income and wages on his Form W-2 for 2008.

Example 2. The same facts as Example 1, except Employer L first discovers the mistake in July 2009. Employer L issues a corrected 2008 Form W-2 for Employee M, and Employee M files an amended income tax return for 2008.

Q-24. If an employer contributes amounts to an employee's HSA that exceed the maximum annual contribution allowed in § 223(b) due to an error, can the employer recoup the excess amounts?

A-24. If the employer contributes amounts to an employee's HSA that exceed the maximum annual contribution allowed in § 223(b) due to an error, the employer may correct the error. In that case, at the employer's option, the employer may request that the financial institution return the excess amounts to the employer. Alternatively, if the employer does not recover the amounts, then the amounts must be included as gross income and wages on the employee's Form W-2 for the year during which the employer made contributions. If, however, amounts contributed are less than or equal to the maximum annual contribution allowed in § 223(b), the employer may not recoup any amount from the employee's HSA.

Q-25. If an employer contributes to the HSA of an employee who ceases to be an eligible individual during a year, can the employer recoup amounts that the employer contributed after the employee ceased to be an eligible individual?

A-25. No. Employers generally cannot recoup amounts from an HSA other than as discussed above in Q&A-23 and Q&A-24. See Notice 2004-50, Q&A-82.

Example. Employee N was an eligible individual on January 1, 2008. On April 1, 2008, Employee N is no longer an eligible individual because Employee N's spouse enrolled in a general purpose health FSA that covers all family members. Employee N first realizes that he is no longer eligible on July 17, 2008, at which time Employee N informs Employer O to cease HSA contributions.

Employer O's contributions into Employee N's HSA between April 1, 2008 and July 17, 2008 cannot be recouped by Employer O because Employee N has a nonforfeitable interest in his HSA. Employee N is responsible for determining if the contributions exceed the maximum annual contribution limit in § 223(b), and for withdrawing the excess contribution and the income attributable to the excess contribution and including both in gross income.

Q-26. Are employer contributions to the HSA of an employee's spouse (who is not an employee of this employer) excluded from the employee's gross income and wages?

A-26. No. The exclusion under § 106(d)(1) is limited to contributions by an employer to the HSA of an employee who is an eligible individual. Any contribution by an employer to the HSA of a non-employee (e.g., a spouse of an employee or any other individual), including salary reduction amounts made through a § 125 cafeteria plan, must be included in the gross income and wages of the employee.

IV. Distributions

Q-27. May an HSA be administered through a debit card that restricts payments and reimbursements to health care?

A-27. Yes, if the funds in the HSA are otherwise readily available. For example, in addition to the restricted debit card, the HSA account beneficiary must also be able to access the funds other than by purchasing health care with the debit card, such as through online transfers, withdrawals from automatic teller machines or check writing. Employers must notify employees that other access to the funds is available. See also Notice 2004-50, Q&A-77 and 79.

Q-28. May an HSA account beneficiary authorize someone else to withdraw funds from his or her HSA?

A-28. Yes. Although an HSA is an individual account, an HSA account beneficiary can designate other individuals to withdraw funds pursuant to the procedures of the trustee or custodian of the HSA. Distributions are subject to tax if they are not used to pay for qualified medical expenses for the HSA account beneficiary, the account beneficiary's spouse, or dependents. See Notice 2004-2, Q&A25. But see Q&A-34, Q&A-35, and Q&A-36 of this Notice regarding prohibited transactions.

Q-29. If the account beneficiary has attained age 65, are Medicare Part D premiums qualified medical expenses?

A-29. Yes. If an account beneficiary has attained age 65, premiums for Medicare Part D for the account beneficiary, the account beneficiary's spouse, or the account beneficiary's dependents are qualified medical expenses. See also Notice 2004-2, Q&A-27, and Notice 2004-50, Q&A-4 and 45, regarding Medicare Parts A and B. See Q&A-6 of this Notice regarding eligibility of Medicare enrollees to contribute to an HSA.

Q-30. If the account beneficiary has not attained age 65, are Medicare premiums for coverage of an account beneficiary's spouse (who has attained age 65) qualified medical expenses?

A-30. No. If the account beneficiary has not attained age 65, Medicare premiums are generally not qualified medical expenses.

Q-31. Are premiums for continuation coverage required under Federal law for the spouse or dependent of an account beneficiary qualified medical expenses?

A-31. Yes. Although qualified medical expenses generally exclude payments for insurance, § 223(d)(2)(C)(i) provides an exception for the expense of coverage under a health plan during any period of continuation coverage.

Q-32. Are premiums for health coverage for a spouse or dependent during a period when the spouse or dependent is receiving unemployment compensation under any Federal or state law qualified medical expenses?

A-32. Yes. Although qualified medical expenses generally exclude payments for insurance, § 223(d)(2)(C)(iii) provides an exception for the expense of coverage under a health plan during a period in which an individual is receiving unemployment compensation under any Federal or state law.

Q-33. Do qualified medical expenses for HSA purposes include the § 213(d) medical expenses incurred by an account beneficiary's child who is claimed as a dependent by the account beneficiary's former spouse?

A-33. Yes. See §§ 152(e) and 213(d)(5).

V. Prohibited Transactions

Q-34. If an account beneficiary borrows funds from his or her HSA, is this a prohibited transaction under § 4975?

A-34. Yes. An HSA is a plan as defined in § 4975(e)(1)(E). An HSA account beneficiary is a disqualified person under § 4975(e)(2). A loan or extension of credit between a plan and a disqualified person is a prohibited transaction. Section 4975(c)(1)(B). Thus, any direct or indirect extension of credit between the account beneficiary and his or her HSA is a prohibited transaction.

Q-35. If a trustee of an HSA lends money to the HSA, is this a prohibited transaction under § 4975?

A-35. Yes. An HSA is a plan as defined in § 4975(e)(1)(E). An HSA trustee is a disqualified person under § 4975(e)(2). A loan or extension of credit between a plan and a disqualified person is a prohibited transaction. Section 4975(c)(1)(B). Thus, any direct or indirect extension of credit between the HSA trustee and the HSA is a prohibited transaction.

Example 1. Bank X is the trustee of an HSA. Bank X extends a line of credit to the HSA. The line of credit is a prohibited transaction under § 4975.

Example 2. Bank Y is the trustee of an HSA. The account beneficiary accesses the funds in the HSA through a debit card. In addition, Bank Y extends a line of credit to the account beneficiary, which is not secured by the account beneficiary's HSA, and amounts in the HSA cannot be used to repay the line of credit.

The line of credit is not a prohibited transaction.

Q-36. If an account beneficiary pledges his or her HSA as security for a loan, is this a prohibited transaction under § 4975?

A-36. Yes. An HSA is a plan as defined in § 4975(e)(1)(E). An HSA account beneficiary is a disqualified person under § 4975(e)(2). A loan or extension of credit between a plan and a disqualified person is a prohibited transaction. Section 4975(c)(1)(B). Thus, any direct or indirect extension of credit between the account beneficiary and his or her HSA is a prohibited transaction.

Example. Individual P is an account beneficiary of an HSA. Bank Z is the trustee of the HSA. Bank Z extends to Individual P a line of credit secured by the HSA.

The pledge securing the line of credit is a prohibited transaction under § 4975.

Q-37. What are the consequences if account beneficiaries or other disqualified persons enter into a prohibited transaction with an HSA?

A-37. Section 223(e)(2) provides that rules similar to the rules of §§ 408(e)(2) and (4) apply to HSAs. Therefore, account beneficiaries may not enter into "prohibited transactions" with an HSA (e.g., the account beneficiary may not sell, exchange, or lease property, borrow or lend money, pledge the HSA, furnish goods, services or facilities, transfer to or use by or for the benefit of himself/herself any assets of the HSA, etc.). If an account beneficiary engages in a prohibited transaction with his or her HSA the sanction, in general, is disqualification of the account. Thus, the HSA stops being an HSA as of the first day of the taxable year of the prohibited transaction. The assets of the beneficiary's account are deemed distributed, and the appropriate taxes, including the 10 percent additional tax under § 223(f)(4) for distributions not used for qualified medical expenses, apply.

If the employer sponsoring the account (or other disqualified person) is the party engaging in a prohibited transaction, then the employer (or other party) is liable for the excise tax, but the account beneficiary is not.

VI. Establishing an HSA

Q-38. When is an HSA established?

A-38. An HSA is an exempt trust established through a written governing instrument under state law. Section 223(d)(1). State trust law determines when an HSA is established. Most state trust laws require that for a trust to exist, an asset must be held in trust; thus, most state trust laws require that a trust must be funded to be established. Whether the account beneficiary's signature is required to establish the trust also depends on state law.

Q-39. May a trustee treat an HSA as established before the date of establishment determined under state law, such as the date when HDHP coverage began?

A-39. No. But see Q&A-40 and Q&A-41 of this Notice concerning the establishment date for HSAs in connection with rollovers, or where a previous HSA was established.

Q-40. When is an HSA established if the funds in the HSA were rolled over or transferred from an Archer MSA or another HSA?

A-40. An HSA that is funded by amounts rolled over or transferred from an Archer MSA or another HSA is established as of the date the prior account was established. Qualified HSA distributions under § 106(e) or qualified HSA funding distributions under § 408(d)(9) do not affect the HSA establishment date. See also Notice 2004-2, Q&A-23.

Example. An account beneficiary established an Archer MSA on October 17, 2000. On May 13, 2004, the account beneficiary rolled the entire amount held in the Archer MSA into an HSA. On January 1, 2008, the account beneficiary has the HSA trustee make a direct transfer of the entire HSA to an HSA with a new trustee.

The establishment date of the HSA with the new trustee is October 17, 2000.

Q-41. On what date is an HSA established if the account beneficiary had previously established an HSA?

A-41. If an account beneficiary establishes an HSA, and later establishes another HSA, any later HSA is deemed to be established when the first HSA was established if the account beneficiary has an HSA with a balance greater than zero at any time during the 18-month period ending on the date the later HSA is established.

Example 1. An account beneficiary established an HSA on March 1, 2007. On June 15, 2007, he withdrew all the funds from the HSA, resulting in a zero balance. On November 21, 2008, he established a second HSA. Because the second HSA was established within 18 months of June 15, 2007, the second HSA is deemed to be established on March 1, 2007.

Example 2. The same facts as Example 1, except that the account beneficiary establishes a third HSA on January 1, 2009. On that date, the second HSA has a balance greater than zero.

The third HSA is deemed to be established on March 1, 2007.

VII. Administration

Q-42. How are HSA administration and maintenance fees withdrawn by the trustee from an HSA reported by the trustee?

A-42. HSA administration and maintenance fees withdrawn by the trustee are reflected on the Form 5498-SA in the fair market value of the HSA at the end of the taxable year. These fees are not reported as distributions from the HSA.

EFFECT ON OTHER DOCUMENTS

Notice 2004-2, 2004-1 C.B. 269, Notice 2004-50, 2004-2 C.B. 196, and Notice 2007-22, 2007-10 I.R.B. 670, are amplified.

DRAFTING INFORMATION ***

Notice 2008-52 (2008-25 I.R.B. 1166)

[**Summary:** The IRS has issued guidance regarding the repeal of the HDHP deductible limit on HSA contributions.]

This notice provides guidance on contributions to Health Savings Accounts (HSAs) under amendments to the Internal Revenue Code by §§ 303 and 305 of the Health Opportunity Patient Empowerment Act of 2006 (the Act) included in the Tax Relief and Health Care Act of 2006, enacted December 20, 2006, Pub. L. No. 109-432.

ANNUAL HSA CONTRIBUTION LIMIT

HDHP deductible limit on annual HSA contributions repealed

For 2004 through 2006, the maximum annual HSA contribution was the lesser of (1) the annual deductible under the high deductible health plan (HDHP) or (2) the statutory maximum under § 223(b)(2)(B). See Notice 2004-2, 2004-1 C.B. 269, Q&A-12. Section 303 of the Act repeals the limit on annual HSA contributions based on the amount of the deductible under the HDHP. For 2007 and later years, the indexed maximum HSA contribution under § 223(b)(2)(A) (for self-only HDHP coverage) and § 223(b)(2)(B) (for family HDHP coverage) determines the contribution limit, without regard to an individual's HDHP deductible. Thus, for 2008, the maximum annual HSA contribution is $2,900 for individuals who have self-only HDHP coverage and $5,800 for individuals who have family HDHP coverage.

Annual HSA contribution limits for 2007 and later years

Section 305 of the Act adds § 223(b)(8) which provides that if an individual is an eligible individual on the first day of the last month of the individual's taxable year (December 1 for calendar year taxpayers), the individual's maximum HSA contribution for the year is the greater of the following:

(1) The sum of the limits determined separately for each month under § 223(b)(2), based on eligibility and HDHP coverage on the first day of each month, plus catch-up contributions for each month, if applicable (see sum of the monthly contribution limits discussion below), or

(2) The maximum annual HSA contribution under § 223(b)(2)(A) or § 223(b)(2)(B) based on the individual's HDHP coverage (self-only or family) on the first day of the last month of the individual's taxable year, plus catch-up contributions under § 223(b)(3), if applicable (see full contribution rule under § 223(b)(8) discussion below).

A testing period applies to the full contribution rule (see discussion of the testing period below). If an individual is not an eligible individual on the first day of the last month of the individual's taxable year (December 1 for calendar year taxpayers), the individual's maximum HSA contribution for the year is determined under the sum of the monthly contribution limits rule under § 223(b)(2). See Example 6 below.

Sum of the monthly contribution limits

Eligible individuals (as defined in § 223(c)(1)) may contribute to HSAs. See Notice 2004-2, Q&A-2; Notice 2004-50, 2004-2 C.B. 196, Q&A-2, 3. Under § 223(b)(1) and (2), the maximum annual contribution to an HSA is the sum of the contribution limits determined separately for each month, based on eligibility and health plan coverage on the first day of the month. For this purpose, the monthly limit is 1/12 of the indexed amount provided under § 223(b)(2)(A) for self-only coverage ($2,900 for 2008) and under § 223(b)(2)(B) for family coverage ($5,800 for 2008). In addition, the maximum HSA contribution is increased by an additional contribution amount (catch-up amount) for individuals age 55 or older as of the last day of the calendar year who are not enrolled in Medicare. The catch-up contribution is also computed on a monthly basis. Section 223(b)(2).

Full contribution rule

New § 223(b)(8)(A) treats an individual who is an eligible individual on the first day of the last month of the taxable year as having been an eligible individual for the entire year and may increase, but not decrease, the contribution limit for such an individual. Thus, in order to make a full contribution for the year under § 223(b)(8), a taxpayer must be an eligible individual on the first day of the last month of his or her taxable year (December 1 for calendar year taxpayers). The eligible individual is also treated as enrolled in the same HDHP coverage (i.e., self-only or family coverage) as he or she has on the first day of the last month of the year. For example, if an individual first becomes HSA-eligible on December 1, 2007, and has family HDHP coverage, he or she is treated as an eligible individual and having family HDHP coverage for all twelve months in 2007. This full contribution rule also applies to catch-up contributions. The full contribution rule applies without regard to whether the individual was an eligible individual for the entire year, had HDHP coverage for the entire year, or had disqualifying non-HDHP coverage for part of the year. However, a testing period applies for purposes of the full contribution rule.

The testing period

The testing period applies to an individual who is an eligible individual on the first day of the last month of the taxable year. The testing period begins on the first day of the last month of the taxable year and ends on the last day of the 12th month following that month. Thus, for a calendar year taxpayer, the testing period is from December 1 of the current year to December 31 of the following year. Section 223(b)(8)(B)(iii). For 2008 HSA contributions, the testing period for calendar year taxpayers begins in December 2008 and ends on December 31, 2009.

Failure to remain an eligible individual during the testing period

If an individual who is an eligible individual on the first day of the last month of the taxable year contributes an amount to his or her HSA greater than the sum of the monthly contribution limits under § 223(b)(1) and (2), and at any time during the testing period, the individual ceases to meet all requirements to be an eligible individual, an amount is included in the individual's gross income and subject to an additional 10 percent tax, unless the failure is due to disability (as defined in § 72(m)(7)) or death.

The amount that is included in the individual's gross income is computed by subtracting the sum of the monthly contribution limits that the individual would otherwise have been entitled to under § 223(b)(1) and (2) from the amount actually contributed. Section 223(b)(8)(B). It is not necessary to distribute this amount from the HSA, and there may be additional adverse tax consequences from such a distribution. See discussion below on distributions not used for qualified medical expenses. Withdrawing this amount from the HSA will not prevent the inclusion of the amount in income or the additional 10 percent tax. However, earnings on the amount are not included in gross income or subject to the 10 percent additional tax, so long as the earnings remain in the HSA or are used for qualified medical expenses.

Unlike the additional 10 percent tax under § 223(f)(4)(A), the additional 10 percent tax under § 223(b)(8)(B)(i)(II) applies regardless of the age of the account beneficiary (i.e., even after age 65).

To remain an eligible individual during the testing period, an individual is not required to keep the same level of HDHP coverage during the testing period. Thus, changing from family HDHP coverage to single HDHP coverage during the testing period does not result in inclusion of amounts in gross income or an additional 10 percent tax. See Examples 8 and 14 below.

Excise tax on excess contributions

Section 4973 imposes a six percent excise tax for each taxable year on HSA contributions in excess of the maximum contribution limit for the year (excess contributions). If the excess contributions for the year and the net income attributable to such excess contributions are withdrawn from the HSA before the last day (with extensions) for filing the federal income return for the taxable year, the amount is not subject to the excise tax for that year. However, an amount included in gross income under § 223(b)(8)(B) because an individual failed to remain an eligible individual during the testing period is not an excess contribution and § 4973 does not apply to this amount. For this reason, the amount cannot be withdrawn under the excess contribution rules.

HSA distributions not used for qualified medical expenses

An HSA distribution not used for qualified medical expenses (as defined in § 223(d)(2)) is included in gross income under § 223(f)(2) and is subject to the additional 10 percent tax under § 223(f)(4) (with certain exceptions), regardless of whether the amount contributed to the HSA under the full contribution limit is included in the account beneficiary's income and subject to the additional tax under § 223(b)(8)(B)(i). See Notice 2007-22, 2007-10 I.R.B. 670 regarding consequences of distributions from HSAs. See Example 9 below.

Establishing HSAs

An individual may establish an HSA at any time on or after the date the individual becomes HSA-eligible. Contributions for the taxable year can be made in one or more payments, at any time prior to the time (without extensions) for filing the individual's federal income tax return for the taxable year. An individual who becomes an eligible individual after January 1 may make the maximum contribution to an HSA on the first day he or she is an eligible individual. Notice 2004-2, Q&A-21. In that case, the individual's contribution is based on the individual's expected coverage on the first day of the last month of his or her taxable year. But see testing period rules above.

EXAMPLES

The following examples illustrate these rules. It is assumed in the examples that the taxable year of all individuals is the calendar year, and that, for purposes of § 223(b)(8)(B)(ii), no individuals are disabled within the meaning of § 72(m)(7) unless otherwise stated.

Example 1. Individual A, age 53, enrolls in family HDHP coverage on December 1, 2008 and is otherwise an eligible individual on that date. A is not an eligible individual in any other month in 2008.

A is an eligible individual with family HDHP coverage on December 1, 2008. A's full contribution limit under § 223(b)(8) for 2008 is $5,800. The sum of the monthly contribution limits is $483.33 (1/12 × $5,800). A's annual contribution limit for 2008 is $5,800, the greater of $5,800 or $483.33

Example 2. Same facts as Example 1, except that A contributes $5,800 to his HSA on December 1, 2008 and ceases to be an eligible individual in June 2009.

The testing period for 2008 HSA contributions ends on December 31, 2009. In 2009, A ceases to be an eligible individual during the testing period. In 2009, A must include in gross income $5,316.67, the amount contributed to the HSA for 2008 minus the sum of the monthly contribution limits ($5,800.00 – $483.33). In addition, the 10 percent additional tax ($532) in § 223(b)(8)(B)(i) applies to the amount included in gross income.

Example 3. Individual B, age 39, enrolls in self-only HDHP coverage on January 1, 2008 and is an eligible individual on that date. B's coverage changes to family HDHP coverage on November 1, 2008 and B retains family HDHP coverage through December 31, 2008. B is an eligible individual from January 1, 2008 through December 31, 2008 and remains an eligible individual through December 31, 2009.

B is an eligible individual with family HDHP coverage on December 1, 2008. B's full contribution limit under § 223(b)(8) for 2008 is $5,800. B's sum of the monthly contribution limits is $3,383.34 ((2/12 × $5,800) + (10/12 × $2,900)). B's annual contribution limit for 2008 is $5,800, the greater of $5,800 or $3,383.34.

Example 4. In 2007, Individual C, age 47, is covered by a general purpose health FSA with a grace period ending March 15, 2008. C enrolls in family HDHP coverage on January 1, 2008. C becomes an eligible individual on April 1, 2008 and remains an eligible individual through December 31, 2009. On April 2, 2008, C contributes $5,800 to his HSA for 2008.

C is an eligible individual with family HDHP coverage on December 1, 2008. C's full contribution limit under § 223(b)(8) for 2008 is $5,800. C's sum of the monthly contribution limits is $4,350 (9/12 × $5,800). C's annual contribution limit for 2008 is $5,800, the greater of $5,800 or $4,350. The testing period for 2008 ends on December 31, 2009. Because C is an eligible individual during the testing period, no amount of the $5,800 contribution is included in C's gross income and C is not subject to the 10 percent additional tax.

Example 5. Individual D, age 57, enrolls in family HDHP coverage on December 1, 2008 and is an eligible individual on that date. D was not an eligible individual in any other month in 2008. D contributes $6,700 to his HSA on December 1, 2008 and remains an eligible individual through December 31, 2009.

D is an eligible individual with family HDHP coverage on December 1, 2008 and remains an eligible individual through December 31, 2009. D's full contribution limit under § 223(b)(8) for 2008 is $6,700 ($5,800 family coverage contribution + $900 catch-up contribution). The sum of the monthly contribution limits is $558.33 ((1/12 × $5,800) + (1/12 × $900)). D's annual contribution limit for 2008 is $6,700, the greater of $6,700 or $558.33.

Example 6. Individual E, age 35, has self-only HDHP coverage and is an eligible individual for the months of May, June, and July 2008.

The full contribution limit under § 223(b)(8) does not apply to E for 2008 because E is not an eligible individual on December 1, 2008. E's contribution limit for 2008 is $725 (3/12 × $2,900).

Example 7. Individual F, age 46, enrolls in family HDHP coverage on January 1, 2008 and is an eligible individual on that date. F contributes $5,800 to an HSA on January 1, 2008. F ceases to be covered by an HDHP on August 1, 2008. On December 15, 2008, F withdraws from the HSA $2,416.67 ($5,800.00 − 3,383.33), plus $45 earnings attributable to the $2,354.16.

F ceases to be an eligible individual on August 1, 2008. The full contribution limit does not apply to F for 2008 because F is not an eligible individual on December 1, 2008, and the testing period in § 223(b)(8)(B)(i) does not apply to F. F's HSA contribution limit for 2008 is $3,383.33 (7/12 × $5,800). The $2,416.67 is an excess contribution for purposes of § 4973, but is not subject to the six percent excise tax under § 4973 because F withdrew the excess contribution and earnings attributable to the excess contribution by the due date, with extensions, for filing her 2008 federal income tax return. F reports the $45 withdrawn earnings as gross income on her 2008 federal income tax return. The gross income inclusion and 10 percent tax in § 223(f)(3) for distributions not used for qualified medical expenses in § 223(f)(2) do not apply because F withdrew an excess contribution.

Example 8. Individual G, age 38, enrolls in family HDHP coverage on January 1, 2008 and is an eligible individual on that date. G's coverage changes to self-only HDHP coverage on September 1, 2008 and he retains that coverage through December 31, 2008. G is an eligible individual for all 12 months in 2008. G contributes $4,833.33 ((8/12 × $5,800) + (4/12 × $2,900)) to an HSA for 2008. G ceases to be an eligible individual on January 1, 2009.

G is an eligible individual with self-only HDHP coverage on December 1, 2008. G's full contribution limit under § 223(b)(8) for 2008 is $2,900. G's sum of the monthly contribution limits is $4,833.33 ((8/12 × $5,800) + (4/12 × $2,900)). G's annual contribution limit is $4,833.33, the greater of $2,900 or $4,833.33. The testing period for 2008 HSA contributions ends on December 31, 2009. G ceases to be an eligible individual during the testing period. Because G's contribution of $4,833.33 is not greater than the sum of the monthly contribution limits, there is no inclusion or additional tax when G ceases to be an eligible individual during the testing period.

Example 9. Individual H, age 25, enrolls in self-only HDHP coverage on June 1, 2008 and is an eligible individual on that date. H is not an eligible individual prior to June 1, 2008. H contributes $2,900 to an HSA on July 1, 2008. H is an eligible individual on December 1, 2008, and continues to be an eligible individual until February 1, 2009. On February 2, 2009, H withdraws $1,208.33 from his HSA. The $1,208.33 distribution is not used for H's qualified medical expenses (as defined in § 223(d)(2)).

H is an eligible individual with self-only HDHP coverage on December 1, 2008. H's full contribution limit under § 223(b)(8) for 2008 is $2,900. H's sum of the monthly contribution limits is $1,691.67 (7/12 × $2,900). H's annual contribution limit is $2,900, the greater of $2,900 or $1,691.67. The testing period for 2008 HSA contributions ends on December 31, 2009. In 2009, H ceases to be an eligible individual during the testing period. In 2009, H must include in gross income $1,208.33, the amount contributed to the HSA minus the sum of the monthly contribution limits ($2,900.00 − $1,691.67). In addition, the 10 percent additional tax ($120.83) in § 223(b)(8)(B)(i) applies to the amount.

The $1,208.33 withdrawn from the HSA is not used for qualified medical expenses and is not a withdrawal of an excess contribution. Therefore, under § 223(f)(2), $1,208.33 is also included in H's gross income and is also subject to the 10 percent additional tax in § 223(f)(4). As a result, H includes $2,416.66 ($1,208.33 with respect to § 223(f)(4) and $1,208.33 with respect to § 223(b)(8)) in gross income in 2009 and an additional tax of $241.66 ($120.83 with respect to § 223(f)(4) and $120.83 with respect to § 223(b)(8)).

Example 10. Individual J, age 27, is eligible for medical benefits through the Department of Veterans Affairs (VA). As a result of medical care (other than disregarded coverage or preventive care) that J received from the VA in January 2008, he is not an eligible individual in January, February, March, or April 2008. J has self-only HDHP coverage and is otherwise an eligible individual from May 1, 2008 through December 31, 2009.

J is an eligible individual with self-only HDHP coverage on December 1, 2008. J's full contribution limit under § 223(b)(8) for 2008 is $2,900. J's sum of the monthly contribution limits is $1,933.33 (8/12 × $2,900). J's annual contribution limit for 2008 is $2,900, the greater of $2,900 or $1,933.33.

Example 11. Same facts as Example 10, except that J also receives medical care (other than disregarded coverage or preventive care) from the VA in October 2008. J is an eligible individual with self-only HDHP coverage in May through September 2008.

The full contribution limit does not apply to J for 2008 because J is not an eligible individual on December 1, 2008. J's 2008 contribution limit is determined under the sum of the monthly contribution limits and is $1,208.33 (5/12 × $2,900).

Example 12. Individual K, age 64, enrolls in family HDHP coverage on April 1, 2008 and is an eligible individual from April 1, 2008 through December 31, 2008. K was not an eligible individual prior to April 1, 2008. K contributes $6,700 to his HSA for 2008 on April 1, 2008. K attains age 65 and enrolls in Medicare on March 24, 2009 and ceases to be an eligible individual.

K is an eligible individual with family HDHP coverage on December 1, 2008. K's full contribution limit under § 223(b)(8) for 2008 is $6,700 ($5,800 family coverage contribution + $900 catch-up contribution). K's sum of the monthly contribution limits is $5,025 ((9/12 × $5,800) + (9/12 × $900)). K's annual contribution limit for 2008 is $6,700, the greater of $6,700 or $5,025. The testing period for 2008 HSA contributions ends on December 31, 2009. In 2009, K ceases to be an eligible individual during the testing period. In 2009, K must include $1,675, the amount contributed to the HSA minus the sum of the monthly contribution limits ($6,700.00 − $5,025) in gross income. In addition, the 10 percent additional tax ($167.50) in § 223(b)(8)(B)(i) applies to the amount.

Example 13. Same facts as Example 12, except that before enrolling in Medicare, K ceases to be an eligible individual during the testing period as a result of becoming disabled. Because K ceases to be an eligible individual due to becoming disabled, no amount is required to be included in income in 2009 or is subject to the additional tax in § 223(b)(8).

Example 14. Individuals L and M, both age 40, are a married couple. L and M enroll in family HDHP coverage on December 1, 2008 and are otherwise eligible individuals on that date. L and M are not eligible individuals in any other month in 2008. L and M divide the contribution limit equally between them. On or after December 1, 2008, L contributes $2,900 to his HSA and M contributes $2,900 to her HSA. On June 1, 2009,

M switches to self-only HDHP coverage and remains an eligible individual through December 31, 2009. L ceases to be an eligible individual in June 2009.

L and M are eligible individuals with family HDHP coverage on December 1, 2008. L and M's combined full contribution limit for 2008 is $5,800. L and M's combined sum of the monthly contribution limits is $483.33 (1/12 × $5,800), or $241.67 each ((1/12 × $5,800) ÷ 2). L and M's combined annual contribution limit under § 223(b)(8) is $5,800, the greater of $5,800 or $483.33. The testing period for 2008 HSA contributions ends on December 31, 2009. During the testing period for 2008, M remains an eligible individual but L ceases to be an eligible individual. Because M is an eligible individual during the testing period, no amount of M's $2,900 contribution is included in M's gross income and M is not subject to the 10 percent additional tax. In 2008, L must include $2,658.33 in gross income, the amount contributed to the HSA minus the sum of the monthly contribution limits ($2,900 − $241.67). In addition, the 10 percent additional tax ($265.83) in § 223(b)(8)(B)(i) applies to that amount.

Example 15. Same facts as Example 14, except M contributes $5,800 to M's HSA and L contributes $0 to L's HSA. No amount is taxable to either L or M.

NO EFFECT ON HSA ESTABLISHMENT DATE

Expenses incurred before an HSA is established are not qualified medical expenses. Notice 2004-2, Q&A-26. Although § 223(b)(8) and this notice provide that certain individuals are treated as eligible individuals on the first day of the taxable year in determining the contribution amount, an HSA is not established before the date that the HSA is actually established. See also Notice 2007-22, 2007-10 I.R.B. 670.

REPORTING

Neither employers nor trustees are responsible for reporting whether an individual remains an eligible individual during the testing period.

EFFECTIVE DATE

Section 223(b)(2)(A) and (B) and § 223(b)(8), allowing full contributions for months preceding the month that an individual is an eligible individual, are effective for taxable years beginning after December 31, 2006.

INTERACTION WITH § 408(d)(9)

See Notice 2008-51, also published in 2008-25 I.R.B.

EFFECT ON OTHER DOCUMENTS

Notice 2004-2 and Notice 2004-50 are modified.

DRAFTING INFORMATION * * *

Notice 2008-51 (2008-25 I.R.B. 1163)

[**Summary:** The IRS has released guidance on qualified HSA funding distribution (a one-time transfer) from an individual's IRA or Roth IRA to an HSA.]

Section 307 of the Health Opportunity Patient Empowerment Act of 2006 (the Act) added § 408(d)(9) to the Internal Revenue Code. The Act is part of the Tax Relief and Health Care Act of 2006, enacted December 20, 2006, Pub. L. No. 109-432. This notice provides guidance on a qualified HSA funding distribution from an individual's Individual Retirement Account (IRA) or Roth IRA to a Health Savings Account (HSA). The qualified HSA funding distribution is a one-time transfer from an individual's IRA to his or her HSA and generally excluded from gross income and is not subject to the 10 percent additional tax under § 72(t).

BACKGROUND

Eligible individuals

Generally, only eligible individuals (as defined in § 223(c)(1)) may contribute to HSAs. Maximum annual HSA contributions are based on an individual's eligibility, age, and health plan coverage.

General rules on taxation of distributions from IRAs

A distribution from an IRA under § 408 generally is included in gross income. If an IRA owner made nondeductible contributions to the IRA, those contributions are recovered on a pro-rata basis and the distribution is partly included in and partly excluded from gross income under the rules of § 408(d) and § 72(e)(8).

A nonqualified distribution from a Roth IRA under § 408A is included in gross income only to the extent that earnings are distributed. A qualified Roth IRA distribution (as defined in § 408A(d)) is excluded from gross income.

If a distribution from an IRA or Roth IRA is made before the IRA or Roth IRA account owner attains age $59\frac{1}{2}$, the distribution also is subject to a 10 percent additional tax under § 72(t) unless an exception applies. These exceptions include distributions made on account of death or disability, and distributions made as part of a series of substantially equal periodic payments for the life expectancy of the IRA holder.

HEALTH OPPORTUNITY PATIENT EMPOWERMENT ACT OF 2006

Tax treatment of qualified HSA funding distributions

Section 408(d)(9) provides, in general, that a qualified HSA funding distribution from an individual's IRA or Roth IRA to that individual's HSA is not included in gross income, if the individual is an eligible individual under § 223(c)(1). Moreover, notwithstanding the pro-rata basis recovery rules under § 72, for purposes of determining the basis in any amount remaining in an IRA or Roth IRA following a qualified HSA funding distribution, the qualified HSA funding distribution is treated as included in gross income to the extent that such amount does not exceed the aggregate amount which would have been so included if there were a total distribution from the IRA or Roth IRA owner's accounts. For example, suppose an individual who has $200 of basis in an IRA with a fair market value of $2,000 makes a qualified HSA funding distribution of $1,500 from the IRA. Immediately after the qualified HSA funding distribution, the individual retains $200 of basis in an IRA that has a fair market value of $500.

If a qualified HSA funding distribution from an individual's IRA or Roth IRA exceeds the aggregate amount which would have been included in gross income if there were a total distribution from that individual's IRA or Roth IRA accounts, the individual's basis in the excess amount (i.e., the amount that would have been excluded from gross income in a distribution to which § 408(d)(9) did not apply) does not carry over to the HSA.

A qualified HSA funding distribution is not subject to the 10 percent additional tax under § 72(t). However, if the qualified HSA funding distribution results in a modification of a series of substantially equal periodic payments that, prior to the modification, qualify for the exception to the 10 percent additional tax under § 72(t)(2)(A)(iv), and such modification results in the imposition of the recapture tax under the rules of § 72(t)(4), the recapture tax applies to the payments made before the date of the qualified HSA funding distribution.

The amount contributed to the HSA through a qualified HSA funding distribution is not allowed as a deduction and counts against the individual's maximum annual HSA contribution for the taxable year of the distribution. In addition, the taxability of these distributions is subject to the testing period rules in § 408(d)(9)(D), discussed below.

Qualified HSA funding distribution only from certain types of IRAs

A qualified HSA funding distribution may be made from a traditional IRA under § 408 or a Roth IRA under § 408A, but not from an ongoing SIMPLE IRA under § 408(p) or an ongoing SEP IRA under § 408(k). For this purpose, a SEP IRA or SIMPLE IRA is treated as ongoing if an employer contribution is made for the plan year ending with or within the IRA owner's taxable year in which the qualified HSA funding distribution would be made.

After the death of an IRA or Roth IRA account owner, a qualified HSA funding distribution may be made from an IRA or Roth IRA maintained for the benefit of an IRA or Roth IRA beneficiary. This distribution will be taken into account in determining whether the required minimum distribution requirements of §§ 408(a)(6), 408(b)(3), and 408A(c)(5) have been satisfied.

Maximum amount of qualified HSA funding distribution

For purposes of § 408(d)(9)(C)(i), a qualified HSA funding distribution from the IRA or Roth IRA of an eligible individual to that individual's HSA must be less than or equal to the IRA or Roth IRA account owner's maximum annual HSA contribution. The maximum annual HSA contribution is based on (1) the individual's age as of the end of the taxable year and (2) the individual's type of high deductible health plan (HDHP) coverage (self-only or family HDHP coverage) at the time of the distribution. For example, in 2008, an IRA owner who is an eligible individual with family HDHP coverage at the time of the distribution and who is age 55 or over by the end of the year is allowed a qualified HSA funding distribution of $5,800, plus the $900 catch-up contribution. An IRA or Roth IRA owner who is an eligible individual with self-only HDHP coverage, and who is under age 55 as of the end of the taxable year, is allowed a qualified HSA funding distribution of $2,900 for 2008.

One-time qualified HSA funding distribution

Generally, only one qualified HSA funding distribution is allowed during the lifetime of an individual. If, however, the distribution occurs when the individual has self-only HDHP coverage, and later in the same taxable year the individual has family HDHP coverage, the individual is allowed a second qualified HSA funding distribution in that taxable year. Both distributions count against the individual's maximum HSA contribution for that taxable year. The distributions must be from an IRA or Roth IRA to an HSA owned by the individual who owns the IRA or Roth IRA or, in the case of an inherited IRA, for whom the IRA or Roth IRA is maintained (i.e., a qualified HSA funding distribution cannot be made to an HSA owned by any other person, including the individual's spouse). IRA or Roth IRA owners are not required to make the maximum qualified HSA funding distribution or to make any qualified HSA funding distribution.

If an individual owns two or more IRAs, and wants to use amounts in multiple IRAs to make a qualified HSA funding distribution, the individual must first make an IRA-to-IRA transfer of the amounts to be distributed into a single IRA, and then make the one-time qualified HSA funding distribution from that IRA.

No deemed distribution date

A qualified HSA funding distribution relates to the taxable year in which the distribution is actually made. The rules in § 223(d)(4)(B) and § 219(f)(3) (contributions made before the deadline for filing the individual's federal income tax return are deemed to be made on the last day of the preceding taxable year) do not apply to qualified HSA funding distributions.

Procedures for making the transfer from an IRA to an HSA

An individual must be an eligible individual (as defined in § 223(c)(1)) at the time of the qualified HSA funding distribution. The distribution must be a direct transfer from an IRA or Roth IRA to an HSA. For example, if a check from an IRA or Roth IRA is made payable to an HSA trustee or custodian and delivered by the IRA or Roth IRA account owner to the HSA trustee or custodian, the payment to the HSA will be considered a direct payment by the IRA or Roth IRA trustee, custodian or issuer to the HSA for purposes of § 408(d)(9).

Testing period rules

If a qualified HSA funding distribution is made from the individual's IRA or Roth IRA to the individual's HSA under § 408(d)(9) and the individual remains an eligible individual during the entire testing period, the amount of the qualified HSA funding distribution is excluded from the individual's gross income and the 10 percent additional tax under § 408(d)(9)(D) does not apply. The testing period begins with the month in which the qualified HSA funding distribution is contributed to the HSA and ends on the last day of the 12th month following that month. Each qualified HSA funding distribution allowed in § 408(d)(9)(C)(ii)(II) has a separate testing period. For testing period purposes, an eligible individual who changes from family HDHP coverage to self-only HDHP coverage during the testing period remains an eligible individual. If at any time during the testing period the individual ceases to meet all requirements to be an eligible individual, the amount of the qualified HSA funding distribution is included in the individual's gross income. The qualified HSA funding distribution is included in gross income in the taxable year of the individual in which the individual first fails to be an eligible individual. This amount is subject to 10 percent additional tax (unless the failure is due to disability, as defined in § 72(m)(7), or death). See § 408(d)(9)(D). Earnings on the amount of the qualified HSA funding distribution are not included in gross income. Amounts included in the IRA or Roth IRA owner's gross income under § 408(d)(9)(D) are not also included in gross income under § 408(d)(1) or (2), nor do the § 72 rules apply (including the additional tax under § 72(t)).

No interaction between testing periods

Section 223(b)(8)(B) provides generally that if an individual fails to remain an eligible individual during the § 223(b)(8) testing period, an amount is included in the individual's gross income (computed by subtracting the sum of the monthly contribution limits that the individual would otherwise have been entitled to under § 223(b)(1) and (2) from the amount actually contributed). The testing period rules in § 223(b)(8)(B) do not apply to amounts contributed to an HSA through a qualified HSA funding distribution. Thus, if an individual remains an eligible individual during the entire § 408(d)(9) testing period, then no amount of the qualified HSA funding distribution is included in income and the 10 percent additional tax under § 223(b)(8)(B) does not apply.

Application of § 223(b)(8)(B) testing period to contributions which are not qualified HSA funding distributions

If an HSA account beneficiary's contributions to his or her HSA in a taxable year include both a qualified HSA funding distribution (or distributions) and other contributions subject to § 223(b)(8), the § 408(d)(9)(D) testing period rules apply to qualified HSA funding distribution (or distributions) and the § 223(b)(8)(B) testing period rules apply to the other contributions. If the individual fails to remain an eligible individual during the § 223(b)(8)(B) testing period, but does remain a qualified individual during the § 408(d)(9)(D) testing period, the amount included in the individual's gross income is the lesser of:

(1) the amount that would otherwise be included under the § 223(b)(8)(B) rules; or

(2) The amount of contributions to the HSA for the taxable year other than the amount contributed through qualified HSA funding distributions.

HSA distributions not used for qualified medical expenses

An HSA distribution not used for qualified medical expenses (as defined in § 223(d)(2)) is included in gross income under § 223(f)(2) and subject to the 10 percent additional tax under § 223(f)(4) (with certain exceptions), regardless of whether the amount contributed to the HSA under the qualified HSA funding distribution is included in the account beneficiary's income and subject to the additional tax under § 408(d)(9)(D). See Notice 2007-22, 2007-10 I.R.B. 670, regarding the consequences of distributions from HSAs.

EXAMPLES

The following examples illustrate these rules. It is assumed in the examples that no previous qualified HSA funding distributions have been made by the individual, and that all distributions are from IRAs and are otherwise included in the IRA owner's gross income. None of the IRAs are ongoing SEP IRAs described in § 408(k), or ongoing SIMPLE IRAs described in § 408(p). For purposes of § 223(f)(4) and § 408(d)(9)(D)(ii), none of the IRA owners or HSA account beneficiaries are disabled. None of the exceptions to the 10 percent tax under § 72(t) apply.

Example 1. Individual A, age 45, enrolls in family HDHP coverage on January 1, 2008, is otherwise an eligible individual (as defined in § 223(c)(1)) as of that date and through December 31, 2009. A's maximum annual HSA contribution for 2008 is $5,800. A owns an IRA with a balance of $2,000. A direct trustee-to-trustee transfer of $2,000 is made from A's IRA trustee to A's HSA trustee on April 2, 2008.

The $2,000 distribution is a qualified HSA funding distribution, and accordingly is not included in A's gross income and is not subject to the additional tax under § 72(t). A's testing period with respect to the qualified HSA funding distribution begins in April 2008 and ends on April 30, 2009. After the qualified HSA funding distribution of $2,000, $3,800 of A's 2008 HSA maximum annual contribution remains.

Example 2. Same facts as Example 1, except that A ceases to be an eligible individual on January 1, 2009. Under § 408(d)(9)(D), in 2009 A must include $2,000 in gross income, the amount of the qualified HSA funding distribution, plus an additional tax of $200 (10 percent of the amount included in income).

Example 3. Individual B, age 57, enrolls in self-only HDHP coverage effective January 1, 2008, is otherwise an eligible individual as of that date and through December 31, 2009. B's maximum annual HSA contribution for 2008 is $3,800 ($2,900 plus the $900 catch-up contribution). B owns an IRA with a balance of $13,550. A direct trustee-to-trustee transfer of $3,800 is made from B's IRA trustee to B's HSA trustee on June 4, 2008.

The $3,800 distribution is a qualified HSA funding distribution. The distribution from B's IRA is not included in B's gross income and is not subject to the additional tax under § 72(t). The qualified HSA funding distribution of $3,800 equals B's 2008 maximum annual HSA contribution. B's testing period with respect to the qualified HSA funding distribution begins in June 2008 and ends on June 30, 2009.

Example 4. Individual C, age 38, enrolls in self-only HDHP coverage on January 1, 2008, is otherwise an eligible individual on January 1, and remains an eligible individual through December 31, 2009. C owns an IRA with a balance of $12,550. A qualified HSA funding distribution of $2,800 is made from C's IRA trustee directly to C's HSA trustee on June 4, 2008.

On August 1, C enrolls in family HDHP coverage. A transfer of $3,000 is made from C's IRA trustee directly to C's HSA trustee on August 15, 2008.

The $2,800 and $3,000 distributions are qualified HSA funding distributions. The distributions from the IRA are not included in C's gross income and are not subject to the additional tax under § 72(t). The qualified HSA funding distributions of $5,800 ($2,800 + $3,000) equal C's 2008 maximum annual HSA contribution. C's testing period for the first qualified HSA funding distribution begins in June 2008 and ends on June 30, 2009 and the testing period for the second qualified HSA funding distribution begins in August 2008 and ends on August 31, 2009.

Example 5. Individual D, age 43, enrolls in family HDHP coverage on January 1, 2008, is otherwise an eligible individual on January 1, and remains an eligible individual through December 31, 2009. D owns an IRA with a balance of $17,500. A qualified HSA funding distribution of $5,800 is made from D's IRA trustee directly to D's HSA trustee on March 18, 2008.

On June 1, D changes from family HDHP coverage to self-only HDHP coverage. The $5,800 distribution from the IRA is not included in D's gross income and is not subject to the additional tax under § 72(t). The qualified HSA funding distribution of $5,800 equals D's maximum annual HSA contribution at the time the transfer occurred. D's testing period begins in March 2008 and ends on March 31, 2009.

Example 6. Individual E, age 50, begins family HDHP coverage and is first an eligible individual on June 1, 2008. E owns an IRA with a balance of $20,000. A direct trustee-to-trustee transfer of $3,500 is made from E's IRA trustee to E's HSA trustee on June 4, 2008. On June 4, 2008 E also contributes $2,300 in cash to his HSA for a total contribution of $5,800. On July 1, 2009, E ceases to be an eligible individual.

The $3,500 distribution is a qualified HSA funding distribution, is not included in E's gross income, and is not subject to the additional tax under § 72(t). E's testing period with respect to the qualified HSA funding distribution begins in June 2008 and ends on June 30, 2009. E remains an eligible individual during the qualified HSA funding distribution testing period. No amount of the $3,500 distribution is included in E's gross income.

The testing period for the $2,300 contribution begins in December 2008 and ends on December 31, 2009. E's full contribution limit under § 223(b)(8) for 2008 is $5,800. E's sum of the monthly contribution limits is $3,383 (7/12 × $5,800). E's maximum annual contribution for 2008 is $5,800, the greater of $5,800 or $3,383.

The amount included in E's gross income and subject to the 10 percent additional tax under § 223(b)(8)(B) in 2009 is $2,417 ($5,800 − $3,383). The cash contribution to E's HSA is $2,300. The amount included in E's gross income and subject to additional tax is $2,300, the lesser of $2,417 or $2,300.

Example 7. Same facts as Example 6, except that the distribution from E's IRA to E's HSA is $1,000 and E contributes $4,800 in cash for a total HSA contribution of $5,800 in 2008.

E remains an eligible individual during the qualified HSA funding distribution testing period. No amount of the $1,000 distribution is included in E's gross income.

E's full contribution limit under § 223(b)(8) for 2008 is $5,800. E's sum of the monthly contribution limits is $3,383 (7/12 × $5,800). E's maximum annual contribution limit for 2008 is $5,800, the greater of $5,800 or $3,383. The amount included in E's gross income and subject to the 10 percent additional tax under § 223(b)(8)(B) is $2,417 ($5,800 − $3,383). The cash contribution to E's HSA is $4,800. The amount included in E's gross income and subject to the additional tax in 2009 is $2,417, the lesser of $2,417 or $4,800.

Example 8. Same facts as Example 6, except that E ceases to be an eligible individual on May 1, 2009.

The $3,500 distribution is a qualified HSA funding distribution, is not included in E's gross income in the year of the distribution, and is not subject to the additional tax under § 72(t). E's testing period with respect to the qualified HSA funding distribution begins in June 2008 and ends on June 30, 2009. E ceases to be an eligible individual during the qualified HSA funding distribution testing period. The $3,500 distribution is included in E's gross income. In addition, the 10 percent additional tax ($350) under § 408(d)(9)(D)(II) applies to the amount.

The testing period for the $2,300 contribution begins in December 2008 and ends on December 31, 2009. E's full contribution limit under § 223(b)(8) for 2008 is $5,800. E's sum of the monthly contribution limits is $3,383 (7/12 × $5,800). E's maximum annual contribution limit for 2008 is $5,800, the greater of $5,800 or $3,383.

The amount included in E's gross income and subject to the 10 percent additional tax in 2009 under § 223(b)(8) is $2,417 ($5,800 − $3,383). The cash contribution to E's HSA is $2,300. The amount included in E's gross income and subject to additional tax is $2,300, the lesser of $2,417 or $2,300.

Example 9. Individual F, age 47, has family HDHP coverage and is first an eligible individual on January 1, 2008. F's maximum annual HSA contribution for 2008 is $5,800. F owns an IRA with a balance of $10,000. A direct trustee-to-trustee transfer of $10,000 is made from F's IRA trustee to F's HSA trustee on September 26, 2008.

The $10,000 contribution exceeds F's $5,800 contribution limit. In 2008, $4,200 ($10,000 – $5,800) is included in F's gross income under § 408 as a taxable IRA distribution. The $4,200 is also subject to additional tax under § 72(t), as well as an excise tax on excess HSA contributions under § 4973.

Example 10. Individual G, age 32, has self-only HDHP coverage and is first an eligible individual on January 1, 2007. G remains an eligible individual through December 31, 2009. G's maximum annual HSA contribution for 2007 is $2,850 and $2,900 for 2008. G owns an IRA with a balance of $4,500. A direct trustee-to-trustee transfer of $1,000 from G's IRA trustee to G's HSA trustee is made on September 6, 2007.

Another direct trustee-to-trustee transfer of $1,500 from G's IRA trustee to G's HSA trustee is made on April 28, 2008. G makes no other contributions to his HSA for 2008.

The $1,000 contribution to G's HSA in September 2007 is a qualified HSA funding distribution, is not included in G's gross income, and is not subject to the additional tax under § 72(t). G's testing period with respect to this contribution begins in September 2007 and ends on September 30, 2008.

The $1,500 contribution to G's HSA in April 2008 is not a qualified HSA funding distribution, is included in G's gross income for 2008 under § 408 as a taxable IRA distribution, and is subject to the additional tax under § 72(t). However, the $1,500 contribution to G's HSA is allowed as a deduction under § 223(a) in 2008, because G remains an eligible individual in 2008 and has not otherwise made contributions to the HSA or had contributions on G's behalf made to an HSA in excess of $1,400 for 2008. No testing period under § 408 applies to the $1,500 contribution.

REPORTING AND WITHHOLDING

Employers are not responsible for reporting whether an employee remains an eligible individual during the testing period.

A qualified HSA funding distribution is not subject to withholding under § 3405 because an IRA or Roth IRA owner that requests such a distribution is deemed to have elected out of withholding under § 3405(a)(2). For purposes of determining whether a distribution requested by an IRA or Roth IRA owner satisfies the requirements of § 408(d)(9), the IRA or Roth IRA trustee may rely upon reasonable representations made by the account owner.

EFFECTIVE DATE

Sections 408(d)(9) and 223(b)(4)(C), allowing qualified HSA funding distributions from IRAs to HSAs, are effective for taxable years beginning after December 31, 2006.

DRAFTING INFORMATION * * *

Notice 2007-22 (2007-10 I.R.B. 670)

[**Summary:** The IRS has released guidance on the procedures for rolling assets from health flexible spending accounts (FSAs) that have grace periods or health reimbursement accounts (HRAs) to health savings accounts (HSAs), as allowed by the Tax Relief and Health Care Act of 2006 (Pub. L. No. 109-432). See chapter 4.]

This notice provides guidance on rollovers from health Flexible Spending Arrangements (health FSAs) and Health Reimbursement Arrangements (HRAs) to Health Savings Accounts (HSAs) under amendments to the Internal Revenue Code by section 302 of the Health Opportunity Patient Empowerment Act of 2006 (the Act) included in the Tax Relief and Health Care Act of 2006, enacted December 20, 2006, Pub. L. No. 109-432. The guidance also provides special transition relief for rollovers completed before March 15, 2007. It is anticipated that additional guidance will be published later under this provision.

As discussed in detail below, the new rules provide, in limited circumstances, for certain amounts in a health FSA or HRA to be rolled over into an HSA and for the rollover to receive favorable tax treatment. Generally, under the new rules, all of the following conditions must be satisfied in order to receive the favorable tax treatment:

- By plan year end—
  - The plan must be amended
  - The employee must elect the rollover
  - The year-end balance must be frozen
- The funds must be transferred by the employer within two and a half months after the end of the plan year and result in a zero balance in the health FSA or HRA.

Under special transition relief provided in this notice for amounts remaining at the end of 2006, however:

- There is no requirement to freeze the year-end balance in the health FSA or HRA, and
- The amendment, election, and transfer must be completed by March 15, 2007.

BACKGROUND

Eligible individuals, as defined in § 223(c)(1) of the Code, may contribute to HSAs. In general, these are individuals who, as of the first day of the month, are covered by a high deductible health plan (HDHP) and by no other health plan that is not an HDHP (with the exception of certain disregarded coverage, including permitted insurance). An individual covered by a general purpose health

FSA or general purpose HRA is not eligible to contribute to an HSA. See Rev. Rul. 2004-45, 2004-1 C.B. 971. If a general purpose health FSA allows reimbursements for expenses incurred during a grace period following the end of the plan year, an otherwise eligible individual participating in the health FSA is generally not eligible to make contributions to an HSA until the first day of the first month following the end of the grace period. The maximum duration of a grace period is until the fifteenth day of the third month following the end of a plan year. See Notice 2005-42, 2005-1 C.B. 1204. Prior to the Act, this rule applied even if the individual's health FSA had no unused benefits as of the end of the prior year (i.e., the balance in the health FSA was zero as of the last day of the plan year). Notice 2005-86, 2005-2 C.B. 1075. However, coverage by an HSA-compatible health FSA or HRA (limited-purpose health FSA or HRA, post-deductible health FSA or HRA, retirement HRA, or suspended HRA), does not affect an employee's eligibility to contribute to an HSA, including coverage during a health FSA grace period. See Rev. Rul. 2004-45.

HEALTH OPPORTUNITY PATIENT EMPOWERMENT ACT OF 2006—GENERAL RULES

Section 302(a) of the Act provides for "qualified HSA distributions" before January 1, 2012. A qualified HSA distribution is a direct distribution of an amount from a health FSA or HRA to an HSA. The distribution (rollover to an HSA) must not exceed the lesser of the balance in the health FSA or HRA (1) on September 21, 2006, or (2) as of the date of the distribution. Thus, an individual who was not covered by a health FSA or HRA on September 21, 2006 may not elect a qualified HSA distribution. Similarly, an individual who participated in a health FSA with one employer on September 21, 2006, and participates in a health FSA with a second employer after that date, may not elect a qualified HSA distribution with respect to the second employer's health FSA.

A qualified HSA distribution must be contributed directly to the HSA trustee by the employer. Qualified HSA distributions may be made from general purpose health FSAs and HRAs, as well as from HSA-compatible health FSAs and HRAs. Only one qualified HSA distribution is allowed with respect to each health FSA or HRA of an individual. Qualified HSA distributions are not taken into account in applying the annual limit for HSA contributions. Qualified HSA distributions are treated as rollovers and thus, are not deductible.

If the individual fails to remain HSA-eligible during the testing period following the distribution, the amount of the rollover is included in gross income and is subject to an additional 10 percent tax. For this purpose, the testing period is defined as the period beginning with the month in which the qualified HSA distribution is contributed to the HSA and ending on the last day of the 12th month following that month. It is not required that an employee be an eligible individual with HDHP coverage in order to have a qualified HSA distribution made on the employee's behalf. However, if an employee is not an eligible individual immediately following the qualified HSA distribution, the amount of the distribution is included in the employee's income and subject to an additional 10 percent tax.

Section 302(b) of the Act provides that only certain health FSA coverage during a grace period is treated as disregarded coverage for the purpose of determining an individual's eligibility to contribute to an HSA. Under new § 223(c)(1)(B)(iii) of the Code, coverage during a grace period by a general purpose health FSA is disregarded if (1) the balance in the health FSA at the end of the prior plan year is zero or (2) the individual makes a qualified HSA distribution of any balance remaining at the end of the plan year to an HSA.

Section 302(b) of the Act only applies to health FSA coverage during a grace period following a plan year. Thus, health FSA coverage during the plan year is not disregarded, regardless of whether the health FSA balance is reduced to zero during the plan year by a qualified HSA distribution or otherwise.

QUALIFIED HSA DISTRIBUTIONS

If an employer wants to provide qualified HSA distributions, the employer must amend the health FSA or HRA written plan. In order to comply with the comparability rules in § 4980G of the Code, the amended plan must offer qualified HSA distributions to any otherwise eligible individual covered by the employer's HDHP. See new § 106(e)(5)(B) of the Code. However, there is no requirement that the health FSA or HRA be terminated in order to provide a qualified HSA distribution. Health FSAs and HRAs must satisfy the nondiscrimination requirements in § 105(h) of the Code.

A qualified HSA distribution may be made at any time prior to January 1, 2012. However, even if the qualified HSA distribution reduces the balance of an FSA or HRA to zero, the health FSA or HRA coverage does not end. If the FSA or HRA is not HSA-compatible, employees can become eligible individuals only after transfers at the end of the plan year of the FSA or HRA that result in either disregarded coverage under 302(b) of the Act, or the termination of the HRA coverage at the end of the plan year. Consequently, qualified HSA distributions from health FSAs or HRAs that are not HSA-compatible and that take place at any time other than the end of a plan year, generally result in the inclusion of the distribution in income and the imposition of an additional 10 percent tax.

The amendments in the Act do not change the requirement that unused amounts remaining at the end of a health FSA's plan year must be forfeited in the absence of a grace period. Notice 2005-42. Thus, if a health FSA does not have a grace period, unused amounts remaining at the end of the plan year are forfeited and generally cannot be transferred through a qualified HSA distribution to an HSA after the end of the plan year. Although the unused amounts can be distributed to an HSA before the end of the plan year, because the health FSA coverage continues until the end of the plan year, an individual covered by the health FSA is not an eligible individual immediately after the qualified HSA distribution, and thus any such qualified HSA distribution is included in income and subject to an additional 10 percent tax. Similarly, an individual without HDHP coverage after a distribution is not an eligible individual after the distribution and thus the qualified HSA distribution is included in income and subject to an additional 10 percent tax. Unless a participant has a change in status as provided in Treas. Reg. § 1.125-4(a), health FSA elections may not be changed during a plan year. Prop. Treas. Reg. § 1.125-1, Q & A-15.

BALANCES DETERMINED ON CASH BASIS

For all purposes, balances are determined on a cash basis. Cash basis means the balance as of any date, without taking into account expenses incurred that have not been reimbursed as of that date. Thus, pending claims, claims submitted, claims received or claims under review that have not been paid as of a date are not taken into account for purposes of determining the account balance as of that date. In addition, the balance as of any date of a health FSA is determined by applying the uniform coverage rule (i.e., maximum reimbursement available for the plan year reduced for prior reimbursements paid as of the date for the same plan year). See Prop. Treas. Reg. § 1.125-2, Q&A-7(b)(2).

HDHP COVERAGE BEGINNING AFTER 1ST DAY OF THE MONTH

An employee who begins HDHP coverage after the first day of the month is not an eligible individual until the first day of the next month. If a qualified HSA distribution is made on behalf of such an employee before the first day of the next month, the employee is not an eligible individual as of the date of the qualified HSA distribution and the amount of the distribution is included in the employee's income and subject to an additional 10 percent tax. Thus, if an employee begins HDHP coverage after the first day of the month, any qualified HSA distribution on behalf of the individual made on or after the first day of the next month avoids immediate inclusion in income.

CONSEQUENCES OF FAILING TO ROLL OVER ENTIRE BALANCE OF GENERAL PURPOSE HEALTH FSA OR GENERAL PURPOSE HRA

An employee with a balance in a health FSA with a grace period or HRA at the end of a plan year is not treated as an eligible individual for HSA purposes on the first day of the immediately following plan year if a qualified HSA distribution does not result in a zero balance in the health FSA or HRA. Because the employee is covered under a health plan that is not an HDHP during the testing period, the amount of the qualified HSA distribution is included in the employee's gross income in the year of the distribution and is subject to a 10 percent additional tax. However, an employee with a balance in an HSA-compatible health FSA or HRA at the end of a plan year remains an eligible individual, if otherwise eligible, regardless of whether a qualified HSA distribution is made.

ADDITIONAL TAX FOR FAILURE TO REMAIN AN ELIGIBLE INDIVIDUAL

If an individual ceases to be an eligible individual during the testing period, the amount of the qualified HSA distribution is included in the gross income of the individual and subject to an additional 10 percent tax. Failing to remain an eligible individual does not require the withdrawal of the qualified HSA distribution, and the amount is not an excess contribution. However, any HSA withdrawal not used for qualified medical expenses is included in income and subject to an additional 10 percent tax (with certain exceptions), regardless of whether the HSA received a qualified HSA distribution that was previously included in the account beneficiary's income and subject to the additional tax. See § 223(f)(4)(B).

PERMANENT RULE—INDIVIDUALS WITH A ZERO BALANCE IN GENERAL PURPOSE HEALTH FSA ON THE LAST DAY OF PLAN YEAR

Under the Act, if an individual has a zero balance in a general purpose health FSA, as determined on a cash basis, on the last day of the health FSA plan year, the individual does not fail to be an eligible individual as of the first day of the immediately following health FSA plan year because of coverage during a health FSA grace period.

PERMANENT RULE—INDIVIDUALS WITH A ZERO BALANCE IN GENERAL PURPOSE HRA ON THE LAST DAY OF PLAN YEAR

An individual with a zero balance in a general purpose HRA, determined on a cash basis, on the last day of the HRA plan year, does not fail to be an eligible individual on the first day of the immediately following HRA plan year, so long as (1) effective on the first day of the immediately following HRA plan year, the employee elects to waive participation in the HRA, or (2) effective on or before the first day of the following HRA plan year, the employer terminates the general purpose HRA with respect to all employees, or (3) effective on or before the first day of the following HRA plan year, with respect to all employees, the employer converts the general purpose HRA to an HSA-compatible HRA, as described in Rev. Rul. 2004-45.

PERMANENT RULE—PLAN-YEAR-END ROLLOVERS FROM GENERAL PURPOSE HEALTH FSA OR GENERAL PURPOSE HRA TO HSA

An employee with a balance in a general purpose health FSA with a grace period or general purpose HRA at the end of a health FSA or HRA plan year (plan year) is treated as an eligible individual for HSA purposes as of the first day of the first month in the immediately following plan year that the individual has HDHP coverage on the first day of the month if:

(1) the employer amends the health FSA or HRA written plan effective by the last day of the plan year to allow a qualified HSA distribution,

(2) a qualified HSA distribution from the health FSA or HRA has not been previously made on behalf of the employee with respect to that particular health FSA or HRA,

(3) the employee has HDHP coverage as of the first day of the month during which the qualified HSA distribution occurs, and is otherwise an eligible individual,

(4) the employee elects by the last day of the plan year to have the employer make a qualified HSA distribution from the health FSA or HRA to the HSA of the employee,

(5) the health FSA or HRA makes no reimbursements to the employee after the last day of the plan year,

(6) the employer makes the qualified HSA distribution directly to the HSA trustee by the fifteenth day of the third calendar month following the end of the immediately preceding plan year, but after the employee becomes HSA-eligible,

(7) the qualified HSA distribution from the health FSA or HRA does not exceed the lesser of the balance of the health FSA or HRA on (a) September 21, 2006, or (b) the date of the distribution, and

(8)(a) after the qualified HSA distribution there is a zero balance in the health FSA or HRA, and the employee is no longer a participant in any non-HSA compatible health plan or (b) effective on or before the date of the first qualified HSA distribution the general purpose health FSA or general purpose HRA written plan is converted to an HSA-compatible health FSA or HRA, as described in Rev. Rul. 2004-45, for all participants.

TRANSITION RULE—QUALIFIED HSA DISTRIBUTIONS FROM GENERAL PURPOSE HEALTH FSA AND GENERAL PURPOSE HRA BEFORE MARCH 15, 2007

An employee with a balance in a general purpose health FSA or general purpose HRA after December 31, 2006 is treated as an eligible individual for HSA purposes as of the first day of the first month in 2007 that the employee has HDHP coverage on the first day of the month if:

(1) the employer amends the health FSA or HRA written plan effective on or before March 15, 2007, to allow a qualified HSA distribution,

(2) a qualified HSA distribution from the health FSA or HRA has not been previously made on behalf of the employee with respect to that particular health FSA or HRA,

(3) the employee has HDHP coverage as of the first day of the month during which the qualified HSA distribution occurs, and is otherwise an eligible individual,

(4) the employee elects on or before March 15, 2007, to have the employer make a qualified HSA distribution from the health FSA or HRA to the HSA of the employee,

(5) the qualified HSA distribution from the health FSA or HRA does not exceed the lesser of the balance of the respective health FSA or HRA on (a) September 21, 2006, or (b) the date of the distribution,

(6) the employer makes the qualified HSA distribution directly to the HSA trustee by March 15, 2007, but after the employee becomes HSA-eligible, and

(7)(a) after the qualified HSA distribution there is a zero balance in the health FSA or HRA, and the employee is no longer a participant in any non-HSA compatible health plan or (b) effective on or before the date of the first qualified HSA distribution, the general purpose health FSA or general purpose HRA written plan is converted to an HSA-compatible health FSA or HRA, as described in Rev. Rul. 2004-45, for all participants.

EXAMPLES * * *

Permanent Rule Examples * * *

Transition Rule Examples * * *

Examples of Additional 10 Percent Tax * * *

NO EFFECT ON HSA ESTABLISHMENT DATE

Qualified medical expenses for HSA purposes are only expenses incurred after the HSA is established. Notice 2004-2, 2004-1 C.B. 269, Q&A-26. While this notice provides that certain individuals are treated as eligible individuals as of the first day of the plan year, those rules do not treat an HSA as established before the actual establishment of the HSA.

State trust law determines when an HSA is established. Most state trust laws require that for a trust to exist, an asset must be held in trust; thus, most state trust laws require that a trust must be funded to be established.

REPORTING

Amounts transferred through a qualified HSA distribution are not reported in box 12 of Form W-2. Employers are not responsible for reporting whether an employee receiving a qualified HSA distribution remains an eligible individual during the testing period. However, employers must report qualified HSA distributions as rollover contributions to the HSA trustee, and the HSA trustee must report the qualified HSA distribution as a rollover contribution on Form 5498-SA.

EFFECTIVE DATE

The provision in the Act allowing qualified HSA distributions from health FSAs and HRAs is effective on or after December 20, 2006, and before January 1, 2012.

EFFECT ON OTHER DOCUMENTS

Published guidance under § 105(b) states that if any person has the right to receive cash or any other taxable or nontaxable benefit under a health FSA or HRA, other than the reimbursement of § 213(d) medical expenses of the employee, employee's spouse or employee's dependents, then all distributions made from the arrangement are included in the employee's gross income, even amounts paid to reimburse medical care. See Rev. Rul. 2006-36, 2006-36 I.R.B. 353; Rev. Rul. 2005-24, 2005-1 C.B. 892; Rev. Rul. 2003-102, 2003-2 C.B. 559; Notice 2002-45, 2002-2 C.B. 93; Rev. Rul. 2002-41, 2002-2 C.B. 75; Rev. Rul.

69-141, 1969-1 C.B. 48. New § 106(e) provides that a health FSA or HRA will not fail to satisfy the requirements of §§ 105 or 106 merely because the plan provides for a qualified HSA distribution. Amounts rolled into an HSA may be used for purposes other than reimbursing the § 213(d) medical expenses of the employee, spouse or dependents. Accordingly, Rev. Rul. 2006-36, Rev. Rul. 2005-24, Rev. Rul. 2003-102, Notice 2002-45, Rev. Rul. 2002-41, and Rev. Rul. 69-141 are modified with respect to qualified HSA distributions described in § 106(e). In addition, Notice 2005-86, 2005-2 C.B. 1075, is modified effective as of December 20, 2006.

DRAFTING INFORMATION * * *

Notice 2005-86 (2005-49 I.R.B. 1075)

[**Summary:** The IRS provides guidance on an individual's eligibility to contribute to an HSA during a cafeteria plan grace period and how an employer may amend the cafeteria plan document to enable a health FSA participant to become HSA eligible during the grace period.]

PURPOSE

This notice provides guidance on eligibility to contribute to a Health Savings Account (HSA) during a cafeteria plan grace period as described in Notice 2005-42, 2005-23 I.R.B. 1204. As discussed below, an individual participating in a health flexible spending arrangement (health FSA) who is covered by the grace period is generally not eligible to contribute to an HSA until the first day of the first month following the end of the grace period, even if the participant's health FSA has no unused benefits at the end of the prior cafeteria plan year. This notice, however, provides guidance on how an employer may amend the cafeteria plan document to enable a health FSA participant to become HSA eligible during the grace period.

BACKGROUND

Cafeteria Plans

Section 125(a) states that, in general, no amount is included in the gross income of a participant in a cafeteria plan solely because, under the plan, the participant may choose among the benefits of the plan. section 125(d) defines a cafeteria plan as a written plan under which all participants are employees, and the participants may choose among two or more benefits consisting of cash and qualified benefits. "Qualified benefits" mean any benefit which, with the application of § 125(a), is not includible in the gross income of the employee by reason of an express provision of Chapter 1 of the Internal Revenue Code, including employer-provided accident and health coverage under §§ 106 and 105(b). A high deductible health plan (HDHP) as defined in § 223(c)(2)(A) can be employer-provided accident and health coverage. A health FSA, which pays or reimburses certain § 213(d) medical expenses (other than health insurance or long-term care services or insurance), is also employer-provided accident and health coverage. The term "qualified medical expenses" as used in this Notice, means expenses which may be paid or reimbursed under a health FSA.

Cafeteria Plan Grace Period

Notice 2005-42, 2005-23 I.R.B. 1204, modifies the application of the rule prohibiting deferred compensation under a cafeteria plan (i.e., the "use-it-or-lose-it" rule). The notice permits a cafeteria plan to be amended, at the employer's option, to provide a grace period immediately following the end of each plan year, during which an individual who incurs expenses for a qualified benefit during the grace period, may be paid or reimbursed for those expenses from the unused benefits or contributions relating to that benefit. A plan providing a grace period is required to provide the grace period to all participants who are covered on the last day of the plan year (including participants whose coverage is extended to the last day of the plan year through COBRA continuation coverage). The grace period remains in effect for the entire period even though the participant may terminate employment on or before the last day of the grace period. But an employer may limit the availability of the grace period to only certain cafeteria plan benefits and not others. For example, a cafeteria plan offering both a health FSA and a dependent care FSA may limit the grace period to the health FSA. The grace period must not extend beyond the fifteenth day of the third calendar month after the end of the immediately preceding plan year to which it relates, but may be adopted for a shorter period.

Interaction Between HSAs and Health FSAs

Section 223(a) allows a deduction for contributions to an HSA for an "eligible individual" for any month during the taxable year. An "eligible individual" is defined in § 223(c)(1)(A) and means, in general, with respect to any month, any individual who is covered under an HDHP on the first day of such month and is not, while covered under an HDHP, "covered under any health plan which is not a high-deductible health plan, and which provides coverage for any benefit which is covered under the high-deductible health plan."

In addition to coverage under an HDHP, § 223(c)(1)(B) provides that an eligible individual may have disregarded coverage, including "permitted insurance" and "permitted coverage." Section 223(c)(2)(C) also provides a safe harbor for the absence of a preventive care deductible. See Notice 2004-23, 2004-1 C.B. 725. Therefore, under § 223, an individual who is eligible to contribute to an HSA must be covered by a health plan that is an HDHP, and may also have permitted insurance, permitted coverage and preventive care, but no other coverage. A health FSA that reimburses all qualified § 213(d) medical expenses without other restrictions is a health plan that constitutes other coverage. Consequently, an individual who is covered by a health FSA that pays or reimburses all qualified medical expenses is not an eligible individual for purposes of making contributions to an HSA. This result is the same even if the individual is covered by a health FSA sponsored by a spouse's employer.

However, as described in Rev. Rul. 2004-45, 2004-1 C.B. 971, an individual who is otherwise eligible for an HSA may be covered under specific types of health FSAs and remain eligible to contribute to an HSA. One arrangement is a limited-purpose health FSA, which pays or reimburses expenses only for preventive care and "permitted coverage" (e.g., dental care and vision care). Another HSA-compatible arrangement is a post-deductible health FSA, which pays or reimburses preventive care and for other qualified medical expenses only if incurred after the minimum annual deductible for the HDHP under § 223(c)(2)(A) is satisfied. This means that qualified medical expenses incurred before the HDHP deductible is satisfied may not be reimbursed by a post-deductible HDHP even after the HDHP deductible had been satisfied. [Editor's Note: The term "post-deductible HDHP" would appear to be incorrect. A "post-deductible FSA" or "post-deductible health FSA" is probably meant.] To summarize, an otherwise HSA eligible individual will remain eligible if covered under a limited-purpose health FSA or a post-deductible FSA, or a combination of both.

OPTIONS AVAILABLE TO AN EMPLOYER

An employer may adopt either of the following two options, which will affect participants' HSA eligibility during the cafeteria plan grace period:

(1) General Purpose Health FSA During Grace Period

Employer amends the cafeteria plan document to provide a grace period but takes no other action with respect to the general purpose health FSA. Because a health FSA that pays or reimburses all qualified medical expenses constitutes impermissible "other coverage" for HSA eligibility purposes, an individual who participated in the health FSA (or a spouse whose medical expenses are eligible for reimbursement under the health FSA) for the immediately preceding cafeteria plan year and who is covered by the grace period, is not eligible to contribute to an HSA until the first day of the first month following the end of the grace period. For example, if the health FSA grace period ends March 15, 2006, an individual who did not elect coverage by a general health FSA or other disqualifying coverage for 2006 is HSA eligible on April 1, 2006, and may contribute 9/12ths of the 2006 HSA contribution limit. The result is the same even if a participant's health FSA has no unused contributions remaining at the end of the immediately preceding cafeteria plan year.

(2) Mandatory Conversion from Health FSA to HSA-compatible Health FSA for All Participants

Employer amends the cafeteria plan document to provide for both a grace period and a mandatory conversion of the general purpose health FSA to a limited-purpose or post-deductible FSA (or combined limited-purpose and post-deductible health FSA) during the grace period. The amendments do not permit an individual participant to elect between an HSA-compatible FSA or an FSA that is not HSA-compatible. The amendments apply to the entire grace period and to all participants in the health FSA who are covered by the grace period. The amendments must satisfy all other requirements of Notice 2005-42. Coverage of these participants by the HSA-compatible FSA during the grace period does not disqualify participants who are otherwise eligible individuals from contributing to an HSA during the grace period.

TRANSITION RELIEF

For cafeteria plan years ending before June 5, 2006, an individual participating in a general purpose health FSA that provides coverage during a grace period will be eligible to contribute to an HSA during the grace period if the following requirements are met: (1) If not for the coverage under a general purpose health FSA described in clause (2), the individual would be an "eligible individual" as defined in § 223(c)(1)(A) during the grace period (in general, is covered under an HDHP and is not, while covered under an HDHP, covered under any impermissible other health coverage); and (3) Either (A) the individual's (and the individual's spouse's) general purpose health FSA has no unused contributions or benefits remaining at the end of the immediately preceding cafeteria plan year, or (B) in the case of an individual who is not covered during the grace period under a general purpose health FSA maintained by the employer of the individual's spouse, the individual's employer amends its cafeteria plan document to provide that the grace period does not provide coverage to an individual who elects HDHP coverage.

EFFECT ON OTHER DOCUMENTS

Notice 2005-42 and Rev. Rul. 2004-45 are amplified.

DRAFTING INFORMATION ***

Notice 2005-83 (2005-49 I.R.B. 1075)

[**Summary:** The IRS provides additional transitional relief for certain health plans with non-calendar year renewal dates, that otherwise qualify as a HDHP, except that the plans provide state-mandated benefits without regard to a deductible or with a deductible below the minimum annual deductible specified in Code section 223(c)(2).]

PURPOSE

This notice provides relief for certain health plans with non-calendar year renewal dates that otherwise qualify as high-deductible health plans (HDHPs), except that the plans provide state-mandated benefits without regard to a deductible or with a deductible below the minimum annual deductible specified in § 223(c)(2) of the Internal Revenue Code.

BACKGROUND AND APPLICATION

Some states require that health plans provide certain benefits without regard to a deductible or with a deductible below the minimum annual deductible specified in § 223(c)(2) (e.g., first-dollar coverage or coverage with a low deductible). These health plans are not HDHPs under § 223(c)(2) and individuals covered under these health plans are generally not eligible to contribute to Health Savings Accounts (HSAs). Notice 2004-43, 2004-2 C.B. 10, provides transition relief that treats health plans as meeting the requirement of § 223(c)(2) when the sole reason the plans are not HDHPs is because of certain state-mandated benefits. For months before January 1, 2006, otherwise eligible individuals covered under these health plans will be treated as eligible individuals for purposes of § 223(c)(1) and may contribute to an HSA. The transition period provided in Notice 2004-43 covers months before January 1, 2006, for state-mandated requirements in effect on January 1, 2004.

Generally, a health plan may not reduce existing benefits before the plan's renewal date. Thus, even though a state may amend its laws before January 1, 2006, to authorize HDHPs that comply with § 223(c)(2), non-calendar year plans may still fail to qualify as HDHPs after January 1, 2006 because existing benefits cannot be changed until the next renewal date. For example, a state amends its laws to authorize HDHPs, effective November 1, 2005. A health plan with a renewal date of July 1, 2005 is required to retain the state-mandated low-deductible coverage for the plan year July 1, 2005 through June 30, 2006 because the benefits can only be modified on the renewal date. As a result, although the state has amended its statute, the health plan will fail to be an HDHP for months after January 1, 2006 (i.e., for the months of January through June, 2006).

Therefore, additional transitional relief is appropriate for non-calendar year health plans. Accordingly, the transition relief in Notice 2004-43 is amplified to provide that for any coverage period of twelve months or less beginning before January 1, 2006, a health plan that otherwise qualifies as an HDHP as defined in § 223(c)(2), except that it complied on its most recent renewal date before January 1, 2006 with state-mandated requirements (in effect on January 1, 2004) to provide certain benefits without regard to a deductible or with a deductible below the minimum annual deductible specified in § 223(c)(2), will be treated as an HDHP. In no event will the additional transitional relief provided in this Notice extend beyond the earlier of the health plan's next renewal date or December 31, 2006.

EFFECT ON OTHER DOCUMENTS

Notice 2004-43, 2004-2 C.B. 10, is amplified.

DRAFTING INFORMATION ***

Notice 2005-8 (2005-4 I.R.B.1)

[**Summary:** The IRS has provided additional guidance on a partnership's contributions to a partner's health savings account and an S corporation's contributions to a 2 percent shareholder-employee's HSA.]

PURPOSE

This notice provides guidance on a partnership's contributions to a partner's Health Savings Account (HSA) and an S corporation's contributions to a 2 percent shareholder-employee's HSA.

BACKGROUND

Section 1201 of the Medicare Prescription Drug, Improvement, and Modernization Act of 2003, Pub. L. No. 108-173, added section 223 to the Internal Revenue Code to permit eligible individuals to establish Health Savings Accounts (HSAs) for taxable years beginning after December 31, 2003. Generally, contributions made to an HSA, within permissible limits, by or on behalf of a taxpayer who is an eligible individual are deductible by a taxpayer under section 223(a). The deduction is an adjustment to gross income (i.e., an above the line deduction) under section 62(a)(19). If an employer makes a contribution, within permissible limits, to the HSA on behalf of an employee who is an eligible individual, the contribution is excluded from the employee's gross income and wages. *See* section 106(d). A partnership may also contribute to a partner's HSA and an S corporation may contribute to the HSA of a 2 percent shareholder-employee (as defined below). The Questions and Answers below discuss the tax treatment of HSA contributions made on behalf of such partners and 2 percent shareholder-employees who are eligible individuals.

QUESTIONS AND ANSWERS

Q-1. What is the tax treatment of a partnership's contributions to a partner's HSA that are treated as distributions to the partner under section 731?

A-1. Contributions by a partnership to a bona fide partner's HSA are not contributions by an employer to the HSA of an employee. *See* Rev. Rul. 69-184, 1969-1.C.B. 256. Contributions by a partnership to a partner's HSA that are treated as distributions to the partner under section 731 are not deductible by the partnership and do not affect the distributive shares of partnership income and deductions. *See* Rev. Rul. 91-26, 1991-1 C.B. 184 (analysis of situation 1, last paragraph). The contributions are reported as distributions of money on Schedule K-1 (Form 1065). These distributions are not included in the partner's net earnings from self-employment under section 1402(a) because the distributions under section 731 do not affect a partner's distributive share of partnership income or loss under section 702(a)(8). The partner, if an eligible individual as defined in section 223(c)(1), is entitled under sections 223(a) and 62(a)(19) to deduct the amount of the contributions made to the partner's HSA during the taxable year as an adjustment to gross income on his or her federal income tax return.

Q-2. What is the tax treatment of a partnership's contributions to a partner's HSA that are treated as guaranteed payments under section 707(c), are derived from the partnership's trade or business, and are for services rendered to the partnership?

A-2. Contributions by a partnership to a bona fide partner's HSA are not contributions by an employer to the HSA of an employee. *See* Rev. Rul. 69-184. Contributions by a partnership to a partner's HSA for services rendered to the partnership that are treated as guaranteed payments under section 707(c) are deductible by the partnership under section 162 (if the requirements of that section are satisfied (taking into account the rules of section 263)) and are includible in the partner's gross income. The contributions are not excludible from the partner's gross income under section 106(d) because the contributions are treated as a distributive share of partnership income under Treas. Reg. § 1.707-1(c) for purposes of all Code sections other than sections 61(a) and 162(a). *See* Rev. Rul. 91-26. Contributions by a partnership to a partner's HSA that are treated as guaranteed payments under section 707(c), are reported as guaranteed payments on Schedule K-1 (Form 1065). Because the contributions are guaranteed payments that are derived from the partnership's trade or business, and are for services rendered to the partnership, the contributions are included in the partner's net earnings from self-employment under section 1402(a) on the partner's Schedule SE (Form 1040). The partner, if an eligible individual as defined in section 223(c)(1), is entitled under sections 223(a) and 62(a)(19) to deduct the amount of the contributions made to the partner's HSA during the taxable year as an adjustment to gross income on his or her federal income tax return.

The following example illustrates the answers in A-1 and A-2.

Example. Partnership is a limited partnership with three equal individual partners, A (a general partner), B (a limited partner), and C (a limited partner). C is to be paid $500 annually for services rendered to Partnership in his capacity as a partner and without regard to Partnership income (a section 707(c) guaranteed payment). The $500 payment to C is derived from Partnership's trade or business. Partnership has no employees. A, B, and C are eligible individuals as defined in section 223(c)(1) and each has an HSA. During Partnership's Year 1 taxable year, Partnership makes the following contributions: a $300 contribution to each of A's and B's HSAs which are treated by Partnership as section 731 distributions to A and B; and a $500 contribution to C's HSA in lieu of paying C the guaranteed payment directly.

Partnership's contributions to A's and B's HSAs are not deductible by Partnership and, therefore, do not affect Partnership's calculation of its taxable income or loss. *See* Rev. Rul. 91-26. A and B are entitled to an above the line deduction, under sections 223(a) and 62(a)(19), for the amount of the contributions made to their individual HSAs. The section 731 distributions to A's and B's individual HSAs are reported as cash distributions to A and B on A's and B's Schedule K-1 (Form 1065). The distributions to A's and B's HSAs are not includible in A's and B's net earnings from self employment under section 1402(a), because distributions under section 731 do not affect a partner's distributive share of the partnership's income or loss under section 702(a)(8).

Partnership's contribution to C's HSA that is treated as a guaranteed payment under section 707(c) for services rendered to the partnership is deductible by Partnership under section 162 (if the requirements of that section are satisfied (taking into account the rules of section 263)) and is includible in C's gross income. The contribution is not excludible from C's gross income under section 106(d) because the contribution is treated as a distributive share of partnership income for purposes of all Code sections other than sections 61(a) and 162(a), and a guaranteed payment to a partner is not treated as compensation to an employee. *See* Rev. Rul. 91-26. The payment to C's HSA should be reported as a guaranteed payment on Schedule K-1 (Form 1065). Because the contribution is a guaranteed payment that is derived from the partnership's trade or business and is for services rendered to the partnership, the contribution constitutes net earnings from self-employment to C under section 1402(a) which should be reported on Schedule SE (Form 1040). C is entitled under sections 223(a) and 62(a)(19) to deduct as an adjustment to gross income the amount of the contribution made to C's HSA.

Q-3. What is the tax treatment of an S corporation's contributions to the HSA of a 2 percent shareholder (as defined in section 1372(b)) who is also an employee (2 percent shareholder-employee) in consideration for services rendered to the S corporation?

A-3. Under section 1372, for purposes of applying the provisions of Subtitle A that relate to fringe benefits, an S corporation is treated as a partnership, and any 2 percent shareholder of the S corporation is treated as a partner of such partnership. Therefore, contributions by an S corporation to an HSA of a 2 percent shareholder-employee in consideration for services rendered are treated as guaranteed payments under section 707(c). Accordingly, the contributions are deductible by the S corporation under section 162 (if the requirements of that section are satisfied (taking into account the rules of section 263)) and are includible in the 2 percent shareholder-employee's gross income. In addition, the 2 percent shareholder-employee is not entitled to exclude the contribution from gross income under section 106(d). *See* Rev. Rul. 91-26.

For employment tax purposes, when contributions are made by an S corporation to an HSA of a 2 percent shareholder-employee, the 2 percent shareholder-employee is treated as an employee subject to Federal Insurance Contributions Act (FICA) tax and not as an individual subject to Self-Employment Contributions Act (SECA) tax. (*See* Announcement 92-16, 1992-5 I.R.B. 53, clarifying the

FICA (Social Security and Medicare) tax treatment of accident and health premiums paid by an S corporation on behalf of a 2 percent shareholder-employee.) However, if the requirements for the exclusion under section 3121(a)(2)(B) are satisfied, the S corporation's contributions to an HSA of a 2 percent shareholder-employee are not wages subject to FICA tax, even though the amounts must be included in wages for income tax withholding purposes on the 2 percent shareholder-employee's Form W-2, Wage and Tax Statement. The 2 percent shareholder-employee, if an eligible individual as defined in section 223(c)(1), is entitled under sections 223(a) and 62(a)(19) to deduct the amount of the contributions made to the 2 percent shareholder-employee's HSA during the taxable year as an adjustment to gross income on his or her federal income tax return. *See* Notice 2004-2, Q&A 19, 2004-2 I.R.B. 269, for employment tax rules for employer contributions to HSAs of employees other than 2 percent shareholder-employees.

DRAFTING INFORMATION ***

Notice 2004-79 (2004-49 I.R.B. 898)

[**Summary:** The IRS has provided guidance on the effect of the Working Families Tax Relief Act of 2004 on the definition of dependent under Code Section 106. For tax years beginning January 1, 2005, the term "dependent" for section 106 purposes will have the same meaning as in Code section 105(b), the IRS said.]

I. PURPOSE

This notice provides guidance regarding the effect of the Working Families Tax Relief Act of 2004 (WFTRA), Pub. L. No. 108-311, 118 Stat. 1166, on the exclusion from the gross income of an employee under § 106 of the Internal Revenue Code (Code) of employer-provided coverage under an accident or health plan.

II. BACKGROUND

Section 201 of WFTRA amended the definition of dependent in § 152, effective for taxable years beginning after December 31, 2004. Pursuant to § 152, as amended, an individual must be either a "qualifying child" or a "qualifying relative" to be a dependent. section 152(c), as amended, provides that an individual must meet relationship, residency, and age requirements to be a qualifying child. In addition, an individual is not a qualifying child if the individual provided over one-half of his or her own support for the calendar year. section 152(c)(3)(A) provides that an individual meets the age requirement if the individual has not attained age 19 as of the close of the calendar year or if the individual is a student who has not attained age 24 as of the close of the calendar year. Under § 152(c)(3)(B), an individual is treated as meeting the age requirement if the individual is permanently and totally disabled (as defined in § 22(e)(3)) at any time during the calendar year.

Section 152(d)(1), as amended, provides, in general, that a qualifying relative is an individual who bears a relationship to the taxpayer described in § 152(d)(2), whose gross income is less than the exemption amount (as defined in § 151(d)), who receives over one-half of his or her support from the taxpayer, and who is not a qualifying child of the taxpayer or any other taxpayer.

Section 207 of WFTRA contains several technical and conforming amendments to Code sections that refer to the § 152 definition of dependent, including an amendment to § 105(b). section 105(b) generally excludes from an employee's gross income employer-provided medical care reimbursements paid directly or indirectly to the employee for the medical care of the employee and the employee's spouse and dependents, as defined in § 152. Under the WFTRA amendment to § 105(b), an individual's status as a dependent for purposes of § 105(b) will be determined without regard to new § 152(b)(1) and (b)(2), which contain certain exceptions to the definition of dependent, and without regard to new § 152(d)(1)(B), which contains the gross income limitation for a qualifying relative. It appears that the intent of Congress in making these conforming amendments was to maintain the current law definition of dependent for purposes of employer-provided medical care reimbursements.

Section 106(a) provides that the gross income of an employee does not include employer-provided coverage under an accident or health plan. Thus, premiums and other amounts that an employer pays on behalf of an employee to an accident or health plan are not included in gross income. Treas. Reg. § 1.106-1 provides that the exclusion from gross income extends to contributions which the employer makes to an accident or health plan on behalf of the employee and the employee's spouse or dependents, as defined in § 152. Because the reference to "dependents" under § 106 appears only in the regulations under that section and not in the statute itself, Congress made no conforming amendments to § 106 in WFTRA.

Under current law, the exclusion under § 106(a) for employer-provided coverage under an accident or health plan parallels the exclusion under § 105(b) for employer-provided reimbursements of medical care expenses incurred by the employee and the employee's spouse and dependents, as defined in § 152. However, as a result of the changes made by WFTRA, the definition of dependent in § 105(b) differs from the definition in the regulations under § 106(a). Accordingly, if the regulations under § 106(a) continued to be applied as currently written after the effective date of section 201 of WFTRA, the value of employer-provided coverage for an individual who is not a qualifying child and who does not meet the gross income limitation for a qualifying relative would have to be included in the employee's gross income. Because the intent of Congress was not to change the definition of dependent for purposes of employer-provided health plans, regulations under § 106 should be revised to provide that the same definition of dependent applies to § 106 as applies to amended § 105(b).

III. APPLICATION

The IRS intends to revise the regulations at 26 C.F.R. 1.106-1 to provide that the term "dependent" for purposes of § 106 shall have the same meaning as in § 105(b). The revised regulations will be effective for taxable years beginning after December 31, 2004.

Taxpayers may rely on this Notice pending the issuance of the revised regulations. Accordingly, an employee may exclude from gross income the value of employer-provided coverage for an individual who meets the definition of a qualifying relative except that the individual's gross income equals or exceeds the exemption amount.

DRAFTING INFORMATION ***

Notice 2004-50 (2004-33 I.R.B. 196)

[**Summary:** Additional guidance on the requirements for HDHPs and HSAs address questions the IRS received after December 2003. This guidance clarifies that for those age 65 or older, Medicare eligibility does make an individual ineligible to contribute to an HSA provided the individual is not actually enrolled in Medicare. The IRS has also provided that employee assistance programs (EAP) that provide short-term counseling regarding such problems as substance abuse, emotional disorders, or financial difficulties, or that provide evidence-based information and case monitoring of care provided by a health plan, or that provide such services as fitness and sports activities are not health plans because they do not provide significant benefits in the nature of medical care or treatment. Therefore, coverage under such an EAP does not render an individual ineligible to contribute to an HSA.]

PURPOSE

This notice provides guidance on Health Savings Accounts.

BACKGROUND

Section 1201 of the Medicare Prescription Drug, Improvement, and Modernization Act of 2003, Pub. L. No. 108-173, added section 223 to the Internal Revenue Code to permit eligible individuals to establish Health Savings Accounts (HSAs) for taxable years beginning after December 31, 2003. Notice 2004-2, 2004-2 I.R.B. 269, provides certain basic information on HSAs in question and answer format. This notice addresses additional questions relating to HSAs.

OUTLINE TABLE OF CONTENTS

The following is an outline of the questions and answers covered in this notice:

I. Eligible Individuals

Q&A 1. Choice between low-deductible health plan and HDHP

Q&A 2. Eligible for Medicare and contributions to HSA

Q&A 3. Eligible for Medicare and catch-up contributions

Q&A 4. Government retiree and enrollment in Medicare Part B

Q&A 5. Eligible for medical benefits from VA

Q&A 6. Coverage under TRICARE

Q&A 7. HDHP and coverage for one or more specific diseases or illnesses

Q&A 8. Permitted insurance and insurance contracts

Q&A 9. HDHP and discount cards

Q&A 10. Employee Assistance Programs (EAPs), disease management programs and wellness programs

Q&A 11. Payroll period other than a calendar month

II. High Deductible Health Plans (HDHPs)

Q&A 12. Family HDHP coverage defined

Q&A 13. State high-risk pools and HDHPs

Q&A 14. Lifetime limit on benefits under HDHPs

Q&A 15. Annual and lifetime limit on specific benefits under HDHPs

Q&A 16. Payments in excess of usual, customary and reasonable (UCR) amounts

Q&A 17. HDHPs without express limit on out-of-pocket expenses

Q&A 18. HDHPs and pre-certification requirements

Q&A 19. HDHPs and increased coinsurance payments

Q&A 20. Cumulative embedded deductibles and out-of-pocket maximum

Q&A 21. Amounts incurred before satisfying deductible and out-of-pocket maximum

Q&A 22. Deductible credit for short year

Q&A 23. Deductible credit after changes in category of coverage

Q&A 24. HDHP deductible and coverage period longer than 12 months

Q&A 25. HDHPs and discounted prices

III. Preventive Care

Q&A 26. Preventive care and treatment of related conditions

Q&A 27. Drugs or medications as preventive care

IV. Contributions

Q&A 28. Contributions on behalf of eligible individuals

Q&A 29. State government contributions and high-risk pools

Q&A 30. Calculating maximum HSA contributions for family coverage

Q&A 31. Contribution rules for family HDHP coverage and ineligible individuals

Q&A 32. Dividing HSA contributions between spouses

Q&A 33. Contribution limit if covered by both HDHP and post-deductible HRA

Q&A 34. Computation of net income on HSA excess contributions

Q&A 35. Withdrawal of nonexcess HSA contributions

V. Distributions

Q&A 36. Distributions for spouse or dependents covered under non-HDHP

Q&A 37. Mistaken HSA distributions

Q&A 38. Use of distributions where both spouses have HSAs

Q&A 39. Deferred distributions for expenses incurred in prior years

Q&A 40. Distributions for qualified long-term care insurance premiums

Q&A 41. Deduction limits under section 213(d)(10)

Q&A 42. Distributions for long-term care services

Q&A 43. Distributions for retiree's self-insured retiree coverage

Q&A 44. Distributions to pay health insurance premiums by individuals with end stage renal disease (ESRD) or disability

Q&A 45. Distributions to pay Medicare premiums

VI. Comparability

Q&A 46. Matching employees' HSA contributions

Q&A 47. Matching contributions under cafeteria plans

Q&A 48. Comparability and health assessments, disease management or wellness programs

Q&A 49. Comparability and health assessments, disease management or wellness programs under a cafeteria plan

Q&A 50. Comparability and catch-up contributions

Q&A 51. Comparability and full-time employees working less than 12 months

Q&A 52. Testing period for making comparable contributions

Q&A 53. Comparability and eligible individuals' coverage under employer's HDHP

Q&A 54. Comparability and after-tax employee contributions

VII. Rollovers

Q&A 55. Frequency of rollovers

Q&A 56. Trustee-to-trustee transfers

VIII. Cafeteria Plans and HSAs

Q&A 57. FSA requirements and HSAs

Q&A 58. Section 125 change in status rules

Q&A 59. HSA offered as new benefit under cafeteria plan

Q&A 60. Accelerated HSA contributions by employer

Q&A 61. Negative elections for HSAs

IX. Account Administration

Q&A 62. Model forms for HSAs

Q&A 63. No joint HSA for husband and wife

Q&A 64. Multiple HSAs

Q&A 65. Permissible investments for HSAs

Q&A 66. Commingling HSA funds

Q&A 67. Prohibited transactions and account beneficiaries

Q&A 68. Prohibited transactions and trustees or custodians

Q&A 69. Administration fees withdrawn from an HSA

Q&A 70. Administration fees and contribution limits

Q&A 71. Administration fees paid directly

X. Trustees and Custodians

Q&A 72. Insurance company qualifying as HSA trustee or custodian

Q&A 73. Limit on annual HSA contributions acceptable by trustee or custodian

Q&A 74. Tracking maximum annual contribution limit for a particular account beneficiary

Q&A 75. Tracking account beneficiary's age

Q&A 76. Return of mistaken distributions

Q&A 77. No restrictions on rollovers from HSA

Q&A 78. Acceptance of rollover contributions

Q&A 79. No restrictions on HSA distributions for qualified medical expenses

Q&A 80. Restrictions on frequency or amount of distributions

XI. Other Issues

Q&A 81. Determining eligibility and contribution limits by employer

Q&A 82. Recoupment of HSA contributions by employer

Q&A 83. HSAs and section 105(h)

Q&A 84. HSA contributions and SECA tax

Q&A 85. HSA contributions and the EIC

Q&A 86. HDHP and cost-of-living adjustments

Q&A 87. HSAs and bonafide residents of Commonwealth of Puerto Rico, American Samoa, the U.S. Virgin Islands, Guam, the Commonwealth of the Northern Mariana Islands

Q&A 88. C corporation contributions to HSAs of shareholders

QUESTIONS AND ANSWERS

I. Eligible individuals

Q-1. If an employer offers an employee a choice between a low-deductible health plan and a high-deductible health plan (HDHP), and the employee selects coverage only under the HDHP, is the employee an eligible individual under section 223(c)(1)?

A-1. Yes, if the employee is otherwise an eligible individual. To determine if an individual is an eligible individual, the actual health coverage selected by the individual is controlling. Thus, it does not matter that the individual could have chosen, but did not choose, a low-deductible health plan or other coverage that would have disqualified the individual from contributing to an HSA.

Q-2. May an otherwise eligible individual who is eligible for Medicare, but not enrolled in Medicare Part A or Part B, contribute to an HSA?

A-2. Yes. Section 223(b)(7) states that an individual ceases to be an eligible individual starting with the month he or she is entitled to benefits under Medicare. Under this provision, mere eligibility for Medicare does not make an individual ineligible to contribute to an HSA. Rather, the term "entitled to benefits under" Medicare means both eligibility and enrollment in Medicare. Thus, an otherwise eligible individual under section 223(c)(1) who is not actually enrolled in Medicare Part A or Part B may contribute to an HSA until the month that individual is enrolled in Medicare.

Example (1). Y, age 66, is covered under her employer's HDHP. Although Y is eligible for Medicare, Y is not actually entitled to Medicare because she did not apply for benefits under Medicare (i.e., enroll in Medicare Part A or Part B). If Y is otherwise an eligible individual under section 223(c)(1), she may contribute to an HSA.

Example (2). In August 2004, X attains age 65 and applies for and begins receiving Social Security benefits. X is automatically enrolled in Medicare. As of August 1, 2004, X is no longer an eligible individual and may not contribute to an HSA.

Q-3. May an otherwise eligible individual under section 223(c)(1) who is age 65 or older and thus eligible for Medicare, but is not enrolled in Medicare Part A or Part B, make the additional catch-up contribution under section 223(b)(3) for persons age 55 or older?

A-3. Yes. See Notice 2004-2, Q&A 14, on catch-up contributions.

Q-4. Is a government retiree who is enrolled in Medicare Part B (but not Part A) an eligible individual under section 223(c)(1)?

A-4. No. Under section 223(b)(7), an individual who is enrolled in Medicare may not contribute to an HSA.

Q-5. If an otherwise eligible individual under section 223(c)(1) is eligible for medical benefits through the Department of Veterans Affairs (VA), may he or she contribute to an HSA?

A-5. An otherwise eligible individual who is eligible to receive VA medical benefits, but who has not actually received such benefits during the preceding three months, is an eligible individual under section 223(c)(1). An individual is not eligible to make HSA contributions for any month, however, if the individual has received medical benefits from the VA at any time during the previous three months.

Q-6. May an otherwise eligible individual who is covered by an HDHP and also receives health benefits under TRICARE (the health care program for active duty and retired members of the uniformed services, their families and survivors) contribute to an HSA?

A-6. No. Coverage options under TRICARE do not meet the minimum annual deductible requirements for an HDHP under section 223(c)(2). Thus, an individual covered under TRICARE is not an eligible individual and may not contribute to an HSA.

Q-7. May an otherwise eligible individual who is covered by both an HDHP and also by insurance contracts for one or more specific diseases or illnesses, such as cancer, diabetes, asthma or congestive heart failure, contribute to an HSA if the insurance provides benefits before the deductible of the HDHP is satisfied?

A-7. Yes. Section 223(c)(1)(B)(i) provides that an eligible individual covered under an HDHP may also be covered "for any benefit provided by permitted insurance." section 223(c)(3)(B) provides that the term "permitted insurance" includes "insurance for a specified disease or illness." Therefore, an eligible individual may be covered by an HDHP and also by permitted insurance for one or more specific diseases, such as cancer, diabetes, asthma or congestive heart failure, as long as the principal health coverage is provided by the HDHP.

Q-8. Must coverage for "permitted insurance" described in section 223(c)(3) (liabilities incurred under workers' compensation laws, tort liabilities, liabilities relating to ownership or use of property, insurance for a specified disease or illness, and insurance paying a fixed amount per day (or other period) of hospitalization), be provided under insurance contracts?

A-8. Yes. Benefits for "permitted insurance" under section 223(c)(3) must generally be provided through insurance contracts and not on a self-insured basis. However, where benefits (such as workers' compensation benefits) are provided in satisfaction of a statutory requirement and any resulting benefits for medical care are secondary or incidental to other benefits, the benefits will qualify as "permitted insurance" even if self-insured.

Q-9. May an individual who is covered by an HDHP and also has a discount card that enables the user to obtain discounts for health care services or products, contribute to an HSA?

A-9. Yes. Discount cards that entitle holders to obtain discounts for health care services or products at managed care market rates will not disqualify an individual from being an eligible individual for HSA purposes if the individual is required to pay the costs of the health care (taking into account the discount) until the deductible of the HDHP is satisfied.

Example. An employer provides its employees with a pharmacy discount card. For a fixed annual fee (paid by the employer), each employee receives a card that entitles the holder to choose any participating pharmacy. During the one-year life of the card, the card holder receives discounts of 15 percent to 50 percent off the usual and customary fees charged by the providers, with no dollar cap on the amount of discounts received during the year. The cardholder is responsible for paying the costs of any drugs (taking into account the discount) until the deductible of any other health plan covering the individual is satisfied. An employee who is otherwise eligible for an HSA will not become ineligible solely as a result of having this benefit.

Q-10. Does coverage under an Employee Assistance Program (EAP), disease management program, or wellness program make an individual ineligible to contribute to an HSA?

A-10. An individual will not fail to be an eligible individual under section 223(c)(1)(A) solely because the individual is covered under an EAP, disease management program or wellness program if the program does not provide significant benefits in the nature of medical care or treatment, and therefore, is not considered a "health plan" for purposes of section 223(c)(1). To determine whether a program provides significant benefits in the nature of medical care or treatment, screening and other preventive care services as described in Notice 2004-23 will be disregarded. See also Q&A 48 on incentives for employees who participate in these programs.

Example (1). An employer offers a program that provides employees with benefits under an EAP, regardless of enrollment in a health plan. The EAP is specifically designed to assist the employer in improving productivity by helping employees identify and resolve personal and work concerns that affect job performance and the work environment. The benefits consist primarily of free or low-cost confidential short-term counseling to identify an employee's problem that may affect job performance and, when appropriate, referrals to an outside organization, facility or program to assist the employee in resolving the problem. The issues addressed during the short-term counseling include, but are not limited to, substance abuse, alcoholism, mental health or emotional disorders, financial or legal difficulties, and dependent care needs. This EAP is not a "health plan" under section 223(c)(1) because it does not provide significant benefits in the nature of medical care or treatment.

Example (2). An employer maintains a disease management program that identifies employees and their family members who have, or are at risk for, certain chronic conditions. The disease management program provides evidence-based information, disease specific support, case monitoring and coordination of the care and treatment provided by a health plan. Typical interventions include monitoring laboratory or other test results, telephone contacts or web-based reminders of health care schedules, and providing information to minimize health risks. This disease management program is not a "health plan" under section 223(c)(1) because it does not provide significant benefits in the nature of medical care or treatment.

Example (3). An employer offers a wellness program for all employees regardless of participation in a health plan. The wellness program provides a wide range of education and fitness services designed to improve the overall health of the employees and prevent illness. Typical services include education, fitness, sports, and recreation activities, stress management and health screenings. Any costs charged to the individual for participating in the services are separate from the individual's coverage under the health plan. This wellness program is not a "health plan" under section 223(c)(1) because it does not provide significant benefits in the nature of medical care or treatment.

Q-11. If an employee begins HDHP coverage mid-month, when does the employee become an eligible individual? (For example, coverage under the HDHP begins on the first day of a biweekly payroll period.)

A-11. Under section 223(b)(2), an eligible individual must have HDHP coverage as of the first day of the month. An individual with employer-provided HDHP coverage on a payroll-by-payroll basis becomes an eligible individual on the first day of the month on or following the first day of the pay period when HDHP coverage begins.

Example. An employee begins HDHP coverage on the first day of a pay period, which is August 16, 2004, and continues to be covered by the HDHP throughout 2004. For purposes of contributing to an HSA, the employee becomes an eligible individual on September 1, 2004.

II. High Deductible Health Plans (HDHPs)

Q-12. What is family HDHP coverage under section 223?

A-12. Under section 223(c)(4), the term "family coverage" means any coverage other than self-only coverage. Self-only coverage is a health plan covering only one individual; self-only HDHP coverage is an HDHP covering only one individual if that individual is an eligible individual. Family HDHP coverage is a health plan covering one eligible individual and at least one other individual (whether or not the other individual is an eligible individual).

Example. An individual, who is an eligible individual, and his dependent child are covered under an "employee plus one" HDHP offered by the individual's employer. The coverage is family HDHP coverage under section 223(c)(4).

Q-13. Can a state high-risk health insurance plan (high-risk pool) qualify as an HDHP?

A-13. Yes. If the state's high-risk pool does not pay benefits below the minimum annual deductible of an HDHP as set forth in section 223(c)(2)(A), the plan can qualify as an HDHP.

Q-14. May an HDHP impose a lifetime limit on benefits?

A-14. Yes. An HDHP may impose a reasonable lifetime limit on benefits provided under the plan. In such cases, amounts paid by the covered individual above the lifetime limit will not be treated as out-of-pocket expenses in determining the annual out-of-pocket maximum. However, a lifetime limit on benefits designed to circumvent the maximum annual out-of-pocket amount in section 223(c)(2)(A) is not reasonable.

Example. A health plan has an annual deductible that satisfies the minimum annual deductible under section 223(c)(2)(A)(i) for self-only coverage and for family coverage. After satisfying the deductible, the plan pays 100 percent of covered expenses, up to a lifetime limit of $1 million. The lifetime limit of $1 million is reasonable and the health plan is not disqualified from being an HDHP because of the lifetime limit on benefits.

Q-15. If a plan imposes an annual or lifetime limit on specific benefits, are amounts paid by covered individuals after satisfying the deductible treated as out-of-pocket expenses under section 223?

A-15. The out-of-pocket maximum in section 223(c)(2)(A) applies only to covered benefits. Plans may be designed with reasonable benefit restrictions limiting the plan's covered benefits. A restriction or exclusion on benefits is reasonable only if significant other benefits remain available under the plan in addition to the benefits subject to the restriction or exclusion.

Example (1). In 2004, a self-only health plan with a $1,000 deductible includes a $1 million lifetime limit on covered benefits. The plan provides no benefits for experimental treatments, mental health, or chiropractic care visits. Although the plan provides benefits for substance abuse treatment, it limits payments to 26 treatments per year, after the deductible is satisfied. Although the plan provides benefits for fertility treatments, it limits lifetime reimbursements to $10,000, after the deductible is satisfied. Other than these limits on covered benefits, the plan pays 80 percent of major medical expenses incurred after satisfying the deductible. When the 20 percent coinsurance paid by the covered individuals reaches $4,000, the plan pays 100 percent. Under these facts, the plan is an HDHP and no expenses incurred by a covered individual other than the deductible and the 20 percent coinsurance are treated as out-of-pocket expenses under section 223(c)(2)(A).

Example (2). In 2004, a self-only health plan with a $1,000 deductible imposes a lifetime limit on reimbursements for covered benefits of $1 million. While the plan pays 100 percent of expenses incurred for covered benefits after satisfying the deductible, the plan imposes a $10,000 annual limit on benefits for any single condition. The $10,000 annual limit under these facts is not reasonable because significant other benefits do not remain available under the plan. Under these facts, any expenses incurred by a covered individual after satisfying the deductible are treated as out-of-pocket expenses under section 223(c)(2)(A).

Q-16. If a plan limits benefits to usual, customary and reasonable (UCR) amounts, are amounts paid by covered individuals in excess of UCR included in determining the maximum out-of-pocket expenses paid?

A-16. Restricting benefits to UCR is a reasonable restriction on benefits. Thus, amounts paid by covered individuals in excess of UCR that are not paid by an HDHP are not included in determining maximum out-of-pocket expenses.

Q-17. Can a plan with no express limit on out-of-pocket expenses qualify as an HDHP?

A-17. A health plan without an express limit on out-of-pocket expenses is generally not an HDHP unless such limit is not necessary to prevent exceeding the out-of-pocket maximum.

Example (1). A plan provides self-only coverage with a $2,000 deductible and pays 100 percent of covered benefits above the deductible. Because the plan pays 100 percent of covered benefits after the deductible is satisfied, the maximum out-of-pocket expenses paid by a covered individual would never exceed the deductible. Thus, the plan does not require a specific limit on out-of-pocket expenses to insure that the covered individual will not be subject to out-of-pocket expenses in excess of the maximum set forth in section 223(c)(2)(A).

Example (2). A plan provides self-only coverage with a $2,000 deductible. The plan imposes a lifetime limit on reimbursements for covered benefits of $1 million. For expenses for covered benefits incurred above the deductible, the plan reimburses 80 percent of the UCR costs. The plan includes no express limit on out-of-pocket expenses. This plan does not qualify as a HDHP because it does not have a limit on out-of-pocket expenses.

Example (3). The same facts as Example 2, except that after the 20 percent coinsurance paid by the covered individual reaches $3,000, the plan pays 100 percent of the UCR costs until the $1 million limit is reached. For the purpose of determining the individual's out-of-pocket expenses, the plan only takes into account the 20 percent of UCR paid by the individual. This plan satisfies the out-of-pocket limit.

Q-18. A health plan which otherwise qualifies as an HDHP imposes a flat dollar penalty on a participant who fails to obtain pre-certification for a specific provider or for certain medical procedures. Is the penalty paid by the covered individual included in determining the maximum out-of-pocket expenses paid?

A-18. No. The penalty is not an out-of-pocket expense and, therefore, does not count toward the expense limits in section 223(c)(2)(A).

Q-19. A health plan which otherwise qualifies as an HDHP generally requires a 10 percent coinsurance payment after a covered individual satisfies the deductible. However, if an individual fails to get pre-certification for a specific provider, the plan requires a 20 percent coinsurance payment. Is the increased coinsurance amount included in determining the maximum out-of-pocket expenses paid?

A-19. No. Under the facts set forth, only the generally applicable 10 percent coinsurance payment is included in computing the maximum out-of-pocket expenses paid. The result is the same if the plan imposes a higher coinsurance amount for an out-of-network provider. See also Notice 2004-2, Q&A 4.

Q-20. Are cumulative embedded deductibles under family coverage subject to the out-of-pocket maximum?

A-20. Yes. An HDHP generally must limit the out-of-pocket expenses paid by the covered individuals, either by design or by its express terms.

Example (1). In 2004, a plan which otherwise qualifies as an HDHP provides family coverage with a $2,000 deductible for each family member. The plan pays 100 percent of covered benefits for each family member after that family member satisfies the $2,000 deductible. The plan contains no express limit on out-of-pocket expenses. section 223(c)(2)(A)(ii)(II) limits the maximum out-of-pocket expenses to $10,000 for family coverage. The plan is an HDHP for any family with two to five covered individuals ($2,000 × 5 = $10,000). However, the plan is not an HDHP for a family with six or more covered individuals.

Example (2). The same facts as Example 1, except that the plan includes an umbrella deductible of $10,000. The plan reimburses 100 percent of covered benefits if the family satisfies the $10,000 in the aggregate, even if no single family member satisfies the $2,000 embedded deductible. This plan qualifies as an HDHP for the family, regardless of the number of covered individuals.

Q-21. Are amounts incurred by an individual for medical care before a health plan's deductible is satisfied included in computing the plan's out-of-pocket expenses under section 223(c)(2)(A)?

A-21. A health plan's out-of-pocket limit includes the deductible, co-payments, and other amounts, but not premiums. Notice 2004-2, Q&A 3. Amounts incurred for noncovered benefits (including amounts in excess of UCR and financial penalties) also are not counted toward the deductible or the out-of-pocket limit. If a plan does not take copayments into account in determining if the deductible is satisfied, the copayments must still be taken into account in determining if the out-of-pocket maximum is exceeded.

Example. In 2004, a health plan has a $1,000 deductible for self-only coverage. After the deductible is satisfied, the plan pays 100 percent of UCR for covered benefits. In addition, the plan pays 100 percent for preventive care, minus a $20 copayment per screening. The plan does not take into account copayments in determining if the $1,000 deductible has been satisfied. The copayments must be included in determining if the plan meets the out-of-pocket maximum. Unless the plan includes an express limit on out-of-pocket expenses taking into account the copayments, or limits the copayments to $4,000, the plan is not an HDHP.

Q-22. If an employer changes health plans mid-year, does the new health plan fail to satisfy section 223(c)(2)(A) merely because it provides a credit towards the deductible for expenses incurred during the previous health plan's short plan year and not reimbursed?

A-22. No. If the period during which expenses are incurred for purposes of satisfying the deductible is 12 months or less and the plan satisfies the requirements for an HDHP, the new plan's taking into account expenses incurred during the prior plan's short plan year (whether or not the prior plan is an HDHP) and not reimbursed, does not violate the requirements of section 223(c)(2)(A).

Example. An employer with a calendar year health plan switches from a non-HDHP plan to a new plan with the first day of coverage under the new plan of July 1. The annual deductible under the new plan satisfies the minimum annual deductible for an HDHP under section 223(c)(2)(A)(i) and counts expenses incurred under the prior plan during the first six months of the year in determining if the new plan's annual deductible is satisfied. The new plan satisfies the HDHP deductible limit under section 223(c)(2)(A).

Q-23. If an eligible individual changes coverage during the plan year from self-only HDHP coverage to family HDHP coverage, does the individual (or any other person covered under the family coverage) fail to be covered by an HDHP merely because the family HDHP coverage takes into account expenses incurred while the individual had self-only coverage?

A-23. No.

Example. An eligible individual has self-only coverage from January 1 through March 31, marries in March and from April 1 through December 31, has family coverage under a plan otherwise qualifying as an HDHP. The family coverage plan applies expenses incurred by the individual from January through March toward satisfying the family deductible. The individual does not fail to be covered by an HDHP. The family coverage satisfies the deductible limit in section 223(c)(2)(A)(i)(II). The individual's contribution to an HSA is based on three months of the self-only coverage (i.e., 3/12 of the deductible for the self-only coverage) and nine months of family coverage (9/12 of the deductible for family coverage).

Q-24. How are the minimum deductible in section 223(c)(2)(A) for an HDHP and the maximum contribution to an HSA in section 223(b) calculated when the period for satisfying a health plan's deductible is longer than 12 months?

A-24. The deductible limits in section 223(c)(2)(A) are based on 12 months. If a plan's deductible may be satisfied over a period longer than 12 months, the minimum annual deductible under section 223(c)(2)(A) must be increased to take into account the longer period in determining if the plan satisfies the HDHP deductible requirements. The adjustment will be done as follows:

(1) Multiply the minimum annual deductible in section 223(c)(2)(A)(i) (as adjusted under section 223(g)) by the number of months allowed to satisfy the deductible.

(2) Divide the amount in (1) above by 12. This is the adjusted deductible for the longer period that is used to test for compliance with section 223(c)(2)(A).

(3) Compare the amount in (2) to the plan's deductible. If the plan's deductible equals or exceeds the amount in (2), the plan satisfies the requirements for the minimum deductible in section 223(c)(2)(A). (Note that the deductible for an HDHP may not exceed the out-of-pocket maximum under section 223(c)(2)(A)(ii).)

If the plan qualifies as an HDHP, an eligible individual's maximum annual HSA contribution will be the lesser of the amounts in (1) or (2) below:

(1) Divide the plan's deductible by the number of months allowed to satisfy the deductible, and multiply this amount by 12;

(2) The statutory amount in section 223(b)(2)(A)(ii) for self-only coverage ($2,600 in 2004) or section 223(b)(2)(B)(ii) for family coverage ($5,150 in 2004), as applicable.

Example. For 2004, a health plan takes into account medical expenses incurred in the last three months of 2003 to satisfy its deductible for calendar year 2004. The plan's deductible for self-only coverage is $1,500 and covers 15 months (the last three months of 2003 and 12 months of 2004). To determine if the plan's deductible satisfies section 223(c)(2)(A) the following calculations are performed: (1) multiply $1,000, the minimum annual deductible in section 223(c)(2)(A)(i), by 15, the number of months in which expenses incurred are taken into account to satisfy the deductible, = $15,000; (2) divide $15,000 by 12 = $1,250; (3) The HDHP minimum deductible for self-only coverage for 15 months must be at least $1,250. Because the plan's deductible, $1,500, exceeds $1,250, the plan's self-only coverage satisfies the deductible rule in section 223(c)(2)(A). The maximum annual HSA contribution in 2004 for an eligible individual with self-only coverage under these facts is $1,200, the lesser of (1) ($1,500/15) × 12 = $1,200; or (2) $2,600.

Q-25. A health plan which otherwise meets the definition of an HDHP negotiates discounted prices for health care services from providers. Covered individuals receive benefits at the discounted prices, regardless of whether they have satisfied the plan's deductible. Do the discounted prices prevent the health plan from being an HDHP as defined in section 223(c)(2)?

A-25. No.

III. Preventive care

Q-26. Does a preventive care service or screening that also includes the treatment of a related condition during that procedure come within the safe harbor for preventive care in Notice 2004-23?

A-26. Yes. Although Notice 2004-23 states that preventive care generally does not include any service or benefit intended to treat an existing illness, injury, or condition, in situations where it would be unreasonable or impracticable to perform another procedure to treat the condition, any treatment that is incidental or ancillary to a preventive care service or screening as described in Notice 2004-23 also falls within the safe-harbor for preventive care. For example, removal of polyps during a diagnostic colonoscopy is preventive care that can be provided before the deductible in an HDHP has been satisfied.

Q-27. To what extent do drugs or medications come within the safe-harbor for preventive care services under section 223(c)(2)(C)?

A-27. Notice 2004-23 sets out a preventive care deductible safe harbor for HDHPs under section 223(c)(2)(C). Solely for this purpose, drugs or medications are preventive care when taken by a person who has developed risk factors for a disease that has not yet manifested itself or not yet become clinically apparent (i.e., asymptomatic), or to prevent the reoccurrence of a disease from which a person has recovered. For example, the treatment of high cholesterol with cholesterol-lowering medications (e.g., statins) to prevent heart disease or the treatment of recovered heart attack or stroke victims with Angiotensin-converting Enzyme (ACE) inhibitors to prevent a reoccurrence, constitute preventive care. In addition, drugs or medications used as part of procedures providing preventive care services specified in Notice 2004-23, including obesity weight-loss and tobacco cessation programs, are also preventive care. However, the preventive care safe harbor under section 223(c)(2)(C) does not include any service or benefit intended to treat an existing illness, injury, or condition, including drugs or medications used to treat an existing illness, injury or condition.

IV. Contributions

Q-28. Who may make contributions on behalf of an eligible individual?

A-28. Although Q&A 11 of Notice 2004-2 only refers to contributions by employers or family members, any person (an employer, a family member or any other person) may make contributions to an HSA on behalf of an eligible individual.

Q-29. May a state government make an HSA contribution on behalf of eligible individuals insured under the state's comprehensive health insurance programs for high-risk individuals (state high-risk pool)?

A-29. Yes. See also Q&A 13.

Q-30. How is the maximum annual HSA contribution limit in section 223(b)(2) determined for an eligible individual with family coverage under an HDHP that includes embedded individual deductibles and an umbrella deductible?

A-30. Generally, under section 223(b)(2)(B), the maximum annual HSA contribution limit for an eligible individual with family coverage under an HDHP (without regard to catch-up contributions) is the lesser of: (1) the annual deductible under the HDHP, or (2) the statutory limit on family coverage contributions as indexed by section 223(g). An HDHP often has a stated maximum amount of expenses the family could incur before receiving benefits (i.e., the umbrella deductible), but also provides payments for covered medical expenses if any individual member of the family incurs medical expenses in excess of the minimum annual deductible in section 223(c)(2)(A)(i)(II) (the embedded individual deductible). The maximum annual HSA contribution limit for an eligible individual who has family coverage under an HDHP with embedded individual deductibles and an umbrella deductible as described above, is the least of the following amounts:

1. The maximum annual contribution limit for family coverage specified in section 223(b)(2)(B)(ii)($5,150 for calendar year 2004);
2. The umbrella deductible; or
3. The embedded individual deductible multiplied by the number of family members covered by the plan.

See Notice 2004-2, Q&A 3, which requires that the embedded individual deductible satisfy the minimum annual deductible for an HDHP.

Example (1). In 2004, H and W, a married couple, have HDHP coverage for themselves and their two dependent children. The HDHP will pay benefits for any family member whose covered expenses exceed $2,000 (the embedded individual deductible), and will pay benefits for all family members after their covered expenses exceed $5,000 (the umbrella deductible). The maximum annual contribution limit under section 223(b)(2)(B)(ii) is $5,150. The embedded deductible multiplied by the number of family members covered is $8,000 (4 × $2,000). The maximum annual contribution which H and W can make to their HSAs is $5,000 (the least of $5,000, $5,150 or $8,000). The $5,000 limit is divided equally between H and W, unless they agree to a different division. See Q&A 32 and Notice 2004-2, Q&A 15.

Example (2). The same facts as Example 1, except the HDHP provides coverage only for H and W. The maximum annual contribution limit under section 223(b)(2)(B)(ii) is $5,150. The umbrella deductible is $5,000. The embedded individual deductible multiplied by the number of family members covered is $4,000 (2 × $2,000). The maximum annual contribution which H and W can make to their HSAs for 2004 is $4,000 (the least of $5,000, $5,150 or $4,000).

Q-31. How do the maximum annual HSA contribution limits apply to family HDHP coverage that may include an ineligible individual?

A-31. The maximum annual HSA contribution for a married couple with family HDHP coverage is the lesser of: (1) the lowest HDHP family deductible applicable to the family (minimum $2,000) or (2) the section 223(b)(2)(B) statutory maximum ($5,150 in 2004). Although the special rule for married individuals in section 223(b)(5) generally allows a married couple to divide the maximum HSA contribution between spouses, if only one spouse is an eligible individual, only that spouse may contribute to an HSA (notwithstanding the treatment under section 223(b)(5)(A) of both spouses as having only family coverage). For an HDHP with embedded individual deductibles see Q&A 30.

Example (1). In 2004, H and W are a married couple and neither qualifies for catch-up contributions under section 223(b)(3). H and W have family HDHP coverage with a $5,000 deductible. H is an eligible individual and has no other coverage. W also has self-only coverage with a $200 deductible. W, who has coverage under a low-deductible plan, is not an eligible individual. H may contribute $5,000 (the lesser of $5,000 or $5,150) to an HSA while W may not contribute to an HSA.

Example (2). The same facts as Example 1, except that, in addition to the family HDHP with a $5,000 deductible, W has self-only HDHP coverage with a $2,000 deductible rather than self-only coverage with a $200 deductible. Both H and W are eligible individuals. H and W are treated as having only family coverage under section 223(b)(5). The maximum combined HSA contribution by H and W is $5,000, to be divided between them by agreement.

Example (3). The same facts as Example 1, except that, in addition to the family HDHP with a $5,000 deductible, W has family HDHP coverage with a $3,000 deductible rather than self-only coverage with a $200 deductible. Both

H and W are eligible individuals. H and W are treated as having family HDHP coverage with the lowest annual deductible under section 223(b)(5)(A). The maximum combined HSA contribution by H and W is $3,000, to be divided between them by agreement.

Example (4). The same facts as Example 1, except that, in addition to family coverage under the HDHP with a $5,000 deductible, W has family coverage with a $500 deductible rather than self-only coverage with a $200 deductible. H and W are treated as having family coverage with the lowest annual deductible under section 223(b)(5)(A). Neither H nor W is an eligible individual and neither may contribute to an HSA.

Example (5). The same facts as Example 1, except that, in addition to the family HDHP with a $5,000 deductible, W is enrolled in Medicare rather than having self-only coverage with a $200 deductible. W is not an eligible individual. H may contribute $5,000 to an HSA while W may not contribute to an HSA.

Example (6). Individual X is a single individual who does not qualify for catch-up contributions. X is an eligible individual and has a dependent. X and his dependent have family HDHP coverage with a $5,000 deductible. The dependent also has self-only coverage with a $200 deductible. X may contribute $5,000 to an HSA while the dependent may not contribute to an HSA.

Q-32. How may spouses agree to divide the annual HSA contribution limit between themselves?

A-32. Section 223(b)(5) provides special rules for married individuals and states that HSA contributions (without regard to the catch-up contribution) "shall be divided equally between them unless they agree on a different division." Thus, spouses can divide the annual HSA contribution in any way they want, including allocating nothing to one spouse. See also Notice 2004-2, Q&A 15.

Example. In 2004, X, an eligible individual, has self-only HDHP coverage with a $1,200 deductible from January 1 through March 31. In March, X and Y marry. Neither X nor Y qualifies for the catch-up contribution. From April 1 through December 31, 2004 X and Y have HDHP family coverage with a $2,400 deductible. Y is an eligible individual from April 1 through December 31, 2004. X and Y's contribution limit for the nine months of family coverage is $1,800 (nine months of the deductible for family coverage (9/12 × $2,400)). X and Y divide the $1,800 between them. X's contribution limit to his HSA for the three months of single coverage is $300 (three months of the deductible for self-only coverage (3/12 × $1,200)). The $300 limit is not divided between X and Y. See also Q&A 23.

Q-33. What is the contribution limit for an eligible individual covered by an HDHP and also by a post-deductible health reimbursement arrangement (HRA)?

A-33. Rev. Rul. 2004-45, Situation 4, describes a post-deductible HRA that does not pay or reimburse any medical expense incurred before the minimum annual deductible under section 223(c)(2)(A)(i) is satisfied. The ruling states that the deductible for the HRA need not be the same as the deductible for the HDHP, but in no event may the HDHP or other coverage provide benefits before the minimum annual deductible under section 223(c)(2)(A)(i) is satisfied. Where the HDHP and the other coverage do not have identical deductibles, contributions to the HSA are limited to the lower of the deductibles. In addition, although the deductibles of the HDHP and the other coverage may be satisfied independently by separate expenses, no benefits may be paid by the HDHP or the other coverage before the minimum annual deductible under section 223(c)(2)(A)(i) has been satisfied.

> **Example.** In 2004, an individual has self-only coverage under an HDHP with a deductible of $2,500. The individual is also covered under a post-deductible HRA (as described in Rev. Rul. 2004-45) which pays or reimburses qualified medical expenses only after $2,000 of the HDHP's deductible has been satisfied (i.e., if the individual incurs covered medical expenses of $2,250, the HRA will pay $250). Because the HRA's deductible of $2,000 is less than the HDHP's deductible of $2,500, the individual's HSA contribution limit is $2,000.

Q-34. An account beneficiary wants to withdraw an excess contribution from an HSA before the due date of his or her federal income tax return (including extensions), to avoid the 6 percent excise tax under section 4973(a)(5). How is the net income attributable to the excess contribution computed?

A-34. Section 223(f)(3)(A)(ii) provides that any distribution of excess contribution to an HSA must be "accompanied by the amount of net income attributable to such excess contribution." Any net income is included in the individual's gross income. The rules for computing attributable net income for excess IRA contributions apply to HSAs. See Treas. Reg. § 1.408-11 and Notice 2004-2, Q&A 22.

Q-35. May an individual who has not made excess HSA contributions treat a distribution from an HSA other than for qualified medical expenses as the withdrawal of excess HSA contributions?

A-35. No. This withdrawal is deemed a withdrawal for non-qualified medical expenses and includable in the individual's gross income under section 223(f)(2). (The additional tax under section 223(f)(4) also applies, unless otherwise excepted).

V. Distributions

Q-36. If an account beneficiary's spouse or dependents are covered under a non-HDHP, are distributions from an HSA to pay their qualified medical expenses excluded from the account beneficiary's gross income?

A-36. Yes. Distributions from an HSA are excluded from income if made for any qualified medical expense of the account beneficiary, the account beneficiary's spouse and dependents (without regard to their status as eligible individuals). However, distributions made for expenses reimbursed by another health plan are not excludable from gross income, whether or not the other health plan is an HDHP. See Notice 2004-2, Q&A 26.

Q-37. An account beneficiary receives an HSA distribution as the result of a mistake of fact due to reasonable cause (e.g., the account beneficiary reasonably, but mistakenly, believed that an expense was a qualified medical expense and was reimbursed for that expense from the HSA). The account beneficiary then repays the mistaken distribution to the HSA. Is the mistaken distribution included in gross income under section 223(f)(2) and subject to the 10 percent additional tax under section 223(f)(4) or subject to the excise tax on excess contributions under section 4973(a)(5)?

A-37. If there is clear and convincing evidence that amounts were distributed from an HSA because of a mistake of fact due to reasonable cause, the account beneficiary may repay the mistaken distribution no later than April 15 following the first year the account beneficiary knew or should have known the distribution was a mistake. Under these circumstances, the distribution is not included in gross income under section 223(f)(2), or subject to the 10 percent additional tax under section 223(f)(4), and the repayment is not subject to the excise tax on excess contributions under section 4973(a)(5). But see Q&A 76 on the trustee's or custodian's obligation to accept a return of mistaken distributions.

Q-38. If both spouses have HSAs and one spouse uses distributions from his or her HSA to pay or reimburse the section 213(d) qualified medical expenses of the other spouse, are the distributions excluded from the account beneficiary's gross income under section 223(f)?

A-38. Yes. However, both HSAs may not reimburse the same expense amounts.

Q-39. When must a distribution from an HSA be taken to pay or reimburse, on a tax-free basis, qualified medical expenses incurred in the current year?

A-39. An account beneficiary may defer to later taxable years distributions from HSAs to pay or reimburse qualified medical expenses incurred in the current year as long as the expenses were incurred after the HSA was established. Similarly, a distribution from an HSA in the current year can be used to pay or reimburse expenses incurred in any prior year as long as the expenses were incurred after the HSA was established. Thus, there is no time limit on when the distribution must occur. However, to be excludable from the account beneficiary's gross income, he or she must keep records sufficient to later show that the distributions were exclusively to pay or reimburse qualified medical expenses, that the qualified medical expenses have not been previously paid or reimbursed from another source and that the medical expenses have not been taken as an itemized deduction in any prior taxable year. See Notice 2004-2, Q&A 31 and also Notice 2004-25, for transition relief in calendar year 2004 for reimbursement of medical expenses incurred before opening an HSA.

Example. An eligible individual contributes $1,000 to an HSA in 2004. On December 1, 2004, the individual incurs a $1,500 qualified medical expense and has a balance in his HSA of $1,025. On January 3, 2005, the individual contributes another $1,000 to the HSA, bringing the balance in the HSA to $2,025. In June, 2005, the individual receives a distribution of $1,500 to reimburse him for the $1,500 medical expense incurred in 2004. The individual can show that the $1,500 HSA distribution in 2005 is a reimbursement for a qualified medical expense that has not been previously paid or otherwise reimbursed and has not been taken as an itemized deduction. The distribution is excludable from the account beneficiary's gross income.

Q-40. May an account beneficiary pay qualified long-term care insurance premiums with distributions from an HSA if contributions to the HSA are made by salary-reduction though a section 125 cafeteria plan?

A-40. Yes. Section 125(f) provides that the term "qualified benefit" under a section 125 cafeteria plan shall not include any product which is advertised, marketed, or offered as long-term care insurance. However, for HSA purposes, section 223(d)(2)(C)(ii) provides that the payment of any expense for coverage under a qualified long-term care insurance contract (as defined in section 7702B(b)) is a qualified medical expense. Where an HSA that is offered under a cafeteria plan pays or reimburses individuals for qualified long-term care insurance premiums, section 125(f) is not applicable because it is the HSA and not the long-term care insurance that is offered under the cafeteria plan.

Q-41. Do the section 213(d)(10) limits on the deduction for "eligible long-term care premiums" restrict the amount of distributions for qualified medical expenses that may be excluded from income under an HSA?

A-41. Yes. "Eligible long-term care premiums" are deductible medical expenses under section 213, but the deduction is limited to the annually adjusted amounts in section 213(d)(10)(based on age). See Rev. Proc. 2003-85 § 3.18, 2003-49 I.R.B. 1184 for the 2004 limits. Thus, although HSA distributions to pay or reimburse qualified long-term care insurance premiums are qualified medical expenses, the exclusion from gross income is limited to the adjusted amounts under section 213(d)(10). Any excess premium reimbursements are includable in gross income and may also be subject to the 10 percent penalty under section 223(f)(4).

Example. In 2004, X, age 41, pays premiums of $1,290 for a qualified long-term care insurance contract. The section 213(d)(10) limit in calendar year 2004 for deductions for persons age 40, but not more than 50, is $490. X's HSA can reimburse X up to $490 on a tax-free basis for the long—term care premiums. The remaining $800 ($1,290-$490), if reimbursed from the HSA, is not for qualified medical expenses and is includable in gross income.

Q-42. Are distributions from an HSA for long-term care services qualified medical expenses which are excluded from income?

A-42. Yes. Section 106(c) provides that employer-provided coverage for long-term care services provided through a flexible spending or similar arrangement are included in an employee's gross income. section 213(d)(1)(C) provides that amounts paid for qualified long-term care services are medical care and section 223(f)(1) provides that amounts paid or distributed out of an HSA used to pay for qualified medical expenses are not includible in gross income. Qualified medical expenses are amounts paid for medical care (as defined in section 213(d)) for the account beneficiary, his or her spouse and dependents. Although section 106(c) applies to benefits provided by a flexible spending or similar arrangement, it does not apply to distributions from an HSA, which is a personal health care savings vehicle used to pay for qualified medical expenses through a trust or custodial account, whether or not the HSA is funded by salary-reduction contributions through a section 125 cafeteria plan.

Q-43. May a retiree who is age 65 or older receive tax-free distributions from an HSA to pay the retiree's contribution to an employer's self-insured retiree health coverage?

A-43. Yes. Pursuant to section 223(d)(2)(B), the purchase of health insurance is generally not a qualified medical expense that can be paid or reimbursed by an HSA. See Notice 2004-2, Q&A 27. However, section 223(d)(2)(C)(iv) provides an exception for coverage for health insurance once an account beneficiary has attained age 65. The exception applies to both insured and self-insured plans.

Q-44. May an individual who is under age 65 and has end stage renal disease (ESRD) or is disabled receive tax-free distributions from an HSA to pay for health insurance premiums?

A-44. No. Section 223(d)(2)(B) provides that health insurance may not be paid by an HSA. However, section 223(d)(2)(C)(iv) provides that payment of health insurance premiums are qualified medical expenses, but only in the case of an account beneficiary who has attained the age specified in section 1811 of the Social Security Act (i.e., age 65).

Q-45. If a retiree who is enrolled in Medicare receives a distribution from an HSA to reimburse the retiree's Medicare premiums, is the reimbursement a qualified medical expense under section 223(d)(2)?

A-45. Yes. Where premiums for Medicare are deducted from Social Security benefit payments, an HSA distribution to reimburse the Medicare beneficiary equal to the Medicare premium deduction is a qualified medical expense.

VI. Comparability

Q-46. Does an employer who offers to make available a contribution to the HSA of each employee who is an eligible individual in an amount equal to the employee's HSA contribution or a percentage of the employee's HSA contribution (i.e., "matching contributions") satisfy the requirement under section 4980G that all comparable participating employees receive comparable contributions?

A-46. If all employees who are eligible individuals do not contribute the same amount to their HSAs and, consequently, do not receive comparable contributions to their HSAs, the section 4980G comparability rules are not satisfied, notwithstanding that the employer offers to make available the same contribution amount to each employee who is an eligible individual. But see Q&A 47 on comparable contributions made through a cafeteria plan.

Q-47. If an employer makes contributions through a cafeteria plan to the HSA of each employee who is an eligible individual in an amount equal to the amount of the employee's HSA contribution or a percentage of the amount of the employee's HSA contribution (i.e., "matching contributions"), are the contributions subject to the section 4980G comparability rules?

A-47. No. The conference report for the Medicare Prescription Drug, Improvement, and Modernization Act of 2003 states that the comparability rules do not apply to contributions made through a cafeteria plan. Conf. Rep. No. 391, 108th Cong., 1st Sess. 840 (2003). Notice 2004-2, Q&A 32 similarly provides that the comparability rules do not apply to HSA contributions made through a cafeteria plan. Thus, where matching contributions are made by an employer through a cafeteria plan, the contributions are not subject to the comparability rules of section 4980G. However, contributions, including "matching contributions", to an HSA made under a cafeteria plan are subject to the section 125 nondiscrimination rules (eligibility rules, contributions and benefits tests and key employee concentration tests). See section 125(b), (c) and (g) and Prop. Treas. Reg. § 1.125-1, Q&A 19.

Q-48. If an employer conditions contributions by the employer to an employee's HSA on an employee's participation in health assessments, disease management programs or wellness programs and makes the same contributions available to all employees who participate in the programs, do the contributions satisfy the section 4980G comparability rules?

A-48. If all eligible employees do not elect to participate in all the programs and consequently, all employees who are eligible individuals do not receive comparable contributions to their HSAs, the employer contributions fail to satisfy the section 4980G comparability rules. But see Q&A 49 on comparable contributions made through a cafeteria plan.

Q-49. If under the employer's cafeteria plan, employees who are eligible individuals and who participate in health assessments, disease management programs or wellness programs receive an employer contribution to an HSA, unless the employee elects cash, are the contributions subject to the section 4980G comparability rules?

A-49. No. The comparability rules under section 4980G do not apply to employer contributions to an HSA through a cafeteria plan.

Q-50. If an employer offers to make available additional HSA contributions to all employees who are eligible individuals and who have attained a specified age or who qualify for the additional contributions under section 223(b)(3)(catch-up contributions), do the contributions satisfy the section 4980G comparability rules?

A-50. No. If all employees who are eligible individuals do not meet the age requirement or do not qualify for the additional contributions under section 223(b)(3), all employees who are eligible individuals do not receive comparable contributions to their HSAs and the employer contributions fail to satisfy the section 4980G comparability rules.

Q-51. How do the comparability rules in section 4980G apply to employer contributions to employees' HSAs if some employees work full-time during the entire calendar year, and other employees work full-time for less than the entire calendar year?

A-51. An employer contributing to HSAs of employees who work full-time for less than twelve months, satisfies the comparability rules if the contribution amount is comparable when determined on a month-to-month basis. For example, if the employer contributes $240 to the HSAs of each full-time employee who works the entire calendar year, the employer must contribute $60 to the HSA of a full-time employee who works three months of the year. See section 4980G(b) and section 4980E(d)(2)(B). See also Notice 2004-2, Q&A 32 on comparability rules for part-time employees (i.e., employees who are customarily employed for fewer than 30 hours per week).

Q-52. What is the testing period for making comparable contributions to employees' HSAs?

A-52. To satisfy the comparability rule in section 4980G, an employer must make comparable contributions for the calendar year to HSAs of employees who are eligible individuals. See section 4980G and section 4980E(d).

Q-53. Under section 4980G, must an employer make comparable contributions to all employees who are eligible individuals or only to those employees who are eligible individuals and are also covered by an HDHP provided by the employer?

A-53. If during a calendar year, an employer contributes to the HSA of any employee covered under an HDHP provided by the employer, the employer is required to make comparable contributions to all eligible individuals with coverage under any HDHP provided by the employer. An employer that contributes to the HSAs of employees with coverage under the HDHP provided by the employer is not required to make comparable contributions to HSAs of employees who are not covered under the HDHP provided by the employer. However, an employer that contributes to the HSA of any eligible individual with coverage under any HDHP, even if that coverage is not an HDHP of the employer, must make comparable contributions to all eligible individuals whether or not covered under an HDHP of the employer. See also Notice 2004-2, Q&A 32.

Example (1). An employer offers an HDHP to its full-time employees. Most full-time employees are covered under the employer's HDHP and the employer makes comparable contributions only to these employees' HSAs. Employee D, a full-time employee and an eligible individual (as defined in section 223(c)(1)), is covered under his spouse's HDHP and not under his employer's HDHP. The employer is not required to make comparable contributions to D's HSA.

Example (2). An employer does not offer an HDHP. Several full-time employees, who are eligible individuals (as defined in section 223(c)(1)), have HSAs.

The employer contributes to these employees' HSAs. The employer must make comparable contributions to the HSAs of all full-time employees who are eligible individuals.

Example (3). An employer offers an HDHP to its full-time employees. Most full-time employees are covered under the employer's HDHP and the employer makes comparable contributions to these employees' HSAs and also to HSAs of full-time employees not covered under the employer's HDHP. Employee E, a full-time employee and an eligible individual (as defined in section 223(c)(1)), is covered under his spouse's HDHP and not under his employer's HDHP. The employer must make comparable contributions to E's HSA.

Q-54. If an employee requests that his or her employer deduct after-tax amounts from the employee's compensation and forward these amounts as employee contributions to the employee's HSA, do the section 4980G comparability rules apply to these amounts?

A-54. No. Section 106(d) provides that amounts contributed by an employer to an eligible employee's HSA shall be treated as employer-provided coverage for medical expenses and excludable from the employee's gross income up to the limit in section 223(b). After-tax employee contributions to the HSA are not subject to section 4980G because they are not employer contributions under section 106(d). See Notice 2004-2, Q&A 12 on aggregation of HSA contributions.

VII. Rollovers

Q-55. How frequently may an account beneficiary make rollover contributions to an HSA under section 223(f)(5)?

A-55. An account beneficiary may make only one rollover contribution to an HSA during a 1-year period. In addition, to qualify as a rollover, any amount paid or distributed from an HSA to an account beneficiary must be paid over to an HSA within 60 days after the date of receipt of the payment or distribution. But see Q&A 78 regarding trustee's or custodian's obligation to accept rollovers. See also Notice 2004-2, Q&A 23 for additional rules on rollovers.

Q-56. Are transfers of HSA amounts from one HSA trustee directly to another HSA trustee (trustee-to-trustee transfers), subject to the rollover restrictions?

A-56. No. The rules under section 223(f)(5) limiting the number of rollover contributions to one a year do not apply to trustee-to-trustee transfers. Thus, there is no limit on the number of trustee-to-trustee transfers allowed during a year.

VIII. Cafeteria Plans and HSAs

Q-57. Which requirements that apply to health flexible spending arrangements (FSAs) under a section 125 cafeteria plan do not apply to HSAs?

A-57. The following requirements for health FSAs under a section 125 cafeteria plan (which are generally imposed so that health FSAs operate in a manner similar to "insurance-type" accident or health plans under section 105) are not applicable to HSAs: (1) the prohibition against a benefit that defers compensation by permitting employees to carry over unused elective contributions or plan benefits from one plan year to another plan year (See section 125(d)(2)(D)); (2) the requirement that the maximum amount of reimbursement must be available at all times during the coverage period; and (3) the mandatory twelve-month period of coverage.

Q-58. Do the section 125 change in status rules apply to elections of HSA contributions through a cafeteria plan?

A-58. A cafeteria plan may permit an employee to revoke an election during a period of coverage with respect to a qualified benefit and make a new election for the remaining portion of the period only as provided in Treas. Reg. § 1.125-4. Because the eligibility requirements and contribution limits for HSAs are determined on a month-by-month basis, rather than on an annual basis, an employee who elects to make HSA contributions under a cafeteria plan may start or stop the election or increase or decrease the election at any time as long as the change is effective prospectively (i.e., after the request for the change is received). If an employer places additional restrictions on the election of HSA contributions under a cafeteria plan, the same restrictions must apply to all employees.

Q-59. Can an employer permit employees to elect an HSA mid-year if offered as a new benefit under the employer's cafeteria plan?

A-59. Yes, if the election for the HSA is made on a prospective basis. However, the HSA election does not permit a change or revocation of any other coverage under the cafeteria plan unless the change is permitted by Treas. Reg. § 1.125-4. Thus, while an HSA may be offered to and elected by an employee mid-year, the employee may have other coverage under the cafeteria plan that cannot be changed, (e.g., coverage under a health FSA), which may prevent the employee from being an eligible individual. See Rev. Rul. 2004-45.

Q-60. If an employee elects to make contributions to an HSA through the employer's cafeteria plan, may the employer contribute amounts to an employee's HSA to cover qualified medical expenses incurred by an employee that exceed the employee's current HSA balance?

A-60. Yes. Where an employee elects to make contributions to an HSA through a cafeteria plan, the employer may, but is not required to, contribute amounts to an employee's HSA up to the maximum amount elected by the employee. While any accelerated contribution made by the employer must be equally available to all participating employees throughout the plan year and must be provided to all participating employees on the same terms, the employee must repay the amount of the accelerated contribution by the end of the plan year. But see Q&A 82 on recoupment of HSA contributions by an employer.

Q-61. Can employers provide negative elections for HSAs if offered through a cafeteria plan?

A-61. Yes. See Rev. Rul. 2002-27, 2002-1 C.B. 925.

IX. Account Administration

Q-62. Are there model IRS forms for establishing HSAs?

A-62. Yes. See Form 5305-B "Health Savings Trust Account" and Form 5305-C "Health Savings Custodial Account."

Q-63. May a husband and wife have a joint HSA?

A-63. No. Each spouse who is an "eligible individual" as described in section 223(c)(1) and wants to make contributions to an HSA must open a separate HSA. Thus, only one person may be the account beneficiary of an HSA. But see Q&A 32 concerning allocating contributions between spouses. See also Q&A 38 concerning reimbursements from spousal HSAs.

Q-64. May an eligible individual have more than one HSA?

A-64. Yes. An eligible individual may establish more than one HSA, and may contribute to more than one HSA. The same rules governing HSAs apply (e.g., maximum contribution limit), regardless of the number of HSAs established by an eligible individual. See also Notice 2004-2, Q&A 12.

Example. For 2004, eligible individual A's maximum contribution to an HSA is $2,400. For 2004, A's employer contributes $1,000 to an HSA on behalf of A. A opens a second HSA and contributes $1,400. If additional contributions are made for 2004 to either of the HSAs, then there are excess contributions to A's HSAs.

Q-65. What are permissible investments for HSAs?

A-65. HSA funds may be invested in investments approved for IRAs (e.g., bank accounts, annuities, certificates of deposit, stocks, mutual funds, or bonds). HSAs may not invest in life insurance contracts, or in collectibles (e.g., any work of art, antique, metal, gem, stamp, coin, alcoholic beverage, or other tangible personal property specified in IRS guidance under section 408(m)). HSAs may, however, invest in certain types of bullion or coins, as described in section 408(m)(3). The HSA trust or custodial agreement may restrict investments to certain types of permissible investments (e.g., particular investment funds).

Q-66. May HSA funds be commingled in a common trust fund or common investment fund?

A-66. Section 223(d)(1)(D) states that the HSA trust assets may not be commingled except in a common trust fund or common investment fund. Thus, individual accounts maintained on behalf of individual HSA account beneficiaries may be held in a common trust fund or common investment fund. A "common trust fund" is defined in Treas. Reg. § 1.408-2(b)(5)(ii). A "common investment fund" is defined in section 584(a)(1).

Q-67. Are there any transactions which account beneficiaries are prohibited from entering into with an HSA?

A-67. Yes. Section 223(e)(2) provides that rules similar to the rules of section 408(e)(2) and (4) shall apply to HSAs. Therefore, account beneficiaries may not enter into "prohibited transactions" with an HSA (e.g., the account beneficiary may not sell, exchange, or lease property, borrow or lend money, furnish goods, services or facilities, transfer to or use by or for the benefit of himself/herself any assets, pledge the HSA, etc.). Any amount treated as distributed as the result of a prohibited transaction will not be treated as used to pay for qualified medical expenses. The account beneficiary must, therefore, include the distribution in gross income and generally will be subject to the additional 10 percent tax on distributions not made for qualified medical expenses. See Notice 2004-2, Q&A 25.

Q-68. Are HSA trustees and custodians also subject to the rules against prohibited transactions?

A-68. Yes. The same rules that apply to account beneficiaries apply to trustees and custodians.

Q-69. If administration and account maintenance fees (e.g., flat administrative fees) are withdrawn from the HSA, are the withdrawn amounts treated as taxable distributions to the account beneficiary?

A-69. No. Amounts withdrawn from an HSA for administration and account maintenance fees will not be treated as a taxable distribution and will not be included in the account beneficiary's gross income.

Q-70. If administration and account maintenance fees are withdrawn from the HSA, does the withdrawn amount increase the maximum annual HSA contribution limit?

A-70. No. For example, if the maximum annual contribution limit is $2,000, and a $25 administration fee is withdrawn from the HSA, the annual contribution limit is still $2,000, not $2,025.

Q-71. If administration and account maintenance fees are paid by the account beneficiary or employer directly to the trustee or custodian, do these payments count toward the annual maximum contribution limit for the HSA?

A-71. No. Administration and account maintenance fees paid directly by the account beneficiary or employer will not be considered contributions to the HSA. For example, an individual contributes the maximum annual amount to his HSA of $2,000. The account beneficiary pays an annual administration fee of $25 directly to the trustee. The individual's maximum annual contribution limit is not affected by the payment of the administration fee.

X. Trustees and Custodians

Q-72. Is any insurance company a qualified HSA trustee or custodian?

A-72. Yes. Any insurance company or any bank (including a similar financial institution as defined in section 408(n)) can be an HSA trustee or custodian. In addition, any other person already approved by the IRS to be a trustee or custodian of IRAs or Archer MSAs is automatically approved to be an HSA trustee or custodian. Other persons may request approval to be a trustee or custodian in accordance with the procedures set forth in Treas. Reg. § 1.408-2(e) (relating to IRA nonbank trustees).

Q-73. Is there a limit on the annual HSA contribution which the trustee or custodian may accept?

A-73. Yes. Except in the case of rollover contributions described in section 223(f)(5) or trustee-to-trustee transfers, the trustee or custodian may not accept annual contributions to any HSA that exceed the sum of: (1) the dollar amount in effect under section 223(b)(2)(B)(ii)(i.e., the maximum family coverage deductible) plus (2) the dollar amount in effect under section 223(b)(3)(B)(i.e., the catch-up contribution amount). All contributions must be in cash, other than rollover contributions or trustee-to-trustee transfers. See section 223(d)(1)(A).

Q-74. Is the HSA trustee or custodian responsible for determining whether contributions to an HSA exceed the maximum annual contribution for a particular account beneficiary?

A-74. No. This is the responsibility of the account beneficiary, who is also responsible for notifying the trustee or custodian of any excess contribution and requesting a withdrawal of the excess contribution together with any net income attributable to the excess contribution. The HSA trustee or custodian is, however, responsible for accepting cash contributions within the limits in Q&A 73 and for filing required information returns with the IRS (Form 5498-SA and Form 1099-SA).

Q-75. Is the trustee or custodian responsible for tracking the account beneficiary's age?

A-75. Yes. However, the trustee or custodian may rely on the account beneficiary's representation as to his or her date of birth.

Q-76. Must the trustee or custodian allow account beneficiaries to return mistaken distributions to the HSA?

A-76. No, this is optional. If the HSA trust or custodial agreement allows the return of mistaken distributions as described in Q&A 37, the trustee or custodian may rely on the account beneficiary's representation that the distribution was, in fact, a mistake.

Q-77. May an HSA trust or custodial agreement restrict the account beneficiary's ability to rollover amounts from that HSA?

A-77. No. Section 223(f)(5) permits the rollover of amounts in an HSA to another HSA, and transfers from one trustee to another trustee.

Q-78. Are HSA trustees or custodians required to accept rollover contributions or trustee-to-trustee transfers?

A-78. No. Rollover contributions or trustee-to-trustee transfers from other HSAs or from Archer MSAs are allowed, but trustees or custodians are not required to accept them. See Notice 2004-2, Q&A 23.

Q-79. May an HSA trust or custodial agreement restrict HSA distributions to pay or reimburse only the account beneficiary's qualified medical expenses?

A-79. No. The HSA trust or custodial agreement may not contain a provision that restricts HSA distributions to pay or reimburse only the account beneficiary's qualified medical expenses. Thus, the account beneficiary is entitled to distributions for any purpose and distributions may be used to pay or reimburse qualified medical expenses or for other nonmedical expenditures. Only the account beneficiary may determine how the HSA distributions will be used. But see Notice 2004-2, Q&A 25 on the taxation of HSA distributions not used exclusively for qualified medical expenses. See also Q&A 80 on restrictions on the frequency or minimum amount of HSA distributions.

Q-80. May a trustee or custodian restrict the frequency or minimum amount of distributions from an HSA?

A-80. Yes. Trustees or custodians may place reasonable restrictions on both the frequency and the minimum amount of distributions from an HSA. For example, the trustee may prohibit distributions for amounts of less than $50 or only allow a certain number of distributions per month. Generally, the terms regarding the frequency or minimum amount of distributions from an HSA are matters of contract between the trustee and the account beneficiary.

XI. Other Issues

Q-81. Are employers who contribute to an employee's HSA responsible for determining whether the employee is an eligible individual and the employee's maximum annual contribution limit?

A-81. Employers are only responsible for determining the following with respect to an employee's eligibility and maximum annual contribution limit on HSA contributions: (1) whether the employee is covered under an HDHP (and the deductible) or low deductible health plan or plans (including health FSAs and HRAs) sponsored by that employer; and (2) the employee's age (for catch-up contributions). The employer may rely on the employee's representation as to his or her date of birth.

Q-82. May the employer recoup from an employee's HSA any portion of the employer's contribution to the employee's HSA?

A-82. No. Under section 223(d)(1)(E), an account beneficiary's interest in an HSA is nonforfeitable. For example, on January 2, 2005, the employer makes the maximum annual contribution to employees' HSAs, in the expectation that the employees would work for the entire calendar year 2005. On February 1, 2005, one employee terminates employment. The employer may not recoup from that employee's HSA any portion of the contribution previously made to the employee's HSA.

Q-83. Is an HSA distribution subject to the nondiscrimination rules of section 105(h)?

A-83. No. For amounts reimbursed to a highly compensated individual by a self-insured medical reimbursement plan to be fully excludable from the individual's gross income under section 105(b), the self-insured medical reimbursement plan must satisfy the requirements of section 105(h). Section 105(h) is not satisfied if the plan discriminates in favor of highly compensated individuals as to eligibility to participate or benefits. Because the exclusion from gross income for amounts distributed from an HSA is not determined by section 105(b), but by section 223(b), section 105(h) does not apply to HSAs.

Q-84. Is a deduction under section 223(a) for contributions to a self-employed individual's own HSA taken into account in determining net earnings from self-employment under section 1402(a)?

A-84. No. The deduction is an adjustment to gross income under section 62(a)(19), and is reportable on the self-employed individual's Form 1040 as an adjustment to gross income. It is not a deduction attributable to the self-employed individual's trade or business so it is not taken as a deduction on Schedule C, Form 1040, nor is it taken into account in determining net earnings from self-employment on Schedule SE, Form 1040.

Q-85. Does an employer's contribution to an employee's HSA affect the computation of the earned income credit (EIC) under section 32?

A-85. No. An employer's contributions to an employee's HSAs are not treated as earned income for EIC purposes.

Q-86. May an HDHP apply any required cost-of-living adjustments under section 223(g) to the minimum annual deductible amounts or maximum annual out-of-pocket expense limits on the renewal date of the HDHP if that date is after January 1?

A-86. Yes. Generally, an HDHP is a health plan that satisfies certain requirements with respect to minimum annual deductibles and maximum annual out-of-pocket expense. These annual amounts are indexed for inflation using annual cost-of-living adjustments. Any required change to the deductibles and out-of-pocket expense limits may be applied as of the renewal date of the HDHP in cases where the renewal date is after the beginning of the calendar year, but in no event longer than a 12-month period ending on the renewal date. Thus, a fiscal year plan that satisfies the minimum annual deductible on the first day of the first month of its fiscal year may apply that deductible for the entire fiscal year, even if the minimum annual deductible increases on January 1 of the next calendar year.

Example. An individual obtains self-only coverage under an HDHP on June 1, 2004, the first day of the plan year, with an annual deductible of $1,000. Assume that the cost-of living adjustments require the minimum deductible amount to be increased for 2005. The plan's deductible is not increased to comply with the increased minimum deductible amount until the plan's renewal date of June 1, 2005. The plan satisfies the requirements for an HDHP with respect to deductibles through May 30, 2005.

Q-87. Are HSAs available to bona fide residents of the Commonwealth of Puerto Rico, American Samoa, the U.S. Virgin Islands, Guam, and the Commonwealth of the Northern Mariana Islands?

A-87. Bona fide residents of the U.S. Virgin Islands, Guam and the Commonwealth of the Northern Mariana Islands may establish HSAs. However, bona fide residents of Puerto Rico and American Samoa may establish HSAs only after statutory provisions similar to sections 223 and 106(d) are enacted.

Q-88. If a C corporation makes a contribution to the HSA of a shareholder who is not an employee of the C corporation, what are the tax consequences to the shareholder and to the C corporation?

A-88. If a C corporation makes a contribution to the HSA of a shareholder who is not an employee of the C corporation, the contribution will be treated as a distribution under section 301. The distribution is treated as a dividend to the extent the C corporation has earnings and profits. The portion of the distribution which is not a dividend is applied against and reduces the adjusted basis of the stock. To the extent the amount of the distribution exceeds the adjusted basis of the stock, the balance is treated as gain from a sale or exchange of property.

EFFECT ON OTHER DOCUMENTS

Notice 2004-2, 2004-2 I.R.B. 269 is changed as follows:

The second sentence of A-2 is changed to read: An "eligible individual" means . . . (3) is not enrolled in Medicare. . . . "

The last sentence of A-12 is changed to read: "In addition to the maximum contribution amount, catch-up contributions, as described in [Notice 2004-2] A-14, may be made by or on behalf of individuals age 55 and older, who are not enrolled in Medicare."

The first sentence of A-14 is changed to read: "For individuals (and their spouses covered under the HDHP) who have attained 55 and are also not enrolled in Medicare. . . . "

The first sentence of the Example in A-14 is changed to read: "An individual attains age 65 and becomes enrolled in Medicare. . . . "

TRANSITION RELIEF

For months before January 1, 2005, a health plan that would otherwise qualify as an HDHP but for the lack of an express maximum on payments above the deductible that complies with the out-of-pocket requirement, as set forth in Q&A 17 and 20 will be treated as an HDHP. Individuals covered under these health plans will continue to be eligible to contribute to HSAs before January 1, 2005.

For months before January 1, 2006, a health plan that would otherwise qualify as an HDHP but for an annual deductible that does not satisfy the rule in Q&A 24 (concerning deductibles for periods of more than 12 months) will be treated as an HDHP if the plan was in effect or submitted to approval to state insurance regulators as of the date of publication of this notice in the Internal Revenue Bulletin. Individuals covered under these health plans will continue to be eligible to contribute to HSAs before January 1, 2006.

DRAFTING INFORMATION ***

Specific issues on HSAs are also discussed in Rev. Rul. 2004-45, 2004-22 I.R.B. 971; Rev. Rul. 2004-38, 2004-15 I.R.B. 717; Rev. Proc. 2004-22, 2004-15 I.R.B. 727; Notice 2004-43, 2004-27 I.R.B. 10; Notice 2004-25, 2004-15 I.R.B. 727; Notice 2004-22, 2004-15 I.R.B. 725.

Notice 2004-43 (2004-27 I.R.B. 10)

[**Summary**: The IRS provides transitional relief for individuals in states where high deductible health plans are not available as a result of state law. Amplified by Notice 2005-83, 2005-49 I.R.B. 1075.]

PURPOSE

This notice provides transition relief for individuals in states where high deductible health plans (HDHPs) as described in section 223(c)(2) are not available because state laws require health plans to provide certain benefits without regard to a deductible or below the minimum annual deductible of section 223(c)(2)(A)(i). The transition relief covers months before January 1, 2006, for state requirements in effect on January 1, 2004.

BACKGROUND

Section 1201 of the Medicare Prescription Drug, Improvement, and Modernization Act of 2003, Pub. L. 108-173, added section 223 to the Internal Revenue Code to permit eligible individuals to establish health savings accounts (HSAs) for taxable years beginning after December 31, 2003. An "eligible individual" under section 223(c)(1) must be covered by a "high deductible health plan" (HDHP). An HDHP under section 223(c)(2) must satisfy certain requirements with respect to minimum annual deductibles and maximum out-of-pocket expenses. However, section 223(c)(2)(C) permits a safe harbor for the absence of a preventive care deductible. An eligible individual may also have certain permitted insurance and permitted coverage under section 223(c)(1)(B).

Notice 2004-23, 2004-15 I.R.B. 725, describes a safe harbor for preventive care benefits that may be provided by an HDHP without a deductible or with a deductible below the minimum annual deductible for an HDHP. In addition, the notice indicates that whether health care required by state law without regard to a deductible is "preventive" will be based on the standards set forth in Notice 2004-23 and other guidance issued by the IRS, rather than on how the benefits are characterized by state law.

Several states currently require that health plans provide certain benefits without regard to a deductible or with a deductible below the minimum annual deductible requirements of section 223(c)(2)(e.g., first-dollar coverage or coverage with a low deductible). These health plans are not HDHPs under section 223(c)(2) and individuals covered under these health plans are not eligible to contribute to HSAs. Because of the short period between the enactment of HSAs and the effective date of section 223, these states have had insufficient time to modify their laws to conform to the standards of section 223. Thus, it is appropriate to provide transition relief that treats HDHPs as qualifying under section 223(c)(2) when the sole reason the plans are not HDHPs is because of state-mandated benefits. During the transition period, otherwise eligible individuals covered under these plans will be treated as eligible individuals for purposes of section 223(c)(1) and may contribute to an HSA.

APPLICATION

For months before January 1, 2006, a health plan which would otherwise qualify as an HDHP under section 223(c)(2), except that it complies with state law requirements that certain benefits be provided without a deductible or below the minimum annual deductible of section 223(c)(2)(A)(i), will be treated as an HDHP for purposes of section 223(c)(2), if the disqualifying benefits are required by state law in effect on January 1, 2004.

DRAFTING INFORMATION ***

Notice 2004-25 (2004-15 I.R.B. 727)

[**Summary:** In general, a qualifying HSA may pay for qualified medical expenses incurred on or after the later of January 1, 2004, or the first day of the month in which the individual became an eligible participant. The IRS has provided relief for individuals who establish health savings accounts (HSA) on or before April 15, 2005. In doing so, it modified prior guidance and provided 2004 calendar year transitional relief allowing qualified medical expenses to be paid or reimbursed by an HSA if even though the HSA account was not in effect at the time the expenses were incurred.]

PURPOSE

[1] This notice provides transition relief for calendar year 2004 for eligible individuals who establish an HSA on or before April 15, 2005 from the requirement that qualified medical expenses may only be paid or reimbursed by an HSA if incurred after the HSA has been established. This notice modifies prior guidance in Q&A 26 of Notice 2004-2, 2004-2 I.R.B. 269.

[2] Section 1201 of the Medicare Prescription Drug, Improvement, and Modernization Act of 2003, Pub. L. No. 108–173, added section 223 to the Internal Revenue Code to permit eligible individuals to establish Health Savings Accounts (HSAs) for taxable years beginning after December 31, 2003. Because of the short period between the enactment of HSAs and the effective date of section 223, many taxpayers who otherwise would be eligible to establish and contribute to HSAs (i.e., generally, individuals covered by a high deductible health plan (HDHP)) have been unable to do so because they cannot locate trustees or custodians who are willing and able to open HSAs at this time.

BACKGROUND

[3] Contributions to an HSA may only be made by or on behalf of eligible individuals as defined in section 223(c)(1)(A). For any month, an eligible individual must, among other requirements, be covered on the first day of the month by a HDHP (as defined by section 223(c)(2)). Although the amount of the contribution to an HSA is based on the number of months an individual is an eligible individual (i.e., is covered by the HDHP), contributions up to the annual maximum limit generally may be made to the HSA as early as the first day of the taxable year and as late as April 15 of the year following the year for which contributions are made. Notice 2004-2, Q&A 21.

[4] On January 12, 2004, Notice 2004-2 was published, providing general guidance concerning HSAs under section 223. The notice provides that distributions from an HSA exclusively to pay or reimburse qualified medical expenses of the account beneficiary, his or her spouse, or dependents, are excluded from gross income. Answer 26 of the notice states that, "The qualified medical expenses must be incurred only after the HSA has been established." However, after an HSA is established, distributions from the HSA exclusively to pay or reimburse qualified medical expenses continue to be excluded from the account beneficiary's gross income whether or not the account beneficiary continues to be an eligible individual. Notice 2004-2, Q&A 28.

TRANSITION RELIEF FOR HSAs ESTABLISHED FOR CALENDAR YEAR 2004

[5] For calendar year 2004, an HSA established by an eligible individual on or before April 15, 2005, may pay or reimburse on a tax-free basis an otherwise qualified medical expense if the qualified medical expense was incurred on or after the later of: (1) January 1, 2004, or (2) the first day of the first month that the individual became an eligible individual under section 223.

EFFECT ON OTHER DOCUMENTS

[6] The rule in the second sentence of Notice 2004-2, Q&A 26, which states that, "The qualified medical expenses must be incurred only after the HSA has been established," is suspended and replaced by the transition relief in this notice. That rule continues to apply to HSAs established for calendar year 2005 and later years.

DRAFTING INFORMATION ***

Notice 2004-23 (2004-15 I.R.B. 725)

[**Summary:** The IRS issued an HSA safe harbor for preventive care benefits provided under an HSA with a list of services and benefits which qualify as "preventive care" under Code section 223(c)(2)(C). The IRS also indicated that "preventive care" will be characterized by reference to the notice and other IRS guidance, instead of state law.]

PURPOSE

[1] This notice provides a safe harbor for preventive care benefits allowed to be provided by a high deductible health plan (HDHP) without satisfying the minimum deductible under section 223(c)(2) of the Internal Revenue Code.

BACKGROUND

[2] Section 1201 of the Medicare Prescription Drug, Improvement, and Modernization Act of 2003, Pub. L. No. 108-173, added section 223 to the Internal Revenue Code to permit eligible individuals to establish Health Savings Accounts (HSAs) for taxable years beginning after December 31, 2003.

[3] Among the requirements for an individual to qualify as an eligible individual under section 223(c)(1)(and thus to be eligible to make tax-favored contributions to an HSA) is the requirement that the individual be covered under an HDHP. An HDHP is a health plan that satisfies certain requirements with respect to minimum deductibles and maximum out-of-pocket expenses. Generally, an HDHP may not provide benefits for any year until the deductible for that year is satisfied. However, section 223(c)(2)(C) provides a safe harbor for the absence of a preventive care deductible. That section states, "[a] plan shall not fail to be treated as a high deductible health plan by reason of failing to have a deductible for preventive care (within the meaning of section 1871 of the Social Security Act, except as otherwise provided by the Secretary)." An HDHP may therefore provide preventive care benefits without a deductible or with a deductible below the minimum annual deductible. On the other hand, there is no requirement in section 223 that an HDHP provide benefits for preventive care or provide preventive care with a deductible below the minimum annual deductible.

PREVENTIVE CARE SAFE HARBOR

[4] Preventive care for purposes of section 223(c)(2)(C) includes, but is not limited to, the following:

- Periodic health evaluations, including tests and diagnostic procedures ordered in connection with routine examinations, such as annual physicals.
- Routine prenatal and well-child care.
- Child and adult immunizations.
- Tobacco cessation programs.
- Obesity weight-loss programs.
- Screening services (see attached APPENDIX).

However, preventive care does not generally include any service or benefit intended to treat an existing illness, injury, or condition (See below for request for comments regarding drug treatments.)

INTERACTION WITH STATE LAW HEALTH CARE REQUIREMENTS

[5] Section 220(c)(2)(B)(ii) allows a high deductible health plan for purposes of an Archer Medical Savings Account to provide preventive care without a deductible if required by State law. However, section 220 does not define preventive care for this purpose. Section 223(c)(2)(C), for purposes of an HSA, does not condition the exception for preventive care on State law requirements. State insurance laws often require health plans to provide certain health care without regard to a deductible or on terms no less favorable than other care provided by the health plan. The determination of whether health care that is required by State law to be provided by an HDHP without regard to a deductible is "preventive" for purposes of the exception for preventive care under section 223(c)(2)(C) will be based on the standards set forth in this notice and other guidance issued by the IRS, rather than on how that care is characterized by State law.

COMMENTS REQUESTED ***

DRAFTING INFORMATION ***

APPENDIX

Safe Harbor Preventive Care Screening Services

Cancer Screening
Breast Cancer (e.g., Mammogram)
Cervical Cancer (e.g., Pap Smear)
Colorectal Cancer
Prostate Cancer (e.g., PSA Test)
Skin Cancer

Oral Cancer
Ovarian Cancer
Testicular Cancer
Thyroid Cancer
Heart and Vascular Diseases Screening
Abdominal Aortic Aneurysm
Carotid Artery Stenosis
Coronary Heart Disease
Hemoglobinopathies
Hypertension
Lipid Disorders
Infectious Diseases Screening
Bacteriuria
Chlamydial Infection
Gonorrhea
Hepatitis B Virus Infection
Hepatitis C
Human Immunodeficiency Virus (HIV) Infection
Syphilis
Tuberculosis Infection
Mental Health Conditions and Substance Abuse Screening
Dementia
Depression
Drug Abuse
Problem Drinking
Suicide Risk
Family Violence
Metabolic, Nutritional, and Endocrine Conditions Screening
Anemia, Iron Deficiency
Dental and Periodontal Disease
Diabetes Mellitus
Obesity in Adults
Thyroid Disease
Musculoskeletal Disorders Screening
Osteoporosis
Obstetric and Gynecologic Conditions Screening
Bacterial Vaginosis in Pregnancy
Gestational Diabetes Mellitus
Home Uterine Activity Monitoring
Neural Tube Defects
Preeclampsia
Rh Incompatibility
Rubella
Ultrasonography in Pregnancy
Pediatric Conditions Screening
Child Developmental Delay
Congenital Hypothyroidism
Lead Levels in Childhood and Pregnancy

Phenylketonuria
Scoliosis, Adolescent Idiopathic
Vision and Hearing Disorders Screening
Glaucoma
Hearing Impairment in Older Adults
Newborn Hearing

Notice 2004-2 (2004-2 I.R.B. 269)

[**Summary:** This guidance contains basic information about HSAs including information on establishing and contributing to HSAs, withdrawals from HSAs, and HSA portability. HSA funds are completely portable, and, similar to IRA funds, can accumulate interest. Unlike flexible spending account funds, unused HSA funds can be rolled over from year to year. The guidance details ways in which tax-advantaged HSA contributions and rollovers can be made and includes a request for comments. Note: Notice 2004-2 was modified by Notice 2004-25, Notice 2004-50, and Announcement 2004-67, reproduced in this appendix.]

PURPOSE

This notice provides guidance on Health Savings Accounts.

BACKGROUND

Section 1201 of the Medicare Prescription Drug, Improvement, and Modernization Act of 2003, Pub. L. No. 108-173, added section 223 to the Internal Revenue Code to permit eligible individuals to establish Health Savings Accounts (HSAs) for taxable years beginning after December 31, 2003. HSAs are established to receive tax-favored contributions by or on behalf of eligible individuals and amounts in an HSA may be accumulated over the years or distributed on a tax-free basis to pay or reimburse qualified medical expenses.

A number of the rules that apply to HSAs are similar to rules that apply to Individual Retirement Accounts (IRAs) under sections 219, 408 and 408A, and to Archer Medical Savings Accounts (Archer MSAs) under section 220. For example, like an Archer MSA, an HSA is established for the benefit of an individual, is owned by that individual, and is portable. Thus, if the individual is an employee who later changes employers or leaves the work force, the HSA does not stay behind with the former employer, but stays with the individual.

This notice provides certain basic information about HSAs in question and answer format, without attempting to enumerate all of the specific rules that apply under section 223.

The notice is divided into five parts. Part I of the notice explains what HSAs are and who can have them. Part II describes how HSAs can be established. Parts

III and IV cover contributions to HSAs and distributions from HSAs. Part V discusses other matters relating to HSAs.

QUESTIONS AND ANSWERS

Set forth below are questions and answers concerning HSAs.

I. *What are HSAs and Who Can Have Them?*

Q-1. What is an HSA?

A-1. An HSA is a tax-exempt trust or custodial account established exclusively for the purpose of paying qualified medical expenses of the account beneficiary who, for the months for which contributions are made to an HSA, is covered under a high-deductible health plan.

Q-2. Who is eligible to establish an HSA?

A-2. An "eligible individual" can establish an HSA. An "eligible individual" means, with respect to any month, any individual who: (1) is covered under a high-deductible health plan (HDHP) on the first day of such month; (2) is not also covered by any other health plan that is not an HDHP (with certain exceptions for plans providing certain limited types of coverage); (3) is not enrolled in Medicare (generally, has not yet reached age 65); and (4) may not be claimed as a dependent on another person's tax return.

Q-3. What is a "high-deductible health plan" (HDHP)?

A-3. Generally, an HDHP is a health plan that satisfies certain requirements with respect to deductibles and out-of-pocket expenses. Specifically, for self-only coverage, an HDHP has an annual deductible of at least $1,000 and annual out-of-pocket expenses required to be paid (deductibles, co-payments and other amounts, but not premiums) not exceeding $5,000. For family coverage, an HDHP has an annual deductible of at least $2,000 and annual out-of-pocket expenses required to be paid not exceeding $10,000. In the case of family coverage, a plan is an HDHP only if, under the terms of the plan and without regard to which family member or members incur expenses, no amounts are payable from the HDHP until the family has incurred annual covered medical expenses in excess of the minimum annual deductible. Amounts are indexed for inflation. A plan does not fail to qualify as an HDHP merely because it does not have a deductible (or has a small deductible) for preventive care (e.g., first dollar coverage for preventive care). However, except for preventive care, a plan may not provide benefits for any year until the deductible for that year is met. *See* A-4 and A-6 for special rules regarding network plans and plans providing certain types of coverage.

Example (1): A Plan provides coverage for A and his family. The Plan provides for the payment of covered medical expenses of any member of A's family if the member has incurred covered medical expenses during the year in excess of $1,000 even if the family has not incurred covered medical expenses in excess of $2,000. If A incurred covered medical expenses of

$1,500 in a year, the Plan would pay $500. Thus, benefits are potentially available under the Plan even if the family's covered medical expenses do not exceed $2,000. Because the Plan provides family coverage with an annual deductible of less than $2,000, the Plan is not an HDHP.

Example (2): Same facts as in example (1), except that the Plan has a $5,000 family deductible and provides payment for covered medical expenses if any member of A's family has incurred covered medical expenses during the year in excess of $2,000. The Plan satisfies the requirements for an HDHP with respect to the deductibles. *See* A-12 for HSA contribution limits.

Q-4. What are the special rules for determining whether a health plan that is a network plan meets the requirements of an HDHP?

A-4. A network plan is a plan that generally provides more favorable benefits for services provided by its network of providers than for services provided outside of the network. In the case of a plan using a network of providers, the plan does not fail to be an HDHP (if it would otherwise meet the requirements of an HDHP) solely because the out-of-pocket expense limits for services provided outside of the network exceeds the maximum annual out-of-pocket expense limits allowed for an HDHP. In addition, the plan's annual deductible for out-of-network services is not taken into account in determining the annual contribution limit. Rather, the annual contribution limit is determined by reference to the deductible for services within the network.

Q-5. What kind of other health coverage makes an individual ineligible for an HSA?

A-5. Generally, an individual is ineligible for an HSA if the individual, while covered under an HDHP, is also covered under a health plan (whether as an individual, spouse, or dependent) that is not an HDHP. *See also* A-6.

Q-6. What other kinds of health coverage may an individual maintain without losing eligibility for an HSA?

A-6. An individual does not fail to be eligible for an HSA merely because, in addition to an HDHP, the individual has coverage for any benefit provided by "permitted insurance." Permitted insurance is insurance under which substantially all of the coverage provided relates to liabilities incurred under workers' compensation laws, tort liabilities, liabilities relating to ownership or use of property (e.g., automobile insurance), insurance for a specified disease or illness, and insurance that pays a fixed amount per day (or other period) of hospitalization.

In addition to permitted insurance, an individual does not fail to be eligible for an HSA merely because, in addition to an HDHP, the individual has coverage (whether provided through insurance or otherwise) for accidents, disability, dental care, vision care, or long-term care. If a plan that is intended to be an HDHP is one in which substantially all of the coverage of the plan is through permitted insurance or other coverage as described in this answer, it is not an HDHP.

Q-7. Can a self-insured medical reimbursement plan sponsored by an employer be an HDHP?

A-7. Yes.

II. *How Can An HSA Be Established?*

Q-8. How does an eligible individual establish an HSA?

A-8. Beginning January 1, 2004, any eligible individual (as described in A-2) can establish an HSA with a qualified HSA trustee or custodian, in much the same way that individuals establish IRAs or Archer MSAs with qualified IRA or Archer MSA trustees or custodians. No permission or authorization from the Internal Revenue Service (IRS) is necessary to establish an HSA. An eligible individual who is an employee may establish an HSA with or without involvement of the employer.

Q-9. Who is a qualified HSA trustee or custodian?

A-9. Any insurance company or any bank (including a similar financial institution as defined in section 408(n)) can be an HSA trustee or custodian. In addition, any other person already approved by the IRS to be a trustee or custodian of IRAs or Archer MSAs is automatically approved to be an HSA trustee or custodian. Other persons may request approval to be a trustee or custodian in accordance with the procedures set forth in Treas. Reg. § 1.408-2(e) (relating to IRA nonbank trustees). For additional information concerning nonbank trustees and custodians, *see* Announcement 2003-54, 2003-40 I.R.B. 761.

Q-10. Does the HSA have to be opened at the same institution that provides the HDHP?

A-10. No. The HSA can be established through a qualified trustee or custodian who is different from the HDHP provider. Where a trustee or custodian does not sponsor the HDHP, the trustee or custodian may require proof or certification that the account beneficiary is an eligible individual, including that the individual is covered by a health plan that meets all of the requirements of an HDHP.

III. *Contributions to HSAs.*

Q-11. Who may contribute to an HSA?

A-11. Any eligible individual may contribute to an HSA. For an HSA established by an employee, the employee, the employee's employer or both may contribute to the HSA of the employee in a given year. For an HSA established by a self-employed (or unemployed) individual, the individual may contribute to the HSA. Family members may also make contributions to an HSA on behalf of another family member as long as that other family member is an eligible individual.

Q-12. How much may be contributed to an HSA in calendar year 2004?

A-12. The maximum annual contribution to an HSA is the sum of the limits determined separately for each month, based on status, eligibility and health plan coverage as of the first day of the month. For calendar year 2004, the maximum monthly contribution for eligible individuals with self-only coverage under an HDHP is 1/12 of the lesser of 100% of the annual deductible under the HDHP (minimum of $1,000) but not more than $2,600. For eligible individuals with family coverage under an HDHP, the maximum monthly contribution is 1/12 of the lesser of 100% of the annual deductible under the HDHP (minimum of $2,000) but not more than $5,150. In addition to the maximum contribution amount, catch-up contributions, as described in A-14, may be made by or on behalf of individuals age 55 and older, who are not enrolled in Medicare.

All HSA contributions made by or on behalf of an eligible individual to an HSA are aggregated for purposes of applying the limit. The annual limit is decreased by the aggregate contributions to an Archer MSA. The same annual contribution limit applies whether the contributions are made by an employee, an employer, a self-employed person, or a family member. Unlike Archer MSAs, contributions may be made by or on behalf of eligible individuals even if the individuals have no compensation or if the contributions exceed their compensation. If an individual has more than one HSA, the aggregate annual contributions to all the HSAs are subject to the limit.

Q-13. How is the contribution limit computed for an individual who begins self-only coverage under an HDHP on June 1, 2004 and continues to be covered under the HDHP for the rest of the year?

A-13. The contribution limit is computed each month. If the annual deductible is $5,000 for the HDHP, then the lesser of the annual deductible and $2,600 is $2,600. The monthly contribution limit is $216.67 ($2,600/12). The annual contribution limit is $1,516.69 (7 × $216.67).

Editors' Note. Q&A 14 was corrected, as shown below, by Announcement 2004-67 (2004-36 I.R.B. 459), which is reproduced in Appendix C.

Q-14. What are the "catch-up contributions" for individuals age 55 or older?

A-14. For individuals (and their spouses covered under the HDHP) who have attained 55 and are also not enrolled in Medicare, the HSA contribution limit is increased by $500 in calendar year 2004. This catch-up amount will increase in $100 increments annually, until it reaches $1,000 in calendar year 2009. As with the annual contribution limit, the catch-up contribution is also computed on a monthly basis. After an individual has attained age 65 and becomes enrolled in Medicare benefits, contributions, including catch-up contributions, cannot be made to an individual's HSA.

Example: An individual attains age 65 and becomes enrolled in Medicare in July, 2004 and had been participating in self-only coverage under an HDHP with an annual deductible of $1,000. The individual is no longer eligible to make HSA contributions (including catch-up contributions) after June, 2004. The monthly contribution limit is $125 ($1,000/12 + $500/12 for the catch-up contribution). The individual may make contributions for January through

June totaling $750 (6 × $125), but may not make any contributions for July through December, 2004.

Q-15. If one or both spouses have family coverage, how is the contribution limit computed?

A-15. In the case of individuals who are married to each other, if either spouse has family coverage, both are treated as having family coverage. If each spouse has family coverage under a separate health plan, both spouses are treated as covered under the plan with the lowest deductible. The contribution limit for the spouses is the lowest deductible amount, divided equally between the spouses unless they agree on a different division. The family coverage limit is reduced further by any contribution to an Archer MSA. However, both spouses may make the catch-up contributions for individuals age 55 or over without exceeding the family coverage limit.

Example (1): H and W are married. H is 58 and W is 53. H and W both have family coverage under separate HDHPs. H has a $3,000 deductible under his HDHP and W has a $2,000 deductible under her HDHP. H and W are treated as covered under the plan with the $2,000 deductible. H can contribute $1,500 to an HSA (1/2 the deductible of $2,000 + $500 catch up contribution) and W can contribute $1,000 to an HSA (unless they agree to a different division).

Example (2): H and W are married. H is 35 and W is 33. H and W each have a self-only HDHP. H has a $1,000 deductible under his HDHP and W has a $1,500 deductible under her HDHP. H can contribute $1,000 to an HSA and W can contribute $1,500 to an HSA.

Q-16. In what form must contributions be made to an HSA?

A-16. Contributions to an HSA must be made in cash. For example, contributions may not be made in the form of stock or other property. Payments for the HDHP and contributions to the HSA can be made through a cafeteria plan. *See* A-33.

Q-17. What is the tax treatment of an eligible individual's HSA contributions?

A-17. Contributions made by an eligible individual to an HSA (which are subject to the limits described in A-12) are deductible by the eligible individual in determining adjusted gross income (i.e., "above-the-line"). The contributions are deductible whether or not the eligible individual itemizes deductions. However, the individual cannot also deduct the contributions as medical expense deductions under section 213.

Q-18. What is the tax treatment of contributions made by a family member on behalf of an eligible individual?

A-18. Contributions made by a family member on behalf of an eligible individual to an HSA (which are subject to the limits described in A-12) are deductible by the eligible individual in computing adjusted gross income. The contributions are deductible whether or not the eligible individual itemizes deductions. An individual who may be claimed as a dependent on another person's tax return is not an eligible individual and may not deduct contributions to an HSA.

Q-19. What is the tax treatment of employer contributions to an employee's HSA?

A-19. In the case of an employee who is an eligible individual, employer contributions (provided they are within the limits described in A-12) to the employee's HSA are treated as employer-provided coverage for medical expenses under an accident or health plan and are excludable from the employee's gross income. The employer contributions are not subject to withholding from wages for income tax or subject to the Federal Insurance Contributions Act (FICA), the Federal Unemployment Tax Act (FUTA), or the Railroad Retirement Tax Act. Contributions to an employee's HSA through a cafeteria plan are treated as employer contributions. The employee cannot deduct employer contributions on his or her federal income tax return as HSA contributions or as medical expense deductions under section 213.

Q-20. What is the tax treatment of an HSA?

A-20. An HSA is generally exempt from tax (like an IRA or Archer MSA), unless it has ceased to be an HSA. Earnings on amounts in an HSA are not includable in gross income while held in the HSA (i.e., inside buildup is not taxable). *See* A-25 regarding the taxation of distributions to the account beneficiary.

Q-21. When may HSA contributions be made? Is there a deadline for contributions to an HSA for a taxable year?

A-21. Contributions for the taxable year can be made in one or more payments, at the convenience of the individual or the employer, at any time prior to the time prescribed by law (without extensions) for filing the eligible individual's federal income tax return for that year, but not before the beginning of that year. For calendar year taxpayers, the deadline for contributions to an HSA is generally April 15 following the year for which the contributions are made. Although the annual contribution is determined monthly, the maximum contribution may be made on the first day of the year. *See* A-22 regarding correcting excess contributions.

Example: B has self-only coverage under an HDHP with a deductible of $1,500 and also has an HSA. B's employer contributes $200 to B's HSA at the end of every quarter in 2004 and at the end of the first quarter in 2005 (March 31, 2005). B can exclude from income in 2004 all of the employer contributions (i.e., $1,000) because B's exclusion for all contributions does not exceed the maximum annual HSA contributions. *See* A-12.

Q-22. What happens when HSA contributions exceed the maximum amount that may be deducted or excluded from gross income in a taxable year?

A-22. Contributions by individuals to an HSA, or if made on behalf of an individual to an HSA, are not deductible to the extent they exceed the limits described in A-12. Contributions by an employer to an HSA for an employee are included in the gross income of the employee to the extent that they exceed the limits described in A-12 or if they are made on behalf of an employee who is not an eligible individual. In addition, an excise tax of 6% for each taxable year is imposed on the account beneficiary for excess individual and employer contributions.

However, if the excess contributions for a taxable year and the net income attributable to such excess contributions are paid to the account beneficiary before the last day prescribed by law (including extensions) for filing the account beneficiary's federal income tax return for the taxable year, then the net income attributable to the excess contributions is included in the account beneficiary's gross income for the taxable year in which the distribution is received but the excise tax is not imposed on the excess contribution and the distribution of the excess contributions is not taxed.

Q-23. Are rollover contributions to HSAs permitted?

A-23. Rollover contributions from Archer MSAs and other HSAs into an HSA are permitted. Rollover contributions need not be in cash. Rollovers are not subject to the annual contribution limits. Rollovers from an IRA, from a health reimbursement arrangement (HRA), or from a health flexible spending arrangement (FSA) to an HSA are not permitted.

IV. *Distributions from HSAs.*

Q-24. When is an individual permitted to receive distributions from an HSA?

A-24. An individual is permitted to receive distributions from an HSA at any time.

Q-25. How are distributions from an HSA taxed?

A-25. Distributions from an HSA used exclusively to pay for qualified medical expenses of the account beneficiary, his or her spouse, or dependents are excludable from gross income. In general, amounts in an HSA can be used for qualified medical expenses and will be excludable from gross income even if the individual is not currently eligible for contributions to the HSA.

However, any amount of the distribution not used exclusively to pay for qualified medical expenses of the account beneficiary, spouse or dependents is includable in gross income of the account beneficiary and is subject to an additional 10% tax on the amount includable, except in the case of distributions made after the account beneficiary's death, disability, or attaining age 65.

Q-26. What are the "qualified medical expenses" that are eligible for tax-free distributions?

A-26. The term "qualified medical expenses" are expenses paid by the account beneficiary, his or her spouse or dependents for medical care as defined in section 213(d) (including nonprescription drugs as described in Rev. Rul. 2003-102, 2003-38 I.R.B. 559), but only to the extent the expenses are not covered by insurance or otherwise. The qualified medical expenses must be incurred only after the HSA has been established. For purposes of determining the itemized deduction for medical expenses, medical expenses paid or reimbursed by distributions from an HSA are not treated as expenses paid for medical care under section 213.

Q-27. Are health insurance premiums qualified medical expenses?

A-27. Generally, health insurance premiums are not qualified medical expenses except for the following: qualified long-term care insurance, COBRA health care continuation coverage, and health care coverage while an individual is receiving unemployment compensation. In addition, for individuals over age 65, premiums for Medicare Part A or B, Medicare HMO, and the employee share of premiums for employer-sponsored health insurance, including premiums for employer-sponsored retiree health insurance can be paid from an HSA. Premiums for Medigap policies are not qualified medical expenses.

Q-28. How are distributions from an HSA taxed after the account beneficiary is no longer an eligible individual?

A-28. If the account beneficiary is no longer an eligible individual (e.g., the individual is over age 65 and entitled to Medicare benefits, or no longer has an HDHP), distributions used exclusively to pay for qualified medical expenses continue to be excludable from the account beneficiary's gross income.

Q-29. Must HSA trustees or custodians determine whether HSA distributions are used exclusively for qualified medical expenses?

A-29. No. HSA trustees or custodians are not required to determine whether HSA distributions are used for qualified medical expenses. Individuals who establish HSAs make that determination and should maintain records of their medical expenses sufficient to show that the distributions have been made exclusively for qualified medical expenses and are therefore excludable from gross income.

Q-30. Must employers who make contributions to an employee's HSA determine whether HSA distributions are used exclusively for qualified medical expenses?

A-30. No. The same rule that applies to trustees or custodians applies to employers. *See* A-29.

Q-31. What are the income tax consequences after the HSA account beneficiary's death?

A-31. Upon death, any balance remaining in the account beneficiary's HSA becomes the property of the individual named in the HSA instrument as the beneficiary of the account. If the account beneficiary's surviving spouse is the named beneficiary of the HSA, the HSA becomes the HSA of the surviving spouse. The surviving spouse is subject to income tax only to the extent distributions from the HSA are not used for qualified medical expenses.

If, by reason of the death of the account beneficiary, the HSA passes to a person other than the account beneficiary's surviving spouse, the HSA ceases to be an HSA as of the date of the account beneficiary's death, and the person is required to include in gross income the fair market value of the HSA assets as of the date of death. For such a person (except the decedent's estate), the includable amount is reduced by any payments from the HSA made for the decedent's qualified medical expenses, if paid within one year after death.

V. *Other Matters.*

Q-32. What discrimination rules apply to HSAs?

A-32. If an employer makes HSA contributions, the employer must make available comparable contributions on behalf of all "comparable participating employees" (i.e., eligible employees with comparable coverage) during the same period. Contributions are considered comparable if they are either the same amount or same percentage of the deductible under the HDHP.

The comparability rule is applied separately to part-time employees (i.e., employees who are customarily employed for fewer than 30 hours per week). The comparability rule does not apply to amounts rolled over from an employee's HSA or Archer MSA, or to contributions made through a cafeteria plan. If employer contributions do not satisfy the comparability rule during a period, the employer is subject to an excise tax equal to 35% of the aggregate amount contributed by the employer to HSAs for that period.

Example: Employer X offers its collectively bargained employees three health plans, including an HDHP with self-only coverage and a $2,000 deductible. For each employee electing the HDHP self-only coverage, X contributes $1,000 per year on behalf of the employee to an HSA. X makes no HSA contributions for employees who do not elect the HDHP. X's plans and HSA contributions satisfy the comparability rule.

Q-33. Can an HSA be offered under a cafeteria plan?

A-33. Yes. Both an HSA and an HDHP may be offered as options under a cafeteria plan. Thus, an employee may elect to have amounts contributed as employer contributions to an HSA and an HDHP on a salary-reduction basis.

Q-34. What reporting is required for an HSA?

A-34. Employer contributions to an HSA must be reported on the employee's Form W-2. In addition, information reporting for HSAs will be similar to information reporting for Archer MSAs. The IRS will release forms and instructions, similar to those required for Archer MSAs, on how to report HSA contributions, deductions, and distributions.

Q-35. Are HSAs subject to COBRA continuation coverage under section 4980B?

A-35. No. Like Archer MSAs, HSAs are not subject to COBRA continuation coverage.

Q-36. How do the rules under section 419 affect contributions by an employer to an HSA?

A-36. Contributions by an employer to an HSA are not subject to the rules under section 419. An HSA is a trust that is exempt from tax under section 223. Thus, an HSA is not a "fund" under section 419(e)(3) and, therefore, is not a "welfare benefit fund" under section 419(e)(1).

Q-37. May eligible individuals use debit, credit or stored-value cards to receive distributions from an HSA for qualified medical expenses?

A-37. Yes.

Q-38. Are HSAs subject to other statutory rules and provisions?

A-38. Yes. HSAs are subject to other statutory rules and provisions not addressed in this notice. No inference should be drawn regarding issues not expressly addressed in this notice that may be suggested by a particular question or answer, or by the inclusion or exclusion of certain questions.

Appendix C

IRS Announcements

Announcement 2006-72 . . . . C-1
Announcement 2004-67 . . . . C-3

Announcement 2006-72 (2006-40 I.R.B. 630)

[**Summary:** The IRS makes corrections to the final regulations (T.D. 9277, 2006-33 I.R.B. 226) that were published in the Federal Register on Monday, July 31, 2006 (71 Fed. Reg. 43056) to fix errors that may be misleading and to provide guidance regarding employer comparable contributions to HSAs under Code Section 4980G. The corrections are effective July 31, 2006.]

* * *

PART 54—PENSION EXCISE TAXES

* * *

§ 54.4980G-0 [corrected]

Par. 2. Section 54.4980G-0 is amended by:

1. Revising the entries for 54.4980G-4 Q-5 and Q-11.

2. Revising the entries for 54.4980G-5 Q-3.

§ 54.4980G-4 Calculating comparable contributions.

* * *

Q-5: Must an employer use the same contribution method as described in Q & A-2 and Q & A-4 of this section for all employees for any month during the calendar year?

* * *

Q-11: If an employer makes additional contributions to the HSAs of all comparable participating employees who are eligible to make the additional contributions (HSA catch-up contributions) under section 223(b)(3), do the contributions satisfy the comparability rules?

* * *

§ 54.4980G-5 HSA comparability rules and cafeteria plans and waiver of excise tax.

* * *

Q-3: If under the employer's cafeteria plan, employees who are eligible individuals and who participate in health assessments, disease management programs, or wellness programs receive an employer contribution to an HSA and the employees have the right to elect to make pretax salary reduction contributions to their HSAs, are the contributions subject to the comparability rules?

* * *

Par. 3. Section 54.4980G-4 is amended by:

1. Revising A-2 paragraph (c) of Example 2.

2. Revising A-2 paragraph (e) of Example 1.

§ 54.4980G-4 Calculating comparable contributions.

* * *

A-2: * * *

(c) * * *

Example 2. In a calendar year, Employer J offers its employees an HDHP and contributes on a monthly pay-as-you-go basis to the HSAs of employees who are eligible individuals with coverage under Employer J's HDHP. In the calendar year, Employer J contributes $50 per month to the HSA of each employee with self-only HDHP coverage and $100 per month to the HSA of each employee with family HDHP coverage. From January 1st through March 31st of the calendar year, Employee X is an eligible individual with self-only HDHP coverage. From April 1st through December 31st of the calendar year, X is an eligible individual with family HDHP coverage. For the months of January, February and March of the calendar year, Employer J contributes $50 per month to X's HSA. For the remaining months of the calendar year, Employer J contributes $100 per month to X's HSA. Employer J's contributions to X's HSA satisfy the comparability rules.

(d) * * *

(e) * * *

Example 1. In a calendar year, Employer K offers its employees an HDHP and contributes on a look-back basis to the HSAs of employees who are eligible individuals with coverage under Employer K's HDHP. Employer K contributes $600 ($50 per month) for the calendar year to the HSA of each employee with self-only HDHP coverage and $1,200 ($100 per month) for the calendar year to the HSA of each employee with family HDHP coverage. From January

1st through June 30th of the calendar year, Employee Y is an eligible individual with family HDHP coverage. From July 1st through December 31st, Y is an eligible individual with self-only HDHP coverage. Employer K contributes $900 on a look-back basis for the calendar year to Y's HSA ($100) per month for the months of January through June and $50 per month for the months of July through December). Employer K's contributions to Y's HSA satisfy the comparability rules.

* * *

Announcement 2004-67 (2004-36 I.R.B. 459)

[**Summary:** Clarified and corrected previously issued guidance to allow HSA contributions (including catch-up contributions) to be made after an individual has attained age 65 provided they are not enrolled in Medicare.]

PURPOSE

This document contains corrections to A-14 in Notice 2004-2, 2004-2 I.R.B. 269, relating to Health Savings Accounts. As published, A-14 of the notice contains errors that may prove to be misleading and are in need of clarification.

CORRECTIONS

The last sentence in A-14 of Notice 2004-2 which currently reads, "After an individual has attained age 65 (the Medicare eligibility age), contributions, including catch-up contributions, cannot be made to an individual's HSA", is corrected to read as follows: "After an individual has attained age 65 and becomes enrolled in Medicare benefits, contributions, including catch-up contributions, cannot be made to an individual's HSA." Additionally, the terms "becomes eligible for" in the first sentence of the Example in A-14 of Notice 2004-2 are replaced by "becomes enrolled in."

Appendix D

IRS Revenue Rulings

Revenue Ruling 2005-25 .... D-1

Revenue Ruling 2005-25 (2005-18 I.R.B. 971)

[**Summary:** The IRS has provided guidance clarifying that an individual with a high-deductible health plan (HDHP) may contribute to a Health Savings Account (HSA) even if his or her spouse has nonqualifying family coverage. So long as the spouse's non-HDHP does not cover the individual, that individual is eligible to contribute to an HSA, and the special rules for married individuals found in Code Section 223(b)(5) do not apply.]

ISSUES

1. Is a married individual who otherwise qualifies as an "eligible individual" eligible to contribute to a Health Savings Account (HSA) under section 223 of the Internal Revenue Code (the Code) if the individual's spouse has non-HDHP family coverage that does not cover the individual?

2. If the individual is eligible to contribute to an HSA, what is the maximum contribution limit?

FACTS

Situation 1

H and W are a married couple and both are age 35. Throughout 2005, H has self-only coverage under a high deductible health plan (HDHP) as defined in section 223(c)(2) with an annual deductible of $2,000. H has no other health coverage, is not enrolled in Medicare and may not be claimed as a dependent on another taxpayer's return. W has non-HDHP family coverage for W and H's and W's two dependents, but H is excluded from W's coverage.

Situation 2

The same facts as *Situation 1*, except that H has HDHP family coverage as defined in section 223(c)(2) for H and one of H's and W's dependents with an annual deductible of $5,000. W has non-HDHP family coverage for W and H's and W's other dependent. H is excluded from W's coverage.

Situation 3

The same facts as *Situation 1*, except that H has HDHP family coverage for H and H's and W's two dependents with an annual deductible of $5,000. W is not covered under H's health plan and has no other health plan coverage.

LAW AND ANALYSIS

Section 223(a) allows a deduction for contributions to an HSA for an "eligible individual." Section 223(c)(1)(A) defines "eligible individual" with respect to any month, as an individual who, in addition to other requirements, is covered under an HDHP on the first day of such month and is not, while covered under an HDHP, "covered under any health plan which is not a high deductible health plan, and which provides coverage for any benefit which is covered under the high deductible health plan." An eligible individual may also have permitted insurance, and certain disregarded coverage in addition to an HDHP. A plan does not fail to be treated as an HDHP merely because it covers preventive care without a deductible.

An HDHP is a health plan that satisfies certain requirements with respect to minimum annual deductibles and maximum annual out-of-pocket expenses. Section 223(c)(2)(A). Family coverage is any coverage other than self-only coverage (e.g., an HDHP covering one eligible individual and at least one other individual (whether or not the other individual is an eligible individual)). Section 223(c)(4) Q&A-12 of Notice 2004-50, 2004-33 I.R.B. 196.

Only eligible individuals may contribute to an HSA. The maximum annual contribution limit is the sum of the limits determined separately for each month. For an individual who is eligible during the entire calendar year 2005, the contribution limit is the lesser of the annual deductible under the HDHP (minimum of $1,000 for self-only coverage and $2,000 for family coverage) or $2,650 for self-only coverage and $5,250 for family coverage. Rev. Proc. 2004-71 § 3.22, 2004-49 I.R.B. 1184.

Section 223(b)(5) provides special rules for married individuals. In general, if either spouse has family coverage, both spouses are treated as having only such family coverage. Also, if each spouse has family coverage under different health plans, both spouses are treated as having family coverage under the plan with the lowest deductible. However, if a spouse has HDHP family coverage and the other spouse has non-HDHP self-only coverage, the spouse with the HDHP family coverage is an eligible individual and may contribute to an HSA up to the amount of the annual contribution limit. Because the other spouse is covered by a non-HDHP and is therefore not an eligible individual, the other spouse may not contribute to an HSA, notwithstanding the special rule in section 223(b)(5) treating both spouses as having family coverage. Q&A-31 of Notice 2004-50.

An eligible individual who attains age 55 before the close of the calendar year may make a catch-up HSA contribution (up to $600 in 2005). Section 223(b)(3).

In *Situation 1*, H has HDHP self-only coverage and no other health coverage, is not enrolled in Medicare and may not be claimed as a dependent on another taxpayer's return. Although W has non-HDHP family coverage, H is not covered under that health plan. H is therefore an eligible individual as defined in section 223(c)(1). The special rules for married individuals under section 223(b)(5) do not apply because W's non-HDHP family coverage does not cover H. Thus, H remains an eligible individual and H may contribute up to $2,000 to an HSA (lesser of the HDHP deductible for self-only coverage or $2,650) for 2005. H may not make the catch-up contribution under section 223(b)(3) because H is not age 55 in 2005. W has non-HDHP coverage and is therefore not an eligible individual.

In *Situation 2*, H has HDHP family coverage for one of H's and W's dependents and W has non-HDHP family coverage for W and H's and W's other dependent. Because the non-HDHP family coverage does not cover H, the special rules in section 223(b)(5) do not affect H's eligibility to make HSA contributions up to H's annual HSA contribution limit. H may therefore contribute up to $5,000 to an HSA (the lesser of the family HDHP deductible or $5,250). W has non-HDHP coverage and is therefore not an eligible individual.

In *Situation 3*, H has HDHP family coverage for H and H's and W's two dependents. H may contribute to up to $5,000 to an HSA (the lesser of the family HDHP deductible or $5,250). Because H's family coverage does not cover W, the special rules under section 223(b)(5) do not apply to treat W as having family coverage. W has no health plan coverage and is therefore not an eligible individual.

HOLDINGS

1. An individual who otherwise qualifies as an eligible individual does not fail to be an eligible individual merely because the individual's spouse has non-HDHP family coverage, if the spouse's non-HDHP does not cover the individual. Accordingly, that individual may contribute to an HSA.

2. The maximum amount under section 223(b) that an eligible individual may contribute to an HSA is based on whether the individual has self-only or family HDHP coverage.

DRAFTING INFORMATION * * *

Appendix E

Department of Labor Releases

Advisory Opinion 2004-09A E-1
Field Assistance Bulletin 2006-02 . . . . E-7
Field Assistance Bulletin 2004-01 . . . . E-12

Advisory Opinion 2004-09A

U.S. Department of Labor
Employee Benefits Security Administration

Office of Regulations and Interpretations

Advisory Opinion 2004-09A
December 22, 2004
Thomas G. Schendt, Esq.
Alston & Bird LLP
601 Pennsylvania Avenue, N.W.
North Building, 10th Floor
Washington, DC 20004-2601

Dear Mr. Schendt:

This is in response to your request for an advisory opinion from the U.S. Department of Labor (the Department) concerning the application of the prohibited transaction provisions under section 4975(c) of the Internal Revenue Code of 1986, as amended (the Code), to certain contributions to health savings accounts (HSAs), as described below.[1]

---

[1] Under Reorganization Plan No. 4 of 1978, 43 Fed. Reg. 47713 (Oct. 17, 1978), the authority of the Secretary of the Treasury to issue rulings under section 4975 of the Code has been transferred, with certain exceptions not here relevant, to the Secretary of Labor. See 5 USC App. at 214 (2000 ed.).

You represent that your client, an insurer (the Company) and its affiliates, offers various health benefit plans in the individual market, including high deductible health plans (HDHPs), as that term is defined in section 223(c)(2) of the Code. In addition, the Company either offers HSAs, as defined in section 223(d) of the Code, to individuals covered by HDHPs issued by the Company, or enters into a contractual arrangement with a specified bank that will offer HSAs to such individuals, as described below.

Your letter contains the following facts and representations.

Factual Scenario I

Under Factual Scenario I, only persons insured under HDHPs issued by the Company in the individual market are able to establish HSAs with the Company. However, a person does not have to establish an HSA with the Company to participate in an individual HDHP with the Company. If a person establishes an HSA with the Company, the Company will serve as both the trustee or custodian and the record-keeper of the HSA. The Company does not provide HSA custodial services in the employer group market.

To encourage participation in the Company's HSA program, the Company will offer an incentive to a person who establishes an HSA with the Company when he or she first enters into an individual HDHP with the Company. This incentive will be in the form of a $100 cash credit by the Company, as trustee or custodian, directly to the individual's HSA. This credit to the HSA will be automatic. The account holder will not be required to make any contribution to his or her HSA to receive the credit to his or her HSA. The credit is dependent on the establishment of an HSA with the Company. The account holder will not be able to divert the money to himself or herself before it is credited to the HSA.

If the person does not establish an HSA with the Company, he or she will not receive any incentive from the Company under this incentive program. Thus, for example, the individual will not receive any incentive from the Company in the form of a credit to an HSA not provided by the Company or in the form of money paid to him or her outside of the HSA. The credit to the account holder's HSA with the Company will be subject to the statutory requirements for HSAs set forth in section 223 of the Code, and the tax treatment of any distributions from the HSA attributable to this credit will be governed by the provisions of section 223(f) of the Code.

With respect to each HSA established with the Company pursuant to this incentive program, the Company represents that any arrangement for services by the Company to the HSA (e.g., as trustee or custodian and/or record-keeper of the HSA) will meet the requirements of section 4975(d)(2) of the Code and the Treasury's regulations at 26 CFR § 54.4975-6.

The Company represents that the premiums payable under the HDHP will not vary based on the individual's choice of HSA custodian or trustee. Thus, the individual's insurance premiums will not be higher or lower as a result of his or her decision to establish an HSA either with the Company or with some other custodian or trustee. The Company also represents that any administrative fees the Company may charge the account holder with respect to his or her HSA will not change (i.e., will not increase or decrease) as a result of the credit to his or her HSA.

The Company states that although the duration of this incentive program has not been determined, it envisions that the incentive program could be used at various times for specified periods of time. The Company also anticipates that the amount of the incentive could change from time to time. However, for purposes of this request, the Company represents that the amount of the incentive will not exceed $100 per person.

Factual Scenario II

Under Factual Scenario II, the Company and its affiliates offer various health benefit plans in the group market, including HDHPs as defined under the Code.

The Company enters into a contractual relationship with a specified bank (the Bank) to provide HSAs for individuals covered by HDHPs issued by the Company. However, an individual does not have to establish an HSA with the Bank to participate in a group HDHP issued by the Company. The Bank serves as the trustee or custodian and the record-keeper of those HSAs and receives remuneration from the Company for its services in that regard. The Company also enters into a contractual relationship with a specified entity (the Vendor) to provide various services in relation to these HSAs, for which the Company compensates the Vendor. Neither the Bank nor the Vendor is a member of the Company's controlled group under sections 414(b), (c) and (m) of the Code.

To encourage the establishment of HSAs with the Bank in connection with group HDHPs issued by the Company, the Bank will offer an incentive to a person who establishes an HSA with the Bank when the Company first covers such person under a group HDHP. This incentive will be in the form of a $100 cash credit from the Bank directly to the individual's HSA. This credit to the HSA will be automatic. The account holder will not be required to make any contribution to his or her HSA to receive the credit to his or her HSA. The credit will be dependent on the establishment of an HSA with the Bank. The account holder will not be able to divert the money to himself or herself before it is credited to the HSA.

If the person does not establish an HSA with the Bank, he or she will not receive any incentive from the Bank under this incentive program. For example, the individual will not receive any incentive from the Company or the Bank in the form of a credit to an HSA not provided by the Bank or in the form of money paid to him or her outside of his or her HSA. The credit to the account holder's HSA with the Bank will be subject to the statutory requirements for HSAs set forth in section 223 of the Code, and the tax treatment of any distributions from the HSA attributable to this credit will be governed by the provisions of section 223(f) of the Code.

With respect to the HSAs established with the Bank pursuant to this incentive program, the Company, the Bank and the Vendor intend that any arrangements for services by the Bank or the Vendor to the HSA (e.g., as the trustee or custodian and/or record-keeper of the HSA) will meet the requirements of section 4975(d)(2) of the Code and the Treasury's regulations at 26 CFR § 54.4975-6.[2]

The Company represents that the premiums charged for the individual's coverage under the group HDHP will not vary based on the individual's choice of HSA custodian or trustee. Thus, the premiums charged by the Company for the individual's coverage under the group HDHP will not be higher or lower as a result of his or her decision to establish an HSA either with the Bank or with some other custodian or trustee. In addition, any administrative fees the Bank or the Vendor may charge the account holder with respect to his or her HSA will not change (i.e., will not increase or decrease) as a result of this credit to his or her HSA.

The Company states that although the duration of this incentive program has not been determined, it envisions that the incentive program could be used at various times for specified periods of time. The Company also anticipates that the amount of the incentive could change from time to time. However, for purposes of this request, the Company represents that the amount of the incentive will not exceed $100 per person.

Advisory Opinions Requested

With respect to Factual Scenario I, you have requested an advisory opinion that the credit to an account holder's HSA will not constitute a prohibited transaction under section 4975(c) of the Code for either the account holder or the Company.

In addition, with respect to Factual Scenario II, you have requested an advisory opinion that the credit to an account holder's HSA will not constitute a prohibited transaction under section 4975(c) of the Code or section 406 of the Employee Retirement Income Security Act of 1974, as amended (ERISA).

Prohibited Transactions under the Internal Revenue Code

Section 4975(e)(1)(E) of the Code defines the term "plan" to include ". . . health savings account described in section 223(d)" of the Code.

A "prohibited transaction" under section 4975(c)(1) of the Code includes, among other things, any direct or indirect:

---

[2] The Company is not requesting, and the Department is not providing, an opinion as to whether any arrangement for services by the Company, the Bank or the Vendor to an HSA will satisfy the requirements necessary for relief under section 4975(d)(2) of the Code and the regulations relating thereto. In this regard, the Department ordinarily does not issue advisory opinions on questions that are inherently factual in nature.

(A)   sale or exchange, or leasing, of any property between a plan and a disqualified person;

(C)   furnishing of goods, services, or facilities between a plan and a disqualified person;

(D)   transfer to, or use by or for the benefit of, a disqualified person of the income or assets of a plan;

(E)   act by a disqualified person who is a fiduciary whereby he deals with the income or assets of a plan in his own interest or for his own account; or

(F)   receipt of any consideration for his own personal account by any disqualified person who is a fiduciary from any party dealing with the plan in connection with a transaction involving the income or assets of the plan.

A "disqualified person" is defined under section 4975(e)(2) of the Code, in pertinent part, to include a person who is a fiduciary or a person providing services to the plan.

Analysis of Factual Scenarios I and II

Under Factual Scenario I, the Company will be a trustee or custodian of the HSA. As such, the Company would be a disqualified person with respect to the HSA.

Under Factual Scenario II, the Bank will be a trustee or custodian of the HSA. As such, the Bank is a disqualified person with respect to the HSA. However, as we understand the facts, the Company would not be a disqualified person with respect to the HSA. In both scenarios, the account holder is a fiduciary and disqualified person with respect to the HSA.

Under both Factual Scenarios, the $100 credit proposed by either the Company or the Bank, respectively, would be a cash contribution to the account holder's HSA. The Department notes that in accordance with IRS Notice 2004-50, Q&A 28, wherein it states that "any person . . . may make contributions to an HSA on behalf of an eligible individual," Code section 223 does not prohibit the Company or the Bank from making such contributions to its customers' HSAs. A cash contribution to a plan is not generally a sale or exchange of property prohibited by section 4975(c)(1)(A) of the Code. Additionally, the cash contribution would not be a transfer of an asset of a plan for the benefit of a disqualified person or an act of self-dealing by either the Company or the Bank under section 4975(c)(1)(D) or (E) of the Code involving the assets of a plan. Therefore, neither the Company's nor the Bank's contribution of a cash credit to the account holder's HSA, as described herein, would be a prohibited transaction under section 4975(c)(1) of the Code.[3]

Similarly, the HSA's receipt of the Company's or the Bank's contribution of a cash credit, under the facts described above, would not be an act of self-dealing on the part of the account holder nor a receipt by the account holder in his or her

---

[3] With respect to contributions or transfers of property to a plan that are considered to be an "exchange," see Adv. Op. 81-69A (July 28, 1981) and the Department's Interpretative Bulletin at 29 CFR 2509.94-3, relating to in-kind contributions to employee benefit plans.

individual capacity of any consideration from a party dealing with the HSA in connection with a transaction involving assets of the HSA. Even though the Company or the Bank, respectively, would make the contribution as an incentive to encourage the account holder's participation in the Company's or the Bank's HSA program, the contribution goes to the HSA and not to the account holder.[4] Therefore, the receipt by the HSA of such cash contributions would not be a prohibited transaction under section 4975(c)(1) of the Code.[5]

Since the Company is not a disqualified person with respect the HSA under Factual Scenario II, the Bank's contribution of the credit to the account holder's HSA would not be a prohibited transaction under section 4975(c) of the Code with respect to the Company.

Finally, with respect to the contribution of any cash credits by the Bank to an account holder's HSA under the facts described above, the same analysis and conclusions would apply, for purposes of the prohibited transaction provisions contained in section 406(a) and (b) of ERISA, to an HSA that would be an "employee benefit plan" covered under Title I of ERISA[6] under the principles discussed in the Department's Field Assistance Bulletin (FAB) 2004-01 (April 7, 2004). Further, in such instances, the fiduciary responsibility provisions of Title I would apply to the selection of service providers to the HSA.

In discussing whether, and under what circumstances, HSA's established in connection with employment-based group health plans would be subject to the provisions of Title I of ERISA, FAB 2004-01 states that generally such HSAs would not constitute an "employee welfare benefit plan" as defined under section 3(1) of ERISA, if employer involvement with the HSA is limited. Specifically, HSAs meeting the conditions of the safe harbor for group or group-type insurance programs at 29 CFR § 2510.3-1(j)(1)–(4) are not considered employee welfare benefit plans within the meaning of section 3(1) of ERISA. However, a finding that an HSA established by an employee is not covered by ERISA does not affect whether an HDHP sponsored by the employer is itself a group health plan subject to Title I. In fact, FAB 2004-01 states that unless otherwise exempt from Title I (e.g., governmental plans, church plans), employer-sponsored HDHPs will be "employee welfare benefit plans" within the meaning of section 3(1) of ERISA and, thus, subject to the fiduciary responsibility provisions of Title I.

---

[4] This distinguishes the arrangement from others that have been found to involve prohibited transactions. See Adv. Op. 89-12A (July 14, 1989) (personal receipt of "free checking" account services by a *customer* from a bank in connection with the investment of assets of the customer's individual retirement account (IRA) in the bank's financial products would constitute a violation of section 4975(c)(1) of the Code.) See also PTE 93-33, 58 Fed. Reg. 31053 (May 28, 1993) (exempting certain arrangements benefiting an IRA account holder).

[5] This advisory opinion does not address payments to the individual account of any person who is a disqualified person for reasons other than as the account holder of an HSA.

[6] Section 3(3) of ERISA defines the term "employee benefit plan" or "plan" as an employee welfare benefit plan (see section 3(1) of ERISA) or an employee pension benefit plan (see section 3(2) of ERISA) or a plan which is both an employee welfare benefit plan and an employee pension benefit plan.

This letter constitutes an advisory opinion under ERISA Procedure 76-1, 41 Fed. Reg. 36281 (Aug. 27, 1976). The letter is issued subject to the provisions of that procedure, including section 10 thereof, relating to the effect of advisory opinions.

Sincerely,

Louis J. Campagna

Chief, Division of Fiduciary Interpretations

Office of Regulations and Interpretations

Field Assistance Bulletin 2006-02

U.S. Department of Labor
Employee Benefits Security Administration

October 27, 2006

Memorandum for: Virginia C. Smith

                       Director of Enforcement, Regional Directors

From: Robert J. Doyle

                       Director of Regulations and Interpretations

Subject: Health Saving Accounts—ERISA Q&As

Background

In general, a Health Savings Account (HSA) is an account established pursuant to section 223 of the Internal Revenue Code (Code) to pay or reimburse the qualified medical expenses of eligible individuals. Although the requirements for tax qualified HSAs are found in the Code, questions regarding the application of the Employee Retirement Income Security Act of 1974 (ERISA) to HSAs arise because employers may establish and contribute to an employee's HSA. On April 7, 2004, the Department of Labor's Employee Benefits Security Administration issued Field Assistance Bulletin (FAB) 2004-01 addressing the status of

HSAs under ERISA. That guidance explained that HSAs generally will not constitute "employee welfare benefit plans" covered by Title I of ERISA where employer involvement with the HSA is limited.

In FAB 2004-01, the Department specifically indicated that employer contributions to HSAs would not give rise to an ERISA-covered plan where the establishment of the HSA is completely voluntary on the part of the employees and the employer does not: limit the ability of eligible individuals to move their funds to another HSA or impose conditions on utilization of HSA funds beyond those permitted under the Code; make or influence the investment decisions with respect to funds contributed to an HSA; represent that the HSA is an employee welfare benefit plan established or maintained by the employer; or receive any payment or compensation in connection with an HSA.

Since the issuance of FAB 2004-01, the Department has received a number of recurring questions about the guidance and the evolving practices regarding the offering of HSAs. The following provides further guidance on many of the frequently asked questions raised with the Department.

Questions And Answers

In the absence of an employee's affirmative consent, may an employer open an HSA for an employee and deposit employer funds into the HSA without violating the condition in the FAB that requires that the establishment of an HSA by an employee be "completely voluntary"?

Yes. The intended purpose of the "completely voluntary" condition in FAB 2004-01 is to ensure that any contributions an employee makes to an HSA, including salary reduction amounts, will be voluntary. HSA accountholders have sole control and are exclusively responsible for expending HSA funds and generally may move the funds to another HSA or otherwise withdraw the funds. The fact that an employer unilaterally opens an HSA for an employee and deposits employer funds into the HSA does not divest the HSA accountholder of this control and responsibility and, therefore, would not give rise to an ERISA-covered plan so long as the conditions described in FAB 2004-01 are met.

If an employer maintains a high deductible health plan (HDHP) for its employees, can the employer limit the HSA providers that it allows to market their HSA products in the workplace or select a single HSA provider to which it will forward contributions without making the HSA part of the employer's ERISA-covered group health plan?

Yes. As stated in FAB 2004-01, an employer may offer an HSA to its employees without establishing an ERISA-covered plan in one of two ways. The employer may rely on the group-type insurance safe harbor in 29 C.F.R. § 2510.3-1(j), in which case the employer cannot make contributions to the HSA, or it may rely on the separate conditions outlined in FAB 2004-01, in which case the employer may or may not elect to make employer contributions to the HSA.

If the employer relies on the group-type insurance safe harbor in 29 C.F.R. § 2510.3-1(j), it cannot "endorse" the HSA provider. In the Department's view, an employer would not be considered to "endorse" an HSA within the meaning of the regulation merely by limiting the HSA providers that it allows to market their HSA products in the workplace or selecting a single HSA provider to which it will forward contributions. Employers may also provide employees general information on the advisability of using an HSA in conjunction with the HDHP without "endorsing" the program. See generally Interpretive Bulletin 99-1, 29 C.F.R. § 2509.99-1.

The separate conditions in FAB 2004-01, though including completely voluntary employee participation and employer neutrality in not representing that the HSA is an employee welfare benefit plan established or maintained by the employer, do not include the group-type insurance safe harbor's prohibition on employer "endorsement." As explained in FAB 2004-01, an employer could limit the HSA providers that it allows to market their HSA products in the workplace or select a single HSA provider to which it will forward contributions and still satisfy the conditions outlined in the FAB without converting the HSA into an ERISA-covered plan.

Would an employer be viewed as "making or influencing" the HSA investment decisions of employees, within the meaning of the FAB, merely because the employer selects an HSA provider that offers some or all of the investment options made available to the employees in their 401(k) plan?

No. The mere fact that an employer selects an HSA provider to which it will forward contributions that offers a limited selection of investment options or investment options that replicate the investment options available to employees under their 401(k) plan would not, in the view of the Department, constitute the making or influencing of an employee's investment decisions giving rise to an ERISA-covered plan, so long as employees are afforded a reasonable choice of investment options and employees are not limited in moving their funds to another HSA. The selection of a single HSA provider that offers a single investment option would not, in the view the Department, afford employees a reasonable choice of investment options.

If contributions to an HSA are made through a cafeteria plan, would the savings that benefit the employer from non-payment of FICA and FUTA taxes on those contributions be considered "payment or compensation received in connection with an HSA" that would subject the HSA to Title I coverage?

No. The Department does not view an employer's non-payment of FICA and FUTA taxes on amounts contributed to an HSA as "payment or compensation" for purposes of the guidance issued in FAB 2004-01.

Can an employer pay the fees associated with the HSA that the employee would normally be expected or required to pay without causing the HSA to become an ERISA-covered plan?

Yes. As stated in the FAB, the mere fact that an employer contributes to an HSA does not result in the HSA being an ERISA-covered plan. Therefore, the Department does not believe that an employer paying fees associated with an HSA that the employee would otherwise be required to pay would make that HSA an ERISA-covered plan.

May an HSA vendor offer an HSA product it offers to the public to its own employees without the HSAs being considered employee benefit plans covered by ERISA?

Yes. Offering HSA products that the employer offers to the public in the regular course of business would not mean the HSA provider established or is maintaining the HSA as an employer to provide benefits to its employees.

If the employer limits the number of HSA vendors to which it will forward contributions, may the employer receive a discount on another product from one of the selected HSA vendors?

No. In the Department's view, receiving a discount on another product from an HSA vendor selected by the employer would constitute the employer receiving a "payment" or "compensation" in connection with an HSA. In the Department's view, the arrangement would also give rise to fiduciary and prohibited transaction issues.

Are HSAs subject to the prohibited transaction provisions of section 4975 of the Internal Revenue Code?

Yes. Although the Department believes that HSAs meeting the conditions of FAB 2004-01 generally will not be ERISA-covered plans, the Medicare Modernization Act specifically provided that HSAs will be subject to the prohibited transaction provisions in section 4975 of the Code. In that regard, the Department's plan asset regulation at 29 C.F.R. § 2510.3-102 states, in relevant part, that "[f]or purposes of [certain specified provisions of ERISA] and section 4975 of the Internal Revenue Code only . . . the assets of the plan include amounts . . . that a participant or beneficiary pays to an employer, or amounts that a participant has withheld from his wages by an employer, for contribution to the plan as of the earliest date on which such contributions can reasonably be segregated from the employer's general assets." (Emphasis added). As a result, employers who fail to transmit promptly participants' HSA contributions may violate the prohibited transaction provisions of section 4975 of the Code. See Code § 4975(c)(1)(D) (prohibited transactions include the "transfer to, or use by or for the benefit of, a disqualified person of the income or assets of a plan").

Do the class prohibited transaction exemptions for owners of individual retirement accounts (IRAs) apply to accountholders of HSAs?

No. The class exemptions issued by the Department for products and services offered owners of IRAs, PTE 97-11, PTE 93-33, PTE 93-1, do not apply to HSA accountholders.

Is it a prohibited transaction for an HSA provider to offer a cash incentive for establishing an HSA with that provider?

No, if the provider deposits the incentive into the HSA. The Department stated in Advisory Opinion 2004-09A that, in certain situations, an HSA provider would not violate the prohibited transaction provisions under Code section 4975(c) or ERISA section 406 where the HSA provider offers an incentive to individuals for establishing an HSA with that provider by depositing cash directly into the individual's HSA. A cash contribution to an HSA generally would not be considered a "sale or exchange of property" or "a transfer of plan assets" for purposes of the prohibited transaction provisions of the Code. Because the cash contribution goes to the HSA and not the HSA account holder, the HSA's receipt of the cash contribution also would not be considered an act of self dealing on the part of the HSA account holder nor a receipt by the HSA account holder in his or her individual capacity of any consideration from a party dealing with the HSA.

May an HSA vendor provide a line of credit for HSA expenses to an HSA accountholder choosing its HSA?

The Internal Revenue Service has issued guidance permitting eligible individuals to use debit, credit, or stored-value cards to receive distributions from an HSA for qualified medical expenses. See IRS Notice 2004-2, Q&A 37. Subsequent guidance by the Service explains that, under section 223(e)(2) of the Code, account beneficiaries, HSA trustees, and HSA custodians may not enter into certain "prohibited transactions" with an HSA. See IRS Notice 2004-50, Q&A 67, 68. For example, an account beneficiary may not borrow or pledge the assets of the HSA or receive a benefit in his or her own individual capacity as a result of opening or maintaining an HSA because such a transaction would constitute a prohibited transfer to or use of the HSA assets by or for the benefit of the account beneficiary. See Advisory Opinion 89-12A. Whether a credit card arrangement between a vendor and owner of an HSA results in a prohibited transaction would depend on specific facts and circumstances. A prohibited transaction would not result merely from an HSA accountholder directing the payment of HSA funds to the credit line vendor to reimburse the vendor for HSA expenses paid with a credit card.

U.S. Department of Labor
Frances Perkins Building
200 Constitution Avenue, NW
Washington, DC 20210

Field Assistance Bulletin 2004-01

U.S. Department of Labor
Employee Benefits Security Administration

April 7, 2004

Memorandum for: Virginia C. Smith

Director of Enforcement, Regional Directors

From: Robert J. Doyle

Director of Regulations and Interpretations

Subject: Health Saving Accounts

Issue

Whether Health Savings Accounts established in connection with employment-based group health plans constitute "employee welfare benefit plans" for purposes of Title I of ERISA?

Background

Section 3(1) of the Employee Retirement Income Security Act of 1974 (ERISA) defines the term "employee welfare benefit plan" in relevant part to mean "any plan, fund, or program . . . established or maintained by an employer . . . to the extent that such plan, fund, or program was established or is maintained for the purpose of providing for its participants or their beneficiaries, through the purchase of insurance or otherwise, (A) medical, surgical, or hospital care or benefits, or benefits in the event of sickness. . . ."

Section 1201 of the Medicare Prescription Drug, Improvement, and Modernization Act of 2003, Pub. L. No. 108–173 (the Medicare Modernization Act), added section 223 to the Internal Revenue Code (Code) to permit eligible individuals to establish Health Savings Accounts (HSAs).[7] In general, HSAs are established to receive tax-favored contributions by or on behalf of eligible individuals, and amounts in an HSA may be accumulated over the years or distributed on a tax-free basis to pay or reimburse "qualified medical expenses." In order to establish an HSA, an eligible individual, among other conditions, must

---

[7] The U.S. Department of the Treasury and the Internal Revenue Service (IRS), which have interpretive and regulatory authority over HSAs under section 223 of the Code, issued general guidance concerning HSAs on December 22, 2003, in I.R.S. Notice 2004-2, and issued additional guidance on March 30, 2004, in I.R.S. Notice 2004-23, I.R.S. Notice 2004-25, Revenue Ruling 2004-38, and Revenue Procedure 2004-22. The Treasury/IRS guidance is available on the Internet at www.treas.gov/offices/public-affairs/hsa.

be covered under a High Deductible Health Plan (HDHP).[8] Contributions to an HSA established by an eligible individual who is an employee may be made by the employee, the employee's employer or both in a given year.[9] Amounts in an HSA may be rolled over to another HSA.[10] If an employer makes contributions to HSAs, the employer must make available a comparable contribution on behalf of all eligible employees with comparable coverage during the same period.[11] However, employers that make contributions to an employee's HSA are not responsible for determining whether HSAs are used for qualified medical expenses or for investing or managing amounts contributed to an employee's HSA.[12]

It is our understanding that a number of employers that currently sponsor ERISA-covered group health plans may wish to add an HDHP option and offer programs designed to enable employees to establish HSAs to pay for medical expenses not covered by the HDHP. Questions have been raised about whether, and under what circumstances, HSAs established in connection with employment-based programs would constitute "employee welfare benefit plans" within the meaning of section 3(1) of ERISA.

Analysis

Congress, in enacting the Medicare Modernization Act, recognized that HSAs would be established in conjunction with employment-based health plans and specifically provided for employer contributions. However, neither the Medicare Modernization Act nor section 223 of the Code specifically address the application of Title I of ERISA to HSAs. Based on our review of Title I, and taking into account the provisions of the Code as amended by the Medicare Modernization Act, we believe that HSAs generally will not constitute employee welfare benefit plans established or maintained by an employer where employer involvement with the HSA is limited, whether or not the employee's HDHP is sponsored by an employer or obtained as individual coverage.

Specifically, HSAs meeting the conditions of the safe harbor for group or group-type insurance programs at 29 C.F.R. § 2510.3-1(j)(1)–(4) would not be employee welfare benefit plans within the meaning of section 3(1) of ERISA.[13] Moreover, although contributions or payment of group insurance premiums by an employer would be a significant consideration in determining whether a group or group-type insurance arrangement is an employee welfare benefit plan

---

[8] See I.R.S. Notice 2004-2, Q&A Nos. 1 and 2.

[9] Id. Q&A No. 11.

[10] Id. Q&A No. 23.

[11] Id. Q&A No. 32.

[12] Id. Q&A No. 30.

[13] Regulation section 2510.3-1(j) excludes from Title I coverage certain group or group-type insurance programs. In general, such programs are excluded from coverage where there are no employer contributions, employee participation is voluntary, the employer does not endorse the program, and the employer receives no consideration in connection with the program, other than reasonable compensation for administrative services actually rendered in connection with payroll deductions. See also 29 C.F.R. § 2509.99-1 relating to payroll deduction IRAs.

under section 3(1), such contributions or payments are not necessarily significant in analyzing the status of HSAs under ERISA. As noted above, HSAs are personal health care savings vehicles rather than a form of group health insurance. For example, funds deposited in an HSA generally may not be used to pay health insurance premiums,[14] and the beneficiaries of the account have sole control and are exclusively responsible for expending the funds in compliance with the requirements of the Code. Because of these differences, we regard court precedent on the significance of employer contributions to group or group-type insurance arrangements as inapposite to HSAs. In the group health insurance context, the employer, whether by choosing an insurance policy or creating a self-funded program, typically establishes the type of benefits provided, the conditions for their receipt, and the manner in which claims will be adjudicated. In the context of HSAs, however, the employer may be doing little more than contributing funds to an account controlled solely by the employee.

Accordingly, we would not find that employer contributions to HSAs give rise to an ERISA-covered plan where the establishment of the HSAs is completely voluntary on the part of the employees and the employer does not: (i) limit the ability of eligible individuals to move their funds to another HSA beyond restrictions imposed by the Code; (ii) impose conditions on utilization of HSA funds beyond those permitted under the Code; (iii) make or influence the investment decisions with respect to funds contributed to an HSA; (iv) represent that the HSAs are an employee welfare benefit plan established or maintained by the employer; or (v) receive any payment or compensation in connection with an HSA.

The mere fact that an employer imposes terms and conditions on contributions that would be required to satisfy tax requirements under the Code or limits the forwarding of contributions through its payroll system to a single HSA provider (or permits only a limited number of HSA providers to advertise or market their HSA products in the workplace) would not affect the above conclusions regarding HSAs funded with employer or employee contributions, unless the employer or the HSA provider restricts the ability of the employee to move funds to another HSA beyond those restrictions imposed by the Code.

Conclusion

HSAs generally will not constitute "employee welfare benefit plans" for purposes of the provisions of Title I of ERISA. Employer contributions to the HSA of an eligible individual will not result in Title I coverage where, as discussed above, employer involvement with the HSA is limited. Finding that an HSA established by an employee is not covered by ERISA does not, however, affect

---

[14] Although the Medicare Modernization Act excludes health insurance from the qualified medical expenses that may be paid from an HSA, there are exceptions for the payment of COBRA premiums, certain insurance for individuals over 65, long-term care insurance premiums and health insurance during periods of unemployment. Code section 223(d)(2).

whether an HDHP sponsored by the employer is itself a group health plan subject to Title I. In fact, unless otherwise exempt from Title I (e.g., governmental plans, church plans) employer-sponsored HDHPs will be employee welfare benefit plans within the meaning of ERISA section 3(1) subject to Title I.

Questions concerning this matter may be directed to Suzanne Adelman, Division of Coverage, Reporting and Disclosure at 202-693-8523.

Appendix F

Annual HSA Limitations

The maximum HSA contribution limits generally apply to an eligible individual with an HDHP and an HSA for the entire taxable year (see chapters 3 and 4). However, an exception is provided for an individual who becomes HSA-eligible after the beginning of a taxable year (see Q 4:38). In general, for tax years beginning after 2006, an eligible individual on the first day of the last month of a taxable year (generally December 31) may be permitted to make the full HSA contribution for the year. An individual who is an eligible individual during the last month of a taxable year is treated as having been an eligible individual during every month during the taxable year for purposes of computing the amount that may be contributed to the HSA for the year. As a result, such individual is allowed to make contributions for months before the individual was enrolled in an HDHP.

If an individual makes contributions under the exception and does not remain an eligible individual during the testing period, the amount of the contributions attributable to months preceding the month in which the individual was an eligible individual which could not have been made but for the provision, is includible in gross income. A 10 percent additional tax also applies to the amount includible. An exception applies if the employee ceases to be an eligible individual by reason of death or disability.

For taxable years beginning in 2009, the HSA maximum annual contribution limit for an eligible individual with self-only coverage is $3,000 and $5,950 for family coverage ($2,900 and $5,800 for 2008). For taxable years beginning before 2007, the annual contribution amount could not exceed annual deductible under the HDHP. The repeal of the annual plan deductible limit is effective for taxable years beginning after 2006.

The 2004–2009 inflation adjustments as well as the base amount for which the numbers are derived (see Q 4:32) are reflected in the following table.

	2010		2009		2008		2007	
	Self-Only	Family	Self-Only	Family	Self-Only	Family	Self-Only	Family
HSA Maximum Annual Contribution	$3,050	$6,150	$3,000	$5,950	$2,900	$5,800	$2,850	$5,650
HSA Catch-Up Contributions (age 55 by end of year)	$1,000		$1,000		$900		$800	
HDHP Minimum Annual Deductible[3]	$1,200	$2,400	$1,150	$2,300	$1,100	$2,200	$1,100	$2,200
HDHP Maximum Out-of-Pocket[4]	$5,950	$11,900	$5,800	$11,600	$5,600	$11,200	$5,500	$11,000

	2006		2005		2004		Base Amount[1]	
	Self-Only	Family	Self-Only	Family	Self-Only	Family	Self-Only	Family
HSA Maximum Annual Contribution	$2,700	$5,450	$2,650[2]	$5,250[2]	$2,600[2]	$5,150[2]	$2,250	$4,500
HSA Catch-Up Contributions (age 55 by end of year)	$700		$600		$500		n/a	
HDHP Minimum Annual Deductible[3]	$1,050	$2,100	$1,000	$2,000	$1,000	$2,000	$1,000	$2,000
HDHP Maximum Out-of-Pocket[4]	$5,250	$10,500	$5,100	$10,200	$5,000	$10,000	$5,000	$10,000

---

[1] These are the base amounts upon which the limits for 2004 and subsequent years are computed. How annual limits are computed and adjusted for inflation (based on the Consumer Price Index (CPI)) is more fully discussed in Q 3:7.

[2] But not more than the annual plan deductible under the HDHP associated with the HSA (for taxable years beginning before 2007). I.R.C. § 223(b)(2)(A)–(B). The contribution limit does not apply to rollovers or transfers from an Archer MSA, FSA, HRA, or an HSA into an HSA.

[3] To be a HDHP, the plan deductible may not be less than the indexed limit. I.R.C. § 223(c)(2)(A)(i). See Q 3:1.

[4] To be a HDHP, the sum of the annual deductible and other out-of-pocket expenses may not exceed the indexed amount. I.R.C. § 223(c)(2)(A)(ii). See Q 3:1.

Appendix G

How Health Savings Accounts[1] Compare to Health Flexible Spending Arrangements (FSAs) and Health Reimbursement Arrangements (HRAs)

---

[1] Health Savings Accounts (HSAs) were passed by Congress as part of the Medicare Prescription Drug, Improvement and Modernization Act of 2003 (Act), which President George W. Bush signed into law on December 8, 2003. HSAs are effective for years beginning after December 31, 2003.

General Description

Health Savings Account (HSA)

- Trust or custodial account used to accumulate funds on a tax-preferred basis to pay for certain medical expenses under Code Section 213(d), as described below.
- Available to individuals covered by a high deductible health plan and no other health plan that is not a high deductible health plan, except for certain "permitted" insurance or coverage.
- Contributions may be made by an employer, eligible individual, or both. Contributions may also be made by any other individual (and would be deductible by the HSA owner).
- An HSA may be offered through a cafeteria plan.

Flexible Spending Arrangement (FSA)

- Employer-sponsored benefit program under which employees receive reimbursement for certain medical expenses under Code Section 213(d), as described below.
- Generally offered as part of an employer's cafeteria plan, but not in conjunction with any other insurance policy.
- Contributions typically made by employees through salary reduction.

Health Reimbursement Arrangement (HRA)

- Employer-sponsored benefit program under which employees may receive reimbursement for medical expenses under Code Section 213(d), as described below.
- May be offered in conjunction with a high deductible or other type of health plan, but this is not required.
- Contributions must be solely from the employer.

	Health Savings Account (HSA)	*Flexible Spending Arrangement (FSA)*	*Health Reimbursement Arrangement (HRA)*
Expenses Eligible for Tax-Free Reimbursement	• Amounts distributed for medical expenses (generally defined under Code Section 213(d)[2]) incurred by the HSA owner and the HSA owner's spouse or dependents (as defined in Code Section 152, without regard to gross income limitations under Code Section 152(d)(1)(B)) are excludable from income, except for amounts distributed to pay health insurance premiums. • However, distributions for expenses of the following types of health insurance	• Amounts may be distributed to reimburse an employee for medical expenses (generally defined under Code Section 213(d)) incurred by the employee and the employee's spouse or dependents, except for: (i) expenses for any type of health insurance premiums and, (ii) expenses for long-term care services.	• Amounts may be distributed to reimburse an employee for medical expenses (generally defined under Code Section 213(d)) incurred by the employee and the employee's spouse or dependents, except for expenses for qualified long-term care services. (Note that premiums for qualified long-term care insurance are reimbursable.)

[2] Code Section 213(d) provides that the term medical care means amounts paid (A) for the diagnosis, cure, mitigation, treatment, or prevention of disease, or for the purpose of affecting any structure or function of the body; (B) for transportation primarily for and essential to medical care referred to in subparagraph (A); (C) for qualified long-term care services (as defined in Code Section 7702B(c)); or (D) for insurance (including amounts paid as premiums under part B of title XVIII of the Social Security Act, relating to supplementary medical insurance for the aged) covering medical care referred to in subparagraphs (A) and (B) or for any qualified longterm care insurance contract (as defined in Code Section 7702B(b)).

	Health Savings Account (HSA)	Flexible Spending Arrangement (FSA)	Health Reimbursement Arrangement (HRA)
	premiums are excludable from income: (i) retiree health insurance premiums (other than Medicare supplemental policies) for individuals who have reached Medicare eligibility, (ii) premiums for COBRA coverage, (iii) premiums for a qualified long-term care insurance contract, or (iv) premiums for a health plan during a period in which an individual is receiving unemployment compensation.		
Distributions For Non-Medical Expenses	• Distributions that are not used for medical expenses are includible in income and subject to a 10 percent additional tax. • The 10 percent additional tax does not apply to amounts distributed in the	• Distributions may not be made for non-medical expenses.	• Distributions may not be made for non-medical expenses.

	Health Savings Account (HSA)	Flexible Spending Arrangement (FSA)	Health Reimbursement Arrangement (HRA)
	event of death, disability, or after an individual reaches Medicare eligibility. • If amounts that would otherwise be taxable HSA distributions are rolled over into another HSA within 60 days, there is no tax consequence associated with the distribution (so long as there have been no other such rollovers in the last 12 months).		
Eligibility	• An individual (or spouse) who is covered by a high deductible health plan and no other non-high deductible health plan that provides benefits covered under the high deductible plan, unless the non-high deductible health plan provides coverage for accidents, disability, dental care, vision care, long-term care or other types of "permitted insurance," as defined below.	• An employee who satisfies the eligibility criteria of the employer and who has made an election under the employer's cafeteria plan.	• An employee who satisfies the eligibility criteria of the employer.

Health Savings Account (HSA)	*Flexible Spending Arrangement (FSA)*	*Health Reimbursement Arrangement (HRA)*
• For 2009, a high deductible health plan is a health plan that has an annual deductible of not less than $1,150 for self-only coverage, and $2,300 for family coverage, with a cap on out-of-pocket expenses (including the deductible) of $5,800 for self-only coverage and $11,600 for family coverage (all indexed for inflation in $50 increments), with the following exceptions related to preventive care and out-of-network expenses. See appendix F.		
• Preventive Care: a plan shall not fail to be treated as a high deductible health plan by reason of failing to have a deductible for preventive care.		
• Network plans: a plan shall not fail to be treated as a high deductible health plan by reason of having an out-of-pocket limitation for		

Health Savings Account (HSA)	*Flexible Spending Arrangement (FSA)*	*Health Reimbursement Arrangement (HRA)*
services provided outside of such network which exceeds the applicable limitations. In addition, such plan's annual deductible for services provided outside of the network is not taken into account in determining the annual contribution limit. • "Permitted Insurance" is defined as: (A) insurance if substantially all of the coverage provided under such insurance relates to (i) liabilities incurred under workers' compensation laws, (ii) tort liabilities, (iii) liabilities relating to ownership or use of property, or (iv) such other similar liabilities as the Secretary may specify by regulations, (B) insurance for a specified disease or illness, and (C) insurance paying a fixed amount per day (or other period) of hospitalization.		

	Health Savings Account (HSA)	Flexible Spending Arrangement (FSA)	Health Reimbursement Arrangement (HRA)
Funding/Tax Aspects	• Individuals who are entitled to benefits under Medicare are not eligible to make contributions. • Account is funded. Earnings grow tax-free. • Contributions may be made either by the employer or the employee, or both, and may be made through a cafeteria plan. • Subject to certain limits, employer contributions are excludable from gross income, and contributions by an eligible individual are deductible in computing adjusted gross income. Contributions are not subject to employment taxes. • Rollovers are permitted from both MSAs and other HSAs. Beginning December 20, 2006, FSAs	• Account is generally not funded. Rather, reimbursements are paid from the employer's general assets. • Contributions are typically made by employees through salary reduction, are excludable from income, and are not subject to employment taxes. • There is no statutory limit to the amount of contributions that may be made; any limits are by plan design.	• Account is generally not funded. Rather, reimbursements are paid from the employer's general assets. • Contributions must be solely employer-paid, are excludable from income, and are not subject to employment taxes. • There is no statutory limit to the amount of contributions that may be made; any limits are by plan design.

	Health Savings Account (HSA)	Flexible Spending Arrangement (FSA)	Health Reimbursement Arrangement (HRA)
	and HRAs may be rolled over to an HSA by direct transfer if the requirements of Notice 2007-22 are satisfied. As of 2007, a one-time transfer from an IRA to an HSA (subject to the maximum annual contribution limit) is permitted.		
Contribution Limits	• Maximum contributions (computed on a monthly basis based on the individual's health coverage) are $3,000 (in the case of self-only coverage) or $5,950 (in the case of family coverage) for 2009; indexed in $50 increments thereafter. • Maximum contribution amounts are decreased by the aggregate amount, if any, paid into an Archer Medical Savings Account (MSA) or another HSA.	• There are no contribution limits.	• There are no contribution limits.

	Health Savings Account (HSA)	Flexible Spending Arrangement (FSA)	Health Reimbursement Arrangement (HRA)
	The maximum contribution amount is increased for individuals who are age 55 or older (again computed on a monthly basis). These individuals may contribute an additional $1,000 in 2009, and in years thereafter.		
Nondiscrimination Rules	• Nondiscrimination rules require an employer who makes contributions into an HSA for any employee to make comparable contributions to HSAs of all comparable participating employees. Failure to do so subjects the employer to an excise tax.	• Nondiscrimination rules prohibit discrimination in favor of highly compensated individuals with respect to eligibility or benefits. (Code Section 105(h)). • Also may be subject to cafeteria plan non-discrimination rules.	• Nondiscrimination rules prohibit discrimination in favor of highly compensated individuals with respect to eligibility or benefits. (Code Section 105(h)).
Carryover of Funds	• Amounts not used for medical expenses by the end of the year may be carried over to future years, and are non-forfeitable.	• Amounts not used for medical expenses by the end of the year are subject to a "use it or lose it" rule that prevents carryover to future years.	• Amounts not used for medical expenses by the end of the year may be carried over to future years. Limits may be imposed by plan design.

	Health Savings Account (HSA)	Flexible Spending Arrangement (FSA)	Health Reimbursement Arrangement (HRA)
Death of HSA owner	• If the surviving spouse is the designated beneficiary of the account, the HSA will be treated as if the spouse is the HSA owner. • If any person other than the surviving spouse is the designated beneficiary, the HSA will cease to be an HSA as of the date of death, and an amount equal to the fair market value of the assets in the account on such date will be includible in the gross income of that person or, in the absence of a designated beneficiary, in the HSA owner's estate. • A deduction is permitted for qualified medical expenses incurred by the decedent before death if paid within one year of death.	• The only amounts that may be distributed upon the employee's death are reimbursements for medical expenses incurred by the employee or by the employee's spouse or eligible dependents prior to the date of the employee's death.	• Upon the HSA owner's death, the account may continue to be used by a spouse or eligible dependents for reimbursement of medical expenses. • When there is no longer a spouse or eligible dependents, the account must be forfeited.

Source: Groom Law Group. Reprinted with permission. Prepared May 13, 2009.

Table of Internal Revenue Code Sections

[References are to question numbers and appendices.]

I.R.C. §

21	2:42
21(b)(1)(B)	2:37, 2:45
22(e)(3)	2:41
23	2:42
24	2:42
32	2:42
35	5:39
35(g)(3)	5:39
61(a)	4:124, 4:184, 4:187
62	2:4, App. A
62(a)(19)	4:60, 4:62, 4:181 4:187, 4:196
71(b)(2)(A)	5:35, 5:36
72	5:44
72(m)(7)	5:74, 6:75
72(t)	5:50
72(t)(1)	4:106, 6:72
105	3:68, 4:74, 5:54, 5:55, 5:62, 6:9
105(b)	2:27, 2:44, 6:9, 6:26
105(h)	2:46, 6:26, App. G
106	2:4, 2:27, 4:74, 5:53, 5:54, 5:55, 5:62, 2:27, 6:9, 6:48, App. A
106(a)	8:12
106(b)(2)	4:82, 4:86
106(b)(5)	4:110
106(c)	1:7, 3:64, 4:20, 6:48
106(d)	2:11, 4:62, 4:71, 4:79, 4:80, 4:82, 4:83, 4:86, 4:91, 4:92, 4:121, 4:124, 4:177, 4:184, 4:187, 4:192, 5:76
106(d)(1)	4:61, 4:71, 7:75
106(d)(2)	4:110
106(e)	4:2, 5:53, 5:71, 5:76
106(e)(1)	5:58, 5:59, 5:60, 5:62
106(e)(2)	4:2, 5:58
106(e)(3)	5:51, 5:84
106(e)(3)(a)	5:53

I.R.C. §

106(e)(3)(b)	5:53
106(e)(3)(B)	5:74
106(e)(4)(A)	4:2, 5:73
106(e)(4)(C)	4:2, 4:81, 5:64, 5:75, 5:88
106(e)(5)(b)	5:57
106(e)(5)(B)(i)	5:67
106(e)(5)(B)(ii)	5:67
125	1:14, 1:15, 2:4, 2:46, 3:64; 3:65, 3:68, 3:69, 3:71, 4:20, 4:21, 4:59, 4:61, 4:70, 4:72, 4:73, 4:85, 4:113, 4:160, 4:169, 4:170, 4:171, 6:2, 6:48, 6:57, 7:72, 8:42
125(a)	4:20
125(b)	4:169
125(c)	4:169
125(d)	4:20
125(d)(2)(A)	4:21
125(d)(2)(D)	3:68
125(f)	4:20, 6:57
125(g)	4:169
129	2:42, 5:55
131	2:42
132(h)(2)(B)	2:44
137	2:42
151	2:42
151(d)	2:43
152	1:20, 1:21, 2:22, 2:35, 2:37, 2:43, 2:45, 6:11, 6:16, 6:27, 6:41, App. A, App. G
152(a)	2:37, 2:38
152(a)(1)	2:37, 2:38
152(b)(1)-(2)	2:37
152(b)(2)	2:37
152(b)(3)	2:38
152(c)(1)	2:39
152(c)(1)(D)	2:39

I.R.C. §

152(c)(3)	2:39, 2:40
152(c)(3)(A)	2:39, 2:42
152(c)(3)(B)	2:41
152(d)	2:38
152(d)(1)	2:43
152(d)(1)(A)	2:43
152(d)(1)(B)	2:37, App. G
152(d)(1)(C)	2:43
152(d)(1)(D)	2:43
152(d)(2)	2:43
152(d)(3)	2:43
152(e)	2:44, 6:36
152(e)(2)	2:44
152(e)(3)	2:44
152(f)	2:38
152(f)(1)(B)-(C)	2:38
152(f)(4)	2:38
152(f)(4)(B)	2:38
152(f)(4)(C)	2:38
152(f)(6)	2:38
152(f)(6)(A)	2:38
152(f)(6)(B)	2:38
162	4:119, 4:183 4:187, 4:191
162(a)	4:124, 4:183, 4:184, 4:187, 4:191
212	6:10
213	4:20, 4:60, 4:66, 4:87 6:29, 6:30, 6:31, 6:32 6:37, 6:39, 6:44, 6:47, 6:51, 6:58, App. A
213(a)	6:28, 6:29, 6:31, 6:40, 6:44
213(b)	6:51
213(d)	2:29, 2:46, 3:16, 4:20, 6:29, 6:36, 6:38, 6:39, 6:48, 6:53, App. G
213(d)(1)	2:30, 6:29, 6:37, 6:51
213(d)(1)(A)	6:32, 6:38, 6:40
213(d)(1)(C)	6:48
213(d)(1)(D)	6:47
213(d)(2)	6:39
213(d)(3)	6:55
213(d)(5)	2:44, 6:36
213(d)(9)(A)	6:40
213(d)(9)(B)	6:40
213(d)(10)	6:56, 6:58
213(f)(1)	6:48
219	App. A
219(d)(2)	5:4
220	1:7, 2:4, 2:45, 4:1, 4:74, App. A
220(3)(B)	2:5
220(c)(2)(B)(ii)	3:56
220(f)(5)	4:92, 5:2, 5:13, 5:14
220(f)(5)(A)	5:6, 5:15
220(f)(5)(B)	5:13
220(f)(8)	5:2
220(i)	1:2
220(i)(2)	2:5
220(i)(3)(B)	2:5
220(j)	1:2

I.R.C. §

220(j)(2)	2:5
220(j)(4)	2:5
223	1:1, 1:5, 1:9, 2:3, 2:4, 2:6, 2:11, 3:4, 3:7, 3:21, 3:25, 3:42, 3:55, 3:68, 4:20 4:74, 4:111, 5:18, 5:31, 6:9, 6:22, 6:28, 6:29, 7:8, 8:17, 8:20, 8:24, 8:35, 8:36, 8:39, 8:42, 8:48, App. A, App. E, App. I
223(a)	4:20, 4:60, 4:62, 4:91, 4:95, 4:181, 4:187, 4:196
223(b)	4:20, 4:30, 4:32, 4:149, 6:26
223(b)(2)	2:1, 2:7, 3:7, 4:6, 4:30, 4:57
223(b)(2)(A)	4:20, 5:68, App. F
223(b)(2)(B)	4:20, 4:50, 4:55, App. F
223(b)(3)	2:1, 4:166
223(b)(3)(A)	4:52
223(b)(3)(B)	4:44, 4:45
223(b)(4)(A)	4:14, 4:31
223(b)(4)(B)	4:14
223(b)(4)(C)	5:3, 5:38, 5:65, 5:66, 5:87, 5:88
223(b)(5)	2:6, 2:9, 4:57
223(b)(5)(A)	4:49
223(b)(5)(B)	4:42
223(b)(5)(B)(i)	4:31, 4:52
223(b)(5)(B)(ii)	4:42
223(b)(6)	4:68
223(b)(7)	2:14, 2:15, 2:17, 4:156
223(b)(8)	1:28, 4:5, 4:6, 4:38, 4:57, 5:50
223(b)(8)(A)	4:38, 4:39
223(b)(8)(A)(i)	4:7, 4:30
223(b)(8)(A)(ii)	4:9, 4:39
223(b)(8)(B)	4:8, 4:39, 5:50
223(b)(8)(B)(i)	4:38, 6:9
223(b)(8)(B)(i)(II)	4:38
223(b)(8)(B)(ii)	4:38, 4:39
223(c)	3:8, 6:3
223(c)(1)	3:55, 3:61, 4:156, 4:187, App. I
223(c)(1)(A)	2:6, 4:20
223(c)(1)(A)(ii)	3:43, 4:20
223(c)(1)(B)	2:8, 3:55, 3:43, 4:20
223(c)(1)(B)(i)	3:43
223(c)(1)(B)(ii)	3:43, 3:55
223(c)(1)(B)(iii)	4:2, 5:53
223(c)(2)	2:6, 2:8, 3:1, 3:22, 3:23, 8:36, App. E
223(c)(2)(A)	3:7, 4:20
223(c)(2)(A)(i)	4:20, App. F, App. I
223(c)(2)(A)(i)(I)	3:1
223(c)(2)(A)(i)(II)	3:1
223(c)(2)(A)(ii)	3:16, App. F
223(c)(2)(A)(ii)(I)	3:1
223(c)(2)(A)(ii)(II)	3:1
223(c)(2)(B)	3:4, 3:43

I.R.C. §

223(c)(2)(3) 2:8
223(c)(2)(C) 3:49, 3:52, 3:55, 4:20
223(c)(2)(D) 3:11
223(c)(2)(D)(ii) 3:11, 3:18
223(c)(3) 2:8, 3:44, 4:20
223(c)(3)(A)(i) 3:45
223(c)(3)(A)(ii) 3:45
223(c)(3)(A)(iii) 3:45
223(c)(3)(A)(iv) 3:45
223(c)(3)(A)(i)-(iv) 3:45
223(c)(3)(B) 3:45, 3:55
223(c)(3)(C) 3:45, 3:55
223(c)(4) 3:40
223(c)(5) 4:1
223(d) . . . . 2:43, 2:44, 4:20, App. E
223(d)(1) 2;20, 7:1
223(d)(1)(A) 2:1, 5:5, 5:32, 5:63, 7:25
223(d)(1)(A)(i) 2:1, 4:1
223(d)(1)(A)(ii) 2:1
223(d)(1)(B) 2:1
223(d)(1)(C) 2:1
223(d)(1)(D) 2:1, 7:16
223(d)(1)(E) 2:1, 6:2
223(d)(2) . . . . App. E
223(d)(2)(A) 2:37, 2:45, 6:27
223(d)(2)(B) 6:42, 6:49, 6:50
223(d)(2)(C) 6:42
223(d)(2)(C)(ii) 6:56
223(d)(2)(C)(iii) 2:31
223(d)(2)(C)(iv) 3:74, 6:49, 6:50
223(d)(3) 2:2
223(d)(4)(A) 5:4
223(d)(4)(B) 4:11
223(d)(4)(C) 4:71
223(d)(4)(D) 4:69
223(d)(4)(E) 7:1
223(e)(1) 4:88
223(e)(2) . . . 6:59, 6:61, 6:62, 6:64, 7:56, App. E
223(f) . . . . 5:35, 7:39, App. E
223(f)(1) 4:92, 5:51, 6:9, 6:20, 6:48
223(f)(2) 4:38, 4:92, 4:106 4:107, 6:60, 6:61,
                                            6:72, 6:74
223(f)(3) 4:38, 4:92, 4:107
223(f)(3)(A) 4:98, 4:100, 4:106, 4:107, 6:72
223(f)(3)(A)(i) 4:97
223(f)(3)(A)(ii) 4:97, 4:99, 4:107
223(f)(3)(B) 4:91, 4:92, 4:107, 5:75
223(f)(4) 4:38, 4:92, 4:106, 5:84, 6:9, 6:72
223(f)(4)(A) 4:39, 4:107, 6:72
223(f)(4)(B) 5:51, 6:74
223(f)(4)(C) 6:74
223(f)(5) . . 4:92, 5:1, 5:2, 5:12, 5:13, 5:18, 5:28,
                                5:31, 5:75, 6:74
223(f)(5)(A) 5:6, 5:15, 5:16
223(f)(5)(B) 5:11, 5:17
223(f)(6) 6:31

I.R.C. §

223(f)(7) 5:33-5:37, 6:74
223(f)(8)(A) 5:22, 5:23, 6:83
223(f)(8)(B)(i) 6:83
223(f)(8)(B)(i)(I) 6:83
223(f)(8)(B)(i)(II) 6:83
223(f)(8)(B)(ii)(I) 6:83
223(f)(8)(B)(ii)(II) 6:83
223(g) 2:1, 4:55
223(g)(1) 3:7, 4:32, 4:33
223(g)(1)(B) 4:30
223(g)(1)-(2) 3:7, 4:32
223(g)(2) 3:7, 4:32
223(h) 7:29, 7:38, 7:40
223(h)(1) 7:38
223(h)(2) 7:38
224 . . . . 2:3, 2:4
262 . . . . 6:32
263 . . . . 4:183, 4:187, 4:191
301 . . . . 4:64
318 . . . . 4:189
401(a) 3:66, 4:112
401(c)(1) 4:71
401(k) . . . . 8:3, 8:5, 8:9, App. E
403(a) 4:110
408 . . . . 5:50, App. A
408(d) 2:1, 5:50
408(d)(3)(A) 5:17
408(d)(8)(B) 5:42
408(d)(9) 4:2, 4:3, 5:3, 5:38, 5:40, 5:53
408(d)(9)(B) 4:3, 5:40, 5:42
408(d)(9)(C)(i) 5:45, 5:48
408(d)(9)(C)(i)(I) 4:3, 5:49
408(d)(9)(C)(ii)(I) 4:3, 5:40
408(d)(9)(D) 5:46, 5:50
408(d)(9)(D)(i) 5:50
408(d)(9)(D)(ii) 5:50
408(d)(9)(D)(iii) 5:50
408(d)(9)(E) 5:47
408(e) 6:62
408(e)(2) 6:59, 6:64
408(e)(4) 6:61, 6:64
408(m)(3) 7:14
408(n) 2:1, 7:22
408(9)(9)(A) 5:44
408A(a) 5:34
409A 4:74
409A(d)(1)(B) 4:74
412 . . . . 4:112
412(a) 4:112
414(b) . . . . 4:145, 6:71, App. E
414(c) . . . . 4:145, 6:71, App. E
414(m) . . . . 4:145, 6:71, App. E
414(o) 4:145
414(q) 1:28, 1:29, 4:115, 4:123
414(q)(1)(B) 4:169
414(s) 4:169

I.R.C. §

419 . . . . 4:111
419(e)(1) 4:111
419(e)(3) 4:111
511 . . . . 4:88
512 . . . . 4:88
584(a)(1) 2:1, 7:16
691 . . . . 6:83
691(c) 6:83
702(a)(8) 4:180, 4:187
707(c) 4:124, 4:176, 4:182-4:187,
4:190, 4:191
731 . . . . 4:124, 4:176-4:181, 4:187
816 . . . . 2:1
848 . . . . 2:4
1274(d) 4:168
1372 . . . . 4:188, 4:189
1372(a) 4:190
1372(a)(1) 4:188
1372(a)(2) 4:189
1372(b) 4:62, 4:188, 4:189
1402(a) 4:63, 4:180, 4:186, 4:187
2056 . . . . 6:85
2503(e)(1) 6:86
2503(e)(2)(A) 6:86
3101(a) 4:72
3101(b) 4:72
3111(a) 4:72
3111(b) 4:72
3121 . . . . 4:194
3121(a)(2)(B) 4:194
3121(a)(5)(G) 4:85
3231 . . . . 2:4
3231(e)(11) 4:82
3306 . . . . 2:4, 5:76
3306(b)(1) 4:72
3306(b)(18) 4:86
3401 . . . . 2:4, 5:76
3401(a)(21) 4:83
3401(a)(22) 4:83
3405 . . . . 6:87
4971(a) 4:112
4972 . . . . 4:113
4972(a) 4:113
4972(d) 4:113
4973 . . . . 2:4, 4:38, 5:75, 7:57, App. A
4973(a) 4:107
4973(a)(5) 4:96
4973(g) 4:92
4973(g)(1) 4:92
4973(g)(2) 4:92
4974(c) 4:106, 6:72
4975 . . . . . . 1:6, 1:9, 2:4, 6:62, 6:68, 7:62, 7:64,
8:18, 8:27, 8:29, 8:30, App. A, App. E
4975(a) 6:67
4975(c) . . . . 6:63, App. E
4975(c)(1) . . . . App. E

I.R.C. §

4975(c)(1)(A) . . . . 6:65, App. E
4975(c)(1)(B) 6:65
4975(c)(1)(C) 6:65
4975(c)(1)(D) . . . . 6:65, App. E
4975(c)(1)(E) . . . . 6:65, 8:30, App. E
4975(c)(1)(F) 6:65
4975(c)(2) 6:68, 6:71, 7:62
4975(c)(6) 6:62, 6:67
4975(d) 6:63, 6:65, 7:62
4975(d)(2) . . . . App. E
4975(d)(17) 6:65
4975(d)(18) 6:63
4975 (d)(20) 6:63
4975(d)(21) 6:63
4975(d)(22) 6:63
4975(e)(1) 6:62, 6:63
4975(e)(1)(E) . . . . 6:71, 8:30, App. E
4975(e)(2) . . . . 6:63, 6:69, App. E
4975(e)(3) 6:63
4975(f)(4) 8:27
4975(f)(6)(B)(ii) 7:62
4975(f)(6)(B)(iii) 7:62
4975(f)(8) 6:65
4975(f)(9) 6:63
4976(a)(1) 4:111
4980B 3:30, 8:20
4980E 4:73, 4:156
4980E(d) 4:114
4980E(c) 4:119, 4:172
4980E(d)(3) 4:115
4980E(d)(4)(A) 4:146
4980E(d)(4)(B) 4:146
4980E(e) 4:145
4980G 1:11, 1:14, 1:15, 2:4, 2:46, 4:73,
4:114, 4:119, 4:156, 4:169, 4:170,
4:172, App. A
4980G(a) 4:118
4980G(b) 4:115, 4:116, 4:119, 4:145, 4:146,
4:156, 4:172
4980(G)(d) 1:28, 1:29, 4:115
5000 . . . . 3:75
5000(b)(1) 3:75
5000(c) 3:75
6051 . . . . 2:4, 4:58
6511 . . . . 2:44
6693 . . . . 2:4, App. A
6693(a)(1) 7:40
6693(a)(2)(C) 7:40
6724(d)(1)(C)(i) 7:40
6724(d)(2)(C)(i) 7:40
6724(d)(2)(W) 7:40
7702B . . . . App. A
7702B(2) 6:56
7702B(b) . . . . 2:31, App. G
7702B(c) . . . . App. G
9832(d)(1) 4:146, 4:154

Table of IRS Announcements and Notices

[*References are to question numbers and appendices.*]

IRS Announcements

92-16, 1992-5 IRB 53 . . . . 4:175
2003-54, 2003-40 IRB 761 . . . . 2:1
2004-2, 2004-2 IRB 322 . . . . 4:59
2004-2, 2004-3 IRB 322 . . . . App. C
2004-67, 2004-36 IRB 459 . . . . 4:43, App. B, App. C
2005-12, 2005-7 IRB 555 . . . . 2:5
2005-59, 2005-37 IRB 524 . . . . 2:1
2006-72, 2006-40 IRB 630 . . . . App. C
2007-20, 2007-20 IRB 1260 . . . . 1:6
2007-44, 2007-19 IRB 1238 . . . . 1:2, 2:5
2007-44, 2008-20 IRB 982 . . . . 7:49

IRS Information Releases (IR)

2008-68 (Apr. 30, 2008) 4:1, 6:74

IRS Notices

96-53, A-9, A-10, 1996-2 CB 219 . . . . 4:15
2002-45, 2002-2 CB 93 . . . . 1:7, 4:20
2002-45, 2002-28 IRB 93 . . . . 4:20
2004-2 . . . . App. E
2004-2, 2004-2 IRB 269 . . . . . . 2:1, 4:11, App. B, App. C
2004-2, Q&A-1, 2004-2 IRB 269 . . . . App. E
2004-2, Q&A-2, 2004-2 IRB 269 . . . . 2:6, App. E
2004-2, Q&A-3, 2004-2 IRB 269 . . . . 2:18, 3:16, 3:27, 3:42, 4:55
2004-2, Q&A-4, 2004-2 IRB 269 . . . . 3:24
2004-2, Q&A-5, 2004-2 IRB 269 . . . . 2:8
2004-2, Q&A-6, 2004-2 IRB 269 . . . . . . 2:8, 3:55
2004-2, Q&A-7, 2004-2 IRB 269 . . . . 3:2
2004-2, Q&A-8, 2004-2 IRB 269 . . . . 2:4

IRS Notices

2004-2, Q&A-9, 2004-2 IRB 269 . . . . 2:1
2004-2, Q&A-10, 2004-2 IRB 269 . . . . 4:16, 7:36, 7:37
2004-2, Q&A-12, 2004-2 IRB 269 . . . . 2:18, 4:30, 4:35
2004-2, Q&A-13, 2004-2 IRB 269 . . . . 4:37
2004-2, Q&A-14, 2004-2 IRB 269 . . . . 4:42, 4:43, 4:46
2004-2, Q&A-15, 2004-2 IRB 269 . . . . 4:57
2004-2, Q&A-16, 2004-2 IRB 269 . . . . . 4:1, 4:18
2004-2, Q&A-17, 2004-2 IRB 269 . . . . 4:60, 4:62, 4:65, 4:66
2004-2, Q&A-18, 2004-2 IRB 269 . . . . . 4:67, 4:68
2004-2, Q&A-19, 2004-2 IRB 269 . . . . 4:72, 4:79-4:87, 4:176
2004-2, Q&A-20, 2004-2 IRB 269 . . . . 4:88
2004-2, Q&A-21, 2004-2 IRB 269 . 2:22, 4:5, 4:90
2004-2, Q&A-22, 2004-2 IRB 269 . . . . 4:93, 4:95, 4:96, 4:98, 4:100, 4:101
2004-2, Q&A-23, 2004-2 IRB 269 . . . . . 2:25, 4:2, 5:1-5:3, 5:10, 5:38, 5:53, 7:33
2004-2, Q&A-24, 2004-2 IRB 269 . . . . 6:1
2004-2, Q&A-25, 2004-2 IRB 269 . . . . . 6:8, 6:11, 6:19, 6:60, 6:61, 6:72
2004-2, Q&A-26, 2004-2 IRB 269 . . . . 2:32, 4:11, 6:9, 6:21-6:23, 6:28, 6:41, 6:44, 6:54
2004-2, Q&A-27, 2004-2 IRB 2 . . . . 2:31
2004-2, Q&A-27, 2004-2 IRB 269 . . . . 6:46, 6:48, 6:49
2004-2, Q&A-29, 2004-2 IRB 269 . . . . 6:12, 6:13, 8:22
2004-2, Q&A-30, 2004-2 IRB 269 . . . . . 4:77, 8:22
2004-2, Q&A-31, 2004-2 IRB 269 . . . . . 6:83, 6:84

IRS Notices

2004-2, Q&A-32, 2004-2 IRB 269 . . . . 4:119,
4:128, 4:149, 4:152
2004-2, Q&A-33, 2004-2 IRB 269 . . . . . 3:65, 4:18
2004-2, Q&A-34, 2004-2 IRB 269 . . . . 4:58
2004-2, Q&A-35, 2004-2 IRB 269 . . . . 4:110, 8:20
2004-2, Q&A-36, 2004-2 IRB 269 . . . . 4:111
2004-2, Q&A 37 . . . . App. E
2004-23 . . . . 3:61, App. E
2004-23, 2004-15 IRB 725 . . . . . 1:25, 3:49, 3:50,
3:52, 3:53, 3:55, 3:56,
4:20, App. B
2004-23, Q&A 55, 2004 IRB 725 . . . . . 5:11, 5:15
2004-25 . . . . App. E
2004-25, 2004-15 IRB 727 . . . . 4:11, 6:22, App. B
2004-43 . . . . 8:36
2004-43, 2004-27 IRB 10 . . . . 1:25
2004-43, 2004-27 IRB 10 . . . 2:6, 3:21, 3:23, 8:36,
8:39, App. B
2004-45, 2004-28 IRB 10 . . . . 1:25, 2:6
2004-50 . . . . 3:15, 4:73
2004-50, 2004-2 CB 196 . . . . 3:55
2004-50, 2004-33 IRB 196 . . . 2:6, 3:4, 3:15, 3:20,
4:30, 4:42, App. B
2004-50, Q&A-1, 2004-33 IRB 196 . . . . 2:13
2004-50, Q&A-2, 2004-33 IRB 196 . . . 2:14, 2:15,
4:43
2004-50, Q&A 3, 2004-33 IRB 196 . . . . 2:18, 4:43
2004-50, Q&A-4, 2004-33 IRB 196 . . . . 2:17
2004-50, Q&A-5, 2004-33 IRB 196 . . . . 2:16
2004-50, Q&A-6, 2004-33 IRB 196 . . . . 2:19
2004-50, Q&A-7, 2004-33 IRB 196 . . . . 3:46
2004-50, Q&A-8, 2004-33 IRB 196 . . . . 3:47
2004-50, Q&A-9, 2004-33 IRB 196 . . . . 3:57
2004-50, Q&A-10, 2004-33 IRB 196 . . . . 3:58
2004-50, Q&A-11, 2004-33 IRB 196 . . . . 2:7
2004-50, Q&A-12, 2004-33 IRB 196 . . 2:18, 3:39,
3:40, 4:42
2004-50, Q&A-13, 2004-33 IRB 196 . . . . 3:5
2004-50, Q&A-14, 2004-33 IRB 196 . . . 3:4, 3:32,
3:37, 4:44
2004-50, Q&A-15, 2004-33 IRB 196 . . . 3:4, 3:33,
3:36, 4:52
2004-50, Q&A-16, 2004-33 IRB 196 . . . . 3:38
2004-50, Q&A-17, 2004-33 IRB 196 . . . . 3:19
2004-50, Q&A-18, 2004-33 IRB 196 . . . . 3:24
2004-50, Q&A-19, 2004-33 IRB 196 . . . . 3:24
2004-50, Q&A-20 (ex 1),
2004-33 IRB 196 . . . . 3:25
2004-50, Q&A-20 (ex 2),
2004-33 IRB 196 . . . . 3:26
2004-50, Q&A-21, 2004-33 IRB 196 . . . 3:16, 3:27
2004-50, Q&A-22, 2004-33 IRB 196 . . . . 3:8, 3:28
2004-50, Q&A-23, 2004-33 IRB 196 . . . . 3:29
2004-50, Q&A-24, 2004-33 IRB 196 . . . . 3:14
2004-50, Q&A-25, 2004-33 IRB 196 . . . . 3:6, 6:16
2004-50, Q&A 26, 2004-33 IRB 196 . . . . 3:55

IRS Notices

2004-50, Q&A-27, 2004-33 IRB 196 . . 3:51, 3:52,
3:54
2004-50, Q&A-28, 2004-33 IRB 196 . . . . . . 4:17,
App. E
2004-50, Q&A-29, 2004-33 IRB 196 . . . . 4:19
2004-50, Q&A-30, 2004-33 IRB 196 . . . 4:53-4:55
2004-50, Q&A-31, 2004-33 IRB 196 . . . . 2:9, 4:56
2004-50, Q&A-32, 2004-33 IRB 196 . . . . 4:57
2004-50, Q&A-34, 2004-33 IRB 196 . . . . . . 4:101
2004-50, Q&A-35, 2004-33 IRB 196 . . . . . 4:108,
6:73
2004-50, Q&A-36, 2004-33 IRB 196 . . . 2:6, 2:33,
6:23
2004-50, Q&A-37, 2004-33 IRB 196 . . 6:78, 6:79,
6:81
2004-50, Q&A-38, 2004-33 IRB 196 . . . . 6:24
2004-50, Q&A-39, 2004-33 IRB 196 . . . . 6:9, 6:25
2004-50, Q&A-40, 2004-33 IRB 196 . . . 6:56, 6:47
2004-50, Q&A-41, 2004-33 IRB 196 . . 3:63, 6:56,
6:58
2004-50, Q&A-42, 2004-33 IRB 196 . . . . . . 3:64,
6:48
2004-50, Q&A-43, 2004-33 IRB 196 . . . . 6:49
2004-50, Q&A-44, 2004-33 IRB 196 . . . . 6:50
2004-50, Q&A-45, 2004-33 IRB 196 . . . . 6:43
2004-50, Q&A-46, 2004-33 IRB 196 . . . . 1:25
2004-50, Q&A-47, 2004-33 IRB 196 . . . 1:25, 4:73
2004-50, Q&A-48, 2004-33 IRB 196 . . . . 4:73
2004-50, Q&A-49, 2004-33 IRB 196 . . . . 4:73
2004-50, Q&A-53, 2004-33 IRB 196 . . . . . . 4:128
2004-50, Q&A-55, 2004-33 IRB 196 . . . . 5:11
2004-50, Q&A-56, 2004-33 IRB 196 . . . . 5:28
2004-50, Q&A-57, 2004-33 IRB 196 . . . . 3:68
2004-50, Q&A-58, 2004-33 IRB 196 . . . . 3:69
2004-50, Q&A-59, 2004-33 IRB 196 . . . . 3:71
2004-50, Q&A-60, 2004-33 IRB 10 . . . . 4:140
2004-50, Q&A-60, 2004-33 IRB 196 . . . . 3:73
2004-50, Q&A-61, 2004-33 IRB 196 . . . . 3:67
2004-50, Q&A-62, 2004-33 IRB 196 . . . . 7:4
2004-50, Q&A-63, 2004-33 IRB 196 . . . . 2:10
2004-50, Q&A-64, 2004-33 IRB 196 . . . . 4:34
2004-50, Q&A-65, 2004-33 IRB 196 . . . 2:1, 7:14,
7:15
2004-50, Q&A-66, 2004-33 IRB 196 . . . . 2:1
2004-50, Q&A 67 . . . . App. E
2004-50, Q&A-68, 2004-33 IRB 196 . . . . . . 7:17,
App. E
2004-50, Q&A-69, 2004-33 IRB 196 . . . . 7:18
2004-50, Q&A-70, 2004-33 IRB 196 . . . . 7:20
2004-50, Q&A-71, 2004-33 IRB 196 . . . . 7:21
2004-50, Q&A-72, 2004-33 IRB 196 . . . . 7:22
2004-50, Q&A-73, 2004-33 IRB 196 . . . . 2:1, 5:5,
5:32, 5:63,
7:24, 7:25
2004-50, Q&A-74, 2004-33 IRB 196 . . . . . . 7:26,
7:27, 7:29

IRS Notices

2004-50, Q&A-75, 2004-33 IRB 196 . . . . 7:30
2004-50, Q&A-76, 2004-33 IRB 196 . . . 6:80, 7:31
2004-50, Q&A-77, 2004-33 IRB 196 . . . 5:1, 5:18,
          5:28, 5:31, 6:6,
          7:32
2004-50, Q&A-78, 2004-33 IRB 196 . . . . 5:8,
          5:18, 5:30, 7:33
2004-50, Q&A-79, 2004-33 IRB 196 . . . 1:25, 6:6,
          7:34, 8:13
2004-50, Q&A-80, 2004-33 IRB 196 . . . 6:14, 7:35
2004-50, Q&A-81, 2004-33 IRB 196 . . . 4:75, 4:76
2004-50, Q&A-82, 2004-33 IRB 196 . . . 1:25, 2:1,
          3:73, 6:2
2004-50, Q&A-83, 2004-33 IRB 196 . . . . 6:26
2004-50, Q&A-84, 2004-33 IRB 196 . . . . 4:63
2004-50, Q&A-86, 2004-33 IRB 196 . . . . 3:9
2004-50, Q&A-87, 2004-33 IRB 196 . . . . 2:11
2004-50, Q&A-88, 2004-33 IRB 196 . . . . 4:64
2004-79, 2004-49 IRB 898 . . . . 2:35, 2:36, App. B
2005-4 . . . . 1:8
2005-1, Q&A 3(c), 2005-2 IRB 274 . . . . 4:74
2005-8, 2005-4 IRB 1 . . . . App. B
2005-8, Q&A-1, 2005-4 IRB 368 . . . . 4:165
2005-8, Q&A-2, 2005-4 IRB 368 . . . . 4:163,
          4:164, 4:166, 4:167
2005-8, Q&A-3, 2005-4 IRB 368 . . . 4:169, 4:171,
          4:173, 4:174,
          4:176
2005-42 . . . . 4:21, 5:79,
          5:84
2005-42, 2005-23 IRB 1204 . . . . 4:20, 4:21, 4:24,
          4:25, 4:26,
          4:27
2005-42, 2005-42 IRB 1204 . . . . 4:21, 4:29
2005-83 . . . . 3:22
2005-83, 2005-49 IRB 1075 . . . . . 1:25, 3:8, 3:23,
          8:36, App. B
2005-86 . . . . 5:78
2005-86, 2005-2 CB 1075 . . . . 5:78
2005-86, 2005-49 IRB 1075 . . . . 1:25, 4:21, 4:29,
          App. B
2007-7, Q&A A-36, 2007-5 IRB 1 . . . . 5:42
2007-22, 45 IRB 670 . . . . 5:53
2007-22 . . . . 5:54, 5:76, 5:83, 5:84,
          5:86, 5:89, App. G
2007-22, 2007-10 IRB 640 . . . . . 5:80, 5:81, 5:82,
          5:83, 5:84
2007-22, 2007-10 IRB 670 . . . . . 2:22, 4:28, 4:29,
          5:51, 5:56, 5:67, 5:68,
          5:69, 5:75, 5:80-5:84,
          5:87, 5:88, 5:89,
          6:9, App. B
2008-48, 2008-36 I.R.B. 586 . . . . 2:27

IRS Notices

2008-51, 2008-25 IRB 1163 . . . . 5:40, 5:42, 5:43,
          5:45, 5:46, 5:49, 5:51,
          5:76, App. B
2008-52, 2008-25 IRB 1166 . . . . 2:21, 2:22, 4:5,
          4:8, 4:9, 4:38, 4:39,
          4:91, 6:9,
          App. B
2008-59, 2008-29 IRB 123 . . . . 2:6, App. B
2008-59, Part 1, 2008-29 IRB 123 . . . . 2:8
2008-59, Q&A 1, 2008-29 IRB 123 . . . . 4:20
2008-59, Q&A 2, 2008-29 IRB 123 . . . . 3:43, 4:20
2008-59, Q&A 3, 2008-29 IRB 123 . . . . 3:43
2008-59, Q&A 4(a), 2008-29 IRB 123 . . . . . . 4:54
2008-59, Q&A 4(b), 2008-29 IRB 123 . . . . . . 4:54
2008-59, Q&A 5, 2008-29 IRB 123 . . . . 2:14, 4:43
2008-59, Q&A 6, 2008-29 IRB 123 . . . . 2:14, 4:43
2008-59, Q&A 7, 2008-29 IRB 123 . . . 3:43, 4:20,
          4:41
2008-59, Q&A 8, 2008-29 IRB 123 . . . 4:20, 4:41,
          4:54
2008-59, Q&A 9, 2008-29 IRB 123 . . . . 2:16
2008-59, Q&A 10, 2008-29 IRB 123 . . . . 3:60
2008-59, Q&A 11, 2008-29 IRB 123 . . . 3:43, 4:20
2008-59, Q&A 12, 2008-29 IRB 123 . . . . . . 3:30,
          4:110, 8:20
2008-59, Q&A 13, 2008-29 IRB 123 . . . . 3:35
2008-59, Q&A 14, 2008-29 IRB 123 . . . . 3:36
2008-59, Q&A 15, 2008-29 IRB 123 . . . . 3:16
2008-59, Q&A 16, 2008-29 IRB 123 . . . . 4:36
2008-59, Q&A 17, 2008-29 IRB 123 . . . . 4:50
2008-59, Q&A 19, 2008-29 IRB 123 . . . . 4:12
2008-59, Q&A 20, 2008-29 IRB 123 . . . . 5:1
2008-59, Q&A 21, 2008-29 IRB 123 . . . . 4:13
2008-59, Q&A 22, 2008-29 IRB 123 . . . . 4:42
2008-59, Q&A 24, 2008-29 IRB 123 . . . . 6:4, 7:74
2008-59, Q&A 25, 2008-29 IRB 123 . . . . 6:2, 6:3,
          6:5, 7:74
2008-59, Q&A 26, 2008-29 IRB 123 . . . 4:61, 7:75
2008-59, Q&A 27, 2008-29 IRB 123 . . . . 6:6
2008-59, Q&A 28, 2008-29 IRB 123 . . . . 6:8
2008-59, Q&A 29, 2008-29 IRB 123 . . . . 6:33
2008-59, Q&A 30, 2008-29 IRB 123 . . . . 6:33
2008-59, Q&A 31, 2008-29 IRB 123 . . . . 6:34
2008-59, Q&A 32, 2008-29 IRB 123 . . . . 6:35
2008-59, Q&A 33, 2008-29 IRB 123 . . . . 6:36
2008-59, Q&A 34, 2008-29 IRB 123 . . . . 6:63
2008-59, Q&A 35, 2008-29 IRB 123 . . . . 6:63
2008-59, Q&A 36, 2008-29 IRB 123 . . . . 6:63
2008-59, Q&A 37, 2008-29 IRB 123 . . . . 6:64
2008-59, Q&A 38, 2008-29 IRB 123 . . . 2:20, 2:25
2008-59, Q&A 39, 2008-29 IRB 123 . . . . 2:23
2008-59, Q&A 41, 2008-29 IRB 123 . . . 2:26, 7:19
2008-59, Q&A 42, 2008-29 IRB 123 . . . . 7:48

Index

[References are to question numbers and appendices.]

A

Accident insurance
exception to requirement of no coverage under other non-HDHP, 2:8
qualified medical expenses, 6:47

Account beneficiaries
defined, 2:1, 2:2
Form 1099-SA, copy provided to, 7:51
use of term, 4:4, 5:1, 8:3

Account fees. *See* Fees

Account holders
use of term, 4:4, 5:1, 8:3

Account owners
advantages of HSAs, 2:45
defined, 2:1, 2:2
Form 1099-SA, copy provided to, 7:51
use of term, 4:4, 5:1, 8:3

Adjusted gross income, 6:30

Advantages of HSAs, 1:12–1:15
to employers, 1:13
to individuals, 1:12, 2:45
persons best suited for, 2:47
retiree health, 1:15

Adverse impact on health
disadvantages of HSAs, 2:46

Adverse selection
disadvantages of HSAs, 2:46

Advisory Opinions
2004-09A
issuance of, 1:11
text of, App. E
ERISA, effect of, 8:29

Age. *See also* Age 55 or older; Age 65
employer relying on representation of employee, 4:76

specified age
attainment of, distributions, 6:7
comparability rule, requirement for contributions, 4:145
10 percent additional tax on distributions, exception to, 6:74
tracking by trustees and custodians, 7:30

Age 55 or older
Medicare, persons eligible for but not enrolled
catch-up contributions, 2:18, 4:43

Age 65
disabled person, under age 65, tax-free distributions, 6:50

Alabama
conforming to Code Section 223, 8:42

Alternate trade adjustment assistance (ATAA), 5:39

Amendments to plan. *See* Plan amendment

American Samoa
HSAs available to residents of, 2:11

Announcements regarding HSAs,
App. C

Archer medical savings accounts (MSAs)
annual contribution limits, 4:31
rollovers, 5:10
comparability rule, 4:120, 4:135
distributions, rollovers to HSAs, 5:1, 5:2, 5:7
all cash or property need not be rolled over, 5:7
proceeds from sale of property, 5:6
same property must be rolled over, 5:6
FSAs, differences, 1:8
HSAs, differences, 1:2, 1:8
replacement of, 2:5

Archer medical savings accounts (MSAs)
(*cont'd*)
  rollovers,   2:25
    annual contribution limits,   5:10
    Archer MSA to Archer MSA rollovers,
      5:13
    one-year rule,   5:13, 5:14
    same property received in distribution,
      5:17
    60-days, completion within,   5:15
    total amount, distribution of,   5:16
  transfers from,   2:25
  as trustee or custodian,   2:1
  trustee-to-trustee transfers,   5:30

ATAA.   *See* Alternate trade adjustment
assistance (ATAA)

Attorney's fees
  ERISA violations by trustees or custodians,
    awarded when,   8:27

Audit requirements
  eligible investment advice arrangements,
    6:66

B

Banks
  Beneficiaries. *See* Account beneficiaries

Beneficiaries
  account. *See* Account beneficiaries
  designated. *See* Designated beneficiaries
  non-spouse beneficiaries, income tax
    consequences,   6:83
  surviving spouse
    income tax consequences,   6:84

Benefits
  nondiscrimination in,   4:149

Best judgment rule,   8:28

Block trades
  prohibited transactions,   6:66

C

Cafeteria plans,   3:65–3:73
  advantages of HSAs,   2:45
  change-in-status rules,   3:69
  comparability rule,   4:149–4:151
    wellness programs and,   4:151
  contributions through,   4:17, 4:18
    grace period rules,   4:21–4:27
  document amended to allow employees to
    fund HSA,   3:66

  employee contributions,   1:14, 4:81
  employer contributions,   4:72, 4:81
    to cover qualified medical expenses in
      excess of HSA balance,   3:73
  FSA requirements not applicable to HSAs,
    3:68
  grace period rules,   4:21–4:27
    caps on amounts,   4:23
    carry over of unused contributions,   4:21
    duration,   4:24, 4:27
    employer provision for,   4:22
    how to adopt,   4:24
    Notice 2005-42,   4:21
    unused benefits,   4:25
  highly compensated employees,   4:149
  HSAs funded by salary reduction
    contributions through,   3:65, 3:66
  interaction between HSAs and health FSAs,
    4:29
  matching contributions through,   4:150
  midyear elections,   3:71, 3:72
  negative elections, use of to enroll
    employees,   3:67, 4:78
  nondiscrimination rules,   4:149
  restrictions on election of HSA
    contributions,   3:70
  structuring of elections as negative
    elections,   4:78

Calendar year basis
  full-time vs. part-time employees,   4:138,
    4:140
  HDHPs,   3:8

California's Assembly Bill 115,   8:41

Cash
  contributions,   4:1
  rollovers,   5:5
  trustee-to-trustee transfers,   5:32

Catch-up contributions,   4:42–4:45
  advantages of HSAs,   2:45
  annual contribution limit,   1:27, 4:30, 4:44
  computation,   4:46
  legislation,   1:29
  maximum amounts,   4:45
  by persons eligible for but not enrolled in
    Medicare,   2:18, 4:43
  spouses,   4:52
  when permitted,   4:42

**Centers for Medicare and Medicaid Services
(CMS),**   1:5

Certificate of creditable coverage
  HIPAA,   8:21
  Medicare Part D,   8:33

**Certification that owner is eligible
individual**
  trustees and custodians,   7:36, 7:37

Change of coverage
COBRA, 3:30
during year
annual contribution limit, 4:6
maximum contribution, 4:6
family coverage, effect of change from self-
only coverage, 3:28, 3:29

Choice
advantages of HSAs, 2:45

Chronic health conditions
COBRA. *See* Comprehensive Omnibus Budget
Reconciliation Act
and employer contributions, 4:73
and proposed changes to HSA rules, 1:27

Clinics, on-site
services provided by, 3:59, 3:60

CMS. *See* Centers for Medicare and Medicaid
Services (CMS)

Code Section 125 cafeteria plans. *See*
Cafeteria plans

Code Section 4980G
comparable contributions under, 4:136,
4:150
waiver of excise tax, 4:152

Collectively bargained employees
comparability rules, 4:127

**Commingling of assets in common investment
funds or common trust funds,** 2:1, 7:16

Community property rules
deductions, effect on, 4:69

Comparability rule
accelerated employer contributions, 4:140
Archer MSAs, 4:120, 4:135
cafeteria plans, 4:149–4:151
Code Section 4980G, 4:136, 4:150
collectively bargained employees, 4:127
controlled groups, 4:125
coverage, categories of, 4:116, 4:117
disease management programs, 4:144,
4:151
employer contributions, 4:114, 4:115,
4:120, 4:121
advantages of HSAs, 2:45
after-tax contributions at request of
employee, not applicable to, 4:121
former employees, 4:131–4:134
excise taxes for noncompliance, 4:119
family HDHP coverage, 4:117
former employees, 4:131–4:134
full-time employees, 4:137–4:148
part-time employees, versus, 4:137
high deductible health plans (HDHPs)
coverage requirements, 4:128–4:130
HSA not established, 4:141
interest rate, 4:148

look-back method, 4:137, 4:139
matching contributions, 4:143
participating employees, 4:115
partnerships, 4:124
part-time employees versus full-time
employees, 4:137
pay-as-you-go basis, 4:137, 4:139
qualified HSA distributions, 5:67
reasonable interest rate, 4:148
same contribution method for employees
working for any month during calendar
year, 4:140
self-employed individuals, 4:122
sole proprietors, 4:123
specified age requirement for contributions,
4:145
testing, 4:122–4:125
categories of employees, 4:126
testing period, 4:118
unionized employees, 4:127
wellness programs, 4:151

Compatible coverage rules
qualified HSA distributions, 5:85, 5:86

**Comprehensive Omnibus Budget
Reconciliation Act (COBRA)**
continuation coverage not required with
respect to HSAs, 4:110
family coverage, change to self-only
coverage, 3:30
General Notices, distribution of for plans
subject to ERISA, 8:20

**Computer model, investment advice program
using,** 6:65, 6:66

Consumer choice
advantages of HSAs, 2:45

Consumer-driven health plans
factors contributing to enactment of HSAs,
1:3
other plans considered to be, 1:7

Continuation coverage
premiums for, 6:34

Contributions, 4:1–4:176
accelerated employer contributions, 4:140
advantages of HSAs, 2:45
annual contribution limit, 4:30–4:41,
App. F
Archer MSAs, 4:31
catch-up contributions, 4:30
computation, 4:46–4:48
eligibility issues, 4:47, 4:48
eligibility on first day of last month of
taxable year, 4:38
eligible individual with family coverage for
entire year, 4:36
embedded individual deductible, 4:54,
4:55

Contributions (*cont'd*)
  annual contribution limit, (*cont'd*)
    enrollment under the exception,   4:40
    exceeded, Form W-2 reporting,   7:74
    family coverage,   4:30, 4:36, 4:49, 4:51,
      4:55
    fiscal year taxpayers,   4:30
    HDHP coverage begun mid-year, effect of,
      4:37
    individual contributions,   1:27
    inflation, indexed for,   4:32, 4:35
    maximum annual contribution,   4:30,
      4:36, 6:4
    multiple HSAs,   4:34
    post-deductible HRA,   4:41
    rollovers,   5:10
    self-only coverage,   4:30
    spouses,   4:49–4:59
    tax penalty, when contribution made under
      last-month exception rule,   4:39
    10 percent additional tax,   4:39
    trustee or custodian, acceptance by,   7:24
    umbrella deductible,   4:53, 4:55
    where individual changes type of coverage
      during eligible year,   4:6
  beginning of year, fully funded plan,   4:4
  on behalf of eligible individual
    deductions,   4:67
    exclusions from income,   4:80
    by state government,   4:19
    tax treatment,   4:79
  cafeteria plans, through. *See* Cafeteria plans
  catch-up contributions. *See* Catch-up
    contributions
  C corporations, deductibility of contributions
    by,   4:64
  comparability rule. *See* Comparability rule
  compensation, eligible individuals not
    required to have,   4:14
  deadline for,   4:90
  domestic partner's health coverage and,
    1:20
  due date for,   4:11
  and effective date,   2:21
  eligibility during the year,   4:7
  eligibility for HSA contributions,   4:17–4:19
  employer. *See* Employer contributions
  excise tax waiver,   4:152
  family coverage,   4:7
  Form 5498-SA, reporting requirements,
    7:42–7:48
  Form 8889, reporting requirements,   7:68
  Form W-2, reporting requirements,
    7:72–7:75
  as fringe benefit,   8:44
  FSA participants, contributions by not
    allowed,   4:20
  full funding of plan, time for,   4:4
    HRA participants, contributions by not
      allowed,   4:20
  individual contributions, deductions for,
    4:60–4:69
    C corporations, deductibility of
      contributions by,   4:64
    community property rules, effect of,   4:69
    contributions made on behalf of eligible
      individual,   4:67
    dependents' contributions,   4:68
    family members, contributions by,   4:67
    itemized deductions,   4:65
    itemized expenses, may not be taken as,
      4:66
    returns, how deductions taken on,   4:62
    self-employed individuals, deductions not
      taken into account in determining net
      earnings,   4:63
  ineligible individuals
    cessation of eligible status during year,
      4:11
    testing period,   4:8–4:10
  institution different from HDHP provider,
    4:16
  interaction between HSAs and health FSAs,
    4:28, 4:29
  and IRAs,   4:15
  itemized expenses, may not be taken as,
    4:66
  January 1 and date for filing, employer
    contributions made during,   4:12
  last date for making contributions,   4:11
  last-month rule,   1:28, 4:4, 4:30, 4:39
    computation of annual contributions,
      4:46
  limits,   1:28
    statutory maximum contribution limit,
      2:1
  making contributions,   4:1–4:16
  maximum annual contribution,   4:30
    change of coverage during year,   4:6
  nondiscrimination in,   4:149
  partnerships. *See* Partnerships, contributions
    by
  percentage of HDHP deductible, based on,
    4:142
  reports
    Form 5498-SA, reporting requirements,
      7:42–7:48
    by individuals, IRS,   4:154, 4:155
  rollovers
    annual contribution limits,   5:10
    trustees and custodians, acceptance,   5:8
  S corporations
    health coverage, impact on,   1:24
  self-only coverage,   4:7
  tax treatment,   4:9, 4:39, 4:153
  testing period,   4:8–4:10

defined, 4:39
ineligible individuals, 4:8, 4:9
timing of, 4:89, 4:90
transfers
from FSA or HRA, 4:2
from traditional IRA, 4:3
trustee or custodian, acceptance by
cash contributions, 7:25, 7:28
exceeding maximum contribution limit,
7:26, 7:27
limitations, 7:24
property, contributions of, 7:25

Controlled groups
comparability rule, 4:125

Correcting distributions
after due date of owner's return, 4:107
after extended due date of individual's federal
income tax return, 4:106
excess contributions, failure to make
distribution, 4:99
taxability of, 4:100

Cosmetic surgery
deductibility, 6:40

Cost-of-living adjustments (COLAs), 1:24

Cost-sharing, advantages of HSAs, 1:13

Court costs
ERISA, consequences of violations by trustees
or custodians, 8:27

Coverage. *See also* Medical coverage and
insurance
change of. *See* Change of coverage
child coverage under HSA or HDHP, 2:27
comparability rule
categories of coverage, 4:116, 4:117
high deductible health plans (HDHPs),
4:128–4:130
compatible coverage rules
qualified HSA distributions, 5:85, 5:86
disregarded FSA coverage, 5:78, 5:79
family coverage. *See* Family coverage
health coverage, impact on HSA
contributions, 1:20
health coverage tax credit
premiums paid with HSA distributions,
5:39
meaningful coverage, 3:4
permitted coverage, 3:45, 3:46
examples of, 3:55
prescription drugs, 3:48
retiree health coverage, 3:74
self-only coverage. *See* Self-only coverage

Creation of HSAs, 2:3

Credit card payments
ERISA, 8:14

Creditor protection, 8:51

Criminal offenses
ERISA, consequences of violations by trustees
or custodians, 8:27

Cross-trading, 6:66

Custodians. *See* Trustees and custodians

Customer Identification Procedures, 8:45

D

Davis-Bacon Act, 8:44

Death
distributions. *See* Death distributions
taxation upon, 2:46

Death distributions, 6:82–6:86
estate tax consequences, 6:85
gift tax consequences, 6:86
income tax consequences, 6:83
10 percent additional tax on distributions,
exception to, 6:74

Debit cards
ERISA exemption, 8:13
HSA with, ERISA, 8:13
restricting payments and reimbursements,
administration through, 6:6

Debt
disadvantages of HSAs, 2:46

Deductibles. *See also* Deductions
embedded individual deductible, 4:54, 4:55
mid-year change of plans, effect of, 3:28,
3:29
umbrella, 4:53, 4:55

Deductions
as adjustment to gross income
S corporation contributions, 4:176
C corporations, contributions by, 4:64
community property rules, effect of, 4:69
contributions made on behalf of eligible
individual, 4:67, 4:79
dependents' contributions, 4:68
employer contributions
federal income tax return, 4:87
for excess contributions
individual contributions, 4:93
family members, contributions by, 4:67
Form 8889, reporting requirements, 7:68
individual contributions, deductions for,
4:60–4:69
C corporations, deductibility of
contributions by, 4:64
community property rules, effect of, 4:69
contributions made on behalf of eligible
individual, 4:67
dependents' contributions, 4:68

Deductions (cont'd)
individual contributions, deductions for, (cont'd)
  excess contributions, 4:93
  family members, contributions by, 4:67
  itemized deductions, 4:65
  itemized expenses, may not be taken as, 4:66
  returns, how deductions taken on, 4:62
  self-employed individuals, deductions not taken into account in determining net earnings, 4:63
  spouse, employer contributions to, 4:61
investment loss, deduction for loss of value of HSA not allowed, 6:10
itemized deductions, 4:65
S corporations, contributions by, 4:171

Deemed distributions
prohibited transactions, resulting from, 6:59–6:71
  block trades, 6:66
  cash incentives to establish HSA and HDHP, 6:71
  Code provisions, 6:62
  cross-trading, 6:66
  definition of prohibited transaction, 6:63
  disqualified person, defined, 6:69
  disqualified person entering into prohibited transaction, 6:64
  electronic communications networks, 6:66
  eligible investment advice arrangements, 6:65, 6:66
  fiduciary, defined, 6:70
  foreign exchange transactions, 6:66
  loans from trustee to HSA, 6:63
  loans, pledging of HSA security for, 6:61
  penalty tax rate, 6:67
  service providers, transactions with, 6:66
  waiver of rules, 6:68

Defined contribution health care arrangements
and HSA enactment, 1:3
other plans considered to be, 1:7

Definition of HSA, 2:1

Dental care insurance
exception to requirement of no coverage under other non-HDHP, 2:8

Department of Labor (DOL)
Advisory Opinions regarding HSAs
  Advisory Opinion 2004-09A, 1:11, App. E
  ERISA, effect of, 8:29
claims procedure rules, compliance by plans subject to ERISA, 8:22
employee welfare benefit plans, 8:6
Field Assistance Bulletins regarding HSAs, 1:11

FAB 2004-01, 8:7, App. E
FAB 2006-02, 8:3, 8:12, App. E
judicial consideration, 8:5
regulatory authority over HSAs, 1:9

Dependents
advantages of HSAs, 2:45
annual contribution limit, family coverage, 4:36
contributions by
  deductibility, 4:68
defined, 2:35–2:37
distributions from dependent care FSA, 5:55
divorce or separation, child claimed as dependent of both parents, 2:44
and GOZA, 2:34, 2:36
qualified medical expenses, distributions used to pay, 6:20
  continuation coverage, 6:34
  divorce, child also claimed as dependent by former spouse, 6:36
  unemployment compensation, 6:35
qualifying children
  age, effect of, 2:40, 2:42
  defined, 2:37, 2:39
  disabled, 2:41
qualifying individuals, defined, 2:37
qualifying relatives, defined, 2:34, 2:38
and WFTRA, 2:35, 2:37

Designated beneficiaries
death distributions, 6:82–6:86
  estate beneficiaries, income tax consequences, 6:83
  estate tax consequences, 6:85
  gift tax consequences, 6:86
  income tax consequences, 6:83
  non-spouse beneficiaries, income tax consequences, 6:83
  surviving spouse beneficiaries, income tax consequences, 6:83
estate as
  value of HSA, reporting of, 5:25
other than surviving spouse as, 5:24
surviving spouse as designated beneficiary, 5:22

Diagnosis, defined, 6:32

Disability
indefinite duration, defined, 6:77
qualifying children, 2:41
substantial gainful activity, defined, 6:76
10 percent additional tax on distributions, 6:74–6:77

Disability insurance
exception to requirement of no coverage under other non-HDHP, 2:8
insurance, 6:47

Disadvantages of HSAs, 2:46
  employers, 1:17
  individuals, 1:16
Disclosure
  ERISA, fiduciary standards for plans subject
    to, 8:27
Discounted prices for services
  HDHPs, 3:6
Disease management programs
  comparability rule, 4:144, 4:151
Distributions, 6:1–6:88
  Archer MSAs, rollovers. *See* Archer medical
    savings accounts (MSAs)
  correcting distributions
    after due date of owner's return, 4:107
    after extended due date of individual's
      federal income tax return, 4:106
    failure to make, 4:99
    taxability of, 4:100
  for cosmetic surgery, 6:40
  death distributions, 6:82–6:86
    estate tax consequences, 6:85
    gift tax consequences, 6:86
    income tax consequences, 6:83
  dependent, payment of qualified medical
    expenses for, 6:20
  divorce, transfers incident to not treated as,
    5:34
  expenses reimbursed by another plan as gross
    income, 6:23
  Form 1099-SA, reporting requirements,
    7:49–7:56
  FSAs, rollovers to HSAs, 5:3
  health coverage tax credit
    premiums paid with HSA distributions,
      5:39
  HRAs, rollovers to HSAs, 5:1, 5:3
  income tax, federal. *See* Income tax, federal
  ineligible individuals
    for qualified medical expenses, excludable
      from gross income, 6:14
  investment loss, 6:10
  IRAs, rollovers to HSAs, 5:1, 5:3
  itemized deductions, 6:44
  for long-term care insurance premiums,
    6:56–6:58
  maximum lifetime distribution rules, 5:48,
    5:49
  for Medicare premiums, 6:43
  medicine and drugs, 6:52–6:55
    Canada, prescription drugs imported
      from, 6:53
    defined, 6:52
    nonprescription drugs, 6:54
    prescribed drugs, 6:55
  for Medigap policy premiums, 6:45, 6:46
  mistake-of-fact distributions, 6:79, 6:81

  MSAs, rollovers to HSAs, 5:1
    all cash or property need not be rolled
      over, 5:7
    proceeds from sale of property, 5:6
  and nondiscrimination rules, 6:26
  to partnerships. *See* Partnerships,
    contributions by
  prohibited transactions, deemed distributions
    as consequences of, 6:59–6:71
    block trades, 6:66
    cash incentives to establish HSA and
      HDHP, 6:71
    Code provisions, 6:62
    cross-trading, 6:66
    definition of prohibited transaction, 6:63
    disqualified person, defined, 6:69
    disqualified person entering into prohibited
      transaction, 6:64
    electronic communications networks,
      6:66
    eligible investment advice arrangements,
      6:65, 6:66
    fiduciary, defined, 6:70
    foreign exchange transactions, 6:66
    loans from trustee to HSA, 6:63
    loans, pledging of HSA security for, 6:61
    penalty tax rate, 6:67
    results of engaging in, 6:60
    service providers, transactions with,
      6:66
    waiver of rules, 6:68
  qualified medical expenses, 2:6, 6:27–6:51.
    See also Qualified medical expenses
  redepositing, erroneous, 6:79
  responsibility for determining, 6:12, 6:13
  restrictions on distributions, 6:14–6:26
    dependent, payment of qualified medical
      expenses for, 6:20
    gross income inclusion, 6:16, 6:19
    qualified medical expenses, distributions
      not used for, 6:16, 6:17
    qualified medical expenses, distributions
      used for, 6:19
    qualified medical expenses, trust or
      custodial agreement, 6:15
    spouse, payment of qualified medical
      expenses for, 6:20
    transitional relief, 6:22
  return of erroneously made distributions,
    6:78–6:81
    mistake-of-fact distributions, 6:78, 6:81
    trustees and custodians, acceptance by,
      6:80
  rollovers, 5:1–5:21
  Roth IRAs, rollovers to HSAs, 5:3
  for self-insured retiree health coverage,
    6:49
  specified age, attainment of, 6:7

Distributions (cont'd)
spousal reimbursement excluded from gross
income, 6:24
spouse, payment of qualified medical
expenses for, 6:20
tax consequences, 6:1–6:11
cessation of eligible status during year,
6:3, 6:5
debit card restricting payments and
reimbursements, administration
through, 6:6
eligibility issues, 6:3, 6:5
excess contributions, 6:4
investment loss, 6:10
maximum annual contribution limits,
recovery of amounts contributed in excess
of, 6:4
qualified medical expenses, 6:9
recoupment of amounts by employer when
employee never eligible individual, 6:3
reimbursements, 6:9
request by employer, 6:2
specified age, attainment of, 6:7
tax-free distribution status, 6:11
when individual permitted to receive, 6:1
withdrawal of funds by authorized
person, 6:8
10 percent additional tax, 6:72–6:77
age, exception for, 6:74
contribution limit, distribution not
violating, 6:73
death, exception for, 6:74
disability, exception for, 6:74–6:77
exceptions, 6:74
rollovers, exception for, 6:74
transfers, exception for, 6:74
transitional relief, 6:22
for transportation expenses, 6:37
trustees and custodians
restrictions on distributions, authority to
place, 6:14
withholding, 6:87, 6:88

Diversification
ERISA, fiduciary standards for plans subject
to, 8:24

Divisibility
advantages of HSAs, 2:45

Divorce
child claimed as dependent of both parents,
2:44
qualified medical expenses, 6:36
child coverage under HSA or HDHP, 2:27
transfers incident to, 5:33–5:38
divorce or separation instrument defined,
5:35
taxable distribution, not treated as, 5:34
as taxable transfer, 5:36

treatment of HSA, 5:37
when permitted, 5:33

Documents, 7:1–7:13
IRS, issued by for establishment of HSA,
7:4
provided by trustee or custodian to HSA
owner, 7:12

DOL. See Department of Labor (DOL)

Domestic partner
health coverage impact on HSA
contributions, 1:20

Drugs. See Nonprescription drugs;
Prescription drugs

E

EAPs. See Employee assistance programs
(EAPs)

Earnings from HSAs
exclusion from gross income, 4:88

Economic Stimulus payments
direct deposits of, 4:1, 6:73

Effective date
and contributions, 2:21

Electronic communications networks
prohibited transactions, 6:66

Electronic media, use of, 8:50

Eligible individuals
age, employer relying on representation,
4:76
compensation, not required to have, 4:14
contributions by, 4:14
defined, 2:6
divorced parents, children of, 2:27
employer responsibility for determining
eligibility, 4:75
medical discount cards, effect of,
3:47, 3:57
Medicare
catch-up contributions, persons eligible for
but not enrolled, 2:18
persons eligible for but not enrolled in
Medicare Part A or B, 2:14
Medicare Part A only, enrollment in, 2:17
military service members
VA medical benefits, effect of, 2:16
Veterans Affairs Department providing
medical benefits, 2:19
nondiscrimination in, 4:149
option to choose plan that is not HDHP,
2:13
qualified medical expenses, responsibility for
determining exclusive use, 4:77

spouses, both must be eligible, 2:6, 2:9
testing period, 5:46
trustees and custodians requiring proof of,
7:36, 7:37

Eligible investment advice arrangements
audit requirements, 6:66
defined, 6:66
notice requirements, 6:66
prohibited transactions, 6:65, 6:66

Embedded individual deductible, 4:54, 4:55

Employee assistance programs (EAPs),
3:58, 3:61
effect on HSA eligibility, 3:47
preventive care safe harbor, 3:61

Employee contributions
cafeteria plans, 1:14, 4:81

**Employee Retirement Income Security Act of
1974 (ERISA),** 8:1–8:30
certificate of creditable coverage, 8:21
claims procedure rules, DOL, 8:22
conditions for exemption, 8:2
consequences of exemption from ERISA,
8:18
contribution limits, 8:17
credit card payments, 8:14
custodial accounts, 8:23
DOL guidance
Advisory Opinion regarding, 8:29
FAB 2004-01, 8:7, App. E
FAB 2006-02, 8:3, 8:12, App. E
judicial consideration, 8:5
employee welfare benefit plans, 8:6
actions representing HSA as employee
welfare benefit plan, 8:6
employer contributions, 4:109–4:113
employer obligations for plans subject to
COBRA General Notices, distribution of,
8:20
encouragement by employer to participate,
8:11
entity as trustee and another as custodian,
8:26
exemption
conditions for, 8:2
consequences, 8:18
FAB 2006-02
guidance, 8:3, 8:12
text of, App. E
fees paid by employer. tax consequences,
8:12
fiduciary standards for trustees and
custodians, 8:24
consequences of violation, 8:27
plans not subject to ERISA, 8:28
401(k) plans, 8:9
group insurance, 8:4, 8:7

incentive payments, 8:29
investment decisions as condition for
exemption, 8:2
single investment trustee with limited range
of investment options, effect of, 8:10
investment rights as condition for
exemption
specific investment options, 8:8
legal obligations if HSA subject to ERISA,
8:19
offer to employee on same terms as offered to
public, 8:15
prohibited transaction rules, applicability,
6:62, 8:30
safe harbor rules, 8:4, 8:7
single option HDHP and HSA, 8:16
Title I, 4:109, 8:51
trustee vs. custodian risk and
responsibilities, 8:25
trusts, 8:23
document, 8:28

Employee welfare benefit plans
actions representing HSA as employee welfare
benefit plan, 8:6
funding of plans, 4:111

Employer contributions, 4:70–4:74
cafeteria plans
election as negative election, 4:78
treatment of, 4:72, 4:81
chronic health conditions, 4:73
comparability rule, 2:45, 4:114, 4:115,
4:120, 4:121. See also Comparability rule
after-tax contributions at request of
employee, not applicable to, 4:121
former employees, 4:131–4:134
ERISA and, 4:109–4:113
excess contributions, deductibility, 4:96
exclusion from gross income, 4:80
FICA taxes, not subject to, 4:72, 4:84
Form W-2 reporting requirements, 4:59
inclusion in gross income, 4:71
income tax withholding, not subject to,
4:83
individual contributions, deductions for
spouse, employer contributions to, 4:61
ineligible employees, deductibility, 4:95
maximum allowable amount for individual,
exceeding, 4:70
nondeductible employer contributions, 10
percent tax, 4:113
nonqualified deferred compensation rules,
4:74
Railroad Retirement Tax Act, 4:72, 4:82
tax advantages, 4:72
treatment of, 4:71

Employers
advantages of HSAs, 1:13, 1:14

Employers (*cont'd*)

age, reliance on representation of employee,   4:76

cafeteria plans. *See* Cafeteria plans

disadvantages of HSAs,   1:17

eligible individuals, responsibility for determining,   4:75

ERISA, obligations for plans subject to, 8:19

COBRA General Notices, distribution of, 8:20

DOL claims procedure rules, compliance with,   8:22

factors to consider before offering HSA with HDHP coverage,   1:21

qualified medical expenses, not responsible for determining exclusive use,   4:77

responsibilities,   4:75–4:78

End-stage renal disease

distributions for health insurance premiums,   6:50

Enrollment

failure to follow applicable rules,   1:22

ERISA.   *See* Employee Retirement Income Security Act of 1974

Establishment of HSA

before becoming effective,   2:22

deposit requirements,   2:24

documentation,   2:24, 7:4

mailing date,   2:24

Model Form 5305-B,   7:4–7:9, 7:11

Model Form 5305-C,   7:5–7:9, 7:11

paperwork and deposit sent, mailing date and,   2:24

previously establishment of HSA by owner, what date HSA considered established, 2:26

qualified medical expenses

expenses incurred prior to establishment of HSA,   2:32

rollovers

from an Archer MSA,   2:25

from another MSA,   2:25

signatures,   2:20

transfers

from an Archer MSA,   2:25

from another MSA,   2:25

treatment as established before date of establishment,   2:23

trustees and custodians

paperwork and deposit sent, mailing date and,   2:24

treatment as established before date of establishment,   2:23

in United States, requirement,   7:10

when considered established,   2:20

Estates

inherited HSAs, reporting of value of,   5:25

Estate tax

death distributions,   6:85

disadvantages of HSAs,   2:46

Excess contributions,   4:91–4:108

account valuation, correcting distributions, 4:105

additional taxes on,   7:57–7:61

adjusted opening balance used in computation,   4:102, 4:103

computations,   4:101–4:104

adjusted opening balance used in computation,   4:102, 4:103

computation period,   4:104

correcting distributions

account valuation,   4:105

after due date of owner's return,   4:107

after extended due date of individual's federal income tax return,   4:106

failure to make,   4:99

taxability of,   4:100

creation,   4:91

deductibility, individual contributions,   4:88

expenses other than qualified medical, distributions not to be treated as withdrawal of excess contributions,   4:108

Form 8889, reporting requirements,   7:68

ineligible employees, deductibility,   4:95

net income attributable to

computation,   4:98

taxability of,   4:98

noncomparable contributions,   4:147

penalties,   2:46

reporting requirements,   4:94

6 percent excise tax

defined for purposes of,   4:92

as penalties,   4:96, 4:97

tax consequences,   6:4

trustee or custodian, responsibilities of, 7:26, 7:27

Excise taxes

comparability rule, noncompliance with, 4:119

distributions, 10 percent additional tax on, 6:72–6:77

age, exception for,   6:74

contribution limit, distribution not violating,   6:73

death, exception for,   6:74

disability, exception for,   6:74–6:77

exceptions,   6:74

permanent rule under Notice 2007-22, 5:84

rollovers, exception for,   6:74

transfers, exception for,   6:74

excess contributions
defined for purposes of, 4:92
penalties, 1:22, 4:96, 4:97
failure to maintain adequate records of
medical expenditures, liability upon, 1:22
failure to make contributions, liability
upon, 1:22
nonconforming group health care plans, HSA
status for excise tax purposes, 3:75
nondeductible employer contributions, 10
percent tax, 4:113
on prohibited transactions
Form 5330, reporting requirements,
7:62–7:64
25 percent tax, 3:75
waiver of, 4:152

Exclusive benefit rule
ERISA, fiduciary standards for plans subject
to, 8:24

Existing illness
preventive care safe harbor, 3:54

Expenses
medical expenses. *See* Qualified medical
expenses
qualified medical expenses, 6:27–6:51. See
also Qualified medical expenses

F

FAB 2004-01, 8:7
text of, App. E
FAB 2006-02, 8:3, 8:12
text of, App. E

**Fair market value, health care charges
below,** 3:60

Family coverage
annual contribution limit, 4:30
computation, 4:49, 4:51, 4:55
eligible individual with family coverage for
entire year, 4:36
December 1, eligibility on, 4:7
deductibles, 1:27
defined, 3:40
effect of change from self-only coverage,
3:28, 3:29
embedded individual deductible,
4:54, 4:55
out-of-pocket expenses, cumulative embedded
deductibles for family coverage subject to,
3:25, 3:26
payment of benefits, when paid, 3:41
self-only coverage vs., 3:39–3:42
umbrella deductible, defined, 4:53, 4:55
who is covered under, 3:42

Federal Unemployment Tax Act (FUTA)
employer contributions not subject to,
1:14, 4:72, 4:86

Fees, 7:18–7:21
attorney's fees awarded when ERISA
violations by trustees or custodians, 8:27
employer, paid by
directly to trustee or custodian, 7:21
tax consequences, 8:12
owner, paid by directly to trustee or
custodian, 7:21
reporting requirements, 7:19
withdrawal from HSA, treatment of, 7:18,
7:20

FICA tax
employer contributions not subject to,
1:14, 4:72, 4:84
two percent shareholders
contributions by S corporations,
deductibility, 4:173, 4:174

Fiduciary standards under ERISA
fiduciary adviser, 6:66
HSA trustee or custodian, 8:24–8:26
prohibited transaction rules
definition of fiduciary, 6:70
fiduciary adviser, 6:66
rules, 6:66

Field Assistance Bulletin regarding HSAs
FAB 2004-01, 8:7
text of, App. E
FAB 2006-02, 8:12
difference from earlier guidance, 8:3
text of, App. E
issuance of, 1:11
judicial consideration, 8:5

Fiscal year taxpayers
annual contribution limit, 4:30

Flat-dollar charges
out-of-pocket expenses, 3:24

Flexibility
advantages of HSAs, 2:45

Flexible spending arrangements (FSAs). *See*
Health flexible spending arrangements (FSAs)

Foreign exchange transactions
prohibited transactions, 6:66

Form 1040
distribution reporting, 6:17, 6:18
Form 8889 attachment, 7:66
HSA rules, 1:11
medical expense reporting, 1:22

Form 1040A
Form 8889 attachment, 7:66

Form 1040EZ
Form 8889 attachment, 7:66

Form 1040NR
distribution reporting, 6:13
Form 8889 attachment, 7:66

Form 1098-SA
trustee-to-trustee transfers, 7:55

Form 1099-SA, 7:49–7:56
beneficiaries, copy provided to, 7:51
boxes, completion of, 7:48
completion of, 7:56
corrected, 7:47
HSA rules, 1:11
owner, copy provided to, 7:51
purpose of, 7:49
rollovers, 5:19
  distribution codes, 5:20
substitute statement, 7:54
time for filing, 7:53
time for providing to recipient, 7:52
year in which distributions to be reported, 7:50

Form 5305-B (Model Form), 7:4–7:9, 7:11

Form 5305-C (Model Form), 7:5–7:9, 7:11

Form 5329, 7:57–7:61
circumstances for filing, 7:58
and joint returns, 7:59
Part VII, how completed, 7:61
purpose of, 7:57, 7:62
time for filing, 7:60, 7:63

Form 5330, 7:62–7:64
disqualified person participating in prohibited transaction, completion upon, 7:64

Form 5498-SA, 7:42–7:48
HSA rules, 1:11
participants, provided to, 5:21
purpose of, 7:43
rollovers, 5:21, 7:43, 7:55
time for filing, 7:45
time for provision to recipient, 7:46
for whom form to be filed, 7:43

Form 5500
filing requirements, 8:19

Form 8889, 7:65–7:68
contributions, reporting, 4:13, 4:59, 7:68
death of owner, completion upon, 7:67
deductions, reporting, 7:68
deemed distributions, reporting requirements, 7:69–7:71
distributions
  for other than qualified medical expenses, reporting requirements, 6:17
  reporting requirements, 6:17
  10 percent additional tax, distributions subject to, reporting requirements, 6:13
excess contributions, reporting, 7:68

HDHP coverage not maintained during testing period, completion where, 7:71
HSA rules, 1:11
individuals, reporting by
  generally, 4:154
  who must file, 4:155
medical expense reporting, 1:22, 1:28
purposes, 7:65
reporting, 5:19, 7:69–7:71
rollovers, 5:19
trustee-to-trustee transfers, 5:29
who must file, 7:66

Former employees
comparability rule, 4:131–4:134
locating, 4:132
qualified HSA distributions, 5:69

Form W-2
employer contributions, reporting requirements, 4:58, 4:59, 4:94, 7:72–7:75
ineligible individuals, 7:74
maximum annual contributions limit exceeded, 7:74
pretax contributions, 7:73
spouse who is not employee of this employer, 7:75

401(k) plans
ERISA, 8:9

Free health care, access to, 3:60

Fringe benefit
contributions as, 8:44

FSAs. *See* Health flexible spending arrangements (FSAs)

Full-time employees
comparability rule, 4:137–4:148
  less than entire calendar year, working full time, 4:138

Funding of plans
minimum funding standards, 4:112
welfare benefit plans, 4:111

FUTA tax
and employer contributions, 1:14, 4:72, 4:86

Future of HSAs, 1:25–1:31
expansion of HSAs, 1:25
proposed changes to HSA rules, reasons for, 1:26

G

General rules. *See* Rules regarding HSAs

Gift tax
advantages of HSAs, 2:45
death distributions, 6:86

GOZA. *See* Gulf Opportunity Zone Act of 2005

Gross income
adjusted gross income, 6:30
deductions
as adjustment to gross income, 4:176
distributions
for expenses already reimbursed by other health care plan not excludable, 6:23
qualified medical expenses, distributions not used for, 6:16
qualified medical expenses, distributions used for, 6:19
employers, contributions by
exclusion, 4:71
inclusion, 4:71
exclusions from, 2:45
qualified medical expenses, 2:28
IRAs
transfers, inclusion in gross income, 5:44
partnerships, contributions by
guaranteed payments, inclusion, 4:167
qualified medical expenses, exclusion from, 2:28
S corporations, contributions by
adjustment to gross income, deduction for, 4:176
exclusion from gross income, 4:172
spouse's qualified medical expenses, exclusion, 6:24

Group health plans
claims procedure rules, DOL, 8:22
nonconforming group health care plans, HSA status for excise tax purposes, 3:75

Group insurance
ERISA, 8:4, 8:7

Guam
HSAs available to residents of, 2:11

Guaranteed payments, partnerships, 4:162, 4:163
guaranteed payment partner, 4:156
inclusion in gross income, 4:167
net earnings from self-employment, inclusion in, 4:166
reports, 4:165

Gulf Opportunity Zone Act of 2005
dependents, 2:34
defined, 2:36

H

Hawaii
availability of HSAs, 2:12, 8:37

HDHPs. *See* High deductible health plans

Health coverage tax credit
premiums paid with HSA distributions, 5:39

Health flexible spending arrangements (FSAs)
annual contribution limit
post-deductible health FSA, 4:41
contributions to HSAs by participants not allowed, 4:20
dependent care FSAs
qualified HSA distributions, 5:55
distributions, rollovers to HSAs, 5:3
generally, 1:7
HRAs, differences, 1:8
HSAs compared, App. G
interaction between HSAs and health FSAs, 4:28, 4:29
limited-purpose health FSA, 4:20, 4:28
mid-year transfers, 5:72
MSAs, differences, 1:8
post-deductible FSA, 4:20
qualified HSA distributions, 5:53, 5:54
allowance for FSAs, 5:62
compatible coverage rules, 5:85, 5:86
dependent care FSAs, 5:55
former employees, balance in account, 5:69
testing period, eligibility issues during, 5:76
transitional relief, 5:79
zero balance FSA, 5:78
reimbursement before minimum HDHP deductible satisfied, 4:20
trustee-to-trustee transfers, 5:38
zero balance FSA, 4:29
qualified HSA distributions, 5:78

Health Insurance Portability and Accountability Act (HIPAA)
certificate of creditable coverage, 8:21
Electronic Standards Regulations, applicability to HSAs, 8:32
nondiscrimination rules, applicability for plans subject to ERISA, 8:18, 8:21
privacy regulations, 8:31, 8:32
applicability to HSAs, 3:76
Electronic Standards Regulations, applicability to HSAs, 8:32

Health insurance premiums
distributions for, 6:42

Health Opportunity Patient Empowerment (HOPE) Act of 2006, 7:4

Health reimbursement arrangements (HRAs)
contributions to HSAs by participants not allowed, 4:20
distributions, rollovers to HSAs, 5:3, 5:6

Health reimbursement arrangements (HRAs)
(*cont'd*)
as eligible individual, 3:62
FSAs, differences, 1:8
generally, 1:7
HSAs compared, App. G
limited-purpose health HRA, 4:20
mid-year transfers, 5:72
MSAs, differences, 1:8
post-deductible HRA, 4:20
qualified HSA distributions, 5:53, 5:54
allowance for HRAs, 5:62
compatible coverage rules, 5:85, 5:86
former employees, balance in account, 5:69
testing period, eligibility issues during, 5:76
transitional relief, 5:79
reimbursement before minimum HDHP deductible satisfied, 4:20
suspended HRA, 4:20
trustee-to-trustee transfers, 5:38

Health Savings Account Act
Pennsylvania, 8:43

Health savings accounts (HSAs). See specific topic

High deductible health plans (HDHPs)
annual deductibles, 3:10–3:15. See also Deductibles
benefits, lifetime limitation on, 3:31–3:33
authority to impose, 3:31
covered benefits, 3:34
payments in excess of UCR not treated as out-of-pocket expenses, 3:38
reasonableness, determining, 3:37
cafeteria plans, 3:65–3:73
calendar year basis, 3:8
cash incentives to create, 6:71
comparability rules
coverage, categories of, 4:116
coverage requirements, 4:128–4:130
family HDHP coverage, 4:117
contributions, 4:5
percentage of deductible, based on, 4:142
post-deductible health FSA or HRA, individual also covered by, 4:41
deductibles, 3:10–3:15. See also Deductibles
changes to, 3:8
satisfaction of, 3:12
transitional rule, 3:15
defined, 3:1
disadvantages of HSAs, 2:46
discounted prices for services, 3:6
domestic partner's health coverage and, 1:20
eligible individuals, defined, 2:6

time that eligibility begins, 2:7
employee assistance programs (EAPs), 3:47, 3:58, 3:61
establishment before becoming effective, 2:22
factors employers should consider before offering HSA with HDHP coverage, 1:21
factors individuals should consider before enrolling in HSA with HDHP, 1:18
family coverage
annual contribution limit, 4:36
comparability rules, 4:117, 4:129
self-only coverage vs., 3:39–3:42
HIPAA privacy, 3:76
history of, 2:6
HSA trustees or custodians only without offering HDHP, 1:6
limited coverage plans, 3:3
long-term care insurance, 3:63, 3:64
meaningful medical coverage, provision of, 3:4
medical discount cards, effect on eligibility, 3:47, 3:57
midmonth, coverage beginning after, 2:7
minimum annual deductible, 3:1, 3:7
transitional relief, 3:21
nonconforming group health plans, 3:75
option to choose plan that is not HDHP, 2:13
out-of-pocket expenses. See also Out-of-pocket expenses
changes to, 3:8
maximum, 3:1, 3:7, 3:11
permitted insurance, 3:44–3:47
plan deductibles, 3:11–3:15
transitional rule, 3:15
post-deductible health FSA or HRA, individual also covered by, 4:41
preventive care. See also Preventive care
safe harbor, 3:49–3:56
providers of, 1:5, 1:6
reimbursement before minimum HDHP deductible satisfied, 4:20
requirements, 3:1–3:9
exceptions to, 2:8
of no coverage under other non-HDHP, 3:43
self-insured medical reimbursement plans sponsored by employers as, 3:2
self-only coverage
effect of change to family coverage, 3:28, 3:29
plan deductibles, 3:12, 3:14
spouses
annual contribution limit, only one spouse covered, 4:50
contributions to HSA, 1:19
state high-risk health plans, 3:5

transitional relief
  state benefit mandates, 8:36
  wellness programs, 3:47, 3:58

Highly compensated employees
  cafeteria plans, 4:149

HIPAA. *See* Health Insurance Portability and Accountability Act

Historical background, 2:3

HOPE Act. *See* Health Opportunity Patient Empowerment (HOPE) Act of 2006

Hospitalization
  out-of-pocket expenses, restriction of benefits to expenses for, 3:36

HRAs. *See* Health reimbursement arrangements

HSA Improvement and Expansion Act of 2007, 1:29

HSA owners
  defined, 2:1
  use of term, 4:4, 5:1, 8:3

HSAs. See specific topic

Husband and wife. *See* Spouses

I

Income tax, federal
  adjusted gross income, 6:30
  disadvantages of HSAs, 2:46
  distributions
    expenses already reimbursed by other health care plan not excludable from gross income, 6:23
  excess contributions taxability of net income attributable to, 4:98
  failure to maintain adequate records of medical expenditures, liability upon, 1:22
  gross income. *See* Gross income
  itemization
    advantages of HSAs, 2:45
    contributions excluded, 4:65
  qualified HSA distributions, deductions, 5:88
  returns, how deductions taken on, 4:62
  withholding
    distributions, 6:87, 6:88
    employer contributions not subject to, 4:83

Individual HSAs, 2:48

Individual retirement accounts (IRAs)
  contributions to, 4:15
  distributions, rollovers to HSAs, 5:3, 5:40
  Economic Stimulus payments, removal of direct deposits, 4:1

gross income
  transfers, inclusion in, 5:44
  rollover to HSA, 5:3, 5:40
  securities laws, guidance, 8:48, 8:49
  SEP IRA, distributions from, 5:42
  SIMPLE IRA, distributions from, 5:42
  transfers
    gross income, inclusion, 5:44
    testing period, 5:50
  as trustee or custodian, 2:1
  trustee-to-trustee transfers, 5:38

Inflation
  annual contribution limit indexed for, 4:32
    statutory annual contribution limits, 4:35
  catch-up amounts indexed for, 4:45

Information returns
  trustees and custodians, filing, 7:29

Inherited HSAs, 5:22–5:27
  designated beneficiaries, surviving spouse as, 5:22
  earnings after death
    penalty not imposed, 5:27
    treatment of, 5:26
  estate as designated beneficiary
    value of HSA, reporting of, 5:25
  rollovers, when permitted, 5:23
  termination where other than surviving spouse as designated beneficiary, 5:24

In-patient care
  out-of-pocket expenses, restriction of benefits to expenses for, 3:36

Insurance. *See also* Medical coverage and insurance
  accident insurance
    exception to requirement of no coverage under other non-HDHP, 2:8
    qualified medical expenses, 6:47
  dental care insurance
    exception to requirement of no coverage under other non-HDHP, 2:8
  disability insurance
    exception to requirement of no coverage under other non-HDHP, 2:8
    qualified medical expenses, 6:47
  end-stage renal disease health insurance premiums, distributions for, 6:50
  HIPAA. *See* Health Insurance Portability and Accountability Act
  life insurance, investment of HSA assets in not permitted, 2:1
  long-term care insurance. *See* Long-term care insurance
  permitted insurance, 3:44–3:47. See also Permitted insurance
  qualified medical expenses, payment for, 2:31

Insurance (*cont'd*)
  vision care insurance
    exception to requirement of no coverage
      under other non-HDHP, 2:8

Insurance company
  as trustee or custodian, 7:22

Interest rate
  comparable contributions, 4:148

Internal Revenue Code (IRC)
  extracts from relevant sections, App. A
  minimum funding standards not applicable to
    HSAs, 4:112

Internal Revenue Service (IRS)
  announcements regarding HSAs, App. C
  notices regarding HSAs, 1:11, App. B
  revenue rulings regarding HSAs, 1:11, App.
    D

Investment contracts, 8:47

Investments
  commingling of assets in common investment
    fund, 7:16
  deduction for loss of value of HSA, 6:10
  ERISA exemption, investment options as
    condition for, 8:2
    single investment trustee with limited range
      of investment options, effect of, 8:10
  how funds may be invested, 7:14
  permissible, 7:14–7:17
  prohibited, 7:17
  restrictions, 7:15

IRAs. *See* Individual retirement accounts

IRC. *See* Internal Revenue Code (IRC)

IRS. *See* Internal Revenue Service (IRS)

Itemization. *See* Income tax, federal

Itemized deductions
  qualified medical expenses, 6:44

J

Joint HSAs, 2:10

Joint returns
  and Form 5329, 7:59

L

Labor Department. *See* Department of Labor
  (DOL)

Last-month rule, 1:28, 4:4, 4:30
  computation of annual contributions, 4:46

Legislative history of HSAs
  factors contributing to enactment, 1:3
  history of HSAs, 2:3

Legislative proposals, leading
  2005-2007, 1:28
  2007-2009, 1:29
  2009-2011, 1:30

Life insurance
  investment of HSA assets in, 2:1, 7:14

Limited coverage plans, 3:3

Loans
  prohibited transactions, when deemed to
    be, 6:61, 6:63
  security for, HSAs may not be pledged as,
    6:61

Lodging expenses
  distributions for, 6:38

Long-term care insurance
  advantages of HSAs, 2:45
  exception to requirement of no coverage
    under other non-HDHP, 2:8
  payment of premiums, 3:63, 3:64
  premiums, distributions for, 6:56–6:58

Long-term care services
  qualified medical expenses, 6:48

Look-back method
  comparability rule, 4:137, 4:139

Loyalty, 8:28

M

Mailing date
  establishment of HSA, 2:24

Maintenance fees. *See* Fees

Mandated benefits
  deductibles below minimum annual
    deductible, 3:21

Matching contributions
  cafeteria plans, 4:150
  comparability rule, 4:143

Meals
  qualified medical expenses, 6:39

Meaningful coverage, 3:4

Medicaid
  eligible individual with family HDHP also,
    4:36
  ineligibility for medical tax deduction, 1:27

Medical coverage and insurance, 3:1–3:76
  benefits, limitation on, 3:31–3:38
    covered benefits, 3:34

hospitalization, restriction of benefits to expenses for, 3:36

in-patient care, restriction of benefits to expenses for, 3:36

lifetime limitations, 3:31–3:33

payments in excess of UCR not treated as out-of-pocket expenses, 3:38

reasonableness of restriction or exclusion, 3:37

separate or higher deductible for specific benefits, 3:35

cafeteria plans. *See* Cafeteria plans

clinics, on-site, 3:59, 3:60

deductibles, 3:10–3:15

transitional rule, 3:15

employee assistance programs (EAPs)

defined, 3:58, 3:61

preventive care safe harbor, 3:61

fair market value, health care charges below, 3:60

family coverage vs. self-only coverage, 3:39–3:42

free health care, access to, 3:60

HDHP requirements, 3:1–3:9

HRAs. *See* Health reimbursement arrangements (HRAs)

long-term care insurance. *See* Long-term care insurance

nonconforming group health care plans, HSA status for excise tax purposes, 3:75

nurse practitioners, 3:59

on-site clinics, 3:59, 3:60

other health plan coverage, 3:43

out-of-pocket expenses, 3:16–3:30

cumulative embedded deductibles for family coverage subject to, 3:25, 3:26

defined, 3:16

family coverage, change to self-only coverage, 3:30

flat-dollar charges, 3:24

hospitalization, restriction of benefits to expenses for, 3:36

in-patient care, restriction of benefits to expenses for, 3:36

limits for, 3:17

mid-year change of plans, effect of, 3:28

non-calendar years, 3:22, 3:23

noncovered expenses, amounts incurred by individual for medical care, 3:27

out-of-network services, 3:18

penalty payments, 3:24

plan deductibles, 3:11

pre-certification, failure to obtain, 3:24

self-only coverage, effect of change to family coverage, 3:29

separate or higher deductible for specific benefits, 3:35

specification of maximum, 3:19

transitional rule, 3:20–3:23

12-months or less, coverage period, 3:23

permitted insurance, 3:44–3:47

examples of, 3:55

plan deductibles, 3:10–3:15

defined, 3:10

limit, adjustment when period lasts longer than 12 months, 3:14

maximum out-of-pocket limitation, taken into account for, 3:11

medical expenses taken into account, 3:12

out-of-network services, 3:11, 3:18

period, deductible, 3:13, 3:14

separate or higher deductible for specific benefits, 3:35

transitional rule, 3:15

prescription drug coverage, 3:48

preventive care safe harbor, 3:49–3:56

employee assistance programs (EAPs), 3:61

privacy rules, 3:76

retiree health coverage, 3:74

security rules, 3:76

Medical discount cards

eligibility, effect on, 3:47, 3:57

Medical expenses

qualified medical expenses. *See* Qualified medical expenses

Medical savings accounts (MSAs). *See* Archer medical savings accounts (MSAs)

Medical service providers

distributions to, 6:20

Medicare

disadvantages of HSAs, 2:46

eligible individual with family HDHP also, 4:36

enrollment in Part A but not Part B, 2:17

ineligibility for medical tax deduction, 1:27

Medigap, 6:45, 6:46

Part A only, enrollment in, 2:17

Part D. *See* Medicare Part D

persons eligible but not enrolled, as eligible individuals for HSAs

catch-up contributions, 2:18, 4:43

termination of eligibility upon enrollment, 2:15

Medicare Advantage Savings Accounts, 1:29

Medicare Part A or Part B. *See* Medicare

Medicare Part D, 8:33, 8:34

certificate of creditable coverage, 8:33

premiums as qualified medical expenses, 6:33

Medicare Prescription Drug, Improvement, and Modernization Act of 2003, 1:5
  and creation of HSAs, 2:3
  enactment of, 2:14
  and HSA effective date, 2:4

Medigap
  defined, 6:45
  premiums as qualified medical expenses, 6:46

Military service
  members covered under TRICARE not eligible for HSAs, 2:19
  VA medical benefits, effect of, 2:16

Minimum funding standards
  HSAs, not applicable to, 4:112

Mistake of fact
  advantages of HSAs, 2:45
  distributions, 6:79

Model Form 5305-B, 7:4–7:9, 7–11

Model Form 5305-C, 7:5–7:9, 7:11

Multiple HSAs
  annual contribution limit, 4:34, 4:35
  contributions, treatment of, 4:35

Mutual funds
  investment of HSA assets in, 7:14

N

New Jersey
  HDHPs that satisfy federal requirements, 8:39

Nonconforming group health care plans
  HSA status for excise tax purposes, 3:75

Nondiscrimination rules
  cafeteria plans, 4:149
  and distributions, 6:26
  ERISA, applicability for plans subject to, 8:18, 8:19, 8:21
  safe harbors, 4:149

Nonprescription drugs
  distributions for, 6:41

Nonqualified compensation plan rules
  contributions to HSAs, 4:74

Non-spouse beneficiaries, income tax consequences, 6:83

Northern Mariana Islands
  HSAs available to residents of, 2:11

Notice 2004-23, 3:55

Notice 2005-42, 4:21

Notice 2005-83, 3:22, 8:36

Notice 2007-22. *See* Permanent rule under Notice 2007-22

Notices
  COBRA General Notices, distribution of, 8:20
  eligible investment advice arrangements, 6:66
  employer contributions, notice to employees, 4:141
  regarding HSAs, 1:11, App. B

Nurse practitioners
  services provided by, 3:59

O

Officers, defined, 4:149

One-time contributions, 1:28

One-time transfers, 2:45

One-year rule for rollovers
  Archer MSAs, 5:12–5:14
  expiration of, 5:12
  general rule, 5:11

On-site clinics
  services provided by, 3:59, 3:60

Out-of-network services
  medical coverage, 3:11, 3:18

Out-of-pocket expenses, 3:16–3:30
  changes to, 3:8
  cumulative embedded deductibles for family coverage subject to, 3:25, 3:26
  defined, 3:16
  disadvantages of HSAs, 2:46
  family coverage, change to self-only coverage, 3:30
  flat-dollar charges, 3:24
  hospitalization, restriction of benefits to expenses for, 3:36
  in-patient care, restriction of benefits to expenses for, 3:36
  lifetime limit on benefits, 3:32
  limits for, 3:17
  maximum, 3:1, 3:7
    cumulative embedded deductibles for family coverage subject to, 3:26
    and lifetime limitations, 3:33
    no maximum provided, transitional relief, 3:20
    payments in excess of UCR not treated as out-of-pocket expenses, 3:38
    and plan deductibles, 3:11
    specification of, 3:19
  mid-year change of plans, effect of, 3:28
  non-calendar years, 3:22, 3:23

noncovered expenses, amounts incurred by individual for medical care, 3:27
out-of-network services, 3:18
payments in excess of UCR not treated as, 3:38
penalty payments, 3:24
pre-certification, failure to obtain, 3:24
self-only coverage
    effect of change to family coverage, 3:29
    family coverage, change to, 3:29
    self-only coverage, change from family coverage, 3:30
separate or higher deductible for specific benefits, 3:35
specification of maximum, 3:19
tax consequences, 1:26
transitional rule, 3:20–3:23
12-months or less, coverage period, 3:23

Overview of health savings accounts, 1:1–1:30
advantages of HSAs, 1:12–1:15
Archer medical savings accounts (MSAs), HSAs based on, 1:2
definition of HSA, 1:1
domestic partner's health coverage and, 1:20
enrollment, failure to follow applicable rules, 1:22
factors employers should consider before offering HSA with HDHP coverage, 1:21
factors individuals should consider before enrolling in HSA with HDHP, 1:18
failure to follow applicable rules
    employers, 1:23
    individual, enrollment, 1:22
federal government agencies regulating, 1:9–1:11
future of HSAs, 1:24, 1:25–1:31
government agencies regulating, 1:9–1:11
HSA trustees or custodians only without offering HDHP, 1:6
as improvement over current health insurance system, 1:4
legislation
    factors contributing to enactment, 1:3
and MSAs
    as based upon, 1:2
    differences between HSAs and MSAs, 1:2, 1:8
proposed changes to rules, 1:26, 1:27
providers of HSAs and HDHPs, 1:5, 1:6
regulation of HSAs, 1:9–1:11
spouses, contributions to HSA, 1:19
states, regulation of HSAs by, 1:10

Owners. *See* Account owners

P

Participation
encouragement by employer, 8:11

Partnerships, contributions by, 4:156–4:167
on behalf of partner, 4:156
comparability rule, 4:124
distributions to partners, 4:157–4:161
    deductibility, 4:161
    reporting requirements, 4:159
    tax treatment, 4:158
guaranteed payments, 4:162, 4:163
    guaranteed payment partner, 4:156
    inclusion in gross income, 4:167
    net earnings from self-employment, inclusion in, 4:166
    reports, 4:165
when permitted, 4:17

Part-time employees vs. full-time employees
calendar year basis, 4:138, 4:140
comparability rule, 4:137

Pay-as-you-go basis
comparability rule, 4:137, 4:139

PBGC. *See* Pension Benefit Guaranty Corporation (PBGC)

Penalties
disadvantages of HSAs, 2:46
ERISA, consequences of violations by trustees or custodians, 8:27
for excess contributions, 4:96
    avoidance of, 4:97
prohibited transactions, deemed distributions as consequences of
    penalty tax rate, 6:67
reports, failure to file, 7:40

Pennsylvania Health Savings Account Act, 8:43

Pension Benefit Guaranty Corporation (PBGC)
health coverage tax credit, 5:39

Pension Protection Act of 2006 (PPA)
eligible investment advice arrangements, 6:65, 6:66

Permanent rule under Notice 2007-22
additional 10 percent tax, 5:84
failure to follow steps, 5:83
grace period extended, 5:82
information provided, 5:84
zero balance
    after distribution, 5:81
    grace period, during, 5:82

Permitted coverage
examples of, 3:55

Permitted insurance, 3:44–3:47
  coverage, 3:45, 3:46
  defined, 3:44
  examples of, 3:55
  exception to requirement of no coverage
    under other non-HDHP, 2:8
  specific diseases or illnesses, 3:46
  workers' compensation considered to be,
    3:45, 3:47

Plan amendments
  qualified HSA distributions, 5:59–5:60

Plan deductibles
  medical coverage, 3:10–3:15
    defined, 3:10
    limit, adjustment when period lasts longer
      than 12 months, 3:14
    maximum out-of-pocket limitation, taken
      into account for, 3:11
    medical expenses taken into account,
      3:12
    out-of-network services, 3:11, 3:18
    period, deductible, 3:13, 3:14
    transitional rule, 3:15

Portability
  advantages of HSAs, 2:45

PPA. *See* Pension Protection Act of 2006
(PPA)

Pre-certification, failure to obtain
  out-of-pocket expenses, 3:24

Premiums
  advantages of HSAs, 1:12, 1:14, 2:45

Prescription drugs
  Canada, distributions for prescription drugs
    imported from, 6:53
  coverage, 3:48
  preventive care safe harbor, 3:51, 3:52

Preventive care. *See also* Preventive care
  safe harbor
  characterization of benefit required by state
    law, 3:56
  examples of, 3:55

Preventive care safe harbor, 3:49–3:56
  benefits permitted, 3:50
  characterization of benefit required by state
    law, 3:56
  defined, 3:49
  employee assistance programs (EAPs), 3:61
  existing illness, treatment of, 3:54
  prescription drugs, 3:51, 3:52
  requirement that HDHP provide, 3:53
  screening services, 3:50, 3:55
  services permitted, 3:50

Privacy rules
  applicability, 3:76
  HIPAA, 8:31, 8:32

Prohibited transactions, 6:59–6:71
  deemed distributions as consequences of. *See*
    Prohibited transactions, deemed distributions
    as consequences of
  ERISA, applicability to plans not subject to
    prohibited transactions rules, 8:30
  excise tax on
    Form 5330, reporting requirements,
      7:62–7:64
    time for filing Form 5330, 7:63

**Prohibited transactions, deemed distributions
  as consequences of,** 6:59–6:71
  block trades, 6:66
  cash incentives to establish HSA and
    HDHP, 6:71
  Code provisions, 6:62
  cross-trading, 6:66
  definition of prohibited transaction, 6:63
  disqualified person, 6:64
    defined, 6:69
  electronic communications networks, 6:66
  eligible investment advice arrangements,
    6:65
    defined, 6:66
  fiduciary, defined, 6:70
  foreign exchange transactions, 6:66
  loans
    pledging of HSA security for, 6:61
    from trustee to HSA, 6:63
  penalty tax rate, 6:67
  results of engaging in, 6:60
  service providers, transactions with, 6:66
  waiver of rules, 6:68

**Promoting Health for Future Generations Act
  of 2007,** 1:29

Pro-rata recovery, 5:47

Protection
  advantages of HSAs, 2:45

Prototype HSAs
  design by plan sponsor, 7:13

Providers of HSAs and HDHPs
  overview of health savings accounts, 1:5, 1:6

Prudent investor rule, 8:28

Prudent man standard
  ERISA, fiduciary standards for plans subject
    to, 8:24

Puerto Rico
  HSAs available to residents of, 2:11

Q

Qualified HSA distributions, 5:52–5:58
  access to funds, 5:77

allowance for both FSAs and the HRA, 5:62

amount limits, 5:68

and annual contribution limitation, 5:65

comparability rule, 5:67

compatible coverage rules, 5:85, 5:86

deduction for amount transferred to HSA, 5:66

defined, 5:52

disregarded FSA coverage, 5:78, 5:79

eligibility issues during testing period, 5:74–5:76

former employee, balance based on FSA or HRA account of, 5:69

ineligibility during testing period, 5:74, 5:75

limited-purpose FSA or HRA, mid-year transfers, 5:72

minimum transfer amount, 5:70

more than one requested, 5:58

offered to all employees, 5:57

one-time basis, 5:61

permanent rule under Notice 2007-22, 5:80–5:84

plan amendment required, 5:59–5:60

property distribution, 5:63

reporting of, 5:89, 5:90

tax-free transfers during year, 5:71

testing period, 5:73–5:76

eligibility issues during, 5:74–5:76

timing issues, 5:71, 5:72

transfer amount, 5:68, 5:69

minimum transfer amount, 5:70

transfer from health care FSA or HRA, on a tax-free basis, 5:53

transitional relief, 5:79

treatment of, 5:64–5:66, 5:87, 5:88

unilateral decision to make distribution, 5:56

zero balance requirement, 5:78

Qualified medical expenses, 2:28–2:33

accident insurance, 6:47

continuation coverage, premiums for, 6:34

cosmetic surgery, 6:41

deductibility, requirements for, 6:32

defined, 2:29, 6:28

dependents. *See* Dependents

determination, responsibility for, 6:12

who is responsible, 6:13

diagnosis, defined, 6:32

disability insurance, 6:47

disabled person, under age 65, tax-free distributions, 6:50

distributions, 6:27–6:51. See also lines throughout this topic

accident insurance, 6:47

continuation coverage, premiums for, 6:34

coordination with medical expense deduction, 6:30

cosmetic surgery, 6:41

deductibility, requirements for, 6:32

deduction as expense under Code Section 213(a) also, 6:31

definition of qualified medical expenses, 6:28

diagnosis, defined, 6:32

disability insurance, 6:47

disabled person, under age 65, tax-free distributions, 6:50

end-stage renal disease health insurance premiums, 6:50

health insurance premiums, 6:42

lodging expenses, 6:38

long-term care insurance premiums, 6:56–6:58

long-term care services, 6:48

meal expenses, 6:39

Medicare Part D premiums, 6:33

Medicare premiums deducted from Social Security benefits, 6:43

Medigap policies, 6:45, 6:46

nonprescription drugs, 6:42

self-insured retiree health coverage, 6:49

transportation expenses, 6:37

types of expenses deductible, 6:29

unemployment compensation also received, 6:35

who must incur expense, 6:27

distributions not used for, withholding, 6:88

end-stage renal disease health insurance premiums, 6:50

excludable from gross income, 2:28

exclusive use, responsibility for determining, 4:77

expenses already reimbursed by other health care plan not excludable from gross income, 6:23

expenses incurred prior to establishment of HSA, not available for, 2:32, 6:21

expenses other than qualified medical, distributions not treated as withdrawal of excess contributions, 4:108

health insurance premiums, 6:42

individual not covered by HDHP, 2:33

insurance, payment for, 2:31

itemized deductions, 6:44

lodging expenses, 6:38

long-term care insurance premiums, 6:56–6:58

long-term care services, 6:48

meal expenses, 6:39

medical care, defined, 2:30

Medicare Part D premiums as, 6:33

Qualified medical expenses (*cont'd*)
Medicare premiums deducted from Social
Security benefits, 6:43
medicine and drugs, defined, 6:52
Medigap policy, 6:45, 6:46
nonprescription drugs, 6:41, 6:42
paid from HSA, 1:27
prescription drugs, 6:55
self-insured retiree health coverage, 6:49
spouses
continuation coverage, 6:34
distributions used to pay expenses, 6:20
expenses excludable from gross income, 6:24
unemployment compensation, 6:35
taxation, 6:9
10 percent additional tax, exceptions, 6:74
time limits on distributions, 6:25
trustees and custodians
determination, responsibility, 6:7
trust or custodial agreement, 7:34
types of deductible expenses, 6:29
unemployment compensation also received,
6:35

Qualifying children
age, effect of, 2:40, 2:42
defined, 2:37, 2:39
disabled, 2:41

Qualifying individual
defined, 2:37

Qualifying relatives
defined, 2:34, 2:37, 2:38

R

Railroad Retirement Act
advantages of HSAs, 1:14

Railroad Retirement Tax Act
employer contributions, 4:72, 4:82

Recordkeeping
income tax liability upon failure to maintain
adequate records of medical expenditures,
1:22
standards, 8:28

Regulation of HSAs, 1:9–1:11

Reimbursements
taxation, 6:9

Reporting requirements, 7:38–7:40. See also
specific forms
additional taxes on excess contributions,
7:57–7:61
contributions
Form 5498-SA reporting requirements,
7:42–7:48

disadvantages of HSAs, 2:46
distributions
Form 1099-SA reporting requirements,
7:49–7:56
for other than qualified medical expenses,
reporting requirements, 6:17
10 percent additional tax, reporting
requirements, 6:13
employer contributions
reporting requirements, 4:58, 4:59,
7:72–7:75
excess contributions, 4:94
additional taxes on, 7:57–7:61
excise tax on prohibited transactions,
7:62–7:64
fees, 7:19
individuals, 4:155
partnerships, contributions by
distributions to partners, 4:159
guaranteed payments, 4:165
penalties for failure to file, 7:40
prohibited transactions, 7:62–7:64
qualified HSA distributions, 5:89, 5:90
rollovers, 5:19
summary plan descriptions, 7:41
time requirements, 7:39
transfers, 5:89, 5:90

Retention of records
disadvantages of HSAs, 2:46

Retiree health
advantages of HSAs, 1:15

Retiree health coverage, 3:74

Revenue Rulings regarding HSAs, 1:11,
App. D

Rollovers, 5:1–5:21. *See also* Transfers
all cash or property need not be rolled
over, 5:7
from an Archer MSA, 2:25
from another MSA, 2:25
cash, 5:5
contributions
trustees and custodians, acceptance, 5:8
Form 1099-SA
distribution codes, 5:20
reporting of contributions, 5:19
Form 5498-SA, 7:43, 7:55
filing, 5:21
participants, provided to, 5:21
reporting of contributions, 5:21
FSA distributions, 5:3
HRA distributions, 5:3
inherited HSAs, 5:23
IRA distributions, 5:3
IRA to HSA, 5:40–5:42
maximum lifetime distribution rules, 5:48,
5:49

MSA distributions, 5:3
  all cash or property need not be rolled over, 5:7
  proceeds from sale of property, 5:6
  same property must be rolled over, 5:6
one-year rule, 5:11
  Archer MSA to Archer MSA rollovers, 5:13
  expiration of, 5:12
  second rollover following, 5:12
pro-rata recovery, 5:47
qualified HSA funding distributions, 5:40–5:42
  examples of, 5:50
  maximum annual contribution limit, 5:45
reporting requirements, 5:19
Roth IRAs
  qualified HSA funding distributions, 5:41
sale of property, proceeds, 5:6
same property must be rolled over, 5:6
second rollover following one-year rule, 5:12
60-days, completion within, 5:15
tax consequences of amount not rolled over, 5:9
tax treatment, 5:43–5:46
10 percent additional tax on distributions, exception to, 6:74
testing period, 5:50, 5:51
total amount, distribution of
  HSA to HSA rollovers, 5:16
  MSA to HSA rollovers, 5:16
traditional IRA to HSA, 5:40–5:42
trustees and custodians
  acceptance by, 7:33
  contributions, 5:8, 5:18
  reporting requirements, 5:20
  restrictions by, 7:32
when permitted, 5:1

Roth IRAs
distributions, rollovers to HSAs, 5:3
Economic Stimulus payments, direct deposits of, 6:73
  removal, 4:1
qualified HSA funding distributions, 5:41
rollovers
  qualified HSA funding distributions, 5:41

Rules regarding HSAs
advantages of HSAs, 2:45
definition of HSA, 2:1
dependents, 2:34–2:44. See also Dependents for detailed treatment
divorced parents, children of, 2:27
effective date, 2:4, 2:21
eligible individuals, 2:6–2:19
establishment of HSA, 2:20, 2:22–2:26. See also Establishment of HSA for detailed treatment
generally, 2:1–2:48
qualified medical expenses, 2:28–2:33

S

Safe harbor
nondiscrimination rules, 4:149
preventive care. See Safe harbor for preventive care

Safe harbor for preventive care, 3:49–3:56
benefits permitted, 3:50
characterization of benefit required by state law, 3:56
defined, 3:49
employee assistance programs (EAPs), 3:61
existing illness, treatment of, 3:54
group insurance programs, 8:4
prescription drugs, 3:51, 3:52
requirement that HDHP provide, 3:53
screening services, 3:50, 3:55
services permitted, 3:50

Sale of property
proceeds, rollovers, 5:6

Savings
advantages of HSAs, 2:45

S corporations, contributions by, 4:168–4:176
adjustment to gross income, deduction for, 4:176
deductibility, 4:171
gross income, exclusion from, 4:172
SECA taxes, 4:175
tax treatment, 4:170
two percent shareholder-employee, 4:168–4:176
when permitted, 4:17

Screening services, 3:50, 3:55

SEC. See Securities and Exchange Commission (SEC)

SECA taxes
S corporations, contributions by, 4:175

Securities and Exchange Commission (SEC)
IRAs, guidance relating to, 8:49
regulation by, 1:9, 8:46

Securities Exchange Act of 1934, 6:47

Securities laws, 8:46–8:49
HSA as security, circumstances, 8:47
investment contracts, 8:47
IRAs, guidance relating to, 8:48, 8:49

Security for loans
HSAs pledged as, 6:61

Security rules
applicability, 3:76

Self-employed individuals
comparability rules, 4:122
deductions not taken into account in
determining net earnings, 4:63
and proposed changes to HSA rules, 1:27

Self-insured medical reimbursement plans sponsored by employers as
as HDHP, 3:2

Self-insured retiree health coverage
distributions for, 6:49

Self-only coverage
annual contribution limit, 4:30
December 1, eligibility on, 4:7
defined, 3:39
family coverage vs., 3:39–3:42
change to family coverage, effect of, 3:29
hospitalization, restriction of benefits to
expenses for, 3:36
in-patient care, restriction of benefits to
expenses for, 3:36
out-of-pocket expenses
family coverage, change to, 3:29
self-only coverage, change from family
coverage, 3:30

Separation or divorce. *See* Divorce

SEP IRAs
qualified funding distributions, 5:42

Service providers, prohibited transactions with, 6:66

Signatures
establishment of HSA, 2:20

SIMPLE IRAs
qualified funding distributions, 5:42

Social Security benefits
Medicare premiums deducted from as
qualified medical expenses, 6:43

Sole proprietors
comparability rule, 4:123

Spousal ownership
advantages of HSAs, 2:45

Spouses. *See also* Surviving spouse
annual contribution limit, 4:49–4:59
catch-up contributions, 4:52
dividing limit between spouses, 4:57
embedded individual deductible, 4:54, 4:55
family coverage for one or both spouses,
4:49
generally, 4:52
only one spouse covered, 4:50
reporting by employer, 4:58
separate health plan, each spouse having
family coverage, 4:51

umbrella deductible, 4:53, 4:55
both spouses must be eligible individuals,
2:6, 2:9
contributions to HSA, 1:19
distributions, qualified medical expenses of
spouse excludable from gross income, 6:24
dividing limit between spouses, 4:57
Form W-2
employer contributions, reporting
requirements when spouse not employee
of employer, 7:75
individual contributions, deductions for
employer contributions to spouse, 4:61
joint HSAs not available, 2:10
qualified medical expenses, distributions used
to pay, 6:20
continuation coverage, 6:34
unemployment compensation, 6:35

Standard deduction, 1:27

State benefit mandates, 8:35–8:37
Hawaii, 8:37
transition relief, 8:36

State Children's Health Insurance Program (SCHIP), 1:27

State government
contributions made on behalf of eligible
individual, 4:19

State high-risk health plans
as HDHPs, 3:5

State law
HDHPs accompanying HSA, 8:35

State tax consequences, 8:38–8:43
Alabama, 8:42
California Assembly Bill 115, 8:41
New Jersey, 8:38
Pennsylvania Health Savings Account Act,
8:43
Wisconsin, 8:39

Stock
investment of HSA assets in, 7:14

Summary plan descriptions, 7:41

Surviving spouse
beneficiaries, income tax consequences,
6:84
inherited HSA, as designated beneficiary of,
5:22

T

TAA. *See* Trade adjustment assistance (TAA)
Tax consequences. See also specific tax
contributions, 4:153

annual contribution limit, 4:39
on behalf of eligible individual, 4:79
death distributions
income tax, 6:83, 6:84
deductions. *See* Deductions
distributions, 6:1–6:11
cessation of eligible status during year,
6:3, 6:5
debit card restricting payments and
reimbursements, administration
through, 6:6
eligibility issues, 6:3
excess contributions, 6:4
investment loss, 6:10
maximum annual contribution limits,
recovery of amounts contributed in excess
of, 6:4
qualified medical expenses, 6:9
recoupment of amounts by employer when
employee never eligible individual, 6:3
reimbursements, 6:9
request by employer, 6:2
return of erroneously made distributions,
tax consequences, 6:81
specified age, attainment of, 6:7
tax-free distribution status, 6:11
when individual permitted to receive, 6:1
withdrawal of funds by authorized
person, 6:8
employer contributions, 4:72
excess contributions, 6:4
correcting distributions, 4:100
excise taxes. *See* Excise taxes
fees paid by employer, 8:12
gross income. *See* Gross income
health coverage tax credit
premiums paid with HSA distributions,
5:39
income tax, federal. *See* Income tax, federal
ineligibility during testing period, 4:9
out-of-pocket spending, 1:26
partnerships, contributions by
distributions to partners, 4:158
prohibited transactions, penalty tax rate,
6:67
proposed changes to HSA rules, 1:26, 1:27
purchase of HSAs, 1:26
rollovers, 5:43–5:46
amount not rolled over, 5:9
S corporations, contributions by, 4:170
self-employed, treatment of, 1:27
standard deduction, 1:27
state tax consequences, 8:38–8:43
unemployed, treatment of, 1:27
workers, treatment of, 1:27

Tax-exempt status
advantages of HSAs, 2:45

Taxpayer Assistance and Simplification Act,
1:29

**Tax Relief and Health Care Act of 2006
(TRHCA),** 1:27
cafeteria plans, grace period rules, 4:21
comparability rule, employer contributions,
4:115
rollovers, traditional IRA to HSA, 5:39
transfers to HSA, 4:2
zero balance FSA, 5:78

Tax shelters
advantages of HSAs, 2:45

Testing period
ineligible individuals, 4:8, 4:9, 5:46
qualified HSA distribution, 5:73–5:76
requirement to remain eligible individual,
4:10
rollovers, 5:50, 5:51
transfers, 5:50, 5:51

Trade adjustment assistance (TAA), 5:39

Transfers, 5:28–5:38. *See also* Rollovers
from an Archer MSA, 2:25
from another MSA, 2:25
contributions
from FSA or HRA, 4:2
by direct transfer
from traditional IRA to HSA, 5:40
disadvantages of HSAs, 2:46
divorce, incident to, 5:33–5:38
divorce or separation instrument defined,
5:35
taxable distribution, not treated as, 5:34
as taxable transfer, 5:36
treatment of HSA, 5:37
when permitted, 5:33
from employer's health FSA or HRA, 4:2
Form 5498-SA, 7:43
maximum lifetime distribution rules, 5:48,
5:49
no limit on number of transfers during
year, 5:28
one-time transfers, 2:45
pro-rata recovery, 5:47
10 percent additional tax on distributions,
exception to, 6:74
testing period, 5:50, 5:51
from traditional IRA, 4:3
trustee-to-trustee transfers. *See* Trustees and
custodians
trust or custodial agreement, restrictions
and, 5:31

Transitional relief
distributions, 6:22
HDHPs, state benefit mandates, 8:36
qualified HSA distributions, 5:79
state benefit mandates, 8:36

Transportation expenses
distributions for,   6:37

TRHCA.   *See* Tax Relief and Health Care Act of 2006 (TRHCA)

TRICARE
military service members under, not eligible for HSAs,   2:19

Trustees and custodians,   7:22–7:37
age of HSA owner, tracking,   7:30
annual contributions
limits which trustee or custodian may accept,   7:24
Archer MSAs as,   2:1
certification that owner is eligible individual,   7:36, 7:37
contributions, responsibility for acceptance of
annual limitation,   7:24
cash contributions,   7:25, 7:28
exceeding maximum contribution limit,   7:26, 7:27
determination whether arrangement is trust or custodial account,   7:3
difference between,   7:2
distributions
amount of distributions, restrictions on,   7:35
determination of use for qualified medical expenses not responsible for,   6:7
frequency of distributions, restrictions on,   7:35
mistaken who returns,   7:31
qualified medical expenses, restrictions on payments of,   7:34
qualified medical expenses, trust or custodial agreement,   6:15
restrictions on distributions, authority to place,   6:14, 6:15
return of erroneously made distributions,   6:80
documents provided to owners,   7:12
eligible individual, certification or proof of, 7:36, 7:37
ERISA
custodial accounts,   8:23
entity as trustee and another as custodian,   8:26
fiduciary standards and,   8:24
risks and responsibilities,   8:25
establishment of HSA
paperwork and deposit sent, mailing date and,   2:24
treatment as established before date of establishment,   2:23
fees paid directly to,   7:21
HSA trustees or custodians only without offering HDHP,   1:6

individual qualifying as,   7:23
information returns, filing,   7:29
insurance company as,   7:22
investments, prohibited,   7:17
IRAs as,   2:1
loans to HSA, prohibited transaction,   6:63
property, contributions of,   7:25
qualified medical expenses, distributions to pay,   7:34
rollovers
acceptance of,   7:33
contributions, acceptance,   5:8
reporting requirements,   5:20
restrictions,   5:18, 7:32
transfers, trust or custodial agreement on,   5:31
trust document,   8:28
trustee-to-trustee transfers
acceptance of,   5:30, 7:33
Form 1098-SA, treatment in,   7:55
FSAs,   5:38
HRAs,   5:38
incident to divorce, not treated as taxable distribution,   5:36
IRAs,   5:38
taxable distributions, not treated as,   5:29

Trustee-to-trustee transfers
acceptance of,   5:30
cash,   5:32
Form 1098-SA, treatment in,   7:55
FSAs,   5:38
generally,   5:29
HRAs,   5:38
incident to divorce, not treated as taxable distribution,   5:36
IRAs,   5:38
trustees and custodians, acceptance by,   7:33

Trusts
HSA offered in form of,   7:1

Two percent shareholders
contributions by S corporations
deductibility
excluded from gross income,   4:172
SECA taxes,   4:175
subject to FICA tax,   4:173, 4:174

U

Umbrella deductible,   4:53, 4:55

Unemployed persons and proposed changes to HSA rules,   1:27

Unemployment compensation
and qualified medical expenses,   6:35

Unionized employees
comparability rule application,   4:127

Unrelated business taxable income,   4:88

USA Patriot Act,   8:45
Customer Identification Procedures,   8:45

Use-it-or-lose it rules,   2:45

V

Vesting
advantages of HSAs,   2:45

Veterans Affairs Department persons eligible for medical benefits through as eligible individuals,   2:16

Virgin Islands
HSAs available to residents of,   2:11

Vision care insurance
exception to requirement of no coverage under other non-HDHP,   2:8

W

Waiver
prohibited transaction rules, of,   6:68

Welfare benefit plans.   *See* Employee welfare benefit plans

Wellness programs,   3:58
cafeteria plans, contributions through,   4:151
eligibility for HSAs, effect on,   3:47

WFTRA.   *See* Working Families Tax Relief Act of 2008 (WFTRA)

Widow(er).   *See* Surviving spouse

Wisconsin HDHPs that satisfy federal requirements,   8:40

Withholding
distributions,   6:87, 6:88
income tax, federal
employer contributions not subject to,   4:83

Workers' compensation permitted insurance, considered to be,   3:45, 3:47

Working Families Tax Relief Act of 2008 (WFTRA)
Archer Medical Savings Accounts,   2:5
dependents,   2:35, 2:37

Written plan documents ERISA, fiduciary standards for plans subject to,   8:24

Z

Zero balance
after distribution,   5:81
exceptions to requirement,   5:78
grace period, during,   5:82